CONTENTS

LIST OF CONTRIBUTORS

Manzoor Alam
Michael J. Bannon
H. H. Blotevogel
J. G. Borchert
Larry S. Bourne
H. J. Buchholz
Harold Carter
L. F. Chaves
Berardo Cori
Etienne Dalmasso
Fany Davidovich
David R. DiMartino
Kazimierz Dziewoński
Manuel Ferrer
M. Reis Ferreira
Frankdieter Grimm
M. Hommel
Sven Illeris
Marek Jerczynski

Piotr Korcelli
G. M. Lappo
J. C. Lilaia
Malcolm I. Logan
A. Simões Lopes
John McKay
Richard L. Morrill
Mauri Palomäki
Yu. L. Pivovarov
Andrés Precedo
I. Schilling-Kaletsch
P. Schöller
James W. Simmons
Robert Sinclair
Igor Vrišer
Olof Wärneryd
James S. Whitelaw
Takashi Yamaguchi

INTRODUCTION

LARRY S. BOURNE AND ROBERT SINCLAIR

Urbanization has been one of the most significant vehicles for the transformation of societies over the last century. All countries to a greater or lesser extent have been affected. Not only has urbanization, as it is traditionally defined, involved a movement of population from rural to urban areas, but it has at the same time reorganized the economic, social, and political structures of every nation state. With this reorganization has come a dramatic shift in the distribution of wealth, in political power, in patterns of production and consumption, and in perceptions of national and cultural identity.

This volume examines one set of dimensions or expressions of this transformation by looking at the urbanization process within the framework of the settlement system. The volume brings together a collection of international papers which illustrate the development and contemporary structure of urban settlements in twenty-two countries of the world. It provides a notably diverse set of studies on settlement systems in both the industrialized western, capitalist societies and in the centrally-planned socialist societies (largely in Eastern Europe), as well as in developing countries.

The unifying concept in these papers is a focus upon *systems of urban settlements*—conceived of as an interrelated and interacting set of urban centres—which effectively present a view of the functional structure of each country's geography. Specifically, the papers examine recent trends in urban growth, city sizes and functions, demographic structure, economic structure, administrative reorganizations and population redistribution within those systems, and the varied responses of government to those trends. Most papers conclude with an assessment of future directions of change in settlement systems.

On Comparative Studies of Urbanization

Comparative studies of urbanization at an international scale are difficult, and relatively rare. Data sources tend to be limited and inconsistent. Direct comparisons of the urban experiences of different countries are handicapped by conceptual and definitional differences concerning what is urban and not urban, by the different reporting practices of national statistical agencies, by contrasting local government organizations, and by the diverse institutional environments within which urbanization has taken place. In some countries, data specific to urbanized areas or to functional urban regions which extend beyond municipal boundaries either do not exist, or are now a decade or more old. Language and writing styles also present barriers to research and the exchange of information.

Despite these difficulties, the study of urban settlement change at the international level is one of the most challenging and rewarding of research pursuits. It is also of immense political and social importance. The UN Conference on Human Settlements (held in Vancouver in 1976) identified an improved understanding of urbanization and the designing of liveable urban settlements, as among the most crucial challenges facing mankind in the remaining years of this century (Ward, 1976).

None of the existing theories of urban growth nor policies of growth control have been shown to have wide applicability outside a limited cultural realm (*see* Abu-Lughod and Hay, 1980 and Pacione, 1981b on the third world experience; Hansen, 1978, Bourne and Simmons, 1978, Hall and Hay, 1980, Pacione, 1981a, and Kawashima and Korcelli, 1982 on the developed capitalist world; and Musil, 1981 on the socialist countries). Too often our explanations of the urban settlement patterns we see evolving around us become strangely irrelevant when they are applied to the experience of other countries. Moreover, it is not true that those varied experiences simply reflect differences in the stage of economic development and industrialization, although these are important determinants of the level and character of urbanization. Indeed, it is now widely accepted that the less developed countries will not necessarily follow the path of urbanization witnessed in the developed countries—either capitalist or socialist. Nor is it true that the path of urban development in the countries of the capitalist and socialist worlds, despite the contrasting roles played by the state, will necessarily diverge in the future.

Conversely, such differences do not mean that there are no common denominators in the processes of urbanization across many (if not all) societies, economies, and types of political systems (see Berry, 1973). Rather, they mean that the mix of common and unique denominators remains to be identified, and evaluated systematically, before any attempt is made to impose a universal explanation for the phenomenon of urbanization.

The Diversity of Urbanization Experience

Despite the sparsity of current literature and the absence of comprehensive data sources at the international level, it is important that we attempt to document the immense diversity in the extent of urbanization with the best and most recent data sources. The following tables and discussion illustrate global levels of urbanization, rates of growth, and city-size distributions for selected countries using recent United Nations statistics (World Bank, 1981). A note of caution is necessary here, however. These statistics, as is acknowledged by the UN itself, are based upon estimates from each country and hence are subject to wide variability in both definition and accuracy. They are, on the other hand, the most recent, consistent, and comprehensive set of data available.

Among individual UN countries, levels of urbanization vary from only two per cent (e.g. Burundi) to well over ninety per cent (or one hundred per cent in the special case of Singapore). However, if averages for groups of countries at different levels of income and stages of economic development are examined, the range in level of urbanization is smaller, but none the less considerable (Table A.1). In this data set the World Bank has grouped countries into four major categories; low-income, middle-income, industrial market economies, and industrial nonmarket or socialist economies, with the additional special category of the small population, but capital-surplus (typically oil-exporting) states. Among the four major

Table A.1: *Levels of Urbanization, Growth Rates and City-Size by Type of Economy, 1980*

	Population* 1980 (millions)	Urban Population				% of Urban Population in Cities Over 500,000	
		% of Total		% Annual Growth			
		1960	1980	1960-70	1970-80	1960	1980
Low-income countries	2,300	15	17	3.8	3.7	31	42
(a) China and India	1,650	n/a	17	n/a	3.2	33	42
(b) Other (34)	650	12	19	4.7	5.0	23	42
Middle-income countries	1,008	37	50	4.1	3.8 ,	35	48
(a) Oil-exporters	334	33	45	4.5	4.3	32	46
(b) Oil-importers	674	39	52	4.0	3.5	36	48
Capital surplus countries	26	37	69	7.4	6.7	22	53
Industrial non market economies	355	49	64	2.5	2.1	23	32
Industrial market economies	675	68	77	1.8	1.3	48	55

*Estimated.
n/a = not available.

Source: Adapted from World Bank, *World Development Report, 1981*. New York: Oxford University Press.

categories, estimated levels of urbanization in 1980 varied from an average of 17 per cent of total population in the low-income countries, to 50 per cent in middle-income countries, 64 per cent in the socialist countries (Eastern Europe only) and 77 per cent in the industrial market economies.

These levels are related not only to differences in levels of income but to each country's type of economy. Industrial economies, particularly capitalist market economies, have tended to produce relatively high levels of urbanization and metropolitan concentration at least initially, because of the benefits of urban agglomeration (Vining, 1982). Within each of these categories, of course, there is wide variability between individual countries because of their differing history, geography and political organization.

Furthermore, the rate of growth in urban population is, in general, inversely related to current levels of urbanization. Annual urban growth rates in the 1970s varied from a staggering 5.0 per cent in the low-income countries (excluding India and China) to 2.1 per cent in the industrial nonmarket countries and only 1.3 per cent in the industrial market economies. Perhaps more critical is the fact that the rates of urban growth in low-income countries have remained high, and in some cases have increased since the 1960s, while those in the industrial world have declined sharply. The continuing potential for explosive urbanization in the future in countries of the developing world, countries least able to manage such growth, is readily apparent.

There appears to be less differentiation between the developing and developed countries in terms of the degree of metropolitan concentration, measured as the proportion of the urban population resident in the largest cities (over 500,000). While the highest proportions are found, as expected, in the industrial market economies (55 per cent), the low- and middle-income countries also show relatively high proportions (42 per cent and 48 per cent respectively). The lowest figures (32 per cent) are recorded in the socialist countries of Eastern Europe, reflecting at least partially the effects of concerted government efforts to decentralize urban growth away from the capital cities and the older industrial heartland and the frequent definitional underbounding of the larger urban areas in those countries.

The principal difference shown between the developing and developed countries rests in the contrasting distribution of cities when ranked by population size. In the developing world, urban population tends to be heavily concentrated in one (the primate) centre or a few large metropolitan agglomerations, and this primacy appears to be increasing. In the developed countries, the city-size hierarchy shows a more even distribution, perhaps moving in the direction of some theoretical rank-size distribution. In those countries with relatively larger urban populations and several major metropolitan agglomerations, the degree of primacy has been reduced. In the last ten years the degree of metropolitan concentration in many industrial countries has stabilized or in some cases declined as part of a process which has been variously labelled as deconcentration, deurbanization or counterurbanization (Berry and Silverman, 1980).

Statistics for individual countries further emphasize the diversity of settlement systems, and also the regularity of the differences identified above. Table A. 2 provides descriptive data for those countries examined in the papers of this volume. Although large parts of the world are under-represented, particularly those of the developing world, real differences in the size of urban population, the number of major urban centres, the rate of growth and the degree of metropolitan concentration are readily apparent. For example, although India has a much lower level of urbanization (22 per cent) than either the USSR (65 per cent) or the United States (73 per cent), it has almost as many urban residents (148 million compared to 174 and 165 million for the USSR and US). All three countries also have among the lowest proportions of their urban population resident in the largest urban area—4 per cent, 6 per cent and 12 per cent respectively reflecting their vast geographic scale and large total population. At the same time, in many countries of Europe, both east and west, the proportion of the urban population resident in cities over 500,000 is declining as the process of deconcentration appears to continue.

Again, the most meaningful single variable in looking to the future is the rate of urban population growth. Despite their small representation in this volume, the high rates of growth in the low- and middle-income countries are strikingly apparent. On the other hand, most of the developed countries show urban growth rates which are converging on zero, indeed several—for example the UK, W. Germany, and E. Germany—have already reached that state. Even with a possible future decline in fertility rates in the Third World, however, the youthful demographic structure of these countries ensures continued rapid urban growth through the rest of this century. The kinds of settlement systems which are likely to evolve in this context will look very different from those in advanced industrial countries which are attempting to adapt to conditions of near-zero population growth (or absolute decline).

Current Forces of Change

The diversity of urbanization experience illustrated by these data underlines, and at the same time reflects, a series of changes which appear to be restructuring most of the world's settlement systems. Descriptions of these changes pervade many of the contributions in this volume, and their spatial impacts upon settlement systems have been analysed and synthesized in a series of recent studies (Bourne, Korcelli and Wärneryd, 1982; Korcelli, 1981; Illeris, 1980; Sinclair, 1982; Van der Berg, 1981; Vining, 1982). In most developed market economies, in addition to an overall declining rate

Table A.2: *Levels of Urbanization, Growth Rates and City-Size: Selected Countries*

Country	Population 1980 (millions)	Urban Population as % of Total Population		% of Annual Growth		% of Urban Population in:				Number of Cities Over 500,000	
						Largest City		Cities Over 500,000			
		1960	1980	1960-70	1970-80	1960	1980	1960	1980	1960	1980
India	673	18	22	3.3	3.3	7	6	26	39	11	36
Mali	7	11	20	5.4	5.5	32	34	0	0	0	0
Brazil	119	46	65	4.8	3.7	14	16	35	52	6	14
Venezuela	15	67	83	4.7	4.2	26	26	26	44	1	4
Ireland	3	46	58	1.6	2.2	51	48	51	48	1	1
Italy	57	59	69	1.5	1.3	13	17	46	52	7	9
UK	56	86	91	0.9	0.3	24	20	61	55	15	17
Finland	5	38	62	3.2	2.7	28	27	0	27	0	1
Japan	117	62	78	2.4	2.0	18	22	35	42	5	9
Australia	14	81	89	2.5	1.9	26	24	62	68	4	5
Canada	24	69	80	2.7	1.7	14	18	31	62	2	9
France	54	62	78	2.4	1.4	25	23	34	34	4	6
Netherlands	14	80	76	1.0	0.6	9	9	27	24	3	3
US	227	67	73	1.7	1.5	13	12	61	77	40	65
Germany W.	61	77	85	1.4	0.4	20	18	48	45	11	11
Denmark	5	74	84	1.5	0.9	40	32	40	32	1	1
Sweden	8	73	87	1.8	1.0	15	15	15	35	1	3
Portugal	10	23	31	1.3	2.9	47	44	47	44	1	1
Spain	22	57	74	2.6	2.2	13	17	37	44	5	6
Poland	36	48	57	1.8	1.7	17	15	41	47	5	8
Hungary	11	40	54	1.7	2.1	45	37	45	37	1	1
USSR	267	49	65	2.8	2.2	6	4	21	33	25	50
Yugoslavia	37	28	42	3.2	2.9	11	10	11	23	1	3
Germany E.	17	72	77	0.1	0.3	9	9	14	17	2	3

Source: Adapted from World Bank, *World Development Report, 1981.* New York: Oxford University Press

of urban population growth and slow economic growth, these changes include:

(1) Revolutionary changes in family formation and household composition, with the ultimate effect of reducing average family and household size. Households are smaller, but there are more of them, so that there has been an increase in the demand for housing and other settlement amenities. Hence, the decline in urban population growth has not thus far been translated into a declining demand for urban infrastructure or most social services. Indeed, until the onset of the current recession in many Western countries, the opposite appears to have been the case.

(2) Changing labour force participation rates, particularly among women, with a corresponding surge in the number of two- (or multi-) income families, have redefined the resources, life styles and behaviour of many households. Not only has this trend increased the wealth and locational flexibility of household units, but it has also increased the overall demand for housing and recreational space (including second homes) and for various commercial and personal services. Higher unemployment rates, on the other hand, have made other households worse off and thus more isolated from the mainstream consumer society.

(3) Basic structural shifts in the economy, with expanding investment and employment in the resource sectors, services and the communications sector and declining employment in manufacturing, have altered the economic base of many urban settlements. Within the manufacturing sector, an increasing proportion of output has been devoted to light, high-technology and consumer-oriented products. These shifts have been accompanied by the continuing revolution in communications technology. The overall spatial implication of such changes has been (*a*) more locational flexibility and (*b*) the declining attraction of the agglomeration economies offered by the older industrial metropolis.

(4) An increasing dominance of major job-providing organizations (e.g., multi-national corporations and large government enterprises), whose locational decision-making practices play an expanding role in restructuring national settlement systems, but which are often detached from the instruments of control available to local and regional governments.

(5) The increasing importance of 'life-style' preferences and environmental amenities, rather than direct economic gain, as factors in migration patterns. These developments, brought about by expanding retirement populations, increased wealth, the expanding role of government transfer payments in relation to total income, and other elements of a mature or 'postindustrial society', are having profound effects upon the settlement systems of most Western countries.

(6) Re-assessments of the availability and costs of energy. In terms of their effects on the structure of settlement systems, these re-assessments have both a consumption aspect—in that they promise substantially to

influence residential, commercial and institutional location decisions—and a production aspect—in that they have brought settlement 'booms' to energy-rich areas, such as those in the western regions of Australia, Canada, and the United States.

(7) Reversals in long-standing national migration patterns, which reflect many of the above changes. The migration of population and jobs from the industrial Northeast and Great Lakes regions to the South and West of the United States probably has received the greatest attention, but this is paralleled by similar shifts in most other Western countries (Vining, 1982). At the same time growth has increased in non-metropolitan areas, often at the expense of the larger metropolitan areas.

These and other changes are well-documented in the pages of this volume, and have received much attention in the recent literature. One attempt to synthesize their spatial impact is shown in Table A.3 (Sinclair, 1982), which relates these changes to various spatial processes operating at different levels of the settlement system.

Equally dramatic changes underlie the urbanization data for low- and middle-income developing countries, although their impact upon settlement systems has been studied less extensively, and their documentation in this volume is restricted by the relative scarcity of contributions. Certainly, however, settlement structures in developing countries are being transformed rapidly by:

(1) The burgeoning population in the younger-age cohorts, which might well constitute a potential for future economic growth, but which today creates an increasing surplus of dependent, unemployed, and underemployed population, often migrating in search of economic opportunity.

(2) Intensive rural-urban migration, often in sequential steps to the local centre, to the regional capital, and eventually to the primate city. This migration is often triggered by a push factor—the lack of opportunity in the countryside—rather than the pull of opportunities in the cities.

(3) A consequent urbanization which in many cases is not a result of either industrialization or economic development, as was the case in more industrialized countries. The result is a burgeoning of urban population, without an equivalent increase in urban productivity, and an increasing polarization between urban and rural areas.

(4) Nevertheless, a relative increase in industrialization has taken place. Generally this growth is due to intentional government economic incentives, or it is dependent on, controlled by, and subservient to, the demands of external capitalist or socialist economies. Each situation has its characteristic influences on the developing settlement system.

(5) In most countries, an increasing amount of government control and regulation emphasizing economic growth and industrial development, but in many cases also specifically oriented toward the planning of urban settlements.

Table A.3: *Spatial Processes within the National Settlement System*

Theme	Underlying Causes	Related Spatial Concepts	Spatial Scale		
			National	Regional	Metropolitan
Zero-sum	Growth in one place means decline elsewhere	Spatial redistribution	'Southern' growth Vs 'Northern' decline	Nonmetropolitan growth Vs Metropolitan decline	Peripheral & selected inner city growth Vs Centre city-inner suburban decline
	Declining population growth-rates	Re-location diffusion	Nonmetropolitan growth Vs Metropolitan decline	Smaller centre growth Vs Large centre decline	
	Increasing mobility				
Expanding Space Demands	Systemwide expansion of settlement space	Expansion diffusion	Settlement expansion	New settlements	Metropolitan spatial expansion
	Rapid household formation		New settlements	Megalopolitan developments	
	Multi-income families		Second home colonies	Second home colonies	
	'Post-shelter' society				

Spatio-social Differentiation	Increasing spatio-social differentiation within system	Expanding mobility Diverse lifestyle motivations	Selective migration Spatial segregation Mosaic pattern	Selective migration streams Interregional & intercity differentiation	Selective migration streams Interarea & intercity differentiation	Social mosaic
System Integration	More intensive system integration	Space–time convergence Postindustrial economy Declining agglomeration economies	Functional decentralization Horizontal linkages Polynodal spatial structure	Interregional functional shifts Increasing number of control points Expanding Role of Smaller Centres	Increasing number of 'activity' centres Polynodal structure	Polynodal functional structure

The very recency and dynamism of the changes outlined here mean that their present and potential impact upon the settlement systems of both developed and developing countries are not adequately documented nor well understood. Certainly we are far from developing satisfactory theories for explaining their complex impacts. It is hoped, however, that the wealth of information contained in the contributions in this volume will fill some of the gaps in our knowledge, and aid in the search for such explanations.

Concepts and Themes

Several distinctive themes act to unify this collection of papers, in addition to their common concern with the processes of global urbanization. First is the focus on the changing settlement pattern, resulting from the transition from a rural to an urban society, from a pre-industrial settlement pattern to an industrial pattern, or from the latter to a service-oriented or post-industrial one. Most of the papers in this volume concentrate upon change, on the dynamic or evolutionary properties of urban settlements, rather than upon detailed examinations of the structure of those settlements at one point in time. Many of the contributors go further, and attempt to project current changes into future settlement patterns.

Second is the focus upon the 'national' settlement system as the principal area of study, an obvious reflection of the importance of the national government, or nation state, in shaping settlement patterns. Such a focus presents considerable difficulty and challenge to the authors in situations where the composition and boundaries of the states themselves have changed drastically in recent decades (e.g. Poland, West Germany, India). Still, even in those situations, the national government has become both a designer of and an outcome of the evolution of urban settlements. In all cases, the nation state is an integral component of and an actor in the process of urbanization rather than an impartial bystander (Simmons and Bourne, 1982; Dear and Scott, 1981; Johnston, 1982).

The third theme is a focus upon a 'system' of urban settlements or an urban 'system'. While few authors actually employ the rich array of concepts and techniques available in the literature on formal systems theory (Bennett and Chorley, 1978), the *idea* of a system permeates most of the papers. The focus upon systems terminology here serves to stress the relatively simple attribute that urban settlements are linked in a complex web of interrelationships and interdependencies. It is those links—involving the movement of people, goods and capital or of growth stimuli—which give meaning to the notion of an urban system (Simmons and Bourne, 1981). In a highly urbanized society these same linkages are the principal means by which a national territory is spatially organized. Through these linkages impulses of growth and change are spread across the nation, wealth is redistributed and political power is redefined. The cities become the *de facto* control points in the national economy and in the territorial power structure.

A final theme, which underlies all the others, is the recognition of the spatial nature of the urban settlement system. All authors, to some degree, utilize measures of basic spatial attributes—spatial patterns, spatial interaction, spatial organization—in their studies. Urban growth and decline are described in terms of places and regions. Maps and spatial models are utilized in all papers. The widespread use of the spatial approach is perhaps a tacit acknowledgement of what a settlement system really is—namely, the impact of man's actions and activities (cultural, social, economic and political) upon the earth's surface.

The Contents

The papers in this volume mirror the diversity of the global experience in general and of the nature and operation of settlement systems in particular. Contributions are included from twenty-two countries, varying in population and size from Ireland and Denmark to India, the US and the USSR. The range in style, content and approach is equally broad, as might be expected given the uniqueness of national settlement systems, the varied backgrounds of the authors and the minimum of restraints imposed by the editors.

Each paper provides a somewhat different perspective on the study of settlement systems. Many of the papers are primarily empirical and descriptive, whereas others are more interpretative and/or theoretical. Some contributors devote considerable space to the role of government policies and planning programmes, whereas others treat the role of government, or the state, as somewhat peripheral. Many papers deal intensively with the historical evolution of the settlement system, whereas others are concerned almost exclusively with the contemporary organization of the system. Moreover, the essentially open definition of the concept of a settlement system allows some contributors to consider the role of small hamlets and rural villages, whereas others examine only the larger metropolitan centres in the system. In the same vein, some contributors have considered it important to deal with the internal or intra-metropolitan structure of cities and processes of change in their analyses, whereas others have paid little or no attention to the intra-urban aspects of the settlement system.

More fundamental differences derive from the diverse analytical and ideological approaches taken by the contributors. Almost the entire spectrum of alternative approaches to the study of urbanization is evident. Some papers offer an approach based upon a more formal use of systems language and concepts. The paper by Grimm on the GDR is a good example. Others take a systematic empirical approach to the study of the urban system, with the papers by Borchert, and Morrill, Sinclair and DiMartino on the Netherlands and the United States respectively, being excellent examples.

Others draw upon specific bodies of theory, such as staple or dependency theory. The latter, for example, links the evolution of a particular settlement pattern to the operation of an international trading system, or more broadly to the international capitalist order (*see* Chaves on Venezuela and Davidovich on Brazil). Here, the terms of trade and the international circulation of capital are seen to be strongly biased toward the demands of larger capitalist economies and the needs of major multinational corporations. This bias in turn defines a settlement system in which the largest centres are enveloped in (and exploited by) the international economic order, while at the same time becoming increasingly detached from smaller centres and rural settlements in the rest of the country.

Quite a different approach to understanding the settlement system starts with the small-scale examination of individual household and firm behaviour (*see* Wärneryd on Sweden). Here, the patterns of settlement we observe at the national or regional levels are viewed as aggregations of such small-scale human behaviour, including the cycles of daily living activities of individual actors. These aggregations, it is argued, can only be understood by first examining their micro-behavioural underpinnings in both space and time. Another approach is to base the discussion of the settlement system upon a framework of administrative (generally hierarchical) components, as Cori does for Italy, while yet another views the settlement system primarily as the outcome of rational planning and the attainment of policy objectives, as in the case of the Lappo-Pivovarov paper on the USSR. Finally, some contributors view the settlement system as an expression of the prevailing cultural atmosphere and the dominant perspectives of individual actors and decision-makers through time, as Morrill, Sinclair and DiMartino do for the United States. In this case the importance of an ideology of social liberalism, of individualism, of the perception of abundance, and of the expectation of continuous growth are stressed.

For the reader the initial impact of this diversity might be one of confusion, and indeed, the collection is somewhat eclectic. At the same time, *this diversity speaks directly to the varied roots from which the phenomenon of global urbanization springs* and to the varied responses of governments, firms and individuals to the problems that result. The editors have resisted the temptation to set out an explicit approach or epistemology for the individual contributors or to impose, *ex post facto*, a single conceptual framework on the resulting papers when no such framework exists. To have done so would have obscured the real diversity and strength of the contributions.

The papers, as previously noted, are also not uniformly representative of the global urban experience. Several continents and major regions of the world, notably Africa, Latin America and Asia, are under-represented. Others, particularly Europe, both east and west, and especially the English-speaking countries, are well represented. This imbalance in representation between the developed and developing worlds, while common to almost all international scientific pursuits, is particularly serious here because it is in the under-represented regions that many of the most serious urban problems of the next two decades will emerge (Ward, 1976). On the other hand, a major strength of this volume is the scope it allows for east-west comparisons within the developed world. In reviewing the contributions from both capitalist and socialist countries, the reader is in a better position to identify those features of urban settlements which are seen to be common to both and those which are unique.

The variation in content, style, and approach among the papers has also meant that there are differences in the nature and use of maps and illustrations. Many authors have produced maps specific to their contributions and original to this volume. Others have relied on maps taken from or adapted from previous publications.

Finally, it should be pointed out that most contributors are not writing in their native language. Although this comprises one of the unique attributes of the volume, it also leads to understandable differences in writing styles. The editors have taken considerable liberties in editing the papers, in an attempt to reduce stylistic and language problems, and in shortening the longer papers to meet the inevitable limitations of space. The editors take full responsibility for the errors thus created.

Background Conditions in the Urbanization Process

Although urbanization, as argued above, is a universal process with many common denominators, the geographical outcomes, or realizations of the process vary greatly in different regions and countries. Clearly, the factors accounting for those differences are many, complicated, and their appearance in combination is specific to each country. In reviewing the papers in this volume, however, a number of such factors appear to be particularly important and universal.

1. *The Geographic Scale.* Settlement systems which develop in countries of continental size (e.g. USSR, US, Canada, Australia) are likely to differ in their spatial structure, internal relationships and degree of regional differentiation, from those which have evolved on a smaller, more regional scale (e.g. most countries in Europe).

2. *The Physical Foundation.* Although the importance of the physical base is so obvious that many authors take the reader's knowledge for granted, it is clear that the settlement system of any country is underlain by that country's unique combination of natural factors—its land and water configurations, landforms, climate, soil patterns, and the location of its mineral resources.

3. *The Historical Foundation of Urbanization.* The roots of the current

settlement network in each country are to be found in both the timing and conditions of initial urban settlement. In Spain, for example, the distribution of urban settlements was largely laid down by the time of the Moorish occupation in the tenth century and in Greece a millennium before that. In Australia and Canada, by contrast, the urban network derives from the arrival and expansion of European colonial settlement in the nineteenth and twentieth centuries.

4. *The Density of the Pre-Urban Settlement Pattern.* Modern urban settlement patterns.are usually, but not always, imposed upon and thus shaped by an existing (and typically rural) settlement pattern. These vary from high density pre-urban settlement, as in India and much of Southern Asia, to very low density patterns as in much of North and South America, Australia, and the USSR east of the Urals.

5. *The Prevailing Mode and Type of Production.* Urbanization is shaped by the dominant type and mode of production—the economic system—prevailing in each country at every stage in the process. Not only do we assume initially that settlement systems will differ between countries with predominantly capitalist and socialist modes of production, but also among countries in which different economic sectors dominate. That is, each major sector, according to its needs, and for purposes of production, distribution and exchange, will generate a particular type of settlement system. Consequently, settlement systems which develop largely on the basis of manufacturing, for example, will differ from those based on service delivery or the exploitation of natural resources or on cultural, transportation and recreational pursuits (Bourne and Simmons, 1978).

6. *Stage of Development.* Within the same type of economic system, urbanization (and the form of the settlement system) will differ depending upon the particular level or stage reached by that country in the evolution from a pre-industrial to a post-industrial society. In most instances stage of development would be measured by employment and occupational trends and by levels of wealth and output.

7. *Degree of External Dependence.* In any system the degree of 'openness' to external influence, and the direction of dependency implied by such external relationships, will strongly influence the internal organization and growth performance of the system. In Canada and Australia, for example, the dependence of their economies upon the external demand for staple products, and in Venezuela and Brazil, their dependence upon foreign capital (as well as the demands of larger capitalist economies), have shaped the pattern of settlement by reducing linkages within the system.

8. *The Prevalent Atmosphere within which Settlement takes place.* The form of the settlement system will ultimately reflect the needs, aspirations, and perceptions of the society in which the settlement process takes place. The individualistic, optimistic, expansive, growth-oriented atmosphere which characterized the settlement of most 'New World' countries had an

influence upon the settlement system which was different or less evident in other, 'older' parts of the world. Even today, the consumption-oriented, amenity-loving attitudes and 'life-style' preferences prevailing in many post-industrial societies give evidence of significantly altering the settlement pattern laid down in a more production-oriented, economically-dominated industrial age.

A Classification of Settlement Systems

While recognizing the uniqueness of the settlement system in each country, it is none the less possible to classify these systems into a limited number of groups based upon combinations of several of the underlying determinants of settlement formation discussed above. Drawing on earlier work by Dziewonski and Jerczynski (1978), at least six types of settlement system can be identified (Table A.4). These six types are based on a cross-classifi-

Table A.4: *A Classification Scheme for Settlement Systems*

Type of Economy and Level of Development	Historical Density of Settlement	
	Sparse Settlement Base	Intensive Settlement Base
A Capitalist/Market Economies	A-1 North America, Australia, Northern Europe e.g., Sweden	A-2 W. Europe e.g., UK, Germany, Japan
B Socialist/Centrally Planned Economies	B-1 USSR (Asia), Africa	B-2 E. Europe, e.g., USSR (Europe), Poland
C Developing/Third World Economies	C-1 Latin America, Africa, Middle East	C-2 S. and S.E. Asia, e.g., India

cation of the prevailing type of economy (capitalist, socialist and developing), and the density of population prior to the formation of an urban settlement system (e.g. intensive vs. sparse). The former is also an explicit differentiation in terms of income level and stage of development, between the developed industrialized world and the so-called Third World.

Further subdivisions of each of the resulting six groups, notably between continental-scale urban systems, such as in Australia and North America and the geographically smaller systems in most Western European countries, could easily be added. The question of geographic scale is also of importance here since it tends to parallel differences in the political organization of the nation state, particularly between the relatively decentralized federal states (e.g. USA, Canada, Brazil, India, Australia) and the more politically centralized states of, for example, Western and Eastern Europe.

The organization of papers in this volume reflects this simple typology, recognizing of course that no single classification is entirely satisfactory.

The papers are presented in three parts, following the A, B, C classification in Table A.4. Part A, Section 1 contains discussions of national settlement systems in developed market economies with low-density settlement, beginning with those of continental dimensions, the United States, Canada and Australia, followed by two related examples, Sweden and Finland, which are low density in character, but on a less-than-continental scale. Section 2 contains the largest number of papers in the collection, and includes discussions of the older and higher-density settlement systems of Western Europe and Japan. Section 3 focuses upon countries of the Mediterranean world, which in many respects represent a transition between the more industrialized parts of Europe and the developing world.

Part B contains the four contributions from the socialist world, all of which are Eastern Europe countries. The continental size and internal diversity of the Soviet Union puts that country in a separate section (Part B, Section 4). Yugoslavia has been placed in Part B, Section 5 with the GDR and Poland, although its size and Mediterranean location might have merited a separate section.

Part C groups the three contributions from the developing world. Two are middle-income countries in Latin America—Brazil and Venezuela—(Part C, Section 6) while the third, India, is our only example from the rich-poor (e.g. low income but culturally-rich) and high density societies of Southern Asia.

REFERENCES

Abu-Lughod, J. and Hay, R., eds. 1980. *Third World Urbanization*. London: Methuen.
Bennett, R. J. and Chorley, R. 1978. *Environmental Systems: Philosophy, Analysis and Control*. London: Methuen.
Berry, B. J. L. 1973. *The Human Consequences of Urbanization*. London: Macmillan.
Berry, B. J. L. and Silverman, L. P., eds. 1980. *Population Redistribution and Public Policy*. Washington, D.C.: National Academy of Sciences.
Bourne, L. S. 1975. *Urban Systems: Strategies for Regulation*. London: Oxford University Press.
Bourne, L. S. 1980. 'Alternative Perspectives on Urban Decline and Population Deconcentration'. *Urban Geography*, 1: 39-52.
Bourne, L. S. and Simmons, J. W., eds. 1978. *Systems of Cities: Readings on Structure, Growth and Policy*. New York: Oxford University Press.
Bourne, L. S., Korcelli, P. and Wärneryd, O. 1982. 'Emerging Spatial Configurations of Urban Systems: A Review of Comparative Experience', *Geographia Polonica*, 48: forthcoming.
Brunn, S. and Wheeler, J., eds. 1980. *The American Metropolitan System: Present and Future*. London: E. Arnold.

Bühr, W. and Fredrick, P., eds. 1982. *Planning Under Regional Stagnation*. Baden-Baden, W. Germany: Nomos Verlagsgesellschaft.

Dear, M. and Scott, A. J., eds., 1981, *Urbanization and Urban Planning in Capitalist Society*. London: Methuen.

Dziewoński, K. 1978. 'Analysis of settlement systems: The state of the art,' *Papers of the Regional Science Association*, 40: 39-52.

Dziewoński, K., ed. 1980. *National Settlement Systems*. 3 Vols. IGU Commission on National Settlement Systems, Polish Academy of Sciences, Warsaw.

Dziewoński, K. and Jerczynski, M. 1978. 'Theory, Methods of Analysis and Historical Development of National Settlement Systems', *Geographia Polonica*, 39: 201-9.

Glickman, N., ed. 1979. *The Urban Impacts of Federal Policies*. Baltimore: Johns Hopkins University Press.

Hall, P. and Hay, D. 1980. *Growth Centres in the European Urban System*. Berkeley: University of California Press.

Hansen, N., ed. 1978. *Human Settlement Systems: International Perspectives on Structure, Change and Public Policy*. Cambridge, Mass: Ballinger.

Illeris, S. 1980. 'Recent Developments of the Settlement Systems of Advanced Market Economy Countries', *Geografisk Tidsskrift*, 78: 49-56.

International Institute for Applied Systems Analysis (IIASA). 1982. *Migration and Settlement*, 3 Vols. Laxenburg, Austria: IIASA.

Johnston, R. J. 1982. *The American Urban System: A Geographical Perspective*. New York: St. Martins Press.

Jones, R., ed. 1975. *Essays on World Urbanization*. London: Philip and Son Ltd.

Kawashima, T. and Korcelli, P., eds. 1982. *Human Settlement Systems: Spatial Patterns and Trends*. Laxenburg, Austria: IIASA.

Klaassen, L. H., *et al.*, eds. 1981. *Dynamics of Urban Development*. London: Gower Publishing.

Korcelli, P. 1981. 'Migration and Urban Change', *WP-81-140*, International Institute for Applied Systems Analysis, Laxenburg, Austria.

Lonsdale, R. and Holmes, J., eds. 1981. *Settlement Systems in Sparsely-Populated Areas: The United States and Australia*. Oxford: Pergamon.

Musil, J. 1981. *Urbanization in Socialist Countries*. London: Croom Helm.

Pacione, M., ed. 1981a. *Urban Problems and Planning in the Developed World*. London: Croom Helm.

Pacione, M., ed. 1981b. *Problems and Planning in Third World Cities*. London: Croom Helm.

Rogers, A. and Williamson, J. G., eds. 1982. *Urbanization and Development in the Third World*. Laxenburg, Austria: IIASA.

Schmal, H., ed. 1981. *Patterns of European Urbanization Since 1500*. London: Croom Helm.

Simmons, J. W. and Bourne, L. S. 1981. 'Urban and Regional Systems - Qua Systems'. *Progress in Human Geography*, 5, 3: 420-31.

Simmons, J. W. and Bourne, L. S. 1982. 'Urban and Regional Systems and the State', *Progress in Human Geography*, 6, 3: 431-40.

Sinclair, R. 1982. 'Changing Spatial Trends at the National, Regional and Metropolitan Levels of the Settlement Systems of Developed Western Countries', *Geographia Polonica*, 48: forthcoming.

Van den Berg, L., *et al.*, eds. 1981. *Urban Europe: A Study of Growth and Decline.* Oxford: Pergamon.

Vining, D. R., Jr. 1982. 'Migration between the Core and the Periphery', *Scientific American*, 247, 6: 45-53.

Ward, B. 1976. *The Home of Man.* New York: Norton.

World Bank, 1981. *World Development Report, 1981.* New York: Oxford University Press.

PART A

SETTLEMENT SYSTEMS IN INDUSTRIAL MARKET ECONOMIES

Section 1: Settlement on New Lands and in Low-Density Regions

1 THE SETTLEMENT SYSTEM OF THE UNITED STATES

RICHARD L. MORRILL, ROBERT SINCLAIR AND DAVID R. DIMARTINO

Introduction

The United States is a large and populous nation, physically and culturally varied: its system of settlement reflects its size and complexity. What are the common images of American settlement?—there is the isolated homestead on the wind-swept plains; the skyscrapers and tenements of New York City; the repetitive uniformity of planned suburbs and trailer parks; the tiny Appalachian hamlet; the tidy and closely spaced villages of the Midwest; and the scenic villages tucked away into New England's mountain valleys.

The settlement system constitutes the places where people live, work, and play. It represents most of the 'built environment'—the imprint of society on the physical landscape. It is the architectural manifestation—in factories, houses, and roads—of the countless location decisions of millions of persons over hundreds of years. It reflects in part the pursuit of the same economic goals—the maximization of the utility of land and the maximization of interaction at least effort—which underlie the location theories of geography; but it reflects as well the perceptions and values of different groups of people at different times.

The Context of Settlement

The settling of America took place within an atmosphere of economic and social liberalism, of relatively unrestrained individualism, of the perception of vast amounts of land and resources, and of the expectation of continuous growth. The government played a role, through the Homestead Act, subsidies to the transcontinental railroads and the like. But compared to many countries, the majority of decisions governing the location, nature, and size of settlements have been individual and private.

The effects of individualism and the lack of centralized control on settlement are pervasive. There is the very privatism of the isolated homestead, a turning away from the idea of the close-knit villages that characterize most of the world. And, in a sense, there is the extension of that idea in the suburbs of low-density, single-family homes that so distinguish American from other cities. There is also the company town, and the hundreds of settlements of as many religious sects, seeking isolation. There is, again in contrast to many countries, the rapid obsolescence in housing, and its replacement. Less obvious, but more critical, there is the high rate of mobility of so much of the population that settlements indeed become temporary abodes, rather than communities. There is the emphasis on private modes of transport, and its manifestation in low densities and in the richness of the road network. There is the mixture of uses, in particular the phenomenon of 'sprawl', the interspersion of idle land, farmland, subdivisions and houses, and the massive dispersion of small businesses along the highways and arterial roads.

The presence of land, resources, and opportunities also was real. There is no question that the relatively high ratio of land to people, even now, and its relatively low cost and ease of transferability, did and still does make possible the isolated homestead, the religious colony, and the extensive suburb of single-family homes.

Finally, there is cultural diversity—race, national origin, religion—that is evidenced in the pattern and nature of settlement. This is the result of a liberal immigration policy, even though that policy might have been based as much upon the need for labour to settle and develop a new land, as upon a true welcoming of diversity.

Settlement Units: Definitions and Data

American settlements generally are perceived as places, rather than as areas or units of government as is common in many nations. The village is an agglomeration of people, not a land division. There is no historically 'ingrained' administrative building block like the 'Commune' or the 'Gemeinde'. Settlement units are underlain by, but do not correspond with the basic system of non-incorporated local administration—the county and township.[1] A partial exception is the New England town or Middle Atlantic borough, but these are perceived as governments, not as settlements.

Data on settlements are drawn primarily from the official Censuses of Population, Agriculture, Wholesale and Retail Trade, Government and Selected Services, Manufacturing, and Transportation. Some suppplementary data are generated by local governments or private firms, particularly in the form of city directories. In addition to the decennial population census, population estimates are made annually for at least the larger places. The dates of the censuses differ, but this does not cause too much difficulty.

The population census publishes limited data (number, age, sex, race) for all levels of legally incorporated places, no matter how small, but only for unincorporated places over 1000 (and only if states have defined them— many have not). Because some states encourage or require incorporation of

---

[1] This local administrative system is more limited in function than in most other countries. The county (parish in Louisiana, borough in Alaska) normally has limited functions, including roads, policing (sheriffs), public health, courts, and some zoning. The township has even more restricted powers, mainly concerning schools. In New England and New Jersey, and to a more limited degree New York and Pennsylvania, the relative importance of the two units is reversed, with the 'town' exercising more powers than the county.

almost all agglomerations, while in other states there are advantages in not incorporating, comparability at the level of the small settlement is poor. The variety of other data (social, economic, financial, political, etc.) is limited for places under 2500, and becomes richer and more refined as governmental units become larger. It is greatest for metropolitan areas with more than 250,000 people.

As in most countries there is only a partial correspondence between the legal entity (village, town and city) and the physical agglomeration of people. The small unincorporated place defined by the Census is closest to the actual agglomeration. An incorporated place variously includes rural territory around it (more common in the South than in the North) or excludes part of the urban settlement around fast growing places. Only around places of 50,000 or more has the Census Bureau endeavoured to define the actual agglomeration,—the 'urbanized areas'. However, many agglomerations over 50,000 have yet to be so defined.

Evolution of Settlement

The evolution of the US settlement system is, compared to most countries, of relatively recent origin. Understanding the *act* of settlement is therefore, in the United States, essential in understanding settlement structure and pattern.

While the native American population was of great significance, it had limited influence upon subsequent European settlement, in part because much of it was non-urban, and in part because the population was largely decimated by European-brought disease (up to 80 per cent of the population). Early European settlement was governed by the pattern of claims and land grants: the Spanish penetrated into Florida and the Southwest; the French into the Great Lakes Region and Louisiana; the British (and others) along most of the Atlantic seaboard. The Atlantic coastal plains filled gradually (1607-1790): in the South a dispersed settlement characterized by a plantation economy dependent on slavery, with a few mercantile–administrative ports (Savannah, Charleston, Norfolk, etc.); in the North a dispersed and village pattern of independent farmers, port towns (Philadelphia, New York, Boston, New Haven), and (in New England) fishing ports (Figure 1.1). Many of those earliest and most easterly ports remain among the top US metropolises over 350 years, and the settlement of a continent, later: New York (Rank 1), Philadelphia (4), Boston (7) and Baltimore (15).

The pace of immigration, the demand for land, and the need for a new nation to settle its newly acquired territory led to a fairly rapid settlement of the territory between the Appalachians and the Mississippi (1787-1820). In the North, settlement was controlled by the Northwest Ordinance of 1787, establishing the basic orthogonal structure of township, range, mile-square section, and local township governance. With wheat production shifting west, the Ohio-Mississippi river ports of Cincinnati, Louisville

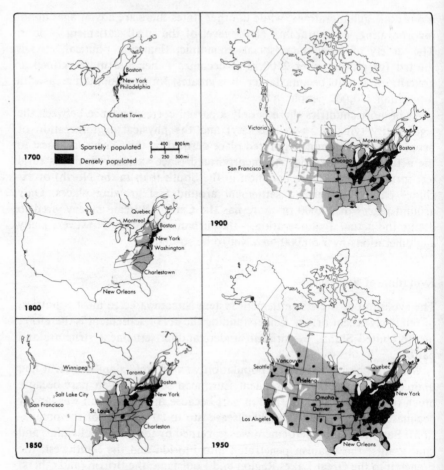

Fig. 1.1 Spread of Settlement, United States and Canada, 1700-1950
      Source: Thoman, Richard, *The United States and Canada*, Figure 1.2, p. 6.

and St. Louis came into prominence. In the South, the slavery-plantation system extended up from the Gulf Coast into Georgia, Alabama and Mississippi.[2] In the Northeast, small-scale industrialization was beginning, especially at locations of water power sites.

The Ante-Bellum period (1810-65) saw the opening of the Erie Canal to the 'West' in 1825, the rapid growth of Albany and Buffalo, and the coming to dominance of New York (although the rival cities of Baltimore and Philadelphia reacted by constructing additional canal systems). Settlement spread into northern Illinois, Wisconsin, and with the Louisiana purchase, across the Mississippi into Missouri and Arkansas, then into Iowa and Minnesota. Liberal land and immigration policies facilitated settlement. The development of the railways after 1840, reaching Chicago in 1852 and

[2] Tennessee, though a slave state, was settled more by independent farmers.

St. Louis in 1863, provided a great impetus to urban growth, agricultural exports, and industrialization, primarily in the North. By 1860 the South had fallen behind the North in wealth, industrial capacity and votes, in spite of the region's cotton-based prosperity. The North's superior power (and victory in the Civil War) resulted in long-term economic subservience of the South for at least sixty years. National imperialism extended US territory to the Pacific (Oregon, 1846), and the Southwest (Texas, 1845). California (1850), with the gold rush, became a new base of settlement.

The period from the Civil War to World War I (1865-1920) was one of growth, vast immigration and assimilation, built upon: (*a*) the continuous settlement of new land (The Homestead Act of 1863): (*b*) exploitation of the resources of the West, both made possible by (*c*) the transcontinental railways, whose construction had been aided by massive land grants; and (*d*) continuing rapid industrialization, especially in the northern core area. The railways (and in the big cities, streetcars) were the creators of and shapers of the settlement system, making possible unity and communication across a vast continent. The old river ports (Louisville, New Orleans, Cincinnati) declined, in part because of the eclipse of the South, but mainly because of the shift from steamboat to railroad. Places like St. Louis and Kansas City quickly made the transition to rail centres. This was the period of vast industrialization, built on coal and steel, furthered by massive immigration, not only from northern Europe (Irish, German, Scandinavian) but toward the end of the century from south and east Europe (Italian, Polish, Russian). While some immigrants moved directly to homesteads on the prairies (Kansas to the Dakotas), many more filled the North's industrial towns and created the nation's first real metropolises. By 1900 New York had 3.5 million people, Chicago 1.7, Philadelphia and Boston 1.3.

After World War I, the growing popularity of the automobile, the development of the highway system (1920s), and rural electrification improved the accessibility of the rural population, and the decline of smaller settlements began. More significant was the start of large-scale suburbanization in the metropolises. Labour unrest, unions, and restrictive laws in northern states started an industrial decentralization to the South, and a new urbanization (Virginia, Carolinas). The growth of the oil industry, though controlled by the North, brought urbanization and capital accumulation in the Southwest (Texas, Louisiana).

Although the Great Depression caused a temporary end to urbanization, a more important long-term influence was the policy of government intervention in agriculture, beginning with the rationalization of Southern agriculture (which had been a semi-feudal sharecropper system since 1865) and the displacement of surplus labour, especially Black sharecroppers. Later the government promoted the decentralization of industry (mainly aircraft) and defence activity during World War II, and thus helped the continuing westward movement and the rapid growth of California and the

West. Industrialization and urbanization began in the South in earnest, although until the 1960s the area's huge rural surplus still went North and West. By the 1960s the North's political and economic control of the nation was broken by the development of regional accumulations of capital (San Francisco, Los Angeles, Dallas, Houston, Atlanta, Miami), by population movements, and by a process of metropolitan and urban deterioration in the North (a complex consequence of social conflicts, suburban sprawl, obsolete plant and infrastructure, and labour productivity problems).

Structure of American Settlement

The Number of and Regional Variation of Settlements

It would be desirable to state how many settlements there are of various sizes, but owing to data limitations, this is not easily done. Table 1.1 provides estimates of the number of agglomerations—that is, distinct urban clusters irrespective of how many incorporated places may constitute them—and Table 1.2, the number of legally defined separate places, classified by major regions.

The most striking contrast is that, whereas a high proportion of the population resides in the rather few largest settlements (74 per cent in 314 metropolitan areas in 1980), there are still a large number of smaller settlements. There is a tendency for a doubling of the number of agglomerations as the size class drops 2 to 2.5 times, even though population aggregates are top-heavy in the larger size classes (reflecting the fact that the larger the place, the less dependent it is upon the population in the immediate rural hinterland).

Regional variation by size of urban place is pronounced, although there is a trend to convergence. The Midwest and South[3] have a larger number of settlements, particularly smaller settlements, and a higher proportion of total population in these settlements—from small urbanized areas to towns, villages and hamlets. The Northeast and West have a more clustered population, with higher proportions of people in metropolises, especially those over one million. Despite having the highest rate of growth, the South still lags in 'millionaire' population (with an 18 per cent share compared to the Northeast's 54 per cent), but has by far the highest proportion of its population in smaller metropolitan areas. The South also has by far the

[3] The terms 'West', 'South', 'Northeast' etc. are utilized throughout this paper, although the authors are aware that they are familiar terms, whose definition is subject to considerable controversy. The general scope of these areas, however, is approximated in the official census Regions used in Table 2: (1) the West Region, comprising the vast Rocky Mountain and Pacific Coast divisions, (2) the South Region, comprising the equally vast South Atlantic, E. South Central, and W. South Central Divisions, (3) the Northeast Region, including New England and the Middle Atlantic states of New York, Pennsylvania and New Jersey, and (4) the North-central Region, including the E. North Central (Gt. Lakes) and W. North Central (Gt. Plains, 'Middle West') Divisions.

Table 1.1: *Number of Settlements or Agglomerations (1980)*

Size Class	Number of Settlements	Population	% of US Population	Metropolitan Areas Number	Metropolitan Areas Population	Metropolitan Areas % of US Population
In Urbanized Areas						
Over 10,000,000	1	15,590,000	6.9	1	16 million	7.1
5-10,000,000	2	16,259,000	7.2	3	20	8.8
2,400,000-5,000,000	7	21,418,000	9.5	8	25	11.1
1-2,400,000	19	26,821,000	11.8	23	35	15.5
500,000-1,000,000	23	15,597,000	6.9	40	26	11.5
250,000-500,000	47	16,202,000	7.2	72	24	10.6
100,000-250,000	110	16,339,000	7.2	139	20	8.8
50,000-100,000	160	10,956,000	4.8	28	2.4	1.1
All Urbanized Areas	369	139,182,000	61.4	314	168	74.0
Other Urban Areas						
25,000-50,000	118[a]	3,784,000	1.7			
10,000-25,000	641	9,699,000	4.3			
5,000-10,000	1071	7,438,000	3.3			
2,500-5,000	1992	6,852,000	3.0			
ALL URBAN	4191	166,955,000	73.7			

Rural Places
Settlements and population according to census statistics

1,000-2,500	4430[b]	7,021,000	3.1			
500-1,000						
200- 500 }	9356[c]	3,901,000	1.7			
Under 200						
Isolated rural		48,617,000	21.5			

Estimated actual numbers of rural settlements[d]

1,000-2,500	5000	7,500,000	3.3			
500-1,000	5000	3,500,000	1.5			
200- 500	10000	3,500,000	1.5			
Under 200	30,000	3,000,000	1.3			
Rural dwellings	14,000,000[e]	42,000,000	18.5			

a Probably actually higher (200?), since only agglomerations over 50,000 have been measured by the census bureau.
b Includes some but not all unincorporated places over 1000.
c Incorporated places only.
d Estimates by the author (Morrill) by extrapolation from states which incorporate most places.
e At least half are rural non-farm families within metropolitan areas.
Source: US Bureau of the Census, 1980

largest number of metropolitan areas, 108 of the nation's 284 (1980). Like the South, the Northcentral region historically has had a more even size distribution and also a lower level of metropolitan, especially large-metropolitan, population than the Northeast or West.

Nevertheless convergence is taking place. The rural-non-farm population is growing more in the Northeast and West than in the South and Midwest. The South is the region of most active metropolis formation, and the South and West are the only regions in which the large metropolitan areas are still expanding vigorously. The convergence is illustrated in overall urbanization figures. Whereas the South has lagged markedly in urbanization in the past, reaching only 49 per cent urban and only 28 per cent 'metropolitan' (urban agglomerations over 50,000) in 1950, compared to the Northeast's 79 per

Table 1.2: *Number of Places by Region, 1980*
(Within or Without Agglomerations)

Places		Northeast	North Central	South	West
(Urban)	Over 100,000	23	39	63	48
	50,000-100,000	75	76	60	79
	25,000-50,000	152	179	181	163
	10,000-25,000	374	479	599	313
	5,000-10,000	524	536	764	357
	2,500-5,000	518	752	1,003	392
	Less than 2,500	257	277	410	72
(Rural)	1,000-2,500	804	1,498	1,560	572
	Less than 1,000	551	4,861	2,866	1,052
	Less than 1,000 (Est.)*	5,000	15,000	20,000	5,000

* Estimates by author (Morrill) by extrapolation from states which incorporate most places.
Source: US Bureau of the Census, Census of Population, 1980

cent and 66 per cent respectively, the South's urban population in the last 28 years has more than doubled and its metropolitan population almost tripled, reaching 67 per cent urban (1980) and 62 per cent metropolitan (1980) (i.e. approaching the levels in the North Central region). The West has doubled in population, and its urban and metropolitan population more than tripled in the same period.

Regional Variation in Stages of Urbanization

The large area and population of the United States have favoured a relatively complete or full size distribution of places from New York to the millions of isolated homes, without the primacy found in so many smaller nations. Although there is a strong trend toward convergence, not all regions are at the same level of development.

Older industrialized regions like the Northeast and California, have perhaps passed their peak level of urbanization (about 85 per cent), and exhibit a 'top-heavy' size distribution. They show a higher-than-average proportion of people in the largest metropolises, and signs of a post-industrial way of life, in the sense of individual abandonment of the 'city' in favour of a return to the 'country'. Other regions, like the Midwest (Western Great Lakes) or the Pacific Northwest are perhaps nearing their peak level of urbanization (about 65-75 per cent), and exhibit a more average size distribution. The South, on the other hand, is in the process of rapid industrialization and urbanization and the population is still, if only for a while, less metropolitan than average.

These 'stages of development' are reflected in the spatial patterns discussed previously. The Northeast and West show a more clustered settlement pattern than the Midwest and South. However, it must be recognized that these variations in spatial pattern also are influenced by environmental conditions (the limited availability of water and/or flat land) and legal specifications (the Northwest Ordinance and subsequent laws governing land disbursement west of the Appalachians tended to impose a greater regularity and dispersal on the landscape).

Figure 1.2 illustrates some typical patterns of settlement: even in the Midwest; more irregular in the East; and clustered in the West.

Functional Variation in United States Settlement.

In a highly developed economy within a physically diverse environment, one expects and finds high levels of functional specialization among places. While the images might not be completely accurate or up-to-date, the public's wide awareness of Detroit as the automobile capital, of Pittsburgh's role in steel, of Butte's in mining, or Las Vegas's in tourism, reveals how vital the economic role of places truly is. The broad functional variation among American cities is attested by the numerous city functional classifications found in the geographic and social science literature (for example: Alexandersson 1956, Berry 1972, Harris 1943, Nelson 1955), and the widespread availability of such studies make it unnecessary to provide such a classification here. However, a few brief comments might be made.

The public may not know the term 'central place', but few would be surprised to discover that by far the largest number of settlements, including most smaller ones (hamlets, villages and towns), exist mainly as service centres for a piece of countryside. Perhaps two-thirds of the national product is, in fact, generated by such central place activities. Although the activities are ubiquitous, the distribution of settlements that are primarily central places is skewed to the Midwest, West, and South—that is, the more sparsely populated and agricultural parts of the nation. In these regions are found true 'regional capitals'—for example Atlanta, Portland, Denver. But perhaps the prototypical American central place is the Midwestern 'town'.

Primarily industrial settlements probably are less prevalent in the United States than in much of Europe and a good proportion of US manufacturing take place in large metropolises with a diverse economic base. Still, there are some thousands of places, from tiny mining hamlets and mill towns to several large metropolises of the Northeast, which are industrial in character. Whereas systems of central places tend toward some regularity or evenness in spacing, industrial and mining settlements tend toward a more clustered or linear pattern, reflecting concentrations of present or past resources and transport arteries.

Governmental activity is relatively decentralized within the American federal system, and public administration is part of the bundle of services in most central places. Nevertheless, as a reflection of the early predisposition to avoid the concentration of economic and political power typified by London and Paris, it was the rule in America to remove the administrative centre from the economic—hence the many small state capitals (e.g., Dover, Delaware rather than Wilmington; Olympia, Wa. rather than Seattle). Washington, DC versus New York is probably the extreme example of this

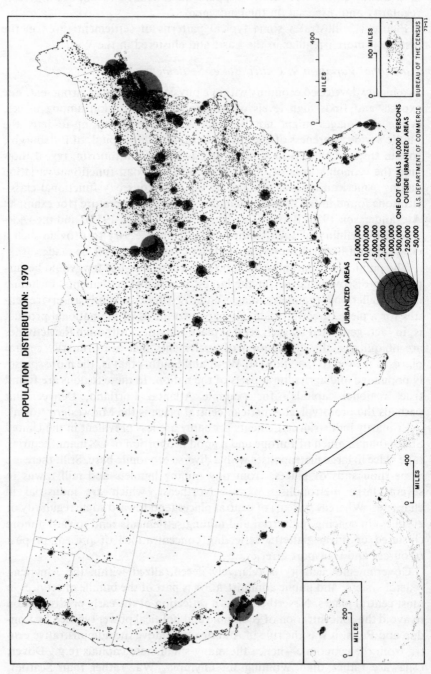

POPULATION DISTRIBUTION: 1970

URBANIZED AREAS

15,000,000
10,000,000
5,000,000
2,500,000
1,000,000
500,000
250,000
50,000

ONE DOT EQUALS 10,000 PERSONS
OUTSIDE URBANIZED AREAS

U.S. DEPARTMENT OF COMMERCE

BUREAU OF THE CENSUS

MILES
0   400

100 MILES
0

200 MILES
0

400 MILES
0

Fig. 1.2   United States Population Distribution, 1970.   Source: US Department of Commerce, Bureau of the Census

separation of functions, but Washington's recent stupendous growth attests to the increasing power of the national government in the American system.

As might be expected, retail trade and specialized services tend to reflect metropolitan populations, and their relative concentration in the largest places is not surprising. Nevertheless, the United States urban system is replete with examples of smaller centres, which have developed exceptional specialized services—for example, Hartford, Connecticut, and Des Moines, Iowa (finance and insurance), Champaign, Urbana, and New Haven, Connecticut (Education), Las Vegas, Nevada, and Orlando, Florida (tourism), Huntsville, Alabama and Norfolk, Virginia (Federal Government), and Charlotte, N. Carolina and Savannah, Georgia (transportation).

Hierarchy of Settlement

The American economy is both highly developed and rather fully integrated—that is with the majority of consumer goods advertised and distributed nationally. The hierarchy of places, from the isolated tavern, drive-in, and service station along the highway, through the village, town, and small city retail centre, to the city, and metropolitan wholesale and retail centre, is well-ordered into eight reasonably distinct levels, culminating in the overwhelmingly dominant financial capital, New York. The major metropolitan areas, perhaps 29 in number, together containing 50 million or 25 per cent of the population of the US, strongly dominate the nation, culturally as well as economically, not only through their control of finance and investment, but through their superior transport services, television, and communications.

Figure 1.3 depicts the basic size structure of metropolitan areas in the United States (less completely shown in the dense Northeast). Because of changes over time, competition among cities, and other factors, the hierarchy is not as clear as it might be. The top is clear—and incomplete. New York (level 8) is pre-eminent, and Chicago and Los Angeles (level 7+) dominate the Midwest and West respectively. For a variety of historic reasons, the South has not yet evolved an equivalent: New Orleans was once dominant, but lost out to a set of rivals. Another level (7-), (San Francisco, Boston, Detroit, Dallas-Fort Worth, Atlanta and Philadelphia), partially intervenes before the basic set of regional metropolises (level 6) of the 1-2,000,000 scale. Each was truncated in potential dominance by growth of a rival.

The set of 20 places at the regional metropolis level (level 6) includes: 6 of a higher importance—Minneapolis, Cleveland, St. Louis, Baltimore-Washington, Houston and Miami; 9 of intermediate importance—Seattle, Portland, Denver, Kansas City, Cincinnati, Tampa, New Orleans, and Pittsburgh; and 6 of lesser rank—Phoenix, Salt Lake City, Milwaukee, Charlotte, San Diego and Buffalo.

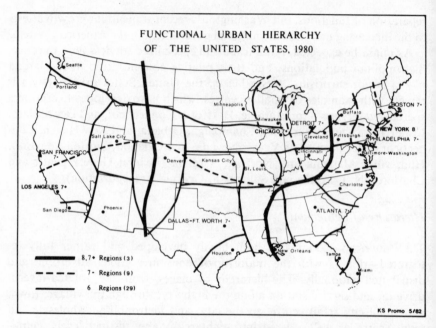

Fig. 1.3   Functional Urban Hierarchy of the United States, 1980

Together, these 29 metropolises comprise the dominant wholesaling, financial, and communication centres of the nation.

At the fifth level are small to medium-sized metropolitan areas, which serve either fairly small hinterlands or are in regions which are sparsely populated (e.g. the mountain West) or less urbanized (parts of the South). It is of interest that the South, which has no single dominant metropolis, has more medium-sized ones, some of which may well move to higher levels in the future.

The functional administrative hierarchy is notably independent of the economic hierarchy. While it is true that places like Boston, Little Rock, Phoenix, and Salt Lake City are the hub of economic and political regions, and that hundreds of county seats are also the economic centres of areas, the system of metropolitan and submetropolitan economic regions commonly violates political (state) boundaries. In such cases, differing state laws and interests complicate dealing with metropolitan-wide problems such as pollution control and transportation. Serious conflicts have developed, leading to efforts to create administrative units capable of approaching the problems of real economic-functional regions.

Social Variation of American Settlements

The United States is a pluralistic society: a nation of diverse racial, ethnic, and religious origins. The 'melting pot' image of American Society (by which each new group is said to assimilate into a homogeneous mixture of values and lifestyles) can be misleading. A more accurate view is that of a social mixture of distinct subgroups which interact, but maintain their own character while contributing to the sum of 'American' society.

That society includes peoples from all parts of the world. All Americans (except for native-Americans—Indians, Eskimos, and Hawaiians) were members of newly arrived immigrant groups at one time or another. All groups found themselves culturally distinct from the mainstream of American society at their time of arrival. Typically the larger, less Anglicized, and less prosperous the entering group, the more threatened the acculturated majority have felt about the possible introduction of new and different values and lifestyles. Generally, newcomers have taken up residence in separate parts of the nation and/or in spatially separate districts within its urban centres.

Euro-American ethnic groups, though culturally and spatially distinct at their time of arrival, have assimilated more readily and rapidly. An acculturation period of one or two generations seems all that was necessary for these immigrants to adopt English as their primary language and to adopt the culture of the majority.

And yet, regional and intra-urban variations in ethnic identities have persisted in the US. Many locations bear the imprint of their European settlers as seen by local customs, place-names, and somewhat distinct landscapes. The colonial period yielded the heritages of the English in New England, the Dutch and German in the Middle Atlantic States, the French in Louisiana, and the Spanish in Florida and the Southwest. The waves of so-called 'Old' Immigrants, who arrived in the nation from northwest Europe before 1880, have also left their ethnic mark. They include the Germans throughout the Midwest, the German Amish and Mennonites of Pennsylvania and Ohio, the Scandinavians of the Western Great Lakes, and the Mormons of the Inter-mountain Basins.

The imprint of immigrant groups shifted from the agricultural interior to the urban centres of the Northeast and Midwest when the so-called 'New' Immigrants entered America from southern and eastern Europe after 1880. American cities, the destination for most New Immigrants, became regionalized into a multitude of distinct ethnic enclaves, often referred to as the 'Little Italys', the 'Poletowns' etc. From these enclaves most Euro-Americans have assimilated into the middle-class, predominantly suburban society of contemporary America. As for the old ethnic neighbourhoods of the central cities, some have been preserved or restored, but many have been occupied and altered by more recent entrants, or by urban renewal policies.

The segregation of non-European groups (both racially and culturally) has been more prolonged and acute. Native-Americans, Asian-Americans, and Afro-Americans have maintained their sub-cultural identities partly because of their social and spatial separation from the rest of American society.

Most native-American groups (1,420,000 persons in 1980) were ultimately separated from the mainstream of American society through the institution of 'reservations' (separate, legally-delimited residential territories). Although a number of reservations have yielded relative security for their residents through the development of important resources, many more have offered their inhabitants only an isolated, disenfranchised and poverty-stricken existence. Native-Americans constitute a locally-significant segment of the population in some regions (particularly those proximate to reservations), such as Maine, Florida, the Dakotas, and the Southwest.

The expanding Asian-American population (reaching over 3,500,000 in 1980) is heavily concentrated in Hawaii, in West Coast cities, and in certain Eastern cities, particularly New York. Japanese are relatively concentrated in Los Angeles and Seattle, Koreans in Los Angeles, Chinese in San Francisco, Portland, and New York, whereas the recently-arrived Vietnamese appear to be congregating in the Gulf Coast and Southern California. Hawaii is unique in having a majority of oriental population. Indeed, Honolulu and many other Hawaiian towns and villages have a Japanese majority.

The most dominant of recent minority groups entering the US has been the complex Latin American group, comprising over 14,600,000 people (6.4 per cent of the US population) in 1980. This group includes: Puerto Ricans, found largely within the East Coast cities (particularly New York); Cubans, predominantly in Florida (especially Miami); Mexican Americans (Chicanos), located mostly in the Southwest but increasingly in other regions; and a mounting number from other Central and South American countries. Many have become segregated into their own urban ghettoes (called *'barrios'* by the Chicanos), and often are more socially, economically and spatially separated than many Afro-Americans.

The largest non-European minority group is the Afro-American, numbering 26,500,000 (11.6 per cent of the US population) in 1980. Blacks are more concentrated in the (formerly plantation) South than in any other region, constituting 18.6 per cent of the Southern population in 1980 and making up the majority of the population in some Southern counties. However, beginning in the Civil War period, and reaching its zenith in the post World War II period, there was a regional migration to Northern and Western cities, which transformed the distribution of the black population. Some Northern cities have black majorities, and the central city 'ghetto' has become a characteristic feature of many Northern and Western cities. In the late 1970s, there was some indication that the northerly migration of blacks had dried up, and indeed, reversed itself.

In absolute numbers the metropolitan areas of New York, Chicago, Philadelphia, Los Angeles, Detroit, Cleveland, St. Louis, Washington, Baltimore, Atlanta, and Houston are most significant. In relative terms, some cities (Detroit, Washington, Atlanta, Gary, Newark, as examples) have black majorities, although no large metropolitan area (census SMSA) has a black majority. There are many small, all-black settlements, particularly in the South.

Although the majority of immigrants into the United States over the last 200 years has had a native tongue other than English, the entrenched power of English has overcome most efforts of ethnic groups to maintain their languages, and has overwhelmed those areas (French Louisiana, Spanish Florida, the Spanish Southwest), where other languages formerly held sway. Today, Spanish is the only significant rival to English, due mainly to the recent large-scale immigration of Latin-American peoples.

Dynamics of the American Settlement System

The United States has no comprehensive national settlement policy either directed or co-ordinated by the national government. Rather, the varied settlement patterns and growth trends have evolved out of the sum total of individual, group and corporate decision-making. The result has been a markedly uneven national development surface.

The growth of the United States settlement system has resulted, in large part, from massive population movements throughout its history. The quest for improved 'well-being' has been the dominant motive for both the influx of large numbers of immigrants and the inter-regional flow of population. Those inter-regional migrations include the historically dominant Westward and rural-urban flows, the more contemporary movements to Northeast and Midwest cities (particularly by Southern Blacks) and to the Southwest (particularly by white Northeasterners) and, most recently, the migration to the so-called 'Sunbelt' (the Southeast and the Southwest), and to 'nonmetropolitan' areas.

Regional Development Trends

The current structure of the American settlement system arose out of the industrial revolution. Industrialization was the catalyst for massive inter-regional population shifts. The mechanization of agriculture created a surplus population in the rural districts of the nation which led to the movement of rural people to urban locations in pursuit of jobs. The same industrialization fostered the concentration of economic activities within urban areas as the result of corporate savings accrued through economies of scale. The net result has been a settlement system with extreme urban agglomeration within specific regions. The Northeast region remains the most urban and industrial. Established as the original industrial 'core' of the nation, historical and institutional inertia have assured its continued pre-eminence. The region has expanded out of its original Eastern Megalopolitan corridor to include a large portion of the eastern Midwest (the southern Great Lakes) region. Though no longer the only well-developed region, it remains an area of concentrated wealth.

The growth of metropolitan centres outside the Northeastern core has accelerated since the midpoint of this century: in the Southwest, the Piedmont South, the Gulf Coast and Florida. That growth may be attributed to the growth or relocation of industries into formerly non-industrial areas (such as the Piedmont South), to the infusion of federal funds (such as the establishment of the aerospace industry in California, Arizona, and Florida), and to the development of regionally important resources (such as the petrochemical industry in Texas and along the Gulf Coast).

The most significant of the recent regional development trends is within the historically disadvantaged and non-metropolitan Southeast. That trend, begun in the early part of this century, accelerated during the 1970s. The recent growth of the South has been attributed partly to the relocation of industry from the North in pursuit of relatively less-costly land, labour, and capital, but other reasons include: an improved connectivity to other regions afforded by the interstate highway network, established since the 1950s and 1960s; the reversal of Afro-American migration patterns, formerly to the North but more recently to the South; federal investments in defence establishments; and the search for 'amenities' by the middle-class and retired elderly.

Urban Development Trends

Economic activities have been concentrated, traditionally, within the urban centres of each of the regions. However, the spatial structure and developmental patterns within each urban centre have become increasingly complex. The trend toward decentralization, which characterizes most American cities today, is not new. Since the turn of the century, urban populations have been moving away from their urban centres. The movement progressed slowly at first, the result of the availability of commuter rail lines, then accelerated with the increased use of the automobile. Likewise, economic activities have been decentralizing for decades, in response to shifting labour supplies, markets, and operating costs. What is new about the current urban decentralization process is its scale. Decentralization has progressed to the point where our largest metropolitan centres now extend well beyond an eighty-kilometre radius from their central cities.

Closely related to the decentralization trend is the more recent trend toward non-metropolitan growth (demetropolitanization). During the 1970s, non-metropolitan counties in the US increased their population by 15 per cent, a rate of growth much greater than that for metropolitan counties (10 per cent). These growth rates represent a reversal of previous trends, but the reversal was foreshadowed before 1970. Analysis of the period 1940 to 1970 demonstrates: that non-metropolitan growth, though less than metropolitan growth, was on the increase; that the positive relationship between initial size of a place and its rate of growth was decreasing in importance; that urban places within SMSAs, but outside urbanized areas, grew more than those within the urbanized areas; and that non-metropolitan counties proximate to metropolitan counties exhibited the greatest rates of non-metropolitan growth.

During the 1970s the trend toward non-metropolitan growth has accelerated (Figure 1.4). In the Northeast-East–North-Central region, non-metropolitan areas grew by 12 per cent while metropolitan territories lost population. Non-metropolitan growth was also faster than metropolitan growth in the Pacific Coast states (33 to 18 per cent). Moreover, for the nation as a whole, non-metropolitan counties with lower population densities grew more than those with higher densities. And, while non-metropolitan counties adjacent to metropolitan counties continue to exhibit the greatest non-metropolitan growth rates (21 per cent), the difference between those and non-adjacent counties (15 per cent growth) is decreasing.

In absolute terms, however, it should be noted that total metropolitan growth in the 1970s (15,000,000) still exceeded non-metropolitan growth (8,300,000). Metropolitan areas still grew more rapidly than non-metropolitan in the W. North-Central states, the South (26 compared to 16 per cent) and in the Mountain states. Indeed, the metropolitan growth of the South, 8,500,000, was over one-third of the nation's total growth of 23,200,000.

The decentralizing and demetropolitanizing trends are, thus, two sides of the same coin. For example, many of the largest metropolitan centres (those with populations in excess of three million) exhibited negative growth rates in the 1970s, especially in the Northeast. However, other metropolitan centres (with populations of 1 to 3 million) have continued to grow, though slowly. Still other metropolises (with populations of less than 1 million) are growing more rapidly than before 1970, particularly in the South and West. It seems clear that what has been labelled by some as 'metropolitan decline' is actually a continuation of metropolitanization at a new scale, so that formerly non-metropolitan counties are experiencing a growth generated in and spilling over from metropolitan counties. In view of these trends, it is appropriate to look at the US metropolis in more detail.

The Nature of Metropolitan Settlement

The most striking aspect of US metropolitan structure is the lack of containment. Urban expansion is a worldwide phenomenon, but in many countries (whether for historical, technological, land resource, aesthetic, or preference reasons), society accepts the idea that urban spatial growth should be contained, or at least planned or regulated. Such an acceptance has hardly affected the form of US cities. Here cities have spread in accordance with the whims of individuals and institutions, and with the transport technology available at any particular period. As a result, American cities encompass large amounts of space, have low densities, have large percen-

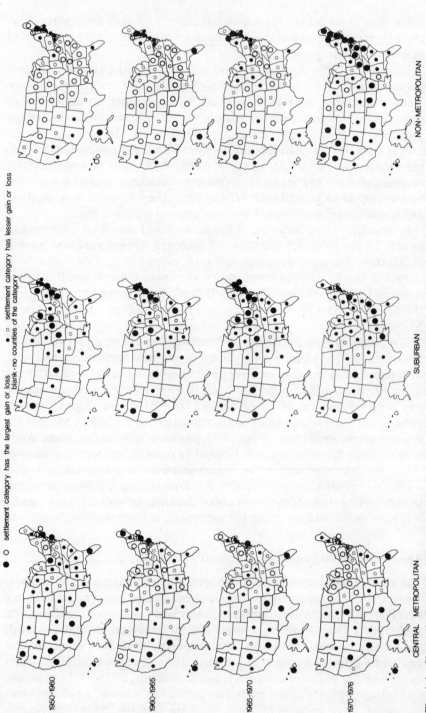

Fig. 1.4   Change in Patterns of In- and Out-Migration in Central Metropolitan, Surburban, and Non-Metropolitan Counties, 1950–76

tages of space devoted to vehicular use, have extensive stretches of unused land, and often show little or no spatial planning. Under such conditions, distinguishing between urban and rural is more difficult than in most other countries.

The spread of US urban agglomerations also has little relationship to political boundaries. American cities tend to be either 'overbounded' or 'underbounded'. The former, found mainly in the West and Southwest (e.g. Oklahoma City), have political boundaries extending well beyond the built-up area. More prevalent are the 'underbounded' cities, where the agglomeration extends well beyond the political limits of the core city. The key to understanding American metropolitan political structure is the incorporated suburb. Although incorporation laws vary from state to state, the rights and powers of the incorporated suburb are universally great and jealously guarded. Those powers include the ability to determine land use, and indirectly the nature of the inhabitants. More important, they include the primary claim to the tax base of individuals and enterprises within their boundaries. This has given rise to the well-known 'Central City-Suburban' dichotomy, to the presence in most metropolitan areas of hundreds of independent jurisdictions (Chicago has 1,214; Philadelphia, 864; and Pittsburgh, 744), and to the overlapping and duplication pattern of decision-making which has prevented an adequate response to metropolitan-wide problems. Although new units constantly are being formed, existing ones tend to become permanent.

The inertia of the urban political net contrasts vividly with the dynamism of the social drama occurring upon and through that net. It is well known that almost 25 per cent of Americans change residence every year and that most of these shifts take place within metropolitan areas. 'Intra-urban migration' is not restricted to individuals. It encompasses the movement of institutions, businesses, industries, and entire social groups. As with most migrations, intra-urban movement is a sifting process. It is the more active, mobile, wealthy, and younger individuals, and the stronger, larger, and more successful businesses which move to what at any time appear to be the more attractive parts of the metropolitan area. Thus a self-perpetuating social and economic differentiation takes place. Because most migration has been in an outward direction, relinquished areas are predominantly in the older central cities. The nature of the political structure means that migrating persons and institutions normally are relieved of the financial responsibility for the upkeep of the areas which they relinquish. The results of this process (e.g. neighbourhood change, property abandonment and instability) are all too apparent on the US metropolitan landscape. The dichotomy between an inert political structure and a dynamic urban society is the source of many of America's urban problems.

Metropolitan Structure

Despite their present polynucleated character, most US metropolitan areas developed around and from a central nucleus. Thus, metropolitan structure can be approached from an historical viewpoint. The form of US cities reflects a series of stages in the development of transport technology. During each of these stages, land use was largely determined by the ability of different uses to pay for desirable (normally accessible) locations. These stages include (1) the 'walking-horse car' stage, lasting till about 1880, (2) the 'streetcar' stage lasting into the 1920s, (3) the 'automobile' stage, from the 1920s to World War II, and (4) the 'expressway' stage, initiated during World War II and continuing at an accelerating pace ever since (Adams, 1970).

Viewing the American metropolis in terms of these four transport stages is helpful in understanding many aspects of urban structure. Each succeeding stage was characterized by greater mobility and decreasing densities. With this greater mobility, and with the passage of time, spatial differentiation has become more pronounced. The transport stage approach also explains many regional variations in the US urban system, because the importance of a particular stage (in influencing a city's structure) depends upon the age of the city. Thus, the characteristics of the pre- and early-streetcar stage are most pronounced in Eastern Seaboard cities. By contrast most Western cities, whose growth took place during the recreational automobile era, exhibit few of these earlier characteristics.

In terms of understanding present-day metropolitan structure, the change from the third stage (the pre-war auto stage) to the fourth (the post-war stage) is of the greatest importance. Essentially this marked the turning-point from city to suburban dominance, from the core-oriented metropolis to the decentralized metropolis of today.

The Core-Oriented Metropolis.   Few topics have received more attention from social scientists than the structure of the core-oriented US metropolis. Permeating virtually all studies are two spatial concepts, the concentric and the sectoral. The concentric concept reflects the fact that the metropolis grew from a central nucleus, so that districts (and their building stock) are progressively younger and less densely spaced with distance from the centre. Because age normally is inversely related to quality, housing quality and desirability improves with distance from the centre. The model has made it easy to conceptualize metropolitan social change as one of outward 'waves' of movement through the different concentric zones. With some significant variations, processes like neighbourhood succession, black ghetto expansion, the spread of blight, the pattern of housing abandonments, and even attempted remedies such as urban renewal and 'gentrification' can be fitted into the concentric idea.

The sectoral concept refers to the tendency for socio-economic and ethno-cultural groups, as well as certain economic activities, to be aligned in a series of pie-shaped wedges around the city centre. This pattern is derived from (*a*) the original establishment and subsequent consolidation of these groups on particular sides of the urban core, (*b*) the axial pattern of many physical lines and barriers (railroads, riverfronts, and traffic arteries), and (*c*) the outward 'directional bias' of intra-city movements and migrations. The sectoral pattern is extended well into the suburbs and indeed, into the metropolitan periphery.

Thus, two co-existent patterns are revealed in an examination of traditional metropolitan structure. Population and housing densities, house age and quality, family size and structure, and a variety of physical and social problems, vary in a concentric pattern outward from the city core, whereas socio-economic, ethno-cultural, and information-perception variables vary sectorally. The generalizations reflect the findings of most factorial ecology and social area analyses, and provide the bases of many models of urban structure. Superimposed upon this structure is the well-known pattern of commercial activities of the American metropolis, comprising the central business district, outlying business districts, neighbourhood shopping streets, isolated store clusters, and different types of arterial ribbons.

The Decentralized Metropolis. Unlike the pre-war core-oriented metropolis, the remainder—the post-war decentralized metropolis—has been less frequently studied, and attempts to model its structure are virtually non-existent. In essence, no acceptable base (such as a historical core) exists upon which to formulate a model. The metropolitan resident of today orients himself toward one of a number of scattered nodes, each of which can be as important as the former central city. The formal pattern of the decentralized metropolis can at best be described as a mosaic. Its functional pattern conveniently can be called polynucleated.

The Mosaic Pattern. The extreme mobility of today's urban population has enabled all but the most disadvantaged groups to seek out, identify with and attach themselves to their preferred areas of metropolitan social space. For the metropolis as a whole, such social areas are found in bewildering variety. Differentiating such areas are not only the traditional factors of socio-economic and cultural-ethnic status, but also those of lifestyles and attitudes. It is possible to discern two general types of such development. The first is the well-established community. Often this community grew upon the nucleus of an early wealthy residential suburb, or a prosperous market centre. It has adapted to changing conditions, and consistently provides a successful mix of services and amenities. A similar development is one evolving around a successful, planned business centre, which later has grown into a well-balanced central place. These constitute the stable and viable parts of suburbia, and their viability tends to be cumulative. They continue to attract upper and middle income residents, as well as a large share of the metropolis's tertiary and quaternary activities.

The second type of suburban area is that which has succumbed to the unfettered, low-density sprawl of the post-war years. Generally no older suburbs existed to serve as nuclei for development. Often heavy industry, seeking cheap rural land, was the trigger for growth. Characteristically, landscape features were obliterated to create monotonous subdivisions. Services and amenities were not adequately provided, so that local shopping centres appear as peripheral afterthoughts rather than integrally planned units. The nature of these areas also becomes cumulative. They tend to attract the poorest housing development, the lower income residents, the less desirable industries, mixed land uses, and facilities which might not be tolerated in more stable parts of suburbia. These two contrasting types of development are spread across the vast extent of American suburbia.

The Polynucleated Functional Structure.   Superimposed upon the social mosaic is the functional structure of the decentralized metropolis. The most important focal points of this structure are the superregional business centres, which have exerted a gravitational pull upon a variety of activities, and have pre-empted all but a few of the functions of the former central business districts. Often originating as élite shopping malls, these centres have gathered offices, professional activities, corporate headquarters, hotels, and entertainment. They have become major centres of social life, and many have developed an out-of-town convention function. They are the new and scattered 'downtowns' of the decentralized metropolis.

The polynodal structure is tied together by freeways. They have become the corridors of economic activity. A traffic flow map of almost any large US metropolitan area emphasizes the multi-directional pattern of movement, and expresses the realities of present-day metropolitan spatial organization.

In summary, it is increasingly clear that today's US metropolitan resident no longer has strong ties (economic, social, or emotional) with any single metropolitan core. In many respects, his outlook is outward, toward the metropolitan periphery, or to some other coalescing metropolitan area. Ultimately it becomes an advantage to locate in the periphery, or in a metropolitan convergence zone. Today, this is an important trend in residential, industrial, and service location, and one of the potent forces shaping today's metropolis. The area between metropolises is often today's growth area. These changes appear to necessitate a redefinition of 'city' or even 'metropolis'. The term 'megalopolis' is an early attempt. Another alternative is the concept of 'urban field'. As yet, however, the political fragmentation of American metropolitan areas has prevented the pragmatic implementation of these conceptualizations.

External Links of the US Settlement System

The US settlement system has worldwide links, reflecting the country's prominent role in the political, economic, military, and cultural affairs of the world during the last three decades. The business, financial, communications, and international (e.g. United Nations) linkages of New York, and the political linkages of Washington clearly place those two cities near the top of the world settlement hierarchy. However, international linkages are not all hierarchical. They also include the far-flung connections of such places as Detroit, an administrative centre of the world auto industry, Boise, Idaho, a headquarters of multinational business corporations, and Lafayette, Louisiana, a 'nerve centre' of the world offshore oil industry. There is no way adequately to measure the extent and configuration of such linkages, although they are perhaps partially revealed in world patterns of airline flows.

There is another more direct kind of international linkage, reflecting the country's position on the North American continent. Clearly the US settlement system extends across its borders, especially into Canada. The long and essential openness of the border, the unimpeded sweep of the plain, the concentration of settlement and exchange throughout the Great Lakes area, the similarity of people, values and life-styles, and (with the exception of the Quebec portion of the border) a common language, have all tended to create a single US-Canadian settlement system. The extension of Spokane's influence into British Columbia; Calgary's into Montana; Winnipeg's into North Dakota and Minnesota; and Montreal and Sherbrooke's into upper New York state and New England are evidence of the continuity of the system.

Relative sparsity of settlement, a language barrier, and greater cultural differences have resulted in lower levels of interaction and investment across the Mexican border. However, along that border are several large twin places which exist *because* of the border, primarily to regulate exchange of labour, or to use labour under provision of special laws (border industries with low-wage labour): Tijuana (San Diego): Mexicali (Calexico); Nogales (Nogales); Cuidad Juarez (El Paso); Piedras Negras (Eagle Pass); Nuevo Laredo (Laredo), and Matamoros (Brownsville).

Future Structure and Patterns of Settlement

Our inclination is to let the future unfold as the actors choose, and indeed, as it will. After all, most past attempts at prognostication are either failures or lucky accidents. Yet if we pretend to know anything at all about human behaviour, values, and adaptation, we have perhaps a responsibility, not to predict or advocate ideal states in distant futures, but rather to indicate a reasonable range of outcomes over a short-to-medium time range. Human history has been one of change. Yet, for the most part, this change has been evolutionary. The weight of history supports the conservative stance: people and societies do not readily forsake the stupendous economic and psychological investment made in existing structures, settlements, and modes of behaviour. Thus the easiest and safest prediction is that the future will not look so different, because people are comfortable with what they know.

The historic patterns have been: (1) the extension of the frontier, (2) a subsequent concentration in towns and cities and metropolises, with this process spreading, at a time lag, behind frontier settlement, (3) local decentralization and (4) national decentralization, or settlement 'on the amenity frontier'. In the United States, all these processes are occurring simultaneously; frontier settlement in Alaska; urbanization and industrialization on the periphery; suburbanization and exurbanization around all cities; and the growth of environmentally attractive 'frontiers' in various parts of the nation. The first is about over, but in our view the second is not—the city is still a valid form of settlement. The second process will continue rivalling the fourth—even though we do not envisage the giant 'ecumenopolises' that Doxiadis described.

So what may we expect, say between now and the year 2000 (i.e. 1980-2000 or 20 years—the last twenty takes us back to but 1960)?

(1) The relative shift southward and westward will continue—of both economic activity and people of all ages, but especially of the retired. The Northeast may drop from its present half of the population to less than 40 per cent.

(2) Urbanization and metropolitan growth will still continue in parts of the South and West, but will have peaked in most urban portions (e.g. Arizona, Colorado, California, Texas, Florida).

(3) Despite rising energy costs, the automobile will still be with us, and 'exurban' residence will be even more common in all parts of the country. This will become possible largely because of a greater decentralization of employment, a larger retired population, and more efficient vehicles. Despite concern for the loss of agricultural land, and environmental pollution, much of this settlement will be highly dispersed. However, the 'post-industrial global village' will not have materialized. Commuting will still prevail.

(4) Despite the exurban flow, cities will not be abandoned. Although some will be in a state of stagnation, many more will have experienced a regeneration, not in numbers, but in quality. In some, the poor will have been pushed out to the present suburbs, and parts of the core will have been reconstructed for the rich (as in the pre-industrial city).

(5) No matter what changes may take place in immigration laws and quotas, the system will continue to be nourished by foreign immigrant streams, which will be dominantly from Latin America, South and East Asia, and the Middle East. The migration chains will, as in the past, lead to the large cities, although the 'points of entry' might be districts scattered widely throughout the metropolis, rather than within the traditional downtown core.

(6) Much of the upper income classes, perhaps as much as a third of the population, will have two or more residences, a city and a country place, or a northern and a southern place.

As in the past, regions and settlements will rise and fall in size and rank. Businesses will fail and be created, relocate or regenerate. Whereas we do not believe that we are moving toward any settlement equilibrium, either by region or between rural and urban, we do see a trend toward regional equalization of well-being (but probably no such convergence within parts of the metropolis). There is a real risk of income, class, or social polarization, a virtual abandonment of the central areas of some cities to the elderly, minorities and the poor. But the patterns will be more subtle, a complex patchwork of classes and cultures within the metropolis, and even the countryside. Our models of metropolitan structure will become even more obsolete.

Some observers feel that people are reacting to the anonymity, powerlessness, and size of modern cities and institutions, and trying to recreate a sense of place, either by creating communities within the city or by moving to smaller settlements. If so, the trend is in part toward an earlier pattern of settlement, perhaps like that which prevailed in the early part of the century, with greater vitality of smaller cities and towns and of urban neighbourhoods. So be it.

REFERENCES

Adams, J. 1970. 'Residential Structure of Midwestern Cities', *Annals of the Association of American Geographers*, 60: 37-62.
Adams, J. (ed.) 1976. *Contemporary Metropolitan America*. Cambridge, Mass.: Ballinger.
Alexandersson, G. 1956. *The Industrial Structure of American Cities*. Lincoln: Univ. of Nebraska Press.
Berry, B. J. L. 1972. *City Classification Handbook: Methods and Applications*. New York: Wiley.
Berry, B. J. L. 1977. *Growth Centers in the American Urban System*. Cambridge, Mass.: Ballinger.
Borchert, J. 1967. 'American Metropolitan Evolution', *Geographical Review*, 57: 301-23.
Dunn, E. S. Jr. 1980. *Development of the U.S. Urban System, Vol 1: Concepts, Structures, Regional Shifts*. Baltimore: Johns Hopkins Univ. Press.
Fuguitt, G. *et.al.*, 1979. *Growth and Change in Rural America*. Washington, D.C.: Urban Institute.
Gottmann, J. 1961. *Megalopolis: The Urbanized Northeastern Seaboard of the United States*. New York: Twentieth Century Fund.
Harris, C. D. 1943. 'A Functional Classification of Cities in the United States,' *Geographical Review*, 33: 86-99.
Nelson, H. J. 1955. 'A Service Classification of American Cities', *Economic Geography*, 31: 189-210.
Pred, A. 1966. *The Spatial Dynamics of US Urban-Industrial Growth 1800-1914*. Cambridge: MIT Press.

48   *Urbanization and Settlement Systems*

Smith, D. 1973. *Geography of Social Well-Being in the US.* New York: McGraw Hill.
Teaford, J. 1979. *City and Suburb: The Political Fragmentation of Metropolitan Areas, 1850-1970.* Baltimore: Johns Hopkins Univ. Press.
Vance, J. 1977. *This Scene of Man.* New York: Harper and Row.
Ward, D. 1971. *Cities and Immigrants: A Geography of Change in Nineteenth Century America.* New York: Oxford Univ. Press.
Yeates, M. and Garner, B. 1980. *The North American City.* New York: Harper & Row.
Zelinsky, W. 1973. *The Cultural Geography of the United States,* Englewood Cliffs, N.J. Prentice-Hall.

2 THE CANADIAN URBAN SYSTEM

JAMES W. SIMMONS AND LARRY S. BOURNE*

Canada provides an interesting illustration of the concept of an urban system and the development of settlement in low-density regions. The significance of the national boundary, the intense functional specialization of regional economies and the importance of exchanges among cities are characteristics shared by many settlement systems, but in other ways Canada's urban system differs markedly from that of most other countries. Distances are vast, and play a major role in determining the pattern of intercity relationships. The population is small; and is concentrated in widely separated nodes. The economic landscape tends to be specialized in one or two dominant—and for the most part primary—activities. The growth and prosperity of any one region is largely determined by market conditions and decisions which are external to the country. The linear shape of the ecumene (or settled territory) makes the pattern of inter-regional dependencies quite explicit, while the close ties with the United States clearly identify the exogenous nature of growth forces.

The Canadian urban system is at once closely bound to the geography of the natural resource base, while being highly artificial in the sense that one can trace much of the landscape back to recent and man-made initiatives, both private and public. No endogenous, cumulative settlement pattern mediates between these alternatives; no centuries-old system of agriculture or industry or transportation exists. Development decisions are taken in the light of current world-wide conditions of technology and commodity markets.

This paper elaborates these various themes in four sections: (1) the basic patterns of the Canadian economic and social landscape; (2) the important linkages among cities, that is the 'organization' of the urban system; (3) the processes of growth and change which transform it; and (4) some of the policy issues and programmes which emerge from the nature of the urban system itself. Throughout the discussion the Canadian example is also used to exemplify more general settlement themes. This paper draws both upon the authors' own work on Canada (Simmons 1974a, b; Bourne, 1975; Bourne and Simmons, 1979) and a collection of papers which examines urban systems in general (Bourne and Simmons, 1978).

Defining the Urban System

The initial description of any spatial system is partly shaped by the definitions of the components of the system and the identification of the significant characteristics for study. The 'cities', as defined in this paper, are not political cities but rather broad 'urban regions' which have been designed explicitly for the analysis of urban system relationships. Their definition embodies two principles. First, the urban regions are spatially extensive and exhaustive, so that they aggregate to comprise the complete settled ecumene (*see* Figure 2.1). Each urban region is centred on an urban node—a city of 10,000 or more population or a census metropolitan area— and includes that part of the regional hinterland economy, such as agriculture or mining, to which the node is more closely linked than with a competing node. The initial unit of aggregation, the county or census division, is sometimes an administrative unit, but basically it is a statistical reporting unit of the Canadian census. These 265 counties are then grouped into 124 urban regions, ranging in size from 20,000 inhabitants to almost 3,000,000. Table 2.1 displays some of the characteristics of the thirty largest centres. Note the very modest differences in population between the definition of these urban regions and the census metropolitan areas.

The other essential component of the definition is the assignment of places to an urban hierarchy (Figure 2.1). Each city is assigned to one of five orders according to its population size and tertiary role. In addition, distance and commercial flows are used to assign each centre to a single higher-order place, thus defining a nested, hierarchical, central place system. As identified here, these linkages represent a convenient hypothesis about how the cities might interact among themselves.

Historical Urbanization

In contrast to most other countries, the Canadian urban system as defined here is highly disaggregated. For the United States, Berry used urban areas with at least 25,000 persons as the basic urban node (Berry, 1973) while Hall *et al* (1973) began with cities of 70,000 or more in their analysis of England and Wales. The decision to include smaller places in Canada arises out of the traditional minimum size threshold of 10,000 for Canadian cities (there were 157 urban places of this size or larger in 1976); and the necessity to cover very large distances (up to 8000 kms), with a relatively small national population (24 million in 1981).[1]

As Figure 2.1 indicates the Canadian urban system includes a 'core' of cities grouped at a reasonably high density in an area stretching from Windsor to Quebec City (*see* Yeates, 1975) and a 'periphery' of widely dispersed cities in the rest of the country, at approximately one-tenth the density (Table 2.2). The former contain the bulk of the industrial and higher-order administrative activities; the latter are mainly devoted to resource gathering and processing.

The definition of urban regions used in this study explicitly rejects the traditional differentiation between urban and rural. In twentieth century

[1]At the time of writing detailed statistics from the 1981 Census were not available.

Table 2.1: *Canadian Urban Regions*

Rank	Urban Region	Population (1976)	Census Metropolitan Area Population (1976)	Growth Rate of Urban Region 1971-6 %	Income per Capita 1976 $	Order in Hierarchy
1	Montreal	2,785,800	2,802,500	2.3	5690	5
2	Toronto	2,699,400	2,803,100	7.5	6965	5
3	Vancouver	1,253,900	1,166,300	9.1	6720	4
4	Edmonton	868,800	554,200	11.9	5910	4
5	Winnipeg	770,600	578,200	6.4	5440	4
6	Quebec	717,500	542,200	7.6	4965	4
7	Hamilton	673,300	529,400	7.7	6160	4
8	Ottawa	603,000	521,300*	10.1	6530	4
9	Calgary	593,400	469,900	15.4	6640	4
10	Halifax	379,100	268,000	6.9	5035	4
11	St. Catharines	365,400	301,900	5.2	5665	3
12	St. John's	327,200	143,400	6.6	3535	3
13	Windsor	310,400	247,600	1.3	6060	3
14	London	303,700	270,400	7.7	5945	4
15	Kitchener	288,500	272,200	13.5	5950	3
16	Victoria	277,700	218,300	13.9	6250	3
17	Oshawa	277,600	135,200	13.9	5930	3
18	Chicoutimi	269,000	128,600	1.2	4030	3
19	Regina	260,000	151,200	3.1	5295	3
20	Trois Rivières	251,200	154,000**	-0.1	4460	2
21	Barrie	242,100	49,200	19.0	5005	2
22	Saskatoon	234,600	133,800	11.7	5300	3
23	Sherbrooke	211,500	104,500	2.0	4405	2
24	Hull	209,500	171,900*	13.1	5200	2
25	Sudbury	205,900	157,000	-1.5	5595	3
26	St. Jerome	188,000	36,500	16.4	5000	2
27	Saint John	171,800	113,000	5.7	4425	3
28	Sydney	170,900	124,100***	0.5	3605	2
29	Moncton	156,900	77,600	12.5	4185	2
30	Thunder Bay	150,600	119,300	3.6	6285	3

* Merged with Hull as Ottawa-Hull CMA   ** Trois Rivières and Shawinigan   *** Sydney and Sydney Mines
Source: compiled by the authors

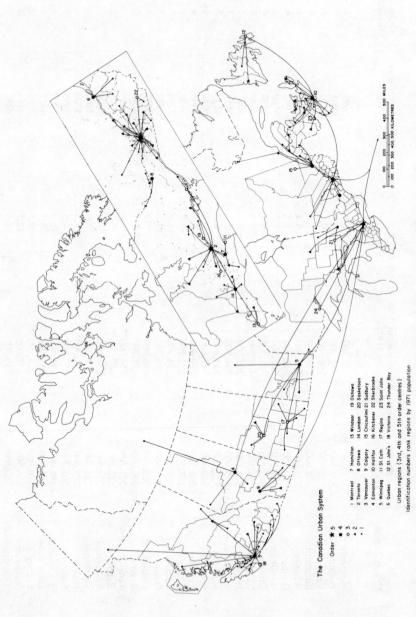

The Canadian Urban System

Order ★ 5
       ● 4
       ○ 3
       ▲ 2
       • 1

1 Montreal	7 Hamilton	13 Windsor	19 Oshawa
2 Toronto	8 Ottawa	14 London	20 Saskatoon
3 Vancouver	9 Calgary	15 Chicoutimi	21 Sudbury
4 Edmonton	10 Halifax	16 Kitchener	22 Sherbrooke
5 Winnipeg	11 St. Cath.	17 Regina	23 Saint John
6 Quebec	12 St. John's	18 Victoria	24 Thunder Bay

Urban regions (3rd, 4th and 5th order centres)

Identification numbers rank regions by 1971 population

Fig. 2.1. The Canadian Urban System: Hierarchic linkages are hypotheses based on various contact patterns

Table 2.2: *The Core and the Periphery in Canada*

	Core[a]	Periphery	Total
Area (km²)	200,500 (2.2%)	9,205,500 (97.8%)	9,406,000
Population (1971)	11,918,000 (55.3%)	9,650,000 (44.7%)	21,568,000
Population Growth, 1961-71	2,183,000 (67.3%)	1,057,000 (32.7%)	3,240,000
No. of Urban Regions	44	80	124
Mean Rate of City Growth, 1966-1971 (S.D.)[c]	7.0% (5.4)	6.0% (11.0)	6.3% (9.4)
Income/capita[b], (S.D.)[c] 1971	$2,380 (490)	$2,070 (560)	$2,158 (560)
Primary Workers[d] (S.D.)[c]	11.2% (4.9)	24.9% (9.9)	20.0% (10.7)
Secondary Workers[d] (S.D.)[c]	23.7% (7.6)	(6.8% (4.5)	12.8% (10.0)
Tertiary Workers[d]	56.7% (4.9)	55.1% (5.7)	55.7% (5.4)

[a] Essentially the southern portions of Ontario and Quebec.
[b] Personal Income from income tax sample. Canada, Revenue Canada. *Taxation Statistics, 1973*. Ottawa.
[c] Standard deviations in parentheses (S.D.)
[d] Canada, Statistics Canada, Census of Canada, 1971. Bulletin 3.4-4 'Industry Divisions by Sex'. Average values for the urban regions of each group.

Canada most of the cultural and economic differentials between the two have lost their meaning. None the less, for the purpose of cross-cultural and temporal comparisons it may be useful to examine the growth of urbanization as shown in Figure 2.2. Here the definition of 'urban' is more conventional, including those people living in cities of over 10,000 or in larger census agglomerations or metropolitan areas as defined in the 1966 Census. In 1976 this included 65.5 per cent of the population.

Canada has always been dependent on a well-developed urban system with external markets. Historically the economy has been dependent on the exploitation of primary resources (or staples) under colonial governments, a process which required the development of networks of forts, ports, and transportation lines. The fur trade, cod fishing, and lumbering each defined their own subsystem (*see* Harris and Warkentin, 1974). In the nineteenth century, agriculture—first in Quebec and Ontario and later (post 1880) in Western Canada—provided a rural alternative; but even then the substantial cash-crop structure of Canadian agriculture, and the rapid mechanization which accompanied its development, also encouraged further urbanization. Even Saskatchewan, the most rural/agricultural province in the country, was 55 per cent urban in 1976.

The graphs in Figure 2.2 indicate the relatively short history of Canadian urban development, with its rapid growth in the last century and a half. The two most intense periods of urbanization occured in the periods of most rapid population growth. Around the turn of the century high levels of immigration fuelled both the settlement of the western prairies and the

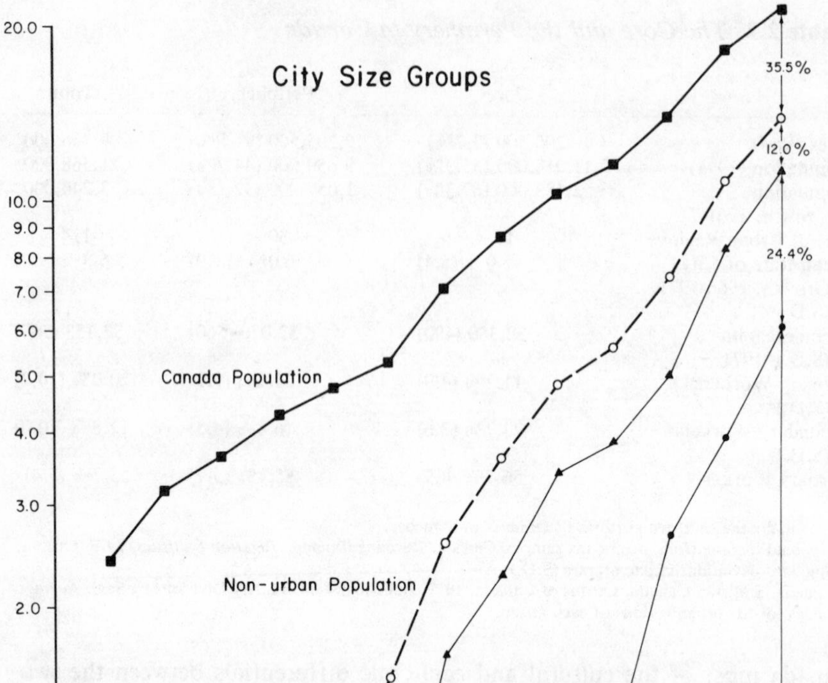

Fig. 2.2 Historical Urbanization
Data assembled by J. W. Simmons, using the 1961 Statistics Canada definitions

industrialization of the older core region. In the period following World War II, massive immigration and a high rate of natural increase, along with a substantial decline in agricultural employment, led to rapid urban growth in almost every region of the country.

City Size and Location

Despite the vast size of Canada its urban places are relatively concentrated in space. We have already mentioned the core region, wherein some 40 per cent of all urban centres and six of the eleven largest centres are located; but even in the periphery, most of the cities are located close to the US border. Accessibility, climate and political development have all contributed to this linear pattern, in which Canadian transportation and communications systems essentially form a single chain of urban centres from east to west.

This chain is anchored by the two highest-order centres, located less than 700 kilometres apart. Toronto and Montreal are now roughly the same size and have been competing for national dominance for over a century. In the last decade, however, Toronto has become the nation's leading financial centre and the cultural headquarters of English-speaking Canada as the space-economy has shifted continuously westward. Montreal is now essentially the cultural and distributional centre for French-speaking Canada, reflecting the regional and linguistic polarization of the nation. The Atlantic Provinces to the east, while historically important, have failed to grow at the same pace as the rest of the country during the twentieth century, and now only Halifax can be included among the major cities of the urban system. Western Canada, in contrast, contains three major nodes—Vancouver, Calgary and Edmonton—that are growing much more rapidly than the system as a whole, as well as Winnipeg, the traditional regional centre of the West, which has now been by-passed.

The Spatial Structure

Canada is characterized by spectacular regional variations in economic base, landscape, and lifestyle. The fisherman of Newfoundland, the automobile factory worker in Ontario, the grain farmer in the West, the office-worker in Toronto's financial district, and the miner on the Canadian shield exemplify the intense spatial variations of the economy. Each major city contains stark symbols of its economic roots. These differences reflect the vast distances from place to place and the restricted economic options, but most of all the openness of the Canadian space-economy to world market conditions.

The starkness of the resulting economic specialization is apparent in Figure 2.3. This map was obtained by classifying those activities that process local raw materials from the manufacturing sector to the appropriate primary sector. The notion of specialization means that at least 10 per cent of total employment is in that sector. Note that virtually no manufacturing beyond primary processing exists outside of the core region. The urban centres in the periphery are almost entirely dependent on the world market conditions for their particular primary specialization—wheat, oil, pulp and paper, or iron ore. The only route to diversification for most centres in the

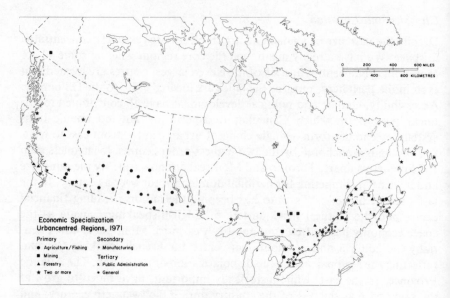

Fig. 2.3   Economic Specialization in Urban Centred Regions, 1971

system is by means of population growth, since larger urban places tend to develop service activities which link together a broad region, thereby encompassing several economic specializations.

Although in the aggregate this relatively small, export-dependent, tariff-protected, and partly foreign-owned economy, living in close proximity to and interdependent with the American giant, has brought high levels of growth and prosperity to Canadians, it has also led to some severe internal problems. The resource-based economy is subject to intense short-term fluctuations. The annual income of the prairie wheat farmer or miner can double or halve within a year, depending on the weather, or the price of wheat, or minerals on world markets.

In either case the uncertainty creates severe personal, and community stress, and hardship, while wasting public investments in infrastructure. In the longer run, technological innovations or the discovery of new resources may lead to severe differences in the rate of growth and level of prosperity among Canadian regions. Figure 2.4 presents the spatial variations in per capita income in 1971, on a map adjusted for the population size of each urban region. Part of this pattern is short-term (e.g. wheat prices); part of the pattern has endured for over 100 years, reflecting the westward movement of population and economic growth; and part of it reflects the higher labour force participation rates and better paying occupations in the larger cities.

The spatial specialization of the economy and the economic disparities it engenders cumulates into frequent inter-regional conflicts. Almost all federal government action is spatially redistributive in some fashion.

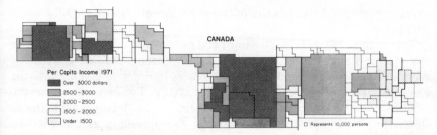

Fig. 2.4   Income Differentials among Urban Regions, 1971

Agricultural subsidies tend to favour the West. Petroleum taxes discrimi-nate against the producing provinces, notably Alberta. Tariffs on imported and lower-priced manufactured goods maintain income for workers in the core region at the expense of the consumers in the periphery. Programmes that explicitly redistribute incomes also lead to divisions among the have and have-not provinces.

Social Characteristics

Although differences in the performance of the economy among the com-ponents of the urban system are a major source of irritation, they are not the only ones. A factor analysis of eighty variables from the 1971 census identified four independent dimensions in the urban system (Simmons, 1978a): the first and most powerful dimension is cultural. It contrasts French-language Canadians, who at that time were also characterized by larger households, lower levels of education, and a different demographic structure; with English-speaking Canadians, particularly those originating from Northern and Eastern Europe who settled in the prairies. The basic separation within this dimension, however, is into two groups: those who speak French and those who speak English. This language grouping leads to parallel networks in almost every medium of communication—the press, radio-television, education, and the distribution of personal and business services.

   The second dimension in the factor analysis is essentially demographic. It differentiates new Northern 'frontier' communities in which rapid in-migration and a large native (Indian, Metis or Inuit) population have led to high levels of natural increase and disproportionately young popula-tions. Factor three combines various measures of economic achievement and very much resembles the income map of Figure 2.4. The final factor identifies the occupational categories linked with city size, such as clerical, managerial, and professional activities. It is of some interest that no core—periphery differentiation of economic attributes emerged clearly in this analysis, indicating that the nature of the economic base does not determine growth or income or social characteristics in this urban system. Each of the various economic bases has the potential for growth under certain market conditions.

This analysis suggests that we must add to conventional measures such as city size and rate of urban growth, less commonly studied patterns of economic achievement and ethnic differences in order to comprehend the complete structure of the Canadian urban system. For better or worse, the result is a complex pattern of political coalitions or cleavages as the focus shifts from issue to issue. For example, the prevailing attitudes to the redistribution of federal funds among the provinces according to their wealth, or 'equalization payments' as they are called, are shaped and reshaped by the patterns shown in Figure 2.4.

The Behaviour of the System

The important feature of any urban system is its organization—the complex network of relationships among cities which transfer growth impulses from one place to another (Simmons, 1978b,c). In Canada, for instance, a bumper wheat crop sold abroad at a good price leads to prosperity in rural Saskatchewan. This prosperity in turn affects a chain of service centres of increasingly larger size, as well as those specific cities containing grain transportation terminals and farm machinery factories. To trace out fully all these relationships would require a complete matrix of inter-regional and intersectoral input - output multipliers, but for Canada even the most rudimentary statistics on the inter-regional movements of goods are unavailable. The organization of the urban system must then be examined indirectly, by looking at some of the available data on inter-city interaction and by evaluating some of the fluctuations in growth relationships among places. The most useful information in the search for organization is our knowledge of the vast ranges of city sizes and levels of accessibility within the system and their obvious relationship to patterns of interaction.

Economic Linkages

The Canadian economy, like that of the other small but relatively highly developed countries, is quite open to external influence. Essentially the nation depends on the export of raw (e.g. wheat, oil, gas, and iron ore) and semi-processed (e.g. newsprint, potash, copper) materials in order to import a wide variety of consumer goods—foodstuffs, manufactured goods from low-income or technologically sophisticated economies, and a variety of tertiary services. Although there is very considerable fluctuation in the amount and character of the exports over the years, they have consistently been dominated by primary goods, and have averaged about 20 per cent of the Gross National Product (GNP).

The economic linkages of the country are anchored, then, by two major transportation subsystems. On the one hand there is a series of ports, water-

ways, railways, and pipelines to ship the various primary products as directly as possible out of the country to some foreign market. Exports occur
largely in peripheral locations (e.g. ocean ports), and often leave relatively
little impression on the space economy (e.g. pipelines or giant ore
freighters). The imported goods, in contrast, arrive much closer to the consumption stage. They, as well as domestic manufactured goods, are
distributed by the central place hierarchy throughout the country. Toronto
and Montreal jointly act as the highest-order centres. Goods are distributed
from there to the next lower order places such as Vancouver, Calgary/
Edmonton, Winnipeg, and Halifax. The pattern of distribution to smaller
places largely resembles the hierarchical structure shown previously in
Figure 2.1.

Within Ontario and Quebec networks of road and rail lines link together
the older manufacturing centres of the core region. Exchanges of parts,
components and raw materials take place largely in a non-hierarchical
fashion (Simmons, 1972), with the pattern of flows dominated by the size of
the urban centre and the nature of the specialization. The clusters of places
surrounding Toronto, from London to Kingston, are particularly closely
linked. Even within the core, however, city size is an important measure,
and the urban hierarchy of Figure 2.1 is a good starting point for tracing the
movement of growth impulses through the Canadian urban system.

The Network of Social Contracts

Given the important role of city size and distance in determining urban
interaction, one expects that flows of information and of people would
follow paths similar to the system of tertiary distribution described above.
There is, however, an additional factor determining social contact, in the
form of a language barrier. McKay (1958) long ago demonstrated its importance in modifying the level of telephone conversation between places.

The best indicator of social contact available is in the flow of migrants
(Figure 2.5). During the period 1966-1971, about 11 per cent of Canadians
changed residence from one urban region to another. Only 14 per cent of
these moves were 'net' moves, resulting in population growth or decline.
The map of migration flows, then, is a good measure of patterns of information, perception of opportunities, and accessibility. The map of largest
outflows identifies that destination most likely to be chosen by a migrant
from a particular centre.

The map confirms the fundamental hierarchical structure suggested
earlier in Figure 2.1. Migrants are most likely to move to the nearest largest
urban centre, the one from which they usually obtain goods and services not
provided locally. Also in evidence is the effect of the language barrier,
which isolates the Montreal urban subsystem. This barrier cuts across Northern New Brunswick and Eastern Ontario. Few major migrant flows cross
this line. The map also contains some other discrepancies from Figure 2.1

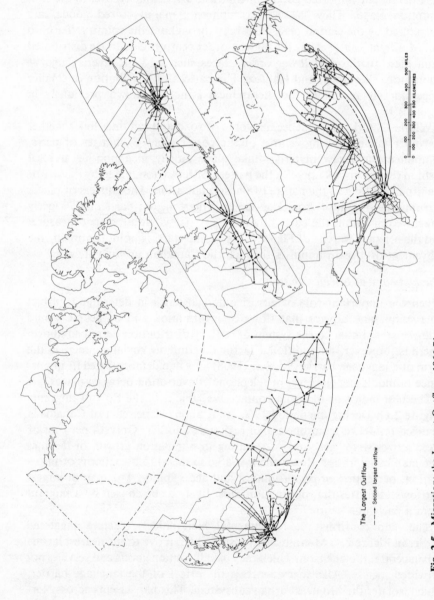

Fig. 2.5 Migration: the Largest Outflow, 1966–71

The Largest Outflow
- - - → Second largest outflow

which may be interpreted as indications of the directions of change in the urban system. Migrants, for the most part, are people looking to the future, and to the extent that the map includes net migrants, it also reflects growth patterns during the period. Edmonton and Vancouver, for instance, may play a larger role in the future settlement system, since they appear to challenge Toronto's dominance in much of Western Canada. Montreal, which grew very little during this period of severe economic and political stress, appears to be losing ground to Toronto in serving the Maritime Provinces. The implications of these linkage changes will be traced out in more detail below.

The Dynamics of Growth

The growth of the Canadian urban system in the past has been highly erratic and largely unpredictable. The fluctuations in time and space of resource production for world markets have been described as a series of regional staple economies wherein the rise and decline of an urban subsystem is determined by the growth or decline of a single primary commodity. These fluctuations have been abetted historically by the ability of Canada to import and export large amounts of both people and capital (e.g. immigrants from Europe, and recently from Asia; emigrants to the US). Over the period 1851-1971 almost 10 million immigrants came to Canada, but almost 7 million emigrants left the country. In any one decade the net migration surplus or deficit can be very large, responding as it does to the aggregate performance of the economy. Within Canada these adjustments have been complemented by massive internal flows of migrants between regions in decline and regions of growth.

Nevertheless, despite the high degree of uncertainty in growth, both nationally and locally, some of the larger cities have achieved considerable stability in their growth rate and population ranking, over the last century. Regional centres like Winnipeg, London, Halifax have tended to remain prominent within their respective regions, although their actual growth rate reflects the growth of the regional economy. The most plausible explanation for this seeming paradox of stable growth amid erratic fluctuations is a kind of spatial dampening process in which random growth impulses from a large number of small urban areas, when aggregated, become a regular growth trend for the regional centre which serves them all.

In any urban system many of the linkages, or interaction coefficients between regions, are effectively zero; that is, there are no direct relationships. In Canada the simplicity of the hierarchical structure, due to the widely-spaced cities, the explicitly external direction of final demand, and the high degree of regional economic specialization, makes the pattern of interdependency relatively simple and weakly defined, at least for that portion of the urban system which is located in the periphery.

Short-Run Growth

Consider changes in the space-economy within a given year. In most local economies a wide range of outputs is possible. The value of the unit of product may vary (e.g. the price of lumber, wheat, oil, newsprint, or gold) and the level of output at any one location may shift due to weather, strikes, trade agreements, or market conditions. Fluctuations of this kind, coupled with the pervasive high rates of unemployment in Canada, create a situation in which there is an excess of productive capacity at most locations and in most sectors. In larger cities, however, the wider range and numbers of activities and the larger service sector tend to average out the variations into a smoother growth trend.

Population growth rates during the census period, 1971-6, range from −11.4 per cent (Dawson Creek, BC) to over 200 per cent (Fort McMurray, Alberta) but as important as the magnitude of the variation in growth rate is its unpredictability. Neither population size, nor accessibility, nor economic specialization, are consistently correlated with urban growth.

The ups and downs in the value of the basic product are transmitted through the local economy by means of a series of multipliers, each of which tends to moderate the impact of output change on the distribution of economic activity. Output affects jobs and wages, jobs and wages in turn affect the service activities, which may expand locally (the non-basic sector) or in more distant and higher-order centres. In the short-run, then, a growth in output, determined by markets external to the country, affects both local and non-local economies.

When these short-run fluctuations in growth are embedded in a national economy in which there is a long record of overall growth, as well as an equally long record of a marked spatial redistribution of economic activity; a powerful short-term growth impulse—or a series of two or three growth impulses—can then set the stage for substantial long-run changes in the space-economy. In the simplest case the level of demand presses on the capacity of local production facilities. A round of expansion in investment, and hiring, is initiated. Second, even if temporary (and no-one knows for sure), a growth sequence creates an environment of reduced unemployment, higher wages, and increased local market size which in turn attracts new workers, new services, and new public investments to that location. Local growth and the expectation of future growth thus begins to attract services, customers, and investment from competing locations. The stage is quickly set for modification to the pattern of interdependency itself.

Long-Run Growth

Over a longer period of time the annual variations in output at various places in the urban system are translated into more permanent changes in the production capacity of regions and in patterns of linkages among sectors and urban places. Technology, investment and migration can alter the pattern of interdependency in a number of ways: the production relationships among sectors themselves, the spatial relationships among a series of central places, the numbers of links in the system, and the city size relationships within the hierarchy.

Almost as soon as the concept of input-output coefficients emerged, their temporal instability became evident. Changes in the organization of production and in the sources of inputs profoundly modify interurban relationships and dependencies. Many examples exist in Canada: the decline in the labour inputs required for agriculture has led to population decline in many parts of the country, although not necessarily accompanied by a decline in the level of income. The sequence of dependence on water power, coal, and oil, for energy, for example, has altered the locational advantages of cities for different industrial activities. Many studies have also documented the redistribution of consumer-oriented activities over time. The diffusion of new technology, and the growing complexity of consumption have shifted the balance of locational advantages towards larger, more centralized cities, although the massive decline of employment in primary and secondary activities and growth in retail and service jobs has partially shielded the smaller centres from decline. Over time then, it is observed that basic-nonbasic multipliers, whether local or extra-local, consistently favour larger places.

In Canada, where distances are still significant cost factors, this pattern is modified in a number of substantive ways. First, access changes affect some places more than others, because of the wide differential in degrees of isolation. Second, and this is particularly true historically, transportation innovations can alter the network of service relationships. A new railroad, or highway, or an enlarged port, may affect several places in a complementary fashion (*see* Spelt, 1955).

At the same time the importance of central place linkages may be declining. Over time, a growing complexity in the pattern of spatial linkages within the urban system has taken place. Larger proportions of goods and services are obtained from outside the local region; complex production relationships link together the cities of the core region in a non-hierarchical fashion. Even in the periphery of the urban system the linear distribution of the regional centres and their increasing size relative to the areas they serve has intensified the importance of intermetropolitan flows.

The other source of change is the differential growth rate of cities. Larger places have more services and better transportation systems, and thus attract trade from a wider area than small places. For instance, the accelerated growth of Calgary and Edmonton in Alberta is rapidly siphoning away much of Winnipeg's service area. The most profound impacts of these competitions occur when a place, which once was a tributary, becomes a competitor. When such a fundamental shift in the hierarchy takes place, the entire urban system is forced to adjust.

For the most part these adjustments simply reflect the ongoing redistribution of economic activity. The shifts from Montreal to Toronto and from Winnipeg to Calgary and Edmonton noted earlier are direct responses to the westward movement of development in North America. Shifts in the organization of the upper levels of the urban hierarchy, at any given time, depend on the particular spatial distribution of growth. The two most rapid periods of urbanization in Canada illustrate the point nicely. The main impetus of growth in the decade 1901-11 was the settlement of Western Canada. The railroads, unlimited immigration, cheap agricultural land, and a world market for wheat generated an almost instantaneous urban subsystem, stretching from Edmonton to Winnipeg. The impact of this growth, channelled through Winnipeg, was transmitted directly to the two highest-order centres—Toronto and Montreal. They, in turn, transferred the effect of the boom to the nearby industrial centres, while non-industrial centres in rural Ontario or the Maritimes were relatively unaffected. The result was rapid growth in one half the urban system and no growth in the rest.

During the 1951-61 period, in contrast, the sources of urban growth were more widely dispersed. Leading the boom was the northward expansion of mining and forest industries, and the widespread growth of the service sector. In one way or another these sources of growth affected almost all regions and urban places. The urban hierarchy was maintained; all urban places grew roughly in proportion. Although the urban system became larger and more complex, it remained essentially the same.

Policy

An ongoing debate exists in the capitalist democracies in the twentieth century as to whether social and economic events are influenced by explicit (and implicit) policy decisions, or if policy simply places a stamp of approval on inexorable economic and demographic processes. Governments claim the credit for prosperity, while blaming recessions on others (e.g. the world economy). The varieties of public intervention are so diverse and often so contradictory that equally plausible arguments can be made in either direction.

Canada, and in particular the development of its space-economy, is no exception to this debate. On the one hand, policy after policy has been aimed at redressing the regional differentials in growth and income, but with little apparent success. On the other hand, it can be argued that numerous political decisions, concerned only indirectly with spatial redistribution, have shaped the Canadian urban system into its present pattern.

The Federal Structure

We can begin with the nation itself, created arbitrarily over a century ago, by means of series of treaties carried out by foreign powers who were preoccupied with issues other than Canada. The political, social and economic pressures exerted first by Britain and, more recently, by the US have given Canada little room to manoeuvre as a nation. The final conditions of the assembly of a series of colonies into the Canadian system were negotiated by Canadians, however, and the British North America Act of 1867 subdivides the nation areally and in terms of political responsibility. The present ten provinces, of widely differing sizes, are each assigned responsibility for the management of public lands, the administration of justice, health services, education and municipal government, and are given jurisdiction over natural resources and economic activities entirely contained within the province. The federal government holds the residual powers.

As in most federal structures, the relative strength of the central government waxes and wanes. The very existence of the provinces has affected the urban system by providing ten political nodes which may (or may not) complement the federal economic policies, which take many of the initiatives in transportation and public facility construction, and which control most of the development of primary activities, including the provision of capital, tax structures, and environmental controls. Relationships between the two levels of government proceed informally on many fronts, most visibly in the form of joint conferences. To the extent that the provinces—particularly the larger ones—can control their own economies, it has been difficult for the federal government to stabilize economic growth over time and space. Two of the major historical policy contributions of the federal government to the urban system have been the introduction of tariffs on foreign manufactured goods, and the creation of integrated national systems for transportation and communications.

The tariffs, imposed after long debate during the early years of the country in the last half of the nineteenth century, were intended to ensure that Canada developed a domestic manufacturing sector. The costs of transportation and the necessary economies of scale ensured that this sector would develop within the more densely-populated core region in Central Canada, as shown earlier. The effectiveness of the national boundary as a barrier to flows of certain commodities determined the growth of several economic sectors, and thus growth at certain locations. In the eagerness to expand the industrial capacity of the country, foreign investment and technology have been welcomed.

Proximity to the United States and the similarities of language, culture, and consumption, have made Canada a fertile breeding ground for the development of multinational organizations. The result, after 100 years, is a national economy closely entwined with US-controlled enterprises in almost every sector. The organization of the Canadian urban system increasingly includes a diffuse pattern of linkages to the US which in turn influences markets, technological diffusion, and the incidence and timing of growth itself. The whole economy appears to be slipping beyond the control of the federal government (Britton and Gilmour, 1978).

The repeated concern of the federal government over the years has been to develop the nation's physical and social infrastructure, to maintain and strengthen the linkages within the urban system. As historians (e.g. Creighton, 1937) have pointed out, the early history of Canada was based on the existence, in the form of the Great Lakes-St. Lawrence drainage system and trade links with Britain, of a commercial network distinct from the United States. In order to maintain these separate structures Canadians have constructed canals, railroads, highways, airlines, and communications networks. The costs have been large, given the distances involved and the paucity of population to be served.

Policy Priorities

Like most peoples, Canadians and their governments are preoccupied with solving day to day problems, rather than shaping the future system. As Bourne (1975) suggests, there are no grandiose national strategies designed to restructure the urban system. None the less a review of current issues of pre-eminent concern gives some indication of what the future may hold. At present, four sets of problems dominate: economic growth, inflation and technology, the distribution of resource revenues, and Quebec's autonomy. Other issues such as Canada's economic relations with the US (the only significant issue in foreign affairs), regional economic disparity, and problems of disadvantaged groups in the population are discussed largely in so far as they relate to these four major ones.

During the 1950s and early 1960s Canada underwent a phenomenal demographic explosion; as high birth rates coupled with rapid net immigration created a significant bulge in the age structure. This bulge is even more pronounced as birth rates and immigration have since sharply declined, a product of changing attitudes, birth control technology, and federal policy, respectively. Twenty years later this concentration of young people entering the labour force, complicated by the rapid increase in the participation rate of women in the labour force, has led to a severe unemployment problem, despite a substantial increase in the number of jobs.

The government's preoccupation with unemployment has led to some unexpected spatial effects, and the re-ordering of other priorities. For example just prior to the current economic recession the federal government introduced a more generous plan of unemployment insurance. As the national unemployment rate has increased to its present level of 10 per cent, transfers from this source now amount to over 3.0 per cent of the GNP. For certain areas (e.g. rural Newfoundland), certain economic sectors (e.g. fishermen) and certain groups in the population, the proportion is much higher. The net effect has been to slow down population redistribution within the urban system, or at least to direct the movement towards locations, such as the west coast, which are also attractive places to live.

At the same time all levels of government are searching for activities

which create new jobs. A growing concern about foreign ownership of
Canadian production facilities has been pushed into the background, in the
search for job-creating capital. A widespread movement to enforce environmental controls on industry has slowed down when it comes into conflict with the provision of jobs. Job-creating growth is now acceptable at
any location, even though the growing concentration of wealth and economic activity in B.C. and Alberta, and in the energy sector in particular, is
the cause of increasing concern. The concept of an optimal settlement
pattern is therefore too imprecise and debatable to compete with these
economic priorities.

In many people's minds Quebec nationalism is as important as the economic problem. From the very inception of the country certain kinds of
political issues have divided Canada on the basis of language. The availability of public sector services in French, and the laggard development of
the Quebec economy are examples of conflicts which have consistently led
the province of Quebec to resist any encroachment on provincial powers by
the federal government. This ongoing problem has been brought into focus
by the election in 1976, and the re-election in 1981, of an avowedly separ-
atist government in Quebec—at a time when the federal government itself
was led by a French-speaking Canadian whose political party is dependent
on a large bloc of Quebec seats to stay in power (Figure 2.6). The most likely
outcome of this confrontation, and the recent (1982) constitutional debate,
will be further devolution of federal powers to the provinces. This in turn
may restructure the Canadian urban system by emphasizing within-province
linkages and institutions, rather than encouraging interprovincial trade and
flows of capital and labour.

The Quebec issue is also explicitly linked to the urban system through the
changing role of Montreal. During the last two decades the city's partici-

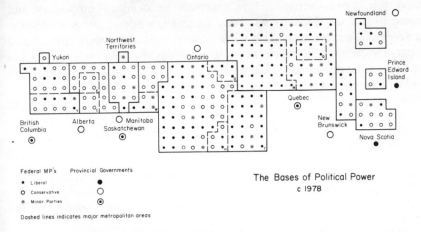

Fig. 2.6 The Bases of Political Power c.1978

pation in the location of head offices, and in the provision of commercial services and information for the nation as a whole has declined, while the links with the French-language urban subsystem in the province have intensified. In the latter process, the control of these services has also switched from English-speaking to French-speaking companies and managers. The net result has been a decline in the rate of growth of the Montreal region, but a rapid upward social and economic mobility for French-speaking Canadians.

The combination of 'growth wherever you can get it', and the trend towards greater provincial power have weakened any national thrust towards the spatial redistribution of income or growth, and it seems unlikely that substantial new additions to the present set of transfer payments will occur. In the decade to come it appears that each part of the country will essentially grow or decline on its own.

Furthermore, if recent growth patterns continue, over the next decade we could witness a significant westward shift in political power, complementing the modifications to the urban system. A continued decline in the relative size of Quebec coupled with the growth (in both population and income) of Alberta and British Columbia might well exacerbate income disparities within the urban system, while decentralizing population growth. Politically it would shift national priorities towards economic issues, particularly those focusing on questions of control and development of the primary and secondary sectors, and on transportation, and away from cultural concerns. The Western provinces are characteristically impatient with the concern over the issue of foreign ownership, and are opposed to tariff protection for the industries of the core region. They prefer to develop processing capacity for their own raw materials to serve both regional and world markets.

In the long run, then, the Canadian political system will respond to the changing pattern of Canadian economic and social development. But it is impossible to over-emphasize how uncertain the location, composition and timing of that development will be. As a small, wealthy, but economically undeveloped nation, Canada is vulnerable to almost any shift in the world economy. New technologies, world wars, droughts, gold rushes, inflation and economic depressions descend upon us at will, each leaving profound and enduring marks upon the Canadian settlement pattern.

REFERENCES

Berry, Brian J. L. 1973. *Growth Centers in the American Urban System*. 2 vols. Cambridge: Ballinger.

Bourne, Larry S. 1975. *Urban Systems: Strategies for Regulation*. London: Oxford University Press.

Bourne, Larry S. and Simmons, James W. (eds.) 1978. *Systems of Cities: Readings* on *Structure, Growth and Policy*, New York: Oxford University Press.

——. 1979. *Canadian Settlement Trends: An Examination of Patterns of Growth 1971-76*. Major Report 15, Centre for Urban and Community Studies, University of Toronto.

Bourne, Larry S. *et al.* (eds.) 1974. *Urban Futures for Central Canada: Perspectives on Forecasting Urban Growth and Form*. Toronto: University of Toronto Press.

Britton, John N. H. and Gilmour, James M. 1978. *The Weakest Link: A Technological Perspective on Canadian Industrial Underdevelopment*. Background Study No. 43. Ottawa: Science Council of Canada.

Creighton, Donald C. 1937. *The Commercial Empire of the St. Lawrence, 1760-1850*. Toronto: The Ryerson Press.

Curry, Leslie and Bannister, Geoffrey, 1974. 'Forecasting Township Population of Ontario, from Time-Space Covariances', in Bourne *et al* (eds.), pp. 34-59.

Gertler, Len and Crowley, Ron. 1977. *Changing Canadian Cities: The Next 25 years*. Toronto: McClelland & Stewart.

Hall, Peter *et al*. 1973. *The Containment of Urban England*. 2 Vols. London: Allen and Unwin.

Harris, R. Cole and Warkentin, John. 1974. *Canada Before Confederation*. Toronto: Oxford University Press.

Innis, Harold Q. 1967. 'The Importance of Staple Products', in W. T. Easterbrook and M. H. Watkins (eds.) *Approaches to Canadian Economic History*. Toronto: University of Toronto Press.

Kerr, Donald P. 1968. 'Metropolitan Dominance in Canada', in Warkentin, J. (ed.) *Canada: A Geographical Interpretation*. Toronto: Methuen, pp. 531-55.

Lithwick, N. Harvey. 1970. *Urban Canada: Problems and Prospects*. Ottawa: Central Mortgage and Housing Corporation.

McKay, J. Ross. 1958. 'The Interactance Hypothesis and Boundaries in Canada', *The Canadian Geographer*, II: 1-8.

Nader, George A. 1975. *Cities of Canada*, 2 Vols. Toronto: MacMillan.

Ray, D. Michael, *et al.* 1976. *Canadian Urban Trends*, Vol. 1. Toronto: Copp Clark.

Robinson, Ira. 1981. *Canadian Urban Growth Trends*, Vancouver: University of British Columbia Press.

Simmons, James W. 1972. 'Interaction in Ontario and Quebec', in L. S. Bourne and R. D. MacKinnon (eds.) *Urban Systems Development in Central Canada: Selected Papers*. Research Publication No. 9, Department of Geography, University of Toronto, pp. 198-220.

——. 1974a. 'Canada as an Urban System: A Conceptual Framework', *Research Paper No. 62*, Centre for Urban and Community Studies, University of Toronto, Toronto.

——. 1974b. 'The Growth of the Canadian Urban System', *Research Paper No. 65*, Centre for Urban and Community Studies, University of Toronto, Toronto.

——. 1975. 'Canada: Choices in a National Urban Strategy', *Research Paper No. 70*, Centre for Urban and Community Studies, University of Toronto, Toronto.

——. 1976. 'Short-Term Income Growth in the Canadian Urban System', *The Canadian Geographer*, XX, 4: 419-30.

——. 1977. 'Migration in the Canadian Urban System: Part I, Spatial Patterns', *Research Paper No. 85*, Centre for Urban and Community Studies, University of Toronto, Toronto.

——. 1978a. 'The Great Canadian Factor Analysis: Dimensions of Variation in the Canadian Urban System', *Research Paper No. 93*, Centre for Urban and Community Studies, University of Toronto, Toronto.

——. 1978b. 'The Organization of the Urban System', in L. S. Bourne and J. W. Simmons. *op. cit.*, pp. 61-9.

——. 1978c. 'Migration in the Canadian Urban System: Part II, Simple Relationships', *Research Paper No. 98*, Centre for Urban and Community Studies, University of Toronto, Toronto.

——. 1979. 'Migration in the Canadian Urban System: Part III', *Research Paper No. 112*, Centre for Urban and Community Studies, University of Toronto, Toronto.

——. 1981, "The Impact of Government on the Canadian Urban System", *Research Paper No. 126*, Centre for Urban and Community Studies, University of Toronto, Toronto.

Simmons, J. W. and Flanagan, P. 1981, "The Movement of Growth Impulses through the Canadian Urban System", *Research Paper No. 120*, Centre for Urban and Community Studies, University of Toronto, Toronto.

Spelt, Jacob. 1955, *Urban Development in South-Central Ontario*, Ossen, Netherlands: Von Gorcum.

Stone, Leroy O. 1967, *Urban Development in Canada*, Census Monograph Ottawa: Dominion Bureau of Statistics.

Yeates, Maurice. 1975, *Main Street: The Windsor-Quebec Corridor*, Toronto: Macmillan.

——. 1981, *North American Urban Patterns*, London: E. Arnold.

* Portions of the research reported here were supported by grants from the Social Sciences and Humanities Research Council of Canada (SSHRCC).

3 THE AUSTRALIAN URBAN SYSTEM

JAMES S. WHITELAW, MALCOLM I. LOGAN
AND JOHN MCKAY

As a product of nineteenth century British colonialism, Australia's settlement and development should display a number of features common to other New World western nations such as Canada, the United States, and New Zealand. Certainly, in the process of stamping out territorial claims, in exploiting natural resources, and in planting administrative port-capitals as bridgeheads to the interior, each country appears—albeit superficially—to have followed a roughly similar path. However, as the last area of continental proportions to be subjected to British imperialism, Australia's development does differ from other former colonies with the result that the evolution of the settlement system has produced some quite unique attributes. Thus, in the case of Australia we have the opportunity of unravelling and elaborating the interplay of certain common processes of urban-economic development within the framework of an island continent which presented a set of resources and environments without precedent in the experience of either the settlers or the colonial administrators.

There would be little debate in the claim that Australia is one of the most highly urbanized countries in the world. This situation has held true since before the turn of the present century. However, it is equally true that most western nations would now be regarded as highly urbanized so that an examination of the Australian urban system prompts rather fundamental questions. Is the urban system that has evolved in Australia—the way it operates, its distributional characteristics and the processes which allow it to function and grow—significantly different from that in other nations? Obviously there are elements common to all national systems, but the presence of these common elements does not imply that all urban systems will operate in quite the same way. Nor would one expect them to 'look' the same given the different historical paths nations have followed and their prospects for the future. It is, therefore, perfectly reasonable to expect differences. Clearly, these differences may have their roots in a wide variety of sources—the ways in which the systems are organized in both spatial and aspatial terms, in the locus of power and decision-making, in the extent to which they are integrated, in the degree of connectedness, in the strengths and directions of the flows of transactions and exchanges between different nodes in the system, in the extent to which their external links make them more or less susceptible to change, and in the degree of domestic control that can be exercised over such change.

In such a situation a study of the Australian urban system can contribute from two perspectives. Understanding of the way in which our system has evolved and now operates places us in a much more confident and informed position to accept or reject policies and programmes designed to bring about change, whether initiated locally or imported from other nations. But it also means that such increased understanding may contribute to the progress of other nations as they search for ways in which to channel and direct their own urban growth process.

This essay does not attempt to be all-embracing or totally comprehensive in its coverage of the Australian urban system. Indeed it is doubtful whether our present state of knowledge would sustain such an intent. Rather it has recognized certain basic themes which contribute to the distinctive manner in which urban Australia has developed and the various dimensions of these themes, explicitly and implicitly, are explored in the following text.

Themes in the Evolution of the Urban System

In an examination of the Australian urban system there is no question but that the highly urbanized state of the nation is the dominant theme. Not only does Australia remain one of the most urbanized nations of the world (except for a handful of city states) but it reached this position many years before Canada or the United States achieved similar levels of urbanization (Table 3.1). Early figures are unreliable and comparisons difficult, but, according to Jackson (1977), census data suggest that even by 1840 when only 11 per cent of the US population lived in towns of 2,500 or more, 30 per cent of the Australian population resided in towns of the same size range. At the turn of the century comparable figures were 40 and 52 per cent respectively. By 1901 some 70 per cent of Australia's urban population was in towns of more than 100,000 and only 16 per cent in towns from 10,000 to 100,000. In contrast, the figures for the United States in 1900 were 47 and 30 per cent respectively (Jackson, 1977). This concentration prompted a

Table 3.1: *Urban Population as a Percentage of Total Population, about 1900*

Country	Year	Minimum Population Counted as Urban	% Urban
Australia	1901	2,500	52
USA	1900	2,500	40
Canada	1901	1,000	35
Australia	1891	10,000	44
Uruguay	1890	10,000	30
Argentina	1890	10,000	28
Chile	1885	10,000	17
Brazil	1885	10,000	10

Source: Jackson (1977), p. 94

contemporary American demographer (Weber, 1899) to highlight 'The most remarkable concentration . . . in that newest product of civilization, Australia, where nearly one-third of the entire population is settled in and about capital cities'. In this sense an urban history pervades much of Australia's entire development as a nation state. But there is much more to this claim than the simple and often misleading arithmetic of calculating the proportion of the population living in towns and cities as compared with those residing in rural environs. The domination of an urban way of life from an early point in the nation's growth sets the scene for understanding much of Australian culture, its economic and political development and its human geography.

Again, the contrast with the United States is an interesting one: settlement came considerably later to Australia when the Industrial Revolution was well advanced and technology allowed long distance transport to work relatively efficiently. In both Canada and the United States on the other hand, an earlier date of settlement and the more primitive level of technology available at that time encouraged a more self-contained and self-sufficient form of settlement. Thus, alongside a lengthy period of urban dominance in Australia's history, in a relative sense, is the fact that in absolute terms the story of European occupance barely spans two centuries. But the important thing is they are the last two centuries during which the development of science, innovations in production, transportation and communications, in the harnessing of inanimate forms of energy, in building and mining techniques, in health and hygiene, and in standards of living for the general populace have all advanced at an unprecedented rate. Throughout almost its entire history of western civilization Australia has participated in the modern era unfettered by institutions, infrastructure, and settlement patterns firmly entrenched by virtue of a long history.

Thus, alongside the urbanized theme sits that of youthfulness. Nowhere are there large tracts of obsolete and decaying residential areas with which to contend. Nowhere are there major pockets dependent on antiquated industry. Nowhere are there vital areas of cities pre-empted by previous development to the extent that advantage cannot be taken of new techniques or processes. Nowhere are the patterns so fixed by inertia that change cannot take place. Indeed, change would have to be coupled with youthfulness as one of the compelling themes of Australian urbanization. Even the fortunes of the major cities have been subjected to quite significant fluctuations over their short history while those of smaller settlements have boomed and waned as first one then another resource has been tapped. But there has been time for the capricious nature of growth to turn the full circle and some towns which experienced boom then decline are now experiencing new and different forms of growth as resort centres, retirement havens, and 'trendy' settings as affluence brings about a reappraisal of their particular qualities.

Another dimension of this youthfulness is reflected in the demographic structure of the country. Immigration has been a potent force in Australia's growth for almost its entire history and waves of migrant intakes have sustained a young population—a process which formed the basis for high rates of natural increase in subsequent periods. A youthful population, of course, has meant continued demand for housing, jobs, and education. It is the towns and cities of Australia which, almost exclusively, have absorbed these demands for consumption.

A third theme contributing to Australia's distinctive urban system has to do with its spatial properties (Figure 3.1). Not only is Australia one of the most highly urbanized of nations, its urban population from the earliest days of settlement has been one of the most concentrated. Australia's high degree of dependency on Britain from the earliest times (for both imports and exports) greatly strengthened the dominance of the port cities, which grew into nodal points for a landward and seaward distribution system. By 1891, at the end of the long boom sparked by the gold discoveries in the 1850s and fanned by the expansion of pastoralism, 38 per cent of the population in the Australian colonies lived in Sydney and Melbourne, and only 14 of the 274 settlements had more than 5,000 people (Linge, 1979a). Even in recent times, 1947-71, metropolitan centralization actually increased; in

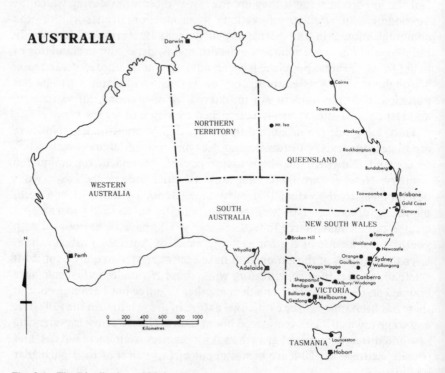

Fig. 3.1 The Distribution of Major Towns in Australia

the case of Sydney from 40 to 60 per cent of the state's population and in the case of Melbourne from 53 to 70 per cent. With only two exceptions each state is overwhelmingly dominated by its port-capital which has led to a situation of extreme primacy at this sub-national scale. In the state of Victoria, Melbourne is now 20 times larger than Geelong, the next largest city; Sydney is eight times larger than Newcastle, and Adelaide is more than 120 times larger than the next city in South Australia.

On the other hand, competition, petty rivalry, and even-handed government policy has prevented the emergence of a strong hierarchical structure (in size terms at least) among the major cities. The marked degree of metropolitan primacy is also a reflection of the environmental conditions in non-metropolitan Australia which were never conducive to a high level of population density in most areas away from a narrow coastal strip. The type of agriculture which emerged under these conditions and in response to world market demands for particular commodities was essentially extensive, low in its labour requirements, and the demand was never there to set up large regional service centres, nor of course were such towns inherited from a by-gone era as they were in Europe. The immediate needs of the rural population could be met by relatively small country towns, while higher-order goods and services were supplied directly from the capital cities. Rose (1967) has termed those direct metropolitan-rural links a colonial relationship, which has replaced the more complex hierarchy of service centres found in older-settled countries. The major urban functions required by the export-oriented agricultural producers were transport, trading, and shipping facilities to transmit goods to the markets of Europe. These were supplied almost solely by the mercantile capital cities. There were, therefore, a number of parallels between the Australian situation and that of Canada as set out by Simmons (1974) utilizing the general framework of staple theory.

The occupational structure of the large cities which emerged, however, has differed from their counterparts in other countries (Table 3.2). They grew essentially as extensions of the European system in the post-Industrial Revolution period and did not evolve through clear-cut developmental

Table 3.2: *Percentage Distribution of Workforce by Occupation Groups, Censuses 1901-1976*

Industry Group	1901	1911	1921	1933	1947	1954	1961	1966	1971	1976
Primary	32.9	30.2	25.8	24.3	17.6	15.1	12.4	10.8	9.0	8.8
Secondary	16.8[a]	19.8[a]	21.2[a]	19.0	27.6	28.0	27.5	27.6	25.0	21.1
Tertiary	50.3	50.0	53.0	56.7	54.8	56.9	60.1	60.6	66.0	70.1

[a] Electricity and gas included in Secondary

Source: Commonwealth Censuses

stages. Their hinterlands were always commercially-oriented and never experienced a prior period of subsistence farming. The cities themselves were commercial or mercantile cities—what McCarty (1970) has called 'pure' products of capitalism—with their growth being determined largely by world economic forces, and their labour forces dominated by service or tertiary, not manufacturing, activities. Services have always been the most important providers of jobs in Australia's urban areas. Definitions of the service sector differ, as do the estimates of the relative importance of the various sectors at different times in Australia's history, but it is clear that during the second half of the nineteenth century Australia had developed an extremely high level of service employment, considerably greater than that found in the United States. Butlin (1964) has estimated that in the 1860s the service sector contributed 42.5 per cent of total gross domestic product. On the other hand large scale secondary industries of a kind comparable to those in the United States in the same period were exceptional in nineteenth century Australia; even as late as 1891 manufacturing was contributing only about 10 per cent of the gross domestic product. Despite huge amounts of government support, manufacturing plants remained small, financed by banks and other financial institutions within the country and owned by individuals, families, or partnerships for the most part (Linge, 1979a). The small and highly fragmented market, with towns separated by great distances, gave a form of protection to local small-scale manufacturers and encouraged a dispersed distribution pattern, and it was not until the 1890s that economies of scale and agglomeration became operational and that the present pattern of metropolitan concentration began to emerge.

Another factor contributing further to the rise of a mere handful of mercantile port cities has been the persistence of the colonial pattern fixed in the last century. The sovereignty each colony exercised over its hinterland led to an almost complete focusing of transactions and flows on their respective port-capitals. Variations in rail gauges, customs, and protectionist policies versus free trade philosophies, recruitment of settlers, incentives for farmers, and encouragement to industry all led to a strongly centralized set of quasi-independent colonies in the nineteenth century having more interaction with Britain than with each other—a further extension of the colonial relationship. The rigidities and rivalries created during this colonial period have been maintained in many aspects of contemporary economic, social, and political life despite eighty years of federation. Indeed, state rights ensured that the federal parliamentary system did not intrude or create much change in the domestic scene until the crisis of the Second World War allowed the central government to take control of personal taxation. Since that time the federal government has participated more directly in internal affairs and its unifying influence has been more strongly felt in issues such as housing, transportation, communications, wage conditions, immigration, health, foreign investment, international marketing, and environmental concerns. All are issues which have a direct significance on the way in which the urban system has grown.

As one component of the evolution of the federal system, the planning and development of Canberra as the national capital has brought the central government into a real participatory role in altering Australia's urban pattern. In fact, Canberra represents one of the few success stories in stimulating the growth of a non-coastal settlement of any significant size since the gold rush days in the state of Victoria in the 1850s and in Western Australia in the 1890s. At the same time it is necessary to note that minerals of different kinds and at different periods have provided the stimulus for numerous specialized mining towns, often in remote areas, throughout the entire history of Australia's urban development.

The construction of Canberra and its successful growth inevitably highlights a further theme (dream might be more appropriate) of significance in a discussion of the Australian urban system. Although often poorly defined and articulated, there has been a long-standing concern in Australia with the issue of decentralization. The movement has taken a number of different forms, but essentially it has been directed at either promoting more uniform settlement and alternatives to metropolitan dominance or as a means of reducing the burgeoning populations of the state primate cities. The popularity of the issue has waxed and waned at different periods and was at its peak in the early 1970s when a federal government department was created with part of its mandate explicitly directed to the stimulation of a number of growth centres outside the orbit of the metropolitan areas. Implicit in the notion of decentralization has been the ideal of creating larger and more viable inland urban centres to offset the growing pressures on the coastal strip while at the same time providing acceptable alternatives to metropolitan living. At the moment such real alternatives do not exist for the great bulk of Australian urban dwellers.

Current Patterns and Recent Changes

Apart from the tragic loss of many thousands of servicemen, Australia emerged from the Second World War remarkably unscathed. Nevertheless the country was confronted with a significant range of problems to resolve, while at the same time the war had created a number of opportunities which could be exploited for the benefit of the economy in general and for urban areas specifically. The war effort had diverted essential materials from domestic consumption so that the metropolitan areas in particular were faced with quite acute housing shortages. Sewerage and water supply schemes had been delayed, non-strategic transport facilities had fallen behind in both equipment and capital works, and there was a shortage of manpower—especially those with skills. In contrast, the shortage of shipping vessels and the uncertainties of supply which plagued both the war and the immediate years following it, created a major stimulus to local manufacturing. Insulated from former competitors, Australia was able to create an artificial market advantage for its local manufacturers despite the absolute small size of its national demand. The first twenty-five years following the war saw Australian manufacturing reach its greatest size in terms of numbers employed. War-damaged and disrupted European economies also created a significant demand for rural produce with all forms of food in short supply. The primary sector had been harnessed to feed the war machine and was able to divert its attention to feeding Europe's civilians when peace was declared. In addition, country towns found that factories, decentralized during the war effort, were significant assets in the immediate post-war period as manufacturers sought cheap and available premises and a supply of female labour. For a few years the attractions of jobs and housing meant that country towns flourished until the metropolitan areas caught up on their backlog of housing and infrastructure and their significant markets and economies of scale allowed these centres to recover their former dominant position over their smaller and uncompetitive rivals.

But perhaps of greatest significance for the cities was the fact that the war, the loss of men, and the associated shortage of skills added to and confirmed Australia's pre-war fear of a declining population. Marriages delayed or abandoned during the depression combined with those disrupted if not foregone by the war reinforced the trend to declining birth rates which had characterized the greater part of the century. Australia became convinced that it had to populate or perish within its Asian region and the conclusion of war signalled the beginning of thirty years of successful and sustained efforts to attract migrants. Overwhelmingly these newcomers became urban dwellers and especially metropolitan residents. After a brief period during which continental European refugees dominated the flows, British migrants formed the bulk of the new settlers for most of these years, but a steady increase in Southern Europeans in the 1960s provided an enriched and broadened Australian culture. Not only did the migrants contribute substantially to the labour force but their demand for housing, consumer durables, education, food, clothing, sport, and leisure boosted domestic production to higher levels with a multiplier effect which created new thresholds for investment and output.

During this prosperous post-war period the Australian economy has undergone quite remarkable change. Primary produce still forms a major anchor for its export base, but a rich and fortuitous suite of mineral resources is increasingly commanding the attention of international investors and markets. Extensive deposits of quality coal in NSW and more especially Queensland, literal mountains of iron ore in Western Australia, oil and natural gas, bauxite, uranium, copper, and mineral sands, have given the mining sector a new lease of life not experienced since the heady and frantic days of the 1850s gold rushes in Victoria. New towns and specialized export ports have been spawned in remote locations but perhaps a greater impact has been felt in the renewed and unparalleled investment in office development in the central cities of the traditional port-capitals. The growth of office jobs—banking, business services, real estate, advertising, investment, legal advice, and so on—has resulted in a major expansion of the tertiary and quaternary sectors of the economy. Again, the bulk of the growth has taken place in the metropolitan areas. Much of the investment capital to fuel this growth has come from overseas.

But there have been costs accompanying this new role in the world community. For much of the post-war period Australian manufacturing (also dominantly metropolitan in location) was fostered behind a barrier of tariffs which protected and subsidized non-economic units with surplus capacity and with no way of realizing adequate economies of scale in the face of a small national market characterized by the duplication of establishments rather than rationalization (Linge, 1979b).

Competition and pressure from a much more open and expanded world community wanting a greater share in the balance of trade between nations has led to a reappraisal and some move away from protection; a quid pro quo if Australia is to have entry to growing markets for her resource-rich products. The cost is being borne by the secondary sector where relative (and in some situations absolute) decline in jobs has had a significant impact on small one-industry country towns, in labour-intensive inner city industries and on the migrant community which has been disproportionately represented in this sector. In addition, automation, machine-controlled production, word processors, and other technological innovations have begun to bite into numerous Australian jobs. Structural change has become a major issue in a country where previously full employment was an ideal ascribed to by all political parties. Today, unemployment in the region of 5 + per cent is rapidly becoming accepted as the norm as problems of achieving gainful employment for the country's youth, migrants, inexperienced, unskilled, and women reaches significant proportions while the nation struggles to adjust to the changed conditions of the late twentieth century. Many of these problems are synonymous with urban life.

A further dimension of the changes being experienced has to do with the growing realization that the ethos of unchallenged growth has to be revised. One major shock came from the conclusions of the National Population Inquiry (1975). Until the mid-1970s Australia had experienced thirty years of unparalleled growth and prosperity. In fact, this growth had been based on the belief that Australia would continue to expand as a result of the combined forces of natural increase and immigration. To a certain extent the downturn in economic growth in the late 1970s was a loss of faith in the belief that Australia's population would continue to increase at the rate of previous decades. The National Population Inquiry showed that previous

estimates of a population of 22 million by the year 2000 were highly optimistic. A more realistic estimate of 17.5 million was put forward. Such a
drastic revision has had major implications for planners of all kinds in
terms of future domestic markets, the size of individual cities, the need for
alternative growth centres, the work-force, housing market, educational
facilities, and changing patterns of consumer demand.

The Urban Pattern

The first census following the war (in 1947) revealed Australia's population
to be 7.56 million of whom almost 32 per cent could be regarded as rural
dwellers (Table 3.3). The metropolitan areas (the six state capitals and
Canberra) accommodated 50 per cent of the nation's population, leaving 18
per cent residing in 'other' urban areas. (In Australia settlements with
populations of 1000 or more are generally defined as urban for census
purposes).

These crude national summaries, of course, mask quite significant variations at the state level, but there is sufficient similarity in the patterns for
such broad generalizations to hold true.

   Thirty years after the war major changes had occurred in the general
pattern of population distribution. The dominance of the metropolitan
areas was a feature of the 1947 pattern and increasing metropolitanization
has been a major trend over the entire post-war period. By 1975, almost
two-thirds of the Australian population resided in the seven capitals. Conversely, the very significant decline in rural population has been an equally
strong trend for the whole period. By 1976 the rural population had been
reduced to one-third of its 1947 share. The picture for the 'other' urban
component is not so simple. The immediate post-war period (1947-54) saw
towns in this class increase their share of national population to one-quarter.
This period has been labelled the 'hey-day' of the country town for reasons
largely suggested in the preceding section. Since that brief period during
which it looked as if the 'other' urban sector could mount a real challenge to
metropolitan dominance this group has remained relatively static, only just
maintaining its proportion. But what is abundantly clear at both the beginning and end of the period is the very high degree of urbanization. In

Table 3.3: *Per Cent Distribution of Urban/Rural Population 1947-76*

	1947	1954	1961	1966	1971	1976
Metropolitan	50.72	54.06	56.26	58.23	60.13	63.83
Other urban	18.14	24.88	25.88	25.13	25.53	22.18
Rural	31.14	21.06	17.86	16.64	14.34	13.89
Total Population (in 000s)	7,561	8,963	10,483	11,531	12,712	13,991

1947, 60 per cent of the population were urban dwellers; but by 1976 more than eight out of ten Australians lived in cities and towns.

When the nation's main urban centres are arranged by rank (Figure 3.2) the country falls into an intermediary position between the idealized conditions of rank-size and primacy. This situation is largely the product of the evolution of the nation's political organization from a set of quasi-independent crown colonies to a federal system of states. Sydney and Melbourne have vied for absolute dominance over the course of their history and are effectively similar in size. They are followed by a group of significantly smaller state capitals—Brisbane, Adelaide, and Perth—which are also roughly comparable in size. Newcastle, Wollongong, Canberra, Geelong, and Hobart create another approximate 'plateau' on the array so that regular systematic size relationships are again negated. Thus when compared to the apparent orderliness of the rank-size relationships of United States cities or the spectacularly primate conditions of Thailand, Japan, Greece, or Sweden, Australia comprises a hierarchical series of similar sized groups of cities.

The picture changes quite dramatically when the size relationships of Australian urban centres are disaggregated to the state scale. At this scale four of the states—NSW, Victoria, South Australia and Western Australia —are all clearly primate with the state capital being substantially larger than the next city in the array, often by a factor of ten or more. The very substantial initial advantage attained by each of the capitals and their subsequent growth and sustained dominance within their own state sub-systems

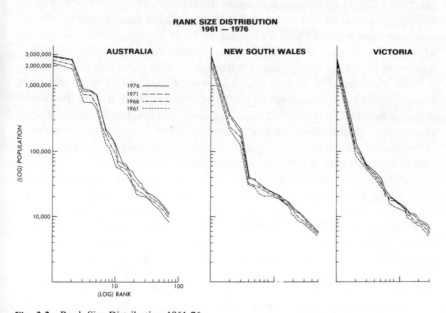

Fig. 3.2 Rank Size Distribution 1961-76

has been explored in previous sections of this paper. The geographical location of Brisbane in the south-eastern corner of its state, its long and fertile coast and its chain of resource-endowed port-towns reduces that capital's dominance. The orientation and access to the main land of Launceston, Tasmania's second largest city, and its command of the productive northern section of the state has, in a similar way, prevented Hobart from achieving clear dominance in that state. What these size relationships do reveal at the state scale is the great inertia that has characterized the urban system since its initiation and the significance of early administrative-political control of each state capital over their former colonial hinterlands. The degree of primacy amongst individual states is highly suggestive of semi-independent sub-systems of urban centres operating at this scale. Federation has been slow to break down these initial patterns and to achieve a high degree of national integration. Indeed, Rose (1966) has argued that, given the timing of settlement and the technology available, it is entirely logical to expect primacy to be the *normal* condition in Australia.

Another view of the population size relationships among Australian urban centres can be obtained from Figure 3.3. Here the rank-size of centres of more than 10,000 inhabitants has been plotted for the period 1961-76. Two features are of major note. The first is the very great stability of ten major cities. Although there have been some modest shifts in their ranks, notably Canberra, this part of the urban system has a momentum and inertia which would require a massive and unprecedented economic disruption to disturb in any drastic way. On the other hand, there has been a surprising degree of turbulence among the smaller centres—especially those with populations of less than 50,000. Centres have been promoted or demoted in rank by very significant margins while a quite substantial number of towns have fallen out altogether (dropping below the qualifying populations of 10,000 or more); many others, of course, have taken their place.

Some care needs to be taken in interpreting Figure 3.3. What has been plotted is the rank of a town so that a change in position over the period does not necessarily mean that a specific town has necessarily lost or gained population. Other towns ranked above or below it may have performed more poorly or better to bring about a change in relative position. In a highly simplistic sense these rank relationships demonstrate one aspect of the urban system—the relative position of towns being dependent upon what is happening to others in the system. However, there are some obvious changes in rank which are clearly explicable. Peripheral metropolitan locations such as Gosford-Woy Woy, Budgewoi-Lake, and The Entrance have experienced rapid promotion through suburban expansion. Resource oriented towns such as Kalgoorlie, Broken Hill, Moe-Yallourn, Morwell, and Lithgow reflect quite rapid responses to the changing fortunes of the minerals on which they are almost solely dependent. It should also be noted that it obviously does not require a very significant increase or decrease in

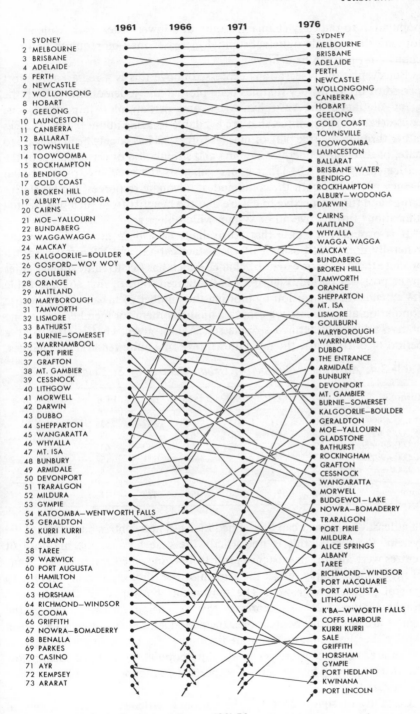

Fig. 3.3 Changes in the Ranking of Towns, 1961-76

population to radically change the rank of a lower-order town while at the top end of the scale quite substantial increases may be required before a change in rank can be achieved.

But despite the reservations expressed above this is a remarkably short period of urban history that has been plotted and it demonstrates both the great volatility of the Australian system and, perhaps more importantly, the considerable opportunities that are available to bring about major changes either through the free play of market forces, as has largely been the case to date, or through deliberate planning and stimulation of certain parts of the settlement system. The latter course suggests the need for some national agency which has both the command of adequate resources, the legislative power and the perspective to ensure that the benefits from such preferential allocations further overall or system-wide objectives.

It is probably the case that Australians have been mesmerized by the generally dominant position of each state capital and have failed to appreciate the degree or extent of change which has occurred to smaller cities in the post-war period. Figure 3.3 has captured some of that change. Table 3.4 extends this dimension by plotting the number of urban centres whose population at six successive censuses qualifies them for membership in one of five arbitrarily defined size classes. Again, given what is effectively a period of thirty years, the table illustrates some quite remarkable changes.

Table 3.4: *Australia—Number of Urban Centres by Size-class 1947-76*

Town Size	1947	1954	1961	1966	1971	1976
1,000-4,999	290	303	315	330	337	353
5,000-9,999	41	69	70	63	67	73
10,000-49,999	29	40	47	53	59	63
50,000-499,999	7	5	8	10	11	13
500,000+	2	4	4	4	5	5
Total:	369	421	444	460	479	507

In at least one sense it can be claimed that 138 new centres have entered the system. Obviously, this is not strictly the case because the majority of centres were already in existence prior to 1947 in some form or other. Some of the changes simply reflect the growth of the whole system in response to general population growth. The movement 'outwards' of the rank-size graphs (Figure 3.2) also expresses this expansion factor. However, the figures are impressive because over the period a number of towns have been 'lost' either becoming incorporated within the orbit of larger contiguous urban areas or because losses in absolute population dropped them below the entry figure. Thus in certain respects the amount of change has been understated.

Certainly of significance for the national settlement system in general has been the 'thickening' of the larger towns. In 1947, only two had populations of more than 500,000 whereas by 1976 five had reached this size. Similarly, towns in the next lower order of 50,000 to 500,000 virtually doubled in number during the period. Given the high degree of primacy in most states the absence of a reasonable number of middle-sized towns is obvious but the table does demonstrate that there has been some in-filling of this previously depleted rank. Even an increase in the membership of the smallest size class by more than one-fifth during a period when this class was clearly losing members to the next highest group shows that Australia has spawned a remarkable number of settlements in the post-war period.

However, despite our inability to examine all 507 of the urban centres contributing to Table 3.4 some general comments can be made regarding the common characteristics of each class. Historically, Sydney and Melbourne have always been the largest of the state capitals and at the beginning of the period they were the only centres with populations of more than half a million. By the end of the period they had been joined by the remaining mainland state capitals—Adelaide, Brisbane, and Perth—all three of which will probably exceed one million by the turn of the century.

In the second group of towns (50,000-500,000), discounting the mainland state capitals which were promoted out of this group during the period, only Hobart, Newcastle, Wollongong, and Geelong were members of the class during the whole time span. In many respects three of these cities are industrial outliers of either Sydney or Melbourne although physically separated from their respective capitals by up to 100 kilometres. All three owe their growth to quite specialized industrial bases and in this context they are all quite vulnerable to major shifts in market demand. The national capital, Canberra, pursued a rapid and planned growth path throughout the period and is now the eighth largest centre in the country with a population hovering on 200,000. Its growth is of interest not only because it represents a major success in stimulating development in an inland location but also because it is now rapidly approaching the size recognized by many observers as the critical lower limit beyond which a self-sustaining mechanism locks in to promote continuing expansion. Whether the same size value applies in Australia, whether it can apply to the rather special functional base of a capital, and whether it will apply in the 1980s under quite changed conditions from those operating in the preceding thirty years remains unanswered. However, the Canberra experience is one that 'managers' of the urban system should be monitoring with close attention as it passes through this size barrier. As Australia's major success in a form of post-war decentralization it is obvious that the Canberra experiment cannot be duplicated in quite the same way, yet it is equally obvious that a real body of expertise has been developed which could be harnessed for creating other growth centres should the need and/or will for such arise.

Other towns to join this second tier in the period include a major residential outlier of Sydney—Gosford; and the Gold Coast and Toowoomba

—both in relatively close proximity to Brisbane. Townsville's military, port, and educational roles have boosted it to third position within Queensland while Tasmania's northern city, Launceston, continues to challenge its state capital for control of that part of the island. Within Victoria the two former gold mining centres of Ballarat and Bendigo command productive agricultural hinterlands and have taken on a number of regional and tourist functions which continue to stimulate their growth.

The third class of towns, those with populations from 10-50,000, have had a much more chequered history over the past thirty years. In some respects this is the most critical size group embracing those centres which have quite substantial investments in infrastructure but which do not have the absolute size or breadth of economic base to insulate them from the possibility of decline should significant changes in the Australian economy occur. This class also includes a much more varied mix of towns in terms of their functional bases than those in classes above or below it.

In fact, rather less than half of the towns in this group have performed quite well in terms of growth for most of the post-war years and in the latest census period (1971-6) have expanded their populations by more than 10 per cent in the majority of cases. Two of the towns, Blue Mountains and Queanbeyan, have benefited from proximity to Sydney and Canberra respectively. In effect, they are both dormitory suburbs of their larger neighbours. Of rather special interest is the performance of Albury-Wodonga. The twin towns lying astride the Murray River were identified as a joint growth centre by the Labour government in 1973 and a co-operative venture involving the states of NSW and Victoria and the federal government led to the creation of the Albury-Wodonga Development Corporation. The Corporation was charged with the task of planning, promoting and guiding the future of the centre. Despite an abrupt and substantial reduction in funding when the federal government was replaced in 1975 and despite the longer-term effects such a reversal of government commitment may have on any future attempts at planned decentralization, the private sector seems to have confirmed the judgement of the previous Labour administration in selecting Albury-Wodonga as an obvious growth point on the corridor between Sydney and Melbourne. While growth is not proceeding as rapidly as originally planned when government support was more plentiful, none the less its population expansion (16 per cent in the 1971-6 period) and the new industries and housing it is attracting suggest that Albury-Wodonga will continue to experience a healthy rate of growth in the immediate future.

Other towns to perform at a satisfactory level of growth in this class include mainly old established and traditional rural service centres such as Wagga Wagga, Tamworth, Armidale, Dubbo, and Orange in NSW; Cairns, Bundaberg, and Gladstone in Queensland; Shepparton and Warrnambool in Victoria; and Bunbury and Geraldton in Western Australia.

On the other hand, somewhat more than half the towns in this class performed quite poorly with some actually losing population for part of if not the whole period since 1947. Almost one-third of those doing poorly— Lithgow, Broken Hill, La Trobe Valley, Mt. Isa, Port Pirie, and Kalgoorlie —have very narrow economic bases. They are almost all specialized towns relying on mining or the processing of minerals for their livelihood. The remaining quality and quantity of their reserves, world prices, and changing technology make their populations vulnerable to the vagaries of markets. Almost all other towns in this group rely on their role as rural service centres to sustain their growth and the bulk of them demonstrated only modest gains. However, a small number—Hamilton, Maryborough, Gympie, and Warwick—have lost population over the two censuses and it would appear that the declining level of demand in their hinterlands combined with increased access to alternative centres has reduced their former viability. Obviously, one doesn't normally expect resource-oriented towns to last for ever, but the decline of rural service centres which generally have evolved over a longer period of time and established a greater air of permanence, gives rise to more serious problems. This is partly because of the time lag between the onset of economic decline and demographic adjustment.

The last two size classes in this analysis—those towns with populations of 1-5,000 and 5-10,000—embrace the largest number of urban centres. More than 80 per cent of all the nodes in the system belong to one or other of these two classes. Unfortunately the large number of centres prevents any discussion of individual members. Certainly, both groups have continued to expand their membership while at the same time promoting a good number to the next class above them. In the most general terms one can only suggest that within these two groups the towns expanding most rapidly have been coastal resort and/or retirement centres and those (often in remote areas of the continent) experiencing a boom as a result of mineral developments. Conversely, those towns experiencing the greatest decline in population have been former boom towns now languishing on their exhausted or uneconomic mineral deposits. Falling between these two extremes and generally struggling to maintain their existing size are the traditional small country towns (usually occupying inland locations) serving their surrounding rural communities. To a degree the major increases in membership of the two classes have taken place in the 'pioneering' and 'frontier' states of Queensland and Western Australia in particular. The longer established and more extensively developed states of the southeast have not experienced the same degree of town proliferation in the post-war period.

Metropolitan Dominance

Except for the cases of Tasmania and Queensland the six state capital cities have always dominated the settlement system within their respective states.

While the degree of primacy has fluctuated somewhat from time to time, the period from 1947 to 1971, one of great economic expansion, witnessed a major increase in metropolitan dominance. During the period, for example, Sydney's share of NSW's population grew from 40 to 60 per cent and Melbourne's share of Victoria's population from 53 to 70 per cent. In the state of Victoria, Melbourne is now 20 times larger than Geelong, the next largest city; Sydney is eight times larger than Newcastle and Adelaide is more than 120 times larger than the next sized city. Overall, by 1976, 64 per cent of the nation's population lived in the six metropolitan areas with a further 22 per cent in the 'other urban' category. The percentage living in the vast expanse of rural Australia had declined to 14 per cent.

As has been implied in the previous discussion this picture of metropolitan dominance needs to be qualified in two ways. In the first place, in the most recent intercensal period, 1971-6, there is clear evidence of a major downturn in the growth rates of the large cities; in fact the rates of growth of Sydney and Melbourne, the two largest cities are now amongst the lowest in the nation (Table 3.5). This is a reflection of changed economic circumstances, higher unemployment levels, lower birth rates, and most importantly, of the decline in immigration.

It is important to note, however, that, unlike some other Western nations, there is no real evidence as yet in Australia of a major shift of the population from the metropolitan cities to smaller urban places; in fact some of the most rapidly growing areas are the statistical divisions abutting the Sydney, Melbourne, and Brisbane metropolitan boundaries. It would also have to be acknowledged that the concept of counter-urbanization is much less appropriate in the case of Australia simply because there are so few centres of any significant size to attract persons seeking a viable alternative to metropolitan living.

The second qualification to be made is that, although a very large proportion of the nation's population lives in large urban areas, and at a state scale there is great primacy, the dominant feature of the settlement pattern

Table 3.5: *Australian Metropolitan Areas, Population Change 1966-76*

	1966	1971	Intercensal Variation Change 1961-71 population	%	1976	Intercensal Variation Change 1971-76 population	%
Sydney	2,447,219	2,725,064	277,845	11.35	2,765,040	39,976	1.47
Melbourne	2,108,401	2,407,914	299,513	14.20	2,479,225	71,311	2.96
Brisbane	716,402	818,423	102,021	14.24	892,987	74,564	9.11
Adelaide	728,279	809,482	81,203	11.15	857,196	47,714	5.89
Perth	500,246	641,800	141,554	28.29	731,275	89,475	13.94
Hobart	119,469	129,928	10,459	8.75	132,524	2,596	2.00
Canberra	93,314	140,864	47,550	50.95	194,517	53,653	38.09
Darwin	21,205	35,516	14,311	67.49	41,374	5,858	16.49

at the national scale is a fairly even spread of large cities around the coast line, that is, a multiple-nucleated national urban pattern. This pattern is a clear reflection of Australia's colonial origins and of the persistence over time of strong state governments and state loyalties, the strength of which distinguishes Australia from the other New World federations such as Canada and the USA.

As is to be expected, the capital cities have played particularly important roles in the economic and social life of the nation. The economic and political activities so heavily concentrated in these cities generate the impulses and linkages which bind the urban places together into a system. Although state loyalties remain very strong in Australia there is evidence of growing national integration, especially in the Sydney-Canberra-Melbourne corridor in the south-east. Nevertheless the distribution of the capital cities around the seaboard, combined with the competitive nature of state development, has produced a good deal of duplication of economic activities from city to city. This has been particularly noticeable in manufacturing industry, which has been a dominant feature of Australia's economic development in the twenty-five years after the Second World War.

During the 1930s some 16 per cent of Australia's GDP was contributed by manufacturing, but by 1950 its contribution had increased to 28 per cent and over 1.3 million workers were employed in manufacturing industry. By 1966, 27 per cent of the nation's workforce was employed in manufacturing. This expansion was generated by a forced disengagement of Australia from the world economy during the war years, and afterwards, by deliberate government encouragement through tariff protection, subsidies, and other measures, and, of course, by the growth of the domestic market. Spatially, manufacturing is even more concentrated in the metropolitan centres than population, because of the size of the capital city markets, the scale economies offered to firms, and the nodality of the transport system in each state.

By 1973, however, severe pressures had built up on manufacturing industry. The oil crisis added to the high production costs that already characterized Australian manufacturing. And, by the early 1970s local exporters were beginning to experience strong competition in Southeast Asian markets by exporters from the low wage countries of Korea, Taiwan and Singapore. Added to these circumstances was a series of technological breakthroughs which made redundant many jobs in manufacturing, and which also threatened jobs in the tertiary sector. Unlike the situation in the 1960s, when the service sector could soak up jobs displaced from manufacturing, the crisis of the 1970s has led to the most extensive and persistent unemployment since the depression of the 1930s. Because of the spatial polarization of economic growth, the current malaise of the Australian economy is immediately apparent in the capital cities especially in NSW and Victoria.

By way of contrast the mineral-rich, but isolated, northern part of the continent is experiencing a development boom. This has given rise to a set of distinctive mining settlements which have but tenuous links to the main centres in the industrial heartland of the south-east. The growth of Brisbane and Perth, however, is directly associated with the inflow of foreign capital to exploit the mineral resources of Queensland and Western Australia.

As significant as manufacturing activity is in the economic base of the cities, it is necessary to emphasize the importance of government as a provider of jobs and as a control mechanism operating through the urban system. Not only is each capital city the seat of state government but it also contains offices of the central government. This means that a large proportion of the tertiary workforce in the CBDs of Australian cities is employed by government, and that each state capital is an outpost of the central government, providing services and managing the various ministries on a state-wide basis.

There is a similar pattern of distribution of control in the private sector. Of the largest 100 companies in 1980, 58 had head offices in Sydney, 34 in Melbourne, four in Brisbane, three in Adelaide and one in Perth. Of the top 50 companies, 24 had headquarters in Melbourne, 23 in Sydney, two in Brisbane and one in Adelaide. The Melbourne based firms are the largest, controlling 60 per cent of the total assets of the top 20 compared with 28 per cent in Sydney. This concentration of head offices has resulted in a pronounced clustering of professional, technical, and administrative occupations in the metropolitan areas, and has reinforced their control function throughout each state sub-system.

Conclusion

The main purpose of this essay has been to identify the ways in which the Australian settlement system is similar to that of other New World nations, but also to point out some of those unique features, arising from such considerations as the timing and nature of the initial settlement, the harsh environment, and the nation's role in the world economy. Australia is not only one of the most highly urbanized nations, but a very high proportion of its population and economic activities are concentrated in its metropolitan centres. These centres are spread fairly evenly around the eastern and southern coastlines and are closely identified with the persistence of strong state governments and state loyalties throughout Australia's history. The export orientation of the agricultural industries has also contributed to the dominance of the port-cities.

But evidence of change in the urban system has become more apparent in the last decade. The rapid growth rates of the metropolitan centres have slowed as the immigration programme has experienced a downturn and as the national economy has been beset by difficulties. Manufacturing industries, whose growth during the long boom from 1945 to 1970 had sustained the increasing dominance of the metropolitan areas, are now in decline. And major technological changes have prevented tertiary activities from being able to absorb the displaced workforce. While there is no evidence of a major shift of the population to the smaller provincial centres, there is evidence of considerable buoyancy in the performance of small centres in the most recent intercensal period. The current boom in the mineral industries in the isolated north and northwest of the continent is also contributing to the development of a set of mining towns with rather weak linkages to other urban places. The state sub-systems, so strong throughout Australia's history, are gradually being integrated into a national system. The current period of economic uncertainty seems to be reflected in turbulence as expressed by the varied growth performances and functions of urban places.

REFERENCES

Butlin, N. G. 1964. *Investment in Australian Economic Development*. Cambridge: Cambridge University Press.

Jackson, R. A. 1977. *Australian Economic Development in the Nineteenth Century*. Canberra: ANU Press.

Linge, G. J. R. 1979a. *Industrial Awakening. A Geography of Australian Manufacturing 1788 to 1890*. Canberra: ANU Press.

Linge, G. J. R. 1979b. 'Australian Manufacturing in Recession: A Review of the Spatial Implications', *Environment and Planning*, 11:1405-30.

Logan, M. I., Whitelaw, J. S. and McKay, J. M. 1989. *Urbanization: The Australian Experience*. Melbourne: Shillington House.

McCarty, J. W. 1970. 'Australian Capital Cities in the Nineteenth Century', *Australian Economic History Review*, X: 107-37.

National Population Inquiry 1975. *Population and Australia: A Demographic Analysis and Projection*. Canberra: AGPS.

Neutze, M. 1977. *Urban Development in Australia*. Sydney: Allen and Unwin.

Rose, A. J. 1966. 'Dissent From Down Under: Metropolitan Primacy as the Normal State', *Pacific Viewpoint*, 7: 1-27.

Rose, A. J. 1967. *Patterns of Cities*. Melbourne: Nelson.

Simmons, J. W. 1974. *Canada as an Urban System: A Conceptual Framework*, Research Paper No. 62, Centre for Urban and Community Studies, University of Toronto.

Weber, A. F. 1899. *The Growth of Cities in the Nineteenth Century*, New York: Cornell University Press.

4 THE SWEDISH NATIONAL SETTLEMENT SYSTEM

OLOF WÄRNERYD

Introduction

Changes in the Swedish settlement system occur daily and hourly as new dwellings are constructed and old ones abandoned. These are micro-events of crucial importance to the individual family but extremely difficult to observe in aggregated data. Over time, however, they have resulted in considerable change. The enclosure reforms which began in the eighteenth century broke up the farming villages and redistributed the farmsteads over larger areas. The rapid population increase during the nineteenth century forced many people into the tilling of new land. With the rapid increase of the rural proletariat and smallholders, the settlement area grew geographically to reach its maximum in the period 1860-70. At the same time industrialization and railway construction pulled the population into small industrial villages, railway junctions, and already existing towns. Emigration, especially to North America, helped to relieve the rural population pressure further; between 1860 and 1920 more than one million Swedes or about 20 per cent of the population left the country (Hägerstrand, 1976).

Large scale urbanization characterized national development in the 1950s and 1960s. More recently there has been an exodus of the population from the largest cities to small villages in their surroundings. The enclosure reforms took around 100 years, the rural urbanization around 50 and the large scale urbanization around 25 years. Projecting this time pattern into the future suggests that the present pattern may be replaced by another in about 15 years.

About Regional Inequalities

After the Second World War, all western industrial societies have in one form or another carried out a policy of economic and social equalization. The central goals of this policy have been to improve the living standard of the large masses of their peoples. Among other goals have been those of full employment and the reduction of the differences in income and living conditions among the different social classes. In order to modify the results of the free market mechanism, the state has moved in strongly as a regulating and governing force. The public sector has increased its control over the use and distribution of resources with the intent of stabilizing the economic and political system. In the process there has been a transition from 'pure' capitalism to a mixed economy. Depending on historical and political differences, individual countries have been more or less successful in these endeavours. In the Nordic countries the development towards a welfare society has gone furthest.

Social and economic equality may be reached in two ways. One is to redistribute the existing goods in the society. The other is to increase the total number of goods and then assign a relatively larger part of these to the poorest groups. But even if combinations of these economic and social equalization policies have in some respects been successful, there are nevertheless tendencies for growing differences between geographical regions to emerge; What is at issue is the identification of the processes generating these regional inequalities (Asheim, 1978).

When the micro-events are added up, they can be seen to have caused large shifts in the settlement pattern on the national scale. Except in the case of the enclosure reforms, it is difficult to give any clear-cut explanation of the shifts. Nevertheless, an attempt will be made in this paper to connect these changes with a number of principles: that change is a continuous process; it results from human beings adjusting to new situations in which each individual tries to survive; it is related to other changes in difficult economic, social, and technical sub-systems (private firms, national boards, regional and local authorities, etc.); and the speed and direction of change can to some extent be influenced by public policy.

Changes in the distribution of population are caused by additive social and ecological processes. Individuals or households are responsible for all the small currents in a never ceasing stream. There are no drastic breaks in this process. The rank ordering of the cities and towns, at least in the upper levels of the urban hierarchy in Sweden (Figure 4.1) has been relatively stable during the last century, but shifts are common amongst localities with less than 10,000 inhabitants. The causes of internal migration are many, such as the development of modern medicine, and of industrial and communication technology. The public sector, private industry, and interest groups have all absorbed this development, but with large differences between sectors and geographical regions. The individual household has responded through increased mobility.

Different policies are part of this picture. For a long time migration was a matter for the individual or for the household, even though labour market and regional policies were designed to promote geographical mobility through various forms of movement subsidies. The idea was to induce people to move to places with good job opportunities. During the last five years, however, attitudes have changed. The right to remain in one's place of birth, education, or work has become an objective of regional policy. Job opportunities are to be spread out to all parts of the country but mainly to the economically disadvantaged places.

In a small country like Sweden which is heavily dependent on foreign trade, it is necessary to allow for constant change in both the industrial and

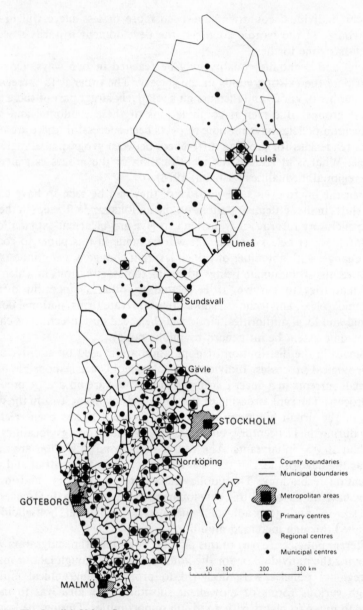

Fig. 4.1 The Swedish Urban System

the public sector. Increased international competition has led to the widespread rationalization of industry. Changes have occurred within almost all private and government owned enterprises in Sweden. Mergers, cooperation, and subcontracting are the rule, and it is inevitable that the location of industrial plants, administrative personnel, and product composition will be influenced. Factories are closing, and employment has been reduced through bans on new hiring. The mobile labour force has nevertheless managed to cope with the new situation. The public sector has also undergone tremendous changes. Social reforms and new education programmes have caused a great expansion in public services. This is especially true of the health sector, but reforms in the administrative division of the country have also been responsible for increases in the number of administrators on the different levels of society.

The forces of specialization also influence the sectoral organization of public services. The geographical concentration and spread of different units within these organizations have had considerable impact on the settlement system. The fact that Sweden has had a fairly stable settlement history is at least partly due to its traditionally decentralized administration. For instance, the growth of the public sector during the last two decades has managed to make up for the employment decrease in industry. The distribution of new jobs within the public sector at the national, regional, and local levels is partially responsible for the fairly even spread of settlement today. The new settlement pattern has grown successively in a process of interdependent adjustments on both the individual and social level. It is not easy to find a clear-cut national strategy which has guided this process. If there is one at all, it is of a late date.

The Historical Growth and Development of the Swedish Settlement System

Between 1850 and 1980 the Swedish population increased from 3.5 million inhabitants to 8.2 million, that is a growth of 4.7 million. Up to 1940, natural increase was greatest in the countryside, while net migration gave negative figures for the countryside and pronounced positive figures for the urban places during the entire period. Since the 1920s, the total rural population has decreased because out-migration has exceeded natural growth. About 350,000 inhabitants lived in the 87 urban places which existed in 1850, making up about 10 per cent of the total population. By 1975 the urban population had grown to 6.8 million or 82 per cent. The term 'urban place' in the context includes all places with more than 200 inhabitants.

Until 1930 Sweden also had an emigration surplus. Substantial immigration occurred during the 1950s and 1960s when Sweden received an immigration surplus of about 250,000 persons. During the same twenty years the natural growth amounted to about 750,000 persons. Despite the strong immigration of the last decades, Sweden has nevertheless experienced a net emigration of about 600,000 for the period 1850-1975; in 1979 about 460,000 were foreign citizens.

Societal Organization and Population Distribution

The data above give us just a crude picture of the development of settlement patterns in Sweden. As a more uncommon way of outlining the biography of a people, the daily life of the individual or the household at three different points in time will be schematized. The intention is not only to demonstrate the adjustment of human beings to social changes but also to show society's own ability to adapt and survive.

The space/time model in Figure 4.2 describes the range of daily activities of a household living in the final stage of pre-industrial society—a society which was still highly regulated. The working population was tied to employers in a personal way, both in agriculture and in the handicraft and trade sectors. Jobs were settled, and mobility was rather limited both in social and geographical terms. Different socio-economic groups and age classes lived near each other in the countryside and in small towns. The agricultural landscape of the villages had been reorganized and the whole cultural landscape had changed. The expanding arable land permitted an increased population, which in turn led to rapid increase in settlement,

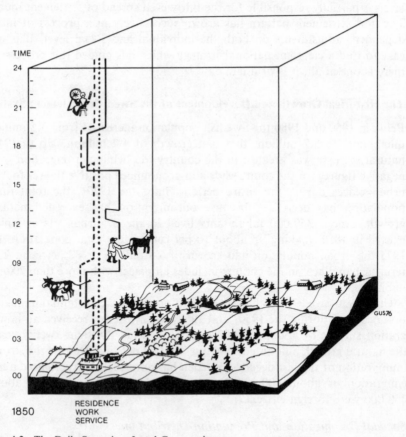

Fig. 4.2   The Daily Space in a Local Community

resulting in, among other things, new settlements in the interior of Norrland.

Around 1870-80 settlement reached its greatest extent in the southern and central parts of Sweden, whereas in Norrland this happened about 30-40 years later. From this period on, the number of houses in the countryside began to decrease. Growth was transferred to towns and villages. Apart from the maximal extent of rural settlement, the highest population density of any time was reached in the towns. In the local community, daily work and other concerns were connected with problems of survival. The places of residence included work places and service functions, and what was needed from outside was not very far away. The whole household took part in the daily duties, and jobs followed in many respects the traditional patterns. What today would be called recreation activities or therapy were natural components of everyday life. Mobility was limited and the frequency of travel was evenly distributed over the whole population. Most people, however, did not own land and had to look for jobs over large areas.

The shift to the next period comprised the transition from a pre-industrial to an industrial society (Figure 4.3). The population increased to about 5.1 million inhabitants with about 30 per cent in towns and other central places. Agriculture decreased its share of total employment and amounted to about 55 per cent. Organizational changes within agriculture together with progress in technology and transport services created the prerequisites for econmic growth and industrialization. The working plan was changed, new occupations and contract work were developed on a larger scale, first in the countryside and then within industry. Socio-economic groups were broken up; even if an extensive poverty problem arose, conditions of life were nevertheless improved for large categories of the population, which was growing rapidly and creating an over-population problem in the countryside. People were looking for jobs (Guteland, *et al.* 1975). Industries were established, primarily in the countryside, in small places and in the vicinity of raw-material and energy resources. At least one member of the household worked in a factory; many preferred to emigrate. The fact that the husband spent his working hours in the factory gave rise to a richer and richer variety of shops, service functions, small workshops and so on. The husband's time which was now unavailable to the household has to be replaced by purchasing the time of other individuals. Although the daily space requirements increased and grew wider, the majority of household members were moving within rather tight geographical boundaries. Towns grew larger, but urbanization was a diffused process, due to the foundation of small industrial places, railway settlements and so on. We can call this process the urbanization of the countryside. The role of trade was also important during this period of urban sprawl. The population pressure within the agricultural sector and the demand for workers by industry redistributed the population to mill towns, factory places, and railway centres.

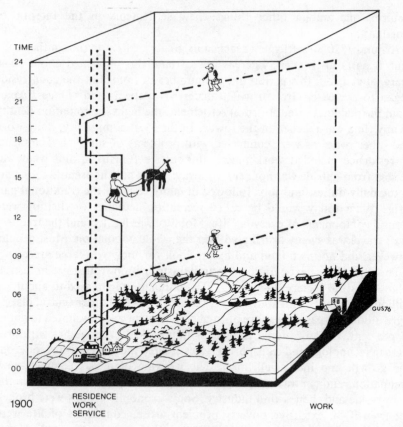

Fig. 4.3   The Daily Space in an Industrial Society

The town and the country had earlier functioned as two quite different units in respect to economic, social, and physical characteristics. Despite the fact that these two units had existed together in two separate spheres, the countryside played the dominating role. To a large extent, this was due to the fact that many of the inhabitants of the small towns lived half as farmers and half as city people. The town was dependent on the products of the rural areas. The role of the town primarily represented the political and administrative powers whose task was to allocate the surplus. With the advent of industrialization, the relationships between the urban places and the rural areas changed. The town took over the dominating role in society, and the manufacturing sector became the principal basis for economic development. During the larger part of the nineteenth century there were few regulations on urban development. The first real building legislation appeared in 1874. However, today's urban system got its fundamental characteristics during this period. The government had no stated policy for the development of the settlement pattern even though subsidies were given to those who wanted to colonize Norrland.

The period after the beginning of industrialization was characterized by increased indusrialization and urbanization. Agriculture was rationalized and people left the countryside to an increasing extent, first for the geographically closest urban places and then for the big cities and towns. A society based on organizations grew up; new views on labour market policy were accepted and an expansion of the public sector occurred. Married women gradually became a factor in labour market policy. As a consequence the tension between household and wage-earning work was brought to light and child care was introduced as a matter of public concern (Guteland, *et al.* 1975). The redistribution of population during this period has perhaps been analysed less than the geographical variations in fertility, but it was no less dramatic. Up to 1920 the natural population growth in the rural areas was more than sufficient to compensate for the 'exile from the countryside'. Through a combination of permanent net migration losses from the rural areas and decreased natural birth rates, however, the rural population diminished more and more in later decades. When foreign emigration ceased, the larger urban places received the vast bulk of migrants. A strong expansion of the urban areas followed and the urban population grew at almost two per cent per annum during the 1930s. During the 1940s growth accelerated to an average of 3 per cent per annum (Guteland, *et al.* 1975).

In total the internal migration amounted to about 10 per cent per annum. In gross terms, this means that about 750,000 persons moved from one commune to another. This mobility rate has remained the same for the last 100 years. Analysis indicates that the largest cities, Stockholm, Göteborg, and Malmö followed the average, while the largest growth occurred in places dominated by metal, textile, rubber, and chemical-technical industries. The other category with high growth included the suburbs around Stockholm (Ahlberg, 1953). Here we also find strong specialization with a more and more diversified division of labour. It was necessary to look for goods and services outside the homes in order to survive. The scattered supply points could be reached by the constantly growing transport system. The car became necessary both for journeys to work and to service centres. In addition, motor vehicles were used to reach recreation areas, to carry children to and from school, and so on (Figure 4.4).

The redistribution of the population which took place during this period has now stabilized. The largest places still are the biggest attraction, but the concentration has taken place more slowly. Immigration to the largest cities has to a large extent been replaced by short distance migration within the urban region. Several cities and towns have even experienced a decreasing population in comparison with smaller places in the vicinity. The result is a marked increase in commuting.

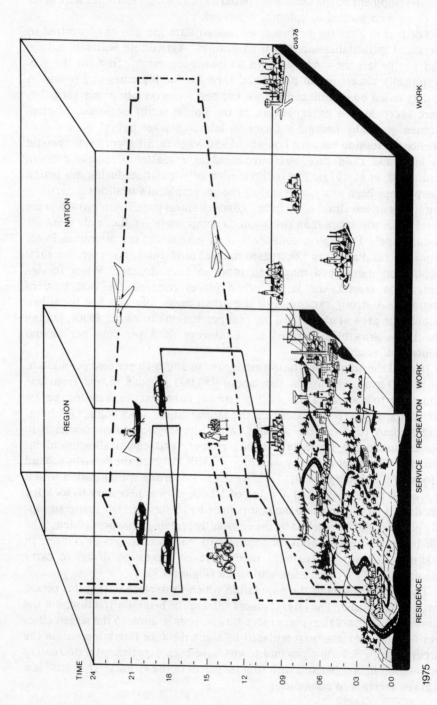

Fig. 4.4 The Daily Space in a Service Society

The 1970s may be named the decade of small urban places, at least as indicated by the changes between 1970 and 1975. In Sweden there are about 1,200 urban places with fewer than 5,000 inhabitants (*see* Table 4.1). All these certainly have not grown, but most of the urban expansion has nevertheless occurred in this size category. During that five-year period, the excess of births amounted to about 140,000 persons, and net immigration to about 40,000. The redistribution of people is the most important factor behind the changes. Although the sparsely populated areas still lose people, it is the larger urban places that yield most of the migrants of today. In total, the three largest cities have lost about 100,000 inhabitants during the last five years.

The small urban places are today places of residence for a little more than 1 million people, and are central places or service centres for more than 1.5 million people living in their vicinities. This means that almost one out of three Swedes is living in or near a small place. These small places are at the same time commuting towns for employees in larger towns and cities. Between 1970 and 1975 the number of commuters increased from about 487,000 to more than 660,000 persons. One of the motives behind this development may be that many people prefer commuting to moving. Liberal tax legislation promotes this behaviour. During the last five years the commuting range has grown even faster.

The decline in the population of the larger urban places did not come as a complete surprise. The difficulties which the urban communities have in satisfying the demand for small houses, villas, or terraced houses—often caused by a lack of suitable land—is one reason. However, the right to deduct journey-to-work costs from taxes, the better possibilities of financing a small house in comparison with renting or buying an apartment, changed views on the environment, and so on, have all contributed to the settlement sprawl (Lewan, 1979).

The concentration of economic activities in certain places in combination with the pricing mechanisms on land results in increasing segregation. As a result, special areas for residence, work, services, administration, education, leisure, have grown up.

This is characteristic of larger urban places where the requirements of efficiency and specialization have gone furthest. One consequence is an increasing need for transport of both persons and goods. This type of mobility goes hand in hand with the rapid expansion of car travel after the Second World War. The separation of residence from work results in increased commuting. Järnegren, *et al.* (1980) have in this context coined the concept of 'daily space' to mark the mobility pattern of the individual during one day and night. This daily space has in general terms expanded over time, but the differences between social groups still remain. Certain special groups, contact-intensive persons, require a national daily space (*see and compare* Figures 4.2, 4.3 and 4.4).

Table 4.1: Size distribution of urban places in Sweden in 1950, 1960, 1970 and 1975

Population in urban places	1950			1960			1970			1975		
	Number	Population in 000s	%	Number	Population in 000s	%	Number	Population in 000s	%	Number	Population in 000s	%
500,000	1	815	17.5	1	957	17.5	1	1,035	15.5	1	995	14.7
100,000-499,999	2	550	11.8	2	671	12.3	2	762	11.5	3	813	12.0
50,000-99,999	7	426	9.1	10	689	12.6	14	1,041	15.6	13	931	13.7
20,000-49,999	19	549	11.8	26	744	13.6	32	998	15.0	33	1,046	15.4
10,000-19,999	36	478	10.3	37	532	9.8	58	829	12.5	58	829	12.2
2,000-9,999	204	822	17.7	231	977	17.9	274	1,109	16.7	304	1,297	19.1
500-1,999	711	659	14.1	624	598	11.0	638	640	9.6	672	655	9.6
200-499	1,076	360	7.7	883	289	5.3	756	242	3.6	700	222	3.3
Total	2,056	4,659	100.0	1,814	5,457	100.0	1,775	6,656	100.0	1,784	6,788	100.0

The sequence of situations shows, at the level of the individual and the household, how our daily routines have changed over a little more than 100 years. The perspective may seem a little narrow, but it is nevertheless in this micro-perspective that one is aware of changes that become evident later at the national level.

The Design of the Swedish Regional Policies

Sweden is well-known for its population statistics which make it possible to trace population development since 1749. Because of this detail, there are a large number of studies and analyses of the changes and redistribution of the Swedish population. Falk (1976) has provided a short and selective reading list, mostly of studies of urban development in Sweden. Urban development as a dynamic factor in the redistribution of the Swedish population has been considered by many geographers. As a consequence, the genesis of urban places is quite well documented, and they have been classified by their occupational characteristics. The focus has been on the structure of the urban system, while there are fewer analyses of the settlement system as a whole.

Many studies indicate that the inertia built into the settlement system continues to be of significance. Of course there have been arguments to the effect that the depopulation of rural areas will create difficulties for the country's food supply. But it is only during the last twenty years that there has been a comprehensive policy for the redistribution of the population. Perhaps this is symptomatic, for there were almost fifty years of heavy emigration before the outflow of people was recognized as a problem (Guteland, *et al.* 1975). What first made the problem acute was the continued depopulation of the rural areas. It was accentuated during the 1940s when other social and economic consequences started to become obvious. Migration to the larger urban places—especially to Stockholm—reinforced the housing shortages, and the point was reached when the state was required to intervene. It was argued that the government should try to influence the mobility of the population especially through its policies of industrial location. Swedish policy thus came to differ from that on the continent and in Britain, where most of the social and economic problems were related to the rapidly growing large cities, by promoting the decentralization of industry.

The above description sets out the situation as it appeared in the late 1940s. If the industrial expansion continued to be concentrated in the few larger cities, the population would probably stagnate or decrease over large areas of the country. It would become difficult to recruit enough labour for the agricultural sector, and forestry. As a consequence, the urban population growth issue assumed national importance. Research and debate on the distribution of the population started immediately after the Second World

War. Geographers contributed many surveys and analyses of the tendencies toward continued depopulation, and of the prospects for retaining enough schools, post offices, shops etc. in the rural areas.

Co-operation between the political and administrative world on the one hand and with the social sciences on the other has a rather long tradition in Sweden. The inquiry into the emigration issue under the leadership of the demographer Gustaf Sundbärg in the first decades of this century is probably still the largest comprehensive study of Swedish society ever carried out. The predominant organizational pattern of cooperation has continued to the present. Numerous government commissions have asked social scientists to contribute background studies. Clearly, such studies tend to function as occasional spotlights, a circumstance which has many disadvantages. As the public sector has widened its scope, the need to arrange more lasting and continuous forms of co-operation has become increasingly obvious. The tendency is now to have mixed-expert groups, where administrators and researchers work in close contact with the respective Ministries. In this manner permanent links have been established between researchers, administrators, and policy makers.

The geographer's traditional surveys of the distribution and location of industry were useful contributions to the government investigations of the early 1950s. The influence of imported theories was strong and new instruments were constructed with the aim of implementing national settlement strategies. Central place theory played an important role, especially in the delimitation of administrative units. This first phase in the national strategy has not passed without controversy. Olsson (1976), for example, makes a rather sharp critique of the unreserved acceptance of central place theory without much examination of the premises behind the theory and its outcome in reality.

Population questions were important during this first phase not only from the political or social point of view, but because they drew attention to the long-term structural changes taking place in society. The large scale urbanization of the 1950s did not appear as a problem during this phase. An active housing policy which aimed at reducing housing shortages was created, and social reforms were gradually implemented to alleviate the inequalities between the classes. Full employment was formulated as a realistic goal, and local islands of unemployment became unacceptable. Related goals for the future settlement pattern were not specified, but the availability of improved statistics at least made it possible to trace the ongoing changes.

This intensified geographical research led to new insights. Great attention was paid to the growth of urban places, and thereby to the accentuated problems of the sparsely populated areas in the northern part of the country. These areas had earlier attracted investments and subsidies of different kinds, but it can nevertheless be said that the location policy in Sweden started in the early 1950s was the beginning of a 'decentralization policy'. The depopulation of certain areas was to be counteracted by an active decentralization policy which directly influenced the location of industry, but indirectly had an impact on all other activities as well. However, the goal could not be to save the population in the sparsely populated and agricultural areas. It was impossible to keep the population in these areas from decreasing.

During the 1950s and the early 1960s, research focused on analyses of regional inequalities. This concern about the need to moderate growth of the large cities, or more correctly, about the consequences of the concentration process, had little impact, however. The concentration process went on. In order to reduce the negative effects for the population in the sparsely populated areas, efforts focused on an active location policy. In 1964, the second location investigation was presented. At this time, the emphasis was on the inertia of the labour force, and on the mobility of firms. It was as part of this policy that society as a whole was given responsibility for the care of the poorer regions. Structural rationalization and economic growth should advance in such a way that individual households would be protected. The new instruments were the promotion of industry through location subsidies and loans tied to the 'support areas' of northern Sweden. No attempts were made to limit the growth of large cities (Guteland, 1976).

The goal of the 1964 policy was economic progress. Continued concentration of the population was therefore looked upon as natural. The labour unions shared this attitude, and accepted the idea that the labour force had to be mobile. Private industry led in development, and it was argued that obstacles should not be put in its way. Foreign workers were imported to make the industrial expansion possible. The concentration of these immigrants in urban places with rapidly growing industry made many towns in the middle of the hierarchy grow. The expansion of the car industry caused growth not only at the main plant, but also in many smaller places all over Sweden. However, in many places one industry came to dominate the labour market, sowing the seeds of later problems. The size of the public sector has also doubled during the last twenty years. This sector is urban oriented, and thus the growth of the urban system was further reinforced. The effects of the administrative process were first felt in Stockholm, but went successively down the hierarchy to the medium size towns.

New policies were presented at the end of the 1960s aimed at national planning for regional balance. The earlier location policy had had small effect on development in the inner part of Norrland, because the bulk of the subsidies ended up in the coastal towns in the north and in some smaller urban places in the south. The new suggestion of the government was to rely more on regional planning and a more definite management of the public sector. However, this sector displays the same tendencies towards the growth of larger units as private industry. Decentralization was therefore implemented in the first phase, for example in the university system, with the creation of four new university branches. The overall goals were expressed in terms of population figures. A measure of a successful regional policy was taken to be reversal of population decline, or the reinforcement of already initiated expansion. The goals were to establish a new regional policy which would indicate where regions of balanced economic growth might be established, and a policy which would indicate where a balanced economic contraction might be reached. This regional policy programme was to cover the entire country, and it was intended that it should create balance in the three largest metropolitan areas as well. First, each individual's welfare would be guaranteed independently without respect to place of abode. The embryo of a 'quality of life' policy was recognised (Guteland, 1976).

This was the first time a comprehensive national policy for the settlement system as a whole had been formulated. The government specified frameworks within which the counties and the regional organizations could operate. A classification of urban places was begun in which the following levels were distinguished: Three large cities, 5-10 metropolitan alternatives, about 150 regional growth centres, service communities, and others. A slower rate of urban growth and extensive commitments to alternative growth centres were also recommended. This was in line with the results arrived at by 'The Urbanization Process', a research project initiated by the Expert Group for Regional Investigations (ERU), in which many geographers took a very active part. Hägerstrand and other investigators proposed that Sweden ought to aspire to an 'equitable' urban system made up of regions with no more than about 100,000 inhabitants each (SOU 1970:14).

To sum up, this policy programme stressed that regional development should be regarded as the result of the interplay between three sectors: households, public authorities, and private enterprises. These three sectors, which are dependent on each other, make their choices through a mutual adjustment process. The economic and structural situation could therefore be affected by the location of the public sector, but also through subsidies to the private and household sectors. As support for this strategy, considerable new research was produced. An important breadth in the approach was gained by engaging several academic disciplines in the work. Most of the results were included in the reports published by the ERU group. A special book *Regioner att leva i* called, 'the Professor's book' contained suggestions about both short and long term changes. A central theme was the regional allocation of increasing wealth in the future, and how it could be understood through research. An ongoing registration of the development of the living standard for different groups was suggested.

Some of the goals which were formulated in the earlier investigation had by then been reached. The out-migration from Norrland had lost strength and the largest cities were not receiving as many migrants as before. However, it has not been verified that it was regional policy that started this process, even though it seems that the policy had contributed to stabilizing the situation. Still the process went on and decreasing employment hit certain regions quite hard. The concentration of administrative activities in Stockholm continued. A new practice emerged in the big cities and large towns where people started to move out to smaller villages in the urban fringe. The proportion of older people in the central areas of the cities grew and the commuting range increased rapidly. The interest of the authorities focused on the labour markets.

A new approach began to characterize the outlook by which the individual was placed in focus. Regional theory thus moved into a fourth phase, having shifted from transport minimization, through profit maximization, and regional balance with perfect competition, to urban system theory[1]. The urban system concept indicates that the resources of urban places and the relations between those places are given especial attention in regional policy (Guteland, 1976). The most striking trend in the future is that the expanding public sector will provide almost all the jobs. One aim of the policy is to create differentiated local labour markets. Another is to create good living conditions in the different urban size categories of today. Perhaps a policy whose main aim is to establish equivalent conditions can be operated within a system of unequally sized places.

The 1972 plan for the development of the regional structure could be regarded as a geographical compromise. Because it must involve a political evaluation of alternative goals, it is important to specify the requirements particularly for the urban system. In a subsequent report some general suggestions were presented about the relative benefits of large and small urban places. The demand that households should be able to move to places where they could find work required a policy of diversified local labour markets (SOU 1974:1).

New concepts were used to distinguish between types of places in the urban system, which were: metropolitan areas, primary centres, regional centres, and local centres. Primary centres were supposed to have a differentiated labour market. Communities with at least 50-100,000 inhabitants were judged to meet the needs of future labour markets. It is significant that much of the net migration during the last decades has been to communities of this size.

There is considerable evidence that the debate on the urban system will continue during the next decades. The expected slow increase of the population, perhaps smaller than one per cent per year up to 1990, suggests that the countryside will continue to be sparsely populated.

---

[1] The concept of an urban system in Sweden includes separate urban places, individual communes or, in some specific cases, groups of communes.

Recent and Continuing Development of the National Settlement System

Changes in the settlement system are related to the requirements and wishes of the population on the one hand, and to the organization and location of the production of goods and services on the other; the public sector, the private sector, and various organizations all play their different roles. The development stages presented before can be expressed in terms of the interdependencies between people and social organization. When as during the industrialization period, society was developing trade and industry throughout the country, people were migrating in search of jobs. During the periods of concentration which characterize the later phase of the urbanization process, once again the population is looking for jobs and accommodation. The location of manufacturing units and public activities in a large number of outlying places has given the migrants a wider set of opportunities to choose among. The out-migration from the larger cities and towns to the surrounding areas indicates that people are moving to new areas of residence, but keeping their jobs in town. The city or town then functions as a meeting place for officials, for the collection and distribution of goods and services, for contract between citizens and authorities, for the search for education and culture, etc.

Most activities in today's society are urban oriented, but families are moving out to smaller villages in the surrounding countryside. 'The human being's first commandment is not logically to let himself be steered from some rational perspective of solidarity but it is to try to keep himself and his nearest alive' (Hägerstrand, 1977, personal communication).

The time picture in Figure 4.3 illustrates the daily activity pattern of a rather typical Swedish household of today, even if it is more and more common that the woman has a part-time or full-time job outside the home. The division of labour has gradually generated a highly determined and rigid pattern. What remains for each household is simply to tie the various pieces together into its own particular life style and activity pattern. One reason why this is possible at all is the increased number of cars. It may be that most households could handle the new situation with an increase in the spatial division of functions and a decrease in the number of service outlets. The inequalities with respect to non-car owners were not widely discussed until the 1960s. When this discussion began, it was through the debate about the quality of life and the related shortcomings in the Swedish welfare system.

Broadly speaking the cures for these shortcomings were said to lie in two directions; one was to decentralize the public sector, for instance through the relocation of administrative boards away from Stockholm to a number of regional centres. The other was to try to increase the mobility of the population. To the first category belong a whole set of other actions as well, for instance, location subsidies, education grants, transport subsidies. The overall aim was to keep already established industries in the declining areas and to induce new ones to move in. To move the 'immobile' households and service outlets closer to each other involved other approaches as well, for instance the use of mobile shops, play schools on wheels, and a rural postal service with linked functions. The drift towards increasingly large administrative units has nevertheless created major problems not only for the private households but also for the local communes. The transport of children to the larger schools, transport service for the elderly and infirm, catering for the sick, and so on are extremely expensive and weigh heavily on the budgets of the communes.

A paradox seems to be emerging from these divergent trends. There are very few indications that the private service sector will break the present trend towards the abandonment of smaller units or the merging of these units into larger ones. Through redistricting and the reform of communes and districts, the majority of public services were located in the local central place. On the national level, several government investigations point to the need for agglomeration in a whole range of sectors. This is said to be necessary if Swedish industry is to hold its share of international markets. Among the most crucial of these industries are steel, and pulp and paper, but the same development seems inevitable in brewing, baking, other food processing industries. At the same time, the population is being spread over larger areas. Permanent residences are being moved to smaller places surrounding the larger cities. The number of vacation houses is expected to increase from 500,000 to 750,000 in ten years. Many prefer to restore old rural houses, but older schools, dairies, and retirement centres are used as well. The construction of new vacation houses, however, is being concentrated in vacation villages in which reasonable public services can be provided, and in which environmental effects can be better controlled.

Regional trends

The picture of the future inherent in the trends which have been described so far is one in which the population continues to spread out while employment opportunities are becoming more concentrated. The high degree of mobility has made all of this possible, but the risk is that we are becoming even more vulnerable to future energy crises. The future structure of the settlement pattern is closely tied to the trends described above. The negative effects which are due to the mismatch between home and work place are being counteracted in a number of ways. However, the data on which these actions are based tend to have only limited time perspectives and to be simple projections from current trends.

In the field of economic policy, the directions are charted in five-year plans. These are continuously updated through the annual national budget, which is the most important tool in the relative distribution of resources among the various sectors. For the local communes there is a counterpart to the five-year plan, but here also it is the annual budget which is the most important steering instrument. It is nevertheless the case that the organizations which represent the various economic sectors are very strong, which means that overall national development to a large extent is determined by these sectors. Both on the regional and the local levels there are detailed plans for development, especially in terms of population numbers and construction permits.

The general attitude has, however, undergone considerable change since the early 1950s. Godlund has written that: 'The overwhelming goal of locational planning in 1951 and 1963 was to increase the gross national product. Now, in the 1970s, economic growth and better resource use continue to be important but they are no longer the only aims. Human values tied to the concept of the quality of life have become increasingly important as both ends and means. At the same time, the population at large has become much more concerned with forming its own life' (1978, p.58).

Even though the general debate draws on concepts of the 'soft-data' type, much of the economy continues to be determined by conventional forces. The hardening of international competition in such traditionally Swedish industries as forestry and steel has also brought considerable adjustment and change. The full employment goal coupled with the basic right to live in one's old milieu has led to a vast assortment of selective policies designed to ease the transition to a post-industrial society. The trend away from the export of raw materials to the production of finished goods has continued, but through increased mechanization the demand for labour has actually decreased. Most of the new employment is within the public sector. Activities within this sector, however, are oriented towards individual households, which means that they should be located where the population is. If the intention is to spread the service outlets accordingly, then there is a need for new organizational forms through which the services can be channelled to the people.

The described changes are typical of most developed countries, but they ought to be analysed in relation to the forecast that the total population will stagnate or even decrease. Throughout the 1970s the population forecasts have continually had to be revised downwards. Up to the year 2000 a very modest population increase is expected; in 1974 the figure for the year 2000 was set at 8.6 million but this has subsequently been lowered to 8.4-8.5 million. The most pessimistic forecast, which does not consider immigration, is for about 8.2 million. Part of this picture is also that the population is growing older and that the future demands on the health and welfare sectors will increase.

In the short term, the goal is still to form a policy in which population and employment are regionally balanced. In a book recently published by the ERU group and entitled *Forming the regional future* there are several indications of the problems which can be expected. For instance, it is argued that the rural population can not decrease any further if the country is to keep an active agriculture and forestry industry (Godlund, 1978). As mentioned earlier, the number of rural residences is increasing, not least through the change of vacation houses into permanent residences. Whether this trend can continue is partly a question of the future energy situation. When compared to the 1960-75 period the future expansion of urban areas will be small. In the light of the expected small population increase, it has been projected that the distribution of population among counties should remain stable. If this goal is achieved, it will mean that the amount of long-distance migration will go down. The contraction of the larger cities is expected to continue. Even if the total number of inhabitants in each county stays roughly the same, local and intra-regional mobility could nevertheless remain high.

At present, there is considerable work in the various communes on the preparation of structural settlement plans. The purpose is to determine for each commune the level of urban growth for 1985-90. The goals for each county can then be divided among the communes. It should be noted that even those communes which expect a decrease in their population are likely to experience an increase in the extent of the built-up area, as the population demands larger living space per inhabitant.

In the introduction it was pointed out how the major shifts in the settlement pattern have tended to accelerate over time. In 1980 we are experiencing new pressures, for example, the impact of higher energy prices on residence preferences. An increasing demand for housing in the central places gives evidence of a concentration of population within the frame of the local communes. At the same time the distribution of the population between the communes or counties is not necessarily affected due to decentralization within the public sector and to employment policies. The inertia of the urban system, and a more and more homogenized labour market in all Swedish communes, influences households, particularly those with two or more working members, to remain in the same area. The transport system allows people to keep up their contact network and long distance commuting is increasing. Together with more free time the choice of residence will become more important and a kind of stabilizing factor in society. As an interesting feature in people's value system one can discern a transition from a rigid career-oriented course of life to a more flexible life with alternating periods of different types of jobs and studies. To meet these social changes society needs to promote a regional policy of diversified and rather large regional labour markets within daily commuting distance. With the development of telecommunications technology more jobs may perhaps be taken care of at home. Conversely the unwillingness to move does worry some politicians and the expanding industries of today.

All of the small steps the individual or the household may take daily or weekly to satisfy their own wishes concerning residence or job do not necessarily coincide with the policy for society as a whole. Both parts have to adjust to new situations. Sweden, as in all other countries, will never experience a stable settlement pattern, but in the long run there is no doubt that energy problems will influence the geographical structure to a great extent.

REFERENCES

Ahlberg, G. 1953. *Befolknigsutvecklingen och urbaniseringen i Sverige 1911-50.* Stockholm.

Asheim, B. T. 1978. 'Regionale ulikheter i levekår'. *Norges Offentlige Utredningar 3.*

Falk, T. 1976. *Urban Sweden. Changes in the Distribution of Population—the 1960s in Focus.* Stockholm.

Godlund, S. 1978. 'Regionalpolitik som idé och realitet.' In *Att forma regional framtid.* Stockholm.

Guteland, G. *et al.* 1975. *Ett folks biografi. Befolkning och samhälle i Sverige fran historia till nutid.* Publica. Uddevalla.

Guteland, G. 1976. 'From Plant location Policy to Settlement System Policy'. *PLAN International Habitat 76.* Stockholm.

Hägerstrand, T. 1976. 'The National Settlement Pattern as Political Problem'. *PLAN International Habitat 76.* Stockholm.

Järnegren, A., Ventura, F., Wärneryd, O. 1980. 'Samhällsutbyggnad och energiförsörjning'. *Byggforskningsrådet. Rapport R52.*

Lewan, N. 1969. 'Arbete och bostad.' Institution för kulturgeografi och ekonomisk geografi, Lunds universitet. *Rapporter och notiser, 3.*

Olsson, G. 1976. *Birds in egg.* Ann Arbor.

NordREFO, 1971. *Ortsystemets framtida utveckling.* Nordiska arbetsgruppen för regionalpolitisk forskning, 1.

Statens Offentliga Utredningar, 1970: *14.* 'Urbaniseringen i Sverige. En geografisk samhällsanalys.'

Statens Offentliga Utredningar, 1974: *1.* 'Orter i regional samverkan.'

5 THE FINNISH NATIONAL SETTLEMENT SYSTEM

MAURI PALOMÄKI

Definition of the National Settlement System in Finland

Main Features of Earlier Studies

The systemic approach to the analysis of national settlement is practically nonexistent in Finland. There are brief reviews of broad concepts produced elsewhere, using Finnish data as case material (Palomäki, 1972). Moreover, there is a long tradition in the analysis of central places, networks, and areas of influence (Mikkonen, 1975). However, from the point of view of the present paper these are narrow in scope and perhaps too thorough and detailed. They form nevertheless a source of material for this report.

The physical aspects of settlement were widely analysed in the 1930s, but after that the field was much neglected with some splendid exceptions. A new stimulus was provided by the growing importance of urbanization and planning. Research on agglomerations (*taajama* in Finnish) attempted to make feasible definitions of agglomerated settlement in a country with a predominantly dispersed rural settlement pattern. This research provided rules for defining the degree of urbanization of agglomerations and their development. Studies of the role of different settlement units, though modest, have used quite advanced methods. Also, attempts have been made to describe the development of Finnish settlement from the beginning of this century to the post-war years, but these have concentrated on small areas of the country, or have been limited in their approach to certain aspects of settlement, or have taken into account only rural or urban areas.

Concepts Used

The settlement system has been defined as: 'a number of settlement units linked together by some significant interactions'. This broad definition, however, needs new concepts to make it more operative for studies on the national level. The following definitions should make it easier to describe the Finnish national settlement system.

Composite Units The composite units of the settlement system have three different elements. The basic element is a group of people, the community. The factors keeping the community together may vary from simple family ties to manifold economic and cultural interdependencies. The size of the community may vary from a few people to the whole nation. The second basic element is the activity through which a community earns its living. There are single-activity communities and multi-activity communities, depending on their size and level of development. The visible element of a settlement unit is the physical settlement. It may consist of a farmstead with the main and auxiliary buildings necessary to the community's activities. In the nucleated settlement, dwelling and production structures are separated, but both are included in the physical settlement, as are the structures necessary for inter-settlement contacts.

Communications   There are many different needs for interaction in a complex settlement system. One group of needs concerns the necessity for moving things, through different kinds of traffic arteries, such as paths, roads, highways, motorways, waterways, railways, and airways. They are called material communications. Another group of needs consists of the necessity and the wish of people to move. The same traffic routes are used, but in another way. These types of movement are called person communications. The third group of needs is concerned with information communications. These needs can be satisfied only partially through person communications. Therefore, a system of information channels, such as mail, telephone, teleprint, newspaper, radio, television, has been developed.

The system of communications penetrates the whole settlement system. It resembles the blood and nerve systems of higher animals. It is present in every settlement unit no matter how small it may be. It can also cross unsettled territories of a country. This is a normal state of affairs in a country like Finland, located at the northern margins of the European ecumene.

Settlement Patterns   When the Finnish people came to what is now Finland during the first millennium AD they pushed the more primitive people into the periphery. They brought farming and permanent settlements. The first towns emerged with the arrival of Christianity from Sweden and, in the eastern extremities of the country, from emerging Russia. Much later, towards the end of the nineteenth century, industrialization favoured town growth, and after the Second World War the urbanization process developed at an accelerated rate. With rising standards of living and mobility came the habit of owning two dwellings. Most city families have a separate summer or vacation home close to nature, especially on shorelines. All these innovations entered the country via the southern, south-western or western coasts. They have since spread out and pushed the older system to the north and east. Partly because of this pattern of innovation diffusion, the present prominent features of the Finnish settlement system can be described in terms of broad zones with the highest intensity values in southern Industrialized Finland. The broad transitional zone of Middle Finland is less industrialized but still industry competes with agrarian occupations for dominance. The rest of the country belongs to Peripheral Finland, where agrarian occupations still prevail. The northernmost tip of the country might be characterized as an area with a nature-oriented settlement system.

Externalities and Environmental Problems The analysis of external influences is essential to the understanding of settlement systems. Sometimes this is very simple as in the case of the natural environment. Geomorphic factors, such as steep slopes, may reject settlement. Micro-climatological factors can lead settlement units to locate on hilltops. Shorelines attract both industry and high-class residential settlement. Large peatbog areas tend to remain outside closed settlement, and certain soils can cause difficulties for road construction. The influence of human activities is more difficult to analyse.

A sudden increase in population obviously calls for adaptation in the settlement system, as was experienced in Finland immediately after the Second World War, when the country received half a million refugees from those territories ceded to the Soviet Union. The problem was solved by settling refugees within existing rural settlements or by steering them to towns.

In the economic sphere, technology, world economic fluctuations, the national economy, and regional variations in production conditions all affect the settlement system. An example is the thinning out of the rural settlement in Northern Finland. Lumbering had been an important side occupation during the time of the saw and the axe. The emergence of the chain-saw diminished the demand for labour. The population of the peripheral settlements fell considerably. Changes in transport technology may also cause changes in the urban settlement's opportunities to grow. An example is the decline of some coastal towns in Finland caused by the decline of coastal shipping and by the increasing importance of highway traffic. The highway usually bypassed these coastal towns and small highway agglomerations began to grow.

Cultural and political changes obviously influence the settlement system. For example, changes in the national schooling system affect the functions of central places, as does the political will to preserve some reserves of untouched nature in the more congested southern parts of the country.

Present Structure of the Settlement System

Main Settlement Units and Subsystems

In Finland there are wide areas with dispersed rural settlement. Typical of such areas are detached houses or groups of two or three houses. However, there are areas with clustered rural settlement, hamlets or villages, especially in South-Western Finland and along the riversides of the Bothnian coast. Very common is a mixed pattern with dispersed settlement and occasional hamlets. Dispersed settlement was formed during the pioneer phase of the region and later in connection with several land enclosures. Hamlets have been formed through the division of the inheritance of big detached landed properties.

The urban counterpart is the *taajama* (official translation: 'urban agglomeration', here termed clustered settlement). In 1970 there were 1045 clustered settlements in Finland. The city-size pattern shows that there is one dominant centre, Helsinki, with half a million people (Figure 5.1). Turku and Tampere each have about 160,000 inhabitants. These are followed by a group of middle-sized cities with 30-100,000 people. Whereas the big clusters are located in the south-western corner, the middle-sized clusters are distributed quite evenly throughout the inhabited part of Finland. There is some tendency toward twin-city formation, mainly in the densely populated and industrialized parts of the country. Examples include: Kotka-Karhula, Lappeenranta-Imatra, Kokkola-Pietarsaari (Peltonen, 1974).

The increasingly high standard of living in post-war Finland has led to a great amount of second-home ownership. This has created a type of settlement which is distributed along sea and lake shores in narrow bands of detached houses. It is dense near cities and in easily accessible places with attractive scenery, and sparser further away in Northern Finland or in peat-bog areas in Southern Finland. This kind of settlement, forming a weekend and holiday refuge for urbanized people, is an important sub-system in the national settlement system.

In Finland, the density of population living in clusters or in dispersed settlement is very low. For the country as a whole it is only 15.5 persons per square kilometre. In the south-western and southern parts of the country there are wide areas with a density of rural population exceeding $20/km^2$. North and eastwards the density diminishes; it is about 15 in the middle lake district and less than 2 in the northernmost county of the country. Within this general picture are great local and regional variations, depending primarily on the amount and productivity of agricultural land in rural areas (Ruotsalo-Aario and Aario, 1977), the nearness of sea or lake shores (Hult, 1962), and on the size and nearness of urban settlement (Ruotsalo-Aario, 1978).

(*a*) *Farms*. In Finland there are about 300,000 farms. Practically all (99 per cent) are privately owned. They average nine hectares of arable land. The biggest farms (averaging more than 14 ha/farm in a commune) are located in Southern, South-Western and Western Finland. The size diminishes eastwards and northwards (6-10 ha) and reaches the lowest values in Northern Finland (below 6 ha/farm arable) (Varjo, 1977, p. 21). The farms are family operated. There are difficulties in getting hired hands, so the population on the farms is generally low (2-4 persons).

The economic base of Finnish farms is a combination of arable farming, dairying, and forestry. Normally the production of a farm is great enough to support a family. On average the share of arable farming is 42 per cent of the total production, that of dairying 36 per cent and forestry 22 per cent, although there is much regional variation. A farm in Finland is very sen-

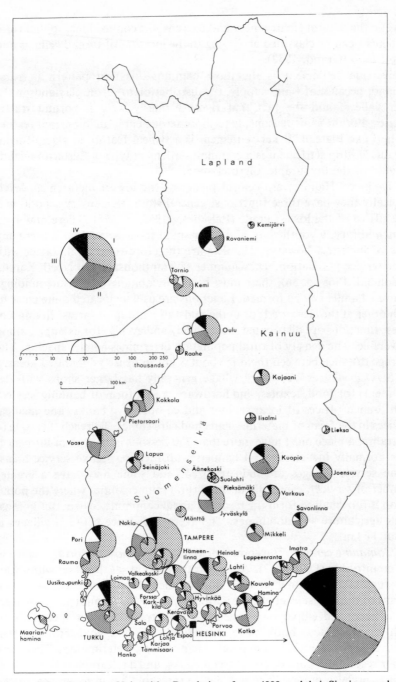

Fig. 5.1 Urban Settlement Units with a Population of over 4000, and their Size in accordance with Numbers of Professionally Employed
I = Industry, II = Trade, III = Transport, and IV = Services
Source: Yli-Jokipii, 1972, p. 8

118 Urbanization and Settlement Systems

sitive to the natural environment and to transport connections, so that rural settlement can be classified according to the location of farm dwellings and arable land (Granö, 1952).

Riverside settlement is the most common location pattern in rural Finland, because of water supply, the distribution of fertile claylands in the river valleys, and the fact that rivers formerly were important traffic arteries. For the same reasons, lake-shore settlement is an important feature in the Lake Plateau. Esker settlement is a typical feature in glacio-fluvial terrain. Hilltop settlement is a common settlement type in Eastern Finland, because of the favourable micro-climate.

(b) *Hamlets*. Hamlets are central places of the lowest hierarchical level. Typically they have three functions: general store, elementary school, and post office of the lowest grade (Palomäki, 1963, p. 165). There may be a branch library, a youth club, and other small services. Seldom is there any kind of industry, however. Hamlets are therefore rural in character with some service population. They number several thousand. In North Karelia (Palomäki, 1968, p. 86), there must be 200 inhabitants in the surroundings before a hamlet can be formed. Functions are usually located quite close to each other at the crossroads or in the midst of a group of farms. In unusual cases, functions are distributed more widely and evenly, for example, along a riverside. The density of rural population determines hamlet spacing. The average distance between them is about 5 km in densely-inhabited areas.

(c) *Service villages*. A service village generally has larger shops with departments for food, textiles, and hardware, a first form of banking services with branch offices of local savings and co-operative banks, and medical services in the form of maternity and child care clinics. To reach this state in centrality, a place must have more than 750 persons in its area of influence. This normally includes 3 to 4 hamlets with their respective service areas. Some service villages are industrialized, and some may have a greater number of services, especially in small rural municipalities where the population is too small to form the basis for a real commune centre. But in most cases agriculture still dominates. The average distance between villages is about 11 km.

(d) *Commune centres*. The commune centre is the most important centre in the countryside (Figure 5.2). Administration begins at this level with local-government (communal council and municipal government), and with organs of the lowest level of state administration such as rural police officer, tax officer, and employment agency. Retail trade includes special shops such as pharmacy, book store, watchmaker's, and goldsmith's shops. Medical services include physician, dentist, and veterinarian. There are junior secondary schools, commercial banks, and a telegraph office. Travel services are also present. The population threshold has in recent years risen to 5000. There are 224 commune centres in Finland quite evenly distributed at about 25 km intervals from each other. The area of influence of each centre consists of one or two rural communes.

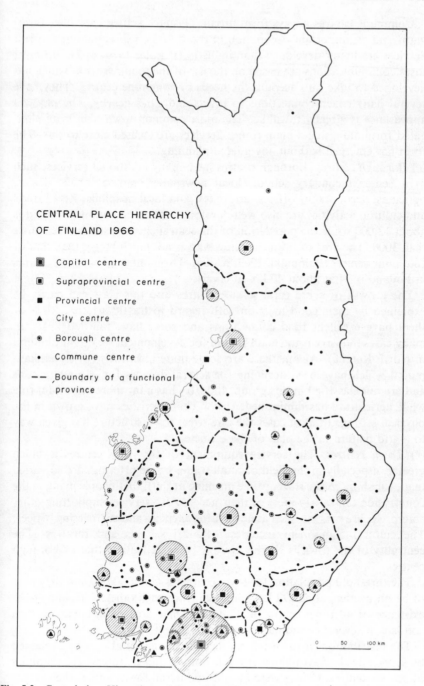

CENTRAL PLACE HIERARCHY
OF FINLAND 1966

▣ Capital centre

▦ Supraprovincial centre

■ Provincial centre

▲ City centre

◉ Borough centre

• Commune centre

—— Boundary of a functional
    province

0   50   100 km

Fig. 5.2 Central place Hierarchy and Centrality of Bigger Places in 1966

Commune centres always form urban, clustered settlements. Yet, farming is still an important occupation in the functions of commune centres. Services are better developed than industry (Peltola, 1976, p. 72). In most cases communications are based on the use of the road network, which has developed to take into account the needs of commune centres. They have several daily coach connections to towns and cities nearby. The physical appearance is already townlike. The most common town plan is an elongated form alongside a main route. Services are located close to this. The form has emerged without any guided planning.

(e) *Borough centres.* Borough centres have many additional services, such as a senior secondary school, local newspaper, motor vehicle dealer, opticians, accountancy offices, attorneys, and local hospitals. Retail trade and cultural activities are also well-developed. The population threshold is about 12,000 while the population of the central cluster itself is often more than 3000. The area of influence, however, is not much bigger than that of commune centres (Palomäki, 1963, p. 206). The number of borough centres in Finland is 74 at about 40 km intervals.

The growth of some rural service centres into this class can partly be explained by their good location with regard to traffic arteries. Most of them have excellent road connections and some have railroad links. In many cases industry is the main reason for development (e.g., Outokumpu in North Karelia). Again, there are some quite old towns (Kristiinankaupunki) which have been declining for several decades for various reasons and are not classified in this group. Industry has a far more important role while agriculture has diminished. Urban characteristics have grown in the physical setting. In most cases the one-street town structure has given way to a grid pattern in the plan of these clusters.

(f) *Town centres.* The service equipment of the town centres is much greater, especially in the field of retail trade, where offerings are so varied (e.g., fur shop, music store, office machine dealer), that people living in the countryside can satisfy most of their needs. Also services supporting other enterprises are present, such as advertising agencies and engineering offices. The cultural component includes technical schools and theatres. The centrality of the town is on the average twice as high as that of borough centres.

The threshold population for town centres is about 60,000 and they tend to be on average about 90 kms distance from each other. This allows the existence of 40 town centres in Finland. Their area of influence in turn consists of several communes.

The distribution of town centres in Finland cannot always be explained by service needs. Savonlinna, Iisalmi, Forssa, and Kemijärvi are examples of service centres. Others were born as industrial towns and as their population has grown they have acquired their service functions. Examples of this type are Pietarsaari, Kemi, Imatra, Hyvinkää, and Hanko (Yli-Jokipii,

1972, p. 8). Some town centres are also important ports, such as Rauma, Maarianhamina, and Hamina. All town centres have good connections to the road network, and all of them have a railway link. Physically their urbanized areas are extensive, there are always several districts within the town, and in most cases also some satellite development. The older ones have had several phases in their morphological development, for example Rauma (Jumppanen, 1973, p. 11).

(g) *Provincial centres.* In Finland provincial centres form an important part of the national settlement system. Administratively many of them have a large number of the so-called middle-level organs. These are, in part, organs of municipal federations, an important feature in the Finnish administration system. In part they are organs of special state administration such as agricultural inspection districts, military districts, and road and waterway construction districts. Eleven (of the seventeen centres) also have organs of the general provincial administration (*lääni* in Finnish). In addition, most of the provincial centres have district offices of the many political parties in Finland. There are furthermore many different kinds of civic organizations which are formed on a provincial basis or have provincial sub-organizations. Wholesale trade emerges into the system at this level. The great national wholesale companies have their distribution and storage divisions organized mainly on a provincial basis. Many other wholesale businesses and the more specialized wholesale-trade functions are organized in the same way. Retail trade is abundant. Provincial centres also have general hospitals with special wards, technical schools and colleges, professional theatres and orchestras, and one or more provincial newspapers. Their population threshold is about 200,000 and the typical distance between them is 200 km. The area of influence consists of the 'functional' province (Palomäki, 1968, p. 284), which to a considerable extent corresponds to the 'conceptual' province in the minds of Finnish people.

Some of the provincial centres are highly industrialized (e.g., Lahti and Pori), but others rely mainly on services (e.g., Joensuu, Seinäjoki, and Rovaniemi). In general, the occupational structure is less specialized than in the town-centre group. The number of connections from provincial centres is larger, and includes air connections. This reflects the need for regular and rapid contact especially with the capital. The Finnish Broadcasting Company has a radio studio network, which corresponds quite well to the provincial divisions of the country. The physical appearance of provincial centres is very much like that of town centres.

(h) *Supraprovincial centres.* The quality of service equipment in supraprovincial centres is rather varied. The main features are that wholesale trade is well developed, that in administration there are on average 28 organs for areas larger than administrative provinces (*läänis*), and that the cultural functions are of a high level (universities or other academic institutions, opera, provincial museums, special museums, and so on). In retail trade highly specialized services are abundant. There are six centres of this level: Helsinki, Turku, Tampere, Kuopio, Vaasa, and Oulu. The population threshold is about half a million people, and the average distance between these centres is 300 km. Their area of influence consists of several provinces. A multi-point minimum travel calculation (Hautamäki, 1972) has shown that the existing supra-provincial central-place network is the best one from a movement point of view. The same result has been obtained in a population-potential simulation model using several factors: population, the distribution of population in the area of influence, the frequency of visits to central places, income level, and distance to centres at the same level.

The occupational structure of supra-provincial cities varies. The degree of industrialization is highest in Tampere and lowest in Kuopio. The service sector is largest in Oulu and that of transport in Turku. All of these centres have an excellent network of communications; coastal centres have ferry and air contacts to Sweden and frequent air contacts with the capital. They all have an influential press as well as TV studios. In their physical outlook these centres differ from the provincial centres mainly through their size and densities. Turku and Tampere belong to the group of large cities in Finland, the others to the upper part of medium-sized cities.

(*i*) *The capital.* Helsinki, the capital of Finland, dominates national life in almost all conceivable ways. Helsinki has all of the politically powerful organs: the parliament, cabinet, and the seat of the President of the Republic. All ministries are located there and all except one of the other central government divisions. Other administrative organs, research institutions, and educational institutions for the whole country can be included in this group. Of the total 111 organs of this kind 101 are located in the capital (Atlas of Finland, 1978, p. 44/311). The political elite, with powerful politicians and party headquarters, are also there. Finnish foreign affairs are handled in Helsinki through embassies or other forms of representations of foreign nations. Helsinki is also a centre of political conferences, especially dealing with international co-operation, educational and research institutions, theatres, opera, orchestras, museums, sports grounds.

In the economic realm, the most important private firms have their headquarters in the capital. All of the powerful commercial banks have their main offices there. Large wholesale enterprises have located even their main storage facilities in the surroundings of Helsinki. The retail trade flourishes with the major department stores and highly specialized sales outlets. Helsinki is the biggest industrial centre in the country, with its industrial structure more varied than elsewhere. However, the dominance of the capital is not as great in the economic field as it is in administration. The occupational structure of Helsinki is, characteristically, service-oriented and, in fact, includes many quaternary activities.

The geographic location of the capital at one end of the country is perhaps awkward for Finns, but Helsinki is close to the economic core area of Finland, and well located, considering Finland's dependence on sea-going trade. Its long history as the capital (since 1812) and the extensive investments intended to enhance its capital functions have made Helsinki a superior central place in Finland, with the rest of the country as its area of influence.

The urban structure of Helsinki reaches far beyond the city limits (Aario, 1951). Greater Helsinki covers the neighbouring municipalities of Espoo, Vantaa, and Kauniainen. The urban settlement of these towns can be interpreted geographically as a cluster of satellites for the capital. If commuting is used as the criterion, Helsinki reaches about 60 km in all directions (Siirilä, 1966). In other Finnish cities the commuting distance at its greatest is about 40 km (Saviranta, 1970). The central parts of Helsinki are quite densely built up, but the outermost parts of Greater Helsinki are still primarily rural in outlook, with intervening urban satellites. Tapiola in Espoo is an exception, because it has been planned according to the new town principle.

Trends and Processes of Change

Population Developments

Population development in Finland resembles that of most industrialized countries. The total number of inhabitants has increased from about 0.8 million in 1800 to close to 5 millions in 1980. In the first half of the nineteenth century rural population dominated with a share of 90 per cent or more. The beginning of industrialization in 1870 meant an increase in the population of towns and other places with preconditions for industry. Yet the rural population kept growing at least until the 1930s, when it levelled off. In 1960, the population living in rural communes abruptly began to decrease. In 1970 the size of the urban population exceeded that of the rural population. Urbanization is still going on. The population growth in Finland has been a result of the birth rate exceeding the death rate, since Finland loses population through emigration mainly to Sweden.

There are differences in the population development in different kinds of settlement units. In ordinary rural communes, according to Hautamäki (1967, p. 79), there are three principal phases of development (Figure 5.3). *Phase I* represents the proportional growth of settlement at the time of a self-supporting agricultural community. The growth was greatest in those peripheral areas where unexploited agricultural reserves still existed. In central districts settlement had reached the saturation point. *Phase II* represents the situation at the initial stage of industrialization. This prevailed during the 1920s. Settlement in peripheral areas of a rural commune continued to become denser, due to agriculture, whereas the expansion of

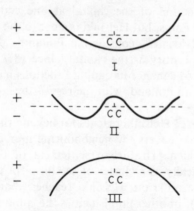

Fig. 5.3 General Phases of Settlement Growth. Change of Settlement in Different Parts of a Commune at Various Stages of Settlement Maturity
Source: Hautamaki, 1967, p. 79

urban occupations accelerated the growth of the centre of communes. Meanwhile agriculture was changing over to a market economy. *Phase III* represents the growth of different parts of the commune at the time of more advanced industrialization. Growth is centripetal: agricultural settlement is withdrawing from peripheral areas, while central districts are growing with the expansion of urban occupations. The centre of the commune is in an advantageous position and nearby villages also continue to grow.

Practically all the towns and cities of Finland have been growing since the independence of the country (1917). This was still true in the late 1960s. The situation has been interpreted that urbanization in Finland is, in Gibb's terminology, in its third phase (Palomäki, 1972). There were signs of the approach of the fourth phase, an even faster growth of the largest cities and stagnation of the smaller ones, but as in other western countries recent years have shown some stagnation in the whole urbanization process.

Changes in the Economy

The reasons for population changes and the development of settlement units are in most cases economic. For instance, a decision to abandon a farm in the periphery of Finland may depend on the ageing of the farmer, who may be a former soldier and who received his farm in 1945 as a cold farm (Mead, 1951), and who, after the clearing of fields and construction of buildings, finds that the economic returns are not sufficient. Moreover, side occupations, such as lumbering and construction works, have also diminished or disappeared (Varjo, 1971). Population decline has also endangered the economic base for hamlets and service villages and even commune centres. The concentration of population in towns and cities, on the other hand, has led to an increase in their service offerings.

These changes have also led to new organizational adaptations. For instance, diminishing rural population density has caused the closing down of permanent stores and the opening of mobile-shop routes. The mobile shops have for some time been very important in Northern Finland (Helle,. 1964) and are growing in the southern parts of the country (Laulajainen, 1967). Another phenomenon is the growing size of retail outlets. This leads immediately to higher population thresholds, and to a diminishing number of sales outlets. It affects rural and suburban retail trade and may cause, in the future, the emergence of new types of retail centres.

In industry two lines of development can be seen. Geographic concentration is still going on. In Southern Finland new jobs continue to emerge and the head offices of large firms still move from smaller centres to Helsinki. On the other hand, there is legislation aimed at developing the underdeveloped parts of the country through subsidizing industrial and other enterprises (Hustich, 1968). The results seem to be favourable, but the time has been short, not more than 15 years, so that the development policy has not led to great changes in the national settlement system of Finland.

Education

Changes in the educational system have also affected settlements. The diminishing of population and decrease in birth rates in rural areas, as elsewhere, have decreased the need for elementary schools. Many schools have been closed down in the hamlets and service-village centres. The rise of the comprehensive school and the disappearance of elementary, civic, and junior secondary schools have strengthened the position of commune centres at the cost of lower-level centres. There are plans for reorganizing the entire secondary level of education with more specialized schools. The cha ge seems again to favour the larger centres. Major changes have also taken place in university-level education. Before World War II, Finland had only three academic centres: Helsinki, Turku, and Jyväskylä. Now there are seven more: Oulu, Tampere, Vaasa, Kuopio, Joensuu, Lappeenranta, and Rovaniemi. This has greatly raised the self-consciousness of the towns and provinces around them. It has in addition strengthened the position of supra-provincial centres, which has led to a political effort to have more towns included in this enviable status.

Politics

In Finland the system of political and administrative centres is to a considerable extent identical to the hierarchical central-place system. The most notable exception is that there is a group of administrative functions which are organized according to the *lääni*-division (12 centres) and not according to the 17 provinces. This class of urban place, which in administration terms is clearly defined, does not exist in other central-place activities. So, there are large cities, for example Tampere, lacking *lääni* administration, and small centres such as Kuovola, Maarianhamina, and Hämeenlinna, having it. This situation reflects the old historical provincial division of the country. There was some modernization in 1960, when the *läänis* of Keski-Suomi and Pohjois-Karjala were formed, but there is still a difference between the *lääni* division and modern functional provinces.

The duties imposed on public administration are growing, creating new administrative organs and regional divisions. In general they follow the system of central places, but when the location of new activities is an important part of regional and national politics, there are also deviations. This has led to a diminishing clarity of central place classes in the administration structure (*Atlas of Finland*, 1978, p. 38/311).

In Finland there are three important changes in the administrative system now being executed or planned. These will have an immediate and strong effect upon the national settlement system. The first is communal reform. It was found in the late 1950s that there were too many small municipalities, which could not carry the burden of increasing communal services. The educational system was growing and both social and medical care demanded greater expenditures. In small communes the number of taxpayers was diminishing, bringing with it higher unit taxes. This led to a situation where small communes became unfavourable locations even for private enterprises. They could not compete effectively, and either closed down their operation or moved to better locations. Population also moved away, and as a result many small communes were no longer viable. After strong political disagreements a communal reform was planned, leading to the amalgamations of many small municipalities.

The discussion of provincial autonomy in Finland began at the end of the eighteenth century, when Finland still belonged to Sweden. The realization of these early ideas was not possible, because after 1808 Finland belonged to the Russian empire. But because the country had a high degree of administrative self-government, the discussion went on.

Since independence in 1917, there have been three proposals for administrative reorganization which are of considerable geographical interest. The first of these, the so-called Tulenheimo Committee's proposal, made a clear distinction between the state-guided *lääni*-administration and the real self-governing provinces. Because of the bilingual character of the Finnish population, Finnish-speaking and Swedish-speaking provinces were defined to be as homogeneous as possible. In cases where this was not easy, such as in the biggest urban areas, there was to be a separation into quite small self-governing areas. The provinces were to contain about 100,000 population. The boundaries were to conform in most cases to the historical provinces. This proposal, however, was never carried through.

One of the latest proposals was made by a committee (*Kunnallisen yhteistoiminnan järjestysmuotokomitea*) in 1970, again emphasizing the self-governing provinces. The regional division is largely the same as the *läänis* of today. The provinces of Satakunta and Pirkanmaa are the only new ones. In this proposal some functional provinces have been united into one administrative province, as for instance in Etelä-Phjanmaa, which consists of three provinces with their main urban centres. Violations of the functional regional structure of Finland are very few. The economic base of the proposed administrative provinces is rather strong, because in only two cases is the population of a province less than 200,000.

Thus one of the main barriers to the renewal of provincial administration, the lack of a suitable regional division, has now been removed. However, discussion is still going on. Some political parties would not like any sort of self-government on a provincial level, while others are of the opinion that the areas ought to be even smaller than in the committee's proposal, that is, they should be formed according to the 'economic provinces'.

The third great political change is the endeavour to lessen the dominance of the capital in the political life of Finland. It is felt in some political circles that too many decisions concerning provinces or even smaller areas are made in Helsinki. The question is, in other words, must all national-level administrative organs be located in the capital city?

The development has taken three principal directions. There are attempts to shift the power of decision-making downward in the existing administrative organization. The development is slowly going on. Some authorities have changed their administrative system so that they have formed new offices for those operations which can better be carried out through a regional organization rather than a central one. This kind of decentralization is only in the beginning phase. The most ambitious plan was to decentralize 26 central government offices from Helsinki to 19 other towns (*Hajasijoituskomitea*, 1974). They were considered to be functions which could operate quite well outside the capital. According to their contact needs and their readiness to move, they were grouped into three categories with plans and schedules concerning relocation. This plan suggested that 6700 jobs should be created in other towns, with Helsinki losing them. There are, of course, many difficulties connected with such a radical plan, that is, the opinions of the families concerned, the need for inner communication systems, the need for construction of offices, and so on. At the time of writing very little of this plan has been realized as the opposition was much stronger than anticipated.

The effect of all these political changes on the Finnish settlement system will be great. The communal reform will concentrate the local administrative power in fewer central places. This will lead to an increase of all activities in the favoured places and a decrease in the number of activities in other places. The rationalizing of administration may, however, benefit all citizens. The decentralization of state government will benefit all central classes of settlement above the provincial level. The dominance of the capital will decrease.

Future Structure and Pattern of the National Settlement System

The Finnish national settlement system has during the post-war years been characterized by rapid urbanization. The present economic and societal situation, however, has stopped it almost completely. The population of Helsinki, for instance, has decreased notably. All large cities grew in the 1960s at an accelerated rate but today they are also in stagnation. Nearly all rural communes lost population in the 1960s to a worrying degree. Today the loss is small or there may even be an increase. Whereas in the 1960s it was interpreted that the process of urbanization had reached the zone of transition between Gibb's phases of population concentration III and IV (Palomäki, 1972), today it is hard to conceive of this development as a phase in the process of urbanization. The country still has a large rural population. The profitability of rural occupations has not improved, and there are few barriers to moving from underdeveloped to developed parts of the country, but the process has come to a standstill. An economic explanation may be found. The unemployment caused by the depression, which continued during the boom, is so great in the urbanized parts of the country that there is little or no attraction for migration.

The Finnish authorities have not (on the level of planning or politics) created any clear picture of the future national settlement system. There have been many attempts to predict the development of important social sectors, such as the economy, but most of these do not have any regional dimension. There are plans that have a regional approach, such as population forecasting by communes, but their main emphasis appears to be in keeping population as it has been. The plans for central-place development show more of a continuation of what has happened before, rather than any radical changes. This supports the author's conclusion that the national settlement system of Finland in the year 2000 will be in its main elements quite similar to what it is today.

REFERENCES

Aario, Leo 1951. *The inner differentiation of the large cities in Finland.* Publicationes Instituti Geographici Universitatis Turkuensis 22, 67pp.
Atlas of Finland, 1978 Folio 311 'Public administration', National Board of Survey and Geographical Society of Finland. Helsinki. p. 44.
Granö, J. G. 1952. 'Settlement of the country'. *Fennia*, 72. pp. 340-380.
Hajasijoituskomitean loppumietintö (1974). 'Virastojen ja laitosten hajasijoittaminen' (Decentralizing the offices and institutions) Committee Report 1974:47. Helsinki. 331pp.
Hautamäki, Lauri 1967. 'Development of settlement in some rural communes in western Finland since 1920'. *Fennia* 96, No. 2. 98pp.

Hautamäki, Lauri 1972. 'Preliminary methods in seeking optimal systems of centres applied to supraprovincial level'. *Fennia* 112. 25pp.

Helle, Reijo 1964. 'Retailing in rural Northern Finland particularly by mobile shops.' *Fennia* 91, No. 3. 120pp.

Hult, Juhani 1962. 'Der Einfluss der Zentren auf die Bevölkerungsdichte ihrer Verkehrsgebiete'. *Fennia* 87, No. 1, 49pp.

Hustich, Ilmari 1968. 'Finland, a developed and an underdeveloped country'. *Acta Geographica* 20. pp. 155-73

Jumppanen, Seija 1973. 'Die innere Differenzierung der Stadt Rauma'. *Fennia* 126. 87pp.

Laulajainen, Risto 1967. 'On the classification of centres'. *Kauppa-korkeakoulun julkaisuja*, sarja C:11:2. 58pp.

Mead, W. R. 1951. 'Cold farm in Finland, resettlement of Finland's displaced farmers'. *Geographical Review* XLI, No. 4. pp. 529-43.

Mikkonen, Kauko 1975. 'Causal analysis of the system of central places and prediction of functional regional structure in the administrative province of Vaasa, Finland'. *Fennia* 138. 162pp.

Palomäki, Mauri 1963. 'The functional centres and areas of South Bothnia, Finland'. *Fennia* 88, No. 1. 235pp.

Palomäki, Mauri 1968. 'Pohjois-Karjalan toiminnallinen aluerakenne'. (Summary: The central place hierarchy in North Karelia, Finland.) Pohjois-Karjalan seutusuunnitelma 1977. Joensuu. pp. 63-90.

Palomäki, Mauri 1972. 'Kaupungistumisprosessin vaikutus taloudellisten ydinalueiden syntymiseen ja siirtymiseen'. (The influence of the process of urbanization on the emergence and shifting of economic core areas). *Proceedings of the Vaasa School of Economics*, Research papers No. 10. 23pp.

Peltola, Olli 1976. 'Vaasan läänin taajamien elinkeinorakenne ja rooli vuosina 1960 ja 1970'. (The occupational structure and role of the settlement clusters in the country of Vaasa). Unpublished master of economics thesis. Vaasa. 98pp.

Peltonen, Arvo 1974. 'Some Finnish double centres: services and interaction'. *Fennia* 130. 83pp.

Ruotsalo-Aario, Ritva 1978. 'Effect of distance from the commune centre on population density in the province of Kuopio in 1967'. *Annales Academiae Scientiarium Fennicae*. Series A., Geologica-Geographica, 125. 19pp.

Ruotsalo-Aario, Ritva and Leo Aario 1977. 'The effect of environmental factors and distance from the functional centre upon the density of rural settlement in the province of Kuopio in 1967'. Annales *Academiae Scientiarum Fennicae*. Series A, Geologica-Geographica 122. 52pp.

Saviranta, Jaakko 1970. 'Der Einpendelverkehr von Turku'. *Fennia* 100, No. 4. 144pp.

Siirilä, Seppo 1966. 'Surr-Helsingin esikaupunkialueet'. (Summary: The suburbs of Greater Helsinki.) *Terra* 78. pp. 90-8.

Varjo, Uuno 1971. 'Development of human ecology in Lappland, Finland, after World War II'. *Geoforum* 5. pp. 47-74.

Varjo, Uuno 1977. 'Maatilatalous'. In Suomen maantiede. Otava. Helsinki pp. 68-86.

Yli-Jokipii, Pentti 1972. 'Functional classification of cities in Finland'. *Fennia* 119. 44pp.

PART A

SETTLEMENT SYSTEMS IN INDUSTRIAL MARKET ECONOMIES

Section 2: Settlement on Old Lands and in Higher-Density Regions

6 THE BRITISH SETTLEMENT SYSTEM: DEVELOPMENT AND CONTEMPORARY CHARACTERISTICS

HAROLD CARTER

Urban Settlement and Administrative Areas

From the early Middle Ages and the time of the Norman Conquest when the chartered borough was widely extended over the country, the basic definition of the town in Britain has been legal and administrative. Indeed, the chartered borough remained the formal urban unit in England and Wales until the early nineteenth century when the rapid changes which followed on the growth of industry revealed how completely outdated the whole administrative system had become. By that period some tiny settlements, indeed some which had disappeared altogether, still enjoyed municipal or urban status, whereas the new industrial towns, such as Birmingham and Manchester, did not. This anachronous situation was dealt with by the Municipal Corporations Act of 1835 which eliminated the decayed boroughs and allowed the new settlements to achieve formal urban status. In addition, a Royal Commission on Municipal Corporation Boundaries aimed 'to limit the borough to what would now be termed the "continuous built-up area". This meant extending the areas of some boroughs and reducing those of others' (Lipman, 1949, p.67).

In spite of this attempt at regularizing the status of urban areas at the beginning of the nineteenth century even greater confusion followed, for the urban population increased even more rapidly in the succeeding decades; by 21.9 per cent between 1851 and 1861, 28.1 per cent between 1861 and 1871, and 2.6 per cent from 1871 to 1881 (Weber, 1899, p.44). In order to solve the particular problems which this rate and extent of growth created, a wide variety of *ad hoc* bodies was created, each exercising authority over the new urban settlements. These bodies undertook such functions as administration of the Poor Law, control of public health and sanitation, development of education, and provision of roads. By the end of the nineteenth century, a complex mass of overlapping authorities had come into being, but with one outstanding principle, the separation of town and country for the purposes of local government.

The reorganization of these chaotic conditions was embodied in the two Local Government Acts of 1888 and 1894. These accepted the separation of town and country and set up three types of urban areas. The first was the County Borough which was entirely autonomous in local government. The minimum population appropriate to this highest rank was greatly contested and proposals ranged widely. Eventually a criterion of 50,000 population at the 1881 census was agreed. Below this, and sharing some functions with the administrative counties, came the Municipal Boroughs which were in principle the survivors of the old chartered boroughs but which in practice included a wide range of the newer towns of the nineteenth century. The members of the third group were given the name 'Urban District'. These Urban Districts possessed no charter and were largely groupings of the new industrial settlements which had grown up during the century and lacked the clear nodal focus of the older towns. Very often they had been governed by various *ad hoc* bodies. The whole administrative system was consolidated by the creation of these somewhat amorphous 'urban districts'.

In England and Wales there emerged from this process, in addition to county boroughs, some 302 Municipal Boroughs and 688 Urban Districts. Until 1974, with but minor boundary changes, these three elements remained as the administrative units for the urban population of England and Wales and were the areas for which population figures were returned in all the censuses of this century, including that for 1971. For reasons of economy no census was held in 1976 and at the time of writing the 1971 figures are the most recent as far as formal census data are concerned. The Office of Population, Censuses and Surveys (OPCS), however, issues estimates for each year.

One consequence of the 1888 and 1894 legislation was to confirm an administrative definition of the urban population with but little provision for adjustment to change and including widely ranging populations from the Greater London total (in 1971) of 7,542,346 down to tiny Urban Districts such as Newcastle Emlyn in Carmarthenshire (now Dyfed) with only 651 people. Once again the system established soon became outdated and owing to its lack of flexibility no consistent relation of physical settlement to administrative boundary was achieved. In response to this situation the Regional Plans Directorate of the Department of the Environment (Department of the Environment, 1974) produced an analysis called *De Facto Urban Areas in England and Wales, 1966* (Figure 6.1 and Table 6.1). This very valuable document identified 1,333 physically separate urban areas using a total population of 3,000 and a density of 0.6 persons per acre (1.5 per hectare) as a qualification. They contained a population of 41.6 millions or 88.3 per cent of the total. This latter proportion varied regionally from 95.9 per cent in the North West to 62.7 per cent in East Anglia.

The situation in Scotland was slightly different. The historical basis provided by the medieval burghs remained largely relevant even after industrialization and it was not until the Local Government (Scotland) Act of 1929 that a major revision took place. By that Act four Counties of Cities were created, equivalent to the English county borough. These were Aberdeen, Dundee, Edinburgh and Glasgow. The remaining urban settlements were divided into 'large burghs' (21) and 'small burghs' (176) differentiated

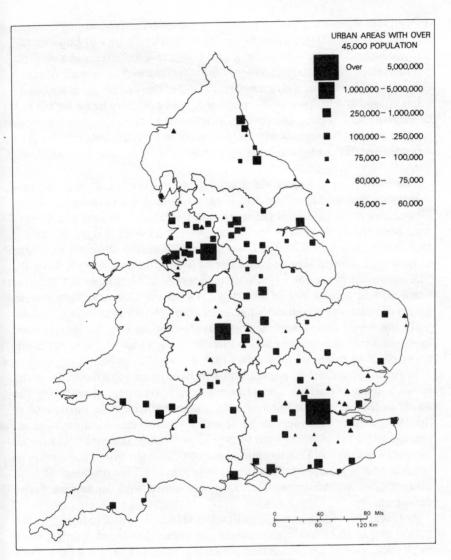

URBAN AREAS WITH OVER
45,000 POPULATION

Over	5,000,000
1,000,000 –	5,000,000
250,000 –	1,000,000
100,000 –	250,000
75,000 –	100,000
60,000 –	75,000
45,000 –	60,000

Fig. 6.1 *De Facto* Urban Areas in England and Wales, 1966
Source: Department of the Environment

by their powers under the local government acts. The same problems of a slowly-changing administratively-based system characterized Scotland as well.

This late nineteenth century system has been completely reformed during the 1960s and 1970s. The London Government Act of 1963 established the administrative area of Greater London covering 1,580 square kilometres and with a resident population of 7.4 millions at the 1971 census, but 6.87 millions according to the 1979 estimate (OPCS monitor, PP1 80/2). It is divided into a second tier of 32 boroughs, with populations ranging between 135,000 and 320,900 (the mean being 227,000), and the City of London, the historic business core, with an area of 2.6 square kilometres and a resident population of only 5,500 but where some 400,000 travel in to work (Central Office of Information, Ref. Pamphlet 1, 1975). This system came into operation in 1965 and in April 1974 a parallel system came into being for the rest of England and Wales. The basic principle was to abandon the nineteenth century attempt to separate town and country so that the new areas are even less adjusted to the physical settlement and much more related to functional areas.

The major conurbations in England were constituted into six new metropolitan counties—Tyne and Wear (including Sunderland as well as Newcastle), West Midlands (Birmingham, the Black Country, and Coventry), Merseyside, Greater Manchester, West Yorkshire (Leeds, Bradford) and South Yorkshire (Sheffield, Rotherham, Barnsley, Doncaster). These in turn were divided into a second tier of Metropolitan Districts, 36 in all. The remainder of the country was divided into Non-Metropolitan Counties, again with a second tier of Districts. Within the Districts there remain parish or community councils which may adopt the status of 'town'. Essentially the whole new system is primarily devoted to effective government based on functional regions and is therefore much less related to the built-up or physical extent of settlements than ever.

In future actual urban populations will have to be constructed from the smallest units for which census population is returned, these being the wards or the parishes or, alternatively, the grid-square basis introduced at the 1971 census. However, in all censuses in this century, up to and including 1971, populations were returned for County Boroughs, Municipal Boroughs and Urban Districts and these constitute the urban population as conventionally measured. This situation produces all the problems of both overbounded and underbounded areas associated with an administrative definition.

At this point, although it will be developed later, it is well to introduce the notion that in an intensively urbanized and highly developed country, small in physical extent, the distinction between what is urban and what is rural now has little meaning. An English megalopolis has come into being, with a distinctive and integrated structure which replaces the older concept of a hierarchy of discrete urban settlements serving purely rural surrounding hinterlands.

The Development of the Urban Hierarchy

In the crudest terms it is possible to consider the growth of the city system in England and Wales in close relation to the administrative system outlined in the previous section. The earliest layer of towns in England was that made up by the Anglo-Saxon burhs, many occupying the sites of former Roman settlements. By 1086 there were some 112 places (including Rhuddlan in Wales) recorded as boroughs (Darby, 1973). Of these London was un- doubtedly the largest, probably followed by York, Lincoln, and Norwich. In the early Middle Ages, after the Norman Conquest, this system was modified and extended. The growth of administration which was based on the shires and executed from the county town, the growth of commerce and trade, and the plantation of new towns, all served to fill out the system. A ranking of towns by size in the late twelfth century based on the average of the 'aids' levied during the reign of Henry II (1154-89) has been carried out (Donkin, 1973), as well as for the years 1334 and 1524 based on Lay Subsidies (Baker, 1973). Although the data are incomplete, and unsatisfactory for a rigorous comparison of ranks, nevertheless a rough ordering can be established. London is at the top of the hierarchy, followed by York, Norwich, Lincoln, Newcastle on Tyne, Bristol, and Exeter.

By the early eighteenth century a complex urban system had emerged taking in the whole country and operating in a hierarchical fashion with a complete coverage of the country by the service areas of the larger provincial capitals and within which nested smaller market towns. Again Darby (1973) identifies the major centres after London, as Norwich, York, Bristol, Newcastle, and Exeter, adding that this situation was much as it had been in 1600. It is possible to regard this system as not only long lasting, since it had emerged during the Middle Ages, but also as extremely adaptable for it has survived beneath the massive transformations of the nineteenth century and of the present. It is true that these centres are no longer in the highest rank of British cities, but along with county towns such as Oxford, Northampton, Gloucester, Shrewsbury, Hereford, Canterbury, and Cambridge, they constitute the traditional provincial capitals, free-standing towns serving well-developed rural areas and characterized both by trade and the industry which developed from it. A. McInnes (1980) has published tables of the populations of leading provincial towns in England at two dates, 1670 and 1750. These are reproduced in Table 6.1.

It is apparent that even by 1750 significant changes were taking place with the rise of Manchester and the entry into the list of Birmingham, Liverpool, Leeds, and Sheffield. These were the great new industrial centres which were superimposed upon and transformed the earlier system of cities which had emerged from the medieval period. Yet the revolutionary nature of this change should not be over-emphasized. Most of the early centres of industry had benefited from the stimulus of developing trade in the pre-industrial period and the process was one of evolutionary transformation rather than a sudden revolutionary break in the pattern of city growth. The global process of urban growth was brilliantly treated by Adna Ferrin Weber (1899) as early as 1899, while a modern treatment of England and Wales set in the context of the evolving city system is to be found in Robson (1973).

Table 6.1: *Ranks and Sizes of the Twenty-Five Leading Provincial Towns in England in 1670 and 1750*

a) *circa* 1670

Norwich	21,000
Bristol	18,000
Exeter	12,500
Newcastle	11,800
York	10,500
Great Yarmouth	9,500
Colchester	9,500
Worcester	8,500
Ipswich	7,500
Canterbury	7,500
Chester	7,500
Plymouth	7,500
Oxford	7,500
Cambridge	7,300
Shrewsbury	7,100
Salisbury	6,700
Coventry	6,500
Hull	6,300
Bury St. Edmunds	5,500
Manchester	5,500
Nottingham	5,500
Leicester	5,000
Hereford	5,000
Tiverton	5,000
Gloucester	4,700

b) *circa* 1750

Bristol	50,000
Norwich	36,000
Newcastle	29,000
Birmingham	23,700
Liverpool	22,000
Manchester	18,000
Exeter	16,000
Plymouth	15,000
Leeds	13,000
Chester	13,000
Coventry	12,500
Ipswich	12,100
Sheffield	12,000
Nottingham	12,000
Hull	11,500
York	11,400
Worcester	10,300
Great Yarmouth	10,000
Sunderland	10,000
Portsmouth	10,000
Bath	9,000
King's Lynn	9,000
Canterbury	8,600
Colchester	8,500
Oxford	8,200

The figures in Table 6.1 are derived chiefly from an analysis of the Hearth Tax returns, the religious census of 1676 and local listings.

Source: McInnes, 1980

In the section of his book devoted to Britain, Weber showed how extensive the transformation has been. One table can be used to illustrate the major changes which have taken place in England and Wales (Table 6.2). A similar transformation has taken place in Scotland (Table 6.3).

The result was that by the middle of the nineteenth century a completely new set of dominant towns had emerged occupying the rank immediately below London (Table 6.4). Only Bristol and Manchester are common to this list and and that for 1670.

Robson (1973) in his study *Urban Growth* was less concerned with the statistical evidence than with the attempt to discern principles relating to the city system and the size distribution of cities within it. After a thorough investigation he concludes,

Even though the generalized patterns do accord with knowledge of the regional economic growth of England and Wales, the details of the spatial patterns can only be interpreted in terms of the particular factor endowments and historical events which underlay the growth of certain towns and the decay of others ... At the national scale, it appears not to be the case that there were regions (or spatial subsystems) which underwent uniformly rapid growth or decline during the nineteenth

Table 6.2: *Percentage of Population of England and Wales in Urban Areas, 1801-91*

Year	London	Other great cities	Cities 20,000-100,000	All cities 20,000+	Urban districts
1801	9.7	0.0	7.2	16.9	—
1811	9.9	2.1	6.1	18.1	—
1821	10.2	3.3	7.4	20.8	—
1831	10.6	5.7	8.7	25.1	—
1841	11.8	6.5	10.6	28.9	—
1851	13.2	9.4	12.4	35.0	50.1
1861	13.9	11.0	13.2	38.2	54.6
1871	14.3	11.5	16.2	42.0	61.8
1881	14.7	14.9	18.4	48.0	67.9
1891	14.5	17.3	21.8	53.6	72.1

Source: Table XIX, A. F. Weber, *The growth of cities in the nineteenth century.*

Table 6.3: *Scotland. Percentage of Population Constituted by Particular Cities*

Year	Glasgow	Cities of 10,000+	Cities of 2,000+
1801	5.1	17.0	
1851	11.5	32.2	51.8
1891	19.4	49.9	65.4

Source: Weber (1899).

Table 6.4: *Largest Cities in England and Wales, 1851*

London	2,363,000	(Metropolis Management Act of 1855 area)
Liverpool	375,955	
Manchester, Salford	367,233	
Birmingham	232,841	
Leeds	172,270	
Bristol	137,328	
Sheffield	135,310	
Bradford	103,310	

Source: Harley (1973).

century. Rather, particular areas showed rapid rates of urban growth because they had a high-than-average number of rapidly growing towns, but at the same time they also had significant numbers which grew at rates similar to or below the national average (Robson, 1973, 126-7).

Robson proceeds finally to suggest that

all that can be said in general terms is that the spatial pattern of nineteenth-century urban growth shows most dramatically the very marked shift from the early boom of the northern textile and metal-working areas and the much later growth of the towns within the South East. Before one could argue that this pattern is suggestive of the early development of a more unitary system focused on London, one would need both more sensitive indicators of the existence of systems, as well as a good deal of non-Euclidean spatial ingenuity (Robson, 1973, 127).

Integral to Robson's problem was the fact that the great cities created by industry were not free-standing towns serving the surrounding countryside but agglomerations created by the exploitation of point resources and backed by the new transport media of canals and railways. Even by the end of the century Weber had noted that the most rapid growth was not taking place in the large cities since population was already moving out to residential suburbs. Through the concentration of population brought about by industrial growth and the dispersal and extension due to suburban development, completely new forms of settlement emerged. These were named 'conurbations' by Patrick Geddes in 1915. 'The neighbouring great towns are rapidly linking up by tramways and streets no less than railways while great open spaces . . . are already all but irrecoverable . . . Some name then for these city regions, these town aggregates, is wanted . . . What of conurbations' (Geddes, 1915, p.14). These new industrial conurbations were coalfield based and since the carboniferous rocks were mainly northern and western in distribution, urbanization was extended to the previously more thinly peopled areas of the country. By the interwar period, therefore, it was possible to consider the urban structure of Britain as dominated by the industrial conurbations and this was tacitly acknowledged in the first postwar census in 1951 by the publication of a volume entitled, *London and Five Other Conurbations* (South East Lancashire, West Midlands, West Yorkshire, Merseyside, Tyneside.) T. W. Freeman (1959) interpreted the whole urban pattern in this way. In addition to the six major centres of the census in England and Wales, he recognized fourteen minor conurbations and seventy-five smaller conurbations and towns.

Change which had been apparent during the 1930s became much more significant after the war. The basic industrial pattern represented by the decline of the heavy and traditional industries concentrated growth in the South East. Again the decline in coal as a fuel released the locational hold which the coalfields had exercised, while road transport and the motorway took over from rail. The result has been the emergence of the English Megalopolis.

It is now apparent that there are three elements in the English urban pattern which can be identified and interpreted. The first of these is the conventional hierarchy where the provision of services for surrounding hinterlands is still the dominant urban role. The second is the industrial conurbation, the creation of point resources though no longer generally sustained by them. The third is the emergent megalopolis in southern and central England, a consequence of the supreme dominance of London re-exerted after the interlude of the Industrial Revolution and partly overlapping the industrial conurbations.

The Hierarchy of Centres

It is still feasible to consider the city system in England and Wales as made up of a series of discrete and identifiable levels. As early as 1944 A. E. Smailes had proposed a hierarchy as in Table 6.5 (Smailes, 1946).

This was an arbitrary and empirical division which recognized six orders of towns. Subsequent work and changes over time have altered this scheme in detail and local studies have also made modifications but it still remains indicative of the urban patterning of the country. To a considerable degree, this ordering of towns can be related to the six highest orders of the seven-fold classification of centres proposed by writers such as Philbrick (1957), and Carol (1960), and derived from Christaller's original work (1933, translated 1966). Even so each order is made up of a wide range of in-dustrial towns, and there is no suggestion that any relationships at this stage can be linked to the predictions of central-place theory as to the number and spacing of centres. It is possible to show, however, how the whole of England and Wales is effectively integrated within a system of serving and controlling centres and covered by a complex of interlocking and over-lapping urban spheres of influence.

At the highest hierarchical levels Kearsley (1971) has re-examined the levels identified by Smailes and has suggested a threefold classification below the level of London. His assessment was based on two studies. The first was of a mass of data relating to higher-order functions which included retail, financial, social, administrative, and professional functions as well as entertainment. The second was a principal components analysis of thirty variables including such measures as the number of department stores, chain jewellers, insurance companies, and chartered accountants. This was followed by a linkage study to provide rankings. The two studies gave

Table 6.5: *The Urban Hierarchy in England and Wales*

The Metropolis	London
Major Cities	e.g. Birmingham, Bristol, Cardiff, Liverpool, Manchester, Newcastle, Hull, Norwich
Cities	e.g. Oxford, Preston, Wolverhampton, Swansea, Gloucester
Major towns	e.g. Bath, Chester, Canterbury, Dover, Shrewsbury, Burton, Halifax
Towns	e.g. Ashford, Bridgwater, Brecon, etc.
Sub Towns	A large number of small towns

Source: A. E. Smailes (1946).

similar results, an hierarchical array in which the *A* centres, as he designated them, included Birmingham, Manchester, Liverpool, Leeds, Newcastle, Nottingham, Bristol, Sheffield, and Cardiff. These can be regarded as the organizing metropoles. Linked to them were the *B* and *C* centres (Figure 6.2) in a structure which indicated a series of sub-systems below the level of London, as capital, although London functions at this level also (Table 6.6).

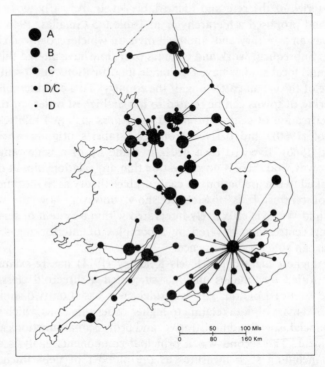

Fig. 6.2 The Upper Ranks of the Urban Hierarchy in England and Wales (*after* Kearsley)

If one of these sub-systems is taken, then the lower hierarchical levels can be indicated and the spread of the national hierarchy to the more rural and thinly peopled parts traced. Thus Figure 6.2 indicates that immediately below the *A* level centre of Cardiff comes the *B* level centre of Swansea. Figure 6.3 reinterprets this relationship in the spatial context of South and West Wales. Immediately below Swansea are the three regional market-towns and administrative centres of Aberystwyth, Carmarthen, and Haverfordwest. If Aberystwyth is taken as representative of this level, then it can be seen that its hinterland covers the western coastal section of mid-Wales. At a lower level this splits into a northern area, served by Aberystwyth, and a southern area served by Cardigan. Lampeter can also be considered to have functions at this level. At a lower order again the smallest urban settle-

Table 6.6: *The Urban Sub-systems of England and Wales* (see also *Figure 6.2*)

Dominant Metropolis	Regional Association
London	S.E. England
Bristol	S.W. England
Cardiff	S. Wales
Birmingham	W. Midlands
Nottingham	E. Midlands
Liverpool	Merseyside and N. Wales
Manchester	N.W. England
Sheffield	South Yorkshire
Leeds-Bradford	West Yorkshire
Newcastle	Tyne-Wear

ments such as Tregaron provide the lowest-order services to immediately surrounding areas. Thus one can conceive of a progression down a firmly nested hierarchy of centres which proceeds: London-Cardiff-Swansea-Aberystwyth-Cardigan-Tregaron, giving a sixfold stratification of centres.

It is interesting to observe that local conditions create modifications. Wales consists of a thinly peopled upland core with a narrow periphery. The result is that its regional centres have never had the opportunity to grow supported by extensive rural areas intensively developed. In consequence there is a level missing, from the above sequence, but a level which can be identified in the *D/C* and *D* centres of Kearsley's ranking of the towns along the English border. The interpolation of a town such as Shrewsbury, between Swansea and Aberystwyth establishes an appropriate grade and a sevenfold system. Here then is a general view of the urban hierarchy in England and Wales interpreted as being made up of discrete levels and effectively covering the whole country in a complex mesh of ranked centres and nested but overlapping tributary areas.

Conurbations

Although the name was coined in 1915 the conurbations were not formally defined until the 1951 census and even then the main criterion was informed local opinion rather than any assemblage of objective data. Those identified in England were Greater London, Merseyside, South East Lancashire, West Yorkshire, West Midlands, and Tyneside. Each was based on a central city, London, Liverpool, Manchester, Leeds, Birmingham, and Newcastle, respectively. There was one conurbation recognized in Scotland, Central Clydeside with Glasgow as the central city, and none in Wales. Outside the central city there was an aureole of smaller industrial towns, although as far as London was concerned they were rather suburban settlements. As the London case suggests, the nature of the organization of these surrounding towns was the consequence of individual growth patterns during the nineteenth and present centuries so that in spatial structure they had little in

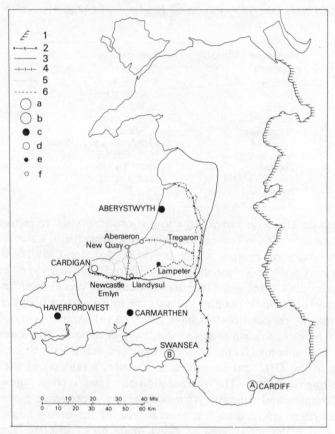

Fig. 6.3 The Urban Hierarchy in West Wales

common. Freeman's book (1959), although now dated, provides a descriptive account of each of the conurbations.

In terms of contemporary socio-economic characteristics an admirable analysis has been carried out (McCullum, 1980). Table 6.7 is taken from his work and sets out a matrix of indices which relates the conurbations' attributes both to the corresponding British average for that attribute and to each other. From a scrutiny of this table he concludes that, 'the various statistical measures analysed ... show that the conurbations, taken as a group, are different from the rest of the country in many important ways ... Equally clear, however, is the evidence which shows how wide are the variations among the seven conurbations, how much they sometimes differ from each other' (McCullum, 1980, 48). Most obviously, Greater London displays characteristics greatly different from the other six. But even within the six McCullum suggests three groups, Clydeside, Merseyside, and Tyneside as one; the West Midlands as a second; and South East Lancashire

Table 6.7: Composite Matrix of Indices for the British Conurbations

	pop. change index 1954-74	% pop. in 15 to 59-64 age group 1971	% households over 5 persons 1971	% male labour force in s.e.g. 1-4 1971	% male labour force in s.e.g. 10-11 1971	% of labour force both parents foreign born 1971	% of total workers in manufacturing 1971	% of total workers in services 1971	% of households in public sector rental 1971	% of households owner occupied housing 1971	% of households lacking basic amenities 1971	% of households overcrowded 1971	% of households with no car 1971
Central Clydeside	84.6	98.7	135.9	81.2	122.0	37.3	111.3	90.6	194.4	51.8	99.4	357.7	136.4
Greater London	77.1	104.7	88.0	120.6	91.2	266.1	78.6	123.6	81.9	83.6	122.2	118.3	109.4
Merseyside	78.4	98.5	131.0	80.6	139.5	49.2	97.7	96.1	109.9	82.6	125.3	116.9	120.8
S.E. Lancashire	88.1	99.5	99.3	96.4	113.2	108.5	125.8	83.3	97.7	105.6	127.8	93.0	118.1
Tyneside	83.8	100.5	98.6	77.0	116.6	23.7	106.7	97.3	143.1	65.2	117.7	135.2	134.2
W. Midlands	94.4	102.2	111.3	85.5	117.1	174.6	155.6	70.9	130.3	93.8	100.0	111.3	104.5
W. Yorkshire	92.1	98.8	93.0	89.7	115.1	123.7	130.1	83.9	101.3	108.3	91.1	97.2	122.0
Average (unweighted)	85.5	100.4	108.2	90.1	116.4	111.9	115.1	92.2	122.7	84.4	111.9	147.1	120.3

Note. In all these indices the GB average is 100.

    s.e.g. = socio-economic groups

    1-4 = managerial and professional occupations

    10-11 = semi-skilled and unskilled workers

Source: McCullum (1980)

and West Yorkshire as the third. Of these the first demonstrates the most 'conurbation-like' features, that is the expected or stereotyped characteristics, whilst the other two show elements of departure.

Some of these features appear in the aggregate population histories of these centres. (Figure 6.4). Central Clydeside, Merseyside, Tyneside, and Greater London show patterns of rapid growth to about 1931, a period of much slower growth to about 1961 and then a rapid decline in growth. South East Lancashire shows the same features but in a much less extreme way, while the shift in the West Midlands came much later. West Yorkshire

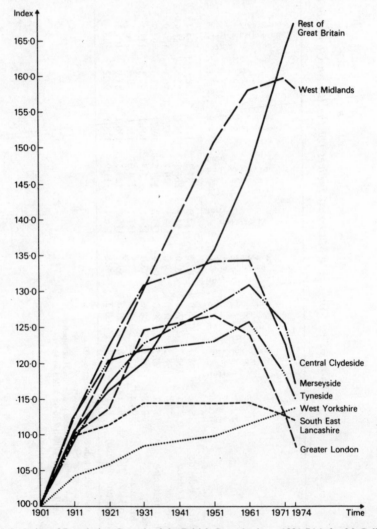

Fig. 6.4   Index of Population Growth of the British Conurbations, 1901-74 (*after* McCullum)

shows a contrasted pattern of slow, continuous growth. These patterns are clearly greatly contrasted with that for the rest of Great Britain but, only in the most general way, delineate common conurbation characteristics.

Any discussion of the national settlement system must take account of these massive agglomerations of population which occurred largely, though not completely, as a result of the rapid growth of heavy industry on the coalfields in the last century. But to discern any common patterns within them is difficult except at the most general level.

Megalopolis England

Beyond the scale of the conurbation lies metropolitan England or what can be called Megalopolis England. This does not imply continuous physical settlement but that the interdependencies and the interlinkages are such that functionally a massive area must be considered as one. The character and anatomy of this feature have been most clearly considered by Peter Hall (1973). He constructs Megalopolis England from two basic functional building blocks. These are:
(1) The Standard Metropolitan Labour Area (SMLA) which is made up of a core containing administrative areas with a density of 5.0 workers per acre (or 12.3 per hectare) or a single administrative area with over 20,000 workers, and a ring comprising contiguous areas which send over 15 per cent of their resident employed workers to the core. To qualify the total population must be over 70,000.
(2) The Metropolitan Economic Labour Area (MELA) which is composed of the SMLA plus contiguous administrative areas which send more of their commuting workers to the SMLA core than to any other core.

When the SMLAs are arranged in rank order the break points can be identified by inspection and ranks established as in Table 6.8.

It will be noted that ranks 1 and 2, here defined on SMLA basis, correspond to the conurbations and ranks 2 and 3 to the Grade *A* cities which were earlier seen as having been identified by Kearsley on a service basis. Virtually the whole of the country comes within the compass of the MELAs and only parts of the South West and Wales really lie beyond their influence. With these building blocks established Hall proceeds to envisage Megalopolis England by constructing from these MELAs a set of contiguous areas which give the maximum concentration of people in relation to their extent (Figure 6.5). In 1961 Megalopolis England so defined contained 56 per cent of the population of England and Wales living on only 7 per cent of the land and at a density of 6,336 per square mile or 2,446 per square kilometre. Again it must be stressed that this is not an area dominated by urban building.

It is a giant urban area only in the sense that here is a large tract of the earth's surface where the great majority of people depend on urban jobs and urban services, and where the impact of these jobs and services, in terms of measurements like

Table 6.8: *Ranking of Standard Metropolitan Labour Areas in England and Wales. After P. Hall (1973)*

---

	1. London	
	2. Birmingham	
	Manchester	
	Liverpool	
	Leeds	
	Newcastle	
	Sheffield	
3. Bristol		4. Stoke
Coventry		Leicester
Nottingham		Cardiff
		Hull
		Portsmouth
		Southampton

(compare with *de facto* urban areas, Table 6.4)

Source: P. Hall (1973)

commuter zones, service areas and the exchange of goods and information, expands to involve each part of the area in a complex series of interactions with other parts (Hall, 1973, p. 320).

The existence of this large-scale feature has implications for the notion of a city system. Within it, extensive commuting means that the town-country dichotomy becomes meaningless while ease of movement to service centres means that traditional hierarchies are likely to disappear. Out-of-town shopping centres in so-called rural surroundings and the growth of hyper-markets undermine the notion of conventional urban service centres. Above all it is characterized by mobility at all scales. Essentially, therefore, a large part of England and Wales must be thought of in terms of this embracing megalopolitan structure which overshadows and integrates the separate pieces of which it is composed.

Changes in the Urban Hierarchy

Like any other urban system, the hierarchy of towns in England and Wales has been, and is being, subject to a number of processes of change operating at different scales both in time and place. Hall (1973, pp. 170-1) has sum-marized the two critical tendencies between 1951 and 1966. The first, he argues, was a regional effect where the dynamism of South East England and the Midlands resulted in a general growth of the metropolitan areas in those regions, whereas the sluggish tendencies in the regional economies in Lancashire and Yorkshire gave rise to poor growth rates. These can be identified on Figure 6.4. The second tendency was a local decentralizing effect where areas peripheral to the Standard Metropolitan Labour Area

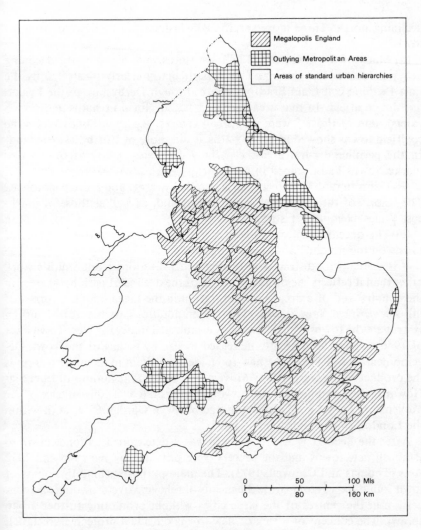

Megalopolis England

Outlying Metropolitan Areas

Areas of standard urban hierarchies

```
0          50         100 Mls
0          80         160 Km
```

Fig. 6.5   The Urban Structure of England and Wales

cores were growing at the expense of the cores. From this summary of
change it is possible to identify three points for discussion: the general
pattern of changes in town rank; the role of new towns; and the decentralizing process.

(i) *The general pattern of change.* The overall pattern of change, irrespective
of rank, within the urban hierarchy of England and Wales between 1938
and 1965 has been studied by R. D. P. Smith (1968). He recorded that in
England out of a total of some 606 centres recognized by Smailes (1944),
some 138 places have risen in status and 78 declined. This general regional
pattern of change confirms Hall's diagnosis of a dynamic south and a

declining north. Three more specific conclusions can be derived from his work.

(*a*) Many of the towns which had lost status were based on the declining heavy industries and mining. This is particularly clearly illustrated by the East Pennine belt from Bradford south through Derbyshire to the Leicestershire coalfield. In that area 18 places had declined in status and only 6 gained, and of those 5 were very small centres. Again in South Wales the coalfield towns showed losses in status as did those of North East England. In the peripheral rural areas, especially of Wales, many of the smaller market towns had declined in rank.

(*b*) Gains in rank were recorded generally by resort and retirement towns. The resorts of the south-west coast of England, as well as those of northeast Wales exemplify this trend.

(*c*) The decentralization process is well marked by the rise in status of towns on the margins of Greater London.

It is difficult to abstract any further generalizations from Smith's work other than it reflects the overall problem of the decline of peripheral areas in the country and of a greater concentration in the megalopolitan core.

(ii) *The British New Towns.* The major additions to the British urban system are the towns which have been established under the New Towns Act of 1946 or have been greatly increased in size by means of the Town Development Act of 1952. The new-town idea in Britain in its modern form is the product of the Garden City Movement based on the notions of Ebenezer Howard. Only two new towns, however, were built as a consequence of the Movement. They were Letchworth and Welwyn Garden City, both within the London sphere (Purdom, 1949).

After the Second World War there was a determined national move to establish new towns and the powers were provided by the 1946 and 1952 Acts (Thomas and Creswell, 1973). The main purpose behind this phase of town founding was to provide the means of relieving overcrowding and congestion at the centres of the large cities without promoting further urban sprawl. The concept of a ring of new towns outside a protected green belt was the dominant theme of early post-war planning (Abercrombie, 1945). This was certainly the *raison d'etre* behind the first generation of London new towns and for those in Scotland about Glasgow. Elsewhere, however, the motives were essentially *ad hoc* and related to the solution of local problems. For example, Cwmbran was established in south-east Wales mainly to provide housing for the new industry locating in the area. Perhaps the most common reason was one which only slowly emerged and this was the use of the new towns as growth centres in declining areas. Scotland's East Kilbride has been regarded as part of a growth-point strategy and this reason has been cited more and more frequently as the basis for development. The new town has in this way become a major element in regional planning strategy and this is most clearly displayed in South East England.

However, the notion of a ring of medium-size new towns outside a green belt has proved far too inflexible and it has been replaced by the notion of growth corridors with new and expanded towns of varying sizes and at varying distances from London. The major period of new-town founding seems now to be over and development is more likely to be directed towards the expansion of existing towns. Even so the new towns have added a very distinctive element to the British city system.

(iii) *Decentralization*. The third distinctive change within urban Britain has been the transfer of population out of the conurbation (or SMLA) cores to the peripheral areas. This has already been noted both in relation to the general changes in town status and to the new-town movement. Hall produces ample evidence to demonstrate this process and concludes, 'the internal dynamics of population in the SMLAs then may be fairly concisely summarized. Both in the 1950s and the 1960s the dominant trend was toward decentralization of population from the core to the ring .... Among big SMLAs there seemed to be a cycle of progress from relative decentralization, to absolute decentralization to decline' (Hall, 1973, pp. 205-6).

(iv) *Changes since 1971*. This has been a major concern of a team at the Centre for Urban and Regional Development Studies at the University of Newcastle. Champion (1980) records that three findings are particularly relevant to post-1971 changes:

(*a*) The broad metropolitan framework has been subject to change during the 1960s so that some 15 new SMLA cores have emerged in two characteristic situations:
1. In areas which have been regarded as outside metropolitan Britain. Examples are Yeovil, Hereford, Canterbury, and Corby.
2. In the outer metropolitan rings of other SMLA cores. Examples are Aylesbury, Basingstoke, Harlow, Hastings, and Crawley, all of which emerged from the outer metropolitan ring of London as it was constituted in 1961.

(*b*) The second feature confirms the pattern of decentralizing already recorded. In particular the cores of the metropolitan counties (virtually the conurbations) showed accelerated decline from 1971 to 1974. The inner rings having increased rapidly in the 1960s fell back in the period 1971-74 when accelerated growth characterized the outer rings.

(*c*) This process of decentralization seems to have reached a peak in the early 1970s but has now subsequently diminished.

The overall impact of these changes traced by Champion indicates considerable re-sorting within megalopolitan England but a retention of its dominance. Economic recession is likely to have its primary impact upon the metropolitan counties furthest removed from the South East.

The Development of the Urban System: Some Generalizations

The major changes in the British city system in recent times were considered in the last section. In this part an attempt will be made to identify the major stages through which the system had evolved to reach its present condition.

The first stage can be called one of *Separation* though in the absolute sense of the complete separation and the absence of interaction between towns it cannot be identified. Even the Roman towns of Britain, as elsewhere in the Empire, were formally and hierarchically organized in an administrative system. But at a time when transport was rudimentary, inter-city competition and the rank ordering of centres which follows from it, was poorly developed. The structuring of the cities into a hierarchy was probably the consequence of the need for an effective system of government and law enforcement rather than of commercial rivalry.

The second stage can be more clearly seen as one of *Competition and Ordering*. As transport became somewhat easier and especially as administration became more effective, so interaction between centres became more important. With interaction came competition and the sorting of cities into some rank order. These early rankings have already been outlined, but it was not until the period 1600-1750 that they become convincing in terms of the modern implications of the concept of a hierarchy. If the highest ranked towns are considered—London followed by Norwich, York, Bristol, Newcastle, and Exeter—two features stand out. These cities were centres of early industry and above all of commerce. They were sea-ports at a time when sea transport was so much easier and effective. They were the major points of assembly and dispersal both of goods circulating internally via the coastal trade and of overseas imports and exports. By the eighteenth century, with improvements in roads and the growth of a network of stage-coach services and of carriers to market, the whole of England and Wales was served by a hierarchy of free-standing towns, and the city system effectively took in the whole national territory.

The third stage can either simply be called *Conurbation* or one of *Revolution in Industry and Transport*. The so-called Industrial Revolution and the coming of the railway completely changed the older system. Both exerted a strong concentrating tendency largely based on the exploitation of point resources. To some extent also the railway permitted the major growth of inland centres though the ports still retained a dominant role. The result was the emergence of a number of conurbations owing little to the provision of services for rural hinterlands and superimposed on top of and reacting with the older hierarchy. The higher-order towns of the earlier period were replaced by these new massive agglomerations based on the cities of Manchester, Birmingham, Leeds, and Sheffield in England, Glasgow in Scotland and Cardiff in Wales.

The next, or fourth stage can be called one of *Integration*. During this the urban system based on the conurbations was gradually modified. In the period after the First World War heavy industry and mining were in a state of decline while a more flexible road transport network grew at the expense of the railway. The result was a confirmation of metropolitan dominance and in particular the relative loss of importance by the outlying and marginal conurbations, such as Tyneside or South Wales. This is a period when the country became dominated by the flow of population into what was called 'the axial belt' which extended from London to Manchester and which Smailes (1946) still identified as an hour-glass shaped feature containing the bulk of urban development. In more local terms this phase corresponded with the beginning of the process of decentralization and suburban sprawl, some of which was contained in what were classified as 'suburban towns' (Moser and Scott, 1961). This marks the filling out of territory, within the axial belt in particular, by physical development and the thickening of the complex urban web.

The fifth stage which brings the process to the present can be called *Metropolis and Megalopolis*. It is dominated by the rapid growth in private car ownership and motorway construction so that its dominant theme is that of mobility. This vast increase in mobility has produced a number of consequences. Place, as such, begins to lose its significance and people live, as Webber (1964) suggests, in a number of realms some of which are aspatial, since contact with the local community or a business contact many thousands of miles away are as easily maintained. In order to meet the demands of the mobile person, and to offset city-centre congestion, out-of-town shopping centres and hypermarkets have developed. These in turn have contributed to the collapse of the established urban hierarchies and a move to specialization almost in the form of the dispersed city. The result is a broad regional organization of a much more complex form than the hierarchical notion of an earlier period. This transformation is certainly not complete even within Megalopolis England, but is still the dominant process and it is accompanied by the decline of the inner city and the gradual dispersal of population into the outer rings of the metropolitan centres. It is perhaps possible to regard England and Wales as composed of three broad urban areas. The first is that which Hall defines as Megalopolis England, the second the outlying conurbations where modification is proceeding at a slower rate. The third area is made up of those remaining territories where the organization is still based on ranked towns and nested spheres of influence.

It is appropriate to set these phases in the growth of the system against the varying nature of formal control. At the earliest stage of separation political power exercised considerable influence. Town founding was a political process, for however much local advantages were exploited the town was primarily the basis of military and administrative control. The second and third phases were marked by the relaxation of such influences and the move to a period of relatively free economic competition. The great upheaval in the urban system at the Industrial Revolution epitomises this era, when changes in rank position were rapid. By the fourth integrative phase, however, political influences were again becoming significant. These were never exerted directly with any formal plan for the evolution of the settlement system, but through regional policy which sought to bolster the declining centres based on heavy industry and coal mining. The present phase has seen planning influences play a dominant part, although again without any formal central-government manipulation of the system. Certainly the Strategic Plans for the counties are concerned with the vitality of centres and their structuring in terms of service provision. Central impacts are, however, exerted through indirect regional policies. Amongst the various influences can be noted:

1. The New Towns Programme
2. Regional policies involving the encouragement of industrial and office employment to move to designated areas
3. The general discouragement of out-of-town shopping centres in an attempt to preserve the existing central areas of towns.

It would be impossible here even to sketch the wide variety of controls. Although these have been far from absolute, and are at present being relaxed, nevertheless the urban system has been subject to considerable modification through central- and local-government planning, but exercised indirectly and in a regional context, rather than directly on the system.

Conclusion

This contribution has attempted to sketch only in briefest outline a descriptive analysis of the settlement patterns of Britain, mainly concentrating on England and Wales, and of the recent changes taking place. In general the situation is one in which changes dependent on mobility have not reached the same stage as parts of the United States, but are equivalent to many highly developed countries where the dominant theme is the emergence of Megalopolis, but where parts of the country remain characterized by former systems.

At this stage it is relevant to introduce, however briefly, attempts to classify British cities with a population of over 50,000 in relation to a wide range of variables. The classic study using component analysis, was that by Moser and Scott published in 1961 but based on data mainly from the early 1950s. Andrews (1971) undertook a more formal cluster analysis of the towns where he criticized Moser and Scott for using descriptive titles for their groups—such as 'mainly resorts, administrative, and commercial towns'—rather than interpretations related to the nature of the extracted components. More recently Grove and Roberts (1980) repeated the analysis using 1970s data. They, like Moser and Scott, extract four components but do not name them. They reject either comparability with Moser and Scott or that their results concur with the standard view that the prime characteristics which differentiate cities in western, industrialized societies are socio-economic status, life-cycle stage, and ethnicity. 'For the 1971 data the first four components show nothing resembling a clear pattern ... We therefore simply list the eight primary variables showing the highest correlations with each component' (Grove and Roberts, 1980, p. 78).

This would seem to confirm the conclusions already set out that megalopolitan structuring does not characterize the whole of Britain; for neither that degree of development of a post-industrial society, nor that stage of mobility have yet been reached. The settlement system is still in transition between its industrial past and its post-industrial future.

REFERENCES

Abercrombie, P. 1945. *Greater London plan, 1944*. London: HMSO.
Andrews, H. F. 1971. 'A cluster analysis of British towns', *Urban Studies*, 8(3): 271-84.
Baker, A. R. H. 1973. 'Changes in the Later Middle Ages', Chap. 5, in: Darby, H. C. *A new historical geography of England*. Cambridge: CUP 186-247.
Carol, H. 1960. 'The hierarchy of central functions within the city', *Annals of the Association of American Geographers*, 50: 419-38.
Census. England and Wales, 1956. *Report on Greater London and five other conurbations, 1951*. London: HMSO.
Central Office of Information, 1975. *Local Government in Britain*, Ref. Pamphlet 1, London: HMSO.
Champion, A. G. 1980. 'Selected aspects of the study of the U.K. settlement system'. Paper submitted to 24th International Geographical Congress, Tokyo.
Christaller, W. 1966. *Central places in Southern Germany*, Englewood Cliffs, NJ: Prentice Hall (Translation by C. W. Baskin).
Darby, H. C. 1973. *A new historical geography of England*, Cambridge: CUP.
Department of the Environment, 1974. *De facto urban areas in England and Wales*, Regional Plans Directorate, London: DoE.
Donkin, R. A. 1973. 'Changes in the Early Middle Ages', Chap. 3, in: Darby, H. C., *A new historical geography of England*, Cambridge: CUP, 75-135.
Freeman, T. W. 1959. *The conurbations of Great Britain*, Manchester: Man. Univ. Press.
Geddes, P. 1915. *Cities in evolution*. New and revised edition, London: Williams and Norgate, 1949.
Grove, D. M. and Roberts, C. A. 1980. 'Principal component and cluster analysis of 185 large towns in England and Wales', *Urban Studies*, 17(1): 77-82.
Hall, P. *et al*, 1973. *The containment of urban England*. Two Vols., London: Allen and Unwin.

Harley, J. B. 1973. 'England circa', Chap. 10, in: Darby, H. C., *A new historical geography of England*. Cambridge: CUP, 529-94.

Kearsley, G. W. 1971. 'The upper ranks of the urban hierarchy', in: *England and Wales*, unpub. Ph.D. thesis, University of London.

Lipman, V. D. 1949. *Local government areas*. Oxford: Blackwell.

McCullum, J. D. 1980. 'Statistical trends of the British conurbations', Chap. 2, in: Cameron, G. C. ed., *The future of the British conurbations*. London: Longman, 14-53.

McInnes, A. 1980. *The English town, 1660-1760*. London: The Historical Association.

Moser, G. A. and Scott, W. 1961. *British towns: a statistical study of their social and economic differences*. London: Oliver and Boyd.

Office of Population Censuses and Surveys, 1979-80. *OPCS Monitor*, London: Govt. Statistical Services.

Philbrick, A. K. 1957. 'Principles of areal functional organization in regional human geography', *Economic Geography*, 33: 299-336.

Purdom, C. B. 1949. *The building of satellite towns*. London: Dent.

Robson, B. T. 1973. *Urban growth: an approach*. London: Methuen.

Smailes, A. E. 1946. 'The urban mesh of England and Wales', *Trans. Inst. Brit. Geogrs*. 11: 84-101.

Smith, R. D. P. 1968. 'The changing urban hierarchy', *Reg. Studies*, 2: 1-19.

Thomas, R. and Creswell, P. 1973. *The new town idea*. Milton Keynes: Open University Press.

Webber, M. M. 1964. 'Urban place and nonplace urban realm', in: M. M. Webber *et al.* (eds.), *Explorations into urban structure*, Philadelphia: Univ. of Pennsylvania Press.

Weber, A. F. 1899. *The growth of cities in the nineteenth century. A Study in statistics* (reprinted 1965), Ithaca, NY: Cornell Univ. Press.

ACKNOWLEDGEMENTS

The author wishes to acknowledge the considerable help and advice of Dr. A. G. Champion and Professor B. T. Robson in the preparation of this chapter.

7 THE FRENCH NATIONAL SETTLEMENT SYSTEM

ETIENNE DALMASSO

Space in France has for a long time been characterized by the close relations which exist between rural areas and towns, with their numerous inter-relations. But the extent of urban domination of the countryside and the strength of inter-urban relations has changed the course of development. France experienced a rather late phase of accelerated urbanization, which increased the dominating role of the towns in spatial organization. The form which this urbanization took served to aggravate spatial imbalances, and consequently led to the implementation of specific policies and demonstrated the need for an extensive study of the French urban system.

Theoretical and Methodological Problems

A study of spatial organization and of the French urban system runs into numerous and different problems, which have not all been equally well resolved.

Problems of Definition

It seems essential to examine briefly the question of the administrative definitions which are the basis of the statistical data, for these do not always coincide with those proposed by geographers or other social scientists.

Towns, Agglomerations, ZPIU. The varied elements of the system of spatial organization in France are defined in relation to the base unit of the administrative division of the country, that is the *commune*. French communes are numerous (36,394) and generally of a small size: hence the necessity for consolidation in order to understand the geographical meaning of many features of their distribution. Nevertheless, even if this is much less significant than in Italy, in the area of just one commune there may be several distinct nucleii, or agglomerations of population as they are called in the census. A population agglomeration consists of neighbouring buildings which form a whole in such a way that none is separated from the nearest building by more than 200 metres, and its population is at least 50 inhabitants. The population of the chief town is that which resides in the agglomeration where the seat of the legal authorities of the commune (that is, the town hall) is situated; other agglomerations are called secondary agglomerations. When a population of 2,000 inhabitants is concentrated in the chief town, it is classified as an urban commune.

While an urban commune can be completely included within the communal boundaries (then called an isolated town), there can also be a population agglomeration of more than 2,000 persons spread over the territory of several communes, thus forming a multi-commune urban agglomeration. For this category, as for an isolated town, the term urban unit is then applied.

The space between the different urban units forms the rural territory, but this remains very heterogeneous. Between the essentially rural and agricultural sectors and the towns, there are intermediate zones where demographic growth is rapid. In some of these areas the majority of the population lives not from agriculture but from industrial activities, often produced by a nearby town. (These communes are classified as rural-industrial.) In other areas the active population works to a large extent in the neighbouring urban unit (dormitory communes). Therefore, if we take into account not only continuity of habitation but also criteria relating to the structure of the active population, daily journeys to work, and the rate of demographic growth, we can then define geographic units larger than the towns and agglomerations which we call zones of industrial and urban settlement (*zones de peuplement industriel et urbain* ZPIU).

These definitions have not always been rigorously applied, especially in the past, and this has given rise to ambiguities in the use of the terms agglomeration, conurbation, urban region, and town.

Urban Network, Urban Infrastructure, Urban System. These terms are often used interchangeably. The concept of an urban system should be understood in the broadest sense, that is to say a set of towns each having a zone of influence in the surrounding rural areas and maintaining between themselves functional relations, whether hierarchical or not. The urban network and the urban infrastructure are concepts which must be understood at a different level. The urban network designates a hierarchical set of centres which provides the administrative, cultural, and commercial services in a region, and which is dominated by a regional metropolis, that is an agglomeration 'endowed with a range of services sufficient to enable the inhabitants of the region to avoid all significant recourse to another more important town which is better equipped than itself' (M. Rochefort). The urban infrastructure constitutes for its part all of the urban networks of a country, dominated by the political (and/or economic) capital, and their interrelations.

Methodological Problems

The study of the French urban system has been conducted using different methods. For a long time an empirical and monographic method prevailed, which produced some remarkable case studies but did not provide a comprehensive view of French towns. Since the 1950s the range of methods available has gradually increased, the need to look at the whole of the urban system has been demonstrated, and methods of statistical analysis have been added to the methods of empirical investigation. Pumain and Saint-Julien (1976) have shown that these works have aimed principally at establishing typologies of towns and proposing hierarchical classifications.

One set of studies attempts to understand the nature of urban functions and their components. This looks at the functional structure of towns, and their diversification or specialization. A second set of studies looks at towns as poles of spatial organization, assessing the extent of the urban zones of influence, and establishing urban hierarchies. Thus, urban agglomerations are shown to have an organizing function, in that they provide the economic agents of towns and their zone of influence with all the services they require. Tertiary activities are considered to be the elements determining the spatial organization. The methods used, however, often produce different, even contradictory, results, in particular with regard to anything concerning the classification of towns according to their activities. Studies of the urban hierarchy are more homogeneous, but much more analysis of relations between the different levels of the urban hierarchy is needed. Even if the classification of centres is satisfactory, knowledge of the flows between one centre and another is incomplete because of the lack of data. This information, however, is essential in order to understand the functioning of the urban system.

Theoretical Problems

The need to explain explicitly the theoretical framework to which one is referring is a very recent development in French geographical literature. However, this does not imply that there has previously been an absence of theoretical concern. To some people the role of the town is to produce and export services. Urban growth, the functional diversity of the centres, and the extent of the integration of the networks are all dependent on exporting activities. This is the application of the theory of the economic base. But if we look at the town as having above all a territorial function, that is to enclose and integrate an area of space, then the significance of industrial activities, which are so important in defining structures of activity and determining the economic base, diminishes in favour of tertiary activities. The level of tertiary activities, measured in terms of quantity, degree of scarcity, and quality of supply, specifies the central places. The theory of central places is widely used in studies on regional urban networks as in those concerned with the urban infrastructure. On the other hand, the theory of growth poles, which assigns to the town the function of production and, equally, the function of spreading growth over the whole of the territory has not been applied precisely, perhaps because of a lack of precision in the concept. Finally, we must note the reference in recent work to the theory of unequal exchange. The idea is that the structure of the spatial system will in future evolve less as a function of the sectoral division of labour than as a function of the levels of qualification and remuneration of labour. A new urban hierarchy would, thus, take form based on specializations in the social structures, with an emphasis on the 'centre' and the 'periphery'.

Development of the System of Spatial Organization—Historical Aspects

The long-standing occupation and development of the French land determined very early the pattern of agglomerations. Nearly all of them are situated on sites which have been occupied for centuries. The town as a factor of spatial organization also appeared very early. This is due to the early existence of settlements, major migratory flows, and the existence of numerous favourable sites in a country of diversified relief. In other respects, we should not ignore the influence of the nearby mediterranean civilizations which are, essentially, urban civilizations. In the course of a long historical evolution several generations of towns have been born and an urban system established which is marked by strong imbalances in the urban hierarchy.

Different Generations of Towns

Since the Gallo-Roman era France has been endowed with a dense set of towns exhibiting a hierarchical order. Although Gallic towns did exist it was nevertheless Roman action which was principally responsible for the urban system of the period. This action was profound and lasting and we should point out that, of the 44 chief-towns or '*civitates*', 26 are today Departmental chief-towns and only 6 have been relegated to the rank of village.

A second generation of towns dates from the Middle Ages, particularly the period from the eleventh to the fourteenth century. The demographic and economic advances, as well as the political transformations of these centuries, brought about a lively urbanization movement, which took place in different ways. While there was a renewal of activity in the Gallo-Roman towns, there was also a creation of new towns in favourable places (at crossroads, or where fairs took place, e.g. Mulhouse). Urban agglomerations were established near castles and monasteries; thus, Chinon, Saumur, and Beaucaire were created around a castle, the seat of manorial political power. Cluny, Moissac, and Aurillac developed from monasteries. Finally, there was the creation of new towns. For example, Saint Louis founded Aigues-Mortes in 1246. A number of these towns were built in the southwest on either side of the frontier between the Kingdom of France and the territories occupied by the English; these are the *bastides* or fortified towns (e.g. Mirande founded in 1282, Villeneuve-sur-Lot in 1264).

From the sixteenth to the eighteenth centuries other towns appeared. France was now a centralized monarchical state practising an expansionist policy. Therefore, towns were created as princely or royal residences (e.g. Versailles in 1671). Also, France conducted wars which brought about the construction of fortress towns like Rocroi in the sixteenth century, or the towns built for Louis XIV by the engineer Vauban (e.g. Neuf-Brisach in 1698). In addition, French colonial expansion encouraged the birth of ports (Le Havre in 1517-1543, Rochefort in 1657, Brest, Lorient, and Sète in 1666).

From then on one can say that, in a sense, the French urban pattern was established. There was a dense body of towns, and the eighteenth century, as the first half of the nineteenth century, saw no notable creations, if some spas and the Napoleonic towns of la Roche sur Yon and Pontivy are excluded. The 'industrial revolution' established heavy industry based on coal and a railway network, but did not actually involve the birth of new towns in any significant number. There was, of course, the construction of mining villages on the coal or iron fields and of railway towns (e.g. La Roche-Migenne) but this was not very significant. In the same way, the growth of thermal spas and tourism created Aix-les-Bains, Vichy, and Deauville for example, but this was not sufficient to change significantly the elements of the urban system. The first half of the nineteenth century, was characterized by economic and demographic stagnation which was not a stimulating factor for urban growth. In fact, France's transition to an industrial economy was achieved with the support of a pre-industrial urban pattern. While the industrialization of the country had as a corollary considerable urbanization, this was achieved more through the growth of the existing towns and the development of the suburbs than by the mushrooming of new agglomerations.

Increasing Imbalances in the System of Spatial Organization

However, this set of towns has not always shown the hierarchical structure which it does today. For long periods it would be more appropriate to speak of an urban 'mesh' than of urban networks. Indeed, functional relations between the towns before the construction of the railways were quite limited. Each centre served a small region without the need for frequent recourse to other centres, given that the division of labour at the national level was not highly developed. The urban pattern, in terms of the population of towns in 1801, shows a very regular distribution over the whole of the country. With the exception of Paris, no town really stands out. There are few regional disparities, with the exception of the west of France where urban centres are almost non-existent.

A century later the situation had changed considerably. During the first half of the century the capital grew considerably as a heavy rural exodus began from the over-populated countryside. The political and administrative centralization of the monarchy and later of the Napoleonic regime made Paris the focal point of these activities and, therefore, of migration. The division of the country into Departments, established during the Revolution, encouraged territorial break-up and a multiplication of chief-towns,

which delayed the growth of medium-sized towns. Moreover, the effects of
the construction of the railways and of industrialization began to be felt.
The railway system has been a powerful agent for the structuring of urban
networks and for the creation of urban hierarchies. Industrialization
occurred mainly on the coalfields and, later, the iron-ore deposits of
Lorraine, while colonization built up certain ports. Regional imbalances,
therefore, were accentuated, and the division between the north and east
of France on the one hand, and the west and south were aggravated. The
urban hierarchy asserted itself through the stagnation of numerous towns
(especially those far from the major railway axes, for example Alençon), the
advancement of some medium-sized towns, and the emergence of some
regional capitals (e.g. Marseille, Bordeaux, Lille, and Lyon). But Paris
asserted itself in an overwhelming way. Everything combined to maintain
this predominance: the effects of the political organization which have
already been noted, a railway system arranged in a star shape with Paris in
the centre which provided the capital with an exceptional locational advantage, plus a growing rural exodus, and the proximity of the industrial
regions.

This imbalance between Paris and the provinces was epitomized in the
famous phrase of J. F. Gravier 'Paris and the French desert', and was maintained during the first half of the twentieth century. From 1901 to 1954,
urbanization continued in spite of slow economic and demographic growth.
It did not result in any real changes, however, but only exaggerated the
contrasts which had emerged in the nineteenth century.

The Present Structure of the System of French Spatial Organization

During the period from the end of the Second World War to the present
day, France has been the scene of profound upheavals. The facts are well-
known and will only briefly be recalled now. The major phenomenon is the
demographic revival due to a strong recovery in the birth-rate, as well as the
return to France of numerous inhabitants of the colonial territories, and
growing foreign immigration. However, this demographic recovery is
tending to diminish today. The crude birth-rate, which went up as high as 21
per cent in 1948 had fallen to 13.6 per cent in 1976. The second fundamental
fact is the transformation of the economic structures of the country.
Industrialization has continued, the system of production has been modernized and economic growth was strong until the recent recession. The result
has been an increase in the rate of employment (especially female employment), an increase in the proportion of wage-earners (82.7 per cent of total
employment in 1975), a decrease in the active agricultural population (9.5
per cent of those in employment) in favour of secondary and, increasingly,
tertiary employment (51.3 per cent of those employed). All this assumes a
very large geographic redistribution of the population with a reduction in
the rural population, the growth of towns, and changes in their structure.

Accelerated Urbanization

(a) *The Increasing Role of the Towns.* For a long time France remained a predominantly rural country. In 1851 the urban population represented only 25.5 per cent of the total population, and in 1901 it had hardly reached 40.9 per cent. It was not until 1928 that the threshold of 50 per cent was reached, which was very late by comparison with other European industrial countries. All this was to change within the space of a generation. In fact, although at the end of the war in 1945 the urban population only represented 53.2 per cent of the national total, urbanization was about to accelerate (Table 7.1).

Table 7.1: *Evolution of the French Urban Population*

Year	Urban population (in millions)	Urban population per cent
1954	28.1	58.6
1962	29.5	63.4
1968	35.5	71.4
1975	38.4	72.9

In reality these percentages are higher if, instead of including only agglomerations, we also take into account the population of the ZPIU. The urban population would then represent 77.3 per cent of the national total in 1962, and 82.5 per cent in 1975. The size of the urban population carries with it an equivalent economic significance, in that 9/10 of output is supplied by the towns. It is worth noting that, once again, this urban growth has not been accompanied by the creation of many new urban sites. A limited number of tourist and industrial agglomerations have been created and the 'new towns' experiment, as we shall see later, has just begun and so far produced only 9 units.

(b) *The Recent Tendency of Urban Growth to Slow Down.* Urbanization has recently, however, shown a distinct tendency to slow down, as can be seen in Table 7.2. This table shows clearly the decline in the rate of population growth in the Paris region which was accompanied by a more rapid growth of small and medium-sized towns. In reality, however, this did not bring about any spectacular changes in the structure of the urban system as determined in the nineteenth century.

The Stability of the System of Spatial Organization

The major feature of the French spatial system remains its stability and the continuance of the imbalances.

(a) *The Continuance of the Imbalances.* French space is characterized by a clear asymmetry between the east and the west and by a profound imbalance between Paris and the provinces. The domination of Paris has created a central space surrounded by a peripheral space.

Table 7.2: *Population Changes in France, 1954-1975*

	Growth Rate 1954-1975 as a percentage	1954-1975	1962-1968	1968-1975
All France	+ 22.4	+ 1.0	+ 1.2	+ 0.8
All rural communes	− 4.4	− 0.6	− 0.3	− 0.2
All urban communes	+ 37.4	+ 1.9	+ 1.8	+ 1.1
Urban units (of less than 5,000 inhabitants)	+ 27.4	+ 1.0	+ 1.3	+ 1.2
Small towns (5,000-20,000 inhabitants)	+ 34.7	+ 1.6	+ 1.7	+ 1.2
Medium-sized towns (20,000-200,000 inhabitants)	+ 48.0	+ 2.3	+ 2.3	+ 1.5
Large towns (200,000 inhabitants and over)	+ 39.4	+ 1.9	+ 2.1	+ 1.0
Paris agglomeration	+ 27.4	+ 1.8	+ 1.4	+ 0.4

This phenomenon can be looked at in many ways. It is perceived in the first instance in the distribution and density of population and towns. Rural space shows strong disparities in population density. The geographical distribution of the small towns shows a lack of uniformity. If the small towns are excluded where the pattern is quite uniform, the distribution of the larger towns or the ZPIU reveals the contrast between the west and the east. The regions of high urbanization are those of the Parisian agglomeration and the Lower Seine, the North, Alsace-Lorraine, the agglomeration of Lyon, and Lower Provence. Elsewhere, the degree of urbanization is smaller and under-urbanization even exists in some areas (south and east of the Paris Basin and south of the Massif Central).

Second, the imbalance is apparent in the distribution of towns according to size. By applying the Zipf criterion to the urban system we can show the anomalies. The divergence between the primate city and the other ag-glomerations is of the most striking nature. The ratio between Paris and the second agglomeration, Lyon, is greater than 7, while it is only 2 or 3 in nearly all the other countries of Europe. The largest French towns do not correspond in size to equivalent towns in neighbouring countries; on the other hand, medium-sized towns are more numerous. On the whole, 'the capital appears abnormally large, while about ten provincial towns appear abnormally small' (Noin, 1976). This situation has changed little from one census to another, as shown in Table 7.3.

This table shows clearly the stability of the whole of the urban system, with a continuing but decelerating decline of the small market towns, the limited but unspectacular decline of Paris which we have already noted, a slight variation in the importance of the small and large towns, and the ad-vance of the medium-sized towns.

These imbalances in the urban hierarchy are accompanied by other

Table 7.3: *Distribution of the Urban Population (percentages)*

	1954	1962	1968	1975
Urban units of less than 5,000 inhabitants	8.3	7.8	7.6	7.7
Small towns	14.0	13.6	13.5	13.7
Medium-sized towns	30.4	30.9	31.6	32.3
Large towns	23.3	23.5	23.8	23.8
Paris agglomeration	24.0	24.2	23.5	22.6

imbalances in the socio-economic structure of the different levels of spatial organization, as can be seen in Table 7.4.

(b) *A Profound Evolution in the Urban System.* Nevertheless, these facts give us an indication that changes are taking place and these trends need to be understood. Pumain and Saint-Julien (forthcoming) have put forward an interpretation of the changes which have affected the urban system of all the agglomerations (with the exception of Paris) with more than 20,000 inhabitants in 1954, for the period 1954-1975. By analysing the main components of residuals when every variable is regressed on itself, these authors have been able to measure both the aggregate and differential changes affecting the urban system. The general processes of change, which include demographic growth, the growth of the tertiary sector, the progressive replacement of declining economic activities and professions, and an increased spending power, have brought about a shift in the urban system which, nevertheless, retains its stability. Thus, by putting together the main aspect of the economic activity of a town, the chief social characteristic, the level of wealth, and the type of demographic development, we can produce a 'profile' of each town.

During this 20 year period there is a noticeable stability in the order of towns ranked according to their 'profile'. The rich, tertiary agglomerations such as Nice and Montpellier, which are still developing, continue to be contrasted with the industrial towns showing population stagnation, such as Lens and Forbach. However, towns grow at different rates from very different initial situations and two opposite, but independent tendencies appear. On the one hand, there is a tendency towards relative homogeneity of urban socio-economic situations; on the other hand, disparities increase as a new principle of differentiation between agglomerations progressively emerges.

The first course tends towards the reduction of disparities in the 'profile'. If the agglomerations have retained their rank and kept the same relative positions with respect to their 'profile', they have also been drawn closer to each other. The growth of the tertiary sector, the spatial redistribution of employment, and the geographical diffusion of expanding sectors of employment, have all resulted in a reduction of heavy specializations (with a

Table 7.4: *Distribution of the Active Population by Sector of Economic Activity in Urban Units, 1968 (in per cent)*

Categories of urban units	Agriculture	Construction	Industry	Transport	Commerce Insurance Banks	Services
Units of less than 5,000 inhabitants	11.9	11.4	34.8	3.2	12.2	26.5
Small towns	7.2	10.4	35.9	3.7	13.2	29.3
Medium-sized towns	2.8	10.4	32.1	4.7	15.8	34.2
Large towns	1.7	9.5	32.9	5.5	15.8	34.6
Paris agglomeration	0.5	8.1	32.7	5.7	15.6	37.4
All urban units	3.1	9.7	33.1	4.9	15.2	34.0

consequent catching-up of tertiary or industrial activities), and diminishing disparities in the socio-economic profile. But, at the same time, new differences have appeared. Towns in the south-east of France have experienced 'functional over-specialization', usually linked to the development of tertiary consumption. Also, there has been a progressive reinforcement of a new structural dimension which is changing the ranking of the urban agglomerations. The towns tend to arrange themselves according to their stage of integration into the general process of development and their different abilities to determine and spread growth, which allows for a differentiation between 'growth centres' and towns on the 'periphery' of the system. These new and original studies, which leave aside the question of the relations of this set of medium-sized and large towns with Paris and the small towns, demonstrate in every case that the main tendency of the system is to perpetuate itself in the same form.

The Different Levels of the Urban System

(a) *The Paris Agglomeration.* Any study of the French spatial system must include a separate section on the Paris agglomeration, even if this leads to a consideration of problems common to other large agglomerations. The situation of Paris is exceptional, however, because of the size of its population, the concentration of activities, its 'supremacy in decision-making' (Beaujeu-Garnier, 1977), and the importance of the methods used to organize this enormous agglomeration.

But we must be very clear about what is understood to be the Paris agglomeration. This term expresses not the administrative but the geographical reality of Paris. At the administrative level, Paris is at the head of a 'region' of 12,000 km², with nearly 10 million inhabitants, and which has been divided into eight Departments since 1964. The town of Paris constitutes a Department by itself and is also a commune in the same way as the others. Since 1976 this region has been called la région de l'Ile de France.

The Paris agglomeration is a shifting reality whose boundaries are constantly extending. Using various criteria such as the continuity of built-up areas, number of inhabitants in the commune, the rate of demographic growth, population density, the proportion of rural life, and daily journeys to work, it is possible to define a Paris agglomeration ('extended agglomeration') covering 1,800 km², divided into 279 communes, inhabited by 8.5 million inhabitants, and divided into two parts. There is the 'restricted agglomeration' (350 km² with 5.3 million inhabitants) consisting of the city of Paris (105 km² with 2.3 million inhabitants) and its immediate suburbs (the inner ring) which are closely bound to Paris. Then there are the outer suburbs ('external zone' or outer ring) consisting of 1,370 km² with 3.1 million inhabitants, which are less densely built-up. On the whole, the extended agglomeration, which is 35 kms wide, forms a genuine urban region with about 30 communes of more than 50,000 inhabitants, more than 90 communes of 20-50,000 inhabitants, and almost as many communes of 10-20,000 inhabitants. In addition, this agglomeration has a regional zone of influence which extends well beyond the Paris Basin. On 0.35 per cent of the national land live 16.2 per cent of the population.

Such a large concentration of people can be explained by the intensity and variety of economic functions. Greater Paris is an enormous centre of production and consumption. The historical reasons for this concentration have already been recalled. At the present time the Paris agglomeration fulfils many different functions. Its industry represents a quarter of the national industry according to manpower (1,650,000 workers) and even more if value of production and innovative capability is considered. Although all branches of industry are present, the refining industries are pre-eminent with metallurgy at the top, particularly the car industry. Of the active population of the agglomeration, 44 per cent are employed in industry. Tertiary activities, therefore, prevail and one of their essential roles stems from the fact that Paris is the political and administrative capital. Government services, those of local organizations and of the semi-public sector employ 900,000 people, of which 25 per cent perform national business, 10 per cent work at a regional level and 65 per cent are concerned with the local needs of the population. To this must be added international functions, with the existence of more than 400 international organizations. The power which is conferred on the seat of government in a country as centralized as France has attracted the headquarters of economic institutions (e.g. head offices of companies, insurance companies, and banks). Thus, Paris has become, overwhelmingly, the foremost French financial centre. Commercial activity is also high because, apart from satisfying the needs of an important local and regional clientele with a much higher purchasing power than the national average, the trade in certain goods is exclusively concentrated in Paris. Finally, the capital is also the main university, cultural, and artistic centre of the country.

This agglomeration is undergoing constant change along very clear lines. The number of inhabitants of the city of Paris is decreasing (it had already declined to 2.3 million inhabitants by 1975). The price of land is so high that renovations or new constructions are only possible for enterprises looking for offices, or for citizens with very high incomes.

Compared to inner Paris, which is becoming middle class, growing old, and where the tertiary sector is increasing, there are the suburbs which are expanding rapidly, with both old areas of communal housing and new planned residential districts (the *grands ensembles*). These suburbs are socially less pretentious, newer, badly supplied with services (despite the introduction of many commercial areas) and over-run with new construction. Most of the expansion occurs near the outer ring, thus taking more land into the urbanized areas.

The need to organize and control the growth of Paris has become imperative during the last few years. In order to do this two methods have been used. To contain the growth of the agglomeration, a policy of industrial and, to a lesser degree, tertiary sector decentralization has been followed, within the framework of regional policy. Some results have been obtained: from 1968 to 1975 the Paris agglomeration showed a total growth of 3.6 per cent while that of all urban communes was 8.1 per cent. The components of population growth are now 86 per cent natural increase and 14 per cent migration (the latter including increasing numbers of foreigners who make up 13 per cent of the population of the agglomeration). Recently the migration balance has become negative.

But there is a limit to this kind of action. Some people believe that the 'de-industrialization' of Paris as well as the diminution of tertiary activities has been too extreme and brutal, and will weaken the international role of the capital. On the other hand, everyone agrees that it is necessary to combat the monocentric nature of the agglomeration, the distortion between a prestigious but often decaying centre, and a chaotic periphery. To this end the *Schéma directeur d'Aménagement et d'Urbanisme de la Région Parisienne* was produced (published in 1965 but amended and approved in 1976). This plan advocated urban expansion along two parallel axes south-east and north-west, tangential to the agglomeration. Aligned along these axes would be five new towns of at least 100,000 inhabitants (Cergy-Pontoise, Saint-Quentin en Yvelines, Evry, Melun-Sénart, Marne la Vallée) each serving a population of 300,000 to one million inhabitants. These new towns would not be dormitory towns but would each have their own life with housing, work, and leisure facilities. Their construction has not been finished and there are many difficulties but, nevertheless, the new towns have come into being. The *Schéma directeur* also envisages a dense network of transport, adding to the 800 kms of motorways and express routes. The *Réseau Express Régional* (RER) now under construction is the masterpiece of this transport system. With the additional aims of creating leisure activities and green spaces, these arrangements represent an attempt to conceive, in a bold and modern way, the development of an agglomeration with manifold problems, and which, because of its exceptional importance, determines the structure of the whole of the national territory.

(*b*) *The Regional Metropoles.* The study of regional 'metropoles' has attracted a lot of attention in France recently, precisely because it is expected that they will combat the growing influence of Paris. Under this term are included a whole set of agglomerations which have in common both that they are large towns (with more than 200,000 inhabitants) and that they exercise the functions of guiding and bringing life to a region. We shall start from the hypothesis that the largest towns have a special role in the organization of space; they are 'poles' of growth because of the external economies generated by virtue of their size. National space will, therefore, be divided into a series of cells made up of 'polarized regions', each with a regional metropolis at its head which will restrict the role of the capital and will govern a series of smaller and less well-supplied towns. But it is exactly this level of the urban hierarchy which is absent in France because centralization has prevented it from being established and expanded, as has happened in Germany, Great Britain and Italy. Armed with this hypothesis, in 1963 the *Commission Nationale d'Aménagement du Territoire* (CNAT) put forward the concept of a policy of 'balancing metropoles'. This policy envisaged accelerating the development of certain towns which had already reached the threshold whereby they could be turned into centres of decision-making, of innovation, of high-order services, and centres for the management of the economic and social life of a region, and would remove the need for constant recourse to the capital. It was hoped that this would lead to a simpler restructuring and balancing of the national space.   ᴧ

The works of Hautreux and Rochefort (1965) have defined the upper level of the French urban infrastructure. Working from a large sample of agglomerations they studied the importance of the tertiary sector, the provision of commercial facilities (number of wholesalers, existence of unusual or specialized trades), the distribution of banks and financial power, the supply of services (the administration of the supra-Department areas, the existence of universities and regional hospital centres, and of certain highly specialized professions), cultural, artistic and sport facilities, as well as the size of the zone of influence. The combination of these various indicators leads to the identification of eight towns which could play the role of a balancing metropolis: Lyon, Marseille, Bordeaux, Lille, Strasbourg, Toulouse, Nantes, and Nancy. Such a classification will of necessity always be somewhat arbitrary, and eventually four more towns were added to the group, i.e. Clermont-Ferrand, Dijon, Nice, and Rennes. Finally, certain agglomerations, the administrative capitals of regions, could equally well be considered to possess the attributes of a regional metropolis. Thus, there are approximately fifteen towns which form the upper level of the urban infrastructure. The object was to endow the chosen towns with a complete range of high-level services and wide-ranging activities. This policy has hardly come into effect yet, but its consideration has led to the clarification of many problems.

In twenty years these towns have expanded greatly and, although very different, they tend to bear a strong resemblance to each other by virtue of their functions and modes of development. Their mix of activities is very close to the average pattern. With the exception of Lyon and Lille they all have a combination of mainly tertiary activities, and their specific characteristics are not very marked. Their 'central place' activities are less important than their production and transit functions. Their social structures vary little and, with the exception of Lille, their social composition is not working class but consists predominantly of wage-earners in the tertiary sector. The role of their administrative machinery is fundamental, for these

towns are centres for an area of influence beyond the level of the Department. But Prost (1965) has shown the close correlation which exists between
the administrative rank of towns and their level of general services. The
introduction of public utilities has immediate results, for instance the
creation of employment, but it also induces further activities. Public policy
can therefore be crucial to capital formation, even in a liberal economic
system.

From the point of view of the spatial development of the regional metropoles, the same trends are seen as in Paris or the smaller towns. Nevertheless, it is easier to observe the developments in the regional metropoles
for they are less complex agglomerations than Paris, and problems relating
to the utilization of space appear in a more compelling manner than in
smaller-sized towns. The major phenomenon is the peripheral growth of the
agglomerations accompanied by a functional and social segregation of
space. The resident population of the city centre decreases while high-level
tertiary activities move in. The logical result of this development is city-
centre congestion leading to further decline. The suburbs, on the other
hand, quickly grow into specialized areas of housing estates and blocks of
flats, eating away at the rural space in a process of 'rurbanization'. These
trends are common to agglomerations with very different structures, such as
the Lille-Roubaix-Tourcoing conurbation and the Lyon agglomeration.

What has been established beyond doubt is that the growth of the large
towns has not had the desired effect of spreading out development, nor of
giving a real structure to space in terms of hierarchical networks. Neither
have they been freed from the domination of Paris and, in addition, they
have lost some of their attraction as a result of congestion and other harm-
ful effects connected with their expansion.

(c) *Medium-Sized Towns*   From 1971 medium-sized towns became a new
priority, since their number and their vitality seemed to single them out as a
specific feature of the spatial system. However, there is no completely
satisfactory definition of a medium-sized town. Statistically a town of
between 20,000 and 200,000 inhabitants in France would fall into this
category, but a larger town can perfectly well have the characteristics of a
medium-sized one. For example, the agglomerations of Toulon (378,000
inhabitants) and Tours (245,000 inhabitants) are not considered to be large
towns. Indeed, medium-sized towns should be defined as those towns with a
considerable demographic weight in relation to the population of the region
and which 'pursue a wide range of functions for the benefit of a hinterland,
and are sufficiently large and urbanized to have a recognised influence'.
(Letter to the Prefects from the Minister of Public Works dated February
1973). These towns vary considerably from one-function towns such as
Royan (tourism), Rochefort (military) and Longwy (industrial) to towns
such as Rodez which are isolated in a rural area, those like Versailles which
belong to a conurbation, and those which are satellites of a metropolis, for
example Elbeuf, a satellite of Rouen. Research on the urban infrastructure

reveals hierarchical differences between these towns. Some have part of the services of a regional metropolis or at least a reasonable level of services: these are the 'regional capitals' or 'regional centres' such as Grenoble, Caen, Limoges. Others, like Perpignan, do not perform a full regional function. They all, however, have an influential administrative function (e.g. chief-town of the Department, a secondary school or university, or a supra-Department public service).

This new dynamism of the medium-sized towns can be observed in most western countries. Their growth rate is higher than that of other urban categories. There are many reasons for this. First, the attempt to make up for the delay in supplying public utilities during the 1960s created employment which then brought about a development of private services and a renewal of the construction industry. Second, the growth of private motoring made the towns more accessible, and by relying on a local population which was already large, certain services were able to extend their influence to the detriment of the small towns and market-towns. Moreover, these towns have attracted either new industries or those resulting from decentralization processes. The development of the industrial system is leading to a reduction in the establishment of giant factories and a move to medium-sized industrial units (i.e. 300 to 1,000 workers). The latter are well-suited to medium-sized towns where wages are often lower than in the large towns. The costs of urbanization are lower than in the metropolises and this results in better services and a better quality of life, for example less pollution and congestion, greater possibilities for participation, and easy access to the countryside. Although they started from very different situations, the development of these towns has been rather heterogeneous. From the spatial point of view their expansion is characterized by the same processes as were noted for the large towns: overcrowding of the centre, large housing estates and blocks of flats in the peripheral areas, and social segregation. The same town planning policy has been applied since the 1967 *Loi d'orientation foncière*. It involves the drawing up of such documents as the *Schémas directeurs d'aménagement et d'urbanisme* (SDAU) which define the public investment objectives for local communities, and the *Plans d'occupation des sols* (POS), which establish ground rights and which can be used to contest claims from third parties. When a large town-planning operation is involved (such as the creation of a new district, restoration, establishment of an industrial zone, etc.) recourse can be made to the same emergency procedures, such as the creation of a *Zone d'Aménagement Concerté* (ZAC). The medium-sized towns encounter the same problems: they find it difficult to acquire land as prices continually rise because of a limited supply and speculation; they face transport problems and difficulties in matching the rate of investments with population growth. But the problems faced by the medium-sized towns are usually less grave than those encountered in large agglomerations.

The range of socio-economic activities is more disparate in the medium-sized towns than in the balancing metropoles; but, with the exception of Montpellier, they have all been through an industrialization phase and most have seen their structures modernized. They have, therefore, become genuine poles of growth, which means that their inhabitants and those living in their zone of influence do not have to turn to the regional metropolis. This allows them to by-pass an intermediary step of the urban hierarchy and to turn directly to Paris when they need an unusual or exceptional service. The spread of medium-sized towns defines, therefore, that part of the territory which Kayser (1975) has called 'non-metropolised space'.

These new facts have been brought out in successive studies and have led to the implementation of a policy on medium-sized towns which was conceived in 1971 and first introduced in 1973. Essentially this has meant a procedure for drafting planning contracts for these towns, an agreement between the State and a commune by which the latter takes charge of the implementation of the three year public utilities programme in return for financial aid from the State. In this way it is possible to envisage a programme which is more comprehensive, original, and flexible in its implementation than those undertaken with annual state subsidies. The first such contract was signed in 1973 with the town of Rodez and today some 50 are being executed.

(d) *Small Towns*　The accelerated urbanization of the last twenty years has involved equally the small towns, and thanks to the work of Laborie (1978) we now have much more information about them. These small towns are elementary urban centres which are incapable of stimulating dynamic expansion since their size does not enable them to generate economies of scale. They are very diverse in character and from the outset we can distinguish rural market towns (urban units with less than 5,000 inhabitants) where the percentage of agricultural workers remains high, and small towns in the proper sense with 5,000 to 20,000 inhabitants. These small towns are spread widely around the country, thus reducing some of the regional contrast between east and west. Some may depend heavily on neighbouring agglomerations, but most have assumed their own individuality. We find centres which are very specialized (fishing, tourism etc.), local centres with a dominant tertiary sector, and a large number of industrial towns. In four out of ten towns the largest sector is industry. The growth of these towns has been ensured by strong migratory movements resulting from the rural exodus of unskilled workers. As in the medium-sized towns, job creation has taken place largely in the tertiary sector. The rural exodus has brought about the disappearance of some rural services and facilities, and this has benefited the small towns. Higher incomes and the expansion of demand for certain consumer goods has created new jobs in the service sector. As the small urban centres and the countryside were catching up on their development, public and private services began to improve and new jobs were thus created. But industry has also played an important role. It is in the small towns that local manufacturing, extractive industries, metal fabricating and processing, and the traditional textile and shoe-making industries are generally located. This is not just the inheritance from an earlier phase of industrialization, but involves new industries which have been attracted by State and local community aid, by the availability of a good infrastructure, and of a labour force with lower wage demands. The location of industry in small towns is therefore one aspect of the new spatial strategies of French capitalism.

Nevertheless, it cannot be said that the small towns enjoy a particularly favourable situation. By contrast with other categories of towns there are clear advantages: spatial segregation is not so evident, the centre of the town is more accessible, the journey from home to work is more convenient, growth is more easily regulated, housing is cheaper, the inhabitants may have a better perception of the town as a whole and participate more easily in local life. But problems remain, and the foremost of these is the dependence of the small towns, which is a double dependence. The small towns depend for survival on changes in their immediate environment. Their influence on the surrounding areas is a function of maintaining a reasonable population level in the rural areas which they dominate, and resisting the competition from services like hypermarkets in the nearby large towns. Their role as a staging post is on the decline. Simultaneously, their dependence is increasing vis-a-vis the industrial corporations which have and continue to locate workshops and factories in them. One small town in three has only one industry and this means that the labour market is restricted to the demand of a limited number of enterprises whose policies are determined by factors which have little to do with the small town in question. The fragility of these small agglomerations and their vulnerability to changes in the macro-economic situation are well known, and this is further demonstrated by the severity of economic crises which sometimes hit them. What is necessary, but is not yet clearly defined, is a specific policy for the small towns.

Rural Space

About 88 per cent of the national territory is rural space but only 14.2 million people, or 27 per cent of the total population, reside there. The rate of decline of the rural population, however, is decreasing. Changes in the classification of communes (rural communes becoming, in statistical terms, urban communes) create the impression of a continuing contraction of rural space, but if we consider the rural population in the framework of the original definition, we find that the depopulation of the countryside which was of the order of 65,000 persons per annum from 1954 to 1962, and near to 50,000 from 1962 to 1968 has now been checked. There was even a gain of 13,561 inhabitants (+ 0.1%) from 1962 to 1968, which is the result of a two-way movement: a continuing fall in the total population of the smallest communes but an increase of 310,000 persons for the communes of 1,000 inhabitants or over. Obviously, there are large regional differences which cannot be studied here. This rural space is no longer occupied by a majority of people employed in agriculture. The population of agricultural households (enumerated according to place of residence) is less than 6 million, with only 2.3 million employed in agriculture; this represents a drop of 3.1 million from 1954 to 1975 (i.e. 150,000 per annum). The French peasantry is becoming an older and smaller group. Non-agricultural workers are a heterogeneous group consisting of those residents of the countryside who work in the towns, those who are employed in service activities for the rural population (commerce, public services, the construction industry), those workers in industrial plants which have been established in the area by an urban firm, and the employees of the tourist industry. The dependence of this rural space on the towns is thus quite clear.

From this situation emerges the need for determined action to maintain, transform, or regenerate the rural areas according to their needs. Apart from the work which aims at the modernization of the agricultural sector, increasing efforts are being made to develop and equip the rural space. In 1970 the *Plan d'Aménagement Rural* (PAR), somewhat similar to the SDAU, was established. Its object was to take a given sector and develop its economic activities, to select public investments and choose their location, and to ensure the preservation of sites and the quality of the environment. The PAR finally produced in 1976 the concept of a *Zone d'Environnement Protégé* (ZEP); this is a rural area for which regulations are established concerning land occupation and land use, in order to protect its agricultural activities and landscape. Also originating in 1976 are the *contrats de pays*, where the *pays* in question is a unit consisting of a number of communes, on average 30, with a total population of 10,000 to 70,000. An agreement is made between this unit and the State with the aim of bringing about the development of the area. The projects undertaken may vary from the construction of an open-air leisure centre, to the installation of a communal television aerial. These diverse initiatives are intended to conserve the rural space and to provide it with an adequate level of services so that the resident population will feel less inclined to emigrate to the towns. The real aim is to check the increase of spatial disparities.

Conclusion

Is it possible, in light of the analysis just made, to make any predictions for the future? The French system of spatial organization has been transformed a great deal since the war. Urbanization, industrialization, and tertiarization have given a new face to the country; yet the fundamental imbalances remain. It is as though regulation had only been introduced in order to perpetuate the old situation. However, various factors have combined to bring about important modifications to the prevailing system. It is tempting to see these changes to be the result of development policies, and while they should not be ignored, the important role played by other factors must be recognized. First, there is the decline in the rate of demographic growth, which is sufficiently large to have necessitated a downward revision of all forecasts. For example, it was predicted that the population of the Paris region would be 14 million in the year 2000 while it is now estimated that this figure will not exceed 12 million. In addition to a declining population growth rate, the economic crisis has also had its dampening effect.

At the same time, however, new attitudes have appeared. The attraction of Paris and the other large towns has clearly diminished, to the benefit of the medium-sized towns. The high price of housing and the constraints of daily life in the large agglomerations are turning an increasing number of people towards the medium-sized towns. Furthermore, regionalist movements are now very much alive in France. The desire to 'live in the country' is clearly stated and is expressed in a wide political debate on regionalization. In other respects, the type of life to which the French aspire attaches great importance to the individual residence or to a place in an old town. Despite imaginative efforts to ensure that the new towns offer varied services, these are only developing slowly. The picture of the near future, then, is one of France with a spatial system slowly evolving and with a very gradual reduction in imbalances.

Territorial planning policies have also moved in the same direction. Measures have been taken either at the sectoral level (e.g. the establishment of mixed-economy companies to modernize the agricultural sector, measures to prohibit the establishment of industry in certain zones, paired with financial help to attract industry to the development zones, and attempts to bring about a dispersion of tertiary activities) or at the national level (rural development policies, special policies for mountain areas, development of the coastline). The new priority given to the medium-sized town is an official recognition of a spontaneous movement. But all of these actions have their limits: one cannot go too far in 'devitalising' Paris; one cannot spread investment expenditure too thinly and one cannot, in a liberal framework, muzzle all private initiatives or secure full public rights over the land. Clearly then, the organization of the French spatial system will be achieved by a series of varied and gradual actions. If there have been some successes, a long and demanding programme of work remains.

REFERENCES

Beaujeu-Garnier, J. 1977. *Paris et la région d'Ile de France*, 2 vol. Paris-Flammarion.
Boudeville, J. R. 1972. *Aménagement du territoire et polarisation*, Paris-M.Th. Génin.

Brunet, R. 1973. 'Structure et dynamisme de l'espace français', *L'Espace géographique*, n° 4, pp. 249-54.

Calmes, R., Delamarre, A., Durand-Dastes, F., Gras, J., and Peyon, J. P. 1978. *L'espace rural français*, Paris-Masson.

Carriere, F., Pinchemel, Ph. 1963. *Le fait urbain en France*, Paris-A. Colin.

Charre, J. G., Coyaud, L. M. 1969/71. *Les villes françaises*, 2 vol. Paris-CRU.

Comby, J. 1977. *Mémento d'urbanisme*, Paris-CRU.

Dalmasso, E. 1976. 'La géographie urbaine en France', in *Human geography in France and Britain*, London, SSRC, pp. 73-7.

Dalmasso, E. 1978. 'Le thème de la croissance urbaine dans les recherches Françaises', in *Urban growth in Japan and France*, Tokyo, pp. 9-27.

Fontanel, C., and Peseux, Ch. 1976. 'Potentiel de la population et réseau urbain en France', *L'Espace géographique*, n° 4, pp. 251-4.

George, P. 1975. *La France*, Paris-PUF.

Gravier, J. F. 1972. *Paris et le désert français*, Paris-Flammarion.

Hautreux, J., Rochefort, M. 1965. 'Physionomie générale de l'armature urbaine française, *Annales de géographie*, pp. 660-7.

Kayser, B. 1975. *L'espace non métropolisé du territoire français*. Paris.

Kayser, B. and J. L. 1971. *95 régions*, Paris-Seuil.

Laborie, J. P. 1978. *Les petites villes dans le processus d'urbanisation*, Thesis, Université de Toulouse, 519 p.

Lajugie, J. 1974. *Les villes moyennes*, Paris-Cujas.

Mathieu, N. 1972. 'Le rôle des petites villes en milieu rural', *Bul. Assoc. géographes frcs*, n° 400-1, pp. 287-94.

Merlin, P. 1976. 'Les villes nouvelles françaises', Paris - La documentation française, *NED* n° 4286.

Monod, J., De Castelbajac, Ph. 1973. *L'aménagement du territoire*, Paris-PUF.

Noel, M., Poitier, C. 1973. *Evolution de la structure des emplois dans les villes françaises*, Paris-Cujas.

Noin, D. 1976. *L'espace français*, Paris-A. Colin.

Pinchemel, Ph. 1972. *La France*, 2 vol. Paris-A. Colin.

Prost, M. A. 1965. *La hiérarchie des villes en fonction de leurs activités de commerce et de service* Paris - Gauthier-Villars.

Pumain, D., and Saint-Julien, Th. 1976. 'Fonctions et hiérarchie des villes françaises: Etudes du contenu des classifications réalisées entre 1960 et 1974', *Annales de géographie*, n° 470, pp. 385-440.

Pumain, D., and Saint-Julien, Th. (n.d.) *Les dimensions du changement urbain en France: système de villes et structures socio-économiques de 1954 à 1975*, (forthcoming).

Pumain, D., and Saint-Julien, Th. (n.d.) *Les transformations récentes du système urbain français*, (forthcoming).

Rochefort, M., Bidault, C., and Petit, M. 1970. *Aménager le territoire*, Paris-Seuil, 144 p.

8 THE SETTLEMENT SYSTEM OF THE FEDERAL REPUBLIC OF GERMANY

P. SCHÖLLER, WITH H. H. BLOTEVOGEL, H. J. BUCHHOLZ, M. HOMMEL, AND I. SCHILLING-KALETSCH

Historical Development

The historical development of the German urban system must be examined in a broader Central European context. This development can be divided into four main periods:

(1) formation of the urban system during the high Middle Ages and its replenishment towards the late Middle Ages (eleventh to fifteenth century),
(2) shifts and additions from early modern times until the beginning of industrialization (sixteenth to early nineteenth century),
(3) growth, intensification and reorganization of the urban system during industrialization (early nineteenth century to the Second World War),
(4) development of the urban system under the influence of the war and the division of Germany (Second World War to 1970).

The urban system of Central Europe essentially arose in the twelfth and thirteenth centuries, when, within a few decades, there developed a dense and differentiated pattern of growth, as well as the founding of new towns. Only in a few cases (for example, Cologne [*Köln*], Trier, Mainz) was this network connected to the late-Roman settlement system, which in the early Middle Ages had become stunted and largely dissolved. Rather the persistence of episcopal sees formed the starting-points for settlement. For the development of the older established class of the high-medieval urban system new impulses were more important: fortified manors (*Burg, civitas*) and/or merchants or market settlements (*Wik, vicus, portus*).

With the founding of Freiburg in Breisgau in 1120 by the Duke of Zähringen, the phase of founding new towns began. Princes and emperors, especially the houses of Staufen and Salien, contributed to the continuous extension of the urban system with an increasing number of new towns every decade. Economic motives were most important for the early foundings, but the towns soon became an instrument for territorial securement and expansion. Most of the early towns founded up to about 1250 developed into larger cities, for example Lübeck (1158), Leipzig (about 1150), and Munich [*München*], (1158) in addition to Freiburg. Together with the older towns, they profited from their initial advantage in comparison to towns founded in the late Middle Ages, although the latter were numerically predominant.

The number of towns founded increased continuously up to 1300, reaching its peak with 220 in the decade between 1290 and 1300, and then declined until 1450 to a level of about ten to twenty foundings per decade.

Only in exceptional cases would these late medieval foundings gain considerable importance. On the one hand the basic structure of the urban system was already established, so that only the lower classes of the urban hierarchy could be completed and consolidated. On the other hand the territorial sovereigns more frequently used the establishment of towns as a means of securing administrative control over their often fragmented territories. As a result strategic factors determined the establishment of towns, for example on mountain ridges, but they often lacked the necessary economic basis for growth.

In early modern times, between about 1500 and 1800, few new towns were established, with the number varying between five and ten per decade. These additions essentially completed the urban system by adding some special functional types. In the fifteenth and particularly in the sixteenth century mining towns were established based on iron and silver ores. In the seventeenth century some towns were founded to resettle protestant refugees. More important were two types of baroque towns: the fortress towns such as Neu-Breisach and Glückstadt, which only reached a moderate size; and the noble residence towns (*Residenzstädte*) like Karlsruhe and Mannheim, which with their famous baroque ground-plans became larger cities.

In spite of these new types of towns, however, the establishment of new towns was itself less characteristic of the urban system as a whole than were shifts and dislocations within the existing pattern. In comparison to the Middle Ages the conditions and factors determining urban growth had changed fundamentally. In Germany the growing power of the princes and other territorial lords not only occurred at the expense of the Emperor but also of the independence of towns. Late-medieval leagues of towns, like the Hanse, were broken up. Urban independence, either as a free imperial city (*freie Reichsstadt*) or as a partly autonomous territorial town, proved to be a handicap for urban development in the age of mercantile economic politics. State and territorial capitals became the centres of urban growth whereas the old free imperial and commercial cities lagged behind the general development or even lost importance and population, particularly if they were cut off from their hinterlands by territorial and customs boundaries.

During the rise of Brandenburg-Prussia (*Preussen*) in the seventeenth and eighteenth century, Berlin became the largest city of Germany with about 200,000 inhabitants (1815), followed by Hamburg with about 107,000 inhabitants. Yet, both cities were surpassed by Vienna (*Wien*) with about 238,000 inhabitants. Since the Middle Ages an extended urban hierarchy had begun to develop in Central Europe. If in 1500 the upper level of this hierarchy was still characterized by about ten commercial and industrial cities of almost the same size, by 1800 this group had been differentiated according to the political and territorial development. As almost equivalent centres, Berlin and Vienna formed the top of the Central European urban system, politically, economically, and culturally. The capitals of other growing German staes ranked on a lower level, for example Munich, Dresden, Stuttgart, Karlsruhe, Brunswick (*Braunschweig*), and Hannover, as well as the large provincial capitals in Prussia. The seaports had a special position. Hamburg took over the position of Lübeck as the most important seaport. In contrast most inland commercial and industrial cities suffered loss of importance, such as Nuremberg (*Nürnberg*), Augsburg, Frankfurt, Dortmund, and Magdeburg. The contrast between the growing state and provincial capitals and declining old free imperial cities can be illustrated by comparing pairs of cities like Munich and Augsburg or Stuttgart and Esslingen (Figure 8.1).

During the Industrial Revolution, particularly between 1870 and 1910, new impulses to the development of the German urban system caused the

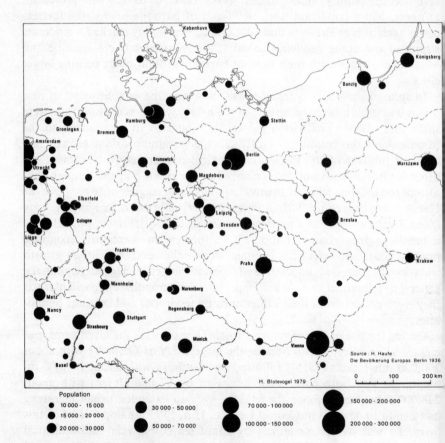

Fig. 8.1   Urban Size Distribution in Central Europe (about 1815)
Source: H. Haufe, *Die Bevölkerung Europas*, Berlin 1936

most fundamental structural changes since the high Middle Ages. The prime factor was industrial growth, which in Germany began relatively late. In the early phase of the Industrial Revolution (the first half of the nineteenth century), the industries most influential in urban growth were the textile industry, with its centres in Saxony (*Sachsen*) and the Rhineland, and the coal mining and iron and steel industry, which was concentrated in the industrial districts on the Ruhr, the Saar, and in Upper Silesia (*Oberschlesien*). Later, other manufacturing industries, in particular mechanical and electrical engineering and clothing, became increasingly important. Agglomeration and urbanization economies as well as market orientation became more important factors of location. A process of circular and cumulative growth meant that the pre-industrial urban system became the location pattern for those industries which were not dependent on raw materials.

In this process the tertiary sector proved to be of great importance both as the non-basic sector serving the industrial population and as a locational factor for further industrial growth. This is exemplified in the superior growth of Berlin which became both the largest industrial city and the leading central-place in Germany. The leading regional centres, such as Munich, Stuttgart, Frankfurt, Cologne, Hannover, Leipzig, Dresden, Breslau, Hamburg, and Königsberg, also became centres of industrial growth which in turn reinforced their importance as central places. This explains why industrialization in Germany did not result in a total transformation of the urban system, but rather in a strengthening and consolidation of the existing pattern. However, it was accompanied by an overall growth in all size classes, fundamental changes of internal structures and functions, and an intensification of inter-urban interactions.

Urban system development in this period was characterized by a growing integration brought about by the improvement of transport conditions and the political and economic unification of Germany, culminating in the founding of the German Empire in 1871. The latter factor contributed to the development of Berlin, which became the dominating economic, political, and cultural centre. But even at the end of this period, when the city's position as the metropolis of the German Empire reached its climax, Berlin did not achieve such a prominent position within the national urban system as either Paris or London. This is because centralization in Germany under the rule of Prussia (i.e., Berlin) was limited by a traditionally strong regionalism, reflected in the strong position of the regional capitals.

Figure 8.2 (1925) can be compared with Figure 8.1 (1815) to show the impact of the urbanization process: a growth of all town-size categories can be observed, which included a ten- to twenty-fold population increase in many cities. The leading position of Berlin becomes obvious, but the size of the leading regional centres also indicates the relatively balanced structure of the urban system.

Although the process of urbanization spread to all parts of Germany,

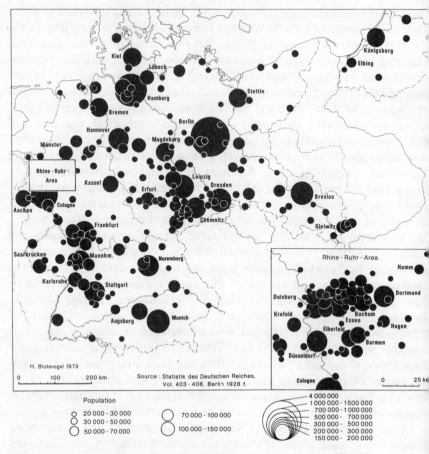

Fig. 8.2   Urban Size Distribution in Germany, 1925
Source: Statistik des Deutschen Reiches, vol. 403-6, Berlin 1928 f.

regional concentrations can be pointed out: apart from the decidedly single-centred agglomerations of Berlin, Hamburg, and Munich, there are the multicentred agglomerations of Rhine-Ruhr, Rhine-Main-Neckar, and in Saxony. The industrial transformation caused a concentration in the formerly more regular urban pattern in Central, Western, and South-western Germany. Mecklenburg, Pomerania (*Pommern*), and East Prussia (*Ostpreussen*) are extensive parts of the German settlement system that were hardly transformed by the process of industrialization.

The development of the German urban system from the Second World War to at least 1960 was mainly determined by effects of the war and the subsequent political division of Germany, which caused a division of the urban system into two systems largely independent of each other. The larger part of the urban network fell to the Federal Republic of Germany, which was formed from the three western-occupied zones and, although physically separate, is connected to West Berlin by many intensive linkages. Other parts of the urban system fell to the German Democratic Republic (GDR), formed by the Soviet-occupied zone and East Berlin. The annexation of the east Prussian provinces of Silesia, Pomerania, and East Prussia by Poland and the Soviet Union resulted in the integration of these former parts of the German urban system into the respective urban systems of those two countries.

The massive migration flows caused by the war and its political consequences decisively influenced the present German urban system. The urban population had already decreased during the war as a result of evacuation and wide-scale destruction by air raids (e.g., Cologne, Wesel). In the course of reconstruction (mainly between 1948 and 1960), the return migration from over-populated rural areas set in. By about 1960 nearly all towns in West Germany had reached their pre-war number of inhabitants.

The east-west political migrations overlapped with and even surpassed rural-urban migrations. More than ten million Germans from the former German eastern provinces and the Soviet occupied zone, later the GDR, came into the Federal Republic, resulting in a general rise in urban population.

The Second World War and the division of Germany formed a decisive turning point in the structure of the urban system. The division into four occupied zones and the subsequent development of two German states put an end to the relatively youthful integration process of the German urban system within the former nation-state. From that time on the urban systems of the Federal Republic and the GDR have developed separately from each other. In the west, new central capital-functions had to be developed. Their distribution among several high-ranking centres, which constitutes a characteristic feature of the present urban system, cannot fully be understood without considering the historical heritage of that system.

The Present Structure of the Urban System

The Spatial Pattern of the Urban System since about 1960

The changes caused by the Second World War were nearly complete by the end of the 1950s. Other development trends then became effective. These trends can be summarized as follows:

(1) Since the 1950s (but still influenced by the migration of refugees), migration from remote rural communities into more urbanized areas increased, particularly into large urban agglomerations.

(2) An out-migration took place from the large cities to rural suburban communities as well as to those towns beyond the immediate suburban fringe which had convenient transportation links to the central city. In addition, manufacturing

industries were transferred to the suburban fringe, whereas tertiary activities and industrial decision-making were more and more concentrated in the cities. This process of selective suburbanization resulted in a spatial expansion of urban land use and caused more intensive interactions (particularly commuting) between suburbia and the city.

(3) After the integration of refugees and expellees had come to its conclusion at the end of the 1950s, a growing labour demand led to the immigration of foreigners into the large cities. This compensated for the out-migration of the German population until the mid-1960s.

(4) Since the mid-1950s an out-migration has taken place from the Ruhr, and later from most other parts of North-Rhine–Westphalia (*Nordrhein-Westfalen*), Northern Germany, and the Saarland to Southern Germany. This migration was not only to the urban agglomerations in South Germany, but also to towns farther away from the larger cities, particularly in southern Baden-Württemberg.

These developments cannot be compared in scope with the immense population shifts of the first post-war period, however. The basic spatial pattern of the urban system was only slightly modified. There are still two major urbanized regions. One is the northern foreland zone of the Central Uplands with two core areas: the large conurbation of the Rhine and Ruhr and the region around Hannover and Brunswick. Northern and eastern Westphalia and southern Lower Saxony (*Niedersachsen*) between these core areas have a dense network of towns, but with only a few larger cities. The other region is the Southwest between the River Saar and eastern Württemberg with the urban agglomerations Rhine-Main, Rhine-Neckar, Stuttgart, Karlsruhe, and Saarbrücken.

This spatial pattern of the present urban system can then be characterized by several basic features:

(1) Due to the separation and division of Berlin, the present urban hierarchy is missing a primate city.

(2) The spatial distribution of the large cities is relatively well-balanced. The conurbations in the urbanized Northwest and Southwest contrast with the country's largest cities Hamburg and Munich in the less urbanized North and Southeast.

(3) The spatial distribution of smaller and medium-sized towns shows particular regional differences. These size-groups consistently have had the highest growth rates since the war. They are concentrated in the urbanized Northwest and Southwest, not only around the large cities but also in areas farther removed (Westphalia, southern and eastern Baden-Württemberg).

(4) Around many large cities are concentrated towns with more than 20,000 residents. Many of the smaller towns in this group have only entered this size-group in the post-war period. The medium-sized towns, several of which have surpassed the threshold of 100,000 residents since the war, are generally historic towns at strategic locations, which often have developed complementary functions. Together with the central city these towns form highly differentiated multi-centred urban agglomerations (e.g., Nuremberg).

(5) By contrast, there are single-centred urban agglomerations consisting of only one central city, with satellites or (sub-)urbanized communities (mostly smaller than 20,000 residents), totally dominated by that central city (e.g., Munich).

(6) A striking exception is the large conurbation at Rhine and Ruhr, the greatest concentration of people on the European continent. This large conurbation consists of several urban agglomerations with quite different structures and functions which have grown together, but have developed remarkably few functional links. It is not the highly-integrated functional unit it seems at first glance. In the Southwest may be the future development of another multi-centred conurbation of similar size at Rhine–Main.

(7) The spatial distribution of metropolitan areas (*Stadtregionen*) with more than 50,000 residents (Figure 8.3) gives an even stronger impression of a relatively well-balanced settlement distribution. Since the smaller towns are now excluded, regional differences in urban density, which essentially depend on the unbalanced distribution of smaller towns, are no longer obvious. These metropolitan areas show a clear size hierarchy which can well be described by a rank size distribution (Beutel 1976).

Some Basic Characteristics of the Urban Economic Structure

Essential differences within the urban system are indicated in the economic structure of towns and cities. The following basic types can be identified (Figure 8.4):

(1) There are few cities dominated by the tertiary sector (over 65 per cent of the labour force). Besides the federal capital Bonn, this type is represented by state or prefectural capitals (e.g., Saarbrücken, Koblenz), university towns (e.g., Giessen), or ports (e.g., Flensburg).

(2) The central cities of half of the large agglomerations are characterized by a dominance of the tertiary sector (55-65 per cent). Hamburg, Bremen, Düsseldorf, Cologne, Frankfurt, and Munich fall into this category. The other cities of this type are again state or prefectural capitals (e.g., Wiesbaden, Kassel), university towns (e.g., Heidelberg), or ports (e.g., Lübeck).

(3) The central cities of the other half of the large agglomerations show a balanced economic structure (manufacturing and tertiary sector each accounting for 45-55 per cent): Hannover, Mannheim, Stuttgart, Nuremburg, and now also Essen and Dortmund, the leading central cities in the Ruhr coalfield.

(4) Cities characterized by manufacturing (55-65 per cent) are concentrated in the urbanized Southwest and Northwest, particularly in the Ruhr coalfield.

(5) Cities dominated by manufacturing (over 65 per cent) are mostly dependent on one particular branch of industry. Half of them are part of urban agglomerations (e.g., Castrop-Rauxel (Ruhr): coal mining; Völklingen (Saar): steel; Solingen (Rhine-Ruhr): cutlery; Ludwigshafen (Rhine-Neckar): chemical industry). The other half are independent cities (e.g., Wolfsburg: cars; Schweinfurt: engineering). Finally there are two groups of smaller towns (not presented in Figure 8.4) in southern Württemberg and in the Central Uplands between the rivers Ruhr and Sieg which are characterized by highly-specialized metal processing industries.

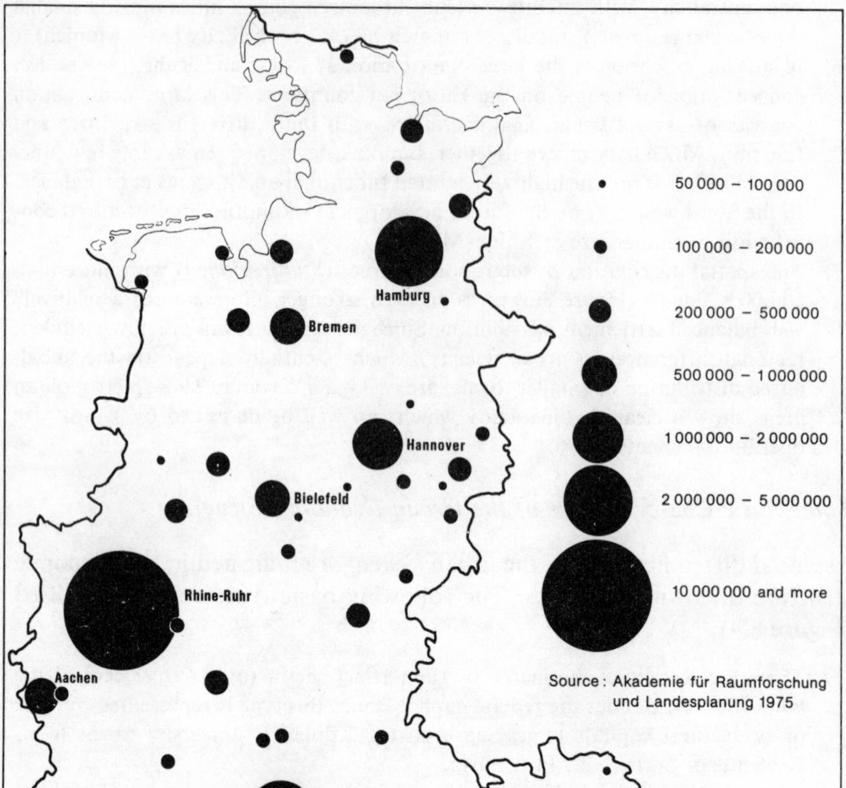

Source : Akademie für Raumforschung
und Landesplanung 1975

50 000 – 100 000

100 000 – 200 000

200 000 – 500 000

500 000 – 1 000 000

1 000 000 – 2 000 000

2 000 000 – 5 000 000

10 000 000 and more

Hamburg

Bremen

Hannover

Bielefeld

Rhine-Ruhr

Aachen

Rhine-Main

Rhine-Neckar

Nuremberg

Saarbrücken

Karlsruhe

Stuttgart

Munich

0   50   100   150 km

M. Hommel 1979

Fig. 8.3. Metropolitan Areas by Population, 1970
  Source: Akademie für Raumforschung und Landesplanung, 1975

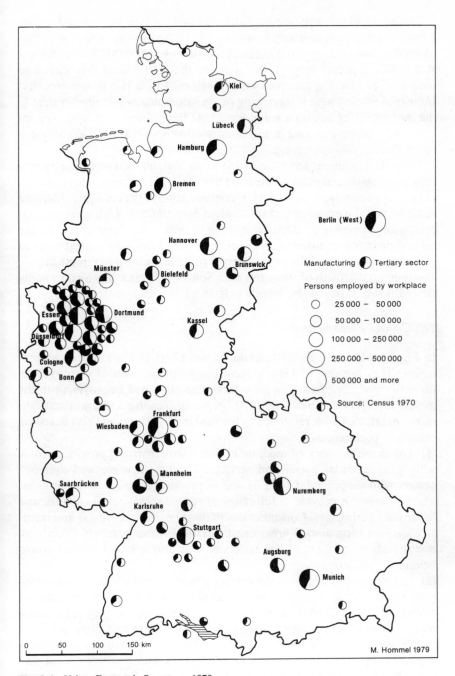

Fig. 8.4 Urban Economic Structure, 1970
Source: Census 1970

The tremendous post-war industrial growth, which had caused an increase in manufacturing employment and resulted in the industrialization of smaller and medium-sized towns in North-Rhine–Westphalia and Baden-Württemberg particularly, slowed down in the 1960s. Since then increased industrial production has been largely achieved by a rise in productivity. Industrial employment is stagnating or even declining, while employment in the tertiary sector has been rising for a long time. These long-term sectoral shifts will continue as long as increased productivity in the tertiary sector is lower than in manufacturing.

These developments have resulted in a considerable 'tertiarization', particularly in the central cities of the large urban agglomerations. This tertiarization was intensified by a process of concentration in the economy. Merging of firms and the expansion of multi-plant corporations resulted in the concentration of economic decision-making in only a few large cities. At the same time manufacturing plants were transferred from the central cities to the suburban zone and the towns beyond (but only seldom to remote areas). The industrial growth of those towns in Southern Germany, which has only slowed down in the 1970s, largely originated in such transfers.

The Central Place System

In Figure 8.5, cities are differentiated according to their degree of centrality. They are ranked mainly according to the number of employees in the tertiary sector (excluding transport), less estimated employment in the middle-level services (based on 1970 Census of Non-Agricultural Establishments data), and with reference to the ranking by Kluczka (1970) based on consumer preferences.

(1) The dense network of medium centres (*Mittelzentren*) provides people with most essential goods and services. Usually they are well-equipped centres with shopping facilities as well as private and professional services. The public sector provides a full range of secondary schools, hospitals, and lesser state authorities. Consumer ties to these centres are regular and intensive, so that their market areas can be defined rather precisely. Nearly all towns with more than 20,000 residents, but also a lot of smaller towns belong to this group.

(2) The network of higher-order centres (*Oberzentren*) which serve as shopping centres for long-term demand and offer specialized services required seldom or only by certain consumer groups. In addition, they are cultural centres (newspaper, theatre, colleges, and university) and often administrative centres for middle-level state authorities. Moreover, they fulfil important functions as locations of wholesaling and industry-related services. Nearly all cities of more than 100,000 residents (except two ports and several manufacturing cities in the neighbourhood of important regional centres) belong to this group.

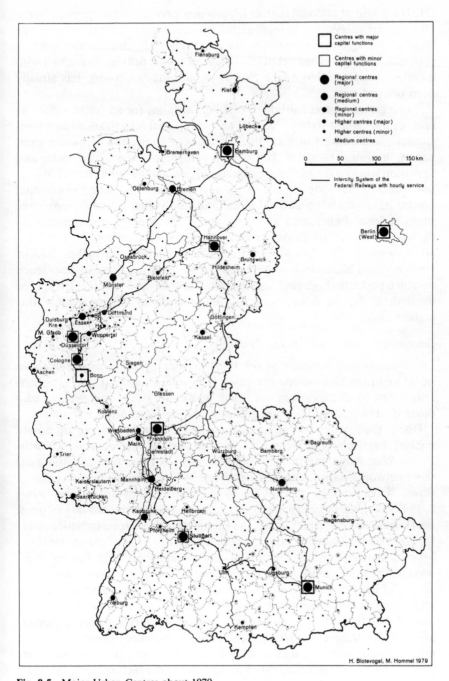

Fig. 8.5   Major Urban Centres about 1970

(3) The group of regional centres (*Regionalzentren*), so characteristic of the German urban system, is represented by the leading central cities of the large urban agglomerations, the state capitals and some former state or provincial capitals. Their relatively balanced spatial distribution, albeit with a certain concentration in the Northwest and the Southwest, has already been pointed out.

The regional centres fulfil high-ranking functions for an entire region: as seats of the highest state authorities and of regional organizations and associations, as locations of executive branches of banks and insurance companies, trading, transport, and service companies, as seats of radio and television stations (or of their regional studios), and of publishers of important regional newspapers, they vary remarkably. Therefore the regional centres have no clearly-defined hinterland. Individual functions may have supra-regional importance and serve the entire country, for example industrial fairs and expositions or certain cultural institutions.

(4) As a result of the loss of Berlin as a national capital, the highest level of the functional hierarchy is represented not by one but by several cities, each of which performs high-ranking functions for the entire country. Except for the federal capital Bonn, only the major regional centres achieve this highest rank.

Interactions within the Urban System

The decentralized structure of the West German urban system leads to an intensive interaction among the cities. The following discussion is necessarily based on an analysis of rail, road, and air transport only because adequate data on capital transfers and information flows are not available.

Due to the spatial distribution of cities, rail and road networks are closely meshed, particularly in the more urbanized parts of the country. In North-Rhine–Westphalia and in the southwest between Frankfurt and Stuttgart, those networks show the highest density as well as the most intensive traffic flows. A considerable part of the total traffic volume arises from direct links between the large urban agglomerations. Between the two largest ones, the Rhine-Ruhr conurbation and the Rhine-Main-Neckar conurbation, traffic flows show maximum values, all the more since most of the traffic flows between the large urban agglomerations overlap there. The Federal Railways has met this continuously growing demand with its recently-developed system of inter-city trains, which provides an hourly service between nearly all regional centres. The development of the road network has emphasized the construction of new motorways between the larger urban agglomerations which bypass smaller agglomerations in between. These new bypass motorways improve the locational quality of cities and towns on the route considerably by establishing rapid direct links to the regional centres. Interactions between the large urban agglomerations have been enhanced by the development of air transport.

As a result, the decentralized urban system of the Federal Republic of Germany is now highly integrated. The distribution of capital functions among the major regional centres means that a considerable part of the total volume of interaction within the urban system comprises direct interactions among those leading cities, which are additionally promoted by moderate distances and highly-developed transport and communication systems. Furthermore, these cities—and thus the urban system of the country as a whole—have intensive interactions with the major urban agglomerations of the neighbouring countries to the west, north, and south, particularly with the Benelux and the Alpine countries, but also with France and Scandinavia.

Present Development Trends

The following tendencies seem to be determining the present development of the urban system:

(1) The period of population growth and ever-stronger economic growth ended in the middle of the 1970s. Population decline or stagnation, and slow growth of the economy are now the basic conditions for change in the urban system.

(2) Migration of economically-active people from remote rural areas to the urbanized areas is continuing, because in a stagnating economy, labour demand usually declines more in remote rural areas than in urbanized areas. More and more this migration is balanced by migration of retired people from urban agglomerations to those remote rural areas which offer beautiful scenery, convenient climate, a traditional rural environment, and other attractions.

(3) Migration from urban agglomerations in the North and Northwest to Southern Germany is continuing. More and more this migration tends toward towns outside urban agglomerations or between them, not only in the more urbanized Southwest, but also in less urbanized Bavaria. The main reason for this migration is the natural and cultural landscape of these areas which makes them attractive not only for retired people, but also for industrialists.

(4) Because of declining labour demand, a substantial number of foreign workers have recently migrated back to their countries. This re-migration is balanced, however, by immigrating families of those foreign workers who decided to stay. Due to this trend and the much higher birth rate of the foreigners, an increase of foreign population in the larger cities can be expected.

(5) The suburbanization process is characterized by an increasing spatial expansion. The motorway network enables people to migrate from the cities to towns beyond the suburban zone, from which they can commute by car in reasonable time to the urban agglomerations. The deterioration of living conditions in many suburban areas, brought about by high land prices, a lack of infrastructure and environmental deterioration, has encouraged more and more people to avoid the suburban zone and move farther out. Suburbia now has declining growth rates. In the long run this movement to 'exurbia' will cause urban agglomerations to grow together along certain development axes, as determined by the spatial arrangement of towns and emphasized by the motorway system.

(6) The decentralized structure of the urban system is stable. There are no tendencies towards stronger centralization and the rise of one primate city. In the course of Western European integration there is a continuous growth of interaction between the large urban agglomerations in this country and in neighbouring countries. This has already brought about a partial integration of the urban systems of the Benelux countries, the Federal Republic of Germany and the Alpine countries. In the long run this process may lead to the development of one decentralized urban system in Western Europe.

Political and Administrative Functions and Centres: Their Role in the Development of the Settlement System

The rise of a developed and differentiated urban system in Germany during the late Middle Ages took place with a dualism of economic and political forces. The more decisively the expanded territorial state developed at the end of the Middle Ages, the more strongly those two forces seemed to fuse: the privilege of holding a market became an instrument of territorial sovereignty; the borough attracted free trade and local market functions.

Nevertheless, in the long run economic forces prevailed in German urban development. The supremacy of trading and service functions remained because the state's power was split up into territories and thus the administrative functions were dispersed. When in the nineteenth century the German territories gained in size and centralizing power, an additional element joined the administrative differentiation, namely the formation of autonomous self-administering corporations. In this way the system of political and administrative centres in Germany remained complicated, multi-levelled and incongruent. The non-uniformity was also strengthened by regional differences, which arose again in the federal system of the post-war period.

The fundamental hierarchy of administrative areas is the community (*Gemeinde*), county (*Kreis*), prefectural district (*Regierungsbezirk*), state (*Bundesland*), and the Federal Republic. For several reasons the county level with the county town is most important for the middle level of the central-place system. Here public and non-public administrative functions extending beyond the community level join with self-governing functions. Except in some regional cases, the county is both a governmental and an autonomous corporation.

Bigger and more important towns are not included in rural counties. In 1965 there existed 137 urban counties (*Stadtkreise*) in comparison to 415 rural counties (*Landkreise*). Before 1945 the threshold for a town to form its own county was 25,000 inhabitants, which was raised to 50,000 inhabitants in the post-war period. In Baden-Württemberg this limit was higher but in Bavaria it was considerably lower. In order to guarantee a balanced regional development, the previously independent towns have been increasingly re-integrated into the surrounding counties in recent years (e.g., Göttingen, Siegen, Herford, and Lüdenscheid). Today only cities over 100,000 inhabitants are able to form a county of their own.

It was the main aim of the local government reform (*kommunale Neugliederung*) to combine and amalgamate the 24,500 communities (1967), of which more than one-third had less than 500 inhabitants, so that they could carry out the functions of a modern service-oriented public administration. Rather than the size of a settlement, the criterion of centrality gained importance: that is, the orientation of local supply areas to central places of the lowest level. Accordingly the concept of counties was adjusted and orientated to central places of the middle level. In this way the number of counties in North-Rhine–Westphalia diminished from 57 to 31, in Rhineland-Palatinate (*Rheinland-Pfalz*) from 39 to 28, and in Schleswig-Holstein from 17 to 12.

In contrast to the counties, the prefectural districts in most states are pure governmental administration units. In formerly Prussian areas they were newly established after 1815 and named after the prefectural town. In Bavaria they were also founded as autonomous corporations with parliamentary bodies. In the course of local government reform, most states were changed into larger units on the middle administrative level. The result was a reduction in the number of prefectural districts and the attempt to coordinate these districts with regional planning districts. This did not succeed everywhere, least of all in North-Rhine–Westphalia where the prefectural district of Aachen was dissolved but the Ruhr conurbation still remained traditionally assigned to three different prefectural authorities.

It is important with respect to the urban system that the prefectural towns in many cases are neither the largest nor the most important urban centres of their districts. An adjustment to the central place hierarchy was not always thought to be necessary. But it is assumed that in future the importance of the prefectural district level will increase because it is the only administrative level where most regional functions come together.

The province (*Provinz*), an important regional institution of the former Prussian State above the prefectural district level, survived with reduced functions only in the state of North-Rhine–Westphalia. Here the self-governing bodies of *Landschaftsverbände* for Westphalia-Lippe and the Rhineland represent old territorial authorities and retain the functions of road construction, social welfare, specialized hospitals, and cultural activities. In other states some administrative relics of traditional territories remain, with special functions for their respective regions and regional centres (Palatinate, Oldenburg, Brunswick).

The Federal Constitution (*Grundgesetz*) of 1949 decisively accentuated the roles of states and state capitals. The cities which gained the most were those which, like Düsseldorf, Hannover, and Stuttgart, became seats of government and leading centres of the new states, or which, like Munich, kept and even enlarged their inherited predominance as capitals of large states. But the states are differentiated with respect to size, wealth, and productivity. Hamburg and Bremen are city states, the Saarland is as small as a prefectural district, and Schleswig-Holstein is the size of the former Prussian province. Rhineland-Palatinate and Hesse with their capitals Mainz and Wiesbaden are centred around the same core area, the Rhine-Main region, which is dominated by the city of Frankfurt. Only Baden-Württemberg, Bavaria, North-Rhine–Westphalia, and Lower Saxony are states of larger dimensions, with greater populations and dominant state capitals.

The centralizing tendency of the states has not been able to eliminate completely the traditional distribution of regional functions, but it is the determining force in post-war development. The extension of parliaments and ministries, of state authorities, special administrations, regional offices, radio and television studios, and state banks, of public organizations, and economic associations is accompanied by the development of cultural functions for which the states have exclusive competence. With the extension of universities, technical colleges, theatres, museums, archives, and collections, the activities of state and municipalities meet. The state capitals are also gaining greater importance in commerce and services.

The Federal Republic of Germany is an extreme case of the decentralization of all leading functions. After the division of Germany and Berlin, the new political centre, Bonn, was chosen as a provisional location, not intended to develop as a dominant capital city. But the decentralization of today is by no means only the result of the weak position of Bonn. The roots are deeper, connected with the strong historical regionalism of Western and Southern Germany. This historical heritage is seen in the strong and differentiated system of higher and regional centres, as reflected in the map of metropolitan areas, but is also alive in the regional links, the hinterland relations of these central cities.

In this sense Bonn, the capital, is a limited governmental city. Even in 1975, 37,800 of the total 58,500 employees of the federal government were located outside Bonn. Berlin (West) with 8,700 persons in 10 leading federal authorities (e.g., Federal Administrative Court) is the second largest centre, followed by Frankfurt (e.g., Federal Bank, Federal Railways) and Wiesbaden (Federal Statistical Office, Federal Criminal Office). Other important federal functions are located in Cologne, Hamburg, Munich, Koblenz, Brunswick, Flensburg, and Hannover. As a result, top level associations with economic and non-economic functions are concentrated not only in and around Bonn but also in the three leading economic centres of the Federal Republic of Germany: in Frankfurt, the main financial, transport, travel, and advertisement centre with the largest airport of Central Europe; in Hamburg, the most important centre for commerce and exports; and in the Rhine-Ruhr conurbation, especially at Düsseldorf with a large number of offices of German and foreign companies and its international fairs.

There are other cities with national functions. The first is Munich, the largest university, research and cultural centre, leading in libraries, theatres, museums, and the film industry. Stuttgart is the leading centre of the publishing industry. Hannover has the most important industrial fair and the Academy of Regional Planning. Cologne has the Lufthansa headquarters, the largest number of insurance companies, and also art galleries and medical organizations. Thus, the pattern of decentralized national functions has eight focal points with long established traditions. Three had been historical free cities: Hamburg, Frankfurt, and Cologne, and five had been territorial capitals of differing historical importance: Munich, Stuttgart, Düsseldorf, Bonn, and Hannover.

Overall, the trend is toward a balanced system of four partial capitals: the three-pole structure of the 'capital region' Bonn-Cologne-Düsseldorf; Frankfurt; Munich; and Hamburg. In the post-war development of Bonn and the 'capital region' mainly political functions were dominant. Frankfurt was able to strengthen its position as the leading financial and organizational centre. During the 1960s Munich used its cultural potential and international image to intensify its role. The future role of Hamburg is related to political integration with the northern states of Lower Saxony, Schleswig-Holstein, and Bremen.

The limited urban role of Bonn has its disadvantages. Bonn is not the intellectual and cultural capital, and not the leading city. It lacks suitable accommodation for international conferences and congresses. It must be recognised only as one out of several cores of a 'capital region' with the greater and more important urban centres of Cologne and Düsseldorf. But the decentralization of the highest functions is favourable for a living regionalism and a well-balanced structure of democratic powers. The federalism which was not very popular in 1949, is now, 30 years later, widely accepted by the public. The persistence of deconcentration within the Federal Republic can be viewed as successful not only for the internal political structure but also for the differentiation and strength of the higher level of the urban system.

Future Structure and Patterns

Until the beginning of the 1970s regional planning was characterized by isolated considerations of the structural properties of areas. The only city-based concept was that of central places with a primary focus on lower-level central places in sparsely populated areas. Even now the impact of the national settlement system upon economic and social development is not fully recognized by planning authorities, either at the federal or the state level.

The planning authorities generally are of the opinion that the existing settlement system is relatively balanced and that it merely needs to be supplemented to adapt it to higher levels of demand for goods and services. However, in the Federal Programme for Regional Planning (*Bundes-raumordnungsprogramm, BROP*), passed jointly by federal and state authorities in 1975, a 'point-axial' development concept was formulated, which may result in changes in the structure of the settlement system. Much depends upon whether authorities allow the elements of the concept—development centres and development axes—to assume a concrete form.

There is agreement that the development centres are to be instruments to reduce regional disparities. They are not to be a system of locations covering the entire Federal Republic spreading development impulses into their respective areas, but locations which should be promoted for a limited period and with specific goals. Two points are particularly controversial: (1) the relationship between the development centres and the system of central places, and (2) the relationship between the development centres with their spheres of influence and the manifold planning divisions of the Federal Republic.

Even if development centres have only an instrumental character, they will influence the existing structure of the settlement system. The planning authorities accept that cities, as agglomerations of population, working places, and infrastructure in locations well integrated into the national transport and communication networks, are of decisive importance for regional development. This opinion, however, is not followed consistently, above all in the diagnosis of regional development. In the *BROP*, the focal areas in which development centres are to be established are determined according to the economic structure and infrastructure of the respective area, but not according to its settlement structure. However, it is acknowledged that existing disparities obviously are related to the settlement system. Moreover, the development centre strategy collides with previous programmes and planning approaches, such as the *Gemeinschaftsaufgabe* (or special programme jointly financed by federal and state governments for the improvement of the regional economic structure). In view of this situation, two alternatives seem possible for the future structure of the settlement system.

The first alternative would be similar to the concept of 'balanced functional regions'. The goal of this concept, which was first formulated by Marx (1975), is to establish equivalent standards of living in all parts of the Federal Republic. It has influenced the formulation of the *BROP* decisively, although it has not been adopted consistently throughout. Marx follows the maxim of 'relative decentralization by regional concentration'. At the same time an essential economic condition is 'a spatial distribution of functions between differently equipped, i.e., differently "endowed" areas' (Marx 1975, p. 2). An economic essential of the balanced functional regions which are to be established is that of efficiently operating regional labour markets forming a system of 'limited agglomerations'.

A theoretical dilemma exists in this strategy, however. The advocates argue from the following principles of polarization theory: (1) the spatial structure of the economy is characterized by a hierarchical system of economically-determined centre-periphery relations, (2) the process of economic growth not only causes spatial inequalities, but also presupposes them, and (3) a spatial redistribution of functions is necessary. At the intra-regional level the strategy is to initiate and intensify the polarization process by directing the population in rural areas towards settlement foci which offer agglomeration economies. On the contrary, at the inter-regional level concentration and polarization are to be reduced. The latter meets the con-stitutional mandate to establish equivalent living conditions, but it contra-dicts the development conditions of the existing socio-economic system.

The problem of this concept is that it attempts to control the polarization process observed at the international, national, and regional level, by limiting it to the regional level only. The strategy does not take into account the fact that urban agglomerations perpetuate their present attractiveness, so that the large urban agglomerations with differing degrees of attractive-ness in the Federal Republic cannot be limited to any particular extent. Leaving aside how it is to be accomplished, the first alternative would con-sist of the following. The Federal Republic is to be covered by a network of large urban centres of similar size whose spheres of influence cover the entire country. Each of these large centres is to exercise four functions:
(1) a stable, differentiated and highly qualified labour market focus;
(2) a high-ranking provider of goods and services;
(3) a settlement focus; and
(4) a focus of self-sustaining development which spreads impulses into its functional region.

These urban centres should form the top level of centres within the point-axial development concept. Medium-sized centres would complement the large centres. They would also perform the four functions mentioned above but at a more modest level. Lower level centres would provide the adjacent area with daily demand. Only the latter could be understood as central places in the classical sense.

The exchange of goods and services between the large urban centres is to be provided by axes of inter-regional importance. In contrast to the centres, these axes are presented in the *BROP*, but no definition of the axes and their functions has been accepted by both the federal and the state governments. This is particularly true of the second-rank axes which are defined by the states to serve as intra-regional connections.

Due to the manner in which the middle- and higher-level central places are defined in the programme and plans of most of the states, any corres-pondence with the medium and large centres discussed above could not be achieved for the entire Federal Republic.

The second alternative accepts the impossibility of defining regions, centres, indicators, and other categories in a consistent manner. Proceeding from existing spatial delimitations and definitions it is conservative and does not lead to fundamental changes. The classical concept of central places would be the basis of regional strategy and the only broadly accepted concept for the settlement system. Consequently, the existing system of central places will not be changed basically by the instrument of development centres. Only those central places which are designated as development centres will be allowed to ascend to the next level. There is likely to be a reduction in the number of central places, which will affect the number of cities now classified as higher-level central places and the number of settlements now classified as lower-level central places. Central places of the middle and higher level will be connected by axes with each other and with their wider spheres of influence.

At the beginning of the 1980s the discussion of concepts has lost much of its importance. It seems probable that the role of the existing large urban agglomerations as centres of innovation and promoters of economic development and the present functional differentiation of the country will be maintained and even reinforced, but without resulting in a uniform distribution of balanced functional regions over the whole country as desired by alternative I. On the other hand, the network of central places will become more widely meshed, particularly in peripheral rural areas, whereas it will be reinforced in areas close to the existing large urban agglomerations, despite the intentions of alternative II.

REFERENCES

Beutel, Jörg, 1976. *Konzentrations- und Verstädterungstendenzen in der Bundes-republik Deutschland.* Meisenheim.
Bundesraumordnungsprogramm (BROP). 1975. Bonn.
Die Entwicklung der Siedlungsstruktur in Europa. 1977. Ed.: Bundesministerium für Raumordnung, Bauwesen und Städtebau. Bonn.
Entwicklungsmöglichkeiten künftiger Siedlungsstrukturen. 1978. Ed.: Akademie für Raumforschung und Landesplanung. Hannover.
Heuer, H. 1975. *Sozioökonomische Bestimmungsfaktoren der Stadtentwicklung.* Stuttgart.
Iblher, P. 1970. *Hauptstadt oder Hauptstädte? Die Machtverteilung zwischen den Großstädten der BRD.* Opladen.
Kluczka, G.1970. *Zentrale Orte und zentralörtliche Bereiche mittlerer und höherer Stufe in der Bundesrepublik Deutschland.* Bonn-Bad Godesberg.
Marx, D. 1975. 'Die Konzeption der ausgeglichenen Funktionsräume'. In: *Ausgeglichene Funktionsräume.* Hannover.
Pehnt, W., ed. 1974. *Die Stadt in der Bundesrepublik Deutschland.* Stuttgart.
Peppler, G. 1977. *Ursachen sowie politische und wirtschaftliche Folgen der Streuung*

hauptstädtischer Zentralfunktionen im Raum der Bundesrepublik Deutschland.
Frankfurt.
Raumordnungsberichte (ROB) der Bundesregierung. 1963, 1966, 1968, 1970, 1972, 1974. Bonn.
Schöller, P. 1967. *Die deutschen Städte.* Wiesbaden.
Stadtregionen in der Bundesrepublik Deutschland 1970. 1975. ed.: Akademie für Raumforschung und Landesplanung. Hannover.
Wild, M. T. 1979. *West Germany: A Geography of its People.* Newton Abbot.

9 THE DUTCH SETTLEMENT SYSTEM

J. G. BORCHERT

The Netherlands is a highly urbanized country, and has an extremely dense settlement pattern. The 1971 census distinguished almost 3,400 settlements, varying in size from small rural hamlets of a few hundred inhabitants to large cities totalling over half a million people. A theoretically even distribution of the settlements over the national territory would yield an average distance between settlements of only 3.4 kilometres. Such a settlement pattern would have a high propensity to develop intensive interactions even if actual distances were experienced in a different way than in larger countries. The implications of geographical scale must be stressed at the outset when discussing the Dutch settlement system.

The approach of this paper is to examine the composition of the settlement system in relation to the urbanization of the country. In examining the dynamic aspects of the settlement system, the analysis is limited largely to migration movements since data on flows of goods and information are, with one exception, unavailable. As there are a number of sources readily available dealing with historical processes, the paper will stress recent developments in the settlement system.

There are strong indications that in recent years the relations between different categories of settlements have intensified. Although it would be an oversimplification to suggest an autonomous development in former days, it will be demonstrated that the recent growth and functioning of smaller settlements is strongly influenced by what is going on in urban areas. The evidence suggests a twofold redistribution of population and economic activities away from the bigger urban centres, at both intra-regional and inter-regional levels. In the second part of this paper, therefore, developments taking place at the urban end of the settlement spectrum will be considered in more detail.

A last section will deal with policy and settlement proposals for future development, as set forth in the *Report on Urbanization* published by the Dutch Government at the end of the 1970s.

Growth and Development of the Dutch Settlement System

Compared with other countries in Western Europe, a large part of the Dutch settlement pattern is of comparatively recent origin. It has been estimated that around AD 400 a few thousand people lived in the whole of the Netherlands. In the northern coastal regions there existed a dense network of early settlements built on artificial refuge mounds (*terpen*) for protection against inundation. This region had a fairly high density of settlement compared with the sandy plains of the eastern districts, where nucleated villages had to await new agricultural methods before receiving concentrations of population in the early Middle Ages (Keuning, 1979). At that time the low-lying areas of the western half of the country consisted mainly of uninhabitable land, apart from some ridges along major rivers and the higher stretches of land at the foot of the dunes.

Until the end of the Middle Ages economic life iñ the Netherlands was limited to the higher areas in the eastern and southern parts of the country. It was in this area that the first cities developed, some, such as Nijmegen, Maastricht, and Utrecht, date back to Roman times. The towns along the river IJssel (Kampen, Zwolle, Deventer, Zutphen) acted as intermediaries between the Baltic on the one hand and the Rhineland and Flanders on the other. Like many other towns to the east of Utrecht, they were members of the Hanseatic League. Utrecht itself was the westernmost city in the Netherlands until the thirteenth century when the reclamation of the marshy areas of the western half of the country had proceeded so far that new cities came into existence. Most of the cities got their charters during the thirteenth century: Alkmaar 1214, Haarlem 1245, Delft 1246, Leiden and Gouda 1272, Schiedam 1275, Amsterdam 1300. In many cases charters were granted in anticipation of future development. Some cities failed to realize their anticipated growth, however, and remained no more than small regional centres.

Cities located on important inland waterways and on crossroads were best able to attract commercial functions. Apart from commercial functions, many cities saw the development of different forms of manufacturing. In the case of Leiden, Haarlem, Delft, and Gouda amongst others, manufacturing was of major importance. At the same time, the countryside was influenced by urban development. Indeed, large-scale reclamation schemes became possible only after a wealthy and enterprising urban bourgeoisie had come into existence. Large stretches of land for reclamation were given out to colonists who reclaimed the area in regular blocks, starting from a canal or dyke. Villages therefore assumed the linear form so typical of polder areas in the western Netherlands.

To supplement the meagre income from agriculture, other forms of production developed in rural places. In fact, the rural population was encouraged by urban entrepreneurs to take on home-based work, especially for the textile industry. During the sixteenth century, however, when export conditions were getting worse, the industrial production in the countryside created serious competition for the urban producers in certain branches. As a consequence, a law of 1531 banned the setting up of new production units outside the cities. There are indications that this law was not strictly applied in all areas, certainly not in rural areas under the jurisdiction of non-urban rulers. Nevertheless the law restricted the possibilities of earning a livelihood in the countryside, and stimulated people to look for jobs in the cities.

The cities attracted people not only from their immediate surroundings, but also from other areas such as Flanders. The great population increase of Dutch cities during the sixteenth century, particularly after 1580, can only be explained by in-migration, since the poor sanitary conditions of cities prevented a natural increase. It has been stated that Holland was already highly urbanized by 1500. Calculations for 1622 show that 54 per cent of the population was concentrated in cities, an unusually high proportion in seventeenth century Europe (Harten, 1972).

Statistical Data on Settlements

The smallest administrative units in the Netherlands are the municipalities, of which, as of January 1, 1979, there were 817. For almost all statistical information, municipalities are used as the basic unit. For the study of settlement patterns, this is unfortunate, as municipalities may comprise several settlements, and urban and rural settlements may be part of the same municipality.

Some statistical data on settlements are provided by the Netherlands Bureau of Statistics for the years a population census was taken (Table 9.1). For most purposes, however, use has to be made of statistical information for municipalities or regions composed of municipalities. If the number of settlements is compared with the number of municipalities (in 1971, 3,377 against 873), some major differences become apparent. These are most pronounced in the case of the smaller places. Almost half of the settlements have a population of less than 500, whereas the number of municipalities in this size group is only four, indicating that the smallest settlements are almost always part of a larger municipality.

In the Netherlands an arbitrary division is made between urban settlements having more than 5,000 inhabitants, and rural settlements with up to 5,000 inhabitants. Using this definition, the urban proportion of the population rose during the last intercensus period 1960-71 from 67.5 to 72.6 per cent, whereas the number of urban settlements increased by 40 per cent to just over 350. Almost half of the urban population is concentrated in only seventeen settlements with populations of over 100,000 inhabitants. The spatial distribution of urban settlements over the national territory is uneven, with a high concentration in the western and central parts of the country. A map of settlements in the Netherlands (Figure 9.1) gives only a generalized picture of the settlement pattern as it exists in reality.

Development of the Settlement Pattern

Analysis of the Dutch settlement system is necessarily based upon data for municipalities, even though the smallest settlements are thereby neglected. Although the proportion of such places has been consistently high over the

Table 9.1: *Dutch settlements by size class*

	Number of settlements			Population (thousands)			Per cent of population		
	1947	1960	1971	1947	1960	1971	1947	1960	1971
URBAN SETTLEMENTS									
Over 500,000	3	3	3	2,032.0	2,430.1	2,293.3	21.1	21.2	17.5
200-500,000	1	2	2	221.6	475.3	496.3	2.3	4.2	3.8
100-200,000	7	9	12	891.6	1,146.2	1,620.7	9.3	10.0	12.4
50-100,000	12	13	15	825.4	954.4	1,037.9	8.6	8.3	7.9
20- 50,000	25	30	54	814.0	927.5	1,523.2	8.5	8.1	11.7
10- 20,000	43	65	89	608.1	901.8	1,235.0	6.3	7.9	9.4
5- 10,000	101	130	177	719.8	906.6	1,235.6	7.5	7.9	9.5
Subtotal	192	252	352	6,112.5	7,741.9	9,442.0	63.6	67.6	72.3
RURAL SETTLEMENTS									
2,000-5,000	275	313	378	865.0	958.5	1,160.8	9.0	8.4	8.9
1,000-2,000	459	521	476	629.7	725.6	664.3	6.5	6.3	5.1
500-1,000	697	712	603	494.6	502.9	427.8	5.1	4.4	3.3
Under 500	2,510	1,949	1,568	553.9	463.3	460.9	5.8	4.0	2.8
Subtotal	3,941	3,495	3,025	2,543.2	2,650.3	2,613.8	26.4	23.1	20.1
OTHER									
Rural dwellings				902.5	985.5	944.1	9.4	8.6	7.2
Vessels				42.1	40.5	21.2	0.4	0.4	0.2
Living-boats				9.3	21.3	23.0	0.1	0.2	0.2
Caravans				12.0	16.3	16.0	0.1	0.1	0.1
TOTAL*	4,133	3,747	3,377	9,625.5	11,462.0	13,060.1	100.0	100.0	100.0

*Including central register of population

Source: Netherlands Bureau of Statistics

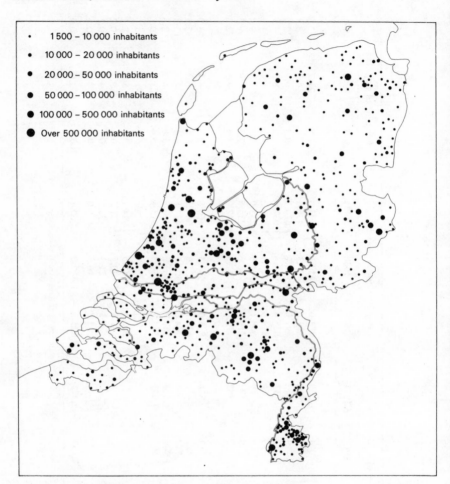

- •   1 500 – 10 000 inhabitants
- •   10 000 – 20 000 inhabitants
- ●   20 000 – 50 000 inhabitants
- ●   50 000 – 100 000 inhabitants
- ●   100 000 – 500 000 inhabitants
- ●   Over 500 000 inhabitants

Fig. 9.1   The Dutch Settlement Pattern, 1970
       Source: Third Report on Physical Planning, 1976, p. 80

years, they have accounted for a fairly small and diminishing proportion of the population. Therefore a discussion based on municipal data will capture the main characteristics of the development of the settlement pattern.

For an unbiased study of the population in different size classes after 1840 (Figure 9.2), a list of permanent municipalities was prepared, comprising all municipalities with at least 5,000 inhabitants in 1970. Account was taken of boundary changes and amalgamations after 1840 by calculating the population data within the 1970 municipal division. The list thus established comprises 502 municipalities or 90.8 per cent of the total population in 1970 (Van der Knaap, 1978).

From these data four general conclusions can be drawn. First, the urbanization process is demonstrated by the steady decline of the lowest size

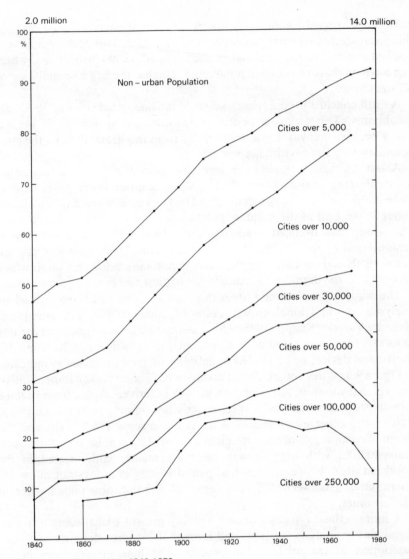

2.0 million   14.0 million

Non – urban Population

Cities over 5,000

Cities over 10,000

Cities over 30,000

Cities over 50,000

Cities over 100,000

Cities over 250,000

Fig. 9.2 City Size Groups, 1840-1979
Source of data: Netherlands Bureau of Statistics

class, which dropped from 53 per cent in 1840 to 9 per cent in 1979. Compared with other European countries the effects of the industrial revolution manifested themselves late and only became apparent after 1870, when massive urbanization took place, and lasting until after the turn of the century. The proportion of the population living in the smallest size group of municipalities decreased from 45 per cent in 1870 to 30 per cent in 1900. Second, the position of the group of small cities is weak throughout the whole period. Although the number of municipalities with 5-10,000 inhabitants increased considerably, the proportion of the population living in this group decreased from 16 per cent to 12 per cent. This development is in marked contrast to the next higher size class, 10-30,000 inhabitants, which increased its share of the total population, and has the largest population of all size classes.

A third conclusion concerns the class of medium-sized cities of 30-50,000 inhabitants. This group is poorly represented during the whole period, partly because many of the municipalities from this group crossed the class boundary into the next higher size class.

A last conclusion reflects the formative period of Dutch urbanization before the turn of the century. The highest size group is composed of only three municipalities (Amsterdam, The Hague, and Rotterdam), which had about 25 per cent of the urban population at the beginning of this century. The group has declined gradually since 1940, although this is partly camouflaged by the fact that Utrecht reached the 250,000 mark at the end of the 1950s and then after twenty years, again sank below this limit, which accounts for the dramatic decrease in the highest size group in recent years.

The study of settlement system development can be complemented by analysing the individual growth paths of municipalities. An example is given by Van der Knapp (1978) who classified each municipality according to its rate of growth based upon an exponential growth curve. By using this short-hand device, he succeeded in defining six growth classes as indicated in Figure 9.3. When the six classes are mapped (Figure 9.4) an impression of the regional variation in population growth is derived. Apart from isolated growth areas connected with specific activities (mining in South Limburg, Philips and other electrotechnical industries around Eindhoven, and the recent development of the municipality of Emmen in the northeast), municipalities with high growth rates are mainly concentrated in the Randstad area. However, the time period is long and does not allow for discrimination between different forms of urbanization taking place at various times.

A more refined typology of municipality growth paths, using a hierarchical cluster analysis (Guffens and Latten, 1979), provides a more precise description of the urbanization process. The high growth rates in the Randstad area are explained partly by an important increase in the formative years of that area around the turn of the century. On the other hand, many municipalities in the vicinity of the bigger cities are shown to have increased in population largely at the end of the study period.

Dynamics in the Urban System

To examine changes in the Dutch settlement system, municipalities are grouped according to criteria related to their main nucleus. The typology uses a fixed set of criteria applied by the Netherlands Bureau of Statistics

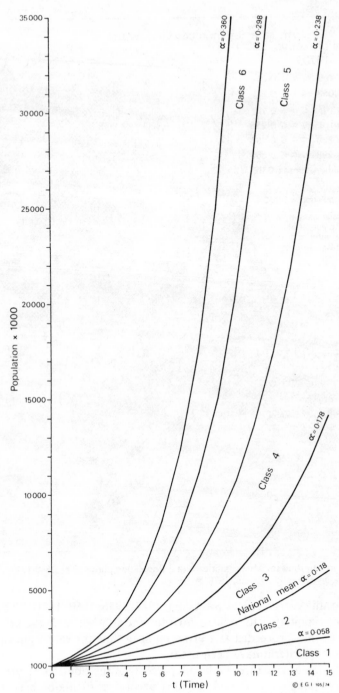

Fig. 9.3 Exponential Growth Behaviour of Dutch Municipalities for Different Values of α
($y = be^{\alpha t}$; $b = 1000$)
Source: Van der Knaap, 1978, p. 62

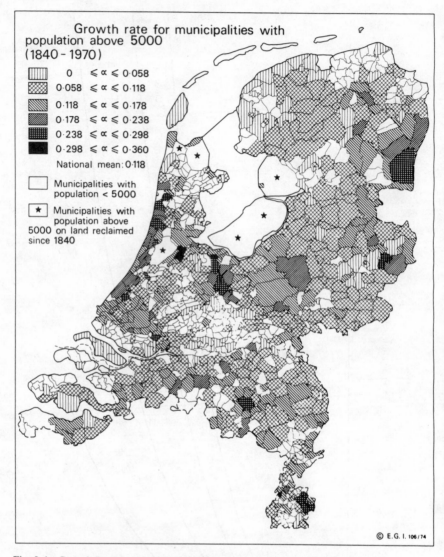

Fig. 9.4   Growth Rate for Municipalities with a Population above 5000, 1840-1970
Source: Van der Knaap, 1978, p. 63

for each of the years a census was taken (1947, 1956, 1960, 1971). The intention of the typology is to indicate how far and in what form the urbanization process has proceeded at a given point in time for each municipality. The following criteria have been used:

(*a*) Employment structure. Only the percentage distribution of the active male population was used, divided according to major branches of economic activity: agriculture, manufacturing, commerce, and transport, and other services.

(*b*) Commuting. In addition to the percentage of employed males not working in their place of residence, a division was made between those born locally and in-migrants, as well as between salaried employees and other wage earners.

(*c*) Physical structure. Inhabitants of the largest nucleated settlement within a municipality were counted both in absolute terms and as a percentage of the total population. Population density was an added characteristic, as was the number of people living in scattered houses. The character of urban places was expressed by the proportion of multi-family houses.

(*d*) Central functions. The presence of administrative and other institutions having a regional function were used.

Applying these criteria, municipalities were classified into three main categories: rural, urbanized rural, and urban. The general characteristic of the rural municipalities is that more than 20 per cent of the active male population is engaged in agriculture. In 1979 almost 30 per cent of the municipalities with 11.9 per cent of the population belonged to this category (Table 9.2).

The second category, urbanized rural municipalities, differs from the first category in that less than 20 per cent of the gainfully employed men earn their livelihood in agricultural occupations. This category accounts for almost 56 per cent of the municipalities with 36 per cent of the total population. It is divided into two sub-categories. The first sub-category has more than 50 per cent of the active male population working in manufacturing industries. The largest nucleated settlement in this sub-category has a population between 5,000 and 30,000 inhabitants. The second sub-category includes all those municipalities that are not really urban in character, with commuters accounting for at least 30 per cent of the total working population. More than 60 per cent of the commuters were born elsewhere, and 80 out of 100 wage earners are salaried employees.

The third main category is composed of urban municipalities, which are characterized both by the structure of their labour force and the physical appearance of the settlement. To be classified as urban, the population density of the built-up area (as opposed to that of the municipality as a whole) has to be at least 2,000 per square kilometre. At least 70 per cent of the population, of which generally less than 10 per cent is engaged in agriculture, has to be concentrated in the built-up area. For smaller centres, inclusion in this category depends upon whether typically urban service functions are performed. Urban centres are divided into five sub-categories according to the number of inhabitants of their built-up area. For the purpose of this paper a further sub-division has been made of urban municipalities with over 100,000 inhabitants, resulting in a total of seven urban sub-categories (Table 9.2; and Steigenga, 1975).

Table 9.2: *Urbanization Characteristics of Dutch Municipalities (1 January, 1979)*

	No. of munici-palities	Population	% of popula-tion	% of area	Population density (inhabitants /km²)
RURAL (Over 20% engaged in agriculture)	241	1,659,342	11.9	40.2	122
URBANIZED RURAL (Less than 20% in agriculture)					
— Industrialized (largest place 5-20,000)	327	3,064,810	21.9	33.8	267
— Predominantly commuting (over 30% commuters; over 60% of commuters not born locally)	129	1,964,645	14.0	8.8	661
— Subtotal	456	5,029,455	35.9	42.6	348
URBAN (Division by size of largest place)					
— 2- 10,000 inhabitants	28	316,046	2.3	2.0	472
— 10- 30,000 inhabitants	43	1,187,840	8.5	5.0	705
— 30- 50,000 inhabitants	16	815,081	5.8	3.3	731
— 100-200,000 inhabitants	16	1,199,792	8.6	2.1	1,677
— 100-200,000 inhabitants	13	1,781,017	12.7	3.5	1,494
— 200-400,000 inhabitants	1	236,053	1.7	0.1	4,336
— 400-800,000 inhabitants	3	1,759,215	12.6	1.2	4,232
— Subtotal	120	7,295,044	52.2	17.2	1,248
TOTAL	817	13,983,841	100	100	413

Note: Classification of municipalities based on the results of the 1971 Census

Data Source: Netherlands Bureau of Statistics

Settlement Type and Population Movement

The classification presented here provides the framework for studying population change in the Dutch settlement system. The method used is shift and share analysis (Perloff *et al.*, 1960). Using this technique an expected growth is calculated for each category of settlements on the assumption that all categories grow at the national rate. The expected growth is then subtracted from the actual change. If the difference is positive the category in question has had a more than proportionate share of growth than would have been expected given national trends (a positive shift). If the difference is negative this indicates a slower than average rate of growth or an absolute loss of population (a relative negative shift or an absolute negative shift).

The results of a shift and share analysis are given in Table 9.3. It should be borne in mind that the Netherlands Bureau of Statistics reclassified many municipalities in 1977 when the results of the 1971 census became available. Therefore, the figures for 1977 and 1978 are not completely comparable with those of earlier years. This is a minor problem because the emphasis here is on a between-group comparison of performance at a certain period rather than on the changing performance of any category through time.

Four main points emerge from Table 9.3. First, the larger urban centres (over 100,000 inhabitants) already had a substantial negative shift during the 1960s, amounting to 13.6 per cent of the 1960 population in this category. For most of the decade the negative shift was relative only, becoming absolute shortly before 1970. This was caused exclusively by the three largest municipalities which reached their maximum size during the late fifties. All other members of this category kept on growing during the 1960s (most of them until 1972).

Second, during the 1960s the municipalities over 100,000 were responsible for over 90 per cent of the total negative shift. The only other category showing a negative shift was the category of 50-100,000 with a small relative negative shift. The table clearly indicates who the gainers were in this period: over two-thirds of the positive shift is accounted for by the urbanized rural group. The rural municipalities had only a modest share during this period.

Third, although suburbanization continued during the first half of the 1970s, the role played by the highest size class did not increase, either in absolute or in relative terms. The average yearly negative shift for this category diminished, and this cannot be explained only by the fact that the size of this category is itself decreasing. Expressed as a percentage of the 1970 population the negative shift had fallen to 11.6 per cent during the 1970s as compared with 13.6 per cent during the preceding decade. If the role of the bigger cities in this shift diminished during the 1970s, that of the category 50-100,000 inhabitants, gained in momentum. The small relative negative shift turned into a substantial absolute negative shift during the first half of the 1970s. If calculated for the full decade this would amount to

Table 9.3: *Population Shifts in the Dutch Settlement System 1960-78*

	Average yearly shift				Share (percentage)			
	1960-9	1970-5	1977	1978	1960-9	1970-5	1977	1978
RURAL MUNICIPALITIES	6,799	31,316	7,364	25,879	12.4	39.6	12.8	43.4
URBANIZED RURAL								
Industrialized	21,758	28,819	15,727	-2,837	39.7	36.5	26.4	-4.7
Commuting	15,120	5,964	9,320	16,186	27.6	7.5	15.6	27.1
Subtotal	36,878	34,783	25,047	13,349	67.3	44.0	42.0	22.4
URBAN MUNICIPALITIES								
2- 10,000 inhabitants	3,995	3,930	14,064	1,922	7.3	5.0	23.6	3.2
10- 30,000 inhabitants	6,494	9,021	11,542	15,581	11.8	11.4	19.3	26.1
30- 50,000 inhabitants	652	-11,258	1,400	102	1.2	-14.3	2.3	0.2
50-100,000 inhabitants	-5,242	-26,496	-3,503	-7,212	-9.6	-33.5	-5.9	-12.1
Over 100,000 inhabitants	-49,576	-41,296	-56,184	-49,621	-90.4	-52.2	-94.1	-83.2
Subtotal	-43,677	-66,099	-32,681	-39,228	-79.7	-83.6	-54.8	-65.8

Note: Classification of municipalities 1960-75 based on the results of the 1960 Census; classification of municipalities 1977 and 1978 based on the results of the 1971 Census

Data Source: Netherlands Bureau of Statistics

Netherlands 213

18.7 per cent of the 1970 population. It can be concluded that the sub-urbanization process during the seventies trickled downward to medium-sized cities.

Finally, there are strong indications that the urbanized rural municipalities are gradually losing their leading position as recipients of the urban exodus. Their function has been taken over partly by the rural municipalities, and partly by the smaller urban centres (10-30,000 inhabitants). This conclusion is reaffirmed if the inland migration pattern between the main categories is analyzed (Figure 9.5). The net in-migration for the urbanized rural municipalities exceeded that for the rural municipalities until 1970. In 1971 and 1972 the figures were almost identical for both groups of municipalities, but after 1972 the relative net in-migration of the

NET INLAND MIGRATION 1963-1977

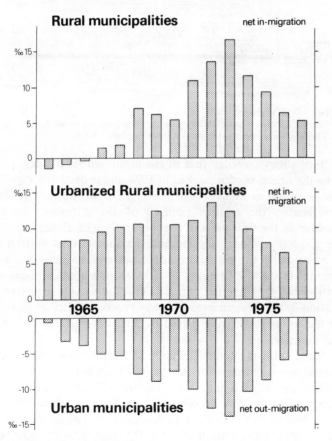

Fig. 9.5   Net Inland Migration 1963-77
Source: CBS. The classification of municipalities is based on the results of the 1960 census; for 1976 and 1977 on the 1971 census

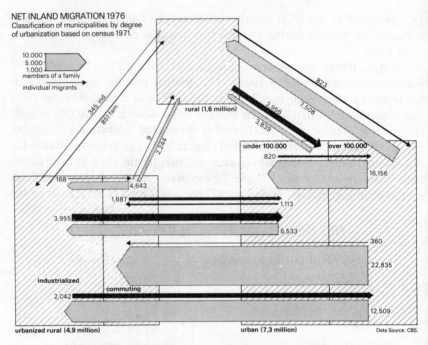

Fig. 9.6   Net Inland Migration, 1976
Classification of municipalities by degree of urbanization based on census 1971
Source of data: Centraal Bureau voor de Statistiek, 1979

rural municipalities exceeded that of the urbanized rural category. At the same time the urban exodus peaked in 1973 and is declining rapidly now.

The observations made so far can be refined in two ways. When differentiated regionally, the relative position of the different categories of municipalities in the four parts of the country bears a close resemblance to the general pattern. Some departures from the national pattern are displayed, however. In the highly urbanized western provinces, for example, urban centres in the size category 30-100,000 have a much bigger share in the negative shift than in other parts of the country. This suggests that suburbanization in the western provinces has proceeded further than in other parts of the country. The role played by the rural municipalities points in the same direction.

The second refinement discriminates between individual migrants and those migrating as a member of the family. If the most recent information on net inland migration is analyzed in this way (Figure 9.6), a clearcut division in migration behaviour becomes evident. The general pattern of migration from municipalities with a high degree of urbanization to lower classified municipalities only holds true for those who are members of a family. Individual migrants form a counter-current in the direction of municipalities with the highest degree of urbanization. Thus some light is shed on the functions performed by different types of settlements for society as a whole. Whereas young individuals are migrating to the bigger cities for educational purposes or to start their careers, those who have formed families are moving to smaller communities with more agreeable housing conditions and a better quality of life. In terms of numbers, the former are far outnumbered by the latter.

Variations in population change are not wholly dependent on migration patterns. Because urban out-migrants tend to be in the child-bearing age groups, there obviously is a relationship between migration and natural population growth. Places with high rates of net in-migration also tend to have high rates of natural increase. The combined effect of migration on the one hand and the interrelated natural population growth on the other will eventually bring about a levelling out of the existing imbalances in the urban hierarchy. Indeed, it may weaken the dominant position of the three largest centres of the Randstad.

Spatial Relationships in the Settlement System

Dutch geographers have studied the dynamic aspects of the settlement system by concentrating on the interactions between places. Most studies were conducted in the framework of central place theory (e.g. Buursink, 1971; Van der Haegen and Van Weesep, 1974). Often the kinds of interactions used are shopping patterns or other linkages that can be visualized in the movements of people to central places. The evidence suggests that this kind of research is more appropriate on a regional rather than a national scale. The interactions are typically of too limited a range to permit firm conclusions about the working of the settlement system as a whole.

Although analysis of interactions at a macro level would be possible with detailed knowledge about flows of people, goods, money and information, data of this kind are seldom available. Therefore, only a limited number of studies can be mentioned which shed some light on the functioning of the Dutch settlement system as a whole.

An interesting example of the study of interaction patterns uses data on telephone traffic between twenty-one district exchanges for the period 1967-74 (Dietvorst and Wever, 1977). Applying graph theory, a hierarchical pattern of the Dutch telephone network was depicted for three successive points in time, both for direct and indirect relationships (Nystuen and Dacey, 1961). A simplified generalization is presented in Figure 9.7. A northern and a southern subsystem are recognized, with the first orientated towards the district exchange of Amsterdam and the second towards The Hague. In addition to the dominating position of the Randstad in the national telephone network, the functional interdependence of the larger cities in the Randstad area is clearly demonstrated. Approximately 50 per cent of the outgoing telephone calls from the exchanges of Amsterdam, Rotterdam, The Hague and Utrecht remain within the Randstad area. This

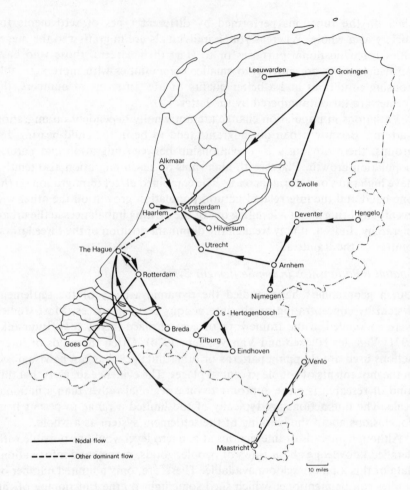

Fig. 9.7   The Hierarchical Pattern of the Dutch Telephone Network, about 1970
Source: Dietvorst & Wever, 1977, p. 76

interdependence has decreased somewhat over the years, whereas relations
with the peripheral districts, notably in the East, have been intensified. All
peripheral districts are strongly linked to the Randstad, with one-third of
their outgoing telephone calls directed to the four exchange centres in that
area. Within the Randstad area there are indications of a weakening of the
position of Amsterdam, with a concomitant rise in the position of Utrecht.

Taken together, the results of this approach suggest that the interrelations
between the different elements in the Dutch urban system are increasing
over time, with the gap between the top three or four cities and the rest
gradually being bridged. A similar conclusion was suggested in the analysis
of migration patterns.

Metropolitan Trends and the Future National Urban System

It has been shown that the traditional pattern of urbanization which results in a concentration of the population in urban centres continued until the end of the 1950s. The first signs of a reversal were shown by the bigger municipalities which started to lose population from the early 1960s onwards, when net out-migration ceased to be compensated by natural growth (Table 9.4). This tendency extended to almost all other municipalities over 100,000 during the early 1970s. It is interesting to note, though, that the last column of Table 9.4 indicates a smaller out-migration in the second half of the 1970s.

To analyse the population development of metropolitan areas, broad statistical urban regions, as defined by the Netherlands Bureau of Statistics, also can be used. These include, in addition to one or two central municipalities, all those urban municipalities sending at least 50 per cent of their commuters to the central municipalities. The classification is based on the results of the 1960 census and are given only for urban regions of at least 100,000 inhabitants (Schmitz, 1966). For the four largest statistical urban regions, a loss of population took place in the period 1974-9 in all but one region. The population loss of the central municipalities exceeded the increase of the urban ring.

Because the definition of statistical urban regions is based on 1960 data, it seems appropriate to attempt a new delimitation using more recent information. The delimitation presented here (Figure 9.8) follows the approach suggested by Hall (1973). Two basic building blocks at the metropolitan scale are used, together forming a Standard Metropolitan Labour Area (SMLA). The SMLA core consists of an administrative area or number of contiguous areas with a 1978 density of at least 1,750 workers per square kilometre and a minimum of 20,000 workers. This density exceeds the one applied by Hall (1973), of 1,235 per square kilometre, to account for the higher overall density in the Netherlands. The SMLA ring consists of administrative areas contiguous to the core and sending at least 15 per cent of their resident employed population to that core.

By applying these criteria, twenty-four SMLAs can be identified, accommodating 59.3 per cent of the 1978 population. A summary of population changes, taking a fixed definition of SMLAs, clearly indicates a slowing down of growth compared with the non-metropolitan population, especially during the seventies.

A more detailed picture can be presented by applying a shift and share analysis to the total of twenty-four SMLAs (Table 9.5). By comparing the percentage shares for 1960-9 with those for 1970-8, a fourfold classification can be developed (Drewett *et al.*, 1976) to characterize the long-term performance of each SMLA. It is interesting that the Rotterdam/The Hague SMLA performed less poorly in the period 1970-8 than in the previous

Table 9.4: *Population Change in Municipalities over 100,000 (yearly average rate per thousand)*

	Population 1979 January 1	Total change				Inland migration			
		1960-4	1965-9	1970-4	1975-8	1960-4	1965-9	1970-4	1975-8
Amsterdam	718,577	-0.9	-9.8	-16.9	-9.6	-8.6	-16.2	-24.0	-21.2
Rotterdam	582,396	-0.4	-13.5	-18.9	-12.3	-8.9	-19.2	-25.0	-20.6
The Hague	458,242	-4.3	-18.6	-21.7	-9.3	-9.2	-20.4	-28.4	-19.6
Utrecht	236,053	11.5	5.4	-19.8	-14.9	-3.6	-5.8	-24.8	-24.0
Eindhoven	192,687	15.1	8.8	3.2	0.1	-0.6	-1.8	-12.4	-6.6
Groningen	160,615	10.7	22.4	-9.3	-6.4	1.8	-1.4	-11.6	-8.6
Haarlem	159,747	3.2	0.5	-9.2	-6.9	6.6	-7.6	-12.4	-12.4
Tilburg	150,751	11.9	9.5	-2.9	-3.2	-2.4	-1.8	-10.0	-9.4
Nijmegen	147,670	15.9	11.5	-2.3	0.3	1.0	-0.2	-10.0	-5.9
Enschede	141,917	14.7	8.6	0.6	0.2	2.2	-3.4	-8.6	-4.3
Apeldoorn	137,244	18.8	20.1	12.3	5.6	6.6	11.6	6.8	2.1
Arnhem	126,998	11.5	5.1	-9.5	0.1	-1.0	-8.4	-15.6	-4.0
Breda	117,521	16.1	7.9	-6.5	0.0	0.2	-0.6	-11.0	-5.1

Data Source: Netherlands Bureau of Statistics

Fig. 9.8 Standard Metropolitan Labour Areas, 1971
(for an explanation of the rank numbers *see* Table 9.5)

decade. Its 'decelerating decline' strengthens the conclusion drawn earlier about the decreasing rate of the urban exodus from the largest urban regions. The second ranking SMLAs may be said to be one phase behind (*compare also* Table 9.4) so that a decelerating decline can be hypothesized for the future. Apart from one or two exceptions such as Heerlen (which has been influenced by an early urbanization associated with the development of coal mining in Limburg), almost all SMLAs still have a positive

220　*Urbanization and Settlement Systems*

Table 9.5: *Population Change in Dutch Metropolitan Areas*

SMLA/by rank	Population 1978	Annual change 1960-9		Annual change 1970-8		Development type
		Shift	Share	Shift	Share	
1 Rotterdam/The Hague	2,363,004	−8,670	−55.5	−5,651	−30.7	Decelerating decline
2 Amsterdam	1,687,581	−5,644	−36.1	−11,673	−63.4	Accelerating decline
3 Utrecht	750,793	1,608	10.3	1,937	10.5	Accelerating growth
4 Eindhoven	397,096	4,067	26.0	3,094	16.8	Decelerating growth
5 Hengelo/Enschede	319,536	650	4.2	1,296	7.0	Accelerating growth
6 Arnhem	288,583	1,046	6.7	594	3.2	Decelerating growth
7 Groningen	267,791	101	0.6	303	1.6	Accelerating growth
8 Nijmegen	235,425	1,373	8.7	993	5.4	Decelerating growth
9 Tilburg	197,142	504	3.2	210	1.1	Decelerating growth
10 Heerlen	176,162	−465	−3.0	−817	−4.4	Accelerating decline
11 's-Hertogenbosch	166,189	978	6.3	1,096	6.0	Decelerating growth
12 Maastricht	156,563	−270	−1.7	1,389	7.5	Accelerating growth
13 Breda	154,465	151	3.4	−135	−0.7	Accelerating decline
14 Leeuwarden	143,709	−583	−3.7	373	2.0	Accelerating growth
15 Dordrecht	143,652	969	6.2	1,010	5.5	Decelerating growth
16 Sittard	109,325	403	2.6	378	2.1	Decelerating growth
17 Almelo	96,183	317	2.0	419	2.3	Accelerating growth
18 Zwolle	92,649	469	3.0	405	2.2	Decelerating growth
19 Gouda	92,124	267	1.7	428	2.3	Accelerating growth
20 Alkmaar	88,588	588	3.8	2,280	12.4	Accelerating growth
21 Oss	86,250	830	5.3	1,097	6.0	Accelerating growth
22 Deventer	79,911	401	2.6	−149	−0.8	Accelerating decline
23 Helmond	72,603	264	1.7	286	1.6	Decelerating growth
24 Roozendaal	69,424	259	1.7	837	4.5	Accelerating growth

Data source: Netherlands Bureau of Statistics

shift, whose relative share is growing in the case of more recently urbanized SMLAs. Some of these SMLAs are obviously in an early phase of urbanization, and are still centralizing. The prevailing theme, however, is one of relative decentralization, during the 1960s in eighteen out of the twenty-four metropolitan areas. Suburbanization at the scale of metropolitan areas is proceeding rapidly. After 1970 more than half of all SMLAs were decentralizing (i.e. their central cores were declining in population).

The suburbanization process has not been restricted to population: economic activities also are leaving the big cities. This applies not only to industrial activities, but increasingly to wholesaling and office functions, which are locating at fairly close distances away from the main centres, preferably inside the city ring of the Randstad area.

In a small country like the Netherlands, suburbanization at the metropolitan level necessarily has implications for the regional redistribution of population and economic activities. Since no less than 62.2 per cent of the total metropolitan population is concentrated in the three western provinces, decentralization from metropolitan areas at the same time implies a movement away from the West. As a matter of fact, the traditionally westward direction of net migration changed from 1961 onwards, and this change gained momentum in the 1970s (Figure 9.9). Ever since the beginning of the 1970s the provinces of North and South Holland have had a monopoly on expulsion in land migration, whereas the neighbouring provinces of Gelderland and North Brabant have been the main overspill areas. Obviously the Randstad is no longer the attractive area it used to be, except for some specific groups in Dutch society.

Urban policy in the Netherlands has been slow to absorb the consequences of the new trends indicated here. For a long time post-war planning aimed at slowing down the development of urban areas in the western provinces, especially of the Randstad area, and stimulating the peripheral regions (Borchert and Van Ginkel, 1979). It has been a declared goal of national planning to bring about a more even distribution of population and economic activities over the different parts of the country at the cost of the West. With the publication of the second report on physical planning in 1966, it was calculated that the share of the western provinces would decrease by the year 2000 to 42.5 per cent if no action were taken. By transferring employment opportunities (including government offices) to outlying areas, this share would be reduced to 33.7 per cent. Even when the first part of the third report on physical planning was presented in 1974 a similar policy was announced, albeit with shifts of a smaller size.

A complete change-over emerged with the publication of the second part of the third report on physical planning (the so-called *Urbanization Report*) in 1976/9. For the first time the consequences of the new trends were recognized. In this report, which deals exclusively with urbanization, measures were announced to improve the quality of life in the urban centres, and at

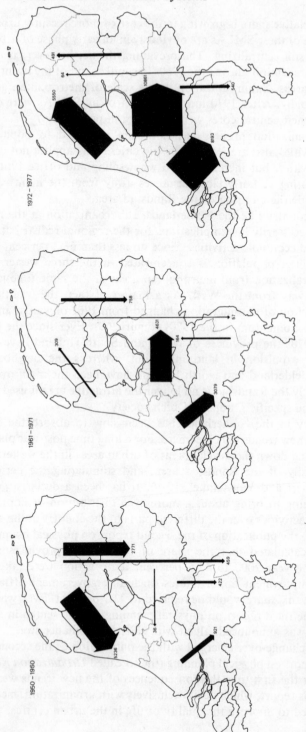

Fig. 9.9 Net Inland Migration (Annual Averages)
Source of data: Netherlands Bureau of Statistics

the same time to enlarge housing capacity in order to accommodate those people who otherwise would leave the Randstad. New building sites would be developed not only in the growth centres (Figure 9.10), but also inside the metropolitan areas. Although the Netherlands still awaits the acceptance of an Urban Renewal Act, much attention has been paid recently to revitalization of the existing urban environment.

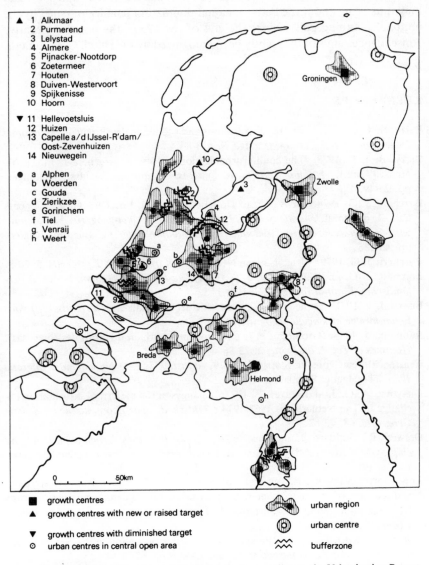

Fig. 9.10 Future Urban Structure of the Netherlands according to the Urbanization Report, 1977

Conclusion

This paper has sketched the structure and development of the Dutch settlement scheme. By concentrating on the changes taking place in the distribution of population, it has been possible to demonstrate that a process of deconcentration is spreading rapidly from the top-ranking metropolitan areas to other elements of the urban hierarchy. Although these tendencies will weaken the dominance of the largest urban areas of the Randstad, and may thus bring about the better regional population balance pursued by the national planning policy since the end of the 1950s, the possible negative consequences have only recently been recognized by the Dutch Government.

REFERENCES

Berry, B. J. L. 1961. 'City size distributions and economic development'. *Economic Development and Cultural Change*, 9: 573-84.
Berry, B. J. L. 1978. 'The counterurbanization process: how general?' In: N. M. Hansen (ed.), *Human settlement systems*. Cambridge, Mass.: Ballinger, pp. 25-49.
Borchert, J. G. 1978. 'De Randstad Holland'. In: J. G. Borchert, G. J. J. Egbers and M. de Smidt, *Ruimtelijk beleid in Nederland; sociaal-geografische beschouwingen over regionale ontwikkeling en ruimtelijke ordening*. Bussum: Romen, pp. 45-186.
Borchert, J. G. 1979. 'Urbanisatie in Nederland'. *Kartografisch Tijdschrift*, 5: 30-3.
Borchert, J. G. and Van Ginkel, J. A. 1979. *Die Randstad Holland in der niederländischen Raumordnung*. Kiel: Hirt.
Buursink, J. 1971. 'De nederlandse hiërarchie der regionale centra'. *Tijdschrift voor Economische en Sociale Geografie*, 62: 67-81.
Buursink, J. 1978. 'Groningue et le developpement urbain du Nord des Pays-Bas'. *Hommes et Terres du Nord*, 2: 73-88.
Centraal Bureau voor de Statistiek, 1979. *Statistiek van de binnenlandse migratie 1976*. The Hague: Staatsuitgeverij.
Dietvorst, A. G. J. and Wever, E. 1977. 'Changes in the pattern of information exchange in The Netherlands 1967-1974'. *Tijdschrift voor Economische en Sociale Geografie*, 68: 72-82.
Drewett, R., Goddard, J. and Spence, N. 1976. *British cities: Urban population and employment trends 1951-71*. London: Department of the Environment (Research Report 10).
Engelsdorp Gastelaars, R. van and Cortie, C. 1973. 'Migration from Amsterdam; a discussion of the movement of employment and residential population away from the municipality of Amsterdam'. *Tijdschrift voor Economische en Sociale Geografie*, 64: 206-17.
Grit, S. and Korteweg, P. J. 'Perspectives on office relocation in the Netherlands'. *Tijdschrift voor Economische en Sociale Geografie*, 67: 2-14.
Guffens, T. F. and Latten, J. J. 1979. *Typologieën van nederlandse gemeenten naar*

bevolkingsgroei. The Hague: Staatsuitgeverij (Monografieën Volkstelling 1971, No. 15A).

Haegen, H. van der and Van Weesep, J. 1974. 'Urban geography in the Low Countries'. *Tijdschrift voor Economische en Sociale Geografie,* 65: 79-89.

Hall, P. *et al.* 1973. *The containment of urban England.* London: Allen & Unwin.

Harten, J. D. H. 1972. *Historische geografie van Nederland.* Utrecht: Department of Geography, University of Utrecht.

Kemper, N. J. 1977. 'The locational efficiency of industries in the southern Amsterdam sub-region'. *Tijdschrift voor Economische en Sociale Geografie,* 68: 211-23.

Keuning, H. J. 1979. *Kaleidoscoop der nederlandse landschappen; de regionale verscheidenheid van Nederland in historisch-geografisch perspectief.* The Hague: Martinus Nijhoff.

Knapp, G. A. van der. 1978. *A spatial analysis of the evolution of an urban system: the case of the Netherlands.* Thesis, Rotterdam University.

Nas, P. J. M. 1976. *Stedeverdelingen, nationale ontwikkeling en afhankelijkheid; een komparatief-kwalitatieve benadering.* Thesis, Leiden University.

Netherlands Bureau of Statistics. 1979. *Statistical yearbook of the Netherlands.* The Hague: Staatsuitgeverij.

Nystuen, J. D. and Dacey, M. F. 1961. 'A graph theory interpretation of nodal regions'. *Papers and Proceedings of the Regional Science Association,* 7: 29-42.

Ottens, H. F. L. 1976. *Het groene hart binnen de Randstad; een beeld van de suburbanisatie in West-Nederland.* Assen: Van Gorcum.

Perloff, H. *et al.* 1960. *Regions, resources, and economic growth.* Baltimore: Johns Hopkins University Press.

Schmitz, J. 1966. 'Stedelijke agglomeraties met 100000 en meer inwoners'. *Maandschrift van het Centraal Bureau voor de Statistiek,* pp. 1042-8.

Steigenga, W. 1975. 'The Netherlands'. In: R. Jones (ed.), *Essays on world urbanization.* London: George Philip, pp. 113-32.

Third Report on Physical Planning. 1976. *Verstedelijkingsnota,* deel 2a: beleidsvoornemens. The Hague: Staatsuitgeverij.

10 THE DANISH SETTLEMENT SYSTEM: DEVELOPMENT AND PLANNING

SVEN ILLERIS

Introduction

In Denmark, research on the national settlement system has been closely connected with national and regional physical planning. After describing the development of the settlement system up to the 1970s, this paper outlines questions about the future settlement system dealt with in the context of regional planning. Planning problems have triggered considerable research on the feasibility and consequences of different future forms of the settlement system. Examples of such studies will also be discussed. Finally, settlement systems principles adopted in the regional planning process—including public participation—will be treated.

Historical Development of the Danish Settlement System

In the ninth and tenth centuries, Denmark already had a dense rural settlement system. In most of the country this system consisted of small villages, but in certain regions included hamlets and isolated farms. The oldest towns seem to have been founded in this period. They were situated at main crossroads, on regional watersheds, or on rivers and inlets—always far from the open sea where attacks from Vikings and pirates could be expected.

The Middle Ages were a period of expansion of both rural and urban settlement. In particular, a system of market towns was established, usually at intervals of about 30 km. Many were small ports. Few of them were of more than local importance, however, and even bishops' seats were rather modest.

The sixteenth, seventeenth, and eighteenth centuries brought few changes in this well-established settlement system. The most important development took place in Copenhagen. In the fifteenth century Copenhagen became the capital of a monarchy including not only the present Denmark, but also Norway, Iceland and parts of South-Western Sweden and Northern Germany. In the seventeenth century the kings gained absolute power. They favoured the growth of Copenhagen, which soon had about half of the total urban population of Denmark.

As a result of major agricultural reforms in the late eighteenth century, the rural settlement pattern changed. Through land reform, all farm holdings were consolidated. Many farms were moved from the old villages to 'enclosed' properties in the open countryside.

In the second half of the nineteenth century, industrialization expanded rapidly. Most of the manufacturing industries located either in Copenhagen or in the most important provincial towns, especially on the east coast of Jutland. Thus, while Copenhagen retained its absolute supremacy in the Danish settlement system, the size distribution of provincial towns became more differentiated, taking on the normal rank-size ordering.

As a reaction to the reduced grain prices in Europe in the 1880s, Danish agriculture quickly switched into specialized animal products. This type of production was highly commercialized. With poor local transport, this led to a dense network of service centres where the farmers could satisfy their expanding needs for consumer goods, and for selling and processing their products (dairies etc.). Thus, between the old provincial towns, a number of new urban settlements developed, often located at railway stations.

The first half of the twentieth century saw few changes in the settlement system. All sizes of towns from the capital to the small urban settlements grew more or less constantly. The big cities had a particularly fast growth in the 1930s, whereas the rural population began to decline not only in relative, but also in absolute terms. In many towns, suburbs developed beyond the administrative boundaries of the central municipalities, though physically contiguous with the built-up areas.

Since 1960 the development of the urban system has changed radically in two ways (Illeris, 1979 and 1980). The first was a rapid growth of scattered settlements in regions surrounding major and medium-sized cities. This was due to the building of one-family houses by commuters, reflecting the substantial increase in car-ownership. It should be noted that legislation since 1949 partially, and since 1970 completely, has prevented house-building in the open countryside. Dispersal has been confined to settlements where house-building has been considered admissible from a conservation point of view, and where at least some services could be provided.

The second change, which has occurred largely since 1970, is an inter-regional shift of both jobs and residences from the Copenhagen region as a whole to small towns and urban settlements all over the country. This tendency could be observed both in the years up to 1973, when there was virtually no unemployment, and since 1974 when there has been very heavy unemployment in all parts of the country.

The distribution of population at different points in time is shown in Figure 10.1, and the most detailed distribution of population growth in Table 10.1. It should be noted that growing areas surrounding the major cities are included in these cities, in such a way that the information primarily illustrates inter-regional development (in Figure 10.1 only from 1960).

The shift in the distribution of population is connected with recent trends in the location of economic activities:

(1) The rapid decline of agricultural employment in previous decades has to some degree levelled out since 1971. This has contributed to a relative stabilization of the population of small villages and scattered farms.

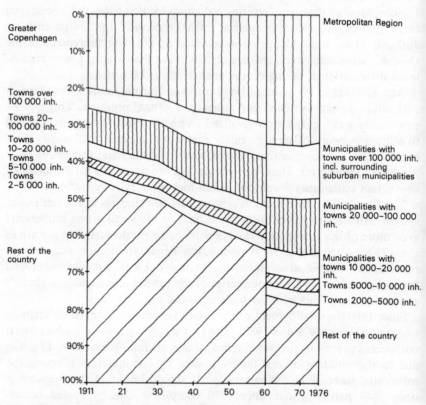

Fig. 10.1   Distribution of Population by Town Size Classes, 1911-76
Towns according to size, 1970; municipalities according to 1970 delimitation

(2) The shift of manufacturing industries from large to medium-size cities —which has taken place for several years, especially in low-wage branch plants—has been extended to small towns. It now appears to include also advanced high-wage branches (Table 10.2).

(3) In private sector services, there has been a similar growth in all size-classes of settlements, except in small villages where shops are closing down. The most dynamic branches (business services) are highly concentrated in the metropolitan areas, but even these branches seem to be following the decentralization of their clients.

(4) In the public sector, two opposing tendencies have been at work for a number of years: within many subsectors, a concentration has taken place into fewer institutions with more specialized functions—for example within hospitals and primary schools. At the same time, the expanding demand for the services of other subsectors has led to a reduction of the threshold population and hence to a more decentralized location pattern. In recent years the concentration tendencies have slowed down, due partly to the high

Table 10.1: *Development of Population 1965-76 by Size-classes of Settlements*

Size 1970	Population (thousands)			Change (per cent)	
	1965	1970	1976	1965-70	1970-76
Metropolitan region of Copenhagen	1678	1753	1761	4.5	0.5
Municipalities with towns over 100,000 + surrounding municipalities	676	721	757	6.7	5.0
Municipalities with towns 10,000-100,000	1019	1071	1107	5.1	3.4
In other municipalities with important out-commuting:[1]					
Settlements 2-10,000	61	66	73	8.2	10.6
Settlements 500-2,000	133	148	182	11.3	23.0
Settlements under 500 and dispersed	466	446	433	−4.3	−3.0
In other municipalities with little out-commuting:[2]					
Settlements 2-10,000	236	256	281	8.5	10.0
Settlements 500-2,000	98	108	125	10.2	16.0
Settlements under 500 and dispersed	400	369	354	−7.8	−4.1
Total	4767	4938	5073	3.6	2.7

[1] Economically-active persons working/economically active persons dwelling = <0.85 in 1970.
[2] Economically-active persons working/economically active persons dwelling = >0.85 in 1970.

Table 10.2: *Manufacturing employment 1973-8*

Size 1970	Employment (thousands)		Change (per cent)
	1973	1978	1973-8
Metropolitan region of Copenhagen	157	124	−21
Municipalities with towns over 100,000 + surrounding municipalities	72	64	−11
Municipalities with towns 20-100,000	81	71	−12
Municipalities with towns 5-20,000	70	70	0
Other municipalities	51	58	+14
Total	431	387	−10

costs of constructing new institutions, and partly to an increased political interest in closer contact between institutions and society. At the same time, local services—such as kindergartens and secondary schools—have become the most important growth sectors all over the country (Table 10.3).

Table 10.3: *Public sector employment 1972-8*

	Employment (thousands)		Change (per cent)
Size 1970	1972	1978	1972-8
Metropolitan region of Copenhagen	219	271	24
Municipalities with towns over 100,000 + surrounding municipalities	72	93	29
Municipalities with towns 20-100,000	73	89	22
Municipalities with towns 5-20,000	66	81	23
Other municipalities	50	74	48
Total	480	608	27

Consequences of Different Settlement Systems

Some of the problems connected with the settlement system are quite old—for example the extreme dominance of Copenhagen over all other Danish towns dates back to the seventeenth century. However, it was only when the Danish Parliament in 1973 passed the Act on National and Regional Planning that the future development of the settlement system became a major research and policy issue.

According to this act, the county councils (in the metropolitan region of Copenhagen, the Metropolitan Council) must prepare regional plans and submit them for approval to the Minister for the Environment. Most notably, the county councils must prepare alternative drafts and organize public debates on these alternatives. In most counties, the public debates took place in the winter 1977/8.

One aspect of these plans is the location of urban growth, in other words the future settlement system. Figure 10.2 shows an example of alternative draft plans. In public debate, the future settlement system was discussed more than any other aspect of the regional plans. Many politicians and planners had expected that such issues would be too abstract for the public to discuss in a meaningful way. However, in most counties the extent and quality of the debate exceeded expectations. The vast majority of those who expressed their opinion at meetings or in writing were in favour of a decentralized settlement pattern.

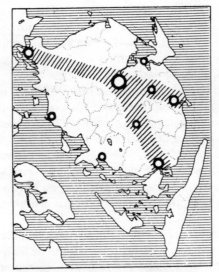

Alternative 'T' focussing on Odense

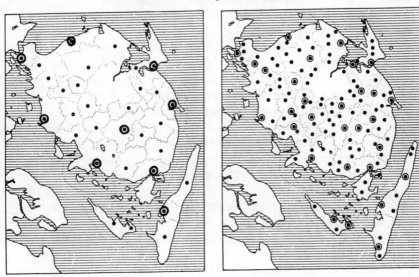

'Coastal town alternative' focussing on
medium-sized towns

'Village alternative'

Fig. 10.2 Alternative Draft Plans for the Future Settlement System in the County of Funen

A settlement system cannot in itself be a political goal. But the development of the settlement system may influence—or even decide—the solution of a broad range of imported political problems, such as: access to jobs, access to services, the limitation of private car traffic, access to the open countryside, the profitablity of private enterprises, the economy and quality of public services, the costs of urban growth, improvement of old urban areas, energy consumption, choice of energy resources, conservation of landscapes or agricultural land and other natural resources, recycling of existing man-made resources (buildings etc.), pollution control, and socio-psychological environment, and quality of life.

Thus, practical planning needs a basis for decisions, in particular extensive knowledge about the conditions and constraints of different settlement systems, and about their conseqences for the above-mentioned questions. However, in the mid-seventies little was known in these fields. Studies that might help fill this gap have now been given high priority. Because of the decentralized growth pattern of the 1970s (people voting with their feet) and the preferences expressed in the public debate, studies on the feasibility and consequences of a decentralized settlement pattern have been particularly numerous.

There are a number of constraints on the planning of future urban growth. First, future population growth seems to be limited. Since 1967 fertility has declined dramatically. According to current forecasts the total population of Denmark will decline from the end of this century. Second, the resources available for house-building and other construction purposes are limited. Third, the existing housing stock and other fixed assets can only be abandoned at a slow rate. For a variety of reasons a good deal of new investment will inevitably be allocated in connection with existing settlements. Consequently about 90 per cent of the population of the year 2000 are already bound to their present municipality.

As a tool for estimating the consequences of developments within these constraints, three alternative models were constructed for the future settlement system. The models expressed the number of people living at various levels of the settlement system, but the location of industries and services would follow the location of residences as closely as possible:

(*a*) A concentration model, in which the bulk of the growth is located in the largest city (cities) of each county (regional centre), with rural municipalities losing population as in the 1960s.

(*b*) A model in which the bulk of the growth is located in medium-sized towns which can supply all frequently needed services and reasonably broad labour-market (district centres). In cases where such towns are farther apart than 15-20 km, a smaller settlement is provided with these functions if possible.

(*c*) A decentralization model, in which as many small settlements as possible are allocated a population of 1,000 persons, which is sufficient for maintaining a school, a shop, and similar services. Calculations show that when the population of the surrounding countryside is included this threshold can be attained in most settlements which today have over 200 inhabitants. In this model a stagnating or reduced population is assumed for the largest cities of the country.

It should be stressed that the models are analytical tools. The central govenment and local authorities possess but limited steering instruments than can ensure the realization of any one of them. The steering tools available are: the location of house building can be restricted through physical planning (zoning); the location of manufacturing industries can be stimulated by regional development subsidies in some parts of the country; land can be purchased and sold for both housing and industrial uses; the location of public institutions can be directly determined by the political authorities also responsible for the planning of the settlement pattern; decisions can be taken regarding transport, energy supply, and other kinds of infrastructure.

The development of the settlement pattern, however, has important consequences for other sectors. With respect to manufacturing industries, the main policy goals are to promote industrial growth in general and in the less-industrialized 'regional development' areas in particular. For some time it has been the opinion of many experts that a 'growth centre' policy for the location of industries would be an appropriate tool for reaching these goals. However, recent studies show that most manufacturing—even technologically advanced high-wage branches—performs quite well in small settlements (Matthiesen, 1980). Thus the justification of a growth-centre policy is questionable.

In the case of services the main policy goals are to provide the greatest number of people with the best services as near to their homes and as cheaply as possible. These goals are contradictory. A concentrated urban growth will supply a large number of people with good, near, and cheap services but will leave the rest of the population with few and distant services. A decentralized growth pattern, on the other hand, will give more equal access to the most frequently used services, but in most regions a poorer supply of the specialized high-quality services. In food retailing, a rapid increase in the threshold population is taking place. Today, the average threshold for a rural grocery is about 300 persons. However, most shopkeepers are elderly people, and a new owner must anticipate investments which demand a higher threshold. It has been estimated that a viable grocery in 1992 will need a population base of about 600 persons (National Agency for Physical Planning, 1981). Within the public service sector similar problems are encountered. A concentration of primary schools has taken place, but in recent years it has slowed down. In the Danish school system, the threshold for an economically viable school is about 1,000 (Koed and Bundsgaard, 1980). However, a further decrease in fertility levels may lead to an increase in the population threshold.

In the case of labour-markets the main policy goals are to give everybody easy access to many jobs in different industries. A concentrated development will give a large number of people easy access to a relatively high number of differentiated jobs. But the population of small settlements will be left with long journeys to work. In a decentralized settlement system, labour markets will be smaller and less differentiated. The population of small settlements will find jobs closer to their home. However, since different firms and institutions demand different kinds of labour-force, this model would only shorten journeys to work to a small degree, and it would cause a good deal of a cross-country commuting (which cannot be carried by public transport).

A policy goal of increasing importance is to keep transport at a minimum. It is intuitively assumed that a concentration of urban growth will minimize the number of man-kilometres required. However, a number of studies carried out in Denmark indicate that the differences in transport volumes between the alternative future settlement patterns are rather modest.

One reason for this result is that if some growth is allocated to small settlements, a number of shops and schools can survive, thus making the trips short for the remaining population who otherwise would have to travel far for these services. Another reason is that growth in larger cities has to take place on their periphery, and the suburban population must travel farther than the average town dweller (Nyvig, 1980). For safety, environmental, and social reasons a shift from private cars to public transport and walking/cycling is desirable. In the case of drastically reduced oil supplies, it might become an absolute necessity. A concentrated settlement pattern will favour walking/cycling and public transport more than a decentralized pattern. On the other hand, a decreased number of passengers from small settlements will make bus services for the remaining population more expensive and/or reduce their quality (Pedersen, 1981).

The relationships between energy supply, energy consumption, and settlement patterns have only been studied in the last few years and conclusions are still very uncertain. On the consumption side, the settlement pattern has minor effects on transport volume. House heating is more important, and might be significantly influenced by the choice of house types. Traditionally, compact house-types are only built in medium-sized and big towns, but they might be considered to increase densities in small settlements.

On the supply side, a combination of different systems is under consideration. Individual oil stoves and individual solar heating systems are independent of the settlement pattern. The same applies for electric heating —fed by nuclear or thermal power plants or windmills—since electricity distribution systems already exist everywhere. It seems to be economically viable to distribute natural gas through pipelines to quite small settlements, depending on the distance from the trunk pipes. District heating is also feasible in rather small settlements. In terms of the total energy requirements of the household, it seems important to recapture waste energy in cooling waters from manufacturing and especially from power plants. In general, a shift from individual stoves to pipe-line distribution systems will favour concentration in the settlement system and increasing densities. But a shift to solar and electric heating in small settlements seems to be equally feasible (Iversen, *et al.*, 1979; Ministry of Energy, 1980).

It has always been a primary policy goal to minimize the costs of urban growth, including road, telephone, electricity, water supply, sewage, district heating and garbage collection systems, the public transport system, the public institutions, etc. There is ample documentation that high densities minimize costs. However, the few studies which compare costs between different settlement systems tend to show that, provided that no building is allowed in the open countryside, total cost differences between alternative growth patterns are insignificant (National Agency for Physical Planning, 1979). It is often important to place growth where there is unused capacity in existing infrastructure, which may be the case in urban renewal areas, but also in rural districts and small settlements.

Conservation of nature and of agricultural land are primary policy goals, which speak against a widespread sprawl of housing. However the differences again are rather modest between the concentrated model and decentralization into a limited number of settlements. Access to the open countryside is often quoted as an important factor in household location preferences. It is evident that distances to recreational areas are greater in a concentrated settlement pattern than in a decentralized one. A significant growth in larger towns will make public land purchases and investments in tourist facilities necessary in the surrounding areas, while such measures are not required in the case of decentralized growth.

The quality of life—including the social, psychological, cultural, health, and physical aspects of the environment—is increasingly stressed in goal statements. It is difficult to estimate the quality-of-life consequences of different settlement patterns in any precise way. Obviously the quality of life is not simply determined by settlement size. However, there is evidence that small settlements offer better conditions than big cities in such respects as social contacts, mortality, and stress. Undoubtedly, growth rates are also important. Fast growth in small settlements will endanger both the social and the physical environment which was the motivation for many people to 'settle there.

In the older parts of Danish cities, there is an urgent need for improvement of the environment, including better housing, more green areas, less traffic, less noise and pollution, etc. In connection with the new planning legislation, the Parliament has decided that densities shall be reduced. A decentralization of growth away from these cities will probably favour the urban renewal goals by minimizing the scope for private investments in economic activities such as retailing, and by minimizing traffic pressures in the older parts of the cities.

It may be concluded that all feasible settlement patterns have both positive and negative consequences. The final choice of a plan will clearly be a decision of a political nature. Research may assist politicians and citizens in exploring the constraints on planning, in analysing the consequences of individual measures, and in assessing their mutual compatibility. But there is no one correct or optimal plan.

The Future Settlement System

After the public debate on the alternative draft plans, the county councils have prepared the final regional plans and, in early 1980, submitted them for approval to the Minister for the Environment. The only firm guideline concerned growth in the Copenhagen region. In 1977, the Minister for the Environment and the Environment Committee of the Government stated that the shift of population growth from the Metropolitan Region of Copenhagen to other parts of the country should continue. The regional authority in question (The Metropolitan Council) was instructed to plan for a reduced population development (Ministry of the Environment, 1977).

The county councils in the rest of the country were influenced by the decentralist preferences expressed by the electorate. On the other hand, they were under pressure from several central-government ministries to plan for a relatively concentrated growth pattern. The above research findings, which gradually became available, tended to weaken the traditional arguments for economies of scale brought about by concentration.

The proposed regional plans represent compromises between these considerations—compromises which are different from county to county. Most county councils have chosen to limit the growth of the major regional centres, but also of small villages without schools. In some counties, however, the lower limit is set lower than in any of the alternative drafts prepared in 1977. The proposed urban network—excluding local centres—is shown in Figure 10.3.

In its annual national planning report to the Parliament, the government in 1979 suggested that the bulk of the growth should be placed in district and municipal centres. During the discussion in parliament the government was encouraged when approving the regional plans to respect the public's wish to ensure the future of small settlements.

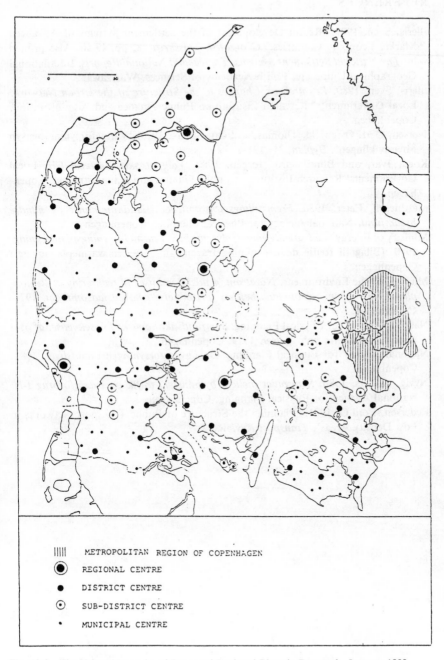

METROPOLITAN REGION OF COPENHAGEN

⬤ REGIONAL CENTRE

● DISTRICT CENTRE

⊙ SUB-DISTRICT CENTRE

· MUNICIPAL CENTRE

Fig. 10.3 The Urban Networks of Proposed Regional Plans in Denmark, January 1980

REFERENCES

Illeris, Sven. 1979. 'Recent Development of the Settlement Systems of Advanced Market Economy Countries.' *Geografisk Tidsskrift* 78, pp. 49-56. Also printed in: *The National Settlement Systems: Topical and National Reports*. International Geographical Union and Polish Academy of Sciences, Warszawa.

Illeris, Sven. 1980. *Research on Changes in the Structure of the Urban Network*. Local Governments' Research Institute on Public Finance and Administration, Copenhagen.

Iversen, Gert, Ostenfeld, Thomas, and Ott, Stefan. 1979. 'Varmeforsyningshensyn i byudviklingen'. *Byplan*, 31: 191-4.

Koed, Ivar, and Bundsgaard, Jørgen. 1980. *Valg af skolestørrelse I-II*. Local Governments' Research Institute on Public Finance and Administration, Copenhagen.

Matthiesen, Peter. 1980. *Fremstillingsvirksomheder i landkommuner og mindre bysamfund*. National Agency for Physical Planning, Copenhagen.

Ministry of Energy. *Vedvarende energi, elvarme m. v. i varmeforsyningsplanlaegning*. 1980. (Bilag til tredje delbetaenkning fra energiministeriets varmeplanudvalg.) Copenhagen.

Ministry of the Environment. *Notat om '4 tidsfølgeskitser til realisering af Regionplan 1973' og om regionplanarbejdets fortsaettelse i hovedstadsomradet*. 1977. Copenhagen.

National Agency for Physical Planning. *Samfundsøkonomiske konsekvenser af øget vaekst i de mindre bebyggelser*. 1979. Copenhagen.

National Agency for Physical Planning. *Dagligvareforsyningen i landsbyer*. 1981. Copenhagen.

Nyvig, Anders. 1980. *Samspillet mellem bymønster, trafik og energiforbrug I-II*. National Agency for Physical Planning, Copenhagen.

Pedersen, Poul O. 1981. 'Planning the Structure of Public Transport Networks in Low Density Areas'. *Transport Reviews*, 1.

11 THE IRISH NATIONAL SETTLEMENT SYSTEM[1]

MICHAEL J. BANNON

Introduction

In Ireland, as in many countries, interest in the national settlement pattern as a system is a relatively new phenomenon and derives much of its impetus from national and regional planning studies which attempt to calibrate the impact of medium and long term changes upon different elements of the system. In this respect the settlement system is seen as highly responsive to changes in factors such as resource utilization, population growth, or migration and is viewed 'as a reflection and/or precondition of the spatial organization of the economy and society of a national territory or even the embodiment of such (Bartels, 1980).

Research into the Irish national settlement system, however, is in its infancy and such research is severely hampered by the lack of data both in respect of the different elements of the system and more especially in respect of flows and exchanges between elements. This paper examines the development of the settlement system to date and attempts to project some of the likely future changes especially in the Dublin agglomeration which dominates the urban system and also occupies 'an intermediate position between the urban and regional scale' (Hansen and Korcelli, 1978).

The Origins of the Settlement Pattern

Recent developments and changes in the settlement system have taken place within a settlement framework which has evolved, and intensified man's control over the environment during a period of 8,000 years. For most of this time, up to about AD 850, the settlement pattern was almost exclusively rural with little evidence of town development, although there is ample evidence of extensive trading, skilled crafts, industrial work, and intellectual endeavour, for which early Christian Ireland was a world focus (Buchanan, 1970). Neither the major royal nor monastic centres of this Celtic period can be said to have been urban in form and, almost without exception, they failed to act as fixing points for later town development.

The urban form of settlement has generally been viewed as an intrusive element in the landscape, often associated with expansive epochs in the

[1] The author wishes to acknowledge the helpful comments of Michael O'Neill on an earlier draft of this chapter.

country's history and with periods of economic and cultural change.[2] The first wave of town building in Ireland followed after the Viking invasions in the mid-ninth century and almost all of the present-day major centres originated in this first period. A second wave of town development can be associated with the Norman invasions in the twelfth and thirteenth centuries. During this period earlier urban foundations were redeveloped and a widespread network of new urban centres was established throughout the South East and East of the country (Graham, 1977).

The third phase of town building can be directly linked to a series of colonial plantation endeavours in the sixteenth and seventeenth centuries (Butlin, 1977). Many of these towns were to flourish subsequently and the ground plans of some, especially those in Ulster, reflected earlier developments in European town planning and were to influence the pattern and layout adopted in many North American towns. As can be seen from Figure 11.1, much of the network of towns had been completed by 1692 and 'Connacht was the only one of the four provinces that could still be regarded as under-urbanized' (Andrews, 1976). By this date the network of towns was also well connected by a system of roads, focusing predominantly on Dublin.

By the end of the seventeenth century, Dublin was a flourishing capital city and together with its suburbs was said to be one of the 'greatest and best peopled towns in Europe' (MacLysaght, 1939). By the year 1700 Dublin was firmly established as the locale of a centralized administration in Ireland and had asserted its primacy within the urban hierarchy; the population of Dublin at that date is put at about 70,000 compared to 25,000 in Cork and 11,000 in Limerick (Butlin, 1965). Throughout the late seventeenth and eighteenth centuries the existing urban pattern was augmented by the creation of numerous new towns and villages as well as the redevelopment or enlargement of existing settlements. Virtually all Irish towns were founded before 1800 and Cullen has said with justification that 'essentially the Irish rural town started as a village planned in the seventeenth or eighteenth centuries which prospered and, by the end of the eighteenth century, had outgrown its modest origins' (Cullen, 1979). An improved network of roads as well as a new canal system linked up the major centres and served to further reinforce the dominance of Dublin.

The story of Ireland from 1801 to 1921 is largely of a country devoid of a resident parliament, of an economy increasingly bypassed by technological and organizational innovations and of a society dominated by unemployment, poverty, and famine, in which mass emigration provided the only available solution (Green, 1969). The contribution of the nineteenth century

---

[2] This view is expressed by Jones-Hughes (1959), pp. 11-27. More recently Simms (1979) amongst others, argues that urban genesis was not just an imported innovation but has to be viewed within the wider context of European trade and political revitalization.

Fig. 11.1 Towns and Principal Roads, c.1692
Source: J. H. Andrews, 'Land and People, c.1685', *The New History of Ireland* (eds. T. W. Moody, F. X. Martin, and F. J. Byrne), vol.III, Clarendon Press, Oxford, 1976, p. 470

lies not in urban growth but in the gradual evolution of administrative reform and innovation in the fields of public health, education, housing, and local government. Thus the Local Government (Ireland) Act, 1898, established the system of local administration which still exists and continues to focus upon Dublin as the control centre. The great achievement of the nineteenth century—the development of the railways—was largely based on the principle of providing 'the greatest amount of accommodation at the least expense of construction and maintenance' (Horner, 1977). In practice this inevitably meant a Dublin-centred system and further reinforced the role of the capital city which, by 1901, was more than five times the size of Cork.

The 1921-59 Period

The period after the granting of Irish independence in 1921 can be divided into two contrasting phases, each with different implications for the settlement system. The first phase up to 1959 represented a continuation of nineteenth century conditions and problems with emigration and economic stagnation as the dominant factors. The second phase beginning in 1958-9 represents a period of unparalleled growth and development.

Between the census years of 1926 and 1961 the population of the country declined by 5.2 per cent as emigration continued. All but five counties lost population over this period and many of the western 'rural' counties lost over one quarter of their population. The aggregate rural population declined by just over 500,000 as agricultural employment declined by 42 per cent. By the 1950s emigration from Ireland was in excess of 40,000 per annum and there were dire predictions that the total population might not exceed 2 million before the end of the century (O'Brien, 1954, pp. 15-45).

The only counties to experience a net growth in population over the 35 year period were those on the east coast where growth was largely explained as a consequence of urban overspill. While the rural population declined, the aggregate urban population increased from 32.3 per cent in 1926 to 46.4 per cent in 1961. The urban population grew by 340,000 of which over 60 per cent was accounted for by the growth of Dublin. In 1926 Dublin City and the adjacent county accounted for only 17.0 per cent of the national population; by 1961 the area contained 25.5 per cent of total population. Outside Dublin urban growth was limited with many towns suffering population decline and economic disinvestment. Even during the 1951-61 decade few towns outside the Dublin area experienced continuous growth and the majority of smaller and more remote towns experienced a continuous loss in numbers. Again between 1956 and 1961 'all size categories of towns under 5,000 suffered a serious loss of numbers' and this decline was widespread except in the East of the country (Bannon, 1975).

As a consequence of population redistribution and the differential impacts of emigration, Ireland was by 1961 a relatively highly urbanized country with a greater share of the population resident in the Dublin ag- glomeration, which offered the functional diversity and range of attractions of a capital city (Schöller, 1978).

The 1959-79 Period

In contrast to the prolonged history of decline, the last twenty years have been years of growth, development, and rapid change. The factors which have led to a dramatic change in Ireland's economic performance since 1958 are many and complex. On the international scene, there was increased demand for consumer goods coupled with a labour scarcity in many indus- trial economies. On the domestic front a new political leadership, a shift in emphasis from agriculture to industrially-led growth, the removal of protec- tionist policies, the introduction of incentives to attract overseas invest- ment, the implementation of a five-year development programme, and an evident willingness to innovate, all combined and helped create the confi- dence necessary for an economic 'take-off'. In consequence Ireland has witnessed twenty years of almost continuous growth and expansion which stands in stark contrast to the preceding century of decline and stagnation.

From 1961 to 1966 continued high levels of natural increase coupled with a halving of the rates of emigration resulted in a 2.3 per cent growth in population. The growth of population, however, was almost entirely con- fined to the larger urban areas and their adjacent rural districts. The more remote western rural areas continued to lose population at rates reminiscent of the 1950s; the aggregate population of smaller town-size groups remained static (Table 11.1), and many smaller towns in the West of the country were unable to retain their 1961 population levels (Johnson, 1968). Growth, whether urban or rural, was largely confined to the East of the country where Dublin increased its population by 72,000 and the East region (see Figure 11.2) grew by 83,000. By 1966 Dublin was almost six times the size of Cork—the second largest city. Writing about the urban pattern of the mid-1960s Forbes described the dominance of Dublin as 'an extraordinary isolated giant' dominating the East and Midlands of the country; she also identified a ridge of medium density urban coverage in the South of the country but showed that the West and North West had little access to urban foci (Forbes, 1970).

With a natural increase rate of 10.1 per 1,000 per annum and emigration at only 3.7 per 1,000, the period 1966-71 witnessed a further 3.3 per cent growth in population. Once again rural population continued to decline but the extent of the territory affected by decline was much less than in the preceding quinquennium and the rate of decline was generally less severe (Parker, 1972). But once again growth was largely confined to the East and South East.

Table 11.1: *Population by Size of Urban Place, Ireland, 1961-71*

Size of Centre	1961		1966		1971		% change in cumulative population of each group	% of total population in each group 1971
	Number of towns	Population	Number of towns	Population	Number of towns	Population		
200-499	255	78,709	256	78,296	199	63,988	− 18.7	2.1
500-1,499	156	131,122	157	131,432	152	129,348	− 1.4	4.3
1,500-2,999	46	104,333	48	107,296	41	89,460	− 14.3	3.0
3,000-4,999	21	84,139	22	88,743	24	91,122	+ 8.3	3.1
5,000-9,999	17	106,311	19	122,684	22	139,060	+ 30.8	4.7
10,000-150,000	14	336,741	14	365,374	16	419,694	+ 24.5	14.1
Dublin area	1	663,389	1	734,967	1	852,219	+ 28.5	28.7
Rural areas	—	1,309,363	—	1,255,210	—	1,193,357	− 8.9	40.0
Total population	—	2,818,341	—	2,884,002	—	2,978,248	+ 5.7	—
% Rural		46.6		43.5		40.0	—	—
% In towns over 200		53.4		56.6		60.0	—	—

Source: *Census of Population*, Dublin Stationery Office, 1966-71. Up to 1971 Dublin is inclusive of suburbs and Dun Laoghaire. The total for 1971 is that for the sub-region, including Dublin City, Dun Laoghaire and County Dublin. In this table the statistics allow both for changes in boundaries and definitional changes by the Central Statistical Office. The 1979 Census of Population does not permit a similar degree of disaggregation.

Region and county boundaries
.... **County boundaries**

DONEGAL

Sligo

NORTH-WEST

NORTH-EAST

Dundalk

Drogheda

WEST

Athlone

MIDLANDS

Dublin

Dun Laoghaire

EAST

Galway

Bray

Ennis

MID-WEST

Carlow

Kilkenny

Limerick

SOUTH-EAST

Tralee

Clonmel

Wexford

Waterford

persons
— 500,000

SOUTH-WEST

Cork

Population of Towns

— 200,000
— 100,000
— 50,000

— 10,000

0   80 Kilometres

Fig. 11.2 Urban Centres and Planning Regions, 1971
Source: Bannon, 1979b

For the first time the 1971 Census showed that the majority of the population were resident in aggregate urban areas and much of the rural expansion could be best explained in terms of the outward expansion of population from larger towns. As Table 11.2 shows, both the number and demographic importance of smaller urban settlements declined and the natural increase and migration patterns reinforced the importance of larger centres, especially Dublin.

The East region had the highest birth rate and the lowest death rate of any region from 1966 to 1971. It was also the only region experiencing net immigration—estimated at 15,000 for the year 1970-1. But unlike the 1961-6 period, when the East region's population grew by more than that of the country as a whole, from 1966 to 1971 the population growth of the East region represented the equivalent of 77.7 per cent of the total population increase and other centres such as Cork, Limerick, Waterford and the North East also grew significantly. The distribution of urban places can be seen in Figure 11.2.

The results of the *Census of Population* 1979 (which are not yet available by city-size category) indicate that developments during the 1970s represented a major change away from trends during the preceding decade. Net emigration was replaced by a positive migration balance of 109,000 during the 1971-9 period (Hughes and Walsh, 1980). Likewise every region experienced a positive migration balance, although only the East and Donegal exceeded the national rate. Natural increase rates remained high, especially in the East region, and all but one county witnessed population growth. As can be seen from Figure 11.3, the pattern of growth was much more wide-

Table 11.2: *Population Changes in the Intercensal Period 1971-1979 for each Planning Region*

Planning Region*	Population		Population Change 1971-79	
	1971	1979	Number	Percentage
East	1,061,914	1,255,533	193,619	+ 18.2
South West	465,655	516,474	50,819	+ 10.9
South East	328,604	366,788	38,184	+ 11.6
North East	174,117	190,231	16,114	+ 9.3
Mid West	269,804	300,802	30,998	+ 11.5
Donegal	108,344	121,941	13,597	+ 12.5
Midlands	232,427	252,137	19,710	+ 8.5
West	258,748	281,857	23,109	+ 8.9
North West	78,635	82,454	3,819	+ 4.9
TOTAL	2,978,248	3,368,217	389,969	+ 13.1

* Regions as mapped in Figure 11.2.
Source: *Census of Population*, Vol. 1, 1979, Table H.

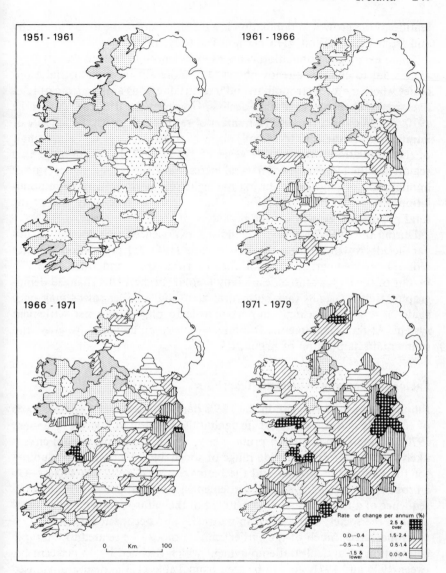

Fig. 11.3 Intercensal Population Changes, 1951-71
Source: Horner and Daultrey, 1980

spread than anything that had happened previously and areas of population decline are few in number and peripherally located. In an analysis of 1971-9 population changes Horner and Daultrey concluded that, generally, growth rates were consistently higher and rates of decline lower in the eastern half of the country; they also argue that the changeover from decline to growth occurred earlier in districts with larger towns, and they conclude that 'one feature of the growth in population is a diffusion down the urban hierarchy and from East to West' (Horner and Daultrey, 1980).

To an extent the population changes experienced in Ireland from 1971-9 are similar to changes already observed in more advanced industrial economies where major metropolitan and industrial regions are in a state of relative or even absolute population decline. However, the Irish case during the 1970s is also quite different in a number of respects; there was a high rate of immigration to the country, family size was relatively large and almost half of the population was under 25 years of age in 1977. In addition the East region had the highest rate of natural increase and the second highest rate of immigration of any region during the eight year period. In fact the population increase of the East region (193,619) represented exactly half of the total population growth for the period.

During the 1959-79 period Ireland has experienced two decades of unparalleled growth. During the first decade (1961-71) population changes reduced the demographic importance of rural areas and small towns in favour of the larger centres, especially Dublin. In the 1970s changed demographic trends suggest that both rural areas and smaller towns may once again have an increasingly important role to play within the settlement system. At the same time the Dublin agglomeration continues to grow and to maintain its position of primacy.

Factors Underlying Settlement Transition

Empirical work by Hannan in the 1960s demonstrated that a complex web of economic and social factors lie behind the decision to migrate (Hannan, 1970). In the Irish context a primate city, which is also the capital city, is likely to offer a relatively wide range of social and economic opportunities for the young, the mobile, and the better educated groups in society. On a broad scale, the changes in the settlement system outlined above are a consequence of a fundamental readjustment of the nature of work and employment in the society as reflected in industrial and occupational data.

As indicated, much of the earlier emigration can be related to the rapid contraction of agricultural employment which declined by 42 per cent between 1926 and 1971. As can be seen from Table 11.3 agriculturally-based employment had declined to less than one fifth of total employment by 1977. This decline had its most serious repercussions on the settlement pattern of the congested, small farming counties of Western Ireland. By contrast the share of jobs in the industrial sector (including building and construction) increased by 26.6 per cent over the period. A considerable amount of the growth of this sector arose from the vigorous industrial development policies pursued by the Industrial Development Authority (IDA) which, over the 1978-82 period, plans to create 75,000 new manufacturing jobs to be located mostly on the IDA's land bank holdings at 120

Table 11.3: *Changes in Employment by Sector 1961-1977*

Sector	1961		1971		1977	
	Number employed	% Share of employ-ment	Number employed	% Share of employ-ment	Number employed	% Share of employ-ment
Agriculture	379,491	36.1	273,079	25.9	217,500	20.8
Industry	257,178	24.4	322,749	30.6	325,500	31.2
Service	415,870	39.5	459,011	43.5	500,400	48.0
TOTAL	1,052,539	100.0	1,054,839	100.0	1,043,400	100.0

Source: *Census of Population* 1961 and 1971 and EEC *Labour Force Survey* of Ireland, 1977.

locations throughout Ireland (IDA, 1979). Such dispersionist industrial policies have clearly contributed to the settlement changes occurring during the 1970s. But it is the service sector which has accounted for the major share of new job creation since 1961 and which has also had the most consistent history of growth since 1926. An analysis of the service sector shows that the growth categories in terms of employment are those associated with the handling of information and having a high proportion of their labour force in white-collar and/or office jobs. Indeed much of the recent change in both industrial and service employment can only be understood in terms of occupational rather than sectoral change (Bannon, Eustace and Power, 1977).

Just over one half of the new jobs created between 1961 and 1971 were white-collar jobs; one in every three new jobs in industry and eight out of every ten new jobs in services created between 1961 and 1971 were office jobs. More recent statistics are not sufficiently disaggregated to identify office employment trends but the aggregated data suggests that the 1960s' trends have continued through the 1970s as well and may have been accelerated by the emphasis placed on the attraction of high technology electronics firms. In terms of spatial distribution, white-collar employment, especially higher grade professional work, is very highly concentrated in the East region and the degree of regional concentration has intensified over time (Table 11.4). An examination of the regional share of office jobs showed a close correlation with the size of the largest urban centre in each region (Bannon and Eustace, 1978).

The high degree of administrative concentration in the East region and specifically within Central Dublin is a reflection of the highly centralized nature of most aspects of Irish life including industry, government, finance, the arts, and even voluntary agencies. The extent of this concentration can be seen from Table 11.5 and is also reflected in both the pattern of goods

Table 11.4: *Regional Distribution of White-collar Work, 1961-71*

Region	NUMBERS EMPLOYED		CHANGE		Percentage Share of Total Change	PERCENTAGE DISTRIBUTION		
	1961	1971	Number 1961-71	Percentage 1961-71		1961	1971	Change in % points 1961-71
East	128,075	163,617	35,542	27.8	59.6	46.7	49.0	+2.3
South West	39,324	46,038	6,714	17.1	11.3	14.3	13.8	-0.5
South East	25,509	29,771	4,262	16.7	7.1	9.3	8.9	-0.4
Mid West	20,461	25,349	4,888	23.9	8.2	7.5	7.6	+0.1
West	17,682	20,670	2,988	16.9	5.0	6.4	6.2	-0.2
Midlands	15,992	18,547	2,555	16.0	4.3	5.8	5.6	-0.2
North East	14,111	16,154	2,043	14.5	3.4	5.1	4.8	-0.3
Donegal	7,161	7,841	680	9.5	1.1	2.6	2.3	-0.3
North West	6,178	6,170	-8	-0.1	—	2.3	1.8	-0.5
TOTAL STATE	274,493	334,157	59,664	21.7	100.0	100.0	100.0	—

Source: Census of Population, Occupation Vols. 1961 and 1971.

Table 11.5: *Miscellaneous Measures of Concentration in the East Region*

Organizations	Total Number in State	Percentage in East Region
Headquarters offices of:		
Central Government Departments	17	100
Embassies accredited to Ireland	22	100
State sponsored bodies	87	86
Commercial State bodies	20	90
Trade, professional and other organizations	503	93
Trade unions	65	93
Largest public quoted companies	50	90
Banking institutions	41	95
Hire purchase firms	41	71
Insurance companies	31	100
Publishing companies	47	89
Advertising agencies	36	97
Full-time university students 1974/75	19,709	64
General service grades in Civil Service of Principal Officer level or above 1976	341	100
Office employees 1971	170,000	59

Source: Administration Yearbook and Diary 1976 and information supplied by the Department of the Public Service.

flows and information flows (Figure 11.4). Describing the pattern of accessibility in Ireland, O'Sullivan states:

Dublin, the centre of the arterial road network, the area of greatest population concentration and growth, is the central focus of this system. Its direct dominance, over-riding the influence of such large centres as Dundalk, Drogheda, and Athlone, spreads deep into the Central Plain and along the East coast. Within a 100 mile radius the influence of Dublin appears to have limited the extent of sub-nodal systems to a few subordinates. Beyond this penumbra there are fairly extensive sub-nodal systems focussed on Waterford, Cork, Tralee, Limerick, Galway, Sligo, and Letterkenny (O'Sullivan, 1968, p.200).

Ireland's urban system compares closely to the theoretical models of urban contact and urban social environments formulated by the European Free Trade Association (EFTA, 1973). Thus, the number of workers in the information sector and the pattern of information flows are both highly focused on Dublin; contact potentials fall off very quickly with distance from Dublin and Dublin has no competitor as a centre for decision-making or related activities (Bannon, 1979a).

The concentration of decision-making work in Dublin means that peripheral urban centres have relatively few of the prestige, highly-paid control functions of either the private or the public sector. Thus such centres are

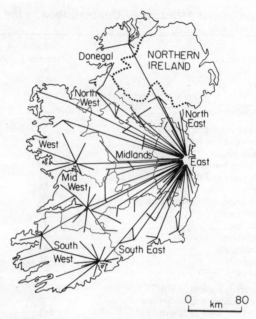

Fig. 11.4 Urban Nodal Structure defined by Telephone Traffic
Source: O'Sullivan, 1968, p. 199

deprived of the entrepreneurial skill and innovative capacity associated with this type of work. They are also deprived of the social advantages and multiplier effects of having a share of national control functions. Empirical communication studies have shown that most recorded communications in Dublin constitute a closed system wherein virtually all the participants are Dublin-based and decisions affecting the whole country are reached and handed down the administrative hierarchy without reference to the periphery. Conversely, office firms in regional centres are required to refer virtually all major decisions to the Dublin-based or overseas headquarters and virtually all subcontracting work and other important linkage benefits are leaked from the periphery to the capital or to overseas (Bannon, 1978a).

Administrative concentration in Dublin has resulted in a major white-collar and office property boom in the city. In the absence of substantial improvements in both roads and telecommunications, few private firms are likely to opt to vacate the environs of the capital. At the same time the government has shown little desire to help the situation either through the relocation of its own decision-making staff or the reorganization and strengthening of local government administration so as to retain and strengthen local decision-making.[3]

[3] While some minor schemes involving the relocation of routine staff have been initiated or planned such relocations do not diminish the degree of control located in Dublin; neither do they appear as part of a clearly defined plan aimed at strengthening the urban system outside the capital.

The importance of Dublin as a centre of administrative control is also paralleled by the importance of the capital city as a centre of retail trade and as the country's highest order central place. Studies conducted in the mid-1960s showed that Dublin was the highest order central place and also that it had almost exclusive and total domination in trade for higher order goods and services within a fifty mile radius. Regional centres have emerged in the South and West but much of the North West of the country is devoid of higher order centres and heavily dependent upon Dublin as the dominant central place (Bannon, 1978b).

Strategies for the Regulation of Urban Development

Faced with the prospect of population and employment growth, the Irish government during the 1960s sought advice on the optimum form of a national strategy for physical development which would be consistent with the existing social and economic policies as proclaimed in the *Second Programme for Economic Expansion, 1964-9*. Opinion was deeply divided between those who saw the economic advantages of concentrating development and those who emphasized the social advantages of dispersal. In an effort to overcome these conflicting views and to arrive at a suitable national strategy consultants were appointed to prepare a report on *Regional Studies in Ireland* (Buchanan *et al.*, 1969). The consultants' report forecast that population could be expected to increase by approximately 500,000 between 1966 and 1986 and they analyzed the likely implications of five development strategies ranging from dispersal to concentration in Dublin. The consultants recommended a regional strategy which had as its main elements:
1) Limitation of the growth of Dublin to its natural increase level only,
2) Promotion of Cork and Limerick as national level centres,
3) Promotion of six other 'regional centres'.
The degree of spatial discrimination and governmental intervention involved in the implementation of the proposals, however, was politically unpalatable. When the government finally supported the urban strategy 'as planning-base figures' some three years later that statement of support was not backed by any policy instruments to enable its implementation. In fact the IDA was simultaneously allowed to embark on a programme of industrial development in 47 'town clusters' comprising some 200 towns and villages (IDA, 1972).

Subsequently, as the economic recession of the mid-1970s adversely affected old established industry, particularly in Dublin, the government admitted abandoning regional policy in favour of nationwide development. Ironically high unemployment rates amongst the less skilled in the Dublin area forced government approval for the IDA to actively promote Dublin as a location for foreign manufacturing investment.

Dublin has proved highly attractive for investment in large-scale high-technology projects, benefiting from the skilled labour pool of the capital city as well as having easy access to universities and research institutes. While the advisory National Economic and Social Council (NESC, 1979) committee continued to press for a regional policy based on a limited number of urban centres there seemed to be little official concern that current policies could further escalate the growth and reinforce the dominance of the Dublin agglomeration.

Growth and Restructuring of the Dublin Agglomeration[4]

The preceding sections have shown that Dublin is central to and dominates any analysis of the Irish urban system. Dublin dominates in terms of size, diversity of economic activity and, above all, it dominates as the control centre of the country and all branches of the economy.

The rapid growth of Dublin can be traced back to the mid-seventeenth century when the city had only a population of about 9,000 (Haughton, 1949). Most of the subsequent 150 years were years of growth and expansion and by 1800 Dublin's population approximated 200,000. Despite the economic stagnation that characterized much of the nineteenth and early twentieth century, Dublin continued to grow; however, much of its population was accommodated in high-density tenement quarters rather than in new suburban growth. Many of the grand seventeenth- and eighteenth-century fashionable developments were to become slums before the end of the nineteenth century and to provide Dublin with its 'inner city' problem in the twentieth century.

The population of the Dublin sub-region has doubled since the establishment of the Irish State in 1921; between 1926 and 1979 the population increased by 48.6 per cent to reach 984,000. The continued growth of the Dublin sub-region does, however, conceal some varying trends within the area. In 1926 just over half of the total population of the sub-region resided in the wards of the eighteenth-century city; since then the population of these wards has declined from 268,000 to less than 100,000 and the population of these inner areas now accounts for a mere 10 per cent of the population of the sub-region. By the 1960s population decline had spread to suburban wards and the areas developed prior to World War II began to register population loss.

[4] Any analysis of demographic or spatial change in Dublin has to deal with a wide range of terms: (1) Dublin City or County Borough administered by the Corporation of Dublin had a population of 544,586 in 1979; (2) The Dublin built-up area including the city, its suburbs and the independent Borough of Dun Laoghaire had a population of 778,000 in 1971 (data not available in 1979 Census); (3) The Dublin sub-region is the name given to the area administered by Dublin city, Dun Laoghaire Borough and Dublin County. With a population of 984,000 in 1979 it is a fast-growing area and roughly corresponds to the Dublin Metropolitan Economic Labour Area; (4) The East Region comprising the Dublin sub-region and the adjacent counties of Meath, Kildare and Wicklow, with population of 1,255,000 in 1979.

The 1979 Census returns demonstrate that most of the wards of Dublin City and Borough of Dun Laoghaire lost population during the 1970s as did some wards within Dublin County. On the other hand wards on the urban periphery, encompassing the new suburbs, experienced very high rates of growth, as did adjacent wards and municipalities beyond the built-up area of the city. The impact of Dublin's growth was being felt more and more widely throughout much of the East region. The results of recent demographic changes have brought about the emergence of clearly defined social areas within the Dublin built-up area.

The suburbanization of Dublin's population has resulted from forces operating in both the public- and the private-sector housing markets. The public authorities saw the surburban development of public housing as the principal means of reducing high densities and overcrowding within the old eighteenth-century city. Likewise the search for low-density private housing favoured the large-scale development of private estates. As a measure of the scale of suburban encroachment upon agricultural land it has been estimated that about 1,000 acres (400 hectares) per year are being lost to urban expansion in the Dublin area (Bannon, 1979). Residential decentralization was also accompanied by a large-scale movement of industry and wholesale uses from the inner city and the port to peripheral estates. Of the 4,000 acres (1600 hectares) currently zoned for industrial development virtually all is located on the urban periphery, mostly to the west of the built-up area. There has also been a major suburbanization of convenience shopping facilities.

The only exception to the decentralizing process has been the rapid expansion of the office industry within the central area. Here new office development has dislocated residential uses, created a boom in property and land, and also intensified the scale of commuting from suburban homes to city centre jobs.

The continuing rapid growth of Dublin coupled with the scale of internal change poses particular problems for those concerned with urban government and management. These problems are made all the more difficult since administrative reforms are long overdue, physical planning is a relatively new art, and resources are inadequate to meet the demands which arise.

Planning the Development of the Dublin Agglomeration

Development planning is implemented by the Planning Authorities through the powers given to them under the Local Government (Planning and Development) Acts 1963 and 1976; there are three planning authorities within the Dublin sub-region and some thirteen within the East region. Rather than dealing with the minutiae of development planning as operated through five-year development plans, this section outlines the overall strategy for the long-term development of the Dublin agglomeration.

Although there were earlier plans for Dublin,[5] the document which has laid the overall basis for development policy has been the *Dublin Regional Report* submitted by Wright in 1967. The report, which examined Dublin within a region of some 30 miles (48 km) radius from central Dublin, forecast that between 1966 and 1986 the population would grow by roughly 300,000 and that about 150,000 new jobs would have to be accommodated in the region. In terms of location, Wright forecast that virtually all this growth would take place adjacent to the existing built-up area and that it should be accommodated in four satellite 'new towns' to the west separated from the existing built-up area and from each other by green wedges of open land. It was envisaged that these 'new towns' would have a high degree of self sufficiency.

Although never formally adopted by the government, the Wright report strategy strongly influenced the development plans for Dublin, especially the plans for Dublin county. More peripheral development is being allowed than was envisaged in the Wright report; nevertheless, the majority of all expected growth is being channelled into these developments to the west of the city broadly in line with Wright's 'new towns'.

The Dublin County Draft Development Plan Review (1980) forecast that the population of the Dublin sub-region may increase from 984,000 in 1979 to over 1,500,000 in 1991. Such a growth in population and labour-force will place very great demands upon the creation of employment and the provision of education and welfare facilities. Thus, the Blanchardstown suburb with a 1979 population of 18,700 may have an ultimate population of 100,000 while Ronanstown may also grow from 27,500 in 1979 to 100,000. The third suburb of Tallaght with 40,000 in 1979 may grow to over 100,000. All three suburban developments are being planned on a neighbourhood unit principle; large tracts of land are being made available for manufacturing and warehousing and in the proposed 'town centres' it is hoped to provide a wide range of convenience and durable goods sales as well as a range of white-collar and office jobs.

The land use strategy will be complemented by a transportation strategy with an eighty-mile-long (128 km) motorway encircling the built-up area and an emphasis on public transport, particularly bus-ways in the centre.[6]

---

[5] In 1916 P. Abercrombie prepared a plan for Dublin entitled *Dublin of the Future*. In 1939 he again prepared a plan entitled *Dublin: A Sketch Development Plan*. The first was strongly influenced by the Beaux Arts School and by the work of Haussmann and Henard in France. In contrast the second plan was dominated by the ideology and thinking of the English green belt planning model.

[6] The transportation strategy follows the recommendations of the report *Transport in Dublin*, An Foras Forbartha, Dublin, 1971, 2 vols.

The development strategy has been designed within the context of growth up to 1986/91 within the Dublin sub-region. Since Dublin has grown more rapidly than anticipated in the 1970s, since much of that growth is happening in areas outside the Dublin sub-region and since growth may continue through into the 1990s there is a clear need for a strategy to determine the scale and location of growth in the longer term and also to offer guidance on the optimum mix of physical, economic, and social programmes to be followed.

Conclusion

This paper has outlined some of the major changes in Ireland's economic fortune and the related changes in the settlement system. During the 1970s all sizes of urban settlements as well as rural areas experienced widespread population growth. Unlike some of the more advanced economies, the 1970s saw the continued growth of the primate, capital city agglomeration which accounted for almost half of the total population increase from 1971 to 1979.

The big issue is whether the pattern of growth experienced in the 1970s is likely to continue or if it is desirable to induce changes in the pattern of growth. For one thing, the rapid spate of house construction in rural areas during much of the 1970s may have been accelerated by specific development policies. These policies have now been reversed on the basis of infrastructure, energy, and environmental costs and the emphasis has shifted to the 'desirability of developing the concept of urban growth' and 'the expansion of towns and villages'.[7]

Much of the growth of smaller towns may have been in large part due to the dispersal policies pursued by the Industrial Development Authority in respect of new manufacturing industry. While such policies have clear social benefits for recipient locations, the equity benefits of such policies may conflict with efficiency objectives at the national level. Unfortunately there has been no objective assessment of the costs and benefits of these development policies to date.

At the other end of the settlement system, Dublin continues to expand, particularly in response to the growth of the information industry; as employment becomes increasingly concentrated in this sector the unique advantages of Dublin as a capital city, and as a centre of research and knowledge, may serve to intensify rather than diminish concentration. While there has been a long debate in Ireland on development centres and while some still argue that 'the growth centre concept is still a valid one in the Irish context' (O'Farrell, 1978), the government has failed to introduce a development centre policy and has confined itself to commenting on the disadvantages of the 'over rapid development of larger urban concentrations'

[7] Department of Environment, *Circular No. P.D. 280*, 1980, 2 pp.

(DOE, 1980). However, it is not without significance that many of those countries experiencing 'counter-urbanization' tendencies during the 1970s, have pursued strong decentralization policies and that much of the migration has been in the form of 'dispersed concentration' to a limited number of small- and medium-sized cities. In the Irish case, reducing the rate of growth of the Dublin agglomeration would depend heavily upon the re-direction of activities in the information sector which, in turn, inevitably entails the pursuit of an urban policy within a context of administrative reform.

Major issues have to be tackled in the absence of adequate knowledge of how the urban system works; little is known about flows within the system or how these may be changing. The little evidence we do have points to a high degree of self sufficiency in the Dublin agglomeration, with other settlements in a largely dependent role. To a large extent policies have been promoted on faith rather than on knowledge. Finally, concern about the size distribution of elements in the settlement system has to be paralleled by a much more active concern about quality of life issues for all social groups in settlements at every size level.

REFERENCES

Andrews, J. H. 1976. 'Land and People c. 1685'. In Moody *et al.* (eds.) *A New History of Ireland*, Vol. III. Oxford: Clarendon Press.

Bannon, M. J. 1973. *Office Location in Ireland: The Role of Central Dublin.* Dublin: An Foras Forbartha.

Bannon, M. J. 1975. 'The Republic of Ireland'. In Jones R. (ed.) *Essays on World Urbanization*. London: George Philip.

Bannon, M. J. 1978a. *Office and White Collar Activities: The Role of Waterford.* Waterford, South East Regional Development Organization (SERDO).

Bannon, M. J. 1978b. 'Processes and Patterns of Urbanization in Ireland', *Geographia Polonica*, 34: 94-6.

Bannon, M. J. 1979a. 'Office Concentration in Dublin and its Consequences for Regional Development in Ireland'. In Daniels, P. W. (ed.) *Spatial Patterns of Office Growth and Location*. New York: John Wiley & Sons.

Bannon, M. J. 1979b. 'Urban Land'. In Gillmor, D. (ed.) *Irish Resources and Land Use*. Dublin: Institute of Public Administration (IPA).

Bannon, M. J. and Eustace, J. G. 1978. *The Role of the Tertiary Sector in Regional Policy: A Comparative Report: Ireland.* Prepared for the EEC.

Bannon, M. J., Eustace, J. G., and Power, M. 1977. *Service Type Employment and Regional Development*. National Economic and Social Council (NESC) Report No. 28.

Bannon, M. J. *et al.* (in press). *Urbanization: Problems of Growth and Decay.* Dublin: NESC.

Bartels, D. 1980. 'Theoretical and Methodological Aspects of Research on National

Settlement Systems', *National Settlement Systems: Topical and National Reports.* Warsaw: Polish Academy of Sciences.

Buchanan, R. H. 1970. 'Rural Settlement in Ireland'. In Stephens, N. and Glasscock, R. (eds.) *Irish Geographical Studies.* Belfast.

Buchanan, C. *et al.* 1969. *Regional Studies in Ireland.* Dublin: An Foras Forbartha.

Butlin, R. A. 1965. 'The Population of Dublin in the Late Seventeenth Century', *Irish Geography*, 5, 2: 51-66.

Butlin, R. A. (ed.). 1977. *The Development of the Irish Town.* London: Croom Helm.

Cullen, L. M. 1979. *Irish Towns and Villages.* Dublin: Easons.

Dublin Corporation. 1975. *Shopping in Dublin: An Analysis of Existing Provision and A Projection of Future Requirements.* Working Paper No. 8.

Dept. of the Environment. 1980. *Circular No. P.D. 280.* Dublin.

European Free Trade Association. 1973. *National Settlement Strategies: A Framework for Regional Development.* Geneva.

Forbes, J. 1970. 'Towns and Planning in Ireland'. In Stephens, N. and Glasscock, R. (eds.) *Irish Geographical Studies.* Belfast.

Graham, B. J. 1977. 'The Towns of Medieval Ireland'. In Butlin, R. A. (ed.) *The Development of the Irish Town.* London: Croom Helm.

Green, E. R. R. 1969. 'Industrial Decline in the Nineteenth Century'. In Cullen, L. M. (ed.) *The Formation of the Irish Economy.* Cork: Mercier Press.

Hannan, D. 1970. *Rural Exodus.* London: Chapman.

Hansen, N. M. and Korcelli, P. 1978. 'The Development of Urban Agglomerations Within the National Settlement System', *Geographia Polonica*, 39: 211-22.

Haughton, J. P. 1949. 'The Social Geography of Dublin', *Geographical Review*, Vol. 39: 257-77.

Horner, A. 1977. 'Planning the Irish Transport Network: Parallels in Nineteenth and Twentieth Century Proposals', *Irish Geography*, 10: 46.

Horner, A. and Daultrey, S. 1980. 'Recent Population Changes in the Republic of Ireland', *Area*, 12, 2: 129-35.

Hughes, J. C. and Walsh, B. 1980. *Internal Migration Flows in Ireland and Their Determinants.* Dublin, Economic and Social Research Institute (ESRI).

IDA. 1972. *Regional Industrial Plans, 1973-7. Part I.* Dublin.

IDA. 1979. *IDA Industrial Plan 1978-82.* Dublin.

Johnson, J. H. 1968. 'Population Change in Ireland, 1961-1966', *Irish Geography*, 5, 5: 470-7.

Jones-Hughes, T. 1959. 'The Origin and Growth of Towns in Ireland', *University Review*, 11, 7: 11-27.

MacLysaght, E. 1939. *Irish Life in the Seventeenth Century.* Quote by M. Jouvain de Rochfort.

NESC. 1979. *Urbanisation and Regional Development in Ireland*, Report No. 45, p. 17.

O'Brien, J. A. 1954. *The Vanishing Irish.* London: W. H. Allen.

O'Farrell, P. N. 1978. 'Regional Planning Policy—An Appraisal'. Dublin, Mimeo (Conference Paper).

O'Sullivan, P. M. 1968. 'Accessibility and the Spatial Structure of the Irish Economy'. *Regional Studies*, Vol. 2: 200.

OECD. 1977. *Regional Policies: The Current Outlook.* Paris: OECD.

Parker, A. J. 1979. 'Ireland: A Consideration of the 1971 Census of Population', *Area*, 4, 1: 31-8.

Ryan, W. J. L. 1967. 'Industrial Development in National Economic Expansion', *Industrial Development and the Development Plan*. Dublin: An Foras Forbartha.

Scholler, P. 1978. 'The Role of the Capital City Within the National Settlement System', *Geographia Polonica*, 39: 223-4.

Simms, A. 1979. Medieval Dublin: A Topographic Analysis', *Irish Geography*, Vol. 12: 25-41.

Wright, M. 1967. *The Dublin Region: Advisory Regional Plan and Final Report*. Dublin: Stationery Office.

12 THE JAPANESE NATIONAL SETTLEMENT SYSTEM

TAKASHI YAMAGUCHI

Theoretical and Methodological Problems

Japan today is an urban-industrial nation. The population engaged in the primary industries is declining rapidly and now stands at less than ten per cent. The number of people engaged in secondary and tertiary industries continues to grow rapidly and has reached about 34 and 52 per cent of the working population, respectively, according to the latest census of 1975 (Table 12.1). In terms of contribution to national income, numbers of

Table 12.1: *Trends in Employment by Industry; 1900-75*

Year	(Percentages) Primary*	Secondary**	Tertiary
1900	70.0	11.8	18.2
1910	63.0	14.9	22.1
1920	53.8	20.5	23.7
1930	49.7	20.3	29.8
1940	44.3	26.0	29.0
1950	48.5	21.8	29.6
1955	41.1	23.4	35.5
1960	32.7	29.0	38.3
1965	24.7	32.2	43.0
1970	19.3	34.0	46.6
1975	13.9	34.1	51.7

Source: Bureau of Statistics

* Agriculture, forestry and fishing
** Mining, construction and manufacturing

people employed, and place of residence, Japan is a nation of people living and working in and around urban industrial concentrations, and more than 75 per cent of the nation's population is now officially classified as urban (Table 12.2).

There are still large areas which remain primarily rural in character, but the general trend almost everywhere in Japan is toward a concentration of population in the urban industrial areas. This trend has been in progress at least since the Meiji Restoration of 1868, although it was temporarily interrupted during World War II. Japan is becoming one vast metropolitan area which has a series of large, medium, and small concentrations of population

Table 12.2: *Numbers of Municipalities and Levels of Urbanization; 1920-75*

Year	No. of Cities	No. of Towns and Villages	Total	% of Total Pop. in Cities	Density of Pop. per sq. km in Cities
1920	83	12,161	12,224	18.0	7,341
1925	101	11,917	12,018	21.6	5,912
1930	109	11,755	11,864	24.0	5,234
1935	127	11,418	11,545	32.7	4,449
1940	168	11,022	11,190	37.7	3,115
1945	206	10,330	10,536	27.8	1,379
1950	254	10,246	10,500	37.3	1,548
1955	496	4,381	4,877	56.1	742
1960	561	3,013	3,574	63.3	720
1965	567	2,868	3,435	67.9	761
1970	588	2,743	3,331	72.1	792
1975	644	2,613	3,257	75.9	830

Source: Ministry of Internal Affairs and Bureau of Statistics

stretching from Hokkaido down to Kyushu, and the rural areas surrounding these concentrations are becoming more and more an integrated part of the national urban system.

Any study of urban areas in Japan is made particularly difficult by ambiguities in the definition of a city, changes in the definition, and in methods of compiling census data on urban population. Especially before the Amalgamation Act of 1953, the lack of an adequate definition made it difficult to determine the number and distribution of real urban areas. The term *shi*, usually translated as 'city', is unsatisfactory, for it refers to an urban administrative district which is often considerably overbounded in terms of the geographical city. There are several conditions necessary for designation as a city, but major consideration is given to a population size of 50,000 or more.

The Bureau of Statistics has recognized this tendency and the officials have gone so far as to develop an urban delimitation called 'Densely Inhabited District' (DID) that theoretically corresponds to the real urbanized area. The DIDs were delineated for the first time in the 1960 census in an attempt to improve the urban-rural classification of population. A DID is defined as an area within a *shi* (city), *machi* (town), or *mura* (village), consisting of a group of contiguous enumeration districts which have a density of 4,000 inhabitants or more per square kilometre and a total population of 5,000 or more.

With this new census category, there is now a fairly realistic definition of an urban area and data have been available for these areas every five years since 1960. In other words, it is now possible and more accurate to say that more than 57.0 per cent of Japan's population is urban, or lives in compact, densely populated communities of more than 5,000 inhabitants. In 1975, the aggregate area of the DIDs was only 2.2 per cent of the total area of

Japan, compared with 27.1 per cent for all *shi*. Some 71.8 per cent of the total *shi* population and 10.6 per cent of the *machi* and *mura* population resided within DIDs in that year (Table 12.3).

Table 12.3: *Proportion of Total Population and Area in DIDs; 1960-75*

Year	Population (%)	Area (%)	Total Population (000s)
1960	43.7	1.03	94.302
1965	48.1	1.23	99,209
1970	53.5	1.71	104,665
1975	57.0	2.19	111,937

Source: Bureau of Statistics

With over 75.0 per cent of the population now resident in the *shi* areas, it goes without saying that the social and economic life of Japan is vested in its cities and in the way these cities operate as an integrated system. Therefore, the subsequent analysis of the national settlement system can be limited to its urban sub-system.

Historical Growth and Development of the Japanese Urban System

Five stages of urbanization have been recognized through the long history of Japan. According to Masai (1978), these stages are ancient, medieval, feudal, modern, and contemporary urbanization; and distinctive systems of urban areas can be seen in each stage. Two of these are treated here.

The Urban System in Feudal Urbanization

It was not until the mid sixteenth century that cities with multiple functions began to appear. Some of the more important feudal clans started to build their castle towns on sites which were defensively and economically important. During the period of more than two and a half centuries of the Tokugawa Shogunate, several factors combined to favour a modest multiplication and growth of urban places. Among the most important of these were the spread of a commercial economy and the differentiation of occupational classes outside the predominantly farming population. Five major highways were constructed which radiated out to the various parts of the country from Edo (now Tokyo), the seat of Tokugawa rule, and sub-highways were built to connect the developing areas of specialized production with the great cities.

Four principal types of city origins may be noted during this period. These are castle towns, post towns, temple and shrine towns, and free ports and markets. Castle and post towns greatly outnumbered the others, but many towns had a combination of more than one function. Among these most of the castle towns (*jokamachi*) are still prosperous today since they were converted intentionally to political-commercial as well as cultural central-places after the end of this period so that they could easily meet the new spatial regime.

Massive urbanization in Japan developed in the seventeenth century when the many dispersed market towns, shrine centres, and military fortresses were displaced by centrally located cities. These coalesced around the castles of the Tokugawa military elite and their political dependents. Such cities dominated the countryside and acted as centres of administration, commerce, and culture.

Edo was by far the largest and most active of the castle towns, exceeding others in both population and functions. By 1700, Edo numbered nearly one million inhabitants. At the same time, Osaka and Kyoto each contained about three hundred thousand people, and ten per cent of the Japanese population lived in cities with over ten thousand inhabitants.

The Urban System in Modern Urbanization

The period between the Meiji Restoration of 1868 and World War II, was characterized by industrialization and the resultant metropolitanization. Japan's economic growth reached the take-off stage at the beginning of the twentieth century followed by that of maturity around 1940. By that time, the major industrial cities had developed in a belt between Tokyo and Nagasaki focusing on the four industrial zones of Tokyo-Yokohama, Nagoya, Osaka-Kobe, and Northern Kyushu.

In the first half of this century, the six metropolises of Tokyo, Osaka, Kyoto, Nagoya, Kobe, and Yokohama were forming as major urban foci in terms of economic, political, and social cohesion, and also in major population movements. Among them, Tokyo's growth was by far the most significant. Within these metropolises, suburban development spread outward along the radiating suburban railways and this trend set the direction for an expanding urban pattern due to metropolitanization. However, during World War II, more than two-thirds of the major cities were almost entirely destroyed. Only a few large cities escaped the air raids. Such was the case of Kyoto as well as Sapporo.

At the beginning of the 1960s, Japan as a whole entered the stage of high mass consumption. The inter-urban as well as intra-urban movements of people and goods continued to be very active and, in 1964, the Japan National Railways' New Tokaido Line (*Shinkansen*) inaugurated its service between Tokyo and Osaka, contributing to the formation of the Tokaido Megalopolis with its bipolar metropolitan nodes (Itoh, 1974). The line was later extended westward to Fukuoka in 1975. This enlarged Japanese Megalopolis includes 9 out of the 10 million-size cities and is intensively connected by the frequent shuttle service of the *Shinkansen* (Table 12.4).

Table 12.4: *Population in the Million-Cities; 1920-75 (in thousands)*

Rank	City	1920	1930	1940	1950	1960	1965	1970	1975A*	1975B**	1975***	Ratio of 1975 B/A
1	Tokyo	3,358	4,889	6,779	5,385	8,310	8,893	8,841	8,644	10,739	8,643	1.243
2	Osaka	1,787	2,478	3,301	2,015	3,012	3,156	2,980	2,779	3,761	2,778	1.353
3	Yokohama	561	702	968	951	1,376	1,789	2,238	2,622	2,370	2,385	0.904
4	Nagoya	660	991	1,415	1,157	1,697	1,935	2,036	2,080	2,379	1,949	1.144
5	Kyoto	725	977	1,119	1,120	1,285	1,365	1,419	1,461	1,572	1,363	1.076
6	Kobe	747	916	1,134	821	1,114	1,217	1,289	1,361	1,412	1,226	1.038
7	Sapporo	145	228	282	394	616	821	1,010	1,241	1,271	1,038	1.024
8	Kita-Kyushu	425	563	819	737	986	1,042	1,042	1,058	1,117	891	1.056
9	Kawasaki	85	148	301	319	633	855	973	1,015	980	972	0.966
10	Fukuoka	233	324	402	488	682	769	872	1,002	1,124	859	1.122
	% of the Total Million-city Pop. to the National Pop.	15.6	18.9	23.0	15.9	20.9	22.0	21.7	20.8	23.9	19.7	

* Resident population
** Day-time population
*** DID population

Source: Bureau of Statistics

Over the last decade, Japan was rapidly urbanizing, and the two most populous metropolitan areas were absorbing a disproportionate share of the national increase in DID population. Japan's inhabitants were becoming increasingly urban, and were also accumulating most rapidly in the two great metropolitan clusters focusing on Tokyo and Osaka.

Present Structure of the Japanese Urban System

Dynamics of Population Growth

It is generally considered that the demographic transition in Japan had its beginning as early as 1920 when the first modern census was initiated. The complete transition from high to low fertility, however, occurred in the decade after World War II. From the time of the first census, the continuity of a drift of population from rural to urban areas has been prevalent. For half a century, two of the nation's principal regions, the Tokyo and Osaka metropolitan areas have continued to experience a net in-migration of population. The basic pattern of population movement has been essentially centripetal in character, with a concentration of migrants from rural areas in the two major metropolitan areas centred on Tokyo and Osaka. Of the two, the Tokyo metropolitan area has held the greater attraction for migrants, but its pull has become relatively much stronger in the post-war period.

Regional differentials in population growth rates, and hence in population redistribution through time, are affected by both internal migration and by regional differences in rates of natural increase. The recent revolutions in demography and population mobility in Japan have subsequently manifested themselves in alterations of important population characteristics such as age structure, the number of dependents, and size of the labour force, and also in the geographical and occupational distributions of the people.

In post-war Japan, the dominant factor in the redistribution process has been migration. This is due partly to the traditionally large regional and prefectural differences in fertility and mortality rates which have declined continuously in the post-war period. However, more fundamental has been the remarkable shift of population from rural to urban and from urban to metropolitan areas (Figure 12.1). Because of this recent massive rural-urban transfer of population, Japan has become strikingly polarized into those areas that are gaining and those that are losing in total population.

The increased concentration of people reflects the operation of two factors, natural increase and net in-migration, that are at a maximum in the highly urbanized regions. Positive proportional growth is now anticipated for only three areas: Tokyo, Osaka, and Nagoya metropolitan areas. The three metropolitan areas together comprise the original Tokaido Megalo-

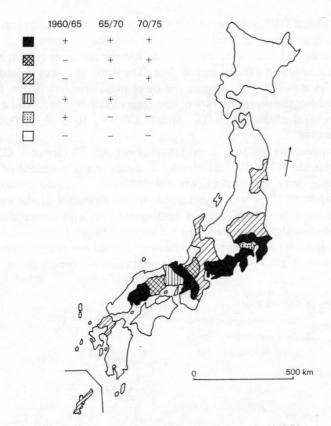

	1960/65	65/70	70/75
■	+	+	+
▨	−	+	+
▨	−	−	+
▥	+	+	−
▦	+	−	−
□	−	−	−

0   500 km

Fig. 12.1 Types of Social Increase in Population by Prefecture, 1960-75

polis, a contiguous urban region representing only about 15 per cent of the nation's land area, but containing some 57 million people, or 55 per cent of the total population.

Dimensions of Urban Functions

As far as the author is aware, no systematic and general research had been done into the way in which Japanese cities differ from, or resemble, one another, or how they interact in forming a system of cities, at least up until the end of the 1970s. A large amount of literature speaks to the increase in urbanization, the changing urban way of life, but without appreciating the variations found both within and between cities.

In 1967 Yamaguchi (1969, 1972) attempted to fill a gap in the knowledge of Japanese cities by developing a parsimonious classification of urban functions. The study included variables on population size and structure, population change, economic and social characteristics, and level of education. The areal units were based mostly on the DIDs. Fifty variables and

189 cities with a DID population in 1960 of 30,000 or over constituted the sample. Using principal component analysis, the underlying common dimensions among cities were examined to test the consistency of the components in relation to parallel sets of data. The study areas comprised three sets of cities grouped according to the three major regions (Core, Southwestern and Northeastern) of Japan, and four sets of cities according to the population sizes of 30,000-50,000, 50,000-100,000, 100,000-250,000, and 250,000 or over.

Four components were extracted from the original 50 variables. Component one was identified with differences in management functions or social status among cities; component two with industrial structure or economic base. Component three was associated with the character of the working population, as a sub-component of component one, and component four with urban centrality in reference to the city size factor (Figure 12.2).

Then, a separate components analysis was carried out for each group of cities mentioned above. The factor of management functions or social

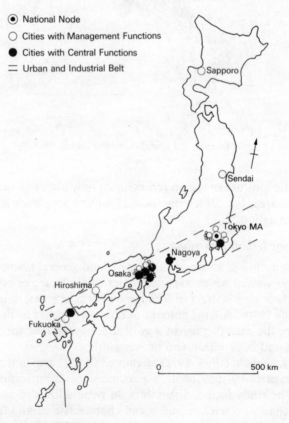

Fig. 12.2 Cities Specialized in Nodal Functions

status was again the dominant factor in all groups except in the case of large cities. For this group of large cities, the urban economic base came out as the dominant component.

All in all, the patterns were broadly similar and a study of factor loadings confirmed that certain variables were commonly related to the two major components. Those variables associated with management functions are education, white-collar occupations, percentages employed in finance and services, and population change in the 1960-5 period. Another group of variables forming the second component, labelled central functions, included the sex ratio and per capita retail and wholesale sales. Significant variables were also grouped by means of a distance matrix. The result revealed that the management functions were most alike in location behaviour, followed by the tertiary group and urban centrality.

Cross-sectional Urban Systems

Hino (1977) also made a study of the Japanese urban system for three time-periods using principal component analysis. The purpose of his paper was to make an overview of the development of the Japanese urban system by means of comparing urban dimensions in 1950, 1960, and 1970. The cities for the 1950 analysis were all 153 cities with a population of over 50,000 in their administrative areas. The cities for the 1960 and 1970 analyses were all cities with a DID population of over 30,000, which numbered 185 in 1960 and 242 in 1960. The input variables for each of the three time-periods comprised five types of data: population size and change, demographic structure, and social, economic, and locational characteristics. The number of input variables for the three time-periods were 34 in 1950, 50 in 1960, and 54 in 1970. The tabulation of data for cities in the three time-periods was based on the city areas in 1970, to avoid the influence of earlier expansions of the administrative areas.

He found the following points were evident through changes in the Japanese urban system since 1950:

(1) social status was extracted as the first component in the three time-periods, but the spatial distribution of the component scores revealed a remarkable contrast between cities located in the two metropolitan areas of Tokyo and Osaka and those cities located outside the two areas. White-collar workers have been concentrating in the former two areas since 1950, and the rate of concentration has also been accelerated since 1960. This interpretation is supported by the fact that the percentage of white-collar workers in the two metropolitan areas, relative to the nation as a whole, has increased continuously since 1950. This concentration reflects the agglomeration of management functions in the largest metropolitan areas.

(2) the ruralism dimension extracted as the second component in 1950 moved down to become the fourth component in 1960 and disappeared in 1970. This phenomenon reflects the significant decline of agricultural

270   *Urbanization and Settlement Systems*

workers in the city areas since 1950 and shows the rapid urbanization of the entire country. That is, the percentages of the labour force in primary industry, self-employed and household sectors, those which had high positive correlations with the ruralism component in 1950, have continuously reduced their variances in association with the decline of agricultural workers. (3) manufacturing activities, which were identified as the third component in 1950 and the second component in 1960, and 1970, have an inverse correlation with variables describing the commercial functions of DID cities in 1970. These functions are represented by variables such as the percentages employed in wholesale and retail sales, in finance, insurance and real estate, and in services. This finding suggests that the negative correlations between variables on manufacturing activities and those on commercial functions were strengthened by an increase in cities specialized either in manufacturing or in commerce after 1960. Rapid post-war industrialization and the functional differentiation among those cities located within the metropolitan regions are major contributors to such a phenomenon.

Many cities, including those in the Pacific Industrial Belt stretching from Southern Kanto to Northern Kyushu, specialize in manufacturing functions, and cities located outside this belt, have developed a specialization in commercial functions. On the other hand, due to the marked functional differentiation among cities included in the metropolitan areas, suburban cities are split into either industrial or residential types.

(4) the city size factor extracted as the fourth component in 1970 was correlated with two variables denoting the wholesale function of cities, such as the wholesale-retail ratio and per capita wholesale sales. This component indicates that differences among cities in per capita wholesale sales became analogous to those of population size in 1970. This has been due largely to the change in the structure of commodity distribution since 1960. Many distribution channels were amalgamated through the policies of large manufacturing concerns, the sales networks of large-scale wholesalers, and the emergence of chain-stores in the retail sector. The expansion of local wholesalers established in medium to small cities stagnated after 1960, and the discrepancy between large and medium-to-small cities in per capita wholesale sales has widened since then.

Internal Migration of Population

Inter- and Intra-prefectural Migration

The annual volume of internal migration in Japan in the early 1920s amounted to a little over two million persons. Although the first census was taken in 1920, reliable time-series data on the origin and destination of migrants are available only from the 1955 census onwards. By 1955, the figure had risen to 5.1 million, to 5.6 million by 1960, and to 8.2 million by 1970 but then down to 7.5 million by 1975 (Table 12.5).

Table 12.5: *Annual Volume of Migration: 1955-75*

Year	Number of people (in 000s)		
	Total migration	Intra-prefectural migration	Inter-prefectural migration
1955	5,141	2,914	2,227
1960	5,653	2,973	2,680
1965	7,380	3,688	3,692
1970	8,273	4,038	4,235
1975	7,544	3,846	3,698

Source: *Annual Report on Internal Migration in Japan*
Derived from the Basic Resident Registers.

Migrants represented 5.7 per cent of the total population in 1955, then 8.0 per cent in both 1960 and 1970 and 6.7 per cent in 1975. This total migrant flow is almost equally divided between that which involves intra-prefectural movements and inter-prefectural ones, usually representing long distance migrants across prefectural boundaries. Both types of mobility showed similar increases during the 1960s with the rate of increase in inter-prefectural migration surpassing that in intra-prefectural migration around 1960; but their positions were reversed around 1965. Although the rate of increase has declined since 1965, the population influx to urban areas has continued to increase, and in 1971, a high of 8.4 million in-migrants was recorded. In general, the number of people migrating short distances from surrounding areas into the prefectural centres and other smaller local centres has been about the same as the number of persons moving greater distances into the largest cities, but the latter type of migration was stimulated by rapid economic growth in the 1960s.

The total magnitude of the more lengthy inter-prefectural migration involved about 4.2 million people in 1971, a slightly greater volume than that which took place within prefectural boundaries. Later, the figure went down to 3.7 million (in 1975) and intra-prefectural migration has surpassed inter-prefectural movement of population since 1972. In 1975, more than half of the total in-migration occurred within 8 of the 47 prefectures, all of them metropolitan in character and therefore offering more attractive employment opportunities. Each of the eight had an annual in-migration exceeding 100,000 persons. Out-migration of more than 100,000 people in 1975 was also characteristic of the same eight metropolitan prefectures.

There are also complex streams of migration existing between the metropolitan prefectures, as well as in the outward movement of inhabitants from the core areas of the large cities to suburban locations, frequently across prefectural boundaries. In considering the increase in inter-prefectural migration, it is instructive to view each separately (Table 12.6).

Table 12.6: *The Annual Volume of Inter-prefectural Migration by Direction of the Flow: 1955-75*

Year	Prefectural migration among metropolitan areas	Migration from metropolitan to non-metropolitan areas	Migration from non-metropolitan to metropolitan areas	Prefectural migration among non-metropolitan areas
	Number of people (in 000s)			
1955	563	385	738	540
1960	706	406	999	568
1965	1,116	705	1,186	685
1970	1,346	870	1,263	757
1975	1,174	901	912	710

The 'metropolitan areas' include the prefectures of Tokyo, Chiba, Saitama, Kanagawa, Aichi, Mie, Osaka, Kyoto and Hyogo.

Source: Annual Report on Internal Migration in Japan
    Derived from the Basic Resident Registers.

1) Migration between metropolitan areas: it began to increase at a slightly later date, but, since 1966, it has accounted for the majority of inter-prefectural migration.
2) Migration from metropolitan to non-metropolitan areas: it began to increase in the early sixties and reached a level of 0.9 million by 1971, a level which was maintained up to 1975.
3) Migration from non-metropolitan to metropolitan areas: it increased in the early sixties and reached a level of 1.2 million by 1963, a level which was maintained until 1972.
4) Migration between non-metropolitan areas: it was the smallest flow among the four types of migration and has stayed at the level of 0.7 million since the late sixties.

The volume of migration, as noted, has declined since 1973. With the shift to more stable economic growth, both inter- and intra-prefectural mobility has declined. Inter-prefectural migration from non-metropolitan to metropolitan areas showed the sharpest drop-off, with the annual inflow increasing by only one quarter between 1970 and 1975. By 1975, the number of persons leaving the large metropolitan areas surpassed the number entering such areas. With the overall drop in the volume of migration, the trend toward further population concentration in the metropolitan areas has been blunted.

Thus, the metropolitan areas, which for more than half a century evidenced a remarkable and consistent increase in net in-migration have, in the recent inter-censal periods of 1965-70 and 1970-5, begun to show a slowing of growth. At the same time, rural regions, where a net out-migration has long been the rule, have shown a reduction in their losses. The net inflow into the three largest metropolitan areas between 1970 and 1975 dropped from 4.7 to 4.0 million. During the same period, only five prefectures experienced a decrease in their populations. The result has been a shrinkage of net out-migration from the rural regions and of net in-migration into the metropolitan areas.

Migration from Metropolitan to Non-metropolitan Areas

A fundamental alteration in the migration stream is the increasing rate of return migration from the metropolitan areas. This rate is currently higher than that of rural out-migration. Return migration from the major metropolitan areas is one of the most recent redistributive movements of population in Japan. The country began to experience this change, often called the 'U-turn phenomenon', around the middle of the 1960s. The basic reason is that the narrowly-defined economic motivation which brought people to the major metropolitan areas in search of employment opportunities has been replaced by a more complex set of processes in which a number of non-economic factors are also considered.

Ishikawa (1978) investigated the stage of internal migration in post-war Japan and the major factors which brought about the recent internal migration trends, including the U-turn phenomenon. These factors were examined by multiple regression analysis, and the following findings were obtained:
1) The recent migration pattern is influenced by more complex and numerous factors than in the past.
2) Inter-metropolitan migration is influenced by more limited factors than migration between metropolitan and non-metropolitan prefectures.
3) The factor of inter-prefectural differentials in per capita income is less valid for explaining any type of migration, but the increase in employment at the destination still plays an important role in migration.
4) Distance is still a strong and stable factor. Migration is determined by the contiguity of areas to a considerable degree.
5) In terms of destination characteristics, the agglomeration of management functions, which has been thought of as a leading factor of urban growth in major cities, does not always play a significant role in attracting in-migrants.
6) Migrants' attitudes, as represented by age groups and levels of education, are important determinants in setting the direction of their migrations.

It has been common, since the end of the nineteenth century, for young people in the rural areas to move to the city temporarily and then to return home to the family business or for marriage at a later date. Consequently, an increase in the number moving to the cities was accompanied by an increase in the number returning to the countryside, though perhaps with a time lag. In recent years, however, a survey made by the Institute of Population Problems, Ministry of Welfare, indicates that most people in metropolitan areas who wish to move in the near future prefer to move within the same metropolitan area. Moreover, the number of people who wish to escape from the deteriorating environment within the metropolitan area also seems to be very small. Accordingly, the intricately interwoven motivations of people in this regard are not so easily discerned. We may be experiencing a return to the traditional pattern whereby only single young people leave their home towns. If this becomes the dominant pattern, and these young people later return to their homes, the distribution of Japan's population as it is now will stabilize (Kawabe, 1980).

Meanwhile, Abe (1980) examined the socio-economic components of return migration from three metropolitan areas to five regional capital cities and clarified the nature of some types of out-migrants. The continuous growth of the regional capital cities depended mostly on in-migration from other areas, especially from the three major metropolitan areas. He identified that the regional capital cities had much closer ties with the major metropolitan areas than with their own hinterlands.

Based on a factor analysis of the socio-economic attributes of in-migrants to these regional capital cities, Abe reached the following rather different conclusions from those in Ishikawa's study. The predominant factor, explaining 40 per cent of the total variance, represents the migration pattern of white-collar workers. In this migration pattern, there are many in-migrants from the three major metropolitan areas to regional capital cities and the distance of such migration is relatively longer. The growth of regional capital cities has actually stimulated the influx of white-collar workers engaged in management functions. The attractiveness of these cities has little effect on the migration stream of blue-collar workers.

The level of migration dropped as Japan's economy entered a period of stabilized growth in the mid-1970s. At the same time, some of the patterns of migration characterizing Japanese society in the pre-war period seem to have re-emerged. Japan today seems to be characterized by a process of population deconcentration with lesser concentrations being formed in the regional or prefectural centres. In short, the Japanese urban system is in the stage of centralized decentralization or of dispersed concentration, a trend which was also confirmed by Glickman's study (1976).

Political and Administrative Functions and Centres

Capital Region

Before World War II, Tokyo was a special prefecture or *fu* with a governor appointed by the central government. It comprised the City of Tokyo as well as many suburban towns and villages. During the war, Tokyo Prefecture and the City of Tokyo were consolidated to form the single local government of Tokyo-TO. Tokyo's size, therefore, presents a problem in definition. There is the ward area of *ku-bu*, which has been enlarged many times. In 1975 the city numbered 23 wards (*ku*) with 8.6 million people. There is also the administrative Tokyo, that is the area of the Tokyo Metropolitan Government, which provides local governmental services for the old city, with its 23 wards, as well as for the suburbs immediately around it. At the 1975 Census, this area had a population of 11.7 million. But outside this limit, rapid population growth has already created the broader Tokyo Metropolitan Region having an estimated population in 1975 of approximately 25 million.

Fukuhara (1977) studied the regional system of the Tokyo Metropolitan Region using principal component analysis and cluster analysis. In this study, he analysed the basic dimensions in the changes of that regional system for 1955, 1960, 1965, and 1970. The study area was made up of 162 cities, wards, towns, and villages focusing on the central business district (CBD) of Tokyo; and 25 variables were used for the analysis. His research findings are as follows:

First, a civic centre has been formed under historical and political conditions. Due to the advantages of concentration, civic functions have increasingly accumulated in a very small area, and some of the functions have been transferred to zones-in-transition or sub-centres. The node of this civic centre has shifted from traditional commercial and industrial functions to more advanced control functions; a trend which was conspicuous during the period of 1955-60.

Second, the civic centre is surrounded by several zones-in-transition where commercial, industrial, and residential functions are intermingled. Surrounding these zones are sub-centres where both business and shopping districts have developed around the terminals of the suburban railways. At present, there are four major sub-centres. Shinjuku in the west and Ueno in the east became sub-centres in 1955 followed by Shibuya in 1960 and Ikebukuro in 1970. Third, the regional system of the Tokyo Metropolitan Region has been greatly influenced by the patterns of railway service and the network configuration of the area.

Reorganization of Administrative Areas

Since the sphere of influence of cities has spread with the expansion of urban functions, the need has arisen for reorganizing the old administrative areas. According to Honjo (1971), the tendency towards reorganization may be observed at two levels. The author, however, has added one more level, the rural community.

Inter-prefecture Level

Prefectures (*ken*), as the largest units of local government, have been the major framework of the local administrative system of Japan. The administrative boundary of the prefecture was generally based on feudal domains before the Meiji Restoration, although several changes had been made in the course of reformation. It has been argued that the areas of prefectures are too small in a period of high spatial mobility in population, and mergers have been proposed from time to time in order to meet the expansion of metropolitan areas.

Inter-municipality Level

It has been recognized that municipalities (*shi, machi,* and *mura*), as the smallest administrative units of local government, and based on traditional communities, are now inadequate in the stage of high spatial mobility. Since they are also too small as administrative bodies to perform the necessary services, the central government has consistently been attempting to reorganize them and enlarge their areal extent (Table 12.2).

Reorganization has taken the form of amalgamation of surrounding municipalities with the larger central cities. With the enactment of the Amalgamation Act of 1953, the Ministry of Internal Affairs of the Central Government decided to encourage such amalgamations far more strongly than before. Such a movement has become a big problem where the regional system was also undergoing a rapid transformation through industrialization. In the 1950s the municipalities were amalgamated mainly for the purpose of improving administrative efficiency, while, in the 1960s, the amalgamations were designed to strengthen administrative capabilities.

Rural Community Level

The prevailing tendency to agglomerate the nation's population has inevitably caused a great change in the lifestyle of people in those rural areas with declining populations. Rural areas have been absorbed by the great wave of urbanization, which in turn stimulates the formation of new rural communities, where places of work and residence are widely separated.

The curtailment of working hours in agriculture through increased productivity, and the increase of off-farm employment opportunities, have caused a rapid growth of part-time farmers. These going-out-type jobs (*dekasegi*), in particular, have brought problems into rural life. These include not only such economic measures as securing the necessary quality of agricultural labour force, but also such social welfare measures as maintenance of better living conditions (Table 12.7). The homogeneity in rural life can no longer be maintained.

In those areas where depopulation is going on, there remains the so-called 'Sparsity Problem' (*kaso mondai*) with an upward shift of age structure. This brings considerable difficulties in maintaining such fundamental conditions for community life as medical and educational services, and local activities for preventing various disasters. As most of these sparsely-populated areas are marginal suppliers of agricultural and fishing products, it may be virtually impossible to solve these problems in the present stage of prevailing urbanization. Therefore, comprehensive social development policies focused on the reorganization of villages and their functions need to be pursued to sustain a reasonable level of community life in rural areas.

Table 12.7: *Types of Agricultural Households by Income Source; 1941-79*

| | | (Percentages) | | |
| | | Part-time* | | |
Year	Full-time	I	II	Total
1941	41.5	37.3	21.2	58.5
1950	50.0	28.4	21.6	50.0
1960	34.3	33.6	32.1	65.7
1970	15.6	33.7	50.7	84.4
1975	12.4	25.4	62.2	87.6
1979	12.5	17.8	69.7	87.5

* Part-time agricultural households are classified into two
categories based on the proportion of income from
agriculture to the total household income.
Part-time I: Income from agriculture is more than 50%.
Part-time II: Income from agriculture is less than 50%.

Source: Ministry of Agriculture

Future Structure and Patterns

Considering the future urbanization of Japan, three distinct patterns can be recognized. In the major metropolitan areas of Tokyo, Osaka, and Nagoya, there is likely to be a remarkable population expansion, due to a high rate of natural increase rather than an in-migration of population. In the regional capitals such as Sapporo, Sendai, Hiroshima, and Fukuoka, both natural and social increases in population will occur simultaneously in accordance with the development of their basic functions as economic and cultural centres for their surrounding districts, resulting in a large increase in total population (Kiuchi and Masai, 1975).

Natural and social increases in population will also continue in other large cities, but, since their present population sizes are small compared with those of metropolitan areas, their future development will be based primarily on the amount of in-migration from other areas. Even in these cities, however, the continued exodus of people to the larger cities may also be expected.

While this is the prospect for most of the large urban areas throughout the country, it is also necessary to consider the creation of new living environments apart from the existing urban system. In order to reorganize and improve the situation in the existing urban system, there have been recommendations for change suggested by different research groups, one of which was the Capital Region Comprehensive Planning Association (1972).

The first proposal is for the widespread dispersal of functions from major metropolitan areas, particularly from Tokyo, to surrounding areas as well as to the regional capitals. In effect, this means the building of new towns with a population of approximately 300,000 in the surrounding upland regions. For industrial development, large-scale industry is to be separated from the major metropolitan areas and dispersed, primarily to under-developed areas, while urban industries are to be established in the lowlands of the more developed areas around cities in keeping with the changing nature of Japanese agriculture. Second, to expand and improve recreational zones in accordance with the changes in life styles, a plan should be made to utilize a combination of recreation and agriculture in rural land use. Finally, for the purpose of achieving these objectives, an effort should be made to increase the nationwide accessibility to all parts of the country through improved transportation and communication networks.

Since population and industry were increasingly concentrated in major metropolitan areas during the period of high economic growth in the 1960s, these areas are now faced with many problems relating to land, water, noise, and safety. Acute limitations caused by this high density have made construction of public utilities difficult, thereby blocking attempts to improve the living environment. Therefore, it is likely that community development in the major metropolitan areas will be limited. In rural areas, however, where an outflow of population is occurring, the population is both declining and ageing. As a consequence, the community spirit which used to be the basis of their unity is also declining, and maintenance as well as improvement of the quality of living environment becomes even more difficult.

In order to solve these fundamental problems, the Economic Planning Agency (1976) set out an economic plan for the second half of the 1970s. The following are some of the recommendations relating to regional systems set out in this plan: first, regional systems throughout Japan must be improved to maintain vigorous local communities. In so doing, it is necessary to encourage the dispersion of population and industry to less-developed areas and to make an effort to further the development of these areas. Second, changes should not be limited to tertiary industries and manufacturing, but management functions within these sectors, namely quaternary industries, should also be dispersed more extensively to areas other than major metropolitan areas. If the trend towards concentration in the major urban areas declines, the proportion of population between urban and rural areas would be kept almost at the same level as the economic functions.

For this purpose, a continuing re-evaluation of past policies including National Comprehensive Development Plans and other programmes for area development of the nation, should be carried on, and associated improvements should be made to maintain the balanced development of regional systems within the framework of the national settlement system.

REFERENCES

Abe, T. 1980. 'Internal Migration and the Japanese Urban System', A Paper presented at the Sapporo Meeting of the IGU Commission on National Settlement Systems, 18 p.

Capital Region Comprehensive Planning Association. 1972. 'The Japanese Land and Life in the 21st Century', *The 4th International Symposium on Regional Development*. Tokyo: JCADR, pp. 94-108.

Economic Planning Agency. 1976. *Economic Plan for the Second Half of the 1970's*. Tokyo: Government of Japan, pp. 74-9.

Fukuhara, M. 1977. 'A Study of Regional Structure of the Tokyo Metropolitan Region', *Journal of Geography*, Tokyo Geographical Society, 86: 18-33. (in Japanese with a summary in English).

Glickman, N. J. 1976. 'On the Japanese Urban System', *Journal of Regional Science*, 16: 317-36.

Hino, M. 1977. 'Fundamental Dimensions of the Japanese Urban System in the Years of 1950, 1960, and 1970', *Geographical Review of Japan*, 50: 335-53. (in Japanese with a summary in English).

Honjo, M. 1971. 'Study of Regional and Urban Development in Japan', *The U.S.-Japan Conference on Regional Development*. Tokyo: JCADR, pp. 5-32.

Ishikawa, Y. 1978. 'Internal Migration in Postwar Japan', *Geographical Review of Japan*, 51: 433-50. (in Japanese with a summary in English).

Itoh, T. 1974. 'The Formation of Japan Megalopolis', *The Bulletin of the Faculty of Education*, Mie University, 25: 93-103.

Kawabe, H. 1980. 'Internal Migration and Population Distribution in Japan', A.J.G. ed. *Geography of Japan*, Teikoku-shoin, pp. 379-89.

Kiuchi, S. and Y. Masai. 1975. 'Japan', *World Urbanization*, IGU Commission on Processes and Patterns of Urbanization, pp. 175-85.

Masai, Y. 1978. 'Urbanization of Japan', *Urban Growth in Japan and France*, Tokyo: Japan Society for the Promotion of Science, pp. 27-36.

Yamaguchi, T. 1969. 'Japanese Cities: Their Functions and Characteristics', *Papers and Proceedings of the Third Far East Conference of the Regional Science Association*, 3: 141-56.

Yamaguchi, T. 1972. 'Parallel Structure of Urban Functions in Japan', *Geographical Review of Japan*, 45: 411-29. (in Japanese with a summary in English).

PART A

SETTLEMENT SYSTEMS IN INDUSTRIAL MARKET ECONOMIES

Section 3: Settlement in the Mediterranean World

13 THE NATIONAL SETTLEMENT SYSTEM OF ITALY

BERARDO CORI

For a long period of time, Italian geographers devoted their attention mainly to rural settlements, especially to rural dwellings (Barbieri and Gambi, 1970). Studies of urban settlements were promoted by Toschi in the 1930s. These were initially studies on individual towns. Comparative studies, or studies of city-territory relationships or of connections between towns, were developed in the 1950s (Toschi, 1966). However, we had to wait until the 1960s and the 1970s for studies on urban networks or settlement systems.

Components of the System

Only 4.5 of 47 million Italians (1979) live in scattered houses, namely houses scattered in the countryside or along the roadside. Another 2 million live in hamlets, that is elementary groups of adjacent or neighbouring houses inhabited by at least five families, but without a 'meeting place'. Over 50 million people live in centres, certainly the main type of settlement to be found in Italy. According to the Italian population census, centres are groups of adjacent or neighbouring houses with roads in between, or some indication of continuity, distinguished by the existence of public services or offices serving the inhabitants of scattered houses, and surrounding hamlets, or other centres.

The relative importance of hamlets and scattered houses has steadily declined during the past century, in keeping with the transformation of Italy from an agricultural to a predominantly industrial country. However, hamlets and scattered houses continue to accommodate large numbers of inhabitants, 20-30 per cent (compared with a national average of 12 per cent) in some regions of northeast and central Italy (e.g. Venetia, Umbria, Marche, Abruzzo) where the survival of agriculture is associated with small estates and direct management (and until recently with sharecropping).

The total number of centres is about 24,000, with an average population of about 2,000 inhabitants. They are combined, for administrative purposes, with the population of hamlets and scattered houses, into slightly more than 8,000 communes. Each commune includes on average three centres and about 850 inhabitants from hamlets or scattered homes, for an average population of 7,000 inhabitants. In Italy, the commune is, at the same time, the smallest administrative unit, the smallest autonomous territorial body, and the smallest unit of statistical surveys. Thus, an analysis of the Italian settlement system, if it is to be complete, must necessarily consider communes and not centres as the basic units of that system.

Functional Sub-systems

Among the 8,080 Italian communes, five functional sub-systems can be distinguished. These are:

(1) *Small non-urban communes* (about 6,000) with a population of less than 5,000 inhabitants. They are not necessarily rural, and may be industrialized, because of the industrialization of the countryside that reached vast areas of central and northern Italy after 1950. However, they do not have the facilities, services and functions to qualify as being urban.

(2) *Non-urban communes of a certain demographic density* (slightly more than 1,500), with a population of more than 5,000 inhabitants. They could also be called agricultural communes, but a larger number of them are industrialized. Within this category, small suburban areas, or even urbanized communes, are often defined as 'urbanized suburbs' or 'incomplete towns'.

Such urbanized areas, although inhabited by populations which because of their standard of living are undoubtedly urbanized, cannot be identified with towns inhabited by actual town populations. The latter are 'nerve centres', distinguished by a certain degree of organization and special functions.

At this point it is more difficult to speak in terms of communes rather than of centres. However, the difficulty is lessened by the fact that the higher the level of the centres, the higher the communal population living in the main centre. Research has revealed 528 true 'urban' communes, in which there are 528 towns. These are towns that have at least three or four of the five functions considered essential to qualify as an urban settlement: that is, commercial, banking, sanitation, educational, and administrative functions. Among this type of settlement, we can also distinguish:

(3) 359 *small towns* (Costa, Da Pozzo and Bartaletti, 1976), namely centres able to supply urban services to a rural *Umland* (not necessarily agricultural), or those endowed with specialized functions (industry, tourism), or involving residential functions (e.g. satellite towns). The dividing line between the small town and the non-urban commune, and that between small towns and medium-sized towns, is functional and not demographic. We have small towns among communes with slightly more than 5,000 inhabitants, and among communes with more than 40,000, up to a maximum of 90,000. However, generally speaking, the most typical population size of the small Italian town is from 10/15,000 to 30,000 inhabitants. Together these small towns have a total population of about 7.5 million inhabitants.

(4) 155 *medium-sized towns*, centres able to organize and govern not only a rural territory but also other small towns (i.e. the beginning of an urban

network). They are identified by the presence of all five of the above-mentioned urban functions, at least three of which are present more consistently than in small towns, and by the control exerted over small towns or over vast territories with several elementary centres. Functions typical of medium-sized towns can be found in some small centres with 20,000 inhabitants, but are more frequent in those with between 30,000 and 200/220,000 inhabitants. Cagliari, Taranto, and Messina (240-270,000 inhabitants) are the largest medium-sized towns. Altogether medium-sized towns accommodate 11.2 million inhabitants.

(5) 14 *large towns* or *regional metropolises* are identified by their important decision-making and cultural functions, by their specialized services, by the extent of their area of influence, and their degree of predominance over other towns. Their population varies from 240,000 inhabitants (Padua) to 2,900,000 (Rome). Although the functional threshold between medium-sized and large towns does not correspond exactly to the demographic one, it is close. The total population of these large towns is 11.3 million inhabitants.

Table 13.1: *Functional Sub-systems of the Italian Settlement System*

	Number	Population (millions)	%
Small non-urban communes <5000 inhabitants	6014	26.8	47
Non-urban communes >5000 inhabitants	538		
Small towns	359	7.5	13
Medium-sized towns	155	11.2	20
Large towns (regional metropolises)	14	11.3	20
Total	8080	56.8	100

The Present Structure of the Settlement System

Territorial Distribution

As we have seen, slightly more than half the Italian population lives in towns (small, medium-sized, and large), the rest in non-urban communes. But the situation varies considerably in the different Italian regions. The most urbanized regions are neither the highly industrialized regions of the Northwest (Piedmont and Lombardy), nor the poorer ones of the South (Molise, Basilicata, Calabria). Instead they are certain regions dominated by large metropolises, such as commercial and tourist Liguria (Genoa), bureaucratic and administrative Latium (Rome), and other regions that became urbanized at an early date, some as far back as the Middle Ages, thanks to the emergence of the *communi* (communes) and the subsequent *signorie* (lordships) (e.g. Tuscany, Emilia, Umbria).

The distribution of Italian towns reveals the dualism between the developed North and the backward South (Figure 13.1). In the North of Italy, there is an average of 20 towns every 10,000 sq. km., against 16 in the South and 12.5 on the Islands. The urban network of northern Italy is more dense, balanced, and continuous than that of the South, where there are only a few metropolises to serve vast areas, or where the presence of very large metropolises is not supported by medium-sized towns. On the whole the continental South and Sardinia appear to have too few medium-sized and large

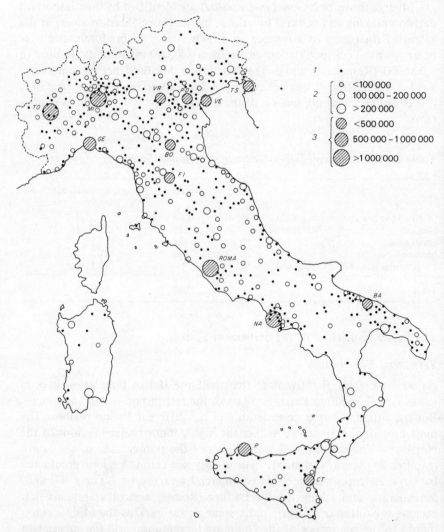

Fig. 13.1 Distribution of Italian Towns, 1979
1 = small towns; 2 = medium-sized towns; 3 = large towns

towns. These accommodate less than 30 per cent of the population, against 40 per cent for the national average. The average minimum distance between medium-sized and large towns is about 33km in the South and Centre-South, and 24km in the North and Centre-North (Table 13.2).

In reality, Italian towns are distributed according to an ancient and stable fabric, whose pattern is strongly influenced by physical relief and above all by natural axes of communication. As Nice (1961) and Compagna (1967) have observed, there exist in northern Italy two important, piedmontian, urban corridors: one at the foot of the Alps, from Turin to Trieste, and the other at the foot of the Apennines, from Asti to Pesaro. In both these corridors towns have arisen at the points where the valleys which cut through the two chains open onto the Po-Venetia plain. A third alignment is that of the median centres of the same plain, from Milan to Venice. These are situated on the line of contact between the upper and lower plain, where the transition from the area of permeable to non-permeable lands produces a line of *risorgive* (springs).

In contrast to these corridors dictated by relief and traffic (later interconnected by transverse axes to create a real urban network), the fabric in the South is more scanty and broken. There are a few centres inland, of no importance and with an irregular layout, but towns facing the sea prevail in number and importance. This is partly due to the presence of small, fertile, isolated plains which are the only hospitable areas in the South. The pattern not only depends on physical features: it also reflects the fact that while central and northern Italy flourished under the urban civilization of the *communi*, the old medieval urban civilization of the South declined under the feudal system which was imposed by the Normans at the end of the eleventh century and remained virtually unchanged for almost eight centuries.

Table 13.2: *The Urban Dualism between North and South*

	Number of towns			Number of towns every 10,000 sq.km.	Number of medium and large towns every 10,000 sq.km.	Average minimum distance between medium and large towns (km)
	Small	Medium	Large			
North and Centre-North	210	99	9	20	7	24
South and Centre-South	149	56	5	15	4	33
Italy	359	155	14	18	6	28

Demographic Behaviour

During the last three decades, the Italian population has increased by about one fifth, from over 47 to about 57 million inhabitants. This increase has been distributed unevenly among the different settlement sub-systems. Non-urban communes had only a slight increase (just over 5 per cent). Small towns had an increase equal to the national average (20 per cent). Medium-sized and large towns grew at a pace that was more than double that of the national average (more than 40 per cent). As a result, the present 169 medium-sized and large towns have a total population of 22.5 million compared with 16 million in 1951.

These differences are not a result of natural demographic trends in the various sub-systems, but rather of a massive internal migration which took place after the Second World War. It was a migration with several different components: (1) long-distance components: from South to North and above all towards the Northwest (at first, also from Northeast to Northwest); (2) shorter-distance components: from the mountains and hills towards the plains, from the hinterland towards the coast, and from the countryside to the towns; (3) a social and professional component: from agricultural work to employment in industry and services (there was a decrease of workers in the primary sector from 37 per cent in 1951 to 17 per cent in 1971, and 14 per cent in 1979). Almost all of these components have contributed towards shifting the population from non-urban to urban communes, and from minor to major centres. They have influenced medium-sized and large towns in particular.

These figures reflect the trends of the post-war decades. The trends of the very recent past, however, are different. From the point of view of natural population growth, the most dynamic are not the medium-sized and large towns, but the medium-sized and small ones. In fact, during the three year period 1976-8, among non-urban communes, only 56 per cent had a positive natural balance (birth rate > death rate). This percentage is slightly higher (57 per cent) in the case of large towns (8 positive and 6 negative cases); but it goes up to 72 per cent in medium-sized and small towns. This shows that medium-sized and small towns are, on the whole, the youngest as far as demographic trends are concerned.

During the same three years migration revealed the following characteristics in the different sub-systems: a positive migratory balance of 61 per cent in medium-sized towns and 62 per cent in small towns; a positive balance of 52 per cent in non-urban communes; and a negative balance in the metropolises (4 positive cases and 10 negative cases).

Thus, compared to the pre-war period, the situation has been reversed. During the pre-war period the mature metropolises underwent a slight natural increase and attracted the largest migratory influx. Today the majority of large cities preserve a youthful demographic behaviour (at a lower rate than medium-sized and small towns) but tend to lose their population. The major poles of attraction have become the medium-sized and small towns.[1]

The Economic Structure

Settlement sub-systems are also differentiated by the economic and professional structure of their active population (Table 13.3).

Table 13.3: *Economic Structure of Active Population in per cent, 1971*

	Primary Sector	Secondary Sector	Tertiary Sector
Non-urban communes	27	46	27
Small towns	18	46	36
Medium-sized towns	9	41	50
Large towns	1	40	59
Italy	17	44	39

This differentiation is not observed in the industrial sector, but it is very evident in the other two sectors. The percentage of agricultural workers clearly distinguishes non-urban communes, though on the whole these communes are no longer predominantly agricultural (on the contrary, they are clearly industrial). Agricultural activity is consistently important in small towns, and still survives in medium-sized towns[2] but has disappeared in large towns.

As the percentage of agricultural population decreases with the increasing level of urbanization, the proportion of the population employed in services increases. Service activity, still less important than industrial activity in small towns (in terms of active population employed), is the main activity in medium-sized towns and is overwhelmingly dominant in large towns.

Contrary to the traditional image of industrialization, however, industrial activity in Italy is concentrated in the minor centres and small towns. Almost two thirds of Italian industrial workers live in these areas. This is the consequence of the development of Italian industrialization in past decades, characterized by labour-intensive, peripheral, decentralized light industry, in which rural labour and the local initiative of entrepreneurs have played important roles.

[1] In forming these conclusions, two provisos should be made: (1) The 1976-8 period saw the return of a large number of emigrants from abroad because of the persistent international economic crisis; (2) A large part of the population leaving the metropolises are probably only leaving for suburban communes.

[2] The importance of using communes rather than centres as units of statistical calculation is here quite evident: small- and medium-sized towns do not fill out the respective communities, which include also rural territories.

Medium-sized and large towns can be considered mature towns, with a strong industrial base serving as a backing to the major activity of the provision of services. More than half the workers employed in services in Italy live in such towns. This high figure is also a reflection of higher tertiary (or quaternary) activities.

National averages conceal quite different regional situations. A 'minimum requirements type' study by Cataudella (1974) on the 'dominant activity' (i.e., the activity having the largest share of the city's basic employment) in Italian towns with more than 50,000 inhabitants, showed that the industrial sector still plays a fundamental role in most towns of northwestern Italy (Figure 13.2). In contrast, the predominance of the tertiary sector is more the prerogative of southern towns. However, this largely re-

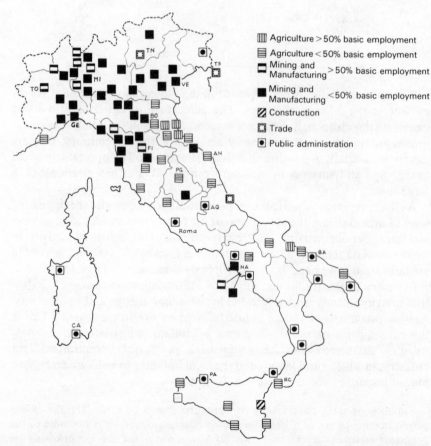

Fig. 13.2 Dominant Activity (according to the minimum requirements method) in large towns and some medium-sized ones, 1961
Source: Cataudella, 1974, modified

flects employment in public administration, a situation akin to the 'masked unemployment' of the Third World. More recent research by Bottai and Costa (1979), using cluster analysis and 1971 census data, partly confirms and clarifies the results of the preceding investigation (Table 13.4).

Table 13.4: *Economic Typology of Italian Large and Medium-sized Towns*

	North and Centre-North	South and Centre-South	Italy
Agricultural towns	14	17	31
Industrial towns	45	8	53
Tertiary towns			
general	22	14	36
mainly trading	11	2	13
mainly transport	10	10	20
mainly administration and services	1	10	11
mainly tourist	5	—	5
Total	108	61	169

Thus, industrial towns are characteristic of the North, as well as trading towns (particularly wholesale and large-scale distribution), and tourist towns. The urban centres in the South are markedly tertiary, specializing in administration (the so-called *buropoli*), professional services, or transport (generally short distance). They also retain agricultural functions to a greater degree than in the North.

City Size Pattern

Italy is a country where the rank-size rule can be applied only approximately. It has three features normally associated with this pattern: a fairly large population, a long history of urbanization, and a complex economic and political structure. Information from three census periods, 1871, 1921, and 1971 suggests an evolution that tends towards the classic rank-size rule pattern (Figure 13.3).

In 1871 the demographic importance of towns from the second rank on is greater than that anticipated by the ideal pattern. Yet there is a fairly constant alignment of values on the graph, arranged along a straight line with an inclination somewhat less than that of the perfect rank-size rule ($q = 0.68$). Towns of rank 3 to 10, with maximum points for Rome, Turin, Florence, and Venice, are further away from this line. These towns had more inhabitants than predicted by the rank-size rule and also by that empirically verified for other Italian towns. Thus, there was a situation of oligarchy, with the most important functions distributed among a few large towns. This obviously reflected the different closed urban networks of the

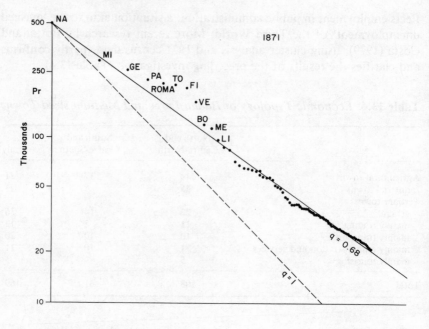

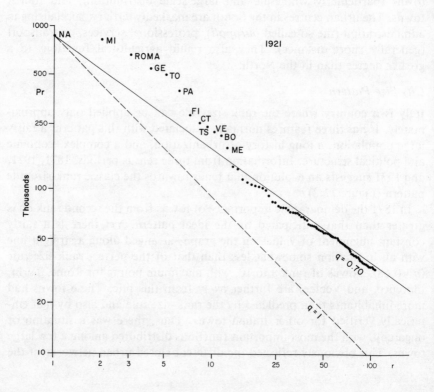

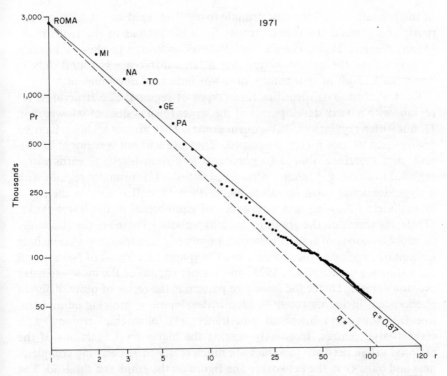

Fig. 13.3   Rank-size Analysis of the Hundred Major Italian Towns, 1871, 1921, and 1971
Source: Cori, 1976

pre-unification Italian states, each with its own capital (which was frequently a true primate city). The decisive historical roles played by the former towns during the *Risorgimento* were also responsible.

After fifty years, the situation had changed very little. The value of q (0.70) was almost identical. The Italian urban network had developed fairly harmoniously, in the sense that the growth rate of the primate town was about equal to the average recorded for the other 99 towns. The divergence begins at the second town (Milan, now with 818,000 inhabitants) and continues until the eleventh or twelfth, with notable values for Rome, Genoa, Turin, and Palermo (i.e. the now growing capital, the other two towns of the already established industrial triangle and the main town of rapidly-growing Sicily, an insular region where the urban system can be considered closed). The oligarchy is accentuated, and is about to expel Naples from its position as the primate city. Naples' growth paralleled that of the system as a whole, and not that of the main towns.

Substantial changes took place from 1921 to 1971. The inclination of the interpolated straight line increases sharply. The q-value increases from 0.70 to 0.87, as does the k-value (i.e. the population of the first town). Contrary to the previous fifty years, towns from rank 2 on have not grown at the rate of the primate town—the *new* primate town. The rapid ascent of Rome has partly reorganized the role of towns from the second to the tenth rank. Milan, Naples, Turin, Genoa, and Palermo continue to show a positive shift from the theoretical values, but a large difference is found only in Turin, as a result of that town's post-war industrial development.

Rank-size analysis identifies three types of regional size structures: (1) regions with a weak development of the larger town (values of q lower than 1), but with a regularity in subsequent grades. They are not highly urbanized regions and/or not highly developed. They are without a regional metropolis and therefore obliged to gravitate, at certain levels, towards extra-regional towns (e.g. Marche, Abruzzo, Umbria); (2) 'primate' regions with a large dominant town (q values higher than 1), deficiencies in the ranks immediately following and a recovery of equilibrium in the lower ranks. (Their alignment on the graph forms a hyperbola.) These are the classically developed regions of Italy (Piedmont, Lombardy, Liguria), but also include Latium (the region of the capital), and Campania (the region of Naples, still the national primate-city in 1921, and former capital of the most extensive pre-unity state). Hence the same size pattern is the result of quite different phenomena, including recent economic development, growing administrative functions, and historical inheritance; (3) 'oligarchic' regions, with several large centres, frequently sharing the higher-level functions of the regional urban network (q values are much closer to 1, denoting completeness and balance in the network). The figure on the graph is a sinusoid. The 'oligarchic' regions are large regions of central and northeastern Italy, with old urban traditions and a recent and scattered industrialization, and also Sicily, one of the most complete and closed Italian sub-systems.

The Metropolises and the Areas of Urban Influence

Research by Mori and Cori in 1969 revealed that 40 towns (14 large and 26 medium-sized) in Italy have regional functions (i.e. with a gravitational pull beyond provincial boundaries. Of these 28 are located in the North and Centre-North, and only 12 in the Centre-South and South, thus confirming the strong urban imbalance which exists between the two parts of the country. Thus, the areas of attraction of regional centres generally have a greater extent in the South than in the North.

Ten large areas of cultural, social and financial influence have been recognized at a higher level. They are dominated either by individual metropolises such as Turin, Genoa, Florence, Rome, Naples, and Bari (which dominate other regional centres), or by polycentric metropolises, which are dependent upon vital regional centres (e.g. Milan with the Lombard towns, or Bologna with the town of Emilia-Romagna), or by multi-metropolitan systems such as the Sicilian (Palermo and Catania with Messina as the regional centre) or the three-pronged Venetian one (Verona, Padua, Venice) or Trieste (plus four regional centres). The greater strength of metropolitan systems in the North and Centre is particularly evident in the cultural field. Universities in the Centre and North continue to attract great numbers of southern students despite the enlargement or creation of several new universities in the South. A study by Caldo and Santalucia (1977) draws attention to the overwhelming strength of publishing houses, opinion weeklies, theatrical, cinematographical, radio and television productions based in the North or in Rome, pointing out that of the 27 Italian daily newspapers with a circulation of over 50,000 copies, only four are southern.

Outside these spheres of influence are the Marche, Calabria, and Sardinia, peripheral regions not sufficiently developed to have their own pole at this level. These regions can reduce their disadvantage by turning, albeit with a distance handicap, to outside metropolises, especially Rome. There still remain some fringe areas, subject to the overlapping influences of several large metropolises, among which the most typical are the provinces of Alessandria and Mantua.

Problems of the Metropolises

In 1871, the present 14 largest Italian cities had 2.6 million inhabitants and contained 9 per cent of the Italian population. By 1921 these figures had risen respectively to 5.4 million and 14 per cent, and by 1951 to 8.1 million and 17 per cent. Today the figures are 11.3 million and 20 per cent. This rate of demographic growth has created a series of problems which have been defined as 'convulsive urbanization'.

The following are examples of these problems, emphasized particularly by Muscara (1976). Urban building has grown enormously. The number of rooms increased at a faster rate than population increase. Assuming a 1951 base at 100 for both inhabitants and rooms, by 1971 the index in Rome was 170 for inhabitants and 300 for rooms, in Milan 135 and 280 respectively, and even in the depressed town of Naples 122 and 289. Improved living conditions have given rise to other effects—foreseeable but not foreseen by the administrators—including a rise in housing and rent costs, the inadequacy of civic services and infrastructures, the deterioration of historic centres, and the emergence of unauthorized suburban districts.

Private motoring has also increased. In 1958, there were 1.4 million private cars in Italy (one for every 35 inhabitants). In 1979 this figure was 17 million, one for 3.3 inhabitants (essentially one per family), with a higher density in the cities. Because urban layouts had been conceived for pedestrians and carriages, the speed of urban traffic flow has been impeded, parking spaces are lacking, and public transport inefficient and insufficient.

Increased motorization is only one aspect of higher living standards. Increased levels of pollution produced by traffic, heating installations, sewage and garbage, and water supply problems in the larger towns particularly in the summer and especially in the South, are other examples.

Administrations have taken only minor remedial steps such as the introduction of purification plants, incinerators, drainage systems, and aqueducts.

The Political-Administrative Functions and the Centres

Historical Development

The administrative organization established when the Italian State was founded in the middle of the nineteenth century was mainly inspired by the French administration, with three districts: the commune, the *circondario* (which corresponded to the French *arrondissement*), and the province. This was to counteract regionalism, inevitable in a state which had only recently been united after centuries of division. All three levels have elected local bodies but as in France, maximum powers were invested in the prefects appointed by the central government.

The model was therefore one of a centralized state. As the prefects as well as all the local officers of the different central administrations (the interior, finance, education etc.) lived in the main provincial towns, these towns were dominated by the tertiary sector, which strongly influenced their demographic and physical development.

This system has remained unchanged during the hundred and more years of Italian unity, the only variations being the abolition of the *circondari* (1927) and the creation of 'regions with a special statute' (1948) in peripheral areas inhabited in part by linguistic minorities. The republican Constitution of 1948 (which replaced the royal statute issued exactly one hundred years earlier) also provided for the institution of 'regions with an ordinary statute', but since this was established much later (1970) it is still too soon to evaluate the influence of this new unit on the system.

We can expect in the near future a growth of bureaucracy and an increase of functions in the regional capitals. Some of these are already metropolises able to fulfil this role (Turin, Genoa, Florence, Naples, Palermo, etc.), others are only medium-sized towns proportionate to the size of their respective regions (Aosta, Campobasso, Potenza), and others must grow as their functions grow (this is already apparent in Cagliari, the main town of a region with a special statute). Disputes about the choice of a region's main town which occurred in Abruzzo between L'Aguila and Pescara, and in Calabria between Cantanzaro and Reggio, are eloquent expressions of what the population expects from a 'main town': not only prestige, but also new jobs, an increase of revenue, and civic and economic development. It is no accident that both disputes broke out in southern regions.

Owing to its administrative history, now more than a hundred years old, the main town of a province is the best example of a settlement stimulated by administrative power and functions. They are the backbone of the medium-sized town category. Some centres still strive to obtain the status of a provincial main town: it was recently obtained by Pordenone, Isernia, and Orisanto, bringing the number of Italian provinces to 95. Several other towns, from Prato to Rimini, are now 'on the waiting list'.

The Capital and Its Role

When Rome was annexed to the Italian State (1871) it was only the fifth town of Italy, exceeded not only by Naples (because of its former European primacy), but also by Milan, Genoa, and Palermo. Conferring on it the function of the capital of a state of a very different size and vitality soon encouraged a vigorous growth. It grew from 212,000 inhabitants in 1871 (0.8 per cent of the Italian population in the present boundaries) to 660,000 (1.7 per cent) in 1921, the year in which Rome became the third city of Italy after Naples and Milan. It overtook Naples in 1931 and Milan in 1936. Officially, the city has now a little less than three million inhabitants, slightly more than 5 per cent of the population of the Italian Republic.

On account of Rome's late development as a capital, no demographic comparisons can be made with other large European capitals. The Italian pattern is not primate. This has economic and social consequences. The predominance of the capital at both the decision-making (choice of siting state industries) and at a cultural level (diffusion of Rome newspapers, university influence), affects only the central-southern and insular half of the national territory. On the other hand, we cannot attribute a similar role in the North to Milan, either in the cultural field (owing to the proximity of other metropolises and medium-sized towns) or economically (because of the relative decentralization of decision-making in Italian private industry). In other words, the stable, efficient urban network of the North reduces the influence of Milan, just as the less mature urban network of the South favours the predominance of Rome.

In this sense Milan and Rome do not share Italy territorially. If anything they divide it vertically, apart from certain common functions. In very simplified form, Rome has the political-bureaucratic function (and is now growing in importance in the economic field, owing to the increasing growth of public expenditure, and to government assistance in the economy), whereas Milan (though some prefer to speak of the 'Milan-Turin ellipse') retains the financial function, certain intellectual functions (publishing), specialized services, and—due to Milan's network of European relations—that of innovation.

The Future Evolution of the System

Projection of the Present System

About ten years ago, a government-sponsored research project, with the name *Progetto 80* (Project for the 80s) was published. This project predicted the consolidation of the interdependent sub-systems of north-western Italy (Turin, Milan, Genoa and the two belts, towards Venice, and along the coast from Genoa to the Arno Valley). Development would be oriented radially around a centre, the triangle of Turin-Milan-Genoa, with ribbon-shaped conurbations along the foot of the Alps towards Venice, along the Apennines towards Bologna and Romagna and along the Tyrrhenian coast towards the Arno Valley. Smaller sub-systems would be isolated by the large northern system and by the Rome-Naples conurbation. These tendencies would lead to the worsening of regional imbalances in the South, which is already backward compared to the rest of the country, and also of a vast area of northeastern and central Italy. There would also be, according to *Progetto 80*: a decrease in the area influenced by actual urban-based organizations and hence an increase in the number of poor and abandoned areas, as well as urban and agricultural degradation; a further concentration of residential settlements, as well as manufacturing industries and services; a general deterioration of the landscape and physical resources in developed and populated areas.

Plans for a Different Development of the Settlement System

In the face of these gloomy prospects, the authors of *Progetto 80*, assuming a fundamental objective of re-establishing an equilibrium, proposed reorganizing the system by dividing it into thirty settlement sub-systems. These are divided into three fundamental types: A, sub-systems founded on present-day metropolises; B, sub-systems of 're-established equilibrium'; C, alternative sub-systems.

A sub-systems are in turn divided into true A sub-systems with a monocentric structure (the sub-systems of Turin, Rome, Naples etc.), and A_1, based on a polycentric structure (the Venetian, Sicilian sub-systems etc.). The former are distinguished by a strong hierarchy of towns, with metropolitan facilities and services concentrated in the main town. They are marked by concentration, congestion, and by a common tendency towards a fairly compact and concentric territorial expansion.

B sub-systems include the peripheral areas of Piedmont, Adige and Garda, western Emilia (linked to Turin, Genoa, and Milan) and areas of southern Latium and the Salernitano (gravitating to Rome and Naples). These systems would balance the tendency towards concentration in stronger areas and assimilate new areas into their already developed metropolitan structures.

C sub-systems would play an *alternative* role to present development trends. At present, they are remote from a metropolitan-type organization. The C group would be the cornerstone of a redistribution of the present settlement system, around which the sub-system of the C_1 group would then be articulated. C_1 sub-systems are presently areas of economic stagnation and weakly developed urban structure. Their development would take place alongside the sub-systems of the *C* group. This would bring about a transition from their present peripheral position to being that of a 'bridge' to more vibrant areas.

Fulfillment of this plan is uncertain, however, given the capabilities shown to date by Italian state and public organizations, not only on the subject of territorial reorganization and long-term planning, but also of the simple management and solution of the most urgent urban problems. After ten years, almost nothing has been done about implementing *Progetto 80* (once defined as a 'dream-book'). But fortunately its catastrophic forecasts have not come about either, thanks to some spontaneous developments (such as the revival of medium-sized and small towns).

REFERENCES

Aquarone, A. 1961. *Grandi città e aree metropolitane in Italia*, Bologna.

Barbieri, G. & Gambi, L. (eds.). 1970. *La casa rurale in Italia*, Firenze.

Bielza de Ory, Y. 1977. 'El systema urbano italiano', *Geographicalia*, 97-123.

Blondel, N. *et al.* 1977. *Les villes italiennes*, Paris.

Bottai, M. & Costa, M. 1979. 'Analisi tipologica delle città italiane', *Studi su Città Sist. Metrop. e Svil. Region.*, 49-87.

Cafiero, S. & Busca, A. 1970. *Lo sviluppo metropolitano in Italia*, Roma.

Caldo, C. & Santalucia, F. 1977. *La città meridionale*, Firenze.

Cataudella, M. 1974. *Il valore di occupazione di base nelle città italiane*, Salerno.

Compagna, F. 1967. *La politica della città*, Bari.

Cori, B. 1976. 'Rank-Size Rule et l'armature urbaine de l'Italie' (with English summary), in Pecora, A. & Pracchi, R. (eds.), *Italian Contributions to the 23rd International Geographical Congress, Moscow 1976*, Roma, 97-109.

Cori, B. 1979. 'La questione urbana in Italia' *Geogr. n. Scuole*, xxiv, 240-7.

Cori, B. 1980. 'La geografica urbana', in Corna-Pellegrini, G. & Brusa, C. (eds.), *La Ricerca Geografica in Italia 1960-80*, Varese, 273-91.

Cori, B. & Cortesi, G. 1976. 'Le reti urbane delle regioni italiane nell' ottica della Rank-Size Rule', *Studi su Città Sist. Metrop. e Svil. Region.*, II, 27-34.

Cori, B. & Costa, M. 1970. 'Les cartes des transports comme élément pour déterminer les zones d'attraction des villes. L'exemple de l'Italie', *Int. Conf. on Transportation Maps*, Budapest: 56-73.

Costa, M., Da Pozzo, C. & Bartaletti, F. 1976. 'The role of Small Towns in the Italian Urban Network', in Pecora, A. & Pracchi, R. (eds.), *op. cit.*: 111-24.

Dematteis, G. *et al.* 1971. 'Le città alpine', *Atti XXI Congr. Geogr. Ital.*, vol. ii, t. ii: 1-395.

Ferro, G. *et al.* 1967. 'Città e campagna in Italia', *Atti XX Congr. Geogr. Ital.*, Roma, vol. ii: 149-416.

Gambi, L. 1973. 'Da città ad area metropolitana', in *Storia d'Italia*, Torino, vol. v: 365-424.

Gentileschi, M. L. 1976. 'Immigration Flows to the Regional Capitals of Italy', in Pecora, A. & Pracchi, R. (eds.), *op. cit.*: 73-80.

Mainardi, R. (ed.) 1971. *Le grandi città italiane. Saggi geografici ed urbanistici*, Milano.

Migliorini, E. 1976. 'Spostamenti di popolazione in Italia nell' ultimo quarto di secolo' (with English summary), in Pecora, A. & Pracchi, R., *Op. cit.*: 61-72.

Mori, A. & Cori, B. 1979. 'L'area di attrazione delle maggiori città italiane' (with English summary), *Riv. Geogr. Ital.*, lxxvi: 3-14.

Muscarà, C. 1976. *La Società Sradicata. Saggi sulla geografica dell'Italia attuale*, Milano.

Muscarà, C. (ed.). 1978. *Megalopoli Mediterranea*, Milano.

Nice, B. 1961. 'Sviluppo e problemi delle grandi città italiane.' *Pubbl. Ist. Geogr. Econ. Univ. Firenze*, x: 1-24.

'Progetto 80: Proiezioni Territoriali'. 1971. a Cura del Centro Studi e Piani Economici, *Urbanistica*, n. 57: 1-60.

Rochefort, R. 1964. 'Le rôle des métropoles dans l'urbanisation de l'Italie', *Inf. Géogr.*, xxviii: 102-8.

Saibene, C. 1975. 'Sedi umane e sviluppo socio-economico nel Mezzogiorno', *Atti XXII Congr. Geogr. Ital.*, Salerno, vol. ii, t. ii: 7-33.

Seronde, A. M., 1976. *Rome, croissance d'une capitale*, Thèse d'Etat, Paris.

Sestini, A. 1958. 'Qualche osservazione geografico-statistica sulle conurbazioni italiane', *Studie in onore di R. Biasutti*, Firenze: 313-28.

Straszewicz, L. 1969. 'Rzym jako metropolia swiatowa', *Przegl. Geogr.*, xli: 623-50.

Toschi, U. 1966. *La città. Geografia urbana*, Torino.

Touring Club Italiano. 1978. *Le Città*, Milano.

Vallega, A. 1971. 'Le proiezioni territoriali del Progetto 80', *Pubbl. Ist. Sc. Geogr. Univ. Genova*, xix: 1-36.

Valussi, G. (ed.). 1978. *Italiani in movimento*, Pordenone.

Vlora, N. R. 1979. *Città e territorio. Distribuzione e crescita urbana in Italia*, Bologna.

14 THE NATIONAL SETTLEMENT SYSTEM IN SPAIN

MANUEL FERRER AND ANDRÉS PRECEDO

The Historical Evolution of the Settlement System

Awareness of the situation of Spain as a crossroads which at the same time remained peripheral to the great diffusion points of Western European culture and Islamic civilization, as well as of the great geomorphological and bio-climatic diversity of the Spanish peninsula, enables us to understand not only the changes which have taken place in the past, but also the extraordinary variety of settlements in the country today.

Ancient and Medieval Spain

Southern Spain almost certainly served as the base of one of the first urban civilizations of the Ancient World, which developed along the Guadalquivir river and in Lower Andalucía. Along the southern coast, a commercial centre was created, joining the Eastern Mediterranean with the Atlantic lands of both the European and African continents. The colonization carried out by the Phoenicians, Greeks, and Carthaginians led to the spread of urban life along the Mediterranean coast, thereby connecting earlier settlements. Hence for the first time we can speak of a Mediterranean axis open to the Atlantic. Andalucía, over twenty centuries ago, was a breeding ground of agrarian activities, of craftsmanship, and of commercial interchanges, which—along with the attraction of mineral resources such as gold, silver, and copper—led to a flourishing of urban life.

When settlements by the Romans began, it was helped by the urban forms established in earlier times. The centre of the peninsula and the North were still, however, in a development stage which was tribal in nature. Rome signified the first attempt at placing the entire peninsula within a single administrative system. The Romans used two prime elements: the provincial organization—which in time underwent notable changes—and the construction of a road network that reached practically all of the peninsula. They also created military base camps, judicial capitals, commercial centres, and other nuclei to be settled by people brought from Rome. Thus the Romans introduced the urban fact into the interior of the country.

A great new epoch came into being with the coming of the Moors who occupied a large part of the peninsula prior to their expulsion via the Christian *Reconquista*. Both events had enormous repercussions from the point of view of settlements. Once more, the southern part of the peninsula was revitalized, and the city came to be considered as the ideal habitat. The high level of urbanization was indeed surprising. The older cities were further expanded, to the extent that Moorish Spain offered levels of the following order: Córdoba, 100,000 inhabitants (possibly the largest city in Western Europe in the tenth century); Sevilla, 40,000; Almería, 27,000; Granada, 26,000; and Málaga, 20,000. This urban growth did not come about through commerce alone, but through industry as well. The Moors in their push towards the North also strengthened other pre-existing cities (such as Visigothic Toledo with 37,000 inhabitants and the Roman cities of Zaragoza and Valencia with 20,000 and 15,000 inhabitants respectively). The Moors followed the Roman example of creating cities of a political and administrative nature along the great routes, for strategic purposes.

Meanwhile, in the north of Spain, a series of groups who shared a Christian background began to organize, and eventually they were to expel the Moors by means of the *Reconquista*. These same groups were to play a prime role regarding the organization of Spain's political, agrarian, and urban territory. At the same time, the old centres of resistance were strengthened with respect to religious, political, administrative, and military purposes.

Around the end of the eleventh century, the *Camino de Santiago* or 'Way of Saint James', by attracting foreign settlers, contributed to the creation of areas of religious pilgrimage and to cultural penetration from Europe. This led to a further integration of the northern and northwestern territories and kingdoms, boosted commerce and crafts, and therefore urban life. A coastal axis was also created along the Cantabrian coast, revolving around fishing activities and commerce. At the end of the twelfth century other axes were created, through commercial routes which joined trade in Flemish, French and English textiles with that in Castilian wools. Later on, Castilian cities took over the functions of storage and distribution of the local wool.

On the Mediterranean-Levantine axis, an urban economy was created in Cataluña in the twelfth century, which was to reach its greatest splendour in the following century, and which was to have as its chief protagonists the cities of Barcelona and Valencia, along with several other cities in the interior of Cataluña. It is interesting to note that from the beginning of the fourteenth century manufacturing centres in wool products existed in Castilla and Aragón, but nevertheless Barcelona was at that time—and is still—the most important centre with regard to the textile industry. We must also point out for this epoch something which has been relevant both in the past and in more recent years: the important role of the Ebro Valley as a development focal point of urbanization.

It is appropriate to mention the further settlement of the southern part of Spain. Towards the beginning of the thirteenth century, settlers from Castilla and León occupied parts of the Southern Meseta which were in large measure empty. This settlement took place on large tracts of land under ecclesiastic and military rule, leading to a type of habitat consisting of large villages. In contrast the occupation of Andalucía and of the

Kingdom of Murcia, which took place half-way through the thirteenth century, was carried out on the basis of the already existing infrastructure. From the end of the fourteenth century, Andalucía once more became important due to its role as a link between the Atlantic and the Mediterranean; between Spain and Northern Africa. Its influence even spread to the Canary Islands. Thus a flourishing economy was created by opening a new commercial route that joined Italy and Flanders via Gibraltar. The shift of European economic activity and interests toward the west, begun in the fifteenth century, also favoured economic growth in this area. It reached its highest point with the opening up of trade with America. The importance of Sevilla with regard to this trade had repercussions in Levante and also in the Basque Country, due to the shift of initiatives and capital from these areas to the Andalusian metropolis. The latter subsequently gained prominence as a competitor to the Italian merchants.

Modern Spain

Following the lines of evolution of the Spanish settlement system, we can establish, in broad form, the characteristics of the rural and urban population of the country in the fifteenth century. Obviously, there was at that time a relative absence of large cities and an abundance of small administrative and economic centres thriving on rural activities. We can establish the following regional schema: Atlantic Spain was an area of dispersed settlement with very few urban nuclei. In the Meseta two clearly distinguishable sub-regions could be found: Castilla la Vieja and León, to the north of the Central Cordillera, where the population tended to be concentrated in small centres, some of which—in the mountainous zones—were in reality hamlets; and others in the Duero Valley which might be called urban nuclei. To the south of the Tajo River, the concentration of the population in larger centres was more evident: large nuclei of several thousand inhabitants appeared as oases dotting the largely empty rural landscape. This phenomenon became more pronounced toward the south.

Near the end of the sixteenth century an official capital was needed for the country. Among the possible cities, Philip II chose Madrid in 1563, and by 1597 its population had grown to 60,000 inhabitants. Thus in the heart of the peninsula, which previously had been little urbanized, there emerged an important focal point which was to have repercussions for future times. In that century Andalucía was to gain even more prominence: Sevilla, thanks to the monopoly it enjoyed in trade with America, grew to become the largest city in the peninsula, with 100,000 inhabitants.

During the seventeenth century, crisis and decadence were the order of the day, both from a demographic and, above all, an economic perspective. The causes of such decadence were epidemics, emigration, and the negative effects of wars, so that the country as a whole, which had 8 million inhabitants in 1600, had only 7 million by the end of the seventeenth century.

Decadence and instability were also to affect the settlement system. The shift of the centre of gravity from Spain to other countries in the European continent also took place; Spain and especially the Mediterranean suffered from the shift which led other countries to gain ground in trade with America. On the regional level, Castilla lost the demographic and economic importance which it had gained in the Early Middle Ages. The only exception of note was the strong dynamism of Madrid, which overtook Sevilla, the previous great Spanish metropolis.

Apart from the demographic and economic revival which Spain enjoyed in the eighteenth century, these hundred years accentuated the fundamental contrast between the more highly populated and urbanized coastal periphery of the country, and the interior spaces. In fact, the decadence which had begun in the previous century continued to affect the latter zone. The agricultural enrichment of the periphery, where new techniques and products—such as corn, potatoes, alfalfa—and the improvement of port facilities had a positive influence on commerce and industry, also positively affected urban life. Also, the proclamation of free trade for all the peninsular ports with regard to business with America acted as a stimulus.

Apart from these events which are specific to this period, we must also bear in mind that the mineral resources of the country are mainly located in the periphery as opposed to the centre. This fact was to have an important effect at the onset of the Industrial Revolution. In the eighteenth century Atlantic Spain prospered, but the greatest and most dynamic growth took place in Levante, where Barcelona soon became the leader due to the technological changes and new markets which affected the Catalonian textile industry. Moreover, Valencia and some Levantine market towns experienced considerable growth as a result of the so-called Agricultural Revolution.

The nineteenth century saw the increasing organization of the Spanish economy around its national capital, Madrid, via a radial road communications network. Madrid became the most nodal of all the Spanish cities. The contruction of the rail networks began in 1848, following a similar pattern and structure to the road network. This was decisive with regard to the unification of the national settlement system and led to the integration of Spain into industrial Europe, in a colonial fashion. Another significant event was the provincial division carried out in 1832. This division was made on the basis of spatial units having a similar population size and did not necessarily take into account either the geographic size of the areas or their history. The institutionalization of the provincial division eventually confirmed the administrative principle with regard to territorial organization and the consolidation of particular cities as capitals of the newly created administrative units. Thus was created the basic spatial framework of the regional sub-system in Spain: the province.

The Industrial Age

The Acceleration of Spatial Imbalances. The industrial revolution introduced two regional areas as great focal points in the country: Cataluña (Barcelona) and the Basque Country (Bilbao), which operated as peripheral sub-centres of the Western European industrial heartland. The consolidation of these two zones, which tended to polarize the economic and urban growth of the country, took place at the time of the First World War, and the zenith of their growth took place during the 1920 and 1930s. In those years the rest of the country maintained a more balanced network within the framework of a traditional hierarchy from the provincial capitals down to the smaller central places.

At this time, the dualism evolved which placed the agrarian areas of the centre and the south in sharp contrast with the industrial areas of the North and Levante. Meanwhile, Madrid continued to gain population and to reaffirm its position as the capital city of the country. Andalucía, having lost its link with America, underwent an economic and financial decline. Still, the considerable urban infrastructure which had accumulated in the south continued to provide a basic network in that part of the country.

In the 1930s another phenomenon began to take effect: massive internal and external migrations. During the nineteenth century up to the First World War, the natural population growth of the country was so great that Spain was unable to absorb and incorporate the entire population increase within its economic framework. In rural areas such as Castilla, Galicia, and Aragón, where there was physical proximity to the new growth points, the migratory effects were most intense. For example, between 1920 and 1930 the rural areas expelled approximately 40 per cent of the country's annual natural growth. The out-migration, which during the nineteenth century was to provincial capitals, shifted during this period in favour of the new growth areas of the country, namely Cataluña, the Basque Country, and Madrid. Nevertheless, in spite of continuing out-migration during subsequent decades, the Spanish population surpassed 35 million inhabitants in 1975.

Development 'At All Costs' and Urbanization. The following facts underly any discussion of the new socio-economic period begun after the Civil War of the 1930s. First was the establishment of an economic development model in which agglomeration economies were emphasized to such a degree that the growth of the three traditional industrial and demographic centres increased the level of polarization.

Second, the spontaneous character of Spanish industrial growth was unable to impede the backwash effect which counterbalanced this trend. Thus from the industrial focal point along the Basque Coast diffusion took place towards the interior of the Basque hinterland. On the other hand,

Barcelona, which until the Spanish Civil War had accommodated the larger part of Cataluña's urban population, experienced a decentralization of growth towards its regional periphery. In the Levante, on the basis of the capital reserves accumulated through its increasingly sophisticated market-oriented agrarian economy and the strengthening of a dispersed artisan tradition, a modern industrial axis came into being along the line of the old Levantine urban network. Hence the Cantabrian and Levantine axes become the most important industrial and urban focal points of the country, based on a simultaneous process of concentration and dissemination.

Third, once the country had been rebuilt after the devastations suffered during the Civil War, the State tried, through a number of different policies and plans, to correct or lessen the imbalance created by a very localized process of industrialization. At the same time, because of the centralist character of the new regime, the State undertook the task of building Madrid industrially, granting all kinds of facilities to both the public (State-owned or State-run) and private sectors. By the 1950s Madrid, with its rapid industrial growth, had added to its importance as the nation's capital. This growth was further enhanced by the advantages of the communications network and by the influx of population, as well as the shifting of the centres of non-political decision-making towards Madrid.

In addition, the State has attempted to carry out regional policies with regard to the intensive agrarian settlements of depressed areas, in Badajoz and Jaén, for example, and to create 'poles' for the promotion and industrial development of other areas. The policy concerning these growth poles—from 1946 to 1976—has had a notable effect in some cases. The State-supported growth poles and those promoted by two provinces enjoying a special status—Navarra and Alava—have helped to boost the spread effects in what was to become the Basque peripheral sub-system. Moreover, this policy has led to the consolidation of industry in some regional metropolises, such as Zaragoza—an urban-industrial bridge between the Basque Country and Cataluña—and Valladolid. Thus, the objective of strengthening interior cities was partially achieved. A different result was achieved in the case of the 8 peripheral poles. The policy of development poles did not strengthen regional urban networks in those areas. Rather, they led to further imbalances.

Fourth, the fact that Madrid has become an enormous demographic and functional centre makes the equally enormous empty spaces of the interior —at least in terms of industry—stand out even more. Except in the case of Valladolid, State policy has attempted to relieve the congestion of the national capital by creating the basic framework for industrial development in neighbouring provincial capitals and in small urban nuclei in the surrounding provinces. The result of this policy has been, by and large, a complete failure. In only a few cases has there been an industrial take-off. Madrid at present is surrounded by two peripheral belts. The first is of dormitory cities and other small cities with a few radial industrial corridors, and the second is an exterior belt which is economically depressed.

Fifth, tourism has been of prime importance in the urbanization process in Spain in recent years. The entire Mediterranean coastline has become dotted with a number of urbanized areas which form a discontinuous but dense line along the coast. Not only has this expanded the urban landscape but it has also given it a special flavour. There has also been, in recent years, a proliferation all over the country of secondary or permanent residential areas in suburban and rural-urban areas, especially near great metropolises.

Finally, three specific phenomena of the rural landscape bear upon the urban fact. First, the rural crisis has influenced more than 80 per cent of the country's *municipios* (lower order administrative units), negatively affecting growth in most of the central places in these zones. Second, in progressive agricultural areas—such as Levante—or in those areas where the industrialization process has penetrated, the improvement of communications and the widespread use of the automobile have led to a progressive extension of commuter movements. This, in turn, has led to a further stagnation of the tertiary capacity of the central places and other service centres. Third, those central places which have been affected by the industrialization process have undergone population growth, but this had not necessarily been accompanied by functional revitalization.

The Present-day Spatial Pattern

As a result of all these processes, a fundamental feature of the distribution of population and urban settlements in Spain is the contrast between the periphery and the interior (Figure 14.1). In brief, this is due to the following factors:

1) the accumulation of population in Andalucía and Levante-Cataluña, brought about by the historical importance of these areas;
2) the location of industry, during the first phase of the Industrial Revolution, in a coastal band in the Cantabrian area and in Cataluña, which left large interior zones such as Aragón and Galacia empty;
3) an intense out-migration from the Spanish interior with the newly created industrial zones along the coast and Madrid being the benefactors;
4) the strengthening of the industrial focal points in the North after the Civil War, the constitution of the Madrid urban area, and the appearance of the Levantine industrial axis.

This second phase has been more intense than the previous one, and has led to virtual depopulation of the interior. However Andalucía, in spite of joining the migratory wave, has maintained its traditionally high demographic indices.

This polarization in turn has led to different demographic, economic, and

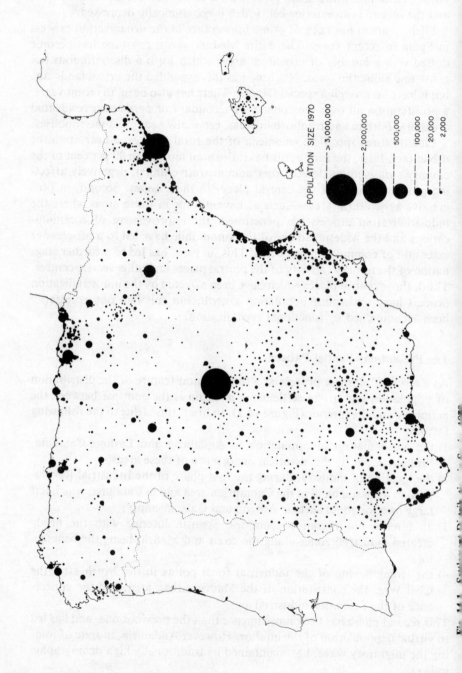

POPULATION SIZE 1970

> 3,000,000

2,000,000

500,000

100,000

20,000

2,000

urban structures on a regional level. To analyse this, we have taken as spatial units the functional regions organized by the respective urban sub-systems, delimited on the basis of inter-provincial transportation flows (Figure 14.2). Of the eleven sub-systems which make up the national settlement system, seven are peripheral, with the coastal provinces operating as 'centres' for the non-coastal provinces, and four are in the interior, and are much less integrated. Within interior Spain, the central urban region — Madrid and its satellite cities — contrasts sharply with the almost complete demographic and urban vacuum found in the remaining interior areas, with the exception of the two metropolises which organize the Castilla-Leon region and Aragón: Valladolid and Zaragoza, respectively.

Population Distribution

The contrast between the peripheral and interior sub-systems rests upon the fact that the former contain 76 per cent of Spain's total population, on only 50 per cent of the total surface area. In the periphery four centres of gravity — Asturias, País Vasco, Cataluña and Levante — contain 58 per cent of the population, with densities which vary between 80.5 inhabitants per square kilometre in the Basque Country and its hinterland, and 160.4 in Cataluña. In the remainder of the periphery, Galicia and Andalucía also have relatively high densities — 87.8 and 68.5 respectively. Conversely, in the interior regions — apart from Madrid — densities are much lower (between 20 and 30).

The three main populated areas in the periphery correspond to three economic regions:

1) The industrial and urban fringe of the periphery which occupies two coastal axes stretching westward and southward from the extreme ends of the Pyrenees: the Cantabrian Axis and the Cataluña-Levante Axis ('developed' Spain);

2) Two dispersed fringes *nebulosa* in the northwest and the south (Galicia and Andalucía respectively) both of a rural nature, although urbanized due mainly to demographic pressure ('developing' Spain);

3) Ample interior spaces, essentially rural and sparsely populated, with only one sub-region — Madrid — standing out ('underdeveloped' Spain).

Urbanization and Ruralization

In the developed part of Spain the accumulation of population has been essentially urban, with great contrasts between dispersed rural areas and urban nuclei. Intensive agriculture also coincides with important urban areas located along the coast. In the parts of Spain which are undergoing change, demographic pressure is found both in rural and urban areas. In some areas we can speak of over-urbanization. In underdeveloped Spain urban areas are relatively unimportant as compared to rural spaces — except for the case of Madrid — and more than half of the *municipios* have fewer than 15 inhabitants per square kilometre.

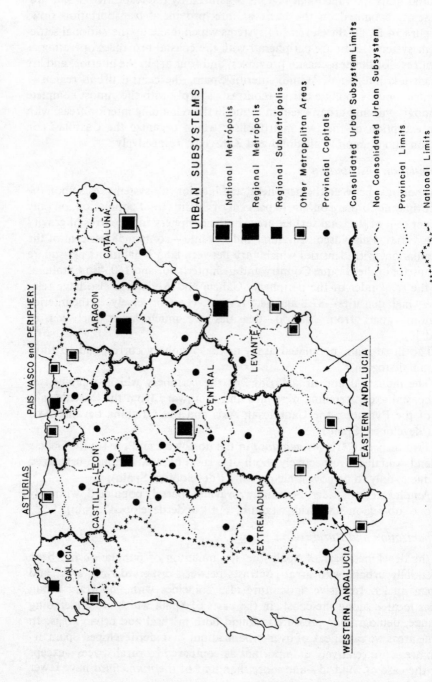

Fig. 14.2 Urban Sub-systems

URBAN SUBSYSTEMS

- National Metrópolis
- Regional Metrópolis
- Regional Submetrópolis
- Other Metropolitan Areas
- Provincial Capitals
- Consolidated Urban Subsystem Limits
- Non Consolidated Urban Subsystem
- Provincial Limits
- National Limits

CATALUÑA
PAIS VASCO and PERIPHERY
ARAGON
LEVANTE
CENTRAL
ASTURIAS
CASTILLA-LEON
EXTREMADURA
EASTERN ANDALUCIA
GALICIA
WESTERN ANDALUCIA

In the developed areas of Spain the population which lives in metropolitan areas and industrial cities ranges from 50 per cent to 75 per cent of the total population. The lowest figures for rural population are to be found in Asturias and País Vasco (3.7 per cent and 6 per cent of the total), whereas the maximum figures correspond to Cataluña and Levante (excluding Murcia) with 11.5 per cent and 16.7 per cent respectively.

Galicia and Andalucía both have rural percentages which closely resemble those found in the interior (40.7 per cent in Galicia, 42.1 per cent in the eastern part of Andalucía and 26.1 per cent in the western part). In these areas the percentage of people residing in metropolitan areas or industrial cities is very low. In the interior, urban population and industrial *municipios* account for only 50 per cent of the total. Completely rural *municipios* house 40 per cent of the population of those areas.

Migratory Movements

The migratory balance in the different regions is shown in Table 14.1. The balance is negative exceeding one million between 1901 and 1970 in the central sub-system (1,302,617 excluding Madrid). In the remaining interior sub-system the number of migrants is close to this figure—between 725,000 and 850,000. In contrast, the balance is positive in Levante (40,000) and very much more so in Cataluña (approximately 2,000,000). The Basque sub-system, due to its outer fringes which are not so developed, shows a negative figure for the period under consideration.

In the 1960s, when the migratory wave reached its maximum, there were positive balances of almost 750,000 in Cataluña, 250,000 in Levante, and more than 200,000 in the Basque Country and its periphery. In contrast, Western Andalucía has been the greatest loser ($-617,199$) along with the Central Region ($-513,310$ excluding Madrid), followed by almost all the rest of the interior regions, Galicia, and Eastern Andalucía (between $-250,000$ and $-300,000$). Basing percentages for the 1961-70 period upon the 1970 population, we can point out more precisely what migration has meant, from a negative point of view, for some of *Spain's functional regions*: close to 30 per cent in the Centre, excluding Madrid, and in Extremadura; approximately 15 per cent in Western Andalucía and in the Castilla-Leon sub-system; around 10 per cent in Eastern Andalucía and Galicia.

Urban Hierarchy

The criterion used to establish different levels of the hierarchy is a functional one. The calculation of centrality is made by taking the number, class, and size of employment in tertiary functions. The result shows a national settlement system that has a bipolar structure. This can be seen by comparing the functional levels obtained with a theoretical distribution of the type $K = 3$ (Table 14.2). Keeping in mind that this model is rather rigid, it still may be useful as a point of reference.

Table 14.1: Demographic Indicators—Functional Regions

Sub-systems	Number of Provinces	Area in km²	1970 Population	Density (per km²)	Migratory Balance 1901-70	Migratory Balance 1961-70	Migrants (1961-70) as percent of 1970 population
Galicia	4	29,434	2,583,674	87.8	−835,770	−229,163	−8.86
Asturias	1	10,565	1,045,635	99.0	−33,459	−31,378	−3.00
Vasco Periferia	7	42,274	3,404,429	80.5	−15,308	+185,685	+5.45
Aragon	3	47,669	1,152,708	24.2	−249,859	−34,563	−2.99
Cataluña	4	31,930	5,122,567	160.4	+2,109,286	+720,523	+14.06
Levante	5	49,480	4,240,594	85.7	+40,454	+220,935	+5.20
East Andalucia	3	28,581	1,975,709	69.1	−807,333	−226,081	−11.44
West Andalucia	5	58,687	3,995,568	68.1	−729,975	−617,199	−15.44
Extremadura	2	41,602	1,145,376	27.5	−549,674	−298,123	−26.02
Castilla-Leon	5	54,494	1,783,597	32.7	−349,116	−276,045	−15.47
Centro (including Madrid)	8	97,647	5,645,550	57.8	+679,812	+174,412	+3.08
Centro (excluding Madrid)	7	(89,652)	(1,852,989)	(20.7)	(−1,302,617)	(−513,310)	(−27.64)
SPAIN (Peninsula only)	47	492,363	32,095,407	65.2	−1,240,942	−410,997	-------

Source: Instituto Nacional de Estadistica. Migratory balance calculated by Alban d'Entremont.

Table 14.2: *The Urban Hierarchy in Spain*

Levels	Categories	No. of Central Places Observed a	b	Theoretical
I	National Metropolises	2	2	2
II	Regional Metropolises	5	7	4
III	Middle Level Metropolitan Areas	13	10	12
IV	Middle Level Cities	43	43	36
V	Small Cities	89	90	108
VI	*Cabeceras Comarcales*	320	320	324

Notes
a   According to method of Ranks
b   According to typical deviation   472   472   486

The centrality of each city in the first three levels according to method of Ranks is as follows:
Level I   Madrid (197.3), Barcelona (131.0);
Level II   Valencia (32.0), Sevilla (26.5), Bilbao (23.8), Zaragoza (19.2), Málaga (16.6);
Level III   Alicante (14.2), La Coruña (13.1), Oviedo (12.5), San Sebastián (12.2), Granada (10.5), Córdoba (10.2), Vigo (10.1), Murcia (9.9), Santander (9.7), Valladolid (9.6), Pamplona (8.3), Cádiz (8.6) and Salamanca (7.9).

These relationships coincide almost perfectly with the metropolitan areas delimited by utilizing demographic, morphological, and spatial criteria; the only difference is that Salamanca, which is not classified as a metropolitan area, does not appear here. The first level is occupied by Spain's two great national metropolises, Madrid and Barcelona. On the second level are large regional metropolises with a population above 500,000 inhabitants, and on the third level, metropolitan areas of a medium size but which still organize the remaining sub-systems. These are in fact the urban centres upon which the Spanish functional space hinges (Figure 14.3).

Spatial Distribution

Though covering the same surface area as the rest of the country, (50 per cent), the peripheral regions contain 65.5 per cent of all the urban settlements and 68.9 per cent of Spain's urban population. Those percentages would be greater were it not for Madrid.

In the coastal periphery there are four times as many metropolitan areas as in the interior. However, there is only 1.8 times more urban population. This is indicative of the polarization or primacy of the interior zones as compared to the polycentricity of the periphery. Of the 7 million inhabitants living in the interior, 4 million are to be found in Madrid.

In the middle urban levels and at the bottom level (small- and medium-sized cities and central places, called *cabeceras comarcales*) there is three times the population in the periphery as compared to the interior. However, the numbers of those settlements in those respective areas are not so

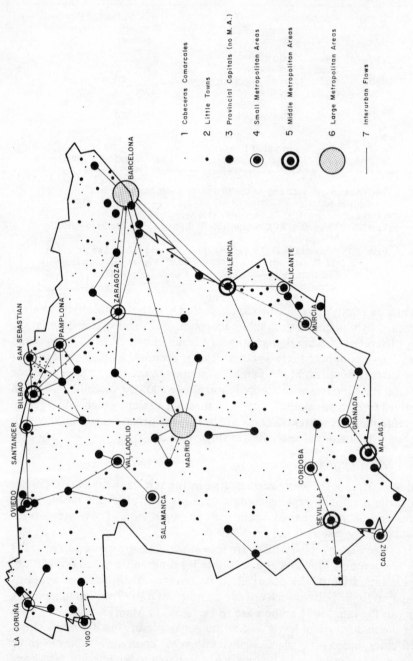

Fig. 14.3   The Structure of the Urban System

divergent: 2.2 and 1.7 respectively. This signifies that in the periphery the *cabeceras comarcales* have maintained their former vitality or else have grown to become small- or medium-sized cities, whereas in the interior they tend to have the same population as before.

In Tables 14.1 and 14.2 it should be emphasized that the contrast between the periphery and the interior is due mainly to the urban concentration in the provinces located along the coast (13,858, 517 inhabitants versus only 2,192,517 in the non-coastal provinces).

Table 14.3 also shows the following contrast: in the periphery the different levels of the hierarchy each contain somewhat similar numbers, whereas in the interior the population in middle-sized and small metropolitan areas comes to less than half of that living in cities at a lower level. This shows the unimportance of the interior metropolitan areas apart from Madrid; that is, in the interior the main elements (medium-sized and small metropolitan areas) which contribute towards equilibrium within the organization of any territory are largely absent.

On the other hand, excluding Madrid, the urban world is very 'ruralized', in the sense that approximately half the urban population inhabits small cities and *cabeceras comarcales*. That is to say, there is a traditional urban milieu which is linked to the rural environment, as compared to the high index of metropolitization found in the periphery. We find the highest percentage of non-metropolitan settlements have all the lower-order functions. The traditional *cabeceras comarcales* have improved their status by means of industry and the subsequent accumulation of population, converting themselves into small- and medium-sized cities which are more fully urban and more strongly integrated within the metropolitan system than within the rural milieu.

Conclusion

In the historical evolution of the settlement system in Spain, the Industrial Revolution constituted a break with earlier patterns. The spatial changes in the traditional settlement distribution occurred in line with locational variations experienced by the diffusion centres of the Mediterranean and Atlantic areas. The industrial phase signified a shifting of the system towards the north of the country, at the same time as contrasts between the periphery and the centre increased, the national capital being the sole exception. The internal inbalances observed today are the result of a very rapid industrialization and urbanization process which provoked huge migratory waves from rural areas and small cities towards three great focal points of industrial accumulation: the Basque Country, Cataluña and Madrid. Other metropolitan areas of regional or sub-regional function also benefited from this process. On the whole, the urban system in Spain is largely bipolar in structure, and possesses a large degree of equilibrium on the national level, whereas on a regional level an enormous lack of equilibrium is the norm.

Table 14.3: *Urban Levels*

Levels	Peripheral Systems		Interior Systems		Total	
	Number	Total Population	Number	Total Population	Number	Total Population
1. Large Metropolitan Areas	1	3,550,970	1	4,012,905	2	7,563,875
2. Middle Metropolitan Areas	4	3,101,288	1	540,308	5	3,641,596
3. Small Metropolitan Areas	11	2,496,984	2	420,518	13	2,917,502
4. Middle Cities	27	2,775,865	16	1,014,034	43	3,789,899
5. Small Cities	64	1,683,680	25	538,777	89	2,222,457
6. *Cabeceras comarcales*	202	2,339,324	118	666,584	320	3,005,968
	309	15,948,111	163	7,193,126	472	23,141,237

Surface Area, Peripheral sub-systems: 250.951 km² (50,96% of total peninsular surface area). Interior sub-systems 241,412 km²

REFERENCES

Aznar, A. 1974. 'Infraestructura y regionalización de las provincias españolas; Una aplicación del análisis factorial'. *Revista Española de Economía*, Madrid, mayo-agosto.

Capel, H. 1973. *La red urbana española 1950-1960*. Universidad de Barcelona.

Casas Torres, J. M. 1973. 'La selección de núcleos de población "cabeceras de comarca" para el bienio 1972-3'. *Revista Geographica.*

Ferrer, M. 1980. 'Introducción al estudio ecológico de las ciudades españolas'. *Homenaje a Floristán Samanes*, Pamplona.

Ferrer, M. 1977. 'Spatial distribution of industrial employment in Spain'. *Geographia Polonica*, Varsovia.

Ferrer, M. 1978. 'Changes in settlement patterns as a result of urbanization in Spain'. *Geographia Polonica*, Varsovia.

Ferrer, M. & Precedo, A. 1980. 'El sistema español de asentamientos'. *Acta Geographica Lovaniensa*, Leuven.

Precedo, A. 1974. 'Galicia: Red urbana y desarrollo regional'. *Boletin de la Real Sociedad Geográfica*, Madrid.

Precedo, A. 1980. 'Los desequilibrios espaciales en España'. *Geographica*, 1980.

Precedo, A. 1980. 'Algunas consideraciones teórico-conceptuales a propósito del estudio del sistema gallego de asentamientos'. *Homenaje a Floristán Samanes*, Pamplona.

Racionero, L. 1978. 'El sistema de ciudades'. *Alianza Editorial*, Madrid.

Ribas i Piera, M. 1976. *Sistemas urbanos y desarrollo regional.* Instituto Nacional de Prospectiva y Desarrollo Económico, Madrid.

15 THE PORTUGUESE SETTLEMENT SYSTEM

A. SIMÕES LOPES, J. C. LILAIA, AND M. REIS FERREIRA

Some Conceptual Issues and Definitions

The study of settlement geography in Portugal has been largely of a static nature, essentially descriptive and basically concerned with population data. More detailed studies have been produced, but they are generally restricted to isolated units (e.g. Gaspar, 1972). Studies of the whole settlement system are rare: apart from a general study devoted to the reorganization of the settlement network (C.E.P. *Centro de Estudos de Planeamento* —Centre for Planning Studies, 1961), these normally consider only some specific urban functions (e.g. C.E.U.H. *Centro de Estudos de Urbanismo e Habitação*—Centre for Housing and Urban Studies, 1977). For both conceptual and operational reasons, the systems approach has not yet been used in the study of settlement geography in Portugal.

The spatial units of reference in Portugal are *cidades* (cities), *vilas* (towns), and *aldeias* (villages).[1] They are to a degree related to the administrative status of urban agglomerations, which in turn depend on the administrative division of the country.

The *distritos* (districts), *municípios* (municipalities), and *freguesias* (parishes) are the administrative divisions. The chief centre of a *distrito* is always a *cidade*. *Municípios* of some importance also have *cidades* as chief centres, otherwise their chief centre will be called a *vila*. *Aldeias* are small agglomerations, and there are still smaller ones called simply *lugares* (hamlets). The country is divided into regions for planning purposes. These regions are groups of *distritos*. They were created during the 1960s and although intended to be provisional, the 1976 Constitution officially established their existence. However, their physical delimitation has not yet been determined. The present structure of the Portuguese settlement system is related to the distribution of natural resources, but this must be seen in historical perspective. The economic and social structure of the whole country is clearly associated with the settlement system, which is also a result of the geographical situation of Portugal. Historical evolution, the distribution of resources, even geograpical situation, all explain why the settlement system is necessarily dominated by two urban agglomerations located near the coast having port cities as their nuclei.

Historical Growth and Development[2]

Portugal became independent during the first half of the twelfth century. Its frontiers are the oldest in Europe. They have also been the most stable.

Since the country is a small part of the Iberian Peninsula, the origin and evolution of its settlement system have many common features with those of Spain. However, geographical factors, notably the country's relative position in Europe, its narrow width (maximum east-west distance of about 200 km), and the great extent of its coastline (832 km), have produced certain distinctive characteristics.

Although some of the most important population centres date from pre-Roman times, it was under Roman influence that an organized movement towards urbanization took place. This organization was based upon the very efficient Roman road system, which also might explain several features of the Portuguese pattern of spatial disequilibrium (Figure 15.1). The barbarian invasion, however, reduced this urbanization trend. It was only with the Moslem occupation that the urbanization movement was renewed, but Arab influence was largely confined to the South.

The Middle Ages was a dynamic period in Portuguese history although population growth was very slight. There was the war against the Moslems to enlarge the national territory, followed by war with other Iberian countries to secure independence; and later maritime expansion. This latter period brought a significant loss of population coupled with an enormous influx of wealth. Centres continued to be built on high defensible sites, whereas the development of commerce influenced the internal organization of the centres. The settlement pattern still showed Roman influence, but urban development was more intense where Moslem influence was greater. At the beginning of the sixteenth century Lisboa had between 50,000 and 60,000 inhabitants, plus 15,000 to 20,000 in its immediate area of influence. This was twice the size of Madrid and more than four times the size of Porto, Portugal's second largest population centre. Primacy, which is a clear feature of the country's present settlement system, was already evident by the end of the fifteenth century.

In modern times maritime expansion has affected the intra-urban organization of almost every city. But the industrial revolution influenced the development mainly of Lisboa, Porto, and one or two other towns. Industrialization, being largely dependent on imports, benefited the port cities and the more densely populated areas. Considering this development, along with the Portuguese road pattern, the railway network, and other development projects of the second half of the nineteenth century, it is not difficult to understand the present settlement pattern, namely the persistent dominance of Lisboa and the enormous imbalance between the littoral region and the interior.

The greatest change in the settlement pattern came about after World War II. Until that time, rural life was found very close to the city centre even in the major cities. Since then, farms have been replaced by buildings, by shanty-towns, by dormitory towns. The development of tertiary industries increased still more the dominance of Lisboa, which must be

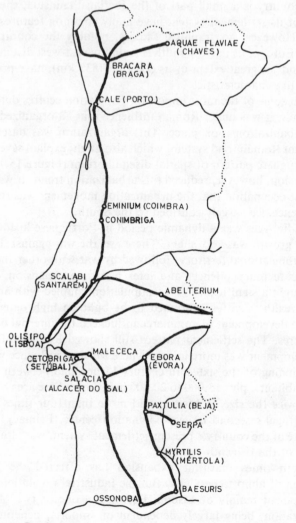

Fig. 15.1 Roman Roads

looked upon as a metropolitan area and no longer as an urban centre with
an influence confined to the corresponding municipality.

There have always been two very distinct settlement patterns in Portugal:
one scattered, the other concentrated. Along the western coast north of
Lisboa, and increasingly northwards, a scattered pattern prevails. In the
South, especially in the interior, the population is concentrated in a few
centres. This is explained by climate, natural resources, road systems, and
by Roman, barbarian, and Moslem influences. As a result, we find most of
the urban population in the littoral region; and this tendency is clearly on

the increase (Table 15.1). The districts of Lisboa and Porto contain the highest proportion of the urban population. Moreover, these districts have been increasing their share (17.9 per cent in 1864, 33.5 per cent in 1970) (Table 15.2). This is mainly a result of the importance of the Lisboa and Porto municipalities (which comprise the former nuclei of these cities). However, the importance of those municipalities has declined since 1930 due to a greater population increase in places close to the main centres which now are regarded as parts of Lisboa and Porto. Until 1950 Lisboa increased faster than Porto. This has changed, however, because the centre of Lisboa has been losing population due to the replacement of housing in some central areas by service industries. The municipality of Porto is expected to show a similar trend in a very short time.

The growth of other centres has not been at a rate which would significantly reduce Lisbon's primacy. There is a large gap between the size of Lisboa (even when we consider only the municipality) and any other population centre (Table 15.3).

Table 15.1: *Urban Population[1] in the Littoral Region[2] in Portugal*

Years	% of total population	% of urban population
1911	13.7	82.7
1940	17.3	82.6
1950	17.4	84.0
1960	19.2	84.7
1970	22.7	86.4

[1] Population in centres with 5,000 inhabitants or more in 1970.
[2] The littoral region includes the districts between Viana do Castelo and Setubal.
Source: *Anuários Estatísticos*, 1965, 1976, Instituto Nacional de Estatistica, Lisboa.

Table 15.2: *Population Growth in Portugal: Lisboa and Porto.*

Years	Total (1) (000s)	Lisboa and Porto districts (2) (000s)	(2)/(1) %	Lisboa and Porto municipalities (3) (000s)	(3)/(2) %	Lisboa municipality (4) (000s)	(4)/(3) %
1864	4,287.0	768.9	17.9	279.6	36.4	190.3	68.1
1878	4,699.0	883.3	18.8	351.4	39.8	240.7	68.5
1890	5,102.9	1,047.1	20.5	447.4	42.7	301.0	67.3
1950	8,510.2	2,276.0	26.7	1,064.6	46.8	783.2	73.6
1960	8,889.4	2,576.3	29.0	1,105.7	42.9	802.2	72.6
1970	8,663.3	2,899.8	33.5	1,076.5	37.1	769.4	71.5
1970/1864	2.02	3.77		3.85		4.04	

Table 15.3: *Population of the Six Largest Towns in Portugal (thousands)*

	1911	1940	1970
Lisboa[a]	435.4	709.2	760.2
Porto[a]	194.0	262.3	300.9
Coimbra	18.4	35.4	56.0
Setubal	25.5	37.1	49.7
Braga	22.2	29.9	48.7
Finchal	20.2	54.9	38.3

[a] The municipality only.

Note. The data in Table 15.2 relate only to resident population and in Table 15.3 to the population of the city or town concerned at the time of the Census Survey.

Sources: *Anuários Estatísticos*, 1965, 1976, INE, Lisboa.

Thus, the growth and development of the Portuguese settlement system just outlined is largely a result of a historical process starting before the Roman occupation and strongly influenced by Portuguese overseas expansion. The capital city was required to play a functional role over an area much larger than the homeland. The pattern of development was mostly based on trade and other service activities, so that the industrial revolution had minimal effects on the socio-economic organization of Portuguese society and settlement. It was only during the 1960s that industrialization and growth had an impact on economic life, this being largely a result of Portuguese membership in the European Free Trade Association (EFTA) and of the colonial war in Africa. These factors, however, have only reinforced the existing unbalanced spatial pattern of development because both have obliged the country to pay more attention to its relations with the outside world than to its internal organization. Portuguese governments have never had the time nor the will to consider seriously the regional development issue. When the issue arose, it received only low priority.

Present Structure of the Settlement System

Until 1960, Portugal had a steady population growth, affected only by a major pneumonia epidemic between 1911 and 1920. The rate of population growth declined after 1940 and reached a negative level during the 1960s, largely as a result of emigration associated with the economic situation and with the colonial war. However, it is believed that the former trend of population growth has been resumed in recent years.

Portuguese economic development is noted for its pattern of spatial disequilibrium: seven districts in the littoral region, with little more than 25 per cent of the total area, contain 66 per cent of the total population, being responsible for 80 per cent of the nation's gross domestic product (GDP) and 90 per cent of the output of manufacturing industries. Two of them (the Lisboa and Porto districts), with less than 6 per cent of the total area, account for more than 40 per cent of the total population and 50 per cent of the GDP. Moreover, even in those districts, the share in population and production of municipalities with an urban character is far greater than the average.

In broad terms, it may be said that the scattered settlement pattern which is dominant in the northern part of Portugal prevails over the whole country. In 1970 there were more than 40,000 hamlets with five households or more, and more than 60 per cent of the total population lived in agglomerations smaller than 2,000 inhabitants. At the same time there is a significant degree of population concentration. Of the 236 agglomerations with 2,000 inhabitants or more, Lisboa and Porto accounted for more than 30 per cent of their combined populations (Table 15.4). Sixty per cent of those agglomerations had fewer than 5,000 inhabitants and combined, they represented only 14 per cent of the population concerned.

Under these circumstances, a high level of urbanization cannot be expected. Small centres dominate the settlement system. They are not well equipped, however, to perform the functions required of them. Most do not reach an adequate threshold population size.

There is an obvious lack of intermediate centres in Portugal. After Lisboa and Porto there is only one agglomeration with more than 100,000 people, and that belongs, as do those immediately following it, to the metropolitan area of either Lisboa or Porto. All centres larger than 40,000 are located in the littoral region (Figure 15.2). There are large inland areas where no centres with 10,000 inhabitants or more can be found. Only the districts of Lisboa, Porto and Setubal have urbanization rates (the percentage of people living in centres of over 10,000) higher than 30 per cent. In some districts, apart from the chief centre of the district, there is no other centre larger than 5,000 population.

Table 15.4: *Agglomerations in Portugal with 2,000 people or more* (*1970*)

Agglomerations by size	Number	%	Population	%
2,000-5,000	143	60.6	429,658	14.1
5,000-10,000	38	16.1	268,524	8.8
10,000-20,000	32	13.6	435,874	14.3
20,000-40,000	11	4.7	278,666	9.1
More than 40,000[a]	10	4.2	578,324	18.9
Porto	1	0.4	301,655	9.9
Lisboa	1	0.4	760,150	24.9
Total	236	100	3,052,851	100

[a] Lisboa and Porto are not included.

Source: Population Census, 1970, INE, Lisboa.

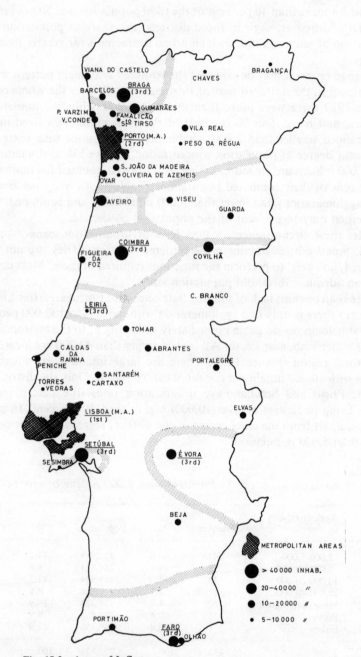

Fig. 15.2   Areas of Influence

The geographical distribution of the urbanization rates by districts conforms to the general disequilibrium pattern and displays a higher degree of population concentration in the South. Lower rates are particularly characteristic of the Northeast region, the location of some of the country's most underdeveloped or depressed areas. The lack of significant urban centres which might play the part of growth poles or growth centres emphasizes the difficulties of stimulating regional development in this area.

Table 15.5 shows the parameters of the rank-size distributions for 1960 and 1970 for centres larger than 5,000 and 10,000 and their respective R^2 coefficients. It is interesting to notice how the α coefficient tends to approach 1.0 along with an increase in ß and a general improvement in the fit. These results should be treated with caution, however, because agglomerations belonging to the metropolitan areas of Lisboa and Porto have been considered separately. Nevertheless, the fact that the municipality of Lisboa has been losing population and that the growth of Porto has been somewhat reduced, help to explain the slight increase in R^2. In this context, the resulting α and ß values can only be accepted as a consequence of proportionately greater growth in centres of intermediate size, which include some of the most important areas of influence of Lisboa and Porto.

Between 1950 and 1960 the Portuguese population increased by 5 per cent. The districts of the littoral region were the only ones to benefit significantly from this increase. Between 1960 and 1970 there was a decrease in population, mostly at the expense of the districts of the interior. However, the loss by the 'country' was much greater than the gain by the 'town' during the 1960s for two reasons: first, the 'country' lost also to foreign countries due to a tremendous increase in emigration; secondly this emigration also caused a significant drain on the population of the urban centres. Figure 15.3, showing results of the analysis of attraction/repulsion rates (the relation between net migration during the period 1960-70 and average population), gives a clearer picture of the situation: only 18 (out of 274) municipalities had a positive rate, and all of these were in the immediate area of influence of Lisboa and Porto.

Table 15.5: *Rank-size Distribution*[a] *in Portugal*

| Lowest size of centres | year | Coefficients | | R^2 |
		α	β	
5,000	1960	0.835	223,100	0.96
	1970	0.913	363,500	0.98
10,000	1960	0.914	272,900	0.94
	1970	0.928	380,400	0.98

[a] The usual distribution is Y.X$^\alpha$ = β where Y is the population and X is the rank.

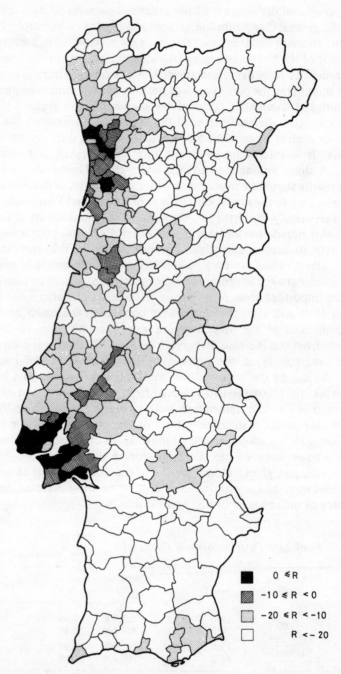

Fig. 15.3 Attraction/Repulsion Rates, 1961-70

Legend:

■ $0 \leqslant R$

▨ $-10 \leqslant R < 0$

▨ $-20 \leqslant R < -10$

□ $R < -20$

These results were to be expected, since there are only two real industrial poles in Portugal—Lisboa and Porto—which, with their neighbouring districts, form two industrial zones. The Portuguese policy of encouraging import substitution during the 1950s, followed by a policy of exporting to the EFTA countries, favoured the location of industry in Lisboa and Porto. They had the basic infrastructures and were able to benefit from unskilled and low-wage labour coming from the 'country'. This labour was employed first in the building industry, then in manufacturing, and later in the non-specialized tertiary sector, as usually happens in cases of 'dependent urbanization'. The metropolitan areas of Lisboa and Porto were also negatively affected, because they could not cope with this influx of people and its impact upon housing needs and the demand for equipment in general. Congestion, in its widest sense, was the result.

There is also the other side of the coin. The inland districts were unable to stem the population drain because they had too little industry to create jobs and services were too poor to assist the people and give them a reasonable life. New industry could not be attracted because the market was small and services could not be provided because population size was low and financial means scarce. Such a population drain has a cumulative impact. As long as congestion increases in Lisboa and Porto, population thresholds are more difficult to reach in the interior areas. Furthermore, it is in these inland areas that the poorest accessibility levels and living conditions are found.

There is no objective basis for identifying units of the settlement system in terms of specific functions. In general it might be stated that Lisboa is mainly a tertiary centre, though manufacturing industries also are of significance. In Porto, the second tertiary centre, manufacturing is more relevant than service industries. Other important centres are mainly concentrations of tertiary activities dominated by public administration, and their importance in the urban hierarchy is largely a result of their administrative status. With few exceptions (such as Covilhã), on a national scale urban centres act as growth poles in the littoral region only, namely where manufacturing industry has been growing. However, on a local, and in several cases on a regional scale, urban centres do act as growth points.

The administrative hierarchy of settlement units is related to their economic, social, and cultural functions and also to size. Using a principal components approach it is possible to classify a sample of settlement units with fewer than 20,000 inhabitants according to several service functions. Correlation analysis indicates a generally high degree of interdependence, which is lower only in the cases of tourism and administrative functions (Table 15.6). There is some evidence that the association becomes closer when larger centres are included. Finally, the analysis also shows a generally significant association between functional importance and size.

Table 15.6: *Interdependence between Urban functions*
(correlation coefficients)

Functions	Correlation Coefficients							
	1	2	3	4	5	6	7	8
1. Administration	1.00							
2. Health	.57	1.00						
3. Education	.56	.70	1.00					
4. Wholesale trade	.68	.86	.70	1.00				
5. Retail trade	.55	.82	.84	.78	1.00			
6. Transport	.59	.82	.66	.78	.77	1.00		
7. Tourism	.36	.60	.57	.55	.76	.62	1.00	
8. All functions	.64	.83	.88	.84	.93	.80	.74	1.00

Source: A. S. Lopes, 1971. *As Funções Económicos dos Pequenos Centros*, Lisboa. (The Economic
Functions of Small Towns and Rural Centres), Oxford, 1970, D. Phil. Thesis.

Urban Agglomerations as Systems

Metropolitan areas as yet have no administrative or political status in
Portugal. They are simply a number of municipalities around Lisboa and
Porto; some of these municipalities do not even belong to the Lisboa and
Porto districts, but to the nearby Setubal and Aveiro districts. Metropolitan
areas do not form planning regions, which as has been seen, merely consist
of groups of districts. In reality, the spatial extents of the Lisboa and Porto
metropolises are closely related to the pattern of labour markets and should
ideally be in conformity with commuter zones. The metropolitan areas are
smaller than such areas.

It has been shown that there is a clear trend towards an increasing proportion of the population living in the metropolitan areas of Lisboa and Porto
(Table 15.2), and that there is a shift in this tendency to favour the areas
immediately surrounding these municipalities. The growth of the old
centres of Lisboa and Porto has slowed down and, in absolute terms both
have declined since 1960. This emphasizes the increasing importance of
suburban areas and the way Lisboa and Porto have expanded into their
immediate surroundings. This is in part a result of immigration from rural
areas. Though no data are available to assess the distance travelled by those
who migrate, migration distances undoubtedly are much greater in the case
of Lisboa (followed by Porto) than for any other centre in Portugal.

The economic pattern is changing within these metropolitan areas.
Taking Lisboa as an example, it is appropriate to separate the part of the
metropolitan area north of the River Tagus from that to the South and to
distinguish between the inner ring and the outer ring. Using this basis, Table
15.7 shows some features of the changing intra-urban employment pattern.

There is a clear trend towards the increasing importance of tertiary
activities everywhere in the region. The more recent expansion of those

Table 15.7: *Employment by Sectors (%) in the Metropolitan Area of Lisboa*

Metropolitan Area	1960			1970		
	Primary	Secondary	Tertiary	Primary	Secondary	Tertiary
NORTH						
inner ring	4.7	35.0	59.6	2.4	31.5	61.1
outer ring	64.0	13.7	20.9	44.8	22.4	25.6
SOUTH						
inner ring	14.7	53.0	31.8	8.7	47.5	40.9
outer ring	42.1	31.0	26.4	27.7	33.3	35.0
TOTAL AREA	9.6	36.5	53.2	5.6	34.0	55.7

Note: Differences from 100% are due to the existence of unspecified categories.

Source: Hejazi. 1978. 'Le Processus d'urbanisation et la croissance économique dans la Région Métropolitaine de Lisbonne', Thèse de doctorat (3me cycle) Paris.

activities in the South explains the faster process of change in that part of the metropolis. The closer to the centre, the greater the importance of services. Industrial expansion has taken place mainly in the outer ring.

The major problems of the metropolitan areas of Lisboa and Porto are similar. They are the outcome of a fast, uncontrolled, and unorganized urban-industrial growth process. In 1970 the suburban population was four times the corresponding population of 1940 in Lisboa and almost three times that in Porto. During this period, especially after 1960, dwellings were largely replaced by services in the city centre; housing was shifted to the suburbs within the limits of the inner ring. Without regional planning, spatial disequilibrium increased. Migration to the major cities accelerated. Congestion became a fact of life and brought with it high management costs.

The major problems of the metropolitan areas may be summarized thus: (*a*) The spread of the urban fabric as a result of a spontaneous urbanization process. This has led to overcrowded suburban areas with very poor accessibility to work places, a saturation in the transport network for which readjustments are nearly always ineffective, and inadequate and inefficient public transport; (*b*) Deterioration in housing conditions, with overcrowding, the continued use of old and sometimes derelict houses, and the growth of shanty-towns. Unauthorized building is common in areas with poorer accessibility, where there is often a complete lack of infrastructure and service facilities; (*c*) Insufficient infrastructure and service equipment. The quality of life is poor, especially in poorer suburban areas, and pollution has increased (rivers, sea, air . . . noise); (*d*) Growing conflict between alternative land uses. Good agricultural areas are invaded by houses and factories. In those areas, soils lose their permeability, rain drainage is affected, and houses are at times unstable. Houses and factories compete in the peripheral zones, whereas services replace houses in the centre.

The intra-metropolitan organization of Portuguese metropolitan areas tends to follow a common pattern: services tend to occupy the city centres, later spreading all over the city; houses move into the periphery; factories also move out into the periphery; recreational areas are scarce, particularly in the city; and cultural life is closely linked to the city centre.

Population densities conform in very broad terms to Clark's law, although average density in the city centre has declined and goes on declining, while density has increased in the periphery. Density is also higher along the industrial axes.

Political and Administrative Functions and Centres

There are two levels of administrative centres in Portugal: those corresponding to the *distrito* and to the *município* levels. Chief centres of districts are also chief centres of municipalities, giving rise to a hierarchical structure in which the capital dominates no more than the chief centre of a district and therefore of a municipality.

The growth of the settlement system is closely related to these administrative functions. The status of a chief centre gives it a level of basic administrative equipment which, through agglomeration and external economies, attracts people and other tertiary and productive activities. It is no surprise to see the higher order centre growing faster. The administrative model is similar throughout the country, with differences occurring mainly in size and importance of the administrative units.

Administrative centres are supposed to achieve certain minimum standards as far as institutions, services, and administrative equipment are concerned; but they are not supposed to conform to any minimum size. It is clear that administrative functions have to be performed all over the country under the most varied accessibility conditions. Therefore, there are undersized chief centres of districts and *municípios* in the interior, even though their area of jurisdiction is larger than those of the littoral region. This raises certain difficulties, since the interior administrative areas are also those where accessibility is generally poorer.

Lisboa and Porto, as noted previously, dominate the national settlement system. Lisboa's dominance has been accentuated by a strong centralizing tendency which has its major expression at the administrative level. Local authorities were greatly dependent on the central government, since only a negligible proportion of their income did not come from the national budget. Things have changed in this respect, but only recently.

This situation helps to explain the Portuguese disequilibrium pattern. With a strongly centralized spatial organization Lisboa acts as the main growth area and, with Porto, gives rise to a narrow zone in the littoral region which is far more highly developed than anything in the interior. This unbalanced situation may be described meaningfully by comparing area, population, GDP, and other measures (Table 15.8). With 0.14 per cent of the total area, the Lisboa and Porto municipalities account for 13.3 per cent of the population, 27.4 per cent of the GDP, 36.2 per cent of those employed in the scientific and liberal professions, and 44.2 per cent of top managerial staff. The proportion of doctors is particularly high.

Future Structure and Patterns of the Settlement System

The spatial organization of Portugal has continuously accentuated the disequilibrium pattern and this is likely to continue. Without some sort of control, Lisboa will accentuate its dominant role, and the interior will fall farther behind the littoral region.

The Portuguese Constitution of 1976 stresses the need for improving the quality of life and for achieving socio-economic development in every part of the country. The Constitution lays down as an objective the correct spatial allocation of social equipment in such a way that people will have social services reasonably accessible to them. Regional policy is to put a strong emphasis on changes in the settlement pattern.

Unfortunately, little has been done. Even the planning regions have not yet been delineated. We believe that a satisfactory spatial organization should have as a long-term objective a hierarchical urban system which uses the basic principles of central place theory. A comparison of the present size of centres and the threshold size demanded by the functional hierarchy would indicate the undersized centres. Short and medium-term economic growth policies should then be designated to create conditions for the growth of those centres. There is no other way to achieve a satisfactory spatial organization, and no other way to attain the social objectives laid down in the 1976 Constitution.

Table 15.8: *Some Indicators of the Spatial Disequilibrium Pattern of Portuguese Settlement (% of the whole country)*

		Area	Population (1970)	GDP (1970)	Doctors (1965)	Scientific professions (1970)	Top managerial staff (1970)
Lisboa	district	3.1	19.5	31.3	41.6	39.2	45.2
	city[a]	.09	9.5	20.9	na	26.8	29.6
Porto	district	2.6	16.2	15.6	19.6	18.0	20.8
	city[a]	.05	3.8	6.5	na	9.4	14.6

[a] Municipality   na = Not available

Sources: *Anuarios Estatísticos,* 1965, 1976, INE, Lisboa.

NOTES

[1] There is no direct correspondence between the usual meaning of cities-towns-villages and *cidades-vilas-aldeias*. The main difference concerns the *vilas* agglomerations, which are very small centres, most of them in rural areas. However, many of the Portuguese *cidades* are no more than towns by European (especially British) standards.

[2] There have been few attempts to study in a systematic way the growth and development of the Portuguese settlement system. *See* O. Ribeiro (1963), upon which much of this section is based.

REFERENCES

C.E.P. (Centre for Planning Studies). 1961. *Rede Urbana do Continente: Hierarquia e Functionamento*, Lisboa.
C.E.U.H. 1977. 'Contribuicões para a organizacão do espaco em termos do funcão bancária', *Cadernos de Análise Regional*, 2. Lisboa.
Gaspar, J. 1972. *A Area de Influência de Evora*, Lisboa.
Ribeiro, O. 1963. 'A Cidade' and 'Portugal' in J. Serrão (ed.) *Dicionario de História de Portugal*, Lisboa.

PART B

SETTLEMENT SYSTEMS IN
CENTRALLY-PLANNED ECONOMIES

**Section 4: Settlement on a Continental Scale, on
New Lands and in Low-Density Regions**

16 SETTLEMENT IN THE USSR

G. M. LAPPO AND Yu. L. PIVOVAROV

Theoretical and Methodological Problems of Studying National Settlement Systems

Geographical publications most often define settlement as the spatial localization of population within a system of populated places. Settlement is treated as an expression of the historically-changing spatial organization of society. It can be assumed that the settlement pattern is determined by the spatial forms of social reproduction (Pokshishevskiy, 1978).

A system of settlement is a spatial combination of places, united by intensive, persistent, and varied connections. An important characteristic of these connections is the stability of their spatio-temporal parameters; their regularity, rhythm, and cyclicity. The formation of settlement systems is a result of the deepening geographical division of labour.

At the national and regional levels the basic framework of settlement is the system of integrally-developed economic centres which ensures the spatial-economic integration of a country or a region. It is composed of a combination of central places of higher hierarchical levels and specialized centres, which determine the spatial organization of the sectors of the national economy. The basic framework of settlement has an integrated character and serves as a mechanism of interconnection and interaction among regions and systems of places. Its development rests on uniform systems of engineering infrastructure, transport, communication, power, and gas supply. Links within the basic framework are the nodes of local settlement systems.

A large urban agglomeration is a compact grouping of urban and rural settlements connected by dense interrelations around a large urban place (in the USSR, as a rule, not less than 250,000 people). An agglomeration represents a combination of the 'daily urban system' bounded by the two-hour travel time isochrone from the centre of the core-city, and the 'weekly urban system', including also an outer and predominantly recreational belt.

An urbanized area is a territory almost completely included within the zones of direct influence of large integrally developed centres. Developed urbanized areas are the most important components of spatio-urban structure. Notable by their structural and functional diversity, these areas constitute the material prerequisites for the new socialist settlement, combining the advantages of urban and rural ways of life.

It is important to study settlement as a component of the spatial structure of the national economy; as one of its sub-systems. Spatio-economic systems (for instance, territorial production complexes) and settlement patterns which are formed on those systems, continue to develop inter-dependently. Hence, the 'complete coincidence of spatial boundaries of territorial-production complexes and settlement systems can be achieved only in certain moments of the dynamic development of both' (Pokshishev-skiy, 1978, p.124).

The evolution of settlement is a successive replacement of individual fields of settlement by settlement networks, and, finally, by settlement systems (Pokshishevskiy, 1978). The transformation of a settlement net-work into a settlement system results from numerous factors, and their role is increasing under the technological revolution. At the local level settlement systems are clearly marked, since 'population' connections here are regular in character. At the macro-territorial level relations became 'generalized' and less easily characterized as the interaction between settlements than as interaction among their elements.

Development of settlement systems is a response to the increasing require-ments of society and its economy. It is a result of technological and social progress, a desire to create an environment favouring the increasing effec-tiveness of activities and the advancement of man.

The distribution of urban population over settlements of different population ranks is defined as the urban structure. Of special importance is the concentration of population in large cities and urban agglomerations. The spatio-urban structure is characterized by the subdivision of the area into parts with different levels of urbanization, the 'pattern' of the major centres, and the spatial distribution of the various forms of settlement (ag-glomerations, urbanized areas, etc.).

The systems approach to studying settlement has deep roots in Soviet science. In the 1930s Davidovich (1934) put forward the concept of designing groups or systems of settlement; he also studied regularities in the formation and development of such systems (1956 and the succeeding publications). Saushkin (1960) brought to light the necessity of analysing the systems of urban places in the USSR which were being formed in the process of the territorial division of labour. Later the systems approach gained broad acceptance, although considerable differences concerning the essence of the systems idea have been revealed.

Active interaction within urban places, between urban places and their suburban zones, the hierarchical composition of the settlements network, and its subordination to the system's national economic base of territorial-production combinations—all speak to the systems character of the geography of settlements. The transition from analysing separate set-tlements to settlement systems is witness to the maturity of the science of settlements.

The following characteristics are essential features of settlement system analysis: (1) complementarity, resulting from the interaction of the system's elements; (2) regular interconnections; (3) a hierarchy of settlements;

(4) stability; (5) interregulation and a proportionality of development; and (6) their amenability to control. Formation of these systems, their levels of development, and their degree of maturity are directly related to the level of economic development, the specifics of the spatial organization of the economy and, in particular, to the level of territorial concentration. Replacement of the combination of relatively autonomous urban places by settlement systems reflects the transition from a 'point' concentration of production to an 'areal' type of concentration.

Three processes are of decisive importance in modern settlement systems: (1) integrated development of an urban place as a complex, multifunctional, socio-economic system; (2) growth of interrelated development among different types of settlements; and (3) formation of the basic settlement framework.

Increasing the systems character of settlement has activated its 'self-development'. The increasingly complex requirements of the system have promoted the emergence of new links in the sub-systems of servicing, and in municipal economic, ecological, spatio-recreational, and construction complexes.

Systems Approach to Studying an Urban Place

An urban place is a functioning part of still more complex spatial socio-economic systems. This is a paradoxical situation: on the one hand, an urban place represents a unity. On the other hand, it is a combination of components, each belonging to other systems, differing in functional structure and territorial pattern, and in management.

An urban place can be treated as a triad of sub-systems: (a) a national economic base (city-forming base); (b) a planning structure with the totality of engineering and social infrastructure facilities; and (c) a population with its structure, dynamics, way of life, etc. The components of the urban economic base, belonging to different sectoral systems, often contradict the interests of the urban place as a national economic unity. This can lead to disproportional development, with possible loosening of the integrity of an urban place (Liubovny, 1977).

Within the set of spatial socio-economic systems which include an urban place as a component, one can differentiate: (1) local settlement systems; (2) a system of urban settlements—central places of hierarchical organization; (3) sectoral production systems of national specialization; (4) an integrated regional urban system; and (5) a macro-system of centres—as the basic framework of a vast territory.

A local system comprises an urban place in full, while in systems defined at other levels it is represented only by its components. The formation of a local system of settlement and the growth of intra-system interactions do not abolish an urban settlement, but modify it. Changes take place in functional and planning structures, in the character of land use, in the direction and rhythm of population movement. That is, the development of an urban place as a part of the system is taking place.

The place of an urban settlement in the system of central places is determined by its role in providing comprehensive services for the population of the hinterland. In sectoral production systems of different economic specialization (for instance, the iron and steel industry, heavy engineering, or the petro-chemical industry) the place of urban settlement is determined by the stage and scales of production and the direction of inter-connections. Some sectoral systems have a multi-level production hierarchy (Pokshishevskiy, 1962).

Considering an urban place as a component of different spatial socio-economic systems helps us to understand the complex dynamics of urban development.

The Formation of the National Settlement System in the USSR

In the first years of Soviet power the composition of urban places was revised and the lag between the economic role of a settlement and its legal status, peculiar to pre-revolutionary Russia, was eliminated. Thus, 106 urban places were changed to urban settlements, 36 to urban-type settlements and 182 rural settlements (which developed on the basis of industrial units and craft industries) received urban status. By the census of 1926 (within the boundaries of that time) there were only 737 urban places. A broader development of the urban network over the national territory was thus a social, economic, and geographic necessity.

Development of new urban settlements in the USSR has included two processes: (*a*) formation of a hierarchical urban network with developed central functions; and (*b*) creation of specialized centres for the leading production industries. Despite the great diversity in the national economic bases of new urban settlements, they (especially in the pre-war period) emerged and developed mainly on an industrial base. The relationship between urbanization and industrialization was clearly manifest.

The requirements of the national economy for new centres was met mainly by old mining and industrial centres, rural regional centres, and old administrative towns, which had lost their urban status. In the process of development they obtained new functions, and accepted newly-built industrial enterprises. Thus a process of 'regeneration' took place, of half-urban, half-rural settlements maturing into actual towns. According to some estimates, about 70 per cent of all urban places formed after 1926 in the USSR had a certain urban embryo (Konstantinov, 1976). Some one hundred urban places, primarily specialized centres, have appeared in previously 'empty' areas.

New town expansion promoted the development of the urban network in the country; it included new areas in the network and settlement became denser in the old developed regions. The integration of urban settlements into agglomerations increased. 'Chains' of towns were formed along the main lines of economic development. By the beginning of 1979 the number of urban places had increased three times as compared to 1926, reaching 2061. All in all 1174 urban places have been created (Figure 16.1).

The emergence and development of new settlements also promoted the advancement of the spatial structure of settlement and the economy through: (*a*) growth control on the largest centres (with the help of satellite settlements and 'counterbalance' settlements); (*b*) more comprehensive use of the potential of those areas with outstanding economic-geographical position; (*c*) the introduction of new resources both in old developed regions and in new ones; and (*d*) the reconstruction of rural settlement. The number of cities has also increased considerably (in 1926—33, in 1959—148, and at the beginning of 1979—273).

At present the settlement system in the USSR is characterized by the following features:
(1) the basic framework of settlement and the spatial structure of the national economy has been formed; 273 cities with population over 100 thousand (1979) accommodate 60 per cent of all the urban population: (2) macro-zones of settlement in the country are manifest, developed under the strong influence of natural conditions; (3) the interrelations between the rural and urban population have been enforced; (4) the concentration of settlement in regions of high economic and social potential has been

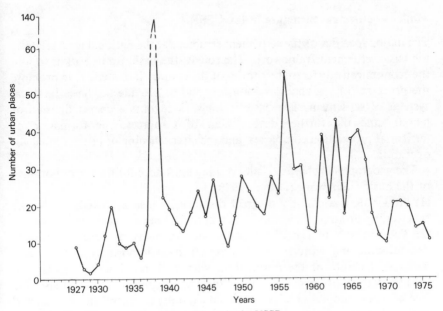

Fig. 16.1 Development of New Urban Places in the USSR

increased; (5) networks of settlements are changing (in areas with favourable conditions) into settlement systems; (6) an accelerating rate of formation of large urban agglomerations is taking place; and (7) the hierarchical character of settlement has become more clearly manifest.

The processes of settlement have positive and negative results. The latter include:
(1) the mono-centrality of urban development (at a regional level), resulting from the inadequate development of other urban settlements; (2) the autonomous character of some urban settlements, because of insufficient integration with the surrounding territory and weak involvement in the general settlement system; (3) insufficient growth control in large and small towns and in large urban agglomerations; and (4) the persistence of considerable regional disparities in services and living conditions.

It is possible to define the following main targets for the improvement of settlement:
(1) Regulation of cities' growth, including the formation of large urban agglomerations; (2) activization of small urban places, by enlarging their economic base and overcoming their social shortcomings; (3) reconstruction of rural settlement, bringing rural living conditions closer to urban ones; (4) further development of the basic settlement framework, to enhance the spatial organization of social life; (5) wholesale use (within ecologically permissable limits) of the economic potential of nodal points in the economy's spatial structure.

Modern Settlement Structure in the USSR

The major specifics of the settlement structure at the national level relate to the basic settlement framework. The role of the basic framework is to join the economically different territories of the country into a unity, to promote the processes of regional development, and to provide the basis for local systems of settlement. The basic framework favours a deeper division of labour, and the further development of resources, the formation of territorial-production complexes, and the strengthening of international co-operation.

The geographical characteristics of the USSR account for the importance of the basic framework (Lappo, 1978):
(1) the USSR is a country of great distances, which are overcome by the functioning of large cities and powerful main lines of transport.
(2) The territory of the USSR has a wide diversity of natural, historic, demographic and national conditions. Of great importance is the multinational structure of the population, with each republic having its own specific pattern of economic and cultural development. This increases the role of cities, and above all, of national capitals, as centres of political and economic consolidation.

The basic framework in the USSR is closely related to the zonal characteristics of the country's natural conditions, and to the peculiarities of the main macro-zones of settlement: (1) extreme north; (2) the middle and economically active; (3) arid; (4) piedmont; and (5) mountainous. Moreover, the nodes of the basic framework are related to certain components of the spatial structure. Among these are: (a) major regions of national importance, developed on the basis of large power and raw materials resources, and the concentration of basic heavy industries; (b) cores of nodal regions, the national bases of scientific and technological development; and (c) belts of population and economic concentration along the main transport axes. Within economically active areas a certain spatial rhythm in the distribution of large centres is observed.

Formation of the basic framework can be described as 'dispersed concentration'. Concentration is displayed in the form of centralization (large, relatively compact cities), agglomerations, and the creation of transport axes. Still more complicated urban formations are developing as agglomeration clusters, for example, in the regions of Samara Luka, Middle Dnieper, the Donbass, Kuzbass, Middle Urals, and Central Russia.

The major aspects of the basic framework are therefore:
(1) the greater involvement of the territory in the network of multifunctional centres; (2) the economic rapprochement of different parts of the country, owing to the nodal and linear concentration of urban settlements; (3) the subdivision of areas with different urban structures, having both highly urbanized and less urbanized territories (Figure 16.2); (4) the enforcement of pre-conditions for the development of large agglomerations; and (5) the increased interaction both within the zones of direct influence of the basic framework nodes, and between them. The main tendencies in the development of settlement are shown schematically by Figure 16.3.

Peculiarities of Regional Settlement System Development

Analysis of the dynamics of regional settlement systems at the republic level reveals the following general tendencies:
(a) advancement of the main urban centre as the result of its prior development. In a number of republics (and regions), however, the leading urban place, carrying out diverse central functions, was often created anew on the basis of a rural settlement or a small town (e.g. the towns of Dushanbe, Cheboksary, Saransk, Shevchenko);
(b) the formation of systems of sub-centres, dominating parts of regions;
(c) advancement of the second ranked urban places. Here the historic past of the area is sometimes manifest (in some cases the second town formerly played the role of a capital (e.g. Samarkand in Uzbekistan, Kaunas in Latvia), or the peripheral location of the main focus (e.g. the location of Baku stimulated the advancement of Kirovabad as the second urban centre for Azerbaijan), or the separation of the territory by mountain ranges (e.g.

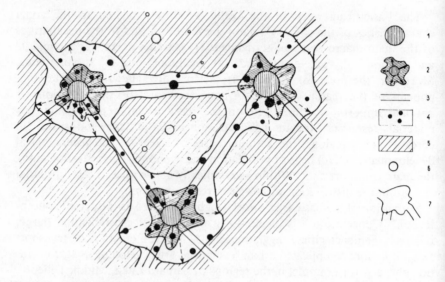

Fig. 16.2   Trends in Settlement Development
(after effects of the basic framework formation)
1. Node-centres of the basic framework (BF), developing multifunctional cities
2. Urban agglomerations, zones of economic concentration, and population inflow, forming in the nodes of BF
3. Main lines—economic axes, forming corridors of moderate concentration
4. Urban settlements in the zone of satellites and in corridors and zones of moderate concentration
5. Inner territories—space between agglomerations
6. Organizational-economic centres—small urban places in spaces between agglomerations
7. Zones of moderate concentration, stabilization, or moderate population growth rates

the development of Osh in Kirgizia, Leninabad in Tajikistan). Often development of the second town is connected with the implementation of major national economic programmes (e.g. owing to construction of a large motor plant, the town of Naberezhnye Chelny became the second urban place of Tataria);

(*d*) formation of agglomerations as the leading nodes of the spatial structure;

(*e*) the development of new urban constellations, among which one can recognize such groups as: resource centres (mining, resort, hydroelectric power, production of construction materials); agro-industrial centres; transportation foci; scientific centres. Typical also is the development of large centres of basic heavy industry—iron and steel, non-ferrous metals, basic chemicals, cement production,—most often designed to meet the requirements of their own republic (Rustavi, Temirtau, Chirchik, Sumgait).

Local Settlement Systems

Local settlement systems being formed in different zones and regions of the

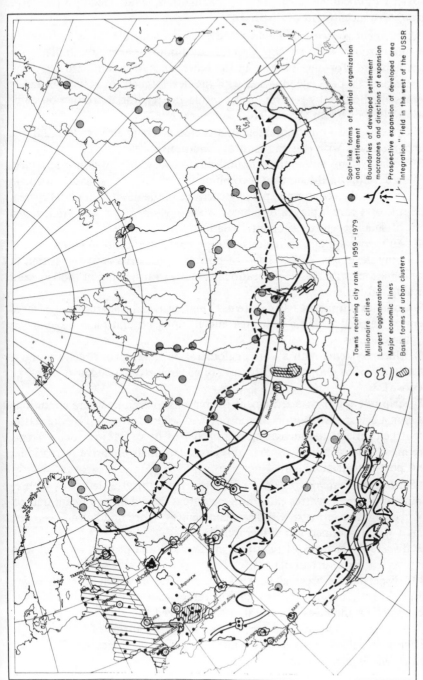

Fig. 16.3 Major Tendencies in Development of Settlement in the USSR

Soviet Union can be, in the first approximation, subdivided into two large groups—concentrated or dispersed.

Settlement Systems of Concentrated Character.   (1) 'Spot' systems in resource zones with extreme natural conditions. These are similar to a 'springboard' for development in the inner parts of a colonized territory. The economic base is connected with the development of resources and is represented either by separate links within the territorial-production complex (TPC) or by an incomplete TPC.

(2) Systems based on a radial line of settlement. These also are found in the resource zones with extreme natural conditions.

(3) Nodal systems within the economically active, older developed territory. These develop on the basis of a combination of centrifugal and centripetal processes in the economy's spatial structure. In the developed nodal system the role of a core is played by a large urban agglomeration surrounded by a belt of smaller centres as counterbalances.

(4) Multi-core systems in regions of high concentration of population and economy developed on the basis of port and industrial activities (often in combination with resort-recreational ones), transportation nodes, and mining industries.

(5) Complex multi-core basin systems. Their basis is the aggregation of large centres, located within a vast area and forming around them large urban agglomerations.

(6) Linear systems with a core-agglomeration developed directly along a clearly manifest geographical feature (e.g. large river, sea coast, strip-like deposit).

(7) Strip-like multi-core settlement formations in regions where conditions favour a linear distribution of centres, and where formation of the settlement belt reflects the increasing complexity of its structures; such systems are mostly characteristic of coastal regions with their intensive recreational and port-industrial activities.

Settlement Systems of Dispersed Character.   (8) grid networks of predominantly small centres extending over areas devoid of significant natural and economic contrasts; with few main centres, more middle-rank centres, and a weakly-defined urban hierarchy.

(9) dispersed networks of relatively hierarchical and proportionate centres (e.g. average-size urban places);

(10) dispersed hierarchical networks of centres, in which large cities are distinguished, but which also have a rather even distribution, and have developed on the basis of central and specialized functions.

The combination of concentrated and dispersed forms of settlements is different in various parts of the country, and this determines the specifics of settlement in each region.

Demographic Aspects of Settlement Systems

In the USSR a wide variety of regional demographic processes may be observed. Specific regional demographic situations have an influence on the formation of settlement systems.

In general the USSR has been characterized since 1960 by a continuous decrease in rates of natural growth (especially notable in the beginning of the 1960s) as a result of decreased birth-rates, changes in age structure (ageing of the population), and advancing qualitative characteristics of population reproduction (e.g. educational level, cultural, health characteristics). The parameters of natural growth and birth rates are highly differentiated among the union republics and large economic regions. In the last two decades this differentiation has been considerably aggravated, especially in terms of natural growth (Table 16.1). The rates of birth and natural growth in Tajikistan have risen considerably, and in Latvia and Estonia have fallen—compared to 1960.

Several types of population growth rates are observed. The major type (covering nearly 80 per cent of the population) is characterized as close to a natural balance, with low, deliberately-controlled birth rates, low mortality, and relatively high rates of population migration. It is represented in the most developed republics (Russian Federation, Ukraine, Byelorussia, the Baltic republics), and is especially characteristic of the majority of regions of European Russia, Latvia and Estonia. According to some demographers this type will spread with time over the rest of the USSR population (Vishnevskiy, 1976; Kvasha, 1978).

Another type is an expanding one, with high birth rates and low mortality, as observed in the indigenous population of the Soviet Central Asian republics, and until recently in Azerbaijan, Kazakhstan, and Armenia (about 18 per cent of the national population). A transitional type is characteristic of Moldavia and Georgia; natural growth in these republics has declined considerably, and in their demographic processes they are coming close to the national norm.

Simultaneously, large disparities in natural growth rates and absolute population increases are observed in some regions, autonomous republics, and urban places, especially in the Russian Federation and Ukraine. Thus, natural growth rates considerably above those of the republics and the national average are observed in most regions of Siberia and the Far East (for instance, 13 per 1000 in the Chita region in 1974, 11-12 per 1000 in the Tumen, Irkutsk, Amur, Sakhalin and Magadan regions, and in Primorskiy territory) and also in some autonomous republics (Daghestan 21.4 per 1000 population, Tuva 19.7, the Checheno-Ingush Autonomous republic 15.1, the Kalmyk Autonomous republic 13.8).[1] In the Ukrainian SSR increased

Table 16.1: *Dynamics of rates of birth, natural growth and population number by union republics**

Republics	Births per 1000 persons		As related to the USSR average (USSR = 100)		Natural growth of population per 1000 persons		As related to the USSR average (USSR = 100)		Dynamics of population numbers 1959-79 (1959 = 100)		
	1960	1978	1960	1978	1960	1978	1960	1978	total	urban	rural
Tajik SSR	33.5	37.5	135	206	28.4	29.2	160	344	191.9	205.0	185.5
Uzbek SSR	39.9	33.9	160	186	33.8	27.0	190	318	189.6	232.7	167.7
Turkmenian SSR	42.4	34.4	170	189	35.9	26.4	202	311	182.0	188.9	176.1
Kirgiz SSR	36.9	30.4	148	167	30.8	22.3	173	262	170.8	196.3	157.9
Azerbaijanian SSR	42.6	24.9	171	137	35.9	18.2	202	214	163.0	181.4	146.5
Kazakh SSR	37.1	24.4	149	134	30.6	17.0	172	200	158.0	194.8	129.4
Armenian SSR	40.1	22.5	161	124	33.3	16.7	187	196	171.9	226.0	117.8
Moldavian SSR	29.3	20.1	118	110	22.9	10.3	129	121	136.8	241.2	106.9
Georgian SSR	24.7	17.7	99	97	18.2	9.7	102	114	124.0	151.8	103.6
Byelorussian SSR	24.4	15.9	98	87	17.8	6.8	100	80	118.8	159.4	84.7
RSFSR	23.2	15.9	93	87	15.8	5.6	89	66	117.0	154.8	75.4
Lithuanian SSR	22.5	15.3	90	84	14.7	5.3	83	62	125.4	197.1	80.3
Ukrainian SSR	20.5	14.7	82	81	13.6	4.0	76	47	118.8	159.4	84.7
Estonian SSR	16.6	14.9	67	82	6.1	2.7	34	32	122.5	151.2	85.2
Latvian SSR	16.7	13.6	67	75	6.7	1.2	38	14	120.8	147.0	86.5
USSR	24.9	18.2	100	100	17.8	8.5	100	100	125.7	163.6	90.8

* Republics are listed according to their natural population growth in 1978.

population growth is taking place in some regions in the southwest and south of the republic (Transcarpathian, Ivano-Frankovsk, Chernovtsy, Crimean, and Kherson regions).

Very low growth and natural increase rates are found in several regions of the North-Western, Central and the Central Chernozem economic regions of the Russian Federation and also in the Ukraine. Natural population growth in the Pskov and Kalinin regions was negative in 1974 (-1.1 and -0.5 per 1000 respectively), in the Novgorod, Smolensk, Kostroma, Yaroslavl, Tula, Orel, Riazan, Kursk, Belgorod, Voronezh, Tambov regions it did not exceed 3.0 per 1000 persons, nor in the Chernigov, Sumy, Poltava, and Kirovograd regions of the Ukrainian SSR. In the majority of the above regions in 1979 the population was below the 1959 level, sometimes by 10 per cent or more (Pskov, Kostroma, Tambov regions), owing to a considerable decrease in rural population.

Low rates of natural increase are characteristic of Moscow (1.4 per 1000 citizens in 1978). For Leningrad, Gorkiy, Kuibyshev, Odessa, Kharkov, and other cities of the RSFSR and Ukraine, birth rates do not exceed 12-15 per 1000. The latter is related in general to the considerable decrease in birth rates in the cities (with population above 500,000) in the RSFSR and some other republics. Hence their population growth is to a considerable extent due to in-migration: it accounts, for instance, for 80 per cent of population growth in Moscow, 75 per cent in Leningrad, and 50 per cent in Tbilisi and Tashkent (Romanenkova, 1980). However, in the republics with high birth rates, this index exceeds 20 per 1000 in the cities as well (e.g. in Dushanbe 25.3 persons per 1000, in Ashkhabad 21.0).

To divide the USSR territory into demo-geographical regions the following five major parameters were used: (1) the percentage of urban population and change according to the censuses of 1959 and 1979; (2) the share of cities in the urban population according to the 1959 and 1979 censuses and its change over these years; (3) population density in 1979—total and rural; (4) population dynamics for 1959-79, in terms of total, urban, and rural population, and (5) indices of natural population growth in 1960, 1965, 1970, and 1974.

The first four indicators are available in the population censuses of 1959 and 1979 for first rank administrative-territorial units (unfortunately these materials are not available for regions). Generalized indices for republics, regions, and areas are also used, although in some cases marked disparities are observed within these administrative-territorial units. This leads to a certain conventionality in attributing individual regions of heterogenous compositions (and also areas, autonomous republics) to one or the other demo-geographical region of the first order.

All five parameters were analysed for 152 administrative-territorial units (9 union republics without subdivision by regions, 17 autonomous SSRs, 8 autonomous regions, 4 autonomous areas, 115 regions and 6 areas).[2] Correlation analysis has corroborated the independent character of the parameters employed. There is little correlation between the percentage of urban population (1979) and the indices of population density and dynamics (the coefficients of linear correlation (r) are respectively -0.08 and $+0.05$). A weak inverse correlation is found between the share of urban population and the rate of natural growth (r = 0.44), and a direct one between the share of urban population and the share of the cities in urban population (r = 0.39). A weak correlation between the indices of urban population and natural growth (given a rather high dispersion of the coefficient in separate regions of the country) is most clearly observed in Soviet Central Asia and Kazakhstan, where several regions with the lowest percentage of urban population have the highest natural growth rate. This association is also notable in many old industrial regions (Centre, Ukraine, Baltic republics, etc.) with a high urban population and low natural growth. It should be taken into account that this correlation could be affected by the absence of region-wide data on population natural growth for some republics (Uzbekistan, Turkmenia, Kazakhstan, Byelorussia). Therefore, in these cases, we had to use the average indices of the natural growth for the respective republics. However, the correlation coefficient between urban population percentage and population natural growth in the USSR is close to the corresponding coefficient (r = 0.43) calculated earlier by Witthauer (1961) for 55 foreign countries.

Comparing statistical data on the above parameters, and taking into account all of the complex of economic-geographical, physiographical, and historic-geographical conditions, 27 demo-geographical regions were delimited. Each of these occupies, as a rule, from 0.8 to 7 per cent of the national territory, and accommodates from 1 to 6 per cent of its population. The leader in terms of area is the Asian North (34.5 per cent), and in population—the Central region 11.3 per cent). A list of demo-geographical regions and some of their parameters are shown in Table 16.2.

To delimit the demo-geographical regions, the settlement regions which were drawn and described in detail by Konstantinov (1967a, 1967b) were used. This regionalization was changed through the subdivision of the first-order regions of Ukraine and Kazakhstan; and the merging of the West of the RSFSR (the Briansk, Kaluga and Smolensk regions), which were small in area and population, into the Central region. Use of the data provided by the 1979 population census and information on natural population movement for 1974, enabled us to redefine the composition of most demo-geographical regions.

Urban Agglomerations as Systems within the National Settlement Systems

Fundamental features of urban agglomeration include the territorial proximity of urban settlements and their complementarity. A special role

Regions	Area '000s km²	Area %	Population in 1979 '000s	Population in 1979 %	Population density 1979 (persons/km²) total	Population density 1979 (persons/km²) rural	Urban population in the regional total % 1959	Urban population in the regional total % 1979	Urban population in the regional total % absolute change	Population of cities in urban total % 1959	Population of cities in urban total % 1979	Population of cities in urban total % absolute change	Population dynamics (1979 as % of 1959) total	Population dynamics (1979 as % of 1959) urban	Population dynamics (1979 as % of 1959) rural
Baltic	275.0	1.2	14.299	5.4	52.0	12.0	65	77	12	67	71	4	127.9	151.8	84.1
Byelorussian	207.6	0.9	9.559	3.6	46.0	20.7	43	55	12	38	60	22	118.7	212.1	77.1
European North	1320.6	5.9	4.286	1.6	3.3	0.8	63	77	14	30	45	15	129.8	157.9	82.0
Northern old agricultural	437.2	2.0	5.348	2.0	12.2	4.7	36	61	25	27	49	22	92.1	159.4	55.1
Central	435.5	2.0	29.584	11.3	67.9	13.8	63	80	17	60	65	5	113.6	144.0	62.2
Southern old agricultural	232.0	1.0	10.051	3.8	43.3	20.3	27	53	26	49	57	8	99.1	193.1	63.7
Volga-Kama	258.3	1.2	10.689	4.1	41.4	17.3	35	58	23	46	65	19	111.8	187.3	71.7
Lower Volga	387.9	1.7	9.336	3.6	24.1	6.7	55	72	17	61	72	11	130.4	169.7	81.4
North Ukraine	183.6	0.8	12.508	4.8	68.1	30.8	34	55	21	37	56	19	114.4	186.6	77.9
South-Western Ukraine and Moldavia	126.3	0.6	10.350	3.9	82.0	48.9	22	40	18	23	44	21	110.6	205.3	84.3
West Ukraine	70.4	0.3	7.123	2.7	101.2	58.6	29	42	13	29	39	10	119.0	174.4	96.7
Black Sea	113.4	0.5	7.134	2.7	62.9	23.7	49	63	14	57	57	0	140.6	181.9	101.5
Southern mining	244.5	1.1	20.671	7.9	84.5	17.6	71	79	8	54	62	8	123.7	138.7	87.6
Urals	710.9	3.2	16.842	6.4	23.7	6.5	61	73	12	48	59	11	110.9	132.8	77.0
West Siberian	1132.2	5.1	13.140	5.0	11.6	3.9	50	67	17	67	69	2	110.4	146.5	74.0
Middle Siberian	1539.8	6.9	5.518	2.1	3.6	1.0	54	72	18	43	56	13	124.6	167.4	74.7
South-Siberian	1045.9	4.7	2.572	1.0	2.4	1.1	45	56	11	38	42	4	126.2	157.6	100.4
Far Eastern	1441.3	6.5	5.136	2.0	3.6	0.9	69	75	6	33	50	17	132.0	144.4	104.2
Asian North	7677.7	34.5	2.650	1.0	0.4	0.1	59	73	14	15	46	31	205.1	252.2	136.5
North Caucasian	254.3	1.2	11.406	4.4	44.9	22.5	37	50	13	40	52	12	137.6	185.8	109.4
Transcaucasian	186.1	0.8	14.075	5.4	75.6	33.8	46	55	9	58	64	6	148.1	178.7	122.1
North Kazakhstan	489.0	2.2	3.740	1.4	7.7	3.9	32	49	17	15	60	45	142.5	216.7	107.2
Central Kazakhstan	738.8	3.3	2.537	1.0	3.4	0.9	65	73	8	40	51	11	172.2	192.5	133.4
West Kazakhstan	728.5	3.3	1.832	0.7	2.5	1.2	42	52	10	—	63	63	171.2	212.7	141.2
East Kazakhstan	395.4	1.8	2.311	0.9	5.8	2.9	45	50	5	39	48	9	133.1	148.6	120.4
South Kazakhstan	365.6	1.6	4.265	1.6	11.7	5.9	43	50	7	70	71	1	178.4	206.3	157.5
Soviet Central Asian	1277.1	5.7	25.480	9.7	20.0	11.8	35	41	6	44	56	12	186.2	217.2	169.7
USSR	22274.9	100.0	262,442	100.0	11.8	4.4	48	62	14	51	60	9	125.7	163.6	90.8

Source: This table was compiled on the basis of the data from: *Naselenie SSSR* (*USSR Population*), *Po dannym Vsesoiuznoi perepisi naselenia 1979 goda.*M., Politizdat, 1980; *Naselenie SSSR* (*USSR Population*), 1973, M., 'Statistika', 1975; *Narodnoie khoziaistvo SSSR v 1978* (National economy of the USSR in 1978). M., 'Statistika', 1979. Data on absolute movement of population are absent in the table, since the above sources give their relative values only (as per 1000 persons). This prevents us from re-calculating them for larger regions.

belongs to the central city, as the very genesis of the system, and as the highest stage of functional development within the system. The central city ensures the fullest use of the potential of the whole agglomeration area—its geographical position, resources, local carrying capacity, and infrastructure.

Agglomeration is a highly urbanized environment offering specific living conditions for its population. It is within the limits of the agglomeration that the weekly cycle of a modern city-dweller takes place. An agglomeration is an area of interrelated settlement, united by common foci of labour and cultural attractions; it is a developed servicing complex able to provide a variety of forms and ways of using leisure time. It is also an area with a deeply modified natural environment, subject to considerable anthropogenic pressure.

An agglomeration is a specific environment adapted for the development of a multi-component production-territorial complex: it provides a grouping of centres, developed engineering and social infrastructure, and a highly qualified labour force. The environment of an agglomeration favours the development of numerous 'growth points', the differentiation of functions, and a deeper specialization of production, science, design, education. All this accounts for the role of agglomerations as centres of development, as well as the emergence of innovations and their diffusion throughout the country.

Urban agglomerations in the USSR have not developed in an uncontrolled fashion, but they have accumulated the results of partial, not always well correlated, departmental decisions, seeking achievements in this or that industry, and not always considering the interests of the agglomeration as a whole. This has led to the need for some kind of regulation.

An essential type of regulation is the impact which agglomerations have on the national economic base, in the form of stimulating some sectors and types of economic activities, while limiting others. The tasks of economic regulation include; (1) elaboration of the general concept of development (e.g. the principal industries and types of activities, general scales of development, major proportions); (2) formation of functional combinations of basic, supplementary, and linkage industries; (3) definition of common trends in the development of the national economy, advancement of the functional structure, and consistent enforcement of interactions to produce the maximal effect.

Strict selection of functions is particularly important for already developed agglomerations. Here functions can be excluded which can be located beyond the limits of agglomerations. This should also activate small and middle-sized towns, allowing for the construction of subsidiaries of large enterprises. Selection of functions envisages; (1) prior development of progressive industries, scientific research, education, information, automatic management systems; (2) creation of an attractive social diversity of labour opportunities and elimination of a one-sided functional structure and; (3) development of central functions.

Role of the Capitals in the Settlement Systems

A special role in the regional system of settlement belongs to the capital cities. Each of the 15 capitals of the Soviet Union republics are noted for their specific character, unique design and ways of development. At the same time, the common features of development of the capitals and their role as major foci in the regional settlement systems are clearly present. Their role is not limited to the performance of political-administrative functions. They contain the management functions of different sectors of the economy.

The functional structure of the capital reflects its specific trends of development. The data below show the tendencies for change for the period 1959-79 (Table 16.3).

Table 16.3: *Functional Structure of the Capitals of the Soviet Union Republics in 1959 and 1979*

Capital Cities	Large functional blocks (in per cent)					
	1959			1979		
	Industry	Other material production	Non-productive sphere	Industry	Other material production	Non-productive sphere
Moscow	37.43	29.38	33.19	30.88	26.18	42.94
Kiev	40.71	30.67	28.62	39.05	28.60	32.35
Tashkent	38.32	33.06	26.62	32.46	32.81	34.74
Baku	35.07	33.95	30.98	—	—	—
Minsk	46.66	30.28	23.06	48.03	25.88	26.09
Tbilisi	36.20	30.86	32.94	32.43	27.72	39.85
Erevan	39.17	33.58	27.25	41.04	26.35	32.61
Riga	48.45	27.22	24.33	47.03	26.84	26.13
Alma-Ata	28.51	39.10	32.39	26.98	36.49	36.53
Frunze	40.35	30.52	29.13	42.08	28.80	29.12
Dushanbe	28.34	41.19	30.48	30.65	35.11	34.24
Vilnius	38.32	30.13	31.56	42.57	27.57	29.85
Tallinn	44.76	31.22	24.02	44.18	33.04	22.78
Kishinev	35.63	33.21	31.16	35.94	30.45	33.61
Ashkabad	25.63	41.19	33.24	22.23	40.58	37.24

A notable feature of the cities is the great diversity in their population composition. In the capitals of the Soviet Central Asian republics and Kazakhstan, especially at the first stage of their development, the task was to attract to these centres (and to urban places in general) the indigenous population. Moreover, the inflow of representatives from different regions of the country favoured the creation of non-traditional branches of the economy, as well as an inter-penetration and mutual enrichment of cultures. Thus, in the development of the capitals two trends were intertwined—the development of the national culture, and a spread of the culture of other republics.

The problems of regulating the growth of the capitals are great. There is the inertia of development. Their functional structure strongly reflects previous stages of development. Inadequate local carrying capacity, the undesirability of expansion of the built-up area over valuable suburban lands, depletion of land and water resources, the high level of concentration already achieved—all are witness to the necessity for rather strict regulation. But regulation is difficult due to the complex task of determining the rational parameters of each capital. The capital is not only the main city of its republic, but also an important node in the national settlement framework and economy (e.g. Riga, Minsk, Tashkent, Baku, and Kiev). In regulating the growth of capitals the following urban places take part: (*a*) the centres heading the republic's economic regions; (*b*) the agglomeration proper; and (*c*) small and average-size towns beyond the limits of the agglomeration.

Future Settlement Structure in the USSR

The principles of future settlement include:
(1) The correlation of settlement with the major aims of society's development; envisaging the creation of favourable conditions for the comprehensive development of human personality, and the growth of labour productivity.
(2) Economic effectiveness; meaning a reduction of expenditure on the rational functioning of the settlement system, and full use of the advantages of concentration.
(3) Ecological prosperity of all forms of settlement; involving a combination of social attractiveness with the favourable state of the natural environment.
(4) The formation of settlement as a component of the national economy's spatial structure; including the spatial progress of urbanization and the projection of population distribution, based upon shifts expected in the spatial structure of the national economy.
(5) Integrity of the settlement system, meaning the interrelation of: (*a*) urban and rural settlement, and (*b*) settlement and the spatial organization of production.
(6) A diversity of forms and systems of settlement; corresponding to different development in different parts of the country, to differences in the national economic potentials of 'points' in socio-economic space, and in the requirements of different groups of the population.
(7) Formation of the basic settlement framework which is the primary task of settlement development.

(8) Systems' character; the objective regularities of the settlement formation which result first of all from the characteristics of the economic base of the settlement. These will be displayed in the regulated division of functions between urban places—the components of the system (principle of hierarchicity), in their interrelated functioning (principle of complementarity), and also in their interrelated development, under which modification of one element of the system produces modifications in other elements.

Future settlement systems will reflect the shifts that will take place in the spatial structure of the national economy, brought about by: (1) the development of resources in the regions of colonization; (2) use of the resources in the old developed parts of the country, especially in connection with the creation of new heavy industry bases; (3) regulation of the existing largest centres through the creation of other towns and agglomerations as counterbalances; (4) further development of the network of central places of high rank; and (5) advancement of foreign economic contacts.

A great impact on the development of the settlement in the USSR will come from the implementation of large complex national economic programmes, in particular, of the plans to create large complexes: Timano-Pecherskiy, KMA, West Siberian, Orenburgskiy, Mangyshlakskiy, Turgai-skiy, Pavlodar-Ekibastuzskiy, Karatau-Jambulskiy, Bratsko-Ust-Ilimskiy, Sayano-Shushenskiy, South Tajik, zone of the new trans-Siberian railway (BAM), etc. These will promote the development of a large group of existing centres and the emergence of large new centres.

Major trends in the advancement of settlement at the national level are: (*a*) the enforcement of relations between urban places and their direct surroundings (increase of centrality, development of complementarity); (*b*) an increase in interaction between the elements of the basic framework; and (*c*) the transition from relatively compact centres and low (at least at the initial stage) development of the zone of satellites, into urban agglomerations, and, under especially favourable conditions, into aggregations of urban agglomerations of strip or basin-like forms.

NOTES

[1] Data on the natural growth of population here and below are cited according to: *Vestnik statistiki* (Journal of Statistics), 1975, No.12.
[2] By the time of the 1979 census in the country there were 15 union republics, 20 autonomous SSRs, 8 autonomous regions, 10 autonomous areas, 121 regions and 6 areas.

REFERENCES

Davidovich, D. J. 1934. *Voprosy planivovki novykh gorodov.* (Problems of planning of new towns), Leningrad.
Gutnov, A. E., *Lzhava I. G.* 1977. *Buduschee goroda.* (Future of towns.)
Kibalchich, O. A., Leizerovich, E. E. 1974. 'Razmeschenie obschectvennogo proizvodstva i rasselenie kak vzaimosviazannye protsessy'. (Distribution of production and settlement as interrelated processes.) In: *Geografia otrasley i raionov SSSR i zarubezhnykh stran.*
Kochetkov, A. V., Listengurt, F. M. 1976. 'Osnovnye polozhenia generalnoi skhemy rasselenia na territorii SSSR'. (Major concepts of settlement over the USSR territory.) In: *Problemy rasselenia naselenia i razvitie neproizvodstvennoi sfery.*
Konstantinov, O. A. 1974. 'Izmenenia v geografii gorodov SSSR za sovetskiy period'. (Changes in the urban geography of the USSR in the Soviet period.) In: *Voprosy geografii,* sb.6.M.
Konstantinov, O. A. 1967a. 'Opyt vyiavlenia raionov rasselenia SSSR'. (An approach to distinguishing the settlement regions of the USSR.) In: *Geografia naselenia i naselennykh punktov SSSR.* L.
Konstantinov, O. A. 1967b. 'Raionirovanie rasselenia SSSR'. (Regionalization of settlement in the USSR.) In: *Nauchnye problemy geografii naselenia.*
Konstantinov, O. A. 1976. 'Rol novykh gorodov v razvitii sistem rasselenia SSSR'. (Role of new towns in the development of the settlement systems in the USSR.) In: *Problemy urbanizatsii i rasselenia.*
Kvasha, A. Y. 1978. 'Nekotorye problemy regionalnogo demograficheskogo analiza'. (Some problems of regional demographic analysis.) In: *Regionalnye demograficheskie issledovania.* Tashkent.
Lappo, G. M. 1978. 'Opornyi karkas territorialnoi struktury narodnogo khoziaistva'. (Basic framework of the territorial structure of the national economy.) In: *Territorialnaia organizatsia proizvoditelnykh sil.*
Lappo, G. 1980. 'Soviet-Polish investigations of urbanization and settlement problems—International cooperation of Geographers'. *Social sciences today.* USSR Academy of Sciences.
Liubovny, V. Ya. 1977. 'Razvitie proizvoditelnykh sil i rasselenie'. (Development of productive forces and settlement.) In: *Izvestia AN SSSR, seria geogr.,* No. 4.
Maergoiz, I. M. 1976. 'Territorialnaia struktura narodnogo khoziaistva i nekotorye podkhody k eio issledovaniu v svete sotsialisticheskoi ekonomicheskoi integratsii'. (Spatial structure of the national economy and some approaches to its studies in the light of socialist economic integration.) In: *Territorialnaia struktura narodnogo khoziaistva v sotsialisticheskikh strinhakh.*
Pertsik, E. N. 1973. *Raionnaia planirovka (geograficheskie aspekty).* (Regional planning (geographical aspects).)
Pivovarov, Yu. L. 1979. *Demogeograficheskie osobennosti razvitia regionalnykh sistem rasselenia v SSSR.* (Demogeographic specific of the development of regional settlement systems in the USSR.) Moskva-Kiev. (Report at IV Soviet-Polish seminar on Urbanization Problems, mimeo).
Pokshishevskiy, V. V. 1962. 'Naselionnye punkty—mestnye tsentry, i problemy ikh sopodchinenia'. (Settlements—local centres and problems of their subordination.) In: *Voprosy geografii,* sb.56.

Pokshishevskiy, V. V. 1978. *Naselenie i geografia. Teoreticheskie ocherki.* (Population and geography. Theoretical essays.)

Romanenkova, G. M. 1980. 'Metodologicheskie osnovy regulirovania demograficheskogo razvitia krupnogo goroda'. (Methodological basis for regulating demographic development of a city.) In: *Izvestia AN SSSR seria ekonom.*, No. 4.

Saushkin, Yu. G. 1960. 'Ob izuchenii sistemy gorodov Sovetskogo Soiuza'. (On studying the urban system of the Soviet Union.) In: *Vestnik MGU. Geografia.*

Vishnevskiy, A. G. 1976. *Demograficheskaia revoliutsia.* (Demographic revolution.)

Witthauer, K. 1961. 'Bevölkerung und natürliche Bevölkerungsbewegung in der DDR. In: *Petermanns geogr. Mitteilungen*, No. 4.

PART B

SETTLEMENT SYSTEMS IN
CENTRALLY-PLANNED ECONOMIES

**Section 5: Settlement on Old Lands and in
Higher-Density Regions**

17 THE POLISH SETTLEMENT SYSTEM

KAZIMIERZ DZIEWOŃSKI, MAREK JERCZYNSKI,
AND PIOTR KORCELLI

Historical Growth and Development

To understand the nature, structure, and changes presently taking place in the national settlement system of Poland, it is necessary to analyse three preceding historical phases of development: the crystallization of feudal settlement; the capitalist transformation of the former feudal system during the political partition of the national territory among three neighbouring empires; and finally the reconstruction of the settlement system within and by the reconstituted Polish state—first from 1918 to 1939 in the capitalist economy of the inter-war years, and then after 1945 under conditions of an evolving socialist society.

The first settlement patterns date from the tenth and eleventh centuries. They represented networks of functional settlement units grouped around the local, in some cases regional, centres of social, economic, and political life. These were tribal in origin, but were subsequently transformed into the seats of a strongly integrated military organization inherited or imposed by force by the then victorious rulers. These regional and local centres served as a basis for the formation of the original boroughs together with their subsidiary and supplementary settlements.

Later, during the period of internal colonization, these districts and provinces were economically developed and strengthened. Then the dense network of towns and villages was established with strong differences in character and structure between urban and rural settlement. This development, however, did not take place simultaneously in all parts of the country. Spatially, the internal colonization and its characteristic forms of settlement spread from the southwestern provinces where they first developed, through the central to the northern and eastern regions. The whole process began at the end of the twelfth century in Silesia and ended in the fifteenth and sixteenth centuries in Masovia and Ducal, Eastern Prussia.

The majority of urban foundations date from that period and the later urban network was relatively stable. However, rural settlement during this whole period and afterwards changed frequently in its structure and patterns, as a consequence of the adoption of various forms of land tenure and successive agrarian reforms. The density of urban locations varied, depending on the amount and productivity of arable land available, as well as on accessible mineral resources and the development of local crafts and industrial production. As a result, the density of urban centres varied from 50 towns per 10,000 sq. km in the mining and industrial south to 15 towns per 10,000 sq. km in the northern lakelands with their extensive areas of preserved forests and woodlands. Average density was about 35 towns per 10,000 sq. km. In addition several larger cities with good transport locations grew up as centres of trade and as seats of national or regional political and ecclesiastical authorities. Some were very rich and prosperous. Their size, however, according to rough estimates, was never greater than 50,000 inhabitants, with most of them not reaching the size of 20,000 or 30,000. One aspect of these urban communities should be stressed. They were based on the grant of individual privileges, which for a very long time were jealously guarded, and their citizens did not possess any consciousness of common urban interests or of the towns' future welfare and growth.

The development of serfdom, with growing burdens imposed on peasants, led to an increasing separation of the rural population and impeded migration to cities and towns, thus limiting their growth and development. Later, the seventeenth and eighteenth centuries brought a specific decline in the urbanization of the whole country (Table 17.1). This was due to the political dominance of the agricultural and rurally-minded gentry, as well as to the decimation of the urban populations and their material wealth by wars, fires, and epidemics.

Table 17.1: *Total Population, Urban and Rural. 1810-1978*

Years	Population* (in millions)			Urban as % of Total
	Total	Urban	Rural	
1810	9.0	2.0	7.0	22.2
1850	14.0	3.1	10.9	22.1
1870	17.5	4.1	13.4	23.4
1897/1900	23.7	6.3	17.4	26.6
1921/1925	26.6	8.7	17.9	32.7
1931/1933	29.8	10.6	19.2	35.6
1939	32.5	12.0	20.5	36.9
1946	23.6	8.0	15.6	34.0
1950	25.0	9.2	15.8	36.9
1955	27.6	12.1	15.5	43.8
1960	29.8	14.4	15.4	48.3
1965	31.6	15.7	15.9	49.7
1970	32.7	17.1	15.6	52.3
1975	34.2	19.0	15.2	55.7
1978	35.1	20.2	14.9	57.5
1979	35.4	20.6	14.8	58.2

* Estimates for years 1810-1939 based on present territory of Poland.

Sources: Statistical characteristics of towns and cities. Dominant functions. *Statystyka Polski No 85*, Central Statistical Office, Warsaw 1977, Table 1, p. 10.
Statistical Yearbook 1980. Central Statistical Office. Warsaw. 1980. Table 2, 52 p. 30.

Nevertheless, from the beginning of the seventeenth century, Warsaw, the national capital, began to develop in a form which some historians call the 'late feudal agglomeration'. In the eighteenth century, specific efforts were made to rationalize, integrate, and spatially concentrate the city which was growing in a dispersed and haphazard way. By the end of the same century, the emerging consciousness of common interests among the urban inhabitants led to demands for economic and political reform in recognition of their status and rights.

The loss of independence and the partition of the national territory between three neighbouring political powers (Prussia, Austria, and Russia) had a deep impact on settlement patterns, due to the very different policies and roads to development pursued by each of the powers. Initially changes were small and slow, but with the development of the capitalist economy, especially in the last decades of the nineteenth century, they were accelerated. The results, as expressed in the settlement patterns, were as follows:

(*a*) Distinct settlement sub-systems were established, more or less integrated with the developing settlement systems of the three occupying states.

(*b*) Where the Polish lands were split and joined into the peripheral regions of those states, separate patterns of central places up to the provincial level were formed out of earlier feudal urban locations. Warsaw, no longer the capital for the whole nation, was reduced to the role of a provincial city and its growth was hampered in comparison to that of similar national capitals. Some subsidiary cultural and economic centres did emerge. The growth of the largest cities was limited: as they were located in the frontier regions they were, almost without exception, turned into military bases and strongly fortified.

(*c*) A process of concentration of urban settlement, by the elimination of the smallest towns, was started in all three parts of the Polish land, but it varied in its rate of advance. The decimation of the feudal urban network was at its strongest in the Congress Kingdom, in the part of Poland under the Tsarist rule, and was almost non-existent in the region under the Prussians, although even there social and economic conditions were eroding the economic bases of a large number of the smallest towns.

(*d*) Industrial settlement began to emerge in areas rich in easily accessible mineral resources (mainly in Upper, but also in Lower Silesia, and in the Carpathians and the Holy Cross Mountains) as well as in and around the largest cities (such as Wroclaw, Poznań, Gdańsk and Szczecin, later also Cracow). In some areas the availability of cheap labour from rural communities and the unhampered access to the Eastern and Far-Eastern markets led to the emergence of strong textile industries with corresponding industrial settlements (e.g. areas of Łodź, Białystok, also Bielsko-Biała). The trends toward concentration, first in industrial production and later in settlement, were clearly visible during the whole nineteenth century, although they were not strongly advanced because of the peripheral character of those industrial centres. However, in Łodź there was a high concentration of both vertical and horizontal industrial organization as well as in housing (though devoid of all sanitary infra-structure, and with very underdeveloped services).

(*e*) Rural settlement underwent some radical changes, while becoming at the same time regionally diversified. These changes were mainly due to two causes: the successive land reforms (carried out in each part of the country in different ways and in different time periods), and the population explosion. The spatial differences caused by this explosion were the result of the underdevelopment of local and regional industrialization and urbanization, as well as of the possibilities, extent, and efficiency of migrations to other provinces and countries. It may be said that in the Prussian part the surplus rural population emigrated to the industrial and urban areas of Western and Central Germany, leaving the rural settlement largely unchanged. In the Austrian and the Russian parts, by contrast, insufficient out-migration led to an overpopulation of rural areas and overemployment in agriculture. This was followed by the fragmentation of peasant holdings and at times the dispersal of rural settlement.

The regaining of independence after the First World War, and the reintegration of the state territory after the First and Second World Wars, are two historical events which have dominated all changes in the national settlement system during the first half of the present century. At the same time the post-war economy and the world economic crisis in the inter-war period severely diminished development, limiting it largely to the elimination of war devastations. However, the economic crisis did not diminish the tendencies towards concentration, both of industry and of urban growth. But in the years immediately preceding the Second World War some efforts were made to instigate the economic development of the country through more imaginative policies.

Thus the basic changes in the settlement system taking place during this period consisted of:

(*a*) the readjustment of central place functions linked to the establishment of the national administration as well as to the reconstruction of transport functions in keeping with the formation of a unified railroad grid;

(*b*) some readjustment among cities and towns with highly-specialized functions. In the more prosperous industries there was a clear tendency towards larger enterprises and geographical concentration; in the stagnating ones there was both dispersal in the location of new factories and amalgamation of old ones; in the declining industries there was concentration, brought about by the elimination of the most antiquated factories and the integration of the remaining ones. Nevertheless, at the end of the inter-war period a planned effort to establish new industries was undertaken—regionally concentrated and locally dispersed, with the Central Industrial Region in the heartland of the country—superimposing a new pattern upon the traditional one;

(c) a dispersal of rural settlement through the creation of rather small, more or less evenly distributed farms in Central Poland, a consequence of agrarian reform and the liquidation of some larger land estates;

(d) the continued process of eliminating the weakest elements in the network of small towns.

The devastations of the Second World War and the resulting change of the national territory have in reality only deepened and ripened these processes.

Out of all these changes a rather clear pattern of settlement has emerged, with a polycentric network of the largest cities only moderately dominated (except in the case of administration and economic management) by the capital—Warsaw— in social, cultural, and political functions, and by the industrial conurbation of Upper Silesia in the economic sphere. Around each of the largest cities both urban and rural regional systems have crystallized. These are widely varied in their hierarchical structure as well as in their degree of concentration or dispersal.

Several types of such regional settlement sub-systems are clearly discernible (Figure 17.1). They are: (a) two major urban agglomerations, one of a metropolitan, monocentric character, Warsaw, and another in the form of an industrial conurbation in the process of transformation into a supraregional megalopolis, integrating the present conurbation of the Upper Silesian Coal District with the surrounding, strongly industrialized and urbanized areas around Cracow, Częstochowa, Opole, and Bielsko-Biała. To these should be added the rapidly developing agglomerations of seaports and cities in the North (Gdańsk and Szczecin); (b) old industrial regions in the mountains and foothills (Sudetes, Carpathians, and the Holy Cross Mountains), now in process of transforming their traditional extractive and textile industries into processing industries; (c) western and northwestern regions with well-developed and balanced hierarchical structures of urban and rural settlement; (d) central regions where the processes of urbanization, strong in the nineteenth century, slowed down in the inter-war period. At present they are again developing, due to the growth of industrial cities based on brown-coal mining, and of the cities on the Lower Vistula. The western part possesses a balanced structure of settlement while the eastern part is characterized by the dominance of the largest cities (Warsaw and Łódź), often at the cost of smaller cities; (e) southeastern regions, without larger cities, but with a well-developed network of middle-sized cities (based either on industrial or central-place functions) and with a dense rural population. The rural areas are characterized by extensive commuting to work in industry or in the transportation sector; (f) northeastern regions with a dominance of the largest (but still not very large) urban centres, where most of the region's factories are concentrated.

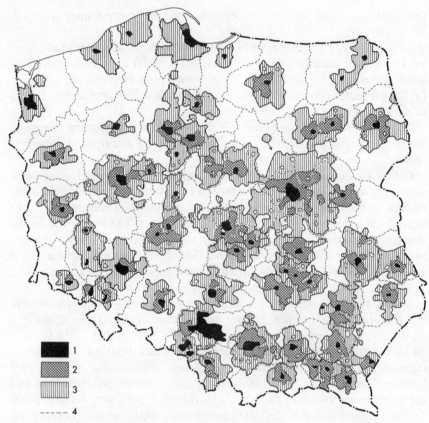

Fig. 17.1   Urban Functional Regions in Poland, 1973
    1. Core areas
    2. Internal zone: out-commuting = 50 per cent of the economically active non-
              rural population
    3. External zone: out-commuting = 10-50 per cent of the economically active non-
              rural population
    4. *Voivod*ship boundaries
    Source: P. Korcelli, D. Bodzak, A. Potrykowska

The Present Structure of the Settlement System

During the last thirty years (i.e. since the Second World War and its after-
math of population exchange, resettlement, and reconstruction problems),
the parallel processes of forced industrialization (carried out under the full
nationalization of industry and a planned socialist economy), and rapid
urbanization have introduced new factors and important modifications into
the Polish settlement system. However, in a situation where the continuous
growth of the national economy has involved successive changes in its structure and where social life has been evolving under the impact of a social
revolution, these factors have themselves been transformed. Although the

national settlement system as a whole has grown and developed, preserving its essential identity and stability, its elements and their characteristic interactions, as well as its dependence on the outside world, have changed. These changes may be described under the following headings:
(1) the growing unity—integration of the settlement system and its essential stability;
(2) the increase in size, functional role, and national importance of urban agglomerations and the feasible limits of their future growth;
(3) the emergence of urban regions and regional settlement patterns;
(4) the changing functions of smaller urban centres;
(5) a transformation in rural settlement—dispersal and concentration, semi-urbanization, and the impact of recreational migration and settlement.

The increasing unity and integration of the national settlement system was due to several factors. Most important was the planned, forced industrialization which from the beginning received top priority among all political, social, and economic goals. Urbanization processes were originally treated only as a subsidiary, indeed unavoidable, consequence of industrialization. Industrialization of a predominantly agricultural and only partly-urbanized country was associated with two characteristic phenomena: the abundance of non-skilled labour and the dearth of capital. These had serious consequences for the location and internal structure of newly-developed industries. Industrial investments were concentrated in the basic industries; complementary and secondary production was left to the existing ones. It was only when disproportions and disruptions in the total economy started to emerge and to threaten national development, that some modifications of these investment policies and corresponding corrective measures were introduced. This rule of thumb also applied to the location of investments in other branches of the national economy, such as transport, housing, community and other services.

The consequences of these policies for the settlement system were that the big developments at new locations were counterbalanced by similar, sometimes even unforeseen and unplanned developments in the old ones and that mutual interactions were extremely strong. The growth of new industrial and urban centres, intended to create a more balanced distribution of productive forces, thus incited additional growth and transformation in the already existing cities and industrialized areas. The net result was that the settlement system was only slightly changed. But the individual industrial and urban centres were pulled together by the increasing specialization of functions, mostly productive functions, although this process was perhaps a haphazard or even random one.

Another important factor in the integration of the settlement system on the national level was a strong centralization of political and economic decisions connected with a planned socialist economy. The administrative functions were of great importance for the development of cities, especially those which had been seats of national or regional governments. It was in them, too, that a large part of industrial investment was concentrated, giving them a polyfunctional character. It should be added that several larger industrial centres also acquired some administrative functions at the beginning of the forced industrialization period. In this way the development of the largest cities was converging. All became importance industrial centres and at the same time administrative capitals.

Recent changes in the territorial administration, shifting from a three- to a two-tier organization, and the subsequent increase of regional units from seventeen to forty-nine, have somewhat blurred the established structure. Although the hierarchical structure does not depend solely on the administrative functions, it is closely related to it.

The higher rate of industrialization in the southern regions produced a specific differentiation in patterns of urbanization and in the subsequent development of the urban network. A large number of specialized industrial towns and villages have been superimposed on the general network of central places. In the North, and to a smaller degree also in the Central regions, the urban population is concentrated in the cities and towns with strongly-developed central-place functions. There is a similar difference in the distribution of the non-agricultural population. In the South the percentage of persons not engaged in agriculture in the rural areas is very high, whereas in the North it is much lower.

However, for the settlement system as a whole, what is perhaps most significant is its essential stability. The last thirty years have not seen the introduction of any major change in the two basic characteristics of this system—its polycentricity and the weak dominance of the capital.

Until the administrative reform in 1975 (Figure 17.2), cities at the lower level—which were the seats of regional administration—clearly dominated in the field of investment and development. Those which were originally solely central places acquired large industrial plants, specialized in production at the national level. Those which had grown up as important industrial centres obtained the full range of specialized higher-rank services, and became important regional central places. It is characteristic that all of them became important centres of higher education.

However, since the administrative reform of 1975, and the increase in the number of administrative regions, the capacity to concentrate the more specialized services and to locate more important industries in regional capitals has diminished. In numerous regions, the previously characteristic functions of the regional capital are now split between several neighbouring, middle-sized cities. With a shortage of investment funds for eventual concentration, at least one generation will pass before the full integration of all regional functions in the regional capital can be expected. It seems that a complete shift in the role of administrative functions has taken place. They are no more a stabilizing factor but rather introduce dynamic changes which transform the whole settlement pattern.

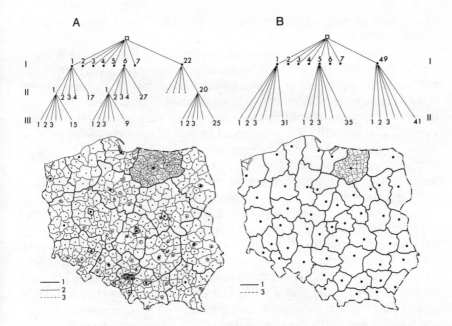

Fig. 17.2 Territorial Organization of Poland before and after the Administrative Reform of 1975

    A.   Territorial organization of Poland in 1970

    I   First order level: 22 *voivod*ships, of which 5 are urban

    II   Second order level: 391 *poviat*s, of which 74 are urban

    III Third order level: 4761 *gromada*s and 775 towns

    1.   *voivod*ship boundaries; 2. *poviat* boundaries; 3. *gromada* boundaries

    B.   Territorial organization of Poland in 1975

    I   First order level: 49 *voivod*ships, of which 3 are urban

    II   Second order level: 2327 *gmina*s and 807 towns

    1.   *voivod*ship boundaries; 3. *gmina* boundaries

The plan for the physical development of the country to 1990 is, with some corrections, based on the existing settlement pattern. Its main goals are stronger industrialization and urbanization of the northern coastal regions as well as the eastern, frontier zone. However, the major long-term innovating factor for the transformation of the existing pattern may be found in the first steps toward the development of a new coalfield and industrial region in the Southeast, with the city of Lublin as its major urban centre.

Urban agglomerations in Poland are a phenomenon of the present century and although their emergence could be observed in the inter-war period, their real growth is connected with recent industrialization and urbanization. At present there is considerable discussion on whether to include all large cities in the term 'urban agglomeration' or to limit its application to cities whose development occupies large areas with dispersed and loose urban settlement. From the latter point of view only a few large cities, together with adjacent towns and suburban zones, conform to the definition.

Another approach to the identification of urban agglomerations is according to their functions, with only secondary consideration given to their size and form of development. Thus, cities named 'urban agglomerations' should play a major role in industrial production, should possess high-rank specialized services, should be subsidiary to the national centres of social, cultural, and scientific life, and should be foci in the diffusion of information. Whatever the definition, there is no doubt that in size and in number urban agglomerations are growing rapidly and play a dominant role in national life, in the economy, and in the settlement system (Table 17.2).

With their rapid growth, the primacy of Warsaw has not been increasing. It is not even the largest among the agglomerations—the Upper Silesian conurbation (depending on delimitation) counts between 3 and 4 million inhabitants in relation to Warsaw's 2 million. However, as a purely urban centre, Warsaw is the largest. Its rapid post-war growth was connected with its reconstruction, and cannot be considered a token of increasing primacy. In the last 15-20 years, Warsaw's further growth was below the general rate of growth of urban population, partly as a result of government containment policy and partly because of its low rate of natural increase.

The plan for physical development to 1990 provides for slower rates of growth for the largest urban agglomerations and for higher increases for the smaller ones. Lately some doubts about their future growth have emerged. The possibilities of their population growth seem now to be more limited than was so far assumed, while other technical and economic thresholds emerge. Their population growth depends to a considerable extent on migration from rural areas. Even now they do not reproduce their popula-

Table 17.2: *Number and percentage of Urban Population in Total Population, 1950-79, by Size of Urban Settlements.*

Size of Urban Settlement (thousands of inhabitants)	Number of Settlements				Urban Population as a Percentage of Total Population			
	1950	1960	1970	1979	1950	1960	1970	1979
Below 5	393	405	359	270	4.3	4.1	3.4	2.3
5-10	159	236	220	186	4.5	5.6	4.8	3.7
10-20	76	138	162	164	4.2	6.4	6.8	6.6
20-50	50	68	97	109	6.2	7.1	8.9	9.5
50-100	12	20	27	39	3.4	4.3	5.7	7.6
100-200	11	13	14	20	6.7	6.4	6.7	8.0
Above 200	5	9	10	15	9.7	14.4	15.9	20.5
Total	706	889	889	803	39.0	48.3	52.2	58.2

Sources: Statistics of towns and urban settlements, Central Statistical Office, Warsaw 1967.
Statistical Yearbook 1972, 1980, Central Statistical Office, Warsaw 1972, 1980.

tion (their rate of natural increase is at present between 3.9 and 8.6 per thousand per annum but the indices of reproduction are below 1). With full depletion of the population reserves of rural areas in sight, the only other existing source of immigrants lies in smaller cities and towns. However, with the evident improvement of living conditions in those cities and towns and with environmental deterioration in the agglomerations, even this source may dry up quickly.

At present Polish urban agglomerations remain attractive magnets both to the population and to the authorities. Their growth will probably proceed, although perhaps at diminishing rates, at least until the end of the present century.

The difficulties of defining the next group of larger cities are equally great. On the basis of population, the next group includes practically all other cities which up to 1975 were seats of regional government. But confusion was introduced when the number of administrative regions was increased from seventeen to forty-nine. Cities which then became new seats of regional government immediately started to press for the same service functions which earlier centres had already obtained.

The hierarchical structures differ regionally depending on whether the urban settlements in the past have developed in more concentrated, balanced, or dispersed patterns. In the first case the number of hierarchical levels in services is smaller and in the latter larger. The provisions of the national plan tend towards a standardization in those hierarchical structures. Only the future will show whether such a goal will be implemented, and to what degree.

In spite of the uncertainties concerning hierarchical levels of urban settlement, the territorial organization of economic, social, cultural, and even political life is becoming increasingly dependent upon the emergence and development of city regions. One type includes the three administrative regions, called urban *voivod*ships, with a distinct organization and powers. In the second type there are some areas outside urban agglomerations with smaller urban centres of their own. In the third, only the urban core of the region is occupied by a larger but easily-accessible city although there may also be some subregional urban centres. The last type may be defined by the existence of several cities fulfilling together the role of main urban centre.

The city regions are informally grouped into larger regional entities which may perhaps be called provinces. Their identity is at present confused but their urban centres are clearly crystallized and may be relatively easily identified as major cultural and scientific as well as economic centres.

Characteristic disarray reigns in the classification of the still smaller cities or towns located outside urban agglomerations. Their range is wide—from regional subcentres to small, ancient market towns and industrial villages. All are too small and too numerous to provide the range of services expected nowadays by urban and adjacent rural inhabitants. In reality they are subsidiary centres within more or less clearly-crystallized city regions. Their economic base is constantly endangered and from time to time they pass through a stage of acute crisis. Such was the situation of the smallest towns in the 1950s, following the nationalization of industry and commerce. In fact nationalization (as well as the earlier war devastations) had introduced a strong need for rationalization both of industry and commerce. In industry this was expressed by the concentration of machinery and production in larger, better-equipped factories, so that the small towns lost a large portion of their plants and workshops. On the other hand, in commerce, nationalization prompted efforts to bring shops nearer to the rural consumers. New shops—more widely dispersed throughout the villages— were organized, and shops in small towns lost a large number of their clients and some of them were closed. Another crisis, this time in the larger small towns, has developed recently with the abolition of territorial administration at the level of *powiat*.

At present three main types of such towns may be identified, although the dividing lines between them are not very distinct. They are: (1) subsidiary regional centres, sometimes called sub-regional centres; (2) local centres—providing basic services to the rural population—usually designated as centres of communes, and finally, (3) industrial villages, usually containing housing estates for workers employed in local industries (usually one large industrial plant). They are not very attractive because of the lack of alternative employment. However, if the industrial plant is really strong, and a growing one, the centre usually excels in the provision and organization of services. These services begin to form an additional place of employment and in turn their existence attracts additional industrial enterprises. In reality industrial villages represent the most active and the most dynamic element in the settlement network at the local and regional level.

The urban part of the Polish settlement system is more or less stable. Changes may be explained in terms of a transformation within the system, rather than through modifications of its structure and pattern. The situation is quite different in the case of rural settlement. The present structure of rural settlement is extremely variegated and even haphazard. Generally speaking, the prevailing tendency has been towards increasing dispersal, although the process has not equally advanced in all parts of the country. However, the almost unanimous opinion of technicians and planners supports concentration and there are some new, growing impulses in this direction. The final outcome of these divergent trends is not very clear and the following description should be considered as tentative.

It is a declared policy of the government that the newly-established rural communes should each have a strong centre for services and social life. However, the number and size of these communes are still fluid. Constant changes and adjustments are being made. In addition the investment funds allocated for such purposes are very limited. It is estimated that by the end of this century only about half of the communes will possess a fully-equipped centre. Even assuming that eventually such facilities will be available, the question remains what will happen to the already existing, rather dispersed services. Some of them will probably vanish, but many may survive as subsidiaries.

As far as housing in rural areas is concerned, the locational tendencies are at present better defined. The larger employers tend to demand the location of housing estates for their employees near the actual site of their work, which in most cases is different from the proposed communal centres. Therefore even the centripetal tendencies in housing lead towards a somewhat dispersed pattern of rural settlement. For the individual farmer—usually a peasant — the traditional tendency or even desire for complete dispersal is characteristic, although it may be partly tempered by technical reasons such as the communal supply of water, electricity, or sewage disposal.

To complicate the situation further, other factors, unconnected with agriculture, have strongly influenced the development of rural areas in many regions. The first is the growth in number and percentage of the non-agriculturally employed in rural areas. This, together with the emergence of 'peasant-workers', has led to new forms of rural settlement, unconnected with agricultural production. The phenomenon was first noted and analysed in Silesia by Golachowski, who named it 'semiurbanization' in contra-distinction to 'suburbanization' as it is known in the western developed countries. The former is connected more with industrialization than with urbanization and in some cases with long-distance commuting to places of work often located in smaller towns outside the urban agglomerations. Its patterns are characterized by ribbon forms (along or in the vicinity of good roads) and by the integration of smaller settlements of various forms (hamlets, villages, colonies, etc.) into extensive settlement complexes with one or several small service centres. There is a question whether this kind of settlement is a transitory or permanent one. With the spread of private ownership, and the growth of the largest cities, such forms of settlement may easily increase.

A similar phenomenon, though emerging in different regions and areas, is the development of settlements connected with tourism and recreation. There are two typical forms. The first is the construction in the countryside, especially in the areas of attractive natural environment and landscape, of tourist hostels and hotels. The second is the building of more or less dispersed cottages and summer houses. Those connected with weekend recreation are usually within easy reach of urban agglomerations, those with summer or winter vacations farther off in the mountains (southern regions) or in lakelands and on the seacoast (northern regions).

Finally, it should be remembered that decisions about the location of the large majority of settlements, specially the urban ones, were taken long ago.

Cities are developed because they are already there, and not for any present environmental advantages. But the natural environment may form a serious obstacle to urban growth, and to overcome it may involve large capital outputs. In Poland, the proper use of the natural environment does improve the effectiveness of the settlement units and the performance of the whole system but, within certain limits, it is not decisive for its existence and functioning.

To sum up, the present state and evolution of the national settlement system in Poland seems to reflect the passage of the nation from the still-prevailing industrialization and urbanization to the next stage of post-industrial development. It is hoped that by the use of the planned economy and physical planning, this passage will be orderly and effective, avoiding the negative aspects evident at present in countries more advanced in development.

Urban Agglomerations as Systems within National Settlement Systems

Traditionally, the structure of a national settlement system has been described by emphasizing the importance either of linkages between individual urban agglomerations, or of intra-regional linkages, that is, those connecting a given agglomeration with its surrounding territory. According to the former interpretation, the main sub-system in a national settlement system would be a set of major urban agglomerations and their mutual relationsips. The latter interpretation assumes that a set of regional sub-systems, each centred around a major urban nucleus, can be distinguished. In Poland, these two interpretations are complementary. There are two spatial dimensions which account for the bulk of linkages in the settlement system. The first dimension, which corresponds to the distance separating major cities and urban agglomerations represents a substantial part of production and organizational links (both on an inter- and intra-industry scale), the principal information exchange channels (national mass media networks), as well as major tourist and scientific contract routes. The second dimension reflects the scale of functional urban regions and contains the bulk of daily and weekly flows between places of residence and places of work, shopping, recreation, social and institutional contacts. Although the first dimension corresponds mainly to production patterns and the latter to consumption patterns, the two spheres do substantially overlap.

Typically, the economic functions of urban agglomerations are highly differentiated, but all are important centres of manufacturing and tertiary activities. Only in the case of the Upper Silesian conurbation do primary functions (mining) play an important, although now a relatively declining, part. Specialized tertiary functions, in particular higher education, scientific research, arts, and culture, dominate in urban agglomerations. In terms of the development level of industry, retail trade and transportation, their per capita indices are close to the average for the whole set of Polish cities.

There are substantial demographic variations among individual urban agglomerations which are explained by differences in their political history and past migrations (Table 17.3). The index of natural increase for the largest urban agglomerations is less than half that for the whole country (between 3.9 per thousand for Łodz *voivod*ship and 5.4 for Warsaw), while for central cities it is still smaller (1.9 per thousand for Łodz, 2.5 for Warsaw, and 3.5 for Katowice in 1973). The bulk of the population increase in urban agglomerations is accounted for by in-migration, which during 1971-75 contributed about 80 per cent of the total growth in the case of Warsaw. Only in the cases of Wrocław and Szczecin (due to the specific population age structure resulting from the post-war resettlement) did in-migration account for less than half of the total population increase. Except for Warsaw and Upper Silesia (and to a certain extent Gdańsk and Gdynia), which attract migrants from all over the country, the migration zones of individual urban agglomerations are clearly of a regional character, and show only limited overlap. Even in Warsaw the majority of migrants come from the nearest *voivod*ships.

Environmental pollution is a critical problem in all urban agglomerations, particularly in the Upper Silesian conurbation. However, protective measures tend to be stronger and better in urban agglomerations than elsewhere. Hence, from the point of view of environmental conditions, urban agglomerations can compete with other large- and medium-size cities in Poland, particularly with centres of heavy industry.

The spread of urban agglomerations, and of urban land use in general, endangers the existing reserves of agricultural land. Due to relatively compact urban forms (one reason being the dominance of multi-family housing), the loss of agricultural land is kept within reasonable limits. Current

Table 17.3: *Internal Migration of Population by Directions, 1951-78*

Years	Migrant Total[b] (in thousands)	by directions (as % of total number of migrants)			
		from rural to urban areas	from urban to rural areas	from urban to urban areas	from rural to rural areas
1951-5[a]	1,396.6	25.7	18.1	27.2	29.0
1956-60	1,343.5	24.0	17.7	23.2	35.1
1961-5	1,006.2	25.9	15.9	22.5	35.7
1966-70	864.9	29.3	13.1	21.9	35.7
1971-5	854.2	34.1	12.1	23.6	30.2
1976-8	943.4	36.3	12.8	28.0	22.9

[a] Incomplete estimate for 1951

[b] Annual average

Source: Internal migration of population to urban settlements and urban agglomerations'. *Statystyka Polski No 123*. Central Statistical Office, Warsaw 1979, Table 3, p. 32.

policies and legislation aim at its further reduction. Another problem is that of water reserves. Two of the largest urban agglomerations (the Upper Silesian conurbation and Łodź) are situated on watershed divides. In the case of a few other urban agglomerations, the scarcity of water may also form a critical barrier to their further expansion. Another growth barrier is developing in the form of the declining migration potential of rural areas. By the 1960s and early 1970s the rural areas of heaviest out-migration have been declining in population.

Policies towards the growth of urban agglomerations have changed during the 1960s and 1970s. Whereas before 1970 growth-limitation measures were widely applied, the later period has been characterized by a selective development approach, following the generally acknowledged rule of 'moderate polycentric concentration'.

The internal structure of an urban agglomeration is determined by its origins, that is, whether the present-day agglomeration has emerged as an expansion of a single large city (the case of Warsaw, Poznań, and Wrocław), or as the integration of a group of self-sustained urban places (the case of Upper Silesia). The morphology of an urban agglomeration depends also on its natural and cultural milieu, as well as on its functions and the degree of planning control over its development.

The planned development of urban areas in Poland since 1945 has been governed by the principle of the separation of major land uses. The rebuilding of the areas destroyed during the Second World War, as well as new construction, has often favoured large industrial and housing estates, increasing the spatial polarization of functions. This has resulted in a substantial increase in the mean distance between dwellings and places of work.

Since the war spatial variations in socio-economic variables within Polish cities have diminished, and residential patterns have changed from concentric-sectoral to mosaic-like. Housing standards and house types have become more or less uniform. However, studies indicate the emergence and persistence of substantial variation in their demographic structures; housing estates developed in successive time periods display specific differences in age and sex structures.

Population densities in Polish cities and urban agglomerations, while generally conforming to the negative exponential rule, display a few specific features. Within the built-up areas, density gradients tend to be less steep than elsewhere, as a consequence of the relatively uniform net residential densities throughout.

The Future Structure and Patterns of the National Settlement System

The future structure and pattern of the national settlement system were not discussed in full until the beginning of the 1970s. The various authors who raised the question ranged from supporters of garden-city ideals, which implied the limited growth of larger cities and their dispersal, to the followers of Le Corbusier's 'La Ville Radieuse', postulating the strong development of highly concentrated large cities. The first plans tackling the problem at the national level (1937, 1947, 1950, 1959) were based upon the moderate and critical extrapolation of past trends and patterns of urban growth, starting from the individual cities and based primarily on forecasts of population, its structure, and migration.

Real discussion started when the critics of the deglomeration policies adopted by the planning authorities in the early 1960s became vociferous at the end of that decade. Two arguments were used. First, the very large cities, representing the largest productive force of the nation, should have the possibility of proper development. Second, the number of smaller centres foreseen by official planners for rapid growth and development was considered to be too high, implying an unnecessary dispersal of efforts and the misuse of resources and investment. Two radical proposals, one based on linear settlement running continuously in several parallel lines from the North to the South, another advocating the concentration of population in cities of a similar size, were rejected as running counter to the real possibilities of economic growth and social development.

In the end a model for urban settlement was formulated in the National Plan for Physical Development to 1990, based upon the advantages of a moderate concentration of population as well as of industries and of services, using the already existing polycentric structure and pattern of urban agglomerations and large cities. The proposed changes involved a more rapid development of middle-sized cities than large ones and of smaller urban agglomerations than the largest existing ones. Spatially a greater growth of industry and cities in the northern and eastern regions was foreseen.

Recently a modification or extension of the model was proposed, stressing the social and economic need for and importance of the polyfunctional character of developed or 'developing' urban centres. However, the polyfunctional character may be obtained only in cities having at least fifty or preferably, a hundred thousand inhabitants. At the same time there is an upper limit to the rational and efficient size of such units, which at present lies somewhere between two and three hundred thousand. The larger cities and urban agglomerations should moreover be subdivided into clearly articulated, relatively autonomous, smaller elements of similar size, each one also of polyfunctional character and structure.

REFERENCES

Central Statistical Office. 1979. 'Internal Migration of Population to Urban Settlements and Urban Agglomerations'. *Statystyka Polski* No. 123, Warsaw.

Dziewoński, K., *et.al.* 1977. *Distribution, Migrations of Population and Settlement System of Poland*, Prace Geograficzne No. 117, Ossolineum, Wrocław-Warszawa-Kraków-Gdańsk.

Dziewoński, K., Jerczynski, M. 1975. 'Urbanization in Poland'. In R. Jones (ed.), *Essays on World Urbanization*. George Philip and Son Limited: London.

Dziewoński, K., Korcelli, P., eds. 1980. *Studies on Migration and Transformations of Settlement System of Poland*. Prace Geograficzne No. 140. Ossolineum. Wrocław-Warszawa-Kraków-Gdańsk.

Dziewoński, K., and Malisz, B. 1978. *The Transformations of Poland's Spatial-Economic Structure*. Studia KPZK PAN No LXII, PWN, Warszawa: 146.

Glówny Urzad Statystyczny 1979. 'Statistical Characteristics of Towns and Cities. Dominant Functions'. *Statystyka Polski* No. 123. Warsaw, (in Polish).

Golachowski, S. 1969. 'Urbanization of Rural Areas in the Opole Voivodship'. In Golachowski, S., *Studia nad miastami i wsiami śląskimi*. Instytut Slaski w Opolu. Opole-Wroclaw: 180-93.

Gontarski, Z. 1980. *Metropolitan Areas in Poland*. Biuletyn KPZK PAN, No 109: 231 (in Polish).

Jerczyński, M. 1973. *Problems of Specialization of the Urban Economic Base of Major Cities in Poland*. Prace Geograficzne No. 97, Ossolineum. Wrocław-Warszawa-Kraków-Gdańsk.

Rykiel, Z. 1978. *The Place of the Macro-Urban Agglomerations in the Socio-Economic Space of Poland*. Prace Geograficzne No. 128, Ossolineum. Wrocław-Warszawa-Kraków-Gdańsk.

Weclawowicz, G., 1977. 'The structure of the socio-economic space of Warsaw in 1931 and 1970'. *Geographia Polonica* no. 37: 201-24.

Zagożdżon, A., 1979. 'Regional and subregional centers in Poland. A general characterization and some methodological problems'. *Acta Universitatis Vratislaviensis No. 513, Studia Geograficzne*, XXXIII. Wrocław: 146.

18 THE SETTLEMENT SYSTEM OF THE GERMAN DEMOCRATIC REPUBLIC: ITS STRUCTURE AND DEVELOPMENT

FRANKDIETER GRIMM

Historical Background

In Central Europe the integration of local and regional settlement systems on a national scale took place during the industrial revolution, that is in the first half of the nineteenth century. Landmarks were the organization of the German Customs Union (*Zollverein*) in 1834, the opening of the first German long-distance railway between Leipzig and Dresden in 1839, and the foundation of the unified German Reich in 1871. In the mid-nineteenth century the territory of the GDR was composed of 14 autonomous German states, the most important being the Kingdom of Prussia with 58.4 per cent of the total area and the Kingdom of Saxony (13.6 per cent). Until the beginning of the nineteenth century, economic and social conditions had been rather uniform with local and regional settlement systems depicting a Christaller pattern of central places. In 1831 the territory of the present GDR was inhabited by 6.0 million people (55 inhabitants per square kilometre).

Despite the relatively even distribution of population, spatial differences existed. Those which turned out to be particularly important at the start of the industrial revolution were:

- an advanced level of manufacturing in the mountains and adjacent regions of the south, especially in Saxony;
- a concentration of economic and political power in the Kingdoms of Prussia and Saxony, which resulted in the development of larger cities (Berlin and Magdeburg in Prussia, Dresden and Leipzig in Saxony);
- the political fragmentation of Thuringia, which hampered the processes of industrialization and concentration;
- a general backwardness of rural districts, especially in the semi-feudal parts of Mecklenburg and Prussia.

In the first decades of the nineteenth century the system still showed the effects of prior development under feudalism and early capitalism. Since that time, the system has been transformed during three main periods:

1. the extensive development of local and regional settlement systems and their integration on the national scale in the second half of the nineteenth century;

2. urbanization and urban sprawl under capitalism at the end of the nineteenth and first half of the twentieth century;

3.   the reconstruction of towns and settlement systems after World War II and their transformation into the national settlement system of a socialist society.

Until the first decades of the present century, the development of settlements on the territory of the GDR had been characterized by rapid population growth and by polarization. Berlin was striking in this respect, reaching close to the 1 million population threshold by 1871. On the other hand, many rural regions remained backward, their settlement systems changed slowly, and they preserved their Christaller-like pattern of central places. Since the first part of the century population growth decreased, and the population has been relatively stable since World War II (1939—16.7 million inhabitants, 1961—17.1, 1975—16.8). The share of the total population in towns and urbanized settlements has increased, whereas the general size distribution and rank of cities has remained comparatively stable (Table 18.1 and 18.2).

Table 18.1: *Share of Population According to Size Groups of Towns in the GDR*

	5,000 to 10,000 inhabitants		more than 10,000 inhabitants	
year	number of towns	percentage of total population	number of towns	percentage of total population
1831	56	6.0	27	12.2
1852	80	7.0	45	17.5
1871	103	7.4	68	26.0
1910	106	5.0	128	35.3
1939	107	4.6	175	51.0
1974	198	8.2	220	54.6

Table 18.2: *Rank-size of the Largest Towns of the GDR*

	1871	1910	1939	1950	1971	1976
Berlin	1	1	1	1	1	1
Leipzig	4	2	2	2	2	2
Dresden	2	3	3	3	3	3
Halle	6	6	6	5	5	4
Karl-Marx-Stadt	5	4	4	4	4	5
Magdeburg	3	5	5	6	6	6
Rostock	11	13	10	9	7	7
Erfurt	8	8	7	7	8	8
Zwickau	12	9	11	8	9	9
Potsdam	9	12	8	10	10	10
Gera	27	15	14	12	11	11
Schwerin	13	20	20	13	13	12

Since World War II, an integrated national settlement system has developed within new frontiers. The system has been transformed, in keeping with the economic and social development of the GDR as a socialist state, by:
- an increasing specialization, co-operation and integration on the national scale;
- a growing percentage of urban population, although this had been already high in 1939;
- the stability of the urban network and the rank-size of large towns;
- an increased development and industrialization of the backward rural regions in the north and east;
- the stagnation of population growth in agglomerated regions;
- the strengthened role of the political administrative centres and their districts (*Bezirk, Kreis*);
- the transformation of rural settlement systems as a result of the rapid reorganization of socialist agriculture and the improved accessibility of neighbouring towns.

The transformation of the last few decades has led to a comparatively well-balanced spatial structure of the national settlement system.

Definitions

In discussing the present settlement system of the German Democratic Republic (GDR), the following definitions are assumed.

1.   Human settlement is a social phenomenon. Settlement units are groupings of people, of houses, of infrastructures. They may be considered as localized communities of people including their architectural environs.

2.   Settlement systems express the human settlement of a certain region. They are composed of spatially separated components (settlement units) which interact with each other in order to realize a common function. The main objective of the system's operation is to provide an optimum spatial organization of population, production, and services (including environment).

3.   National settlement systems comprise the human settlement of a nation (state). They are characterized by the spatial specialization and interaction of settlement units (elements, sub-systems) in the fields of economy, politics, social, and cultural affairs. Traditionally, settlement systems have been treated mainly as social systems. Thus, the concept of national settlement systems needs an extension not only in space but also in content.

4.   National settlement systems are complex, requiring a subdivision into more manageable sub-systems. These may be derived from the most important functions of the system: social goals and economic goals. Therefore it is possible to separate two different sub-systems:

(*a*) the B settlement system which aims at the fulfilment of social goals (B = *Bedürfnisse*);

(*b*) the E settlement system which aims at the fulfilment of economic goals

5. There is only one settlement system (sub-system) which by definition can be limited to towns (or urban agglomerations). This sub-system exerts a unique function. It is the national urban system of political, economic, and social superstructure. Other 'urban sub-systems' are parts of the national spatial socio-economic system. They are not systems on their own.

Present Settlement Structure

The B Settlement System

The B settlement system reflects the immediate realization of the requirements of human life and work. Its function is to realize the social needs of a nation: labour, housing, retail trade, education, health service, culture, etc. Elements of the system are people (communities) at their places of residence and work. Many relationships of B settlement systems are translated into reality by direct contacts among people. Therefore daily communication in space is of dominating significance (Grimm, 1980, p. 11, 12).

The B settlement system, its elements, sub-systems, and relations are the best-known parts of the settlement system of the GDR. This knowledge is based upon empirical investigation of commuting to work, retail trade centres, centres of health service, etc. Among these, data on commuting to work are most significant and most reliable.

Centres.   The most important towns in the B settlement system are those which are within the reach of everyday traffic circulation. In the GDR their pattern is rather dense. Often it is similar to the spatial pattern of *Kreis* towns (i.e., the politico-administrative centres of *Kreises* or districts). Grimm and Hönsch (1974) classified the towns of the GDR according to their position as social centres for their hinterlands (Table 18.3, Figure 18.1). The spatial pattern of centres shows the comparatively even distribution of centres of everyday social interaction (*Kreis* centres) and the less equal distribution of centres of higher rank. It illustrates the success of the government policy stressing social harmonization in all parts of the country.

The similarity of politico-administrative status and social importance for the hinterland may be exemplified by *Kreis* towns (Grimm, 1974): The 191 *Kreis* towns of the GDR are the political and in most cases the social centres of their *Kreis*es. Most have less than 20,000 inhabitants. In addition to their politico-administrative function nearly all *Kreis* towns perform a group of further functions which are closely linked with their administrative status: *Kreis* office of political parties, of the trade union, of various political, social, and cultural organizations; *Kreis* centres of education with a secondary school and adult college; the editorial office of the special newspaper for the *Kreis*; *Kreis* centre of economy and trade with insurance offices,

Table 18.3: *Types of Towns According to their Importance for their Hinterland* (see *Figure 18.1*)

Type of Town	Description of hinterland
1. Berlin the capital	many highly specialized functions extend over several *Bezirks*
2a. Major centres	many highly specialized functions extend beyond their own *Bezirk*
2b. *Bezirk* centres[1]	many specialized functions extend over their own *Bezirk*
3a. Regional centres	several specialized functions extend beyond the area of a *Kreis*
3b. *Kreis* centres	many functions and relations extend over a *Kreis*
4a. Partial *Kreis* centres	some functions and relations extend over a *Kreis*
4b. Local centres	functions and relations extend to neighbouring communities

[1] There is a strict distinction in terminology between *Bezirk* town (administrative centre) and *Bezirk* centre (administrative and complex social centre). The same applies to the distinction between *Kreis* town and *Kreis* centre.

Source: Grimm and Hönsch, 1974.

offices of banks, and savings banks. As a rule about 50 different functions are located in every *Kreis* town of the GDR. Most everyday political, social, and cultural activities are performed within the framework of a *Kreis*.

Normally a *Kreis* town can be easily reached by all citizens living in that *Kreis*. Every community is connected with the *Kreis* town by public transport, mainly by bus. Eighty-one per cent of all the GDR citizens live in *Kreis* towns (and *Bezirk* towns) or within 40 minutes travelling time from them. Only four per cent live outside the 60 minute boundary. Therefore, the *Kreis* towns of the GDR are the decisive centres of everyday life, with visits to the institutions listed above, the exchange of local news with the aid of the *Kreis* newspaper, the organization of cultural and sports events in the *Kreis* framework, and other activities. In most cases the *Kreis* town is the main centre of commuting because of the diversity of jobs offered, and because of well developed traffic connections between *Kreis* and *Kreis* town. The present administrative division of the GDR has led to a stable, well-balanced integration of settlement systems within the *Kreis* framework. The even distribution of towns promotes the equalization of working and living conditions in accordance with the political and social aims of socialist society.

A few small *Kreis* towns in rural regions cannot meet all the social and economic requirements necessary for a real centre of a *Kreis*. A few *Kreis* towns in agglomerated regions are 'specialists' and perform the function of a 'normal' *Kreis* town only to some extent (e.g., Flöha near Karl-Marx-Stadt, Freital near Dresden). Except for these few cases the *Kreis* towns are the decisive centres for general working and living conditions. However, other towns in the *Kreis*es can be important. In a few cases another town is

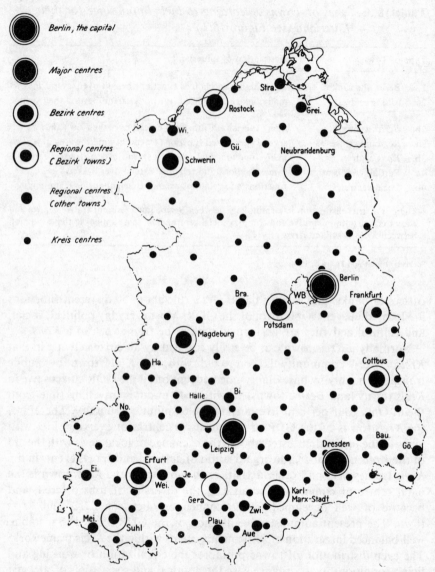

Fig. 18.1 Classification of Urban Settlements in the GDR according to their Importance to their Hinterlands

even bigger and more important than the *Kreis* town, and sometimes efficient co-operation between two towns exists (Wittenberge/Perleberg, Hermsdorf/Stadtroder).

Spatial Relationships. As far as the number of persons is concerned, journeys to work are the most extensive form of interaction in B-settlement systems. Every third worker in the GDR is a commuter (i.e., works outside his commune of residence). The main reason for commuting to work is the access to diversified jobs; an additional cause is housing shortage in towns. Interesting jobs requiring higher qualifications are mainly offered in towns and in large industrial enterprises. On the other hand, living conditions are often more convenient in the countryside. Commuters aim at an optimal combination. They constitute the adaptation between rapid changes in industrial structure and the comparatively stable pattern of places of residence.

The vast majority of commuters make daily journeys to work. The number of weekly commuters is limited. Due to the well-balanced spatial and social structure of the GDR the number of commuters is lower than in many other industrialized countries. The main centres of commuting are the major cities and large industrial plants such as the Leuna and Buna works (near Halle and Merseburg), or the chemical plants at Bitterfeld and Wolfen. Nearly all commuting centres of any importance are situated in the south with the exception of Berlin, Magdeburg, and Rostock.

The extent of the commuting zones depends on the quality and diversity of jobs offered in the centres and on the location of neighbouring towns. The usual travelling time of commuters to small towns does not exceed 20 minutes. Medium-sized towns have developed commuting zones up to 60 minutes travelling time. Commuters to big cities often spend more than one hour commuting. For example, 25.6 per cent of all commuters to Leipzig live at a distance of more than 60 minutes (Halle 24.8 per cent, Karl-Marx-Stadt 23.1 per cent; including weekly commuting). There are differences in the hinterlands of small, medium-sized, and large towns. The commuting zones of large and medium-sized towns are composed of several zones of intensity, and in the outer zones there are additional commuting sub-centres.

Apart from the attractiveness of a town itself, the size and intensity of commuter areas are influenced by the situation of neighbouring centres. Overlapping commuter sheds exist in the industrialized south of the GDR, that is between Leipzig and Halle, and between Erfurt, Weimar, and Jena. Nevertheless, even in the south the major cities and towns show clearly delimited commuting zones. Outside the industrialized regions the zones are larger and there is no overlapping. The differences become clear when comparing the hinterlands of towns of equal numbers of commuters: commuters to Rostock (north) live in 316 communes (communes where at least 5 per cent of all out-commuters work in Rostock), whereas commuters to Zwickau (agglomeration region, south) live in 76 communes; the same applies to Magdeburg (301 communes) in comparison with Halle (83). There are also regional differences in commuting which reflect differences in industrialization. Most communes in the southern districts are characterized by commuting, whereas the share of commuters in rural districts is lower. However, commuting to towns is developing rapidly in previously rural districts, so that these spatial differences are lessening.

Moreover, internal commuting in the large co-operative farms is increasing, but is not recorded by the official statistics.

Most commuting is on a local/micro-regional scale, covering at most several *Kreis*es, and is important for the integration of this level of the settlement system. But long-distance commuting may also be important. It is directed toward the major cities, mainly Berlin and Leipzig, and to new industrial centres during the period of construction, such as Schwedt (chemical plants), and Greifswald (nuclear power station). Although the number of long-distance commuters is smaller than the number of day-trip commuters, the former contributes to the integration of the settlement system on a macro-regional and national scale.

The network of retail trade has developed according to the requirements of the population, so that shopping facilities tend to correspond with the number of inhabitants of the town and its area. Analyses of the turnover of industrial consumer goods have shown the overwhelming importance of the capital, the *Bezirk* towns, and a few regional and tourist centres. Interaction patterns between town and hinterland have some similarities to those of commuting to work. Due to increasing personal wealth and increased mobility (cars, buses) the service areas of large- and medium-sized towns have been enlarged to the disadvantage of small towns. Retail trade fosters the integration of settlement systems on a local scale as well as on the scale of a *Kreis* or even several *Kreis*es. Administrative relations are less important than in other spheres of social infrastructure, but there are trends toward increased administration even in the retail trade.

Under socialism the spatial extent of many social interactions are laid down by the Government. They may be called territorially-fixed relations (Grimm, Krönert, Lüdemann, 1975). Examples of such relations on the national scale are radio, television, and newspapers of national importance, all of which are located in Berlin. Examples on the *Bezirk* scale are health services (*Bezirk* hospital), *Bezirk* newspapers, and many activities in culture and sport. Examples on the *Kreis* scale are discussed above. Territorially-fixed relations are of particular importance in the B settlement system of the GDR, and their share is increasing.

Some forms of interaction in B settlement systems are partly territorially-fixed, partly flexible. In education, for example, the lower levels of the structure are organized in accordance with administrative areas (e.g., creches, nursery schools, pre-school classes), whereas the higher levels are more or less territorially flexible (e.g., job training, Technical Institutes, Engineering Institutes, Technical and Engineering Colleges, Universities).

City-hinterland Regions.   A synthesis of the various relations and interactions in B settlement systems has led to the concept of city-hinterland regions (Krönert, 1977). Krönert defined the city-hinterland region as a spatial unit consisting of a centre (city, town) and its hinterland, integrated by the movement and interaction of people. The city (town) has priority as the political, economic, social, and cultural centre of the region. City-hinterland regions can be interpreted as sub-systems of the B settlement system, as local/micro-regional, and meso-regional settlement systems. The size and structure of city-hinterland regions depend mainly on the functions, size, and attractiveness of the central town. In addition, they are influenced by the general structure of the region, its population density, industry, and secondary centres, and by the distance to towns of equal or higher rank. Specific zones of intensity of city-hinterland interaction can be distinguished, especially in the case of large and medium-sized towns. Krönert (1977) found that every main class of towns (Table 18.3) corresponds to a specific zoning of hinterlands with *Bezirk* centres and regional centres having three hinterland zones, *Kreis* centres and partial *Kreis* centres, two zones, and local centres only one zone.

Berlin, the major centres, and the *Bezirk* centres have developed the largest hinterlands, composed of three zones of contact intensity. Zone 1 is the zone of intensive interaction, of intensive commuting, and of many forms of daily interaction between town and hinterland. The cities provide the basic requirements of the people living in the zone, and they are the primary places of work for commuters. Zone 1 surrounds the central city, with an average radius of 25 kilometres (for Berlin) and 16 kilometres (other centres). It generally involves the area of one Kreis and extends up to neighbouring *Kreis* towns. Although there are still daily journeys to work, most interaction between the central city and zone 2 is periodic. Sub-centres (mainly small towns) are found in zone 2, and are the centres of daily interaction for the people living there. In most cases zone 2 is not ring-shaped, as is the case with zone 1, but is shaped by communes arranged around sub-centres (local centres).

Zone 3 has only special forms of interaction with the city, such as the commuting of specialist workers, low frequency shopping, advanced education, or theatre. Zone 3 extends outside the *Kreis* of its central city, into areas where the neighbouring *Kreis* towns have developed their own zones 1 and 2. Zone 3 is mainly connected with the central city by relations between the larger city and the adjacent *Kreis* towns.

The hinterlands of regional centres and *Kreis* centres are composed of two zones, each smaller than those of the large cities. The average radius of zone 1 amounts to 11 kilometres around the regional centres, and 9 kilometres in the case of large *Kreis* centres (towns of more than 40,000 inhabitants). The average radius of zone 2 is 14.5 kilometres (regional centres) and 12.5 kilometres (*Kreis* centres). The limits of zone 2 often coincide with the administrative boundary of a *Kreis*. Regional centres develop functions and forms of interaction with one or two neighbouring *Kreis* towns. These relations may be considered as a first stage of a third zone.

Local centres (small towns) have only one small hinterland zone. Interaction is limited to serving the elementary needs of the people, such as shopping (durable goods), general polytechnical school, or cinema. Small towns are centres of short-distance commuting and are often the seats of management of large co-operative farms and of associations of communes (*Gemeindeverband*). At the same time local centres are sub-centres in the hinterland of centres of a higher rank (zone 2) and promote contacts between the central town and the individual communes of zone 2.

In summary, empirical evidence as well as general experience show that the national B settlement system is a complex of local/micro-regional systems, generally providing the social requirements of people. Therefore the network of *Kreis* centres is most important for the social harmonization of the GDR society. The integration of the B settlement system on the national scale is mainly put into practice by information flows, with other relations such as tourist trips, distant commuting to work, and so forth. The hierarchical structure of the B settlement system of the GDR is strongly influenced by the politico-administrative spatial organization of the country.

The E Settlement System

The E settlement system is based upon the processes of production and services. It is the function of that system to guarantee a high national product including services. Elements of the system are the places of production and infrastructure (communities of working people, plants, offices, etc.) and the places of residence of manpower. Relations within the E settlement system are those which realize the economic functions of the system. They are translated into reality by flows of commodities, persons, and information. Therefore E settlement systems are not characterized by dominance, although there is a certain dominance on the national scale (Grimm 1980, p. 12).

Compared with the B settlement system, knowledge of the E system is limited. Often economic functions and relations are not included in research work on settlement systems. Towns and their attributes as places of production and services are represented in many maps of the *Atlas der DDR* and in the two volumes of *Ökonomische Geographie der DDR* (Kohl, Jacob, *et al.* 1974, 1976). Knowledge of interaction is mainly based on analyses of railway goods traffic (Wehner, 1976), business trips, telephone calls (Schnack and Thomas, 1980), and others. Among these the data on goods traffic are most informative.

Local E-systems in Rural Regions. Many local/micro-regional E settlement systems in rural districts are determined by the spatial organization of agriculture. In the GDR crop cultivation is done by large co-operative farms (*LPG Pflanzenproduktion*), each covering many settlements (10-20 communes) and 4,000-5,000 hectares of arable land. Two or three co-operative animal husbandry farms (*LPG Tierproduktion*) work with the crop farm on the same territory. As a result of the industrialization and concentration of agricultural production, most work is performed in a few settlements, (e.g., offices of the co-operative farms, large livestock units, barns and store-houses, machinery depots, vocational schools).

The present settlement pattern of the GDR is a result of historical devel-opment based upon agricultural production. Today it is being transformed to meet the demands of socialist, industrialized, and large-scale agriculture. Many villages and hamlets are now merely places of residence. Much inter-action in rural settlement systems is a result of the gap between the disper-sion of rural settlement and the concentration of agricultural production. In a very short time, commuting to work has taken a dominant role in GDR agriculture. Some case studies have shown that 30-40 per cent of all persons employed in agriculture are commuters, working outside their residential settlement. The predominant distance for agricultural commuting amounts to 2.5-4.0 kilometres, but 10 per cent of agricultural commuting reaches 10 kilometres or more. Besides commuting, the operation of agricultural technology, as well as the management of the large farms, support the inte-gration of local E settlement systems over the territory of a co-operative farm, while social and cultural facilities develop in the central town or village of the local system.

Often the integration of a local E settlement system on the scale of a co-operative farm is supplemented by the formation of an Association of Communes (*Gemeindeverband*) within the same territory. These associ-ations cover the majority of all rural districts in the GDR. Each association comprises about one third of the rural parts of a *Kreis*. Most are units of less than 5,000 inhabitants (40 per cent of all associations) or of 5,000-10,000 inhabitants. Associations of Communes are concerned prin-cipally with the realization of social goals and must be considered B systems, but these are interwoven with local E systems in cases where the co-operative farms and Associations of Communes are spatially identical.

Local E-systems in Industrialized Regions. Because of the diversity of industrial production, E settlement systems in industrialized districts are less homogeneous than the rural systems, and there is little coincidence between B and E systems. Some aspects of coincidence may be shown using the example of a comparatively isolated *Kreis*. Sonneberg (29,000 inhabi-tants) is situated near the southern frontier of the GDR. Its hinterland is identical with its *Kreis* and comprises the Southern Thuringian Forest and adjacent lowlands. The *Kreis* of Sonneberg (65,000 inhabitants) covers 300 square kilometres and is delimited by the State frontier and by mountains. The Sonneberg region is connected with other parts of the GDR only by two railways and two roads. Analyses of telephone calls, commuting to work, and other spatial interaction have indicated that the district is comparatively self-contained. Because of the predominance of light industry, the volume of inter-regional goods transport is moderate.

For centuries the Sonneberg district has specialized in the production of toys, and this has affected the development of the settlement system. In former times the toy industry was dispersed, with main production done by outworkers in the town as well as in many villages of its hinterland. The interaction between Sonneberg and its hinterland was that of production, the delivery and supply of raw materials, and final products. Every home was a place of production. During the last two decades, the toy industry has changed from a dispersed outwork form to one of concentrated production in plants. These plants are located in Sonneberg and a few additional communes. As a result, the interaction pattern of delivery and supply has been replaced by commuting to work from the dispersed settlement network to fewer places of production.

The places of production interact with each other and form the production backbone of an E settlement system. Sonneberg, as the centre of the region, contains the majority of industrial production. It is also the seat of the management of the toy industry (for the region as well as of the whole toy industry of the GDR), of wholesale trade, of job training for the toy industry, and of a museum of toys. Other industrial branches have located their plants in Sonneberg, some initiated by the toy industry; including the production of electric household-appliances (related to the production of model railways), radios, ceramics, ready-made clothes, and others. Some branches have changed from a pattern of spatial dispersion to one of concentration (e.g., china), others were concentrated in Sonneberg from their early beginning (e.g., radios). Large nationally-owned enterprises develop services for their staff such as cultural centres, medical care, retail shops, and others, and therefore are involved in social systems, too. At present Sonneberg has less than a half of the inhabitants but two thirds of the employed persons of the region.

The concentration of industry in the *Kreis* towns has brought about an integration of an E settlement system in the *Kreis*. In the case of Sonneberg this coincides with the B settlement system of the *Kreis*, which has developed in a similar way to the B systems of many other *Kreis*es. This coincidence is exceptional, however, and caused by the isolation of the region. The majority of the industrialized *Kreis*es of the GDR are incorporated into larger regions. Their E settlement systems, if they exist, are less self-contained. The spatial coincidence of B systems and E systems in average industrialized *Kreis*es, should it be present, is limited to labour markets.

E-systems in Agglomerated Regions. The nature of E settlement systems in agglomerated regions may be discussed using the example of Leipzig-Halle, a region of heavy industry. Leipzig (570,000 inhabitants) and Halle (306,000 inhabitants, including Halle-Neustadt) are the centres of a region of 2.0 million people which is the very heartland of the southern GDR. Both cities rank high in economic management trade (e.g., Leipzig Fair) and research, as well as in leading branches of industry. The situation of Leipzig and Halle at one of the most important junctions of the traffic network of central Europe has resulted in the development of many characteristic urban branches of industry such as mechanical engineering, chemicals, and printing. The concentration of people in Leipzig, Halle and several towns of 50,000 inhabitants has also led to a high degree of mobility and the availability of qualified labour, and the region is thus able to meet the changing requirements of industry.

Special features have resulted from the main production functions of the region, the chemical industry (Leuna and Buna works, and others) and energy industry (lignite opencast mining, power stations). Because of the large area required, and of environmental problems, the large plants in the chemical industry are situated as far as possible from Leipzig and Halle, as is energy production. Therefore both cities are places of work for their inhabitants and in-commuters as well as places of residence for out-commuters to the chemical and energy industries. These large works have developed extensive social facilities and are important social centres in the Leipzig-Halle agglomerated region.

The intense interaction of goods, persons, and information is closely interwoven and forms the unique E settlement system of the agglomerated region of Halle and Leipzig. Nevertheless there is no equivalent B settlement system because Leipzig and Halle have developed different, though partly overlapping, B systems. In the last few decades, population and economic activity has concentrated in Leipzig, Halle and a few other places. The number of inhabitants in settlements outside cities, towns and urbanized belts has been decreasing partly because of the abandonment of settlements in areas of opencast mining. The unattractive landscape of the surrounding lowland is an additional reason for the concentration and lack of urban sprawl.

The GDR as a National E-system. Data on goods traffic and telephone calls are good indices of the structure of the national E settlement system. Data on goods traffic show the material co-operation of production whereas data on telephone calls emphasize the interconnections of information and management. In general the E settlement system of the GDR turns out to be a well integrated whole. Its core regions are the southern district (Saxony, Thuringia) and Berlin, the capital.

The pattern of mass goods traffic is dominated by coal transport, originating in the regions of extraction (Cottbus, Halle, Leipzig) and covering all the territory of the GDR. The pattern of other kinds of goods traffic is heterogenous and it is difficult to determine the limits of sub-systems. The existence of E-settlement sub-systems are suggested by the analyses of railway traffic in machinery and equipment: Leipzig-Halle-Bitterfeld, Magdeburg and neighbouring towns; Dresden-Karl-Marx-Stadt-Zwickau, Cottbus and neighbouring towns; Berlin and neighbouring towns; Erfurt and neighbouring towns. Telephone calls, on the other hand, emphasize integration on the national scale and the dominance of Berlin,

Leipzig-Halle, and Dresden. They also reflect the importance of the politico-administrative organization of the country even in the economic field.

The GDR may be considered a unique E settlement system on the macro-regional scale. Yet there is a second macro-regional E settlement system, that of the industrialized zone of the south, enclosing the *Bezirks* of Karl-Marx-Stadt, Dresden, Leipzig, Halle, Erfurt, Gera, Suhl, and parts of Magdeburg and Cottbus. The macro-regional E settlement system of the south is in close contact with Berlin, the capital.

In summary, the E settlement system of the GDR is first of all integrated on the national scale. Some spatial sub-systems are discernible: on the macro-regional scale the industrialized zone of the south; on the meso-regional scale some E systems like the agglomerated region of Leipzig, Halle, and Bitterfeld; on the local/micro-regional scale the E systems of large co-operative farms and other units. The hierarchical structure of the E settlement system is less strict than that of the B system, but some similarities are evident.

The Urban System of the Economic Superstructure

The urban system of the national economic superstructure exerts a unique function: the management of political, economic, and social affairs. Elements of this system are the towns/urban agglomerations where the offices of superstructure are located. Interrelations in the system are the spatial interactions between the towns/urban agglomerations, or more specifically between the people working there in the fields of superstructure. The main centres are the large urban agglomerations.

Politico-administrative Organization

Politico-administrative centres and the administrative division of the territory are important in socialist countries like the GDR for administration and politics as well as for the economy. The administrative structure of the GDR consists of three hierarchical levels: Berlin, the capital; 15 *Bezirks* and their *Bezirk* towns; and 191 *Kreis*es and the *Kreis* towns (Figure 18.2).

Berlin, the capital, is the leading political, social, and economic centre of the GDR, the seat of the parliament (People's Chamber, *Volkskammer*), of the central institutions of the government (Council of ministers, ministries), and of the central bodies of the Socialist Unity Party of Germany (SED). The leading position of Berlin as a social centre is indicated by the fact that all broadcasting and television stations are located there, by the publishing of newspapers (all newspaper publishing houses of national importance are in Berlin), by its central position in science (seat of the Academy of Sciences of the GDR), and in art (leading theatre of the GDR). Berlin has the national airport of the GDR (Berlin-Schönefeld). Because of the relatively small size of the GDR, Berlin is also in constant contact with all towns and

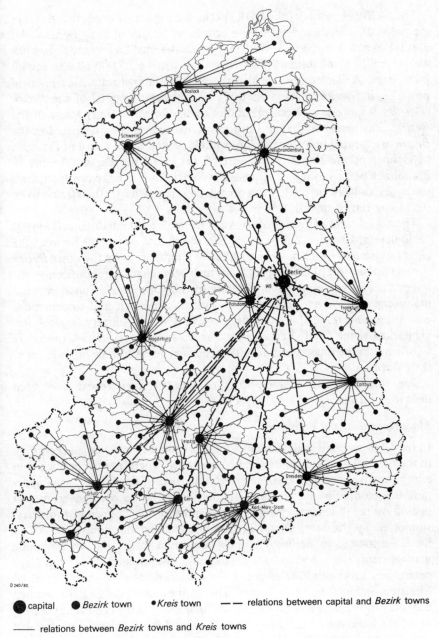

capital ● *Bezirk* town ● *Kreis* town ── ── relations between capital and *Bezirk* towns

── relations between *Bezirk* towns and *Kreis* towns

Fig. 18.2 The Politico-Administrative Structure of the Urban System of the GDR

villages of the country, especially with the *Bezirk* towns, by direct express trains. Every morning newspapers published in Berlin are available even in the remotest parts of the country.

The 14 *Bezirk* towns of the GDR (Berlin is a separate *Bezirk*, the 15th) are the political, social, and partly the economic centres of their *Bezirks*. An average *Bezirk* town has 100,000-200,000 inhabitants, an average *Bezirk* has 0.8-1.5 million inhabitants and covers an area of 5,000-10,000 square kilometers. A *Bezirk* town is also the seat of the institutions of political power in its *Bezirk*; *Bezirk* assembly (*Bezirkstag*); Council of the *Bezirk* (*Rat des Bezirkes*); and central bodies of the Socialist Unity Party of the *Bezirk*. Furthermore, many institutions of central significance for the *Bezirk* are located in its towns: for example, the editorial board of the main newspaper of the *Bezirk*; the Court of Justice of the *Bezirk*; the *Bezirk* Planning Commission; and others. The *Bezirk* town is linked with all *Kreis* towns by railway or bus. They permit day-trip visits to the *Bezirk* town (including return travel).

The actual sizes of *Bezirk* towns vary from 570,000 inhabitants (Leipzig) to 40,000 inhabitants (Suhl). There is a significant difference between the eight largest cities with more than 200,000 inhabitants and the other *Bezirk* towns with up to 110,000. Apart from their administrative significance, the importance of the large cities is determined by specialized functions on a macro-regional or national scale in industry, research and information, education, and trade, for example, Leipzig (German Library, agricultural exhibition of the GDR, Leipzig Fair), or Rostock (port). *Bezirk* towns are significant in the integration of settlement systems within the boundaries of their *Bezirks*.

The functions and characteristics of the 191 *Kreis* towns have been described earlier.

Management of the Economy

In the GDR as in all socialist countries, the economy is managed according to the principles of a socialist planned economy. Therefore the political and administrative centres and the territorial division of the country are important for economic management. In the GDR the decisive governmental institution for the management of the economy is the Council of Ministers, supported by the State Planning Commission and the ministries. All of them are located in Berlin. The most important institutions of economic management, the associations of nationally owned enterprises, and large enterprises in key industries are directly subordinated to the Council of Ministers and its supporting bodies. The institutions of the socialist planned economy in the *Bezirks* and *Kreises* are analogous to the central apparatus, and they have their seats in *Bezirk* towns and *Kreis* towns. The socialist planned economy is linked by specialization and co-operation within the frontiers of the administrative units (national territory, *Bezirk*, *Kreis*). Therefore a considerable amount of functional interaction, such as co-operation in industry and construction engineering, information flows, business trips, telephone calls, takes place within a *Bezirk* (and within a *Kreis*). They have an integrating effect upon E settlement systems.

On the other hand, the management of the economy depends on its own specific principles. It is allied to the spatial distribution of production, which in many cases is not in spatial conformity with the administrative divisions of the country. The main centres of industry in the GDR are the agglomerated regions of Berlin, Leipzig-Halle, Dresden, and Karl-Marx-Stadt-Zwickau. They are the main centres of the economic superstructure as well.

The management of industrial branches and of large industrial enterprises (groups of plants) is performed by the Associations of Nationally-Owned Enterprises (*Vereinigung Volkseigener Betriebe*, or VVB) and by industrial combines (*Industriekombinate*). Most of these are in Berlin, Leipzig, and Karl-Marx-Stadt (Table 18.4). The VVB associations are spatially more concentrated than the combines: 57 VVB associations are located in 19 cities, 128 combines are located in 67 cities and towns (1978). Their locations do not correspond with the administrative status of the towns, and 3 *Bezirk* towns have neither a VVB nor a combine.

The combination of political-administrative structure, on the one hand, and the location of the VVB associations and industrial combines on the other, yields a general model of the national urban system of the economic superstructure with two groups of centres:

(*a*) Berlin, Leipzig, Karl-Marx-Stadt, Dresden, Halle and Magdeburg as the most important centres of economic superstructure of industrial branches (an extended variant includes about 70 towns);

(*b*) Berlin, the capital, and 14 *Bezirk* towns (an extreme variant would include all *Kreis* towns).

Table 18.4: *Spatial Distribution of the Leading Institutions of VVB Associations and Industrial Combines (1978) (Percentage of National Total)*

	VVB (%)	VVB and combines (%)
Berlin	23.0	14.0
Leipzig	16.0	11.0
Karl-Marx-Stadt	11.0	8.6
Dresden	7.0	6.5
Halle	8.8	4.3
5 cities total	66.0	45.0
other towns in agglom. regions	12.0	13.0
agglom. regions total	78.0	58.0

Note: VVB (*see* text)

The economic superstructure is closely linked with production. Therefore, this urban system is accompanied by many other economic relations between the cities and the urban system described above and is partly representative of the co-operation of economic regions (i.e., for the basic structure of the spatial system of economy of the GDR). A summary of the spatial organization of the urban system of the GDR is best shown by a map of telephone calls (Figure 18.3), the general structure of the impacts behind these interactions is shown in Figure 18.4.

The Combined Settlement System

B settlement systems, E settlement systems, and the urban system of the economic superstructure are linked together in many ways to form a unique socio-economic spatial system of human settlement in the GDR: the combined national settlement system. Its base and general background is the political, economic, social, and cultural unity of the GDR. Supported by a well-developed system of communications, and by a high degree of mobility, the national settlement system acts to unite the densely populated industrialized regions of the South, the less populated central and northern districts, and Berlin, the capital.

The B systems and E systems are interlocked at various levels of the national settlement system. Both systems converge in their basic elements, places of residence and places of economic activity. In urban agglomerations such as Magdeburg, Rostock, and Schwerin, B systems may be spatially similar to E systems. The same may apply in rural districts where a small town plays a central role in a B system (Association of Communes) and an E system (co-operative farms). In exceptional cases this even applies to industrialized regions (e.g., Sonneberg).

The urban system develops similar spatial patterns to B and E systems in terms of the political and administrative organization of the country and related spatial structures, including the territorially-fixed relations (B settlement systems), and the governmental part in the management of the socialist planned economy (E system). On the other hand, there are fundamental differences between B systems and E systems. Although the main basic units of both systems are identical, some other units are not, such as the units of elementary supply, of services, and others. They are only components of B systems.

A general outline of the settlement system of the GDR can only be descriptive, and at this time the application of a systems approach will mainly be limited to B systems, E systems, and to the national urban systems. At the top of the system is Berlin, supported by 14 *Bezirk* towns which are equally distributed over the territory of the GDR, and supplemented by some 'specialists' centres such as Weimar (culture) and Greifswald (university). Of the first order, beside Berlin, are Dresden (culture, science), and Leipzig (science, sport, culture), and most important

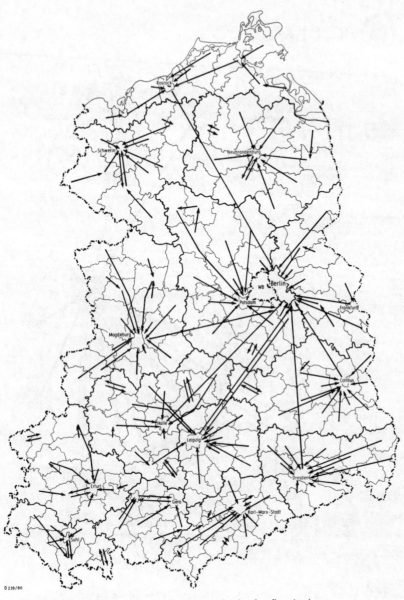

D 239/80

◄——— dominating telephone flow (the most extensive leaving flow is shown
for each town/region under consideration)

Fig. 18.3 Telephone Calls as an Indicator of Relations in the Urban System of the GDR
Source: Schnack and Thomas

among the other *Bezirk* towns are the *Bezirk* centres (Grimm and Hönsch,
1974). Berlin and the *Bezirk* towns co-operate with the *Kreis* towns (Grimm,
1974, guaranteeing an equal basic level of working and living conditions in
all parts of the GDR.

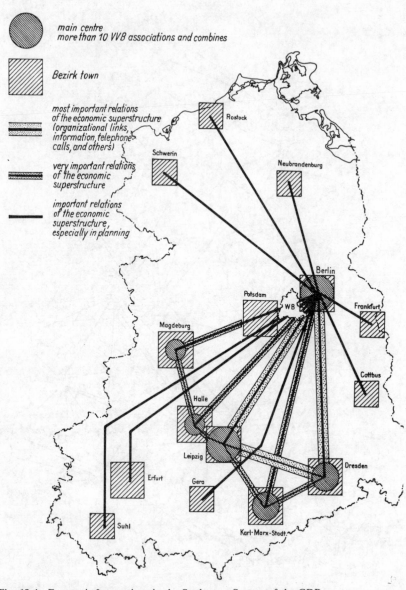

Fig. 18.4 Economic Interactions in the Settlement System of the GDR

In the sphere of economic goals, the main partners of Berlin are the large cities of the southern agglomerations, primarily Leipzig and Karl-Marx-Stadt. On the whole the spatial pattern of E systems reflects the spatial differences of the productive forces. At the same time, the *Bezirk* towns co-operate with the capital as partners in the economic use and development of all parts of the national territory. The general structure of the national settlement system reveals the dichotomy and unity of the socio-economic aims of socialist society and the GDR as a whole.

Future Development

The settlement system of the GDR has developed into a stabilized spatial unit with a high degree of industrialization and urbanization. The size of the national population has been constant, and because of the age structure, it will be constant or decrease in the years to come. Therefore the settlement system will preserve and stabilize its essential identity, at least until the beginning of the twenty-first century, although there will be some internal changes.

The future development of the settlement system will be influenced mainly by two factors: development of productive forces, and development of the requirements and habits of the people.

1. Owing to the high degree of industrialization already achieved, and to the constant total population size, programmes for the further development of productive forces will concentrate upon the perfection of the current structure (Programme of the SED). This will also result in a stabilization of the settlement system as a whole.

2. At present the housing programme (1976-90) is the central feature of the socio-political programme (the SED). Because most new apartments will be constructed in large and medium-sized towns, it will result in an increasing urban population. Besides the housing programme, there will be other changes in the social sphere, produced by growing national wealth, an increasing amount of free time, and increasing dependence on motor transport.

Considering these goals and trends, the following changes in the settlement system will be most important:

1. The growing unity and integration of the national settlement system of the GDR is part of the increasing specialization and co-operation of production and services on a national scale. Specialization in formerly backward regions, their increasing co-operation with traditional industrialized districts, and the increasing volume and scope of GDR transport are indications of this integration as is the nationwide scope of recreation. National integration is promoted by the strong position of Berlin, by the approved administrative organization of the territory, and by the railway and *autobahn* network with Berlin and Leipzig-Halle as its centres of gravity. Some aspects of integration, on the other hand, will become less important, such as migration on a national scale.

2. The increasing importance of urban agglomerations will be strengthened by the housing programme: the concentration of most housing construction in less than 100 towns will bring about increased rural-urban migration and the further growth of large and medium-sized towns.

3. There will be an increasing integration of single *Kreises*, neighbouring *Kreises*, and single *Bezirks*. The increasing unity of *Bezirks* will continue in the next few decades, with a growing integration in the *Bezirks* which have been less integrated up to now. The integration of *Kreises* will also continue, but owing to the concentration of industrial investments and housing construction in a few towns, and to increasing mobility, not all *Kreis* towns will grow in importance. The settlement systems of the larger *Kreis* centres will grow, and several small *Kreis* towns and their *Kreises* will become integrated parts of these systems. Krönert (1977) proposed the development of a basic network of about 130 towns based upon service demands, and of about 150 towns based upon production and service requirements. These proposals are close to the concepts of the State Planning Commission (Kluge, 1974).

4. The concentration of industry in towns and the industrialization of agriculture will result in a transformation of rural settlements and settlement systems. The number of inhabitants of most villages will decrease due to rural-urban migration. Most villages have already become the places of residence for out-commuters, whereas the share of those with agricultural occupations has decreased. The development of a village depends primarily upon the accessibility of neighbouring towns or other places of work. Remote and small hamlets will be abandoned. The small towns will be the economic and social centres of local settlement systems with an increasing share of the inhabitants of the system within the town itself. This trend will be promoted by the organization of Associations of Communes.

The planning of settlements and settlement systems in the GDR is integrated into the socialist management of production and infrastructure. The spatial development of the society is influenced by means of investments in industry and infrastructure. On the national scale, this is regulated by the programme for the development of productive forces (e.g., energy programme, traffic programme) and of the required facilities (e.g., housing programme), as well as by government recommendations for the unification of the settlement programme, of *Bezirks* and *Kreises*. Settlement planning in a *Bezirk* is carried out by extensive proposals elaborated by the Offices for Regional Planning (*Büros für Territorialplanung*). These programmes are the very backbone of the settlement planning strategy in the GDR. The programmes for the development of the *Kreises* are incorporated into the *Bezirk* plans.

These changes will last at least up to 1990. Following the realization of the GDR housing programme, one of the main motives for present migration—the housing shortage—will become unimportant. Other motives such as quality of work and environmental conditions will become more important.

ACKNOWLEDGEMENTS

The author gratefully acknowledges the comments and help of Professor Dr. D. Scholz, Martin Luther University Halle; Drs. Krönert, H. Neumann, and R. Schmidt; and G. Taege, R. Thomas and B. Weyrich, Collaborators at the Institute for Geography and Geo-ecology of the Academy of Sciences of the GDR (Leipzig).

REFERENCES

Böhnish, R., Mohs, G. and Ostwald, W., 1976. *Territorialplanung*, Berlin.

Grimm, F., 1974. 'Die Kreisstädte der DDR und ihre Rolle im Siedlungssystem', *Geogr. Berichte* 19, 4: 229-47.

Grimm, F. and Hönsch, I., 1974. 'Zur Typisierung der Zentren in der DDR nach ihrer Umlandbedeutung', *Peterm. Geogr. Mitt.* 118, 4: 282-8.

Grimm, F., Krönert, R. and Lüdemann, H., 1975. 'Aspects of urbanization in the German Democratic Republic', in: *National Settlement Strategies East and West*, IIASA Conference Proceedings Laxenburg (Austria).

Grimm, F., Lüdemann, H. and Weinhold, P., 1975. 'Selected Bibliography on Problems of Urbanization and the Development of Settlement Systems in the GDR (1970-1974)', in: *National Settlement Strategies East and West*, IIASA Conference Proceedings, Laxenburg (Austria): 193-219.

Grimm, F., 1980. 'The nature of national settlement systems', Report to the IGU Commission on National Settlement Systems, Leipzig.

Jahn, H. and Taege, G., forthcoming 'Nutzung der Reisendenstromerhebung zum Eisenbahnfernverkehr innerhalb der DDR für Untersuchungen zu gebietlichen Wechselbeziehungen', *Wissensch. Mitteil. d. Inst. f. Geogr. u. Geoökologie*, Leipzig.

Kluge, K., 1974. 'Die Bedeutung der Siedlungskategorien für die Planung der Siedlungsstruktur' *Peterm. Geogr. Mitteil.*, 118, 4: 255-60.

Kohl, H., Jacob, G., et al., (eds.), 1974, 1976. *Okonomische Geographie der DDR*, 2 vol. Gotha/Leipzig.

Krönert, R., 1977. 'Stadt-Umland-Regionen von Groß-und Mittelstädten der DDR', *Geogr. Berichte* 22, 2: 255-60.

Lindner, W., 1979. *Komplexe Verkehrsentwicklung im Territorium*. Berlin.

Lüdemann, H., Grimm, F., Krönert, R. and Neumann, H. (eds.) 1979. *Stadt und Umland in der DDR*. Gotha/Leipzig.

Schnack, H. and Thomas, R., forthcoming 'Fernsprechströme zwischen Städten, Gebieten und ihre Aussagemöglichkeit für räumliche Wechselbeziehungen' *Wissensch. Mitteil. d. Inst. f. Geogr. u. Geoökologie*, Leipzig.

Strenz, W., 1976. 'Entwicklungstendenzen in der regionalen Verteilung der Bevölkerung im Prozeß der industriellen Revolution des Kapitalismus auf dem heutigen Territorium der DDR', *Jahrbuch f. Wirtschafts-geschichte* a/I: 161-83.

Wehner, W., 1976. 'Zustandsformen territorialer Produktionsverflechtungen in der DDR' *Wissenschaftl. Abhandl. d. Geograph. Gesellschaft der DDR*,, 13: 137-47.

Atlas der Deutschen Demokratischen Republik. 1976, 1981, 2 volumes Gotha/Leipzig.

Programm der Sozialistischen Einheitspartei Deutschlands, (Programme of the SED) 1976. Berlin.

19 THE YUGOSLAV NATIONAL SETTLEMENT SYSTEM

IGOR VRIŠER

Yugoslavia came into existence in the year 1918 with the union of the Kingdom of Serbia, the principality of Crna Gora (Montenegro), and the Yugoslav provinces of the Austro-Hungarian monarchy. The union has joined several nations and ethnic minority groups with very different ethnic, linguistic, and cultural characteristics. With the introduction of the socialist system after the Second World War, the people and regions of Yugoslavia underwent an intensive socio-economic transformation. The social transformation was reflected also in the transformation of the settlement system.

Historical Development of the Settlement System

A system of settlements originated in the Ancient period, when the settlements of the Illyrians, Celts, and Greeks came into existence. It was, however, in the Roman period that a more permanent network was formed. The Romans also founded numerous military camps, many of which later became towns. The system of settlements in the Roman period was thus composed of three elements: the Old Celtic-Illyrian villages; colonization settlements; and urban places (*Zgodovina naradov Jugoslavije*, 1953). The settlement system underwent considerable changes following the disintegration of the Roman empire and settlement by the Slavs in the early Middle Ages. The old system was best preserved in the East within the Byzantine vassal states: Macedonia, southern Serbia, and Kosovo. In contrast to the western part of Yugoslavia that was heavily latinised during the Roman period, this eastern part retained the characteristics of the Greek and later Byzantine culture. In the western part that was gradually included into the medieval Holy Roman Empire or into the Hungarian-Croat kingdom, western cultural influences slowly became predominant.

A special system of settlements began to form in a large part of the present Yugoslav territory of Serbia, Macedonia, Bosnia and Hercegovina, Montenegro) following the Turkish invasions and the destruction of the Slav states during the fourteenth and fifteenth centuries. Settlements in these regions still contained some elements of the old Roman and Byzantine order but were at the same time incorporated in the Islamic culture and in the Turkish feudal order. The far-reaching consequences of the Turkish period have not yet been entirely eradicated.

The system of settlements during the era of Turkish feudalism was of several kinds. Predominant in the agricultural countryside was the *timar* ownership system with its differentiation into farms belonging to the Christian *raja* (*Baština*), or to muslims (*čiftluk*), and the landholdings belonging to the ruler (*has*), or to the muslim ecclesiastical domain (*vakuf*). Rural settlements were villages and hamlets (of the old *Vlah* type), larger loose villages (of the *Šumadija* type), and the manors belonging to a *spahi* or a *beg* (*Zgodovina naradov Jugoslavije*, 1959). Urban settlements, which were later reinvigorated during the sixteenth and seventeenth centuries by the revival of trade, consisted of market-towns (*varošica, kasaba*) and towns (*varoš, grad*). During the second half of the eighteenth century and in the nineteenth century the Turkish feudal state retreated, due to worsening economic and social conditions, the Turkish-Austrian wars, and the liberation struggle of the Balkan peoples.

Social and economic conditions in the western half of Yugoslavia, which had become the 'military march' of Christian Europe, deteriorated as Turkish power declined. The Dalmatian towns, which had already come under Venetian rule, lost their hinterlands in the Balkans. The Croat and Slovene towns, performing the function of middlemen in the area between the Alpine and Pannonian lands, Northern Italy and the Adriatic, were in a state of decay. Many had become fortresses or were founded with such a purpose. Only toward the end of the seventeenth and in the eighteenth century did economic revival take place as the Habsburg monarchy gained strength. Slavonia and Vojvodina were again acquired, and the Turkish domain was pushed back to the Sava-Danube line. Serbian refugees and colonists from Habsburg lands were systematically settled in the newly acquired territories. The large villages of Vojvodina came into existence during that time. The rural settlements in the entire area dominated by the Habsburg monarchy began to undergo change during the second half of the nineteenth century because of the abandonment of feudal duties and the development of transportation, handicrafts, and early manufacturing industries.

These changes first became apparent in the northwestern regions (Slovenia, Istria, western Croatia), but spread in the second half of the nineteenth century and in the early twentieth century to Dalmatia, Slavonia, and Vojvodina (Mirkovic, 1958). Gradually the change affected also Bosnia and Hercegovina, occupied by the Austro-Hungarian empire in the year 1878, and Serbia, liberated from Turkish rule after several uprisings and wars (1878, 1913). The socio-economic transformation in rural areas provoked a strong emigration. The agricultural population moved to towns or to America. The towns grew because of modest industrialization, the development of commercial and administrative functions, and improvement in communications. However, they still remained relatively small and few had more than ten thousand inhabitants. Only the largest urban settlements had between thirty and one hundred thousand inhabitants (Sarajevo, Ljubljana, Subotica, Zagreb).

Considerable change occurred in the system of settlements in the newly established Serbian state. The traditional migratory flows from the mountainous interior to the fertile lowlands were enhanced with the departure of the Turkish feudal lords. The Serbian government fostered internal colonization in rural areas and the development of towns. Even some new towns were planned and built.

In the year 1918 Yugoslavia was among the least developed and least urbanized countries in Europe. Conditions did not improve in the period between the world wars. The system of settlements persisted in its traditional structure. Urbanization progressed slowly. At the time of the first Census of population (in 1921) the degree of urbanization was only 13.16 per cent. It was no more than 15.1 per cent in the year 1931. At the same time there was a general stagnation in rural areas because of economic crisis, agricultural overpopulation, emigration, social differentiation, and marked underdevelopment.

The Political-Administrative Status of Settlements

In 1945 Yugoslavia was transformed into a federated republic. Ethnic composition, historical tradition, and community feelings were considered in the reorganization. The social system was also changed with the introduction of socialism. Extensive decentralization was carried out in the political-administrative structure and self-management was introduced. Citizens acquired great independence in the management of their affairs in particular within the local communities and communes. At the same time a conscious and planned development of the country was initiated. The economic development policy was based on intensive industrialization.

The results of these social, political, and economic changes began to be reflected, at first slowly but later more fundamentally, in the social and economic structure of all Yugoslav regions. They have triggered some far-reaching socio-economic processes: reduction in agricultural employment, urbanization, destratification of the peasant class, and the formation of new social strata (working class, urban dwellers).

The political-administrative structure was changed several times in the post-war period. The commune (*Opština*) has become the basic unit. It was meant to be a well-defined socio-economic unit (functional region). Large cities were also divided into communes although associated in 'urban communities'. Because of the large size of the communes (about 40,000 people and 500 km^2 on the average), and in order to achieve more self-management, the communes were subdivided into local communities (*mjesna zajednica*). There were, in the year 1978, 518 communes and 11,752 local communities in Yugoslavia. Apart from these political-territorial units, a smaller territorial unit, the settlement, is still used for statistical purposes. There are altogether 27,568 settlements. The terms 'town' and 'district', still used in legal documents during the first post-World War II decade, became superfluous.

The former categorization of settlements was abandoned in the new administrative system, but since the need for a classification remained, the Federal Statistical Office introduced a new typological classification of settlements. It ran into great difficulties in application because of the marked regional differences in the size and character of settlements. Small settlements are predominant in the northwestern part of Yugoslavia, in Bosnia and Hercegovina, and in Montenegro. Towns there are also smaller. The settlements in Slavonia, Vojvodina, Serbia, Kosovo, and Macedonia are mainly large and compact. Towns are much larger but contain large agricultural populations, raising doubts about their urban character.

Two criteria were therefore used by the Federal Statistical Office in the classification of settlements: the number of inhabitants; and the percentage of non-agricultural population (Table 19.1, Figure 19.1).

Three categories of settlements were discerned: urban, mixed, and rural (Macura, 1954). These criteria are not the most appropriate and were frequently criticized, but they are still used for lack of a better alternative.

Using these methods of classification, it was possible to define in 1971 495 urban settlements (1.8 per cent), 2,961 mixed settlements (10.7 per cent), and 24,568 rural settlements (87.5 per cent) out of the total of 27,568 settlements. In that year 7,915,000 people were living in urban settlements (38.6 per cent), 2,928,000 people in mixed settlements (14.3 per cent), and 9,679,000 people in rural settlements (48.1 per cent) (Table 19.2).

Table 19.1: *The Size and Structure of Yugoslav Settlements in 1971*

Federal units	Percentage of settlements in size classes						average size of settlement
	Number of inhabitants						
	below 300	300- 599	600- 1199	1200- 4999	5000- 14999	over 15000	
Yugoslavia	52.7	21.8	15.8	8.4	0.9	0.4	744
Bosnia/Hercegovina	49.1	24.3	17.3	8.5	0.6	0.2	633
Montenegro	69.5	18.2	9.1	2.4	0.6	0.2	420
Croatia	56.5	23.1	13.3	6.2	0.6	0.2	663
Macedonia	44.4	25.7	19.3	9.2	0.6	0.8	971
Slovenia	82.5	11.7	3.7	1.7	0.3	0.1	287
Serbia	21.5	27.8	29.2	18.4	2.3	0.8	1390
Serbia proper	21.4	28.7	31.2	16.6	1.5	0.6	1253
Vojvodina	4.0	7.7	15.1	53.9	15.3	4.0	4328
Kosovo	27.1	31.4	27.9	12.8	0.3	0.5	866

Source: Rančić, 1975.

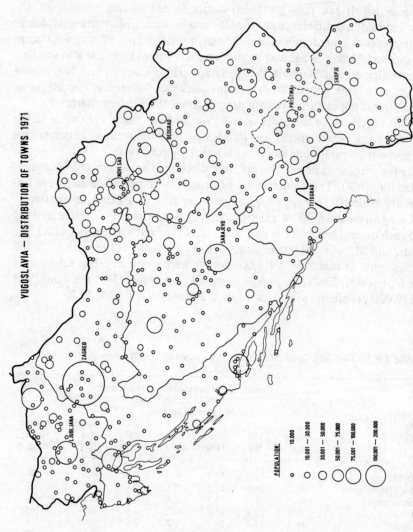

Fig. 19.1 Distribution of Towns in Yugoslavia, 1971
Source of data: Federal Statistical Office

Table 19.2: *The Development of Urbanization in Yugoslavia*

Federal units	Years	Total population (000s)	Urban population (000s)	Population in urban settlements %	Population in mixed settlements (000s)	Population in mixed settlements %	Population in urban + mixed settlements %
Yugoslavia	1921	12545	1642	13.1	—	—	—
	1931	14534	2194	15.1	—	—	—
	1948	15842	2743	17.3	—	—	—
	1953	16999	3688	21.7	1076	6.3	28.0
	1961	18549	5252	28.3	2028	10.9	39.2
	1971	20522	7915	38.6	2928	14.3	52.8
Bosnia/Hercegovina		3746	1045	27.9	739	19.7	47.6
Montenegro		529	182	34.4	82	15.5	49.9
Croatia		4426	1816	41.0	716	16.2	57.2
Macedonia		1647	793	48.1	95	5.8	53.9
Slovenia		1727	650	37.6	406	23.5	61.1
Serbia		8446	3429	40.6	890	10.5	51.1
Serbia proper		5250	2141	40.8	373	7.1	47.9
Vojvodina		1952	953	48.8	396	20.3	69.1
Kosovo		1243	335	26.9	121	9.7	36.7

Source: Census of Yugoslavia 1953, 1961, 1971. Beograd 1959, 1965, 1975.

Socio-economic Development of Post-War Yugoslavia and the Transformation of the Settlement System

The great changes in the economy of the country have led to a considerable social and geographical transformation. The agricultural population has been considerably reduced from 76.6 per cent in the pre-war period to 38.2 per cent in 1971. Reduction in agricultural dependence was most pronounced in the more developed republics where the percentage of the population engaged in agriculture was greatly reduced: to 20.4 per cent in Slovenia, to 32.3 per cent in Croatia, and to 39.0 per cent in Vojvodina. The accelerated industrialization has attracted to the factories the larger part of this agricultural population that was leaving their small farms (with an average size of only 3.8 hectares). The proportion of the employed population engaged in manufacturing industries was therefore increasing from one census to another: it was 7.9 per cent in the year 1953 and as much as 17.7 per cent in the year 1971. It was highest in Slovenia (32.3 per cent) and in Croatia (18.6 per cent), and lowest in Kosovo (11.7 per cent), Macedonia (14.7 per cent), and Serbia proper (14.8 per cent).

The socio-economic development has led to numerous migrations. In 1971, only 60 per cent of the entire population of the country was still living in the place of birth. In urban settlements this share was only 42 per cent. Migrations—apart from those to foreign countries—were largely directed towards towns. (Žuljíc, 1973; Ginić, 1967; Vrišer, 1977)

The urbanization and consolidation of the state has changed the rank size distribution of settlements. In 1921 this distribution was still a markedly irregular one. However, the size distribution in 1971 for the fifty largest towns was already fairly regular. Deformations appear only between the fiftieth and hundredth towns with a greater share of small towns in the respective set.

The socio-economic transformation of post-war Yugoslavia was also reflected in the functional orientation of Yugoslav towns. Analyses carried out on the basis of the economically active population in the year 1953 have revealed that orientation to tertiary or quaternary activities was predominant (Vogelnik, 1961). According to data provided by the 1971 Census, industry (together with construction, handicraft, and mining) has become the main function of the 495 towns in Yugoslavia. Forty-nine per cent of the urban population was dependent on these activities. The share for the tertiary activities (transportation, commerce, catering, tourism, and communal utilities) was 21.5 per cent and for the quaternary activities (administration, social services), 21.8 per cent. The share for agricultural (primary) activities remained comparatively high with 7.1 per cent.

The socio-economic classification was carried out according to the structure of the economically active population. A town was classified according to whether the share (per cent) of a certain activity group was above the average for that group in all Yugoslav towns. These percentages were: primary activities (P) 7.09 per cent; secondary activities (S) 49.52 per cent; tertiary activities (T) 21.53 per cent; and quaternary activities (Q) 21.84 per cent.

According to this rather rough classification the majority of the urban places in Yugoslavia (495 altogether) were oriented to secondary activities (113 towns), primary activities (60 towns), tertiary activities (20 towns), and quaternary activities (10 towns). As many as 203 towns had a double orientation and 41 towns a triple orientation. There were marked differences between the federal units. Thus, Slovene towns are mainly oriented to industrial activities. Many towns of Vojvodina are agriculturally oriented. In Kosovo most towns show a double orientation to either primary-quaternary or primary-tertiary activities. In Croatia many towns show tertiary orientation because of the developed transportation and touristic functions.

The socio-economic development of Yugoslavia has made possible a gradual stabilization of the network of central places and of their areas of influence (Vrišer, 1971). An analysis of central places carried out in 1968 has shown that the system consists of 1,358 central places. It was possible, on the basis of their qualitative attributes (the number and composition of central functions) as well as quantitative characteristics (the number of people employed or active in service activities), to establish six hierarchical levels (Table 19.3). The lower level of provision of central functions is represented by centres of the I and II levels; that is by the centres of local communities and of administrative communes together with some other settlements (industrial villages and tourist centres). The middle level is represented by central places of the III and IV levels; in most cases these are the seats of former districts which offer more demanding services. The higher level is represented in this classification by the centres of provinces (V level) and republics (VI level) and, of course, by the national capital of Belgrade (VII level).

The network of central places, however, was not uniform throughout Yugoslavia. In the more developed and densely inhabited northwestern and western areas the network was denser, with more centres at the lower levels. In the less developed and more sparsely populated areas (Southern Serbia, Kosovo, Macedonia, the Dinaric areas) the network of lower order centres

Table 19.3: *The Central Places in Yugoslavia*

		Lower		Service level Middle		Higher		
	Total	I	II	III	IV	V	VI	VII
Number of centres	1358	915	310	88	28	12	4	1

was much looser and the role of the centres of the middle level more pronounced.

The areas of influence of central places reflected their position on the hierarchical level (Vrišev, 1973) (Figure 19.2). It was possible to establish by means of an extensive questionnaire survey concerning the provision of goods and services to local communities that, in 1968, 466 towns and other settlements offered complete provision at the basic level (the micro-regional centres). The remaining 29 urban settlements (out of the total of 495) did not form independent service areas around them. The provision at the middle level was performed by 189 centres (the meso-regional centres) which were, in general, central places of the III, IV, and higher levels but also, because of exceptional circumstances, 56 settlements of the II level. The provision at the higher level was performed by 17 centres (the macro-regional centres) at the V to VII hierarchical level.

The main foci of the Yugoslav network of settlements were the cities and towns that could have been classified as centres at the higher level (hierarchical levels V, VI, and VII): Belgrade (level VII), Zagreb, Sarajevo, Skopje, and Ljubljana (level VI), Novi Sad (level V/VI), followed by Maribor, Rijeka, Split, Osijek, Banja Luka, Mostar, Tuzla, Subotica, Priština, Niš, and Titograd (level V). Rogić (1973) as well as Hamilton (1968) arrived at similar conclusions (including also Bitola in this category).

Vrišer (1973) has also shown that some centres were too small and poorly equipped with central functions and had therefore not been able to dominate their areas of influence. Some regions lacked an adequate centre, although they should have had one, considering their area and population. Such areas were western Slavonia, north-central Bosnia, the Drina basin, and southwestern Serbia.

The following factors were mainly responsible for the formation of the urban system: the number and density of population, accessibility, consumption patterns, and administrative division. The number and density of population were in direct relation to the number and size of towns and to their hierarchical position. Deviations from this rule occurred in some areas (Kosovo) because of economic underdevelopment. Improved communications and motorized transportation have increased the accessibility to centres but have also led to a certain differentiation among towns. The rise of living standards and consumption, together with industrialization, have strengthened the basic lower level of centres (micro-regional centres) and made their distribution more dense while they were destroying the original pattern of the system that had existed in a predominantly agrarian society. Because of the long-lasting and important role of the public administration, the numerous elements of the administrative order are still present in the structure of settlements.

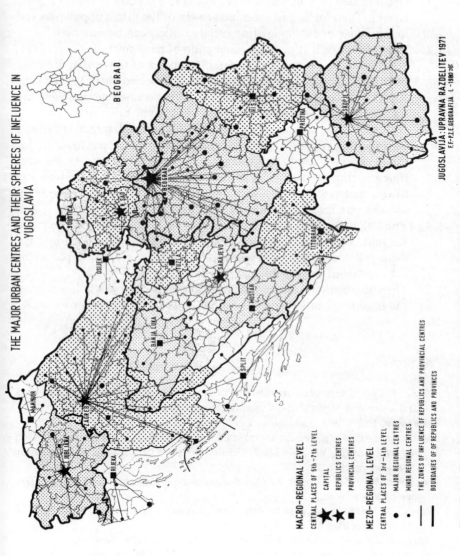

THE MAJOR URBAN CENTRES AND THEIR SPHERES OF INFLUENCE IN
YUGOSLAVIA

BEOGRAD

JUGOSLAVIJA : UPRAVNA RAZDELITEV 1971
F.F-Z.E.GEOGRAFIJA L -1980 %

MACRO−REGIONAL LEVEL

CENTRAL PLACES OF 5th −7th LEVEL
★ CAPITAL
★ REPUBLICS CENTRES
■ PROVINCIAL CENTRES

MEZO−REGIONAL LEVEL

CENTRAL PLACES OF 3rd −4th LEVEL
● MAJOR REGIONAL CENTRES
• MINOR REGIONAL CENTRES

▬ THE ZONES OF INFLUENCE OF REPUBLICS AND PROVINCIAL CENTRES
▮ BOUNDARIES OF OF REPUBLICS AND PROVINCES

Fig. 19.2.   The Major Urban Centres and their Spheres of Influence in Yugoslavia

The Future of the System of Settlements

In attempting to assess the future of the settlement system, the following characteristics and development trends can be discerned.

1. Urbanization of Yugoslavia is still weak (38.6 per cent of the total population). Therefore a further rapid growth of the urban population and, in particular of the population of large cities, can be expected.

2. The predominant functional orientation of most towns is to secondary activities. There is still a considerable number of towns that are economically dependent on agriculture. It is expected that the one-sided functional orientation will be reduced with increased development and that orientation to tertiary activities will become more pronounced.

3. Increased consumption, improved accessibility, widespread car ownership and the expansion of manufacturing industries, tends to strengthen the network of the basic (lower) level of central places. At the same time the role of large cities is also being enhanced. The middle-sized towns, that used to have a dominant role in the provision of goods and services, are losing their former function.

4. The Yugoslav urban system has been for years a bi-polar one (Belgrade-Zagreb). The modern development, based upon socialist self-management and decentralization, tends to favour other centres, in particular, the capitals of the republics.

5. The socio-economic development of post-war Yugoslavia has reduced the traditional rural-urban dichotomy that used to be so pronounced.

REFERENCES

Ginić, I. 1967, *Dinamika i struktura gradskog stanovništva Jugoslavije.* Beograd. (Dynamics and Structure of Yugoslav Urban Population).

Hamilton, F. E. 1968. *Yugoslavia.* London.

Macura, M. 1954, 'Kriterium za razgraničenje gradskog i seoskog stanovništve', *Statistička revija*, VI, 3/4: 371-7. ('Un critère pour délimitation des population urbaine et rurale').

Mirkovic, M. 1958. *Ekonomska historija Jugoslavije.* Zagreb. (The Economic History of Yugoslavia).

Rančić, M. 1975. 'Naselja po veličini i tipu', *Jugoslovenski pregled*, XIX, 3. ('The Size and Typology of Yugoslav Settlements').

Resultats définitifs du recensement de 31. janvier 1921, 1929. Sarajevo.

Resultats définitifs du recensement de 31. mars 1931, 1940. Sarajevo.

Rogić, V. 1973. 'Regionalizacija Jugoslavije', *Geografski glasnik.* 35: 13-28 (Regionalization of Yugoslavia).

Statistički godišnjak SFRJ, 1955-1979. Beograd. (Statistical Yearbook of Yugoslavia).

Vogelnik, D. 1961. *Urbanizacija kao ordraz privrednog razvoja FNRJ*. Beograd. (Urbanization in Yugoslavia as an Expression of its Economic Development).
Vrišer, I. 1971. 'The Patterns of Central Places in Jugoslavia', *Tijdschrift voor Economische en Sociale Geografie*, 62, 5: 290-300.
Vrišer, I. 1973. 'Vplivna območja jugoslovanskih mest in drugih središč', *Geografski vestnik*, XLV: 21-45 ('The Areas of Influence of Yugoslav Cities and Towns').
Vrišer, I. 1977. 'Urbanizacija občin v luči faktorski analize', *Geografski vestnik*, XLIX: 131-8 ('The Urbanization of Yugoslav Communes in the Light of Factor Analysis').
Zgodovina narodov Jugoslavije. 1953. I: 50-4. Ljubljana. (The History of Yugoslav Nations I).
Zgodovina narodov Jugoslavije. 1959. II: 33-40. Ljubljana. (The History of Yugoslav Nations II).
Žuljíc, S. 1973, *Urbanizacija no području Jugoslavije*. Zagreb. (The Urbanization of Yugoslavia).

PART C

SETTLEMENT SYSTEMS IN THE DEVELOPING WORLD

Section 6: Settlement on New Lands and in Low-Density Regions

20 BRAZILIAN URBAN SETTLEMENT

FANY DAVIDOVICH

This paper is a geographical re-interpretation of Brazilian urbanization. Its main motivations are: (i) a theoretical concern for the problem of what is urban in the country; (ii) a concern for presenting the urban system as the spatial component of social development.

Most studies carried out on the Brazilian urban system have been formal and descriptive, and include centrality studies, rank-size approaches, and centre-periphery models. Such contributions do not explain Brazilian urbanization in its specific form. A more 'comprehensive' theoretical approach is necessary; one which interprets space as an expression of social processes and as the result of an historical evolution.

An urban system cannot be defined exclusively by the relationships and interdependences among cities at a given moment. These interactions must be included in a spatial context that is larger than that of the urban system itself. Moreover, the interactions of the urban system must be understood as relationships that have developed over time. In addition, the dynamics of the urban system should be related to processes of social change and cannot merely be identified with the functionality inherent in a systemic organization.

This paper is primarily an attempt at developing a new conception of the Brazilian urban system (Figure 20.1). Its aim is to look at the levels and spatial dimensions of the urbanization process. It does not consider the particular social, economic, political, and ideological interpretations of this process. It assumes that what is urban expresses itself in different spatial forms and that these forms can also express the social structure.

Considerations about Brazilian Urbanization

Spatial Characteristics

The complex spatial structure of urbanization reflects the development of a new phase of Brazilian economic growth. With a capitalistic-industrial base, this new phase represents a rupture with the preceding economic base supported by the exportation of primary goods for the international market. By the forces of its technological features and the intense urbanization promoted by it, the new phase has affected social and spatial structures throughout the country. The main changes may be summarized in the following items:

(i) The cumulative urban-industrial process has integrated the national economy into the world capitalist system. This has replaced the so-called

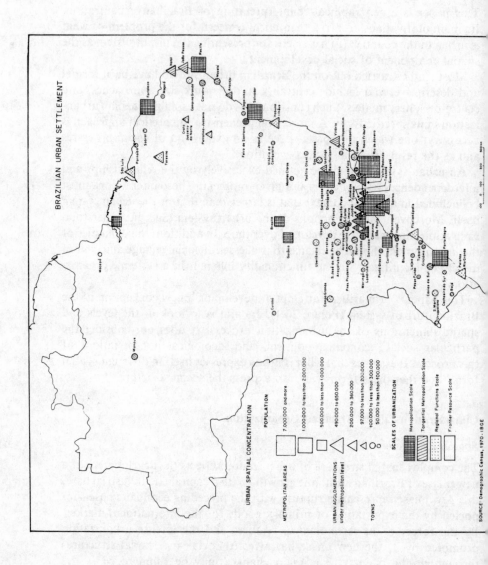

BRAZILIAN URBAN SETTLEMENT

URBAN SPATIAL CONCENTRATION

POPULATION

METROPOLITAN AREAS

- 7.000.000 and more
- 1.000.000 to less than 2.000.000
- 500.000 to less than 1.000.000

URBAN AGGLOMERATIONS
under metropolitan level

- 490.000 to 650.000
- 200.000 to 360.000

TOWNS

- 97.000 to less than 300.000
- 100.000 to less than 300.000
- 50.000 to less than 100.000

SCALES OF URBANIZATION

- Metropolization Scale
- Tangential Metropolization Scale
- Regional Functions Scale
- Frontier Resource Scale

SOURCE: Demographic Census, 1970 - IBGE

'comparative advantages' that were a feature of previous phases of territorial occupancy. It is useful to point out that this economic-growth model did not bring stability to the urban system. It developed at the cost of imbalances, at times in the balance of payments, at times in prices and exchange rates, and at the expense of the intensification of social inequalities in the spatial structure. In fact, the expansion of the capitalist system in the country has been accomplished through oligopolistic forms of entrepreneurship, involving a State sector and a private sector with a strong component of multinational firms.

Such expansion became articulated, above all, in the Southeastern region, where a massive urban-industrial concentration offered the most favourable conditions to achieve economies of scale and agglomeration. In fact, the Southeast combined both the requirements demanded by the production sector, represented by levels of capitalization, financial capacity, and efficiency, and those demanded by the consumption sector, as represented by market density. The Southeast region has brought about a 'destructuring' of traditional regions, primarily through the progressive elimination of local activities as they are replaced by goods coming in from the Southeast. This is especially the case of the Northeast.

(ii) The development of industrial capitalism has expanded the urban basis of the system. In the course of the last decades, the growth of population in cities and small towns has intensified. In 1970, the urban population made up 56 per cent of the overall population compared to 31 per cent in 1940. In addition to demographic changes, the process of urbanization has brought other movements of surpluses towards the urban-industrial sector. These include flows of financial resources and goods. They not only reflect flows from the countryside, but also have an urban origin, in that the mobility of people among cities of different sizes has become substantial.

The enlargement of the urban sector has been mainly expressed in agglomerations and in an increasing number of large cities, with a decrease in the importance of small localities. The group of centres which each used to represent 0.05 per cent of the Brazilian urban population grew by 144 per cent between 1950 and 1970. Cities which used to represent between 1.01 and 2.00 per cent of the overall Brazilian population, grew by 781 per cent during the same period. This category of centres contained about 10 per cent of the Brazilian urban population in 1970, whereas in 1950 it contained only 3 per cent. At that time, this represented an urban size of 500,000-1,000,000 inhabitants (Porcaro, 1977).

Such reorganization of the national urban space is related to a changing territorial division of labour, involving greater economic efficiency. Thus, there are tendencies leading to the destructuring of some traditional regionalisms. New spatial structures reflect greater interdependences of the productive system, similar to what has happened in countries of advanced capitalism. The result is the 'contraction' of economic space as reflected in the form of urban concentration. Such a compacting of the urban space is contrary to the traditional dispersed forms of urban distribution.

The National Dimension

With the increasingly urban basis of the economic system, the spatial structure has taken on a national dimension as opposed to the traditional regional organization of the territory. The urbanization process not only reflects industrial development, but also the presence of mercantile and financial capital. Thus there are sharp differentials between the main urban concentrations of the country.

Between 1950 and 1970 industrial production increased at an annual rate of 8 per cent. Along the São Paulo-Rio de Janeiro axis, the national concentration of industrial employment increased during that period from 57 per cent to 62 per cent. The share of the Northeast in the employment capacity of the country dropped.

In spite of these differentials the large urban concentrations form a highly integrated set, maintaining greater interaction with each other than with centres in their respective areas of influence. The new national dimension of urbanization is reinforced by the integration of the industrial economy, the radiating core of which is the São Paulo-Rio de Janeiro axis.

These interactions are aided by policies undertaken by official planning agencies. Such planning intervenes in the allocation of resources and in the promotion of large-scale production. It represents a political and economic instrument of a very centralized political power. The improvement in access to the country's entire territory by means of internal highways has promoted urban concentration. Such an improvement responds to the demand for remote natural resources needed for the industrial economy and for exports. It also concurs with the need to supply food for the home market.

Within this new urban framework it is possible to distinguish several forms of cities: (i) those directly involved in the urban-industrial economy, which implies changes in the previous spatial structure of cities. These are the changes which have resulted in the present metropolitan areas and urban agglomerations; (ii) those that involve the growth of cities in areas with a capitalistic development of agricultural activities; (iii) those in areas of older occupancy, which at times show some deteriorating or declining trends.

The new spatial structure also implies the creation of new cities. It is necessary to distinguish centres that arose from spontaneous or officially-induced industrial implantation and those that arose from the expansion of the resource frontier. It is also important to distinguish those cities founded with the purpose of consolidating the advance toward the interior, for example Belo Horizonte in the past, Goiânia in a following period and more recently Brasília.

The distribution of the principal urban concentrations along the coastal strip is the main configuration of the system (Geiger and Davidovich, 1974).

At present, this 'coastlining' of the urban system can be understood as an 'extension of the centre'. According to de Oliveira and Reichstul (1973), the subsidized deconcentration of industries from the core area toward other agglomerations (largely located along the coastline), has as its main purpose the continuation of profits for capital concentrated in the Southeastern region.

Scales of Urbanization

The Concept

The assumption underlying scales of urbanization is that they correspond to different dimensions of one and the same process. According to Harvey (1973), the urban system must be understood as a whole, and is moved by unequal rhythms through which the different parts adjust to changes. Thus, big cities more rapidly acquire resources, activities, and innovations than smaller places. Big cities converge, small cities diverge.

In Brazil, the differentiated parts of the urban structure and their unequal rhythms are influenced by urban-industrial development. From this point of view, when we refer to scale of metropolitization, we are dealing with multiple subdimensions of the industrialization process. We imply that the largest concentrations develop among each other more intensive interactions than with their regions. A scale involving small dispersed centres, in turn, may show great economic inertia and a weak articulation in the regional economy. Thus, the scales are defined by the integration of certain types of urban centres corresponding to the main socio-spatial structures developed or supported by the dominant economy. The scales are not uniform. In each the interactions generated by this economy can be perceived in different ways and intensities.

This approach further implies the notion of synchronicity of the system and of the co-existence of different dimensions of 'urban' structure in the country. Thus, it stresses not only the relative position of cities, but also the role played by them in the different forms of production organization.

Thus, different sizes of cities in the Brazilian urban system are not examined according to the 'rank-size' model. Several centres with over 200 thousand inhabitants act to integrate rings or spaces peripheral to the metropolitan areas. Often state capitals assume the position of an extension of the metropolitan core to the extent that they are involved in the process of induced industrialization. (For example, João Pessoa (Paraíba) and Natal (Rio Grande do Norte) in relation to Recife, the regional metropolis of the Brazilian Northeast, or Aracaju (Sergipe) in relation to the metropolitan area of Salvador (Bahia)). Moreover, centres with a population of less than 20 thousand inhabitants, located in 'urban regions' may perform specialized functions which are not related to the rural sector. This situation can be observed in areas near to the metropolis of São Paulo. Some centres in turn, have an appreciable proportion of rural population, such as the *bóia-fria* (rural workers hired by the day) in the state of São Paulo and in other regions of the country.

The notion of scales of urbanization leads, therefore, to the analysis of cities as components of spatial structures related to forms of production organization, and not as isolated points or autonomous unities. The notion of scale implies, too, an image of fluidity and is thus more compatible with the fluidity of social relations (Harvey, 1973). It would, therefore, be more adequate to express the idea of space in movement rather than the notion of a sub-system, which tends to imply fixed categories and activities.

In their spatial configuration, subdimensions of the scales of urbanization may involve physical continuity and discontinuity and structures with greater or lesser density of centres. Such subdimensions can be identified within the axes of urban concentration, in the aggregates of centres in dense agriculture regions, in the arrangement of agglomerations along some highways, and in the scattered distribution of places in certain areas.

Indicators

Indicators used in this analysis are: (i) urban size; (ii) population dynamics; (iii) income conditions; (iv) industrial activity position. Except in the case of population dynamics, which refers only to a particular group of urban centres, these indicators refer to a set of ninety (90) observation units, for which data were available at the municipal level (Table 20.1).

Urban Size covers centres of over 50,000 inhabitants in 1970. Three types of urban areas are included: metropolitan areas, urban agglomerations below the metropolitan level, and other cities. The urban size measure allows us to assess theoretical postulates such as the connection between the size of centres and their economical relevance.

Income Conditions are based upon the average monthly income of those economically-active people with earnings. The characterization of centres follows the classification provided in Davidovich and De Lima (1976). Centres were identified according to: Situations of Precariousness (1, 2, and 3); Intermediate Situations (1, 2, and 3); and Favourable Situations (1, 2, and 3).[1]

The Indicator, Industrial Activity Position, is taken as proxy for the position of the urban centres within the national economy. The ratio, Value Added in Industry/Personnel Occupied in Industry (Industrial Census, 1970), was utilized as a simple measure of productivity. High indices expressed a superior position.

Finally, Population Dynamics Measures refer to the urban growth rate recorded between 1960 and 1970. The figures reported in Table 20.1 comprise the same set of centres.

Interpretation

(i) 'The Scale of Metropolitization' comprises the main urban concentrations of the country. The delimitation of this scale was based on criteria reported in an earlier paper (Barat and Geiger, 1973) identifying areas of immediate metropolitan influence. They correspond to the areas contained within circles of different radii calculated as a proportion of the population of each metropolis, namely São Paulo = 84 km, Porto Alegre, Salvador, Fortaleza, Belém, and Curitiba each between 75 and 78 km, approximately. The scale in question is thus defined by the largest urban size, comprising about 63 per cent of a total of 44,654,079 inhabitants.[2] The relationship between population and economic relevance is the same as for income conditions. In fact, the highest levels are recorded in the metropolises, rather than in the centres of their respective regions. The most favourable situations are, nevertheless, found in the Centre-South, especially in the state of São Paulo.

But the largest urban size is not necessarily correlated with a higher level of industrial productivity. The latter is found in centres which specialize in capital goods such as petrochemicals in the agglomeration of Santos (SP), and iron and steel in the agglomeration of Volta Redonda (RJ). In turn, the relationship between urban size and demographic growth shows that large concentrations which might be expected to manifest a certain stability, do not reach such a condition. The metropolitan areas of São Paulo (SP) and Belo Horizonte (MG) still show demographic growth above the national average. The centres of greater industrial productivity show more demographic stability in the same period.

The economic and social contrasts among the centres included in this scale reflect the problems of the regions where they are located. Their inclusion in the same scale of urbanization reflects the interdependence brought about by the industrial economy of the country, interdependences that imply social and spatial disparities.

(ii) 'The Scale of Tangency to Metropolitization' comprises centres in the process of integration into metropolitan structures. These centres feature conditions of transition, between the changes which they are experiencing, and the permanence of traditional regional functions.

The degree of metropolitization of these centres may be related to: (1) their geographical location near the periphery of metropolitan areas. Socio-economic contrasts (income levels, industrial activity) between these centres are derived from the conditions of the metropolitan nuclei with which they are connected; for example, superior conditions are found in those connected with the metropolitization of São Paulo, such as Ribeirão Preto and Bauru; (2) the role played by local entrepreneurship in the development of nation-wide industries; for example German colonization in the south of Brazil; (3) the particular intervention of federal action, which influences the

Table 20.1: *Scales of Urbanization*

1. Scale of metropolitization

Centres	Urban population 1970	Classes by growth 1960/70	% Growth 1960/70	Position by income of econ. active population	Estimate of value added by industry (VTI) Cr$ 000s	VTI/ people employed in indus.
SOUTHEAST						
1. AM* São Paulo	8,139,730	4	97.86	Favourable 3	22,889,998	25.43
2. Agl.** Santos	626,746	3a	57.92	Favourable 3	845,725	40.90
3. Agl. Campinas	491,632	4	87.73	Favourable 3	1,068,649	25.71
4. Agl. Jundiaí	194,556	4	93.55	Favourable 2	599,136	23.50
5. Agl. Sorocaba	202,609	3b	63.01	Favourable 2	308,238	16.34
6. Agl. São José dos Campos	240,260	5	125.31	Favourable 2	666,751	26.47
7. Agl. Taubaté	152,986	3b	71.70	Intermediate 2	104,876	14.50
8. Agl. Guaratinguetá	140,001	3a	50.34	Intermediate 2	110,354	20.75
9. Agl. Americana	97,334	4	86.81	Favourable 2	252,712	15.15
10. Piracicaba	125,384	3a	55.43	Favourable 1	198,998	16.77
11. Limeira	77,094	3b	70.35	Favourable 1	187,290	20.63
12. Rio Claro	69,192	3a	42.52	Favourable 1	59,448	15.00
13. AM Rio de Janeiro	7,080,661	3a	52.23	Favourable 3	6,847,066	23.06
14. Agl. Barra Mansa - Volta Redonda	226,955	3a	49.90	Favourable 2	816,450	55.74

15. Nova Friburgo	74,003	2	37.81	Precarious 2	79,742	10.77
16. Teresópolis	53,447	4	80.93	Precarious 2	27,275	15.87
17. Juiz de Fora	218,856	4	75.11	Intermediate 1	160,566	13.02
18. AM Belo Horizonte	1,605,306	4	98.84	Intermediate 3	1,197,526	19.67
19. Sete Lagoas	61,001	3b	68.04	Precarious 2	40,990	18.12
SOUTH						
1. AM Porto Alegre	1,531,257	3b	66.13	Favourable 3	1,869,565	17.26
2. AM Curitiba	821,233	3b	73.95	Favourable 3	575,666	15.19
CENTRE-WEST						
1. Agl. Brasília	516,082	5	484.33	Favourable 3	61,236	13.76
2. Agl. Goiânia	501,007	5	150.79	Intermediate 3	133,352	14.55
NORTHEAST						
1. AM Salvador	1,147,821	3b	62.92	Intermediate 3	610,293	22.49
2. Feira de Santana	126,972	5	106.08	Precarious 1	32,284	10.25
3. AM Recife	1,791,822	3a	55.29	Intermediate 1	858,609	15.97
4. AM Fortaleza	1,036,779	4	76.12	Precarious 1	270,302	10.86
NORTH						
1. Belém	655,901	3b	60.70	Intermediate 3	156,544	11.65
TOTAL	28,006,127 (78.68% of Total Urban Pop.)					

* AM — Metropolitan Area
** Agl. — Agglomeration

2. Scale of Tangency to Metropolitization

Centres	Urban population 1970	Classes by growth 1960/70	% Growth 1960/70	Position by income of econ. active population	Estimate of value added by industry (VTI) Cr$ 000s	VTI/ people employed in indus.
SOUTHEAST						
1. Ribeirão Preto	191,472	3b	64.84	Favourable 1	119,419	13.73
2. Bauru	120,229	2	41.05	Favourable 2	51,142	13.40
3. Araraquara	82,621	2	42.26	Favourable 1	116,599	30.00
4. São Carlos	74,767	3a	49.50	Intermediate 3	116,076	16.04
5. Franca	86,863	4	83.86	Precarious 2	103,111	11.17
6. Poços de Caldas	51,783	3b	60.36	Intermediate 3	58,271	17.93
7. Divinópolis	69,873	3b	68.19	Precarious 2	38,516	12.69
8. Agl. Ipatinga	121,762	5	193.05	Favourable 2	447,235	52.00
9. Agl. Vitória	358,183	4	98.11	Intermediate 3	126,928	16.68
10. Barbacena	57,767	2	37.77	Precarious 2	24,861	12.83

SOUTH						
1. Caxias do Sul	108,082	4	78.33	Favourable 2	224,702	15.18
2. Joinville	54,073	4	75.65	Favourable 1	314,258	17.92
3. Blumenau	85,944	4	84.46	Favourable 1	210,164	12.82
4. Tubarão	82,006	3b	72.43	Intermediate 2	18,030	13.14
5. Criciúma	50,334	5	115.74	Favourable 2	63,096	11.10
6. Ponta Grossa	114,889	3a	47.67	Intermediate 3	72,623	13.21
7. Paranaguá	51,462	4	85.60	Favourable 2	—	—
NORTHEAST						
1. Agl. João Pessoa	326,197	3a	58.23	Precarious 1	69,666	11.34
2. Agl. Natal	278,881	3b	67.52	Intermediate 1	63,686	11.96
3. Agl. Aracaju	189,238	3b	61.58	Intermediate 1	41,136	9.84
4. Maceió	243,009	3a	58.51	Intermediate 1	61,622	10.35
5. Caruaru	100,985	3a	56.53	Extremely Precarious	13,768	5.14
NORTH						
1. Manaus	283,635	4	84.16	Favourable 1	169,763	19.73
TOTAL	3,193,985 (8.93% of Total Urban Pop.)					

3. Scale of Regional Functions

Centres	Urban population 1970	Classes by growth 1960/70	% Growth 1960/70	Position by income of econ. active population	Estimate of value added by industry (VTI) Cr$ 000s	VTI/ people employed in indus.
SOUTH						
1. Agl. Pelotas - Rio Grande	324,357	2	25.14	Precarious 2	230,875	17.90
2. Bagé	56,980	1	18.88	Intermediate 1	23,083	16.70
3. Uruguaiana	60,155	2	24.40	Intermediate 1	8,168	10.17
4. Santa Maria	120,510	3a	53.16	Intermediate 2	26,456	13.87
5. Cachoeira do Sul	49,987	2	29.30	Precarious 2	20,347	11.70
6. Passo Fundo	69,062	3a	46.01	Intermediate 2	34,736	14.34
7. Itajaí	54,073	2	39.04	Intermediate 2	29,881	13.68
8. Lages	82,006	5	133.56	Precarious 2	104,755	17.85
9. Londrina	156,352	5	110.97	Intermediate 2	120,876	22.85
10. Maringá	100,847	5	138.82	Intermediate 2	84,485	30.79
11. Agl. Florianópolis	227,223	4	87.72	Intermediate 3	30,193	8.26
SOUTHEAST						
1. Presidente Prudente	91,474	3b	69.22	Intermediate 2	65,219	21.63
2. Marília	73,217	2	41.38	Intermediate 2	82,156	20.07
3. Araçatuba	85,616	3a	59.84	Intermediate 2	66,839	27.46
4. S. José do Rio Preto	108,433	3b	63.12	Intermediate 3	43,313	13.65
5. Barretos	52,976	2	32.61	Intermediate 1	34,723	19.96
6. Uberaba	108,259	3a	50.25	Precarious 2	36,240	11.57
7. Uberlândia	110,289	3a	55.95	Intermediate 1	93,699	32.43
8. Campos	155,169	2	35.75	Precarious 2	115,554	13.55
9. Cachoeiro Itapemirim	58,918	3a	49.27	Precarious 1	51,290	13.29
10. Montes Claros	81,657	5	101.40	Precarious 1	41,744	31.36
11. Governador Valadares	124,904	4	77.18	Precarious 2	29,994	13.18
12. Teófilo Otoni	64,718	3a	57.80	Extremely Precarious	14,922	19.98

NORTHEAST

1. Vitória da Conquista	82,230	4	75.79	Precarious 1	7,131	9.04
2. Jequié	62,147	3a	54.76	Extremely Precarious	6,170	7.44
3. Alagoinhas	53,817	2	40.71	Precarious 1	3,962	6.66
4. Agl. Itabuna - Ilhéus	220,692	3a	49.93	Precarious 1	21,710	12.64
5. Agl. Petrolina - Juazeiro	122,900	5	101.38	Precarious 1	15,784	11.15
6. Campina Grande	162,554	2	39.86	Precarious 1	54,177	12.13
7. Mossoró	77,199	4	98.80	Extremely Precarious	17,596	7.56
8. Sobral	51,835	3b	60.57	Extremely Precarious	17,793	10.66
9. Agl. Crato - Juazeiro do Norte	167,043	3a	48.91	Extremely Precarious	19,213	10.46
10. Parnaíba	57,030	2	42.75	Extremely Precarious	5,197	8.82
11. Agl. Teresina	257,380	4	92.24	Precarious 1	14,477	5.82
12. Agl. São Luis	302,609	3a	52.92	Precarious 2	42,210	15.48

CENTRE-WEST

1. Campo Grande	130,615	5	102.00	Intermediate 3	44,682	19.17
2. Cuiabá	83,638	4	92.00	Intermediate 3	6,004	7.39

NORTH

1. Santarém	102,431	4	95.07	Extremely Precarious	5,192	9.06

TOTAL	4,351,302 (12.16% of Total Urban Pop.)				116,403	57.45

4. Scale of the Frontier of Resources

1. Macapá	51,422	4	86.41	Favourable 1		
TOTAL	35,772,836 (100%)					

industrial and administrative sectors, as illustrated by the cases of Vitoria (ES), Natal (RN) and Manaus (AM).

The highest urban size recorded in this scale is approximately 300 thousand persons. High urban growth rates are characteristic, but, contrary to the situation in the Scale of Metropolitization, the highest population increases were in centres of more recent iron and steel development, such as Ipatinga (MG). Effects of urban growth of the major centres manifest themselves differently in the localities of the Tangency Scale. The intense polarization of São Paulo certainly exercised an influence upon population change in centres related to it, in fact, a significantly lower increase. Agglomerations touching the metropolitization of Porto Alegre (RS) or that of Curitiba (PR) recorded higher urban growth than those main centres.

(iii) 'The Scale of Regional Functions' refers to centres with mainly commercial activities involving goods and services, including the state-capital function. These are central places that develop within dominantly mercantile structures and are distinguished from more industrial centres. These centres are based upon the regional economies, with their respective demographic densities, areas of influence, income levels, natural resources, and types of production. They are relatively small (less than 250,000 inhabitants, in the most populous centres), and the largest concentrations are found in the Northeastern and South regions. Cities with 100,000 inhabitants are more frequent in this scale and are located mainly in the Southeast.

These centres vary greatly in terms of urban growth. Some centres recorded large relative increases up to 100 per cent. Such increases are due to rural affluence. Teresina (PI), Mocoró (RN), Campo Grande (MT), or Montes Claros (MG) are examples. In the north of the State of Paraná, the high urban growth recorded by Londrina and Maringá is related to capitalistic changes introduced into the agrarian structure. Other centres have experienced little growth, Pelotas-Rio Grande and Bagé (RS), for instance, have structural characteristics peculiar to traditional cattle-breeding areas which have predominantly low demographic densities. Some cities situated in older and relatively stagnant agricultural areas also recorded little population increase. This suggests the inability of these centres to revitalize the agrarian activities of surrounding areas as well as the competition of more dynamic agglomerations. Cities such as Cachoeira do Sul (RS) and Itajaí (SC) in the South region, or Campos (RJ) and Cachoeiro do Itapemirim (ES) in the Southeast, or else, Crato and Juazeiro do Norte (CE) and Campina Grande (PB) in the Northeast might also be mentioned. The polarization of the metropolis of São Paulo is certainly expressed in the moderate urban growth rates of the centres located in the Western plateau of São Paulo, such as Marília, Aracatuba, São José do Rio Preto.

(iv) 'The Scale of the Resource Frontier' involves very small urban sizes. The exception is Macapá (AP), which reached around 50,000 inhabitants in 1970. This centre has privileged conditions, due to the presence of technically advanced enterprises, such as the mining of manganese.

A common feature of the centres included in this scale is their role in support of the development of the interior. Great distances separate this scale from the metropolitan centres. Included are both new urban nuclei that mark a pioneering advancement and developing places at the rear of such advancement.

The most recent centres are located mainly along the Belém-Brasília highway and the São Paulo-Cuiabá (MT)-Porto Velho highway. Important urban occupancy is observed in some stretches of the Amazonian periphery, such as those found in North Mato Grosso and Goiás, in Rondônia, and in Southeastern and Centre-Western Para. Some of these centres recorded a relatively explosive rate of urban growth (over 1000 per cent) between 1960 and 1970, especially in the state of Mato Grosso. Nevertheless, urban life in these areas is nearly always ephemeral, as growth may be followed by a fast decline. However, certain towns have a more stable urban position, such as Imperatriz (MA) or Araguaína (GO), having developed some important regional functions.

Behind the frontiers, the dynamics of urbanization is variable. In some areas an intense growth can still be noted, as seen in Northwestern, Western, and Southeastern Paraná. In turn, the rate of urban increase is lower in areas where cattle breeding has replaced farming, such as in the valleys of the rivers Mearim and Pindaré (MA) and the region of Mato Grosso de Goiás (GO).

Final Remarks

The scales of urbanization presented here reflect an urban system subject to very rapid changes. They also point to social inequalities and some disparities in the territorial distribution of the centres. Two kinds of considerations are worthy of mention: one concerns the scales of urbanization themselves. The other concerns their implications for strategies of national urban policy.

The urban-industrial economy has introduced changes into the functions of the cities, which in turn leads to a differentiation of certain subdimensions in the scales of urbanization. In the state of São Paulo, it is possible to identify a polynucleated urban area. In turn, in the Western plateau of the state of São Paulo (*planalto ocidential paulista*), the advance of a capitalistic agriculture and the decline of the rural population have gone a long way to modifying the previous system of central places. Hierarchies based upon traditional regional functions have undergone modifications with respect to a well-balanced distribution of goods and services between the cities and to the rapid emptying out of population in their areas of influence. In the Northeast, greater accessibility to the capitals has lead to the decline of traditional centres and has intensified the tendency to urban primacy, as in Ceará, Alagoas or Sergipe.

The scales of urbanization elicit a number of hypotheses. In general, the scales used to be arranged longitudinally, from the coastline to the interior.

It might now be hypothesized that income patterns get more precarious the greater the distance from the centres of their respective regions.

The scales of urbanization also have implications for urban policy. There should be different strategies for each scale, considering the peculiarity of the problems in each. Investments, resources, and policies ought, therefore, to be applied accordingly. Thus, in the Scale of Metropolitization, where economic growth accumulates in the largest centres, strategies ought to involve problems of equity. Priority also should be given to the rational use of urban soil. In the Scale of Tangency to Metropolitization, where there are varied economic and social conditions, the strengthening of links of the centres with the metropolitan sector should be emphasized. At the Scale of Regional Functions, priorities should be directed to the consolidation of the economic bases of the centres and of their respective areas of influence. The dominant question is how to link the urban sector with the rural sector, by the integration of the urban activities—including agro-industry—with the rational organization of the agrarian space and the exploitation of natural resources.

At the Scale of the Resource Frontier, strategies involve the need to eliminate problems of conflicting land tenure. It is here that the interests of the modern capitalistic enterprise conflict with the traditional occupants of the soil, including the remaining Brazilian aborigines.

Finally, the interactions among the scales of urbanization must be recognized and a national dimension must be given to the structuring of space. Urban policy must consider the influences that cities exercise over others within the urban system. In particular, the interactions promoted by the national metropolises may be interpreted as intersections on all scales of urbanization. These intersections may be expressed in complementarities, divisibilities and other forms of articulation within the prevailing economy. Their optimization would imply strategies aimed at expanding the efficiency-equity dimension of the system. It is desirable that such optimization should incorporate the social experiences of local and regional levels.

NOTES

[1] Situations of Precariousness, which refer to the prevalence of earnings below 200 cruzeiros per month, comprise variations such as Extreme Precariousness, Precarious Situation 1 and Precarious Situation 2; Intermediate Situations, refer to a progressive distinction of the earnings from 200-400 and from 400-1000 cruzeiros per month. There are three degrees—1, 2, 3. Favourable Situations show the share of the highest income groups, (again differentiated into 3 categories).

[2] The total urban population of those centres with over 5,000 inhabitants in 1970.

REFERENCES

Barat, J. and Geiger, P. P. 1973. 'Eśtrutura Econômica das Areas Metropolitanas Brasileiras', *Pesquisa e Planejamento Econômico*, Vol. 3, No. 3.

Chaves, L. F. 1973. 'Análisis descriptive del patrón de asentamiento en Venezuela y sus cambios bajo el impacto de le urbanización', *Revista Geografica* (Universidad de los Andes/Merida, Venezuela).

Davidovich, F. 1977. 'Indústria, In Geografia do Brasil', *Região Sudeste*, IBGE, Rio de Janeiro.

Davidovich, F. and B. De Lima, O. M. 1975. 'Contribuicão ao estudo de aglomeracoes urbanas no Brasil', *Rev. Brasileira de Geografia*, Ano 37, No. 1.

Davidovich, F. and B. De Lima, O. M. 1976. 'Análise das Aglomeracões Urbanas no Brasil', *Rev. Brasileira de Geografia*, Ano 38, No. 4, Rio de Janeiro.

Faissol, S. 1972. 'A Estrutura Urbana Brasileira: uma visão ampliada no contexto do processo brasileiro de desenvolvimento econômico', *Rev. Brasileira de Geografia*, Ano 34, No. 3.

Faissol, S. 1973. 'O Sistema Urbano Brasileiro: uma análise e interpretacao para fins de planejamento', *Rev. Brasileira de Geografia*, Ano 35, No. 4, Rio de Janeiro.

Geiger, P. P. and Davidovich, F. 1974. 'Reflexóes sobre a evolucáo da estrutura espacial do Brasil, sob efeito da industrializacáo', *Rev. Brasileira de Geografia*, Ano 36, No. 3, Rio de Janeiro.

Geiger, P. P., Davidovich, F., Rua, J. and Ribeiro, L. A. 1973. 'Concentracáo urbana no Brasil: 1940-1970', *Pesquisa e Planejamen to Econômico*, Vol. 2, No. 2, IPEA.

Harvey, D. 1973. *Social Justice and the City*, London: Edward Arnold.

de Oliveira, F. and Reichstul, H. P. 1973. 'Mudancas na divisão interregional do trabalho no Brasil', *Estudos Cebrap* (4), São Paulo.

Porcaro, R. M. 1977. 'Industrializacáo e Tamanho Urbano', *Rev. Brasileira de Geografia*, Ano 39, No. 1.

Santos, M. 1971. *La specificité de l'espace en pays sous-developpé: qualques aspects significatifs*, IEDES, Document de travail No. 28, Paris.

Tolosa, H. C. 1973. 'Macro-economia da urbanizacão brasileira', *Pesquisa e Planejamento Econômico*, IPEA, Vol. 3, No. 3, Rio de Janeiro.

21 THE SETTLEMENT SYSTEM OF VENEZUELA

L. F. CHAVES

Definition of the National Settlement System

An interpretation of the national settlement system of Venezuela is only possible using the conceptual framework of a peripheral capitalist social formation. Within peripheral capitalist society, two basic organizations of national settlement systems may be recognized: dendritic and polarized. These two patterns do not exclude each other, since the dendritic organization implies a polarization of the economy towards an external focus, an imperial metropolis, a viceregal submetropolis, or the central capitalist economy.

In a socio-economic space in which several dendritic systems are juxtaposed, as was the case in Venezuela from the eighteenth century to the beginning of the present century, the rank-size curve is characterized by a gentle slope, due to the relatively small size differences among the export centres. From the last quarter of the nineteenth century, Caracas stood out alone among the remaining places, having about twice the population of the second largest settlement. However, the second and third ranked settlements (Cumaná and Maracaibo at the eve of the nineteenth century, but Valencia and Maracaibo around the middle of the century) have always had almost equal populations which were not much larger than those of the urban settlements in the following ranks. The sixth-ranked settlement has always had between one quarter and one sixth of the population of the first. From the sixth or seventh rank down, the slope of the rank-size curve decreases further. The tenth-ranked settlement still ranged between one quarter and one sixth of the population of the first (Chaves, 1964) (Figure 21.1).

When a national market developed in Venezuela, a polarization in space took place in a manner described in the centre-periphery model (Friedmann, 1966). A strong national centre (the capital) appeared, followed by a strong sub-centre in the West (Maracaibo), and a set of agglomerations playing the role of less important regional sub-centres. This structure was evidenced by the rank-size curve which, in 1971, showed a steep slope in the interval between the first and third ranked city (Caracas-Maracaibo and Valencia) and continued with the 'ideal' slope between the third and the thirty-first centres. The remainder (i.e. the 'tail') of the curve went down suddenly (Chaves, 1974: 42-3) (Figure 21.2), a fact which is probably related to a disfunctionality in the urban centres having less than 35,000 inhabitants. The spatial policy of the National Government (5th National Plan), based

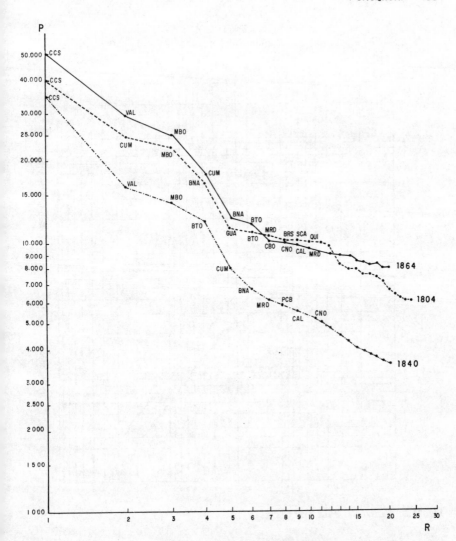

Fig. 21.1 Evolution of the Rank-Size Curve during the Nineteenth Century

on a strengthening of the main regional centres, will probably widen the gap between the regional centres and the smaller sized centres.

In a peripheral capitalist economy based on the export of raw materials and exotic products, the process of spatial differentiation has a selective-cyclical character, determined by fluctuations in international demand. In those areas in which the raw material or food is produced, a central place cluster may appear, which then becomes integrated into the general dendritic system. In Venezuela from about the middle of the eighteenth century to the beginning of the nineteenth century, a cluster of central places appeared in the basin of Lake Valencia, followed by another in the Western

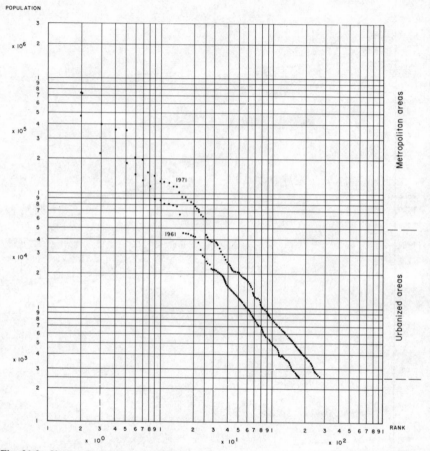

Fig. 21.2 Venezuela: Rank-Size Curves

Llanos. Toward the end of the nineteenth century, an increase in the demand for coffee and cacao generated the growth of central places and settlements specialized in transport functions in the Northeast and the Andes. During the time of the predominance of petroleum, other settlements have arisen whose functions are not those of a central place, but are more specialized, especially in the East (Oriente) and in the basin of Lake Maracaibo. At the end of each cycle, many central places and transport centres lost their former importance. The development of national market, associated with a modern net of highways, creates a national demand for food and raw materials, encouraging growth in selected areas. This leads to the creation or re-activation of agro-industrial settlements. Doubtless this will make the formation of the national settlement system less dependent on the fluctuations in the international market for raw materials and tropical foodstuffs.

Besides the economic dimension of the spatial system there is also a social dimension, characterized by traits such as consumption and housing patterns. A correlation between the economic and the social spatial system may be postulated. In fact, each system is a result of the same process—the reproduction and widening of the capitalist mode of production. In this process, the pre-capitalist modes of production become integrated and subordinated to the dominant mode of production. Differing from the process of reproduction of the capitalist countries, in the underdeveloped countries this process was unable to absorb the labour which deserted the countryside and the traditional industries. Some consequences of this influx were the growth of unemployment and underemployment and the so called 'tertiarization of the economy' through the absorption of the excess active population in insufficiently remunerated services. Several authors, including McGee (1971), as well as Santos (1972), have postulated the existence of a 'lower' sub system or circuit (also called the informal sector by Friedmann and Wulff, 1976). The existence of this circuit leads to a massive growth of the non-basic sector of the urban economy. The distribution of the lower circuit and of the 'culture of poverty' is related to the hierarchy of settlements as the ubiquitous functions are characterized as belonging, to a large degree, to the 'lower tertiary sector'. It is also characterized by high proportions of inadequately remunerated but actively employed population. In contrast, metropolises show high remuneration levels. High remuneration is also found in those centralized industries (located as a direct function of the settlement size as well as an inverse function of the distance to the capital), and in several highly technical and sporadically-located industries such as the petroleum industry.

Within the national settlement system there is a vertical and horizontal differentiation in the geographic patterns of poverty. According to data obtained in 1971 by the Mereavi survey, families having monthly incomes under 1,500 bolivars comprised a little under 60 per cent of the population in the capital (metropolitan area of Caracas), 60-75 per cent in the big agglomerations of the Central Seaboard (Valencia, Maracay), as well as in Maracaibo and Ciudad Guayana, and 76-80 per cent in the agglomerations of Barquisimeto, Barcelona-Puerto La Cruz, San Cristóbal, Maturín, and Valera. In the intermediate sized cities (occasionally in some large peripheral cities, such as Cumaná and Ciudad Bolívar) levels of 80-85 per cent were predominant and in the smallest cities there were even cases of 90 per cent and more. Horizontal differentiation is also evident, with relatively low percentages in some oil cities, such as Ciudad Ojeda (76 per cent), Anaco (74 per cent), Punto Fijo (75 per cent), and El Tigre (78 per cent), or in industrial cities of the Coastal-North-Central region such as La Victoria (77 per cent), Cagua (74 per cent), and Charallave (74 per cent), or in some central places, more particularly in those having administrative and social functions (Figure 21.3).

The most recent tendencies of the national settlement system in Venezuela point toward global metropolization. Between 1961 and 1971 the largest part of the territory lying north of the rivers Boconó, Apure, and Orinoco was losing population from the countryside. To the south of these rivers, the territory was becoming intensively settled in the Western Llanos, between the Boconó, Apure, and Arauca rivers, as well as along the Orinoco. To the north of that line the territory has become metropolized, in a process whose characteristics were: the loss of population in the central business districts of the main metropolises and a strong loss of rural population around the agglomeration, essentially due to the change of category of settlements passing into a suburban classification. The dynamics of growth of non-metropolitan central places were maintained at a low tempo. Due to the expansion of the capitalist mode of production outward from the regional metropolises, central places have become satellites of the latter. Generally speaking, there is a trend to the formation, to the north of the line Boconó-

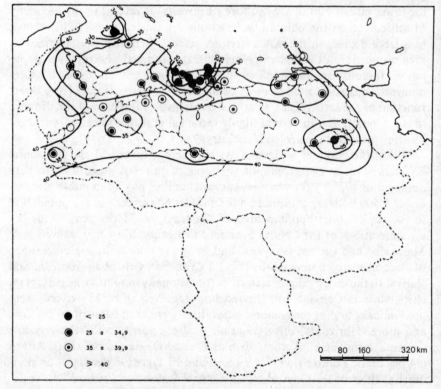

Fig. 21.3 Percentage of Families having Incomes of less than 500 Bolivars, 1971

Apure-Orinoco and in northeastern Guayana, of a mosaic of metropolitan systems, with a megalopolis in active formation in the Coastal North-Central region. (Chaves, 1974)

Historical Growth and Development of the Settlement System

Unlike such countries as Mexico and Peru, the indigenous societies in pre-Columbian Venezuela were only able to organize themselves as village communities, whose geographical base might be relatively weak (nomadic community) or more stable (sedentary community). In the latter case hamlet clusters or even true village settlement systems could emerge under the leadership of the village of the principal *cacique*—the head of a government having theocratic traits—as was the case among the Caquetio of the North-west (Sanoja and Vargas, 1974: 175). The most important villages later became the basis for Spanish settlements (Coro, Mérida, etc.).

The colonial settlement system had as its basis the colonial social formation, integrated by the slave-mercantilist hacienda and Indo-Hispanic modes of production (the latter being of a tributary nature). The colonial formation functioned spatially by having the Spanish metropolis as its focus and the Mexican and Peruvian sub-metropolises as secondary foci. The peripheral spaces of the Spanish Empire, such as Venezuela, were dependent on the metropolis and on one of the sub-metropolises (in the case of Venezuela there was a strong dependence on the Mexican sub-metropolis). Inside these peripheral spaces there were export-oriented areas of slave-hacienda and less mercantilized areas of agricultural production based on the tributary mode of production (*encomiendas, repartimientos*-missions). Areas of mining production were also incorporated into the central economies.

Venezuela, as a peripheral space, was organized as a supplier of the metropolis and the sub-metropolis as early as the beginning of the sixteenth century, when two well-developed, dendritic systems were already formed: the Western system included La Grita, Pedraza, Barinas, Guanare, Mérida, Trujillo, Gibraltar, and Maracaibo, with the last town being the export port to Cartagena, in present-day Columbia. In the West-Central region, Nirgua, Barquisimeto, El Tocuyo, and Carora were integrated into a dendrite confluent to Coro; but some flows from Nirgua were addressed to Valencia. In the coastal North-Central region there were only small circuits between Nirgua, Valencia, and Borburata, as well as San Sebastián, Caracas, and Caraballeda.

The dendritic system became developed in the next two centuries when the pioneering front advanced toward the Orinoco River. This advance was, to a considerable extent, a task accomplished by Roman Catholic missionaries. A new dendrite developed along the river net of the Orinoco basin. Barinas, Pedraza, and Guanare, among other cities in the Western Llanos, became integrated into this dendrite, converging in the first instance, on Puerto de Nutrias, then on San Fernando de Apure and Angostura (the present-day Ciudad Bolívar).

At the beginning of the nineteenth century, clusters of central places arose in the valley of the Tuy River, Caracas, Aragua, and Carabobo (in the Coastal North-Central region) and in the Western Llanos. To a lesser degree the phenomenon of urban clustering arose in the valleys of the Yaracuy, Turbio, and Tocuyo rivers (present states of Lara and Yaracuy). When the slave and tributary components of the colonial formation reached a crisis in the first half of the nineteenth century (culminating when Independence was consolidated between 1821 and 1823), Venezuelan society became one of the big landlords exploiting their lands with the labour of '*peones*', '*vecinos*', '*colonos*', partners, and tenants. The landlord class was associated with a class of German traders who controlled the export trade in the main port cities. Due to the maturation process of the capitalist system, which happened in the last quarter of the nineteenth century, the exporting *latifundista* mode of production became subordinate to foreign capitalist investment and was integrated into the peripheral capitalist formation. A strong increase occurred in the demand for coffee and cacao in international markets. Venezuela developed new areas of coffee production in the Andes and, to a lesser degree, in the Eastern region (Caripe), and of cacao production, especially in the East (Peninsula of Paria). Additionally, gold extraction was developed in the mines of El Callao (state of Bolívar). Thus the Andean states—as well as Sucre and Bolívar—which in 1873 contained 18.8 per cent of the Venezuelan population, had 27.5 per cent by 1920.

At this time, two factors also promoted a policy of railway construction: (1) the interest of the Venezuelan state in bringing export products to international markets, which was coincident with the interest of the buyers in lowering transportation costs from the production areas; and (2) the interest of large financial groups in central capitalist countries in investing in peripheral countries. Big banking groups (such as the *Norddeutsche* Bank and the *Discontogesellschaft* of Germany) participated, as well as manufacturing groups (such as Krupp of Essen). The government of Guzmán Blanco was one of the most prodigal in the granting of railroad concessions, especially in the 1880s.

The coffee and cacao cycle now made central places conspicuous, some having important commercial and financial functions, such as in the Andes, the Northeast, and Guayana. However, the population remained essentially rural. From 1873 to 1920 the number of local cities having 10,000 or more inhabitants increased from six to seven and the ratio of population in them increased from 8.3 to 8.5 per cent. At the beginning of the nineteenth century there were more settlements with over 10,000 inhabitants than in 1920.

At the end of the First World War, the United States replaced Europe as the leading exporter of capital to Venezuela. Petroleum investment became more important than investments in agricultural production: coffee and cacao became less important export commodities. The exploitation of oil brought about consumption patterns which contributed to a national market, even though the population still remained predominantly rural. In some cities of the Coastal North-Central region, administrative and/or military functions developed: Caracas, Maracay, Los Teques, San Juan de Los Morros, etc. The states of Aragua, Carabobo and Miranda, which saw their share in the Venezuelan population reduced from 19.2 to 14.6 per cent during the years 1873 to 1926, began to increase their share again between 1926 and 1936 (from 14.6 to 15.4 per cent). These developments brought an increase in urbanization. The number of localities having 10,000 or more inhabitants increased from 7 in 1920 (comprising 8.5 per cent of the total population) to 22 in 1941 (comprising 23.2 per cent of the total population). Whereas between 1920 and 1936 (Comezian times) rural-urban migration was 68,000 persons, between 1636 and 1941 (post-Comezian times) it was 174,000 persons (Páez Celis, 1975: 49).

The embryo of urban Venezuela grew to maturity in the next decades. Data collected by Corrales and Giordani have shown (*see* graph by Travieso, 1972: 70) the changes occurring during the Second World War, when a rise in the production of oil (beginning in 1942) was accompanied by a rise in manufacturing production. The rise in oil production and export continued its strong growth until 1958-62, when a stabilization took place.

With the increase in oil production, the Venezuelan state (with the Hydrocarbons Law of 1943) obtained a series of new, heretofore unknown benefits (de la Plaza, Rísquez-Iribarren and Güerere Añez, 1973: 51-62). The increase in petroleum income was responsible for the construction of an infrastructure. In fact, this time period corresponds with the construction of the modern highways, uniting the dendritic system into which the Venezuelan space had been divided.

The number of localities having 10,000 and more inhabitants increased from 22 in 1941 (23.2 per cent of the total population) to 37 in 1950 (36.4 per cent) and to 72 in 1961 (47.2 per cent). During this time the Venezuelan population moved out of a predominantly rural condition. Beginning in the intercensal period 1941-50, the annual urbanization rates were maintained at over 30 per thousand. The growth of the urbanization levels in the decennial intercensus periods have been over 10 per cent and the growth of urban population as a ratio of the total population has been over 90 per cent. The urban population absorbed almost all the intercensus growth or even took population from the countryside (in relative as well as absolute numbers). The shift of population was not only vertical (i.e., toward the highest ranks in the hierarchy), but there was a horizontal displacement toward the oil production centres of the Coastal North-Central region (Otremba, 1954).

About 1958 there was a decrease in investment in oil, followed by a relative stabilization in production. The oil producing states began to lose their relative importance in the aggregate national economy. As a matter of fact, in Monagas the gross territorial product per capita in 1970 (Gerbasi, 1971) had decreased since 1953 (Uslar Pietri, 1958), from 5,966 to 2,434 bolivars. Zulia was displaced from the third to the eighteenth and Monagas from the fifth to the penultimate state. The above states, which in 1961 held 20.6 per cent of the Venezuelan population, contained only 19.6 per cent in 1971.

On the other hand, the Federal District increased its GTP per capita from 4,312 bolivars to 5,069 bolivars, Aragua from 1,580 to 3,584 bolivars, Miranda from 1,410 to 7,310 bolivars and Bolívar from 1,511 to 3,427 bolivars. The states of the Coastal North-Central region, between 1961 and 1971, increased their share in the national population from 15.8 to 19.2 per cent which was larger than the increase of the Federal District (16.7 to 17.4 per cent) while Bolívar increased its share from 2.8 to 3.6 per cent. The basis for this growth was industrialization by import substitution.

In this stage the metropolitization process had its beginnings. In 1961, five settlements having 100,000 or more inhabitants (Caracas, Maracaibo, Barquisimeto, Valencia, and Maracay) accounted for 27.0 per cent of the Venezuelan population; in 1971, sixteen settlements of this size accounted for 39.2 per cent and one half of the Venezuelan population was concentrated in 33 settlements having 50,000 and more inhabitants. If metropolitan areas are considered instead of individual settlements, by 1971 50.5 per cent of the Venezuelan population was concentrated in fifteen metropolitan areas having 100,000 inhabitants or more. As a matter of fact, the construction of highways suggests that the incorporation of former cities and towns into metropolitan areas is actually higher than is shown by the statistical data.

The most conspicuous fact is the megalopolization of an extensive area between the states of Carabobo and Miranda. In Caracas, after a big leap in the previous stages, growth has become more moderate. In the basin of Lake Valencia, Maracay and Valencia have, with Ciudad Guayana, the highest relative growth among the big Venezuelan metropolises, but the highest rate occurs in the minor cities, located between the two metropolises. According to one estimate for 1971, about one third of the Venezuelan population resided in that densely settled and urbanized area (Chaves, 1974:46).

In addition to the megalopolis, large urban complexes have tended to develop around Maracaibo, the polycentric oil-producing conurbation, as well as the new manufacturing city of El Tablazo. In other areas, there are minor city clusters (Margarita, the valley of Yaracuy as well as the area of Carúpano, in the state of Sucre), with the most conspicuous urban growth occurring in Ciudad Guayana, whose population increased 370 per cent between 1961 and 1971.

The present tendencies suggest that in 1981 Venezuela has about 85 per cent of the urban population in settlements which have 2,500 and more inhabitants. The growth of the urbanization level, which has been in decline over the intercensus period, will decrease to only 9 or 10 points. From this moment onwards, Venezuela will enter the mature stage of the urbanization process; the next increases, following Davidovich's rule, will become progressively smaller.

It is likely that, for 1981, the population in agglomerations (metropolitan areas) having 100,000 and more inhabitants will reach two thirds of the total population. The policy of industrial deconcentration is summarized as follows: (*a*) promotion of the departure of manufacturing plants from the metropolitan area of Caracas; (*b*) non-encouragement of industrialization in Aragua, Carabobo, and Miranda; (*c*) special inducements for industrialization in the conurbations of the interior, such as Maracaibo, Barquisimeto, Barcelona-Puerto La Cruz, Ciudad Guayana, and the axis San Cristóbal-La Fria. The problem of the stagnation of minor cities which is evidenced by the existence of a truncated rank-size curve (Friedmann and Alonso, 1964:148.), has been disregarded by the national government. These settlements are likely to become incorporated into the expanding metropolitan economies either as suburbs or as satellites.

The Present Structure of the Settlement System

Travieso and his collaborators postulate the theory of the underdevelopment pole, a core area of dependent growth. According to this model, an underdeveloped country in the stage of industrialization through import substitution, as is the case of Venezuela, is characterized by a centre where final manufacturing industries are based on the import of semi-finished products. These inputs, added to the final product of the national market, generate profits for transnational companies and conglomerates (Travieso, 1972:100, 118).

We have postulated that the dependent capitalist economy is diffused from a centre (in this case the national capital), as a direct function of the size of the receiving settlement and as an inverse function of its distance from the diffusing settlement. The industrialization process arrives more quickly at the nearer settlements, even if small; at longer distances only the larger settlements are affected. Díaz Gonzalez showed with 1971 data that six out of the nine industries considered depended in their spatial distribution on the size of settlement/distance ratio to Caracas (1975:28-29). This explains the formation of a heartland based on manufacturing as well as the emergence of a process of megalopolization.

Inside the Venezuelan socio-economic space, the megalopolis is characterized by the most complete range of services in the national settlement system as well as by the maximum industrial diversification. Functional diversification depends on the presence of a big market, which attracts the investment of the transnational companies and conglomerates. Inside the megalopolis, a particular spatial distribution of functions exists. For instance, Maracay is a pole for the manufacturing of textiles and Valencia for the vehicle industry and related industries. In the minor cities, the specialization may be even greater. The fact that almost three quarters of the value added in manufacturing is produced in an area which contains only about one third of the population (i.e., the megalopolis), clearly points up deficiencies in the interior regional metropolises, at least in manufacturing.

After the regional metropolises, in the urban hierarchy, are intermediate sized cities (15,000-50,000 inhabitants) providing central functions. In large part they are being transformed into satellites, or specialized settlements, agro-commercial, or administrative. Finally, the smallest settlements (i.e., the 'tail' of the rank-size curve), have tended to become dormitory places or other types of suburbs, as they are not able to compete efficiently with larger sized settlements. Those which are not able to become satellites due to their relative isolation, vegetate by fulfilling a few ubiquitous functions.

Urban Agglomerations as Systems within the National System

With Venezuela having about 66 per cent of its population in metropolitan areas of 100,000 inhabitants or more, 75 per cent in metropolitan areas of 50,000 inhabitants or more and 85 per cent in urban centres having 2,500 inhabitants or more, a functional model of the national settlement system should be based on large conurbations, not on individual cities. Some conurbations are closely integrated with others, thus resulting in true conurbations and even megalopolises, while others remain relatively independent, as centres of regions.

The megalopolis is formed by two big sub-systems. The first is the polycentric conurbation integrated by the metropolitan area of Caracas (estimated at about three million inhabitants in 1981). Included are two big metropolises having more than 100,000 inhabitants each: the Central Seaboard (La Guaira, Maiquetía, Catia La Mar, Macuto, Caraballeda, and Naiguatá) and Ciudad Fajardo (Guarenas-Guatire) as well as two metropolises having more than 50,000 inhabitants: Los Teques and Ciudad Losada (Middle Tuy). The second sub-system is formed by the twin agglomerations in the basin of Lake Valencia: Maracay (with Turmero, San Mateo, Palo Negro, and Cagua) and Valencia with the port and manufacturing metropolis of Puerto Cabello-Morón having more than 100,000 inhabitants and Guacara, with over 50,000 inhabitants. Between Cuacara and Maracay are two other urban centres, San Joaquín and Mariara. In 1981 the urban agglomeration formed around Valencia and Maracay had over 1,000,000 inhabitants. Between the sub-systems of Lake Valencia, the metropolis of La Victoria, and the polycentric conurbation of Caracas, are the manufacturing cities of the upper Tuy (El Consejo, Las Tejerías and Paracotos). The cities of western Carabobo (Bejuma, Miranda, and Montalbán) and southeastern Yaracuy (Nirgua), as well as the cities of northern Cojedes (Tinaquillo, Tinaco, San Carlos) are actually satellites of Valencia. The towns of eastern Falcón may be mentioned as 'vacation suburbs'. In the west (Occidente) Maracaibo, which reached one million inhabitants in 1981, is associated with Altagracia, and includes the manufacturing complex of El Tablazo, which attained 50,000 inhabitants, and may even have reached 100,000. To the south, on the eastern shores of Lake Maracaibo, there are two petroleum cities, Cabimas and Lagunillas-Ciudad Ojeda, each having over 100,000 inhabitants. The complex polycentric conurbation is complemented with minor cities, such as Santa Rita, Mene Grande, Bachaquero, and La Victoria, to the south of Lagunillas-Ciudad Ojeda.

Another important sub-system is the continental Central-West, including such cities as Barquisimeto, with over half a million inhabitants, Acarigua-Araure, with over 100,000 and San Felipe, with over 50,000. Barquisimeto, growing beyond its traditional boundaries, is extending toward Cabudare and Los Rastrojos. In the state of Yaracuy, an urban cluster, including San Felipe-Corcorote, Chivacoa and Yaritagua appears as a 'bridge' between the Central-Western system and the megalopolis. Between and around Vabudare and Acarigua-Araure, settlements are growing dynamically, and many will be influenced by the construction of the Central-Western highway.

The next sub-system is Guayana with two cities having over 100,000 inhabitants, Ciudad Guayana and Ciudad Bolívar. The growth forces have been mining, hydroelectricity, iron and steel, and electro-chemicals. Another subsystem is Falcón, with a metropolis having more than 100,000 inhabitants (Punto-Fijo–Carirubana–Punta Cardón–Cardón) and another having more than 50,000 inhabitants (Coro).

The remaining socio-economic space is formed by a mosaic of ungrouped metropolises. In the Northeast the most important metropolitan aggregate is Barcelona-Puerto La Cruz, including Guanta, Lecherías and Pozuelos, with about 250,000 inhabitants. The other more or less autonomous metropolitan areas are Cumaná, Maturín, and El Tigre-San José de Guanipa-San Tomé, each having more than 50,000 inhabitants.

In the Southwest, the most important metropolitan aggregate is San Cristóbal-Táriba-Palmira, which has transformed Rubio into a satellite and is integrating San Juan de Colón, La Fría, and other minor towns into the so-called 'San Cristóbel-La Fría axis', planned as one of Venezuela's big centres of manufacturing. Other important conurbations are those of Valera-Trujillo and Mérida-Ejido, each having more than 100,000 inhabitants, as well as Guanare and Barinas, each having more than 50,000 inhabitants. Although functional autonomy is postulated for these metropolises, the existence of dependency relations with Barquisimeto (especially in the case of Guanare and Barinas), Maracaibo, and San Cristóbal is obvious.

In any urban economy, there are two sectors: basic or exogenous, and non-basic or endogenous. In a dependent urban economy, however, the relationship between the two sectors is distinctive. With a high degree of foreign investment, resultant capital-intensive technology, and the export of profits, the capacity of the exogenous sector to generate employment in the endogenous sector (the multiplier effect), is limited. Therefore a subsector or circuit emerges independent of the exogenous sector for its functioning.

Within the 'lower circuit', there are high indices of underemployment and unemployment and a proliferation of employment in the tertiary sector (Chaves, 1973a). In a 1976 report the Council for National Economy estimated that in the poor districts ('*barrios*'), more than 50 per cent of the population was unemployed. Moreover, an estimated 72 per cent of the total labour force in the 'lower circuit' is concentrated in seven economic branches: agriculture, construction, retail, government services, domestic services, other personal services, and not well specified activities. In addition, there are manufacturers of the handicraft or repair type which, strictly speaking, belong to the tertiary and not to the secondary sector. The proportion of employment in the 'lower circuit' tends to decrease in the metropolitan economies, due to the presence of sporadic functions whose employment is related to the city size (by a power function whose exponent is over 1) and to the relatively high concentration of employment in the 'upper circuit'.

Summarizing, the megalopolis furnishes the metropolitan functions, especially those having the highest rank in the hierarchy (only found in Caracas) as well as the market-oriented industries developed on the basis of technological dependency. Manufacturing of durable consumer goods, or the processing of intermediate goods are found side-by-side with the traditional industries, which essentially produce non-durable goods. Both the intermediate and the semi-finished goods are predominantly of foreign origin. In counterbalance, there are some industries of a particular geographical orientation, such as the agro-industries or the fishing industries, intermediate industries such as petro-chemicals, iron and steel, and oil refining, and/or services to the petroleum industry. Commerce and transport may be important as intermediaries between an agricultural and mining hinterland and the industrialized economies of the megalopolis. Non-metropolitan settlements, especially those of intermediate size (15,000-50,000 inhabitants), both central and non-central, have tended to become complements of the metropolitan economies.

The inner differentiation of the Venezuelan metropolises is not essentially different from that of the Western metropolises. However, the social dimensions of the metropolitan space have not been extensively studied. Acosta (1973) has proposed several hypotheses to explain the location of the so-called *'barrios de ranchos'* (shanty towns). According to her, these *'barrios'* are located in areas whose physical characteristics are so unfavourable that their profitable exploitation is almost impossible, even under conditions of private property. Other factors influencing the distribution of *'barrios de ranchos'* are nearness to (1) the main routes leading into the city; (2) developments of popular housing; (3) industrial areas and other workplaces; (4) high class housing (being a possible workplace in which 'marginal' people may provide domestic services). Andressen (1970, 1972) shows that these factors may, at least initially, have some significance in the population density in the *'barrios de ranchos'* of Caracas: the significance of distance to the conurbation centre and of topography was shown statistically for the first stage of development (1959), but there is also a correlation with distance to workplaces. Acosta also shows that the *'barrios de ranchos'* are of relatively minor importance in the cities of the North-Central Coastal region, the more immediately neighbouring areas of the West Central region, in the Far North, a part of the Eastern Llanos, and the northeastern corner of Guayana, as well as the Andes. At least in part, this distribution corresponds to areas having more family groups based on marriage. By contrast, in the cities of the Llanos and a part of the Northeast, with family groups based on consensual coupling, the *'barrios de ranchos'* are relatively more important (50 per cent or more of total houses). The internal organization of Venezuelan cities has some common traits. For instance, the area neighbouring the central business district is a zone of old houses whose high rent cannot be paid by one family alone. They are transformed into boarding houses for students and/or migrants. As another instance, when the available municipal lands become exhausted, there is speculation, manifested in the presence of relatively large areas of vacant land rapidly increasing in value.

The scarcity of housing and land has led the state to create urban neighbourhoods of single or multi-family housing far from the city centre, where the land cost is lower but the cost of installation of services is higher. Land developers profit, receiving services at low cost for private housing developments near the neighbourhoods built and serviced by the State. Some municipal councils with large financial resources have bought land on the outskirts of the city, making their future growth more rational (e.g., Ciudad Guayana). But in the case of municipal councils with smaller resources (e.g., Mérida), the State has been obliged to interfere directly through the acquisition of land, drawing on a special national fund. This policy is presently being revised. Now higher-cost land which is more accessible for the extension of services, is preferred. In sum, structural schemes produced in the developed countries are difficult to apply to Venezuela. Models would have to take into account the extensive land occupation by squatters, the monopoly of land ownership, and land speculation by landlords and urbanizers, as well as State policies promoting social development.

Political and Administrative Functions and Centres— Their Role in the Development of the National Settlement System

An analysis of Venezuelan administrative history reveals two models of administrative organization, corresponding to different social formations and to different settlement systems. In the first place there is the province-city-state formation (Brewer-Carías and Izquierdo Corser, 1977:30), administratively centralized and politically as well as militarily decentralized, which is typical of the colonial *latifundista* and even of the agricultural stage of the peripheral capitalist formation. It is also typical of the dendritic structure and functioning of the socio-economic space, with which a truncated shallow slope rank-size curve is associated. This was the situation in 1804 (Figure 21.1). Later on the central places in the north grew and the curve took a different form. The second model, beginning with the rural-oil producing stage of peripheral capitalism, corresponded to an incipient capitalist stage, controlled by a military apparatus which was the guarantee for the foreign investment in the face of the regional *caudillos*. In these circumstances space tended to be polarized by the national capital and other cities constituting the regional base for a central bureaucratic-military complex. Thus, the rank-size curve not only increased its slope but also tended to become truncated again.

The present stage of the reproduction and extension of the capitalist mode of production, is one in which the population tends to be organized in a system of metropolitan systems covering the largest part of the most populated area of the country, and in which the State has been transformed (through transnational companies and national monopolies), into an essential factor of social (including spatial) formation. Thus, the centralist structure of the State tends to become obsolete. This is due not only to excessive centralization which creates diseconomies of scale, making the system function less efficiently, but also because the spatial enlargement of the capitalist mode of production leads to decentralization. The regionalization of development has been adopted as a goal by the State and this also implies a decentralization and deconcentration of investment. To accomplish this goal, regional development corporations have been created which also have planning functions. But a programmed decentralization is difficult to implement because the execution must be realized through obsolete politico-territorial entities.

Future Structure and Patterns of the National Settlement System

It is evident that an inevitable and irreversible process of the metropolitization of the Venezuelan population is occurring. In some urban clusters (Margarita, Yaracuy), the principal centres are united with secondary centres (Punta de Piedras, Chivacoa) and minor urban settlements to create integrated but diffuse metropolitan complexes. To the south of Lake Maracaibo another autonomous nucleus may emerge in El Vigía, if the construction of a motor road for fast traffic does not lead to the formation of a bicentric conurbation at Mérida-El Vigía. In some cases, the State itself has contributed to the transformation of urban clusters into urban agglomerations (as in the case of Ciudad Losada and Ciudad Fajardo). There are still some cities, such as San Carlos (state of Cojedes) or the aggregate Caicara-Cabruta (on the banks of the Orinoco River) that, because of their location may, in future, become centres of some importance.

In addition, with the policy of industrial deconcentration, the National Government tends to favour the big urban centres of the interior. The discovery of big oil deposits between the Portuguesa river and the delta of the Orinoco river and between the Orinoco and the line Calabozo-Valle de la Pascua-El Tigre-Maturín (Orinoco belt) in an area relatively sparsely settled and urbanized, may lead in the future, when oil exploitation begins, to the strengthening of some centres in the periphery of the belt as well as to the creation of new settlements. It is also possible that the Programme for the Alto Llano Occidental (PIALLO), and for the 'High Western Llanos', for the agricultural development of the territory in the zone contiguous to the Andes and the Western Llanos, the Portuguesa, and the Arauca rivers, may intensify the settlement in the Western Llanos and create new urban settlements in that area.

If we exclude physically difficult areas such as: (1) mountainous zones (Perijá, the Andes, Serranía del Interior etc.); (2) semi-arid zones (Falcón and Lara); (3) flat areas subject to inundation (Low Llanos and the Deltas of the Orinoco and Catatumbo rivers); (4) arid plains (the Gulf of Venezuela); and, (5) mesas having poor soils (Eastern Llanos), the remaining territory of Venezuela is easily accessible to large urban agglomerations. We should point out that land reclamation may lead to the expansion of the settled area, and result in the creation of new central places, which may become integrated into the megalopolis.

Under conditions of strong metropolitization, increases in commuting will also lead to the conversion of small towns into suburbs. The growth of minor cities will be encouraged more by the transfer of metropolitan investments to the suburbs rather than through productive investment.

One of the problems associated with the development of national settlement systems is that of the organization of local administration. We believe that there is no clear and/or distinct orientation which integrates a policy of territorial organization at municipal and regional level.

REFERENCES

Acosta L. M., 1973. 'Urbanización y clases sociales en Venezuela'. *Revisto Interamericana de Planificación*, 7, 26: 22-44.
Andressen, R., 1970. 'Densidad de población en las áreas de ranchos de Caracas y su

relación con el número de viviendas, topografía y distancia al centro de la ciudad'. *Revista Geográfica*, 19, 24-5: 5-25.

Andressen, R., 1972. *Densidad de población en las áreas de ranchos de Caracas y su relación con el número de viviendas, topografía y distancia al centro de la ciudad.* Mérida.

Brewer-Carias, A. R. and Izquierdo Corser, N., 1977. *Estudios sobre la regionalización en Venezuela.* Caracas, Universidad Central de Venezuela, Ediciones de la Biblioteca.

Chaves, L. F., 1964. *La Ciudad venezolana de mediados del siglo XIX.* Universidad de Los Andes, Facultad de Ciencias Forestales.

Chaves, L. F., 1973a. *Estructura funcional de las ciudades venezolanas.* Mérida, Universidad de Los Andes, Facultad de Ciencias Forestales, Instituto de Geografía y Conservación de Recursos Naturales.

Chaves, L. F. 1973b. 'Análisis descriptivo del patrón de asentamiento en Venezuela y sus cambios bajo el impacto de la urbanización'. *Revista Geográfica*, 14, 1-2: 5-51.

Chaves, L. F. 1974. *Proceso y patrón espacial de la urbanización durante el período 1961-1971.* Mérida, Universidad de Los Andes, Facultad de Ciencias Forestales. Instituto de Geografía y Conservación de Recursos Naturales.

Chossudovsky, M., 1977. *La miseria en Venezuela: mapa de la pobreza en Venezuela.* Valencia (Venezuela), Vadell Hermanos.

Diaz Gonzalez, R. 1975. *Clasificación de las ciudades venezolanas según la estructura espacial de la oferta de la actividad económica, 1971.* Mérida, Universidad de Los Andes, Facultad de Ciencias Forestales, Escuela de Geografia.

Friedmann, J., 1966. *Regional development policy: a case study of Venezuela.* Cambridge, Mass.: MIT Press.

Friedmann, J. and Alonso, W., (ed.) 1964. *Regional development and planning: a reader.* Cambridge, Mass.: MIT Press.

Friedmann, J. and Wulff, R., 1976. 'The urban transition: comparative studies of newly industrializing societies'. *Progress in Geography: international review of current research*, 8: 1-93.

Funes, J. C. (ed.) 1972. *La ciudad y la región para el desarrollo*, Caracas, Comisión de Administración Pública de Venezuela.

Gerbasi, J., 1971. 'El Impacto del proceso de desarrollo en el nivel de vida de los venezolanos'. *Diario El Nacional.* 3 de agosto de 1971, D2.

Humboldt, A. von, 1965. *Biafe a las regiones equinocciales del Nuevo Continente.* Caracas, Ediciones del Ministerio de Educación, Dirección de Cultura y Bellas Artes, 5 v.

McGee, T. G., 1971. *The urbanization process in the Third World: explorations in search of theory.* London, C. Bell and Sons.

Otremba, E., 1954. 'Entwicklung und Wandlung der venezolanischen Kulturlandschaft unter der Herrschaft des Erdöles', *Erdkunde* 8, 3, 169-88.

Paez Celis, J., 1975. *Ensayo sobre demografía exonómica de Venezuela.* 2nd ed. Caracas, eduven.

Plaza, S de la. Risquez-Iribarren, W., and Guerere Añez, V., 1973, *Breve historia del petróleo y su legislación en Venezuela.* Caracas, Crafiunica.

Pollak-Eltz, A., 1976. *La familia negra en Venezuela.* Caracas, Monte Avila Editores.

Sanoja, M. and Vargas, I., 1974. *Antiguas formaciones y modos de producción venezolanos: notas para el estudio de los procesos de integración de la sociedad venezolana (12,000 A.C.-1,900 D.C.)* Caracas, Monte Avila Editores.

Santos, M. 1972. 'Los dos circuitos de la economía urbana en los países subdesarrollados', in: Funes, J. C. (ed.) *op.cit.* 1972: 69-99.

Travieso, F. 1972. *Ciudad, región y subdesarrollo.* Caracas, Fondo Editorial Común.

Uslar Pietri, A. 1958. *Sumario de economía venezolana para alivio de estudiantes.* Caracas, Fundación Mendoza.

Venezuela. Corporación de Los Andes, 1971. *Estudio de la base económica de Valera.* Mérida.

Venezuela. Presidencia de la República, 1976. 'V Plan de la Nación' *Gaceta Oficial de Venezuela*, Año 103, mes 6, N 1860. Extraordinaria (11 de marzo), 2-95.

PART C

SETTLEMENT SYSTEMS IN THE DEVELOPING WORLD

Section 7: Settlement on Old Lands and in Higher-Density Regions

22 THE NATIONAL SETTLEMENT SYSTEM OF INDIA

MANZOOR ALAM

Although many of the urban settlements in India are of great antiquity, a national settlement system only emerged during the period of colonial rule in the mid-nineteenth century with the building of the railway network. This network increased the mobility of goods and people, reduced physical distances between settlements, and enhanced their interdependence. The evolution of a national settlement system was further reinforced with the rapid development of a road transport system in India in the post-Second World War period. While recognizing the fact that recent factors are more relevant to an understanding of the settlement system-forming processes in India, the national system can be better appreciated if it is examined in historical perspective, because of the antiquity of the country's urban civilization.

Historical Growth and Development

The origin of the settlement pattern lies far back in the early valley-stage civilization (Basham, 1971). Valuable information regarding the distribution of settlement units lies scattered in various mythological and religious literature and in records of archaeological research. One can conclude on the basis of these sources that by about the fourth century BC, the whole subcontinent had come to possess a fairly large number of settlements of varying functional character. More than 600 settlement units (163 towns and 441 villages), spread over the whole country, have been referred to in ancient Puranic and Buddhist literature alone as existing by AD 700 (Law, 1954).

Villages were the fundamental socio-economic units. Various size-groups of villages were recognized—*Gamaka* (small), *Gama* (ordinary), *Nigamagama* (big), *Dvaragama* (suburban), *Panchhantagama* (a frontier/border village) (Dube, 1967). These units ranged in size from 2-3 house clusters to villages of a thousand families. That considerable thought had been given to the study of villages differentiated on the basis of their form (such as openbowl, circular etc.), is evident in Jain canonical texts (Mukerjee, 1972).

Functional categorizations of villages have also been made. Puranic literature refers to villages as *Grama* (without market), *Pura* (with market), *Durga* (fort), *Pattana* (port), *Ghosa* (milkmen settlement), *Khata* (agricultural), and *Khamata* (near markets). There are many references in the Tamil Sangam literature (the earliest *Sangam* is dated 3,000 BC) to the territorial organization of the peninsula into five geographic divisions and the associated characteristics of communities and settlements in these regions. Here again functional categories of settlements and their spatial structures are described. Studies of ancient Tamil poetry of the earliest Sangam period lead us to the conclusion that peninsular India must have had even by this time a well organized and clearly demarcated settlement structure consisting of numerous well planned *nagarams* (towns) and *gramas* (villages). Madurai, Vanji, Poompuhar, for example, which exist today, date back to Sangam days (Basham, 1971).

As seen in the works cited above, the fertile, alluvial plains of the Indo-Gangetic system and riverine tracts, and the coastlines in peninsular India were dotted with numerous settlements. As agricultural communities prospered, accumulated wealth, and acquired technology and power, the political system and trade activities came to play a prominent role in shaping settlement patterns. Settlements located in appropriate sites developed into capitals or commercial towns. But political systems were subject to frequent changes which were reflected in the changing location of capital cities, fortresses, or defence towns.

Urban centres date back to prehistoric days, but there is no record of continuity in the urban tradition, at least where urban form or distribution is concerned (Smailes, 1968). What is clear and well substantiated is that cities of the historic period were expressions of imperial expansion and the intrusion of conquerors who sought security in urban concentrations. The fortresses and trading posts attracted accretions of indigenous peasant communities. Thus one can conclude that ancient urban centres acted as nodes which integrated communities and settlements directly or indirectly within the jurisdiction of the authority housed in the urban centre. As both agriculture and trade were the chief economic activities large numbers of market towns came to be established in pre-industrial India. In the south especially, trade connections across the Indian Ocean led to the emergence of many littoral kingdoms, such as the Kalinga, Pallava, Chera, and Pandyan, each with its capital city and leading ports. Port towns and inland towns, well connected with each other through natural routes, added another component to the settlement structure of this early period in South India.

Periods of political stability also stimulated religious and cultural activities. Religious establishments such as temples, monasteries, and *dargahs* (shrines of Muslim saints), and cultural centres like universities added to the importance of the settlements, transforming them into urban status. The construction of national highways, well maintained with shade-giving trees and rest houses, stimulated inter-regional traffic and many *serai* towns came into existence (Sinha, 1976). But it is the capital cities which dominated and organized the settlement system in any region with roads converging on/and radiating from them. These roads served administrative, military, trade, religious, and cultural traffic and stimulated the growth of new towns as well. It is during Moghul rule, especially in Akbar's reign (1556-1605), that a systematic division of the country led to a proliferation of administrative and garrison towns all linked to the capital city, Agra, by national highway (Naqvi, 1969). Western India and the Deccan showed a spurt in the growth of urban centres (new forts and administrative headquarters) as a result of Shivaji's (1646-1680) defence and administrative measures and the rise of Deccan kingdoms on the break-up of the Bahmani Kingdom.

The later Maratha kingdoms (1680-1707), the Sultanates of Eastern India and the Deccan, each added to the complexity of the urban mosaic in this period. But in general the earlier pattern formed by the administrative headquarters of the provinces or *Subas* (made up of major urban nodes, and sub-nodes of market towns within an agriculture-oriented economy), was not much disturbed. It can be said to underlie even the present regional settlement pattern in many parts of the country. The earlier urban centres, with a much reduced jurisdiction, still serve as nodes of mini-settlement systems.

Urbanization Factors During the Colonial Period 1757-1946

The break-up of the Moghul Empire, expansion of British political control over India after 1757, the development of rail and canal networks since the mid-nineteenth century, the commercialization of crop culture, the emergence of the expatriate settlements of Calcutta, Bombay, and Madras as the key ports of India and as centres of finance, banking, and industry, and the political division of the country into British India and princely India, each with distinctly different political and economic systems, markedly influenced India's urban mosaic during the colonial period.

The expansion of British political control gave a new dimension to urban development in India. Unlike the feudal cities of medieval India which were largely consumption-oriented the British introduced production-based urban centres with a monetary-based economic system typical of the development of towns in a capitalist society. The concentration of investment in industries and commerce in and around the port towns of Calcutta and Bombay led to their development as powerful urban magnets and primate cities. While the fort towns represented the defence settlements during the medieval period, the British established a large number of unwalled garrison towns or cantonments as discrete urban units exclusively for the use of the armed forces of the British rulers. These were located either adjacent to the existing towns and formed part of the urban complex, such as in Meerut, Poona, Allahabad, and Bangalore, or were founded as independent new towns such as Secunderabad, Sagar, Mhow, and Kamptee.

The greatest incentive to urbanization during the colonial period was provided by the twin and almost simultaneous development of the rail network and the irrigation canal systems during the mid-nineteenth century (Schwartzberg, 1978). During the initial phase of rail development (1853-75)

Bombay was linked with its agriculturally productive hinterland, which also possessed canal irrigation facilities, and with strategically important towns such as the capital cities of major princely states, Baroda, Hyderabad, Gwalior, Bangalore. By 1925 a mature rail network had emerged serving the cotton belt of India, and the canal irrigation areas of the Cauvery and Krishna-Godavari deltas in the south and the Indo-Gangetic plains in the north. By then Calcutta, Bombay, Madras, and Delhi were interlinked. The emergence of these rail lines re-oriented the inland trade routes of India, and encouraged new centres of production, trade, and commerce. The railway system was focused around Calcutta and Bombay primarily to serve the defence and commercial needs of the colonial powers in India. The railway lines were also instrumental in inducing the growth of a number of independent towns. The influence of the railway network on the distribution of towns and their size is underlined by the fact that, except for the hill towns of Shillong and Srinagar, all large towns with populations exceeding 100,000 are located along the rail lines.

The introduction of the modern canal system between 1850-1900, in the Cauvery and Krishna-Godavari deltas in South India and in the Indo-Gangetic plains in the north, laid the foundation for commercial agriculture and, supported by the rail network, stimulated the development of market settlements and agro-industrial based urbanization. Numerous towns in the Punjab (Bhatinda, Jalalabad) and Rajasthan (Suratgarh, Padampur) are the outcome of the transformation of purely agriculture-based rural settlements into a system of urban market centres based on agricultural surplus. Canals could not generate extensive urbanization without the supporting facilities—largely the railways—for the bulk movement of surplus agricultural products. Thus the major commercial towns of India, excluding the million population cities, such as Vijayawada, Kumbakonam, Hapur, Ludhiana, are located both in the canal-irrigated zone and along the railways. Agriculturally prosperous pockets in India are positively correlated with a well-established canal and rail network, have a fairly high level of urbanization, are noted for large clusters of medium to small size urban centres, and possess a well articulated system of settlement. This is fairly well susbtantiated by the settlement systems of the Punjab (Bhat, 1976) and the Krishna-Godavari deltas (Alam, 1976).

The introduction of tea plantations in Assam in the early nineteenth century and the cultivation of cash crops such as jute and cotton exclusively for export, created new pockets of economic prosperity and urban development (Munsi, 1980). They generated the rise of the plantation settlements of Shillong and Darjeeling and induced the growth of small and medium-sized urban settlements in the cotton belts of Maharashtra and Tamilnadu. Sholapur and Coimbatore are good examples of towns in this category.

The emergence of industries based on cash crops—jute and cotton— around the expatriate port cities of Calcutta and Bombay and the concentration of export-import trade and banking in these cities, supported by the rail and road network which linked them to their hinterlands, induced hyper-concentration of urban centres around these cities leading to the formation of conurbations. Consequently, Calcutta and Bombay became the most attractive urban settlements for job seekers. They eventually emerged as primate cities within their respective urban systems, commanding an extensive and productive hinterland. Barring a few isolated inland industrial towns such as Kanpur, Ahmadabad, and Coimbatore, the major manufacturing belts were focused around these two ports and, to a minor degree, around the port of Madras in south India.

Another important factor influencing the pattern and character of urbanization in India was the political division of the country, prior to Independence in 1947, into British India and Princely India. The Princely states of India were essentially consumer-oriented societies and were marked by their low level of agricultural and industrial development and consequent low level of urban development. Being a feudal society the development was concentrated in the capital cities, and therefore, most of them had a primate-city pattern of development. These primate cities in the Princely states developed as parasites on their agricultural hinterlands. In British India urbanization had spread outside the primate cities of Calcutta and Bombay into those relatively better developed prosperous areas based on either plantation agriculture or cash crops and supported by canal irrigation. Even the district headquarters in British India had gained urban status with a tertiary economic base. Hence, in 1901, those cities with populations exceeding 100,000 were concentrated in British India (Figure 22.1).

Post-Independence Urbanization Factors

In the post-Independence period the introduction of Five Year Development Plans since 1951, as well as the creation of new states and the multiplication of administrative districts and *taluqs/tahsils* (lower revenue administrative units) in each state, has led to the rise of new capital cities for the newly created states and to an increasingly wide scatter of urban settlements supported largely by a weak tertiary base (Alam, Rao, and Gopi, 1974).

The impact of the Five Year Development Plans has left its mark on the urban pattern of the country, but this has been more an incidental outcome of the implementation of sectoral programmes than the consequence of any clearly defined goals of urban development. The increased tempo of economic development, particularly of industries in the inland centres along railway lines, was conducive to both the rise of new towns and the accelerated growth and development of old established towns. The expansion of the road network and road transport, which facilitated the collection of agricultural surpluses at market centres and their distribution to centres of

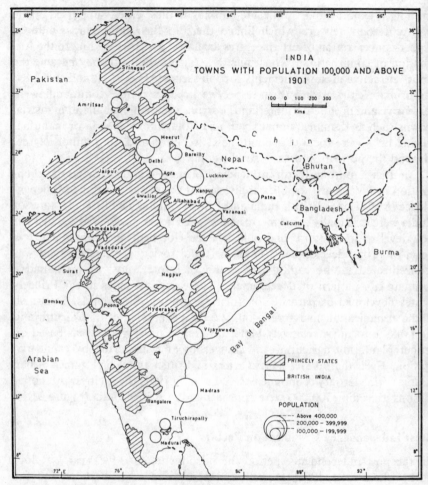

Fig. 22.1   Towns with a Population of 100 000 and above, 1901

consumption, led to the emergence of a number of *mandi* (small growth centres) towns, such as Hapur in Uttar Pradesh and Anakapalli in Andhra Pradesh, and reinforced the growth of existing urban settlements. The urban network has spread further in India with the extensive development of major irrigation and multi-purpose projects in Bihar, Rajasthan, Andhra Pradesh, and Karnataka.

The planners' emphasis on large-scale mineral and industrial development has had two types of spatial consequences. First, the stepping up of mining exploration, prospecting, and exploitation resulted in the rise of a large number of mining towns, such as Khetri in Rajasthan, Neyveli in Tamilnadu, and Kothagudem in Andhra Pradesh. Second, the large industrial complexes, together with associated residential developments, either provided the nucleus of new towns in the hitherto economically backward regions (Rourkela, Bhilai) or were established as suburban settlements on the peripheries of large towns, such as Bharat Heavy Electricals' Townships on the periphery of Bhopal and Hyderabad, New Bombay near Bombay, Gandhinagar near Ahmedabad, and Faridabad and Ballabhgarh near Delhi. These new settlements were instrumental in the accelerated growth of their senior settlements, but they were equally responsible for complicating their planning and development problems.

Urban Pattern of India and Metropolitan Development 1901-71

Although rural settlements (525,938 in 1971) far outnumber the urban settlements (2636 in 1971), the settlement systems of India are dominated by the urban settlements. It is largely through these urban settlements that the settlement systems of India are being integrated (Figure 22.2). During the period 1901-71 the number of urban settlements increased by 42 per cent from 1851 to 2636, but the urban population increased by the much larger margin of 322 per cent. Towns in the upper three categories (25,000 + inhabitants) recorded the highest increase both in the number of settlements and in population (Table 22.1). As can be seen from the table, these settlements constitute approximately 33 per cent of all urban settlements, but contain over 80 per cent of the urban population. The concentration of population in the metropolitan or Class I settlements with populations exceeding 100,000 is most marked. These settlements constitute only a minor fraction (5.6 per cent) of the total number of urban settlements (in 1971), yet they dominate the urban population. The share of metropolitan population in the total urban population has been rising progressively since 1931, and by 1971 it had almost reached 50 per cent. The concentration of population in metropolitan settlements is further emphasised by the fact that this handful of large settlements contained over 10 per cent of the nation's total population in 1971. The explosive rise in the proportion of the metropolitan population is indicative of a distinct trend towards a greater concentration of investments and developmental activities in such settlements.

While it is observed that as a class the large-sized urban settlements have registered higher growth rates, the growth rates of individual cities are not strongly related to their size. This is borne out by an examination of the size-category distribution of towns with growth rates of 50 per cent and above. None the less the fact remains that the large-sized towns are growing at a relatively faster rate than the towns in all lower rank orders. They have collectively contributed over 63 per cent of the total increase in urban population during the decade 1961-71 (Table 22.2).

The declining trend in the growth rate of small towns as a class, though not unique to India, is causing grave concern in view of the poor industrial and economic base of most of the metropolitan cities. It is all the more

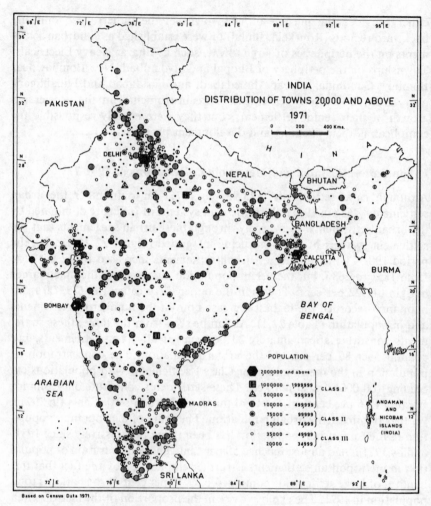

Fig. 22.2   Distribution of Towns with a Population of 20 000 and above, 1971
Source of data: Census, 1971

disturbing that despite their weak economic base they are able to attract large numbers, indeed most migrants, resulting in phenomenally high growth rates (Table 22.3).

Dominance of Metropolitan Settlements at the State and National Levels

The development of metropolitan settlements in each state of India is strongly influenced by the state's political, social, and economic conditions. There is, therefore, a wide variation among the states in the proportion of metropolitan to total urban population, as is shown in Table 22.4. None the less, except for a few states, the urban pattern at the state level is dominated

Table 22.1: *Growth in Number of Towns & Urban Population by Size Category of Towns*

	Number of Towns				Population			
	1901		1971		1901		1971	
	Number	% of Total Towns	Number	% of Total Towns	Pop. in '000	% of Total Urban Population	Pop. in '000	% of Total Urban Population
All Classes	1851		2636		25,852		109,094	
I 100,000+	25	1.35	148	5.61	5,692	22.02	53,381	48.93
II 50,000-99,999	42	2.27	183	6.94	2,948	11.48	14,712	13.49
III 25,000-49,999	136	7.34	582	22.08	4,382	16.95	19,947	18.28
Total of I to III	203	10.97	913	34.63	13,022	50.37	88,040	80.70
IV 10,000-24,999	395	22.34	873	33.12	5,847	22.62	13,961	12.80
V 5,000-9,999	756	40.84	678	25.72	5,752	20.63	6,197	5.68
VI <5,000	497	26.85	172	6.55	1,650	6.38	8,952	0.82
Total of IV to VI	1648	89.03	1723	65.37	12,829	49.73	29,116	19.30

Source: Compiled from Census of India, General Population Tables, 1971

Table 22.2: *Distribution of Urban Settlements with High Growth Rates by Size Class, 1971*

Size Class	A No. of Towns	B No. of settlements with growth rate of over 50 per cent	B as Percentage of A
I	148	65	43.91
II	185	40	21.85
III	582	98	16.84
IV	873	105	12.02
V	678	48	7.08
VI	172	22	12.79
All Classes	2638		

Table 22.3: *India: Urban and Metropolitan Population, Growth Per Annum (in per cent)*

Period	Total Population Growth	Total Urban Population Growth	Metropolitan Population Growth
1901-31	0.6	1.0	1.4
1931-51	1.5	4.3	9.5
1951-71	2.6	3.7	7.8

Source: Census of India, 1971, India: Final Population Tables

by the metropolitan settlements. Further, the share of metropolitan population in each state, except West Bengal, has increased, in many states phenomenally. The decline in West Bengal is minimal.

The tendency towards primate city development is most notable at the state level. The leading cities of all the states have, by and large, maintained a high level of primacy. Table 22.4, giving the three city index of primacy, reveals that primacy is pronounced: (i) in states with expatriate settlements which originally linked India commercially with Britain, (ii) in states with a strong feudal background and, (iii) in the peripheral states where all development activities are concentrated in a single city.

Rank-Size Distribution System of Urban Settlements in Indian States

The Indian urban system covers a diversified culture and economy which is clearly reflected in the system itself and particularly in the size distribution of its urban settlements. At the national level the distribution has been consistently log-normal from the beginning of this century. This is because the settlement system of India has been treated as mono-nodal with Bombay

Table 22.4: *Proportion of Metropolitan Population to Urban Population and Three City Index of Primacy by States, 1961 and 1971*

States	Capital/First Ranked Cities	1961		1971		Per Capita income 1969-1970 (rupees)
		Proportion of Metropolitan to urban population	Index of primacy	Proportion of Metropolitan to urban population	Index of primacy	
1. Andhra Pradesh	Hyderabad	40.58	3.7	45.41	3.3	544
2. Assam	Shillong	11.00	7.92	12.66	5.02	586
3. Bihar	Patna	35.15	0.7	32.32	0.9	402
4. Gujarat	Ahmedabad	42.42	2.10	54.09	1.7	740
5. Haryana	Chandigarh	8.07	—	12.82	—	N.A.
6. Himachal Pradesh	Simla	—	2.59	—	1.45	N.A.
7. Jammu & Kashmir	Srinagar	65.54	—	66.79	—	503
8. Kerala	Cochin-Ernakulam*	26.96	0.60	42.32	0.59	643
9. Madhya Pradesh	Indore*	31.56	0.60	41.06	0.67	495
10. Maharashtra	Bombay	60.49	2.9	64.76	3.5	736
11. Manipur	Imphal	—	11.50	—	6.97	N.A.
12. Karnataka	Bangalore	36.77	2.40	45.37	2.10	545
13. Orissa	Bhubaneshwar	13.19	—	30.04	—	571
14. Punjab	Amritsar	37.71	0.80	39.90	0.86	1002
15. Rajasthan	Jaipur	37.83	0.90	40.95	1.50	478
16. Tamil Nadu	Madras	37.76	2.4	43.80	2.7	591
17. Uttar Pradesh	Kanpur*	50.45	0.80	53.05	0.80	497
18. West Bengal	Calcutta	55.48	14.0	54.91	14.5	706
India		44.50	—	48.93	—	590

* non-capital cities
N.A.: Not available

Sources: Census of India: General Population Tables 1961 and 1971.

and Calcutta included as part of the same system. If the urban settlement system of India is disaggregated and examined at the state level three distinct rank-size distributions can be identified:

(1) primate city distribution
(2) log-normal city distribution
(3) decentralized or polynucleated distribution

Primate City Distribution

The states which exhibit this pattern of distribution include Andhra Pradesh, West Bengal, Maharashtra, Tamilnadu, Karnataka, Gujarat, Kashmir, Manipur, Meghalaya, and Nagaland (Figure 22.3a). These states have as their capital or primate cities, centres which were formerly (i) the expatriate colonial ports such as Bombay, Madras, and Calcutta, (ii) the headquarters of plantation agricultural areas (Shillong) and (iii) the capital cities of the erstwhile princely states such as Hyderabad (Hyderabad State), Bangalore (Mysore State), and Srinagar (Jammu and Kashmir), or the capital cities of the newly constituted backward hill states. In this category Ahmedabad, the capital of Gujarat state, is the solitary exception, being one of the early industrial nodes of India.

Log-Normal Distribution

In this category are included the states of Uttar Pradesh and Rajasthan (Figure 22.3b). They have distinct but not overwhelmingly dominant first-order cities in their respective states. It has recently been observed, however, that Jaipur is tending to emerge as a primate city.

Decentralized or Polynucleated Distribution

The states which conform to this pattern are Madhya Pradesh, Bihar, Orissa, Kerala, and Punjab (Figure 22.3c). The settlement system seems to be decentralized, focused around two or more major cities. It has not yet crystallized around any single metropolitan city. The states in this category, with the exception of Punjab, which has a high level of economic development, are relatively less developed economically as is reflected in their low per capita income (Table 22.4).

Dominance of National and Regional Metropolises

The dominance of the national and regional metropolises in the economy of the country is evident from the fact that the nine 'million' cities together contain nearly 25 per cent of the country's total working population. The concentration in the more productive and profitable sectors of 'Manufacturing other than household', 'Trade and Commerce', and 'Transport and Communication' are more marked. The four national metropolises Calcutta, Bombay, Delhi, and Madras and the other 'million' cities together contribute 30.7 per cent and 38.3 per cent respectively to the total urban workforce in large-scale manufacturing, 19.5 and 26.7 per cent respectively in construction, 22.5 per cent and 29.1 per cent respectively in trade and commerce, 23.9 per cent and 31.0 per cent in transport and communication, and 20.13 per cent and 28.31 per cent in other services.

The intensity of this concentration of economic activities in the nine 'million' cities is evident from their control over national commodity flows, trade and commerce. These nine cities together contributed in 1974-5 over 30 per cent of the total trade of India, 45 per cent of total manufacturing and 30 per cent of the country's construction trade. In addition they are the centres of concentration of the quaternary functions since they are the main or regional headquarters of most of the national banks, of multi-national firms, and of the regional offices of the government of India. For instance, Hyderabad City which is the capital of Andhra Pradesh and its political, administrative, and judicial headquarters, has five universities, a large number of research institutes of national and international importance, the headquarters of the Andhra Bank and the State Bank of Hyderabad, and the regional headquarters of the Reserve Bank of India and most of the nationalized banks. It also has the regional sales offices of a number of national commercial agencies. With this concentration of high-order tertiary and quaternary functions Hyderabad will continue to be both primate and parasitic for it is linked more strongly with large urban centres outside the state than with the settlements in its own region. The present national policy seems to be to concentrate economic power in these cities and is strongly supported by the system of air and fast train services, and by bank deposits and advances (Table 22.5).

National Metropolises and Metropolitan Systems of India

At the national level the economy of the country is spatially organized by four metropolitan cities—Bombay, Calcutta, Madras and Delhi. The transportation system of India is also focused around these four metropolises which have, therefore, assumed national importance. While interacting strongly themselves, they also have a core area of their own metropolitan dominance within which they shape and direct the economic activities of their respective urban sub-systems. It is therefore wrong to assume the metropolitan system of India to be mono-nodal and to define its size distribution on that basis (Berry, 1971). Of the four national metropolitan centres, the first three were developed as expatriate settlements in the early eighteenth century by the British rulers. Although Delhi has an ancient origin, New Delhi was built by the British as the new capital of India in 1911.

(a) Primate City Distribution

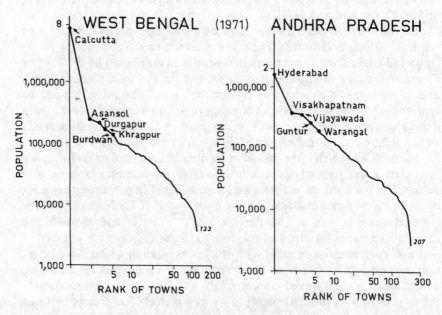

(b) Log-normal Distribution

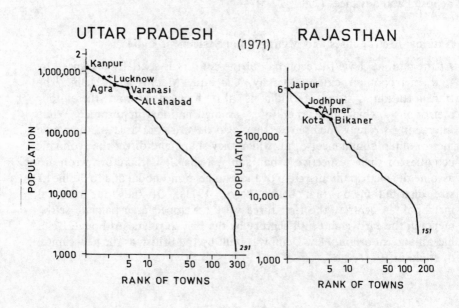

(c) <u>Decentralised Distribution</u>

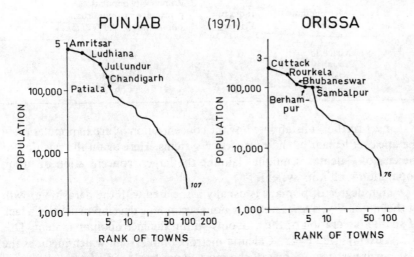

Fig. 22.3   Rank-size Distributions in Selected Indian States, 1971

Table 22.5: *Distribution of Deposits and Advances of Scheduled Commercial Banks (as on 31st December, 1975)*

Rs. 00,000

City	Number of Offices	Deposits	Advances
1. Delhi	595	128,001	118,659
2. Calcutta	490	134,649	122,666
3. Kanpur	112	14,321	7,669
4. Ahmedabad	233	21,335	24,196
5. Bombay	729	217,078	203,666
6. Hyderabad	203	21,040	14,991
7. Bangalore	290	24,471	33,290
8. Madras	351	43,580	57,687
9. Poona (D)	138	15,854	11,861
Nine city Total	3,141	620,329	594,685
All India	20,050	1,371,073	1,007,345

Source: *Banking Statistics—Basic Statistical Returns*, Volume 5, December 1975, Reserve Bank of India

City Primacy

A primate city growth pattern is discernible in all of the four metropolitan systems of India, but is most pronounced in the Calcutta metropolitan system (Table 22.6). In the other metropolitan systems there is not much difference in their indices of primacy. The primate city pattern of these four

Table 22.6: *Three City Index of Urban Primacy, 1971*

Metropolitan System	Index of Primacy	Primate city population as percentage of total urban population of the system
Calcutta	6.4	35.37
Bombay	1.7	21.70
Madras	1.3	15.68
Delhi	1.7	16.09

systems is further substantiated by the concentration of urban population in the apex settlement of their respective systems. Here again the position of the city of Calcutta is unique claiming the largest concentration of urban population within its system.

A high degree of primacy is usually associated with the parasitic growth of the major city, a low level of regional economic development, and a lack of spatial integration of the economy within the metropolitan system. This is best exemplified by the Calcutta metropolitan system which includes the vast north-east region, one of the most underdeveloped areas in the country. Besides, political factors also seem to have contributed significantly to the high primacy of Calcutta. As a result of the partition of the country in 1947 the whole of East Bengal, which was formerly part of the Calcutta metropolitan system, was separated from it. This disturbed the structural integration within the metropolitan system acquired during the pre-partition period. The entire transport system had to be reorganized; but still continues to be weak. This further distorted the settlement system focused on Calcutta and accentuated its primacy. The other metropolitan systems were not much affected by this political division of India.

Inter-Settlement Distances

An analysis of inter-settlement distances helps to achieve a better understanding of the hierarchical system of settlements. In a well-developed and functionally integrated hierarchy of settlements the number of settlements increases and inter-settlement distances tend to decline regularly from the higher to the lower levels of hierarchy. Any significant deviation would mean distortion in the system of settlements.

It may be observed, however, that in a dynamic system of settlements the inter-settlement distances within the same size range do not remain constant. This is corroborated by an earlier study of settlements with populations of 100,000 and above (Alam, Rao and Gopi, 1974). The straight line inter-settlement distances by size class for the settlements in all four metropolitan systems are given in Table 22.7 highlighting two distinguishing features common to them all. In all of the systems between the size ranges

Table 22.7: *Metropolitan Systems of India: Number of Settlements and Inter-Settlement Mean distances between Settlements of Same Size Class, 1971*

Population Size	Madras System		Calcutta System		Bombay System		Delhi System	
	Number of towns	Average distance in kms	Number of towns	Average distance in kms	Number of towns	Average distance in kms	Number of towns	Average distance in kms
Above 2,000,000	1	—	1	—	1	—	1	—
1,000,000-1,999,999	1	—	—	—	3	616	—	399
500,000-999,999	2	170	1	—	2	335	5	213
100,000-499,999	31	122	30	231	36	187	32	287
75,000-99,999	10	268	12	319	13	298	15	203
50,000-74,999	38	160	25	249	36	232	34	211
35,000-49,999	42	175	37	188	40	226	42	159
20,000-34,999	104	117	88	160	124	155	105	

100,000-499,999 and 75,000-99,999 the number of settlements has declined and distances have increased with a fall in the size range. This is contrary to the accepted principles of the hierarchical ordering of settlements and is presumably due to the clustering of settlements in higher size ranges which has developed in the economically prosperous pockets of the country. This substantiates the earlier results obtained through the analysis of rank-size graphs, regarding the skewed development of the hierarchy of settlements in the four metropolitan systems. The Madras and Delhi metropolitan systems suffer from similar distortions in the size class 35,000-49,999 producing a rise in the inter-settlement distances above the preceding size class. These inter-settlement distance distortions are a reflection of the wide disparities in levels of regional development which distort the hierarchy of settlements. It must be emphasized that the four metropolitan systems of India should be considered as emerging systems. There are bound to be distortions in these settlement systems until they reach the stage of maturity. A mature settlement system with a well-articulated hierarchy can develop only if regional disparities are minimized and a rural-urban continuum is fully established.

Distortions in the Settlement System

The settlement system of a country develops in response to its politico-economic system and level of economic development, and tends to organize the integration of the agrarian sector with the urban and industrial sectors. Such factors as the economic structure of India, the break in the historical continuity of its evolving settlement system due to political factors, wide inter-regional disparity in levels of development, the inadequacy of linkages between urban centres and their surrounding rural areas and consequent malfunctioning of the supply and distribution system, the dysfunctional development of urban settlements, the haphazard development of services in the urban and rural settlements, and misconceived development strategies and policies of private and public sectors, have tended to disrupt and distort the evolution of the settlement system and thereby prevent the spatial integration and optimization of the economy and a proper articulation of a settlement hierarchy.

The settlement system is deemed to be distorted if: (1) the distribution is marked by a significant clustering of large-sized settlements in pockets or corridors of development, (2) such settlements are disproportionately more numerous, and (3) the inter-settlement distance range of such settlements is much less when compared to the settlements in the lower size range. These are symptomatic of weaknesses in the linkages among the middle and lower orders of the urban settlements implying thereby a breakdown of the information system. Therefore, they cease to function as effective links in the chain of settlement systems and tend to become ineffective centres of urban activities.

Conclusion

Distortions in the settlement system of the developing countries and particularly that of India were the direct outcome of the policy during colonial
rule to concentrate investments and high-order administrative and political
functions in a few large urban centres. This resulted in their hypertrophy
and prevented the formation of the systems of towns embracing the entire
settled territory of the country, and also the formation of regional urban
sub-systems (Raza and Atiya, 1976).

The colonial capitalistic system also induced the growth of monopolistic
production and finance capitalism which have 'taken control of the primate
metropolitan hierarchy in India. Hence, it is subject to behaviour exactly
according to the law of the capitalist accumulation and concomitant forms
of urbanization' (Chakraborty, 1978). The control of monopolistic production and finance capitalism of the metropolitan economy has continued
even after Independence and, therefore, the pattern of urban and metropolitan development in independent India is not much different from that
in colonial times. Such a metropolitan growth arrests the wider diffusion
of technology, causes stagnation of the hinterland economy, prevents
adequate articulation of a hierarchical system of settlements, and induces
the exodus of people from surrounding rural areas and middle-order urban
centres to the metropolitan centres. To generate a more dynamic system of
urban and metropolitan development and to rectify the distortions in the
system of settlements, the government must intervene to provide dis-
incentives to the growth of metropolitan settlements, accelerate the growth
and development of the middle-order urban centres, and initiate a public
policy to promote the percolation of developmental impulses to the lowest
level of settlements in the system.

ACKNOWLEDGEMENTS

The author acknowledges with grateful thanks the assistance given by Dr. K. N.
Gopi, Miss C. K. Aruna, and Miss Zubaida Begum, in the preparation of this
chapter.

REFERENCES

Alam, S. M. *et al.*, 1976. *Planning Atlas of Andhra Pradesh*, Hyderabad: Govt. of
Andhra Pradesh.
Alam, S. M., Rao, R. M. and Gopi, K. N., 1974. 'Trends and Patterns of Metro-
politan Development in India'. Occasional Paper No. 3 Center for Urban Re-
search, Department of Geography, O.U., Hyderabad.
Basham, A. L., 1971. *The Wonder that was India*, London: Fontana.

Berry, B. J. L., 1971. 'Internal Structure of the City', in Larry S. Bourne, *Internal Structure of the City*, London.

Bhat, L. S., 1976. *Micro Level Planning*, New Delhi: K.B. Publications.

Chakraborty, S. C., 1978. 'Development and Primate Metropolis: Some Value Questions', in Alam-Ram Reddy, *Socio-Economic Development Problems in South and South-East Asia*, Bombay: Popula Prakasha: 76-104.

Dube, B., 1967. 'Geographical Concepts in Ancient India', *National Geographical Society of India*, Varanasi.

Law, B. C., 1954. *Historical Geography of Ancient India*, Paris: Société Asiatique de Paris.

Mukerjee, A. B., 1972. 'Rural Settlements in Sivalik Hill Tract of Punjab', *N.G.J.I.*, XVIII, pp. 57-63.

Munsi, S. K., 1980. *Geography of Transportation in Eastern India Under the British Raj*, Calcutta: K. P. Bagchi & Co.

Naqvi, H. K., 1969, *Urban Centers of Industries in Upper India (1556-1803 A.D.)*, Bombay; Asia Publishing House.

Raza, M. and Atiya, H., 1976. 'Characteristics of Colonial Urbanization—A Case Study of Satellitic Primacy of Calcutta (1850-1921)', in Alam-Pokshishevsky, *Urbanization in Developing Countries*, Hyderabad: Osmania University, 1976: 187-209.

Schwartzberg, J. E. *et al.*, 1978. *A Historical Atlas of South Asia*, Chicago: University of Chicago Press.

Sinha, S. N., 1976. *The Mid-Gangetic Region in the 18th Century*, Allahabad: Shanti Prakashan.

Smailes, A. E., 1968. 'The Indian City—A Descriptive Model', IGU Symposium on Urban Geography, Varanasi.

INDEX